OPERATION: MEMORIES

OPERATION: MEMORIES

Incredible Stories of
World War II Veterans

as told to:
Evelyn I. Gregory

The following persons have given permission for parts of their story
to be taken directly from their own books and writings. They are gratefully
acknowledged as follows:

Hassel, Walter, *In my Country's Service*, Vantage Press, Inc.,

Robinson, Samuel, *The Way it Was, Robinson's Chronicle,* unpub. 1990,

Duchscherer, James P., *At War with the 365th, an unorthodox View
of World War II in France.* self-pub. 1993

Chapin, William P.G., *Milkrun, Prisoner of War, 1944, An American Flier
in Stalag 17B.* Special Permission, Windgate Press.

Parker, Kermit R. Autobiographical notes from *Kermit's Story (His Childhood)*
and *Kermit's Story (Adulthood).*

Irving J. Mills, **Log,** dated April 8, 1945 through May 2nd, 1945. Death march
from Stalag 17 prison.

Arnold, Robert Bruce, anectdote about General Henry Harley 'Hap' Arnold.

Poetic Quotations of Charles A. Lindbergh, reprinted with permission of Scribner
from *The Spirit of St. Louis,* by Charles A. Lindbergh, copyright 1953 and 1981.

DEDICATION

To the memory of those who died on the battlefields,
in or from planes, ships, submarines,
or in the prison camps of World War II.
Thanks to the men and women who have carried the scars
and injuries received from all circumstances in the war.
This dedication salutes the veterans of World War II of America
especially the Veterans of Foreign Wars Bear Flag Post #13,
Sonoma, California.

Acknowledgements

Thanks to the forty-eight Veterans of World War II and their three special guests (two veterans of the Korean War and one Pearl Harbor Survivor) for this distinguished book of "firsts". More importantly, my gratitude for friendship and trust on your part for helping bring *Operation:Memories* into being. You overwhelmingly shared Logs, diaries, pictures, mementos, scrap books, autobiographies and sections of your self-authored books as well as your experiences. Through your generosity and your lives, the reader can find the positive as well as negative qualities of the historical World War II.

To Donald Gregory, a professional Computer Analyst and first generation Sonoman who has not only set the style and finesse design of this book on the computer for the writer, his mother, but has kept the glitches from becoming problems. To Joyce Gregory for help with the computer cover artwork.

The same vote of thanks goes to Carolyne Weasner, former Librarian for being the first person to read the work, who corrected a few spelling words and cancelled a lot of commas. Her enthusiasm has matched the author's own in the awe of the contents. She is presently the President of the Sonoma Valley Historical Association.

This book would not be complete without the inclusion of General H.H. 'Hap' Arnold. It was a great privilege to have Robert Bruce Arnold, Grandson of the General provide us with a story and a background of this honorable leader of World War II.

I am indebted to Frank Gregory and the Sonoma County Library System for use of rare and interesting books as extra research on World War II events and subjects. The vote of thanks is extended to the Research Librarians in the Sonoma branch of the Library.

In conclusion, I would express deep appreciation for the cooperation of the Veterans of Foreign Wars, Vernon Dearing, Commander 1990-1994 of Bear Flag Post 1943.

Table of Veteran's Stories

Foreword

"Anticipation ran riot! This was Walt's idol....He was about to be a guest on the K.C. Headwind! This was Walt's hero of America. Here he, Walt was but 21 years old and all of a sudden he was going to be with the great aerial navigator of all times! Lindbergh was going to be escorted by the Headwind's Crew and Walt was going to be Lindbergh's Navigator!!"

'Fate' or the 'Guardian Angel' has been present not only in the lives of the people of this book but in the very concept of the book itself. One January morning of 1994, words came so clearly, "write a World War II Memories book from oral interviews." Where else to contact a Veteran but at the Veterans of Foreign Wars? After a two month delay, who should visit? It was another Walter. He wondered if the author would like to include his little known story in *Operation Memories* about the British Ship Queen Mary. At that very moment this incredible adventure began and has like a tea bag steeped full measure continued strong for eleven more months. History, humor, heartbreak, love, intensive battles, education and music names just a few elements shared by over fifty people. They lived from "sea to shining sea" in America and in Hawaii before World War II. They are now retirees in the wine country town of Sonoma, California.

No boundary on earth was too great for these war stories to originate. A cargo of gold was brought from Africa to New York. Betty, decoding a secret message knew an important two-piece package was arriving with officers to be protected near San Francisco. Those packages and Officers were placed on the USS Indianapolis for destination Tinian Island in the Pacific. Mules and men were extremely taxed transporting guns and supplies over the exquisitely described Himilaya Mountains in Burma. Adventures equally impressive took place on six continents, all oceans, in the air and under the seas.

Collected by Vincent were details of a secret invasion of Devon, England. William, as a child with his family was forced into Auschwitz Prison in Poland. Today, William is known internationally as the renouned Vice-Chairman of the Holocaust Museum of Washington D.C. He helped design and plan the museum. Proudly presented is Sonoma's Five Star General H.H. 'Hap' Arnold. One more story from Hap's illustrious career as architect of the Air Force and as member of President Roosevelt's Chief of Staff comes to life.

A poignant memory by a prisoner-of-war shows the resilience exhibited by Irv and other prisoners in their behavior in a German Prison Camp. Even in adversity, their joy of life and hope in America shown through. Below is just one entry from Irv's private *LOG* of the death march from Stalag 17 until the Airman's rescue by the American Army. We have first privilege to bring the complete text of the *LOG* copied from hand written notes dated April 8th until May 2nd, 1945.

"(No Jerry Chow yet) Mountains are beautiful but hard on feet. Last night 9 men to a loaf of bread that is all. Ran out of G.I. chow about 4 days ago and am living (?) Anyone of the Four Horsemen could get us. Happy Birthday!" Some days, the men on this march received no food at all and were pressed onward by machine-gun to walk still another 24 miles per day. Many stumbled and fell in the rain. It was Irv's birthday when he wrote the quote.

Many birthdays and traditional holidays passed by when these Veterans of World War II were in cold and inhospitable places. Many buddies died on uncompromising battlefields. Graveside details are explained in both the Pacific and European regions. Sometimes these brown and blue clad individuals were having fun. Peggy danced to romantic music in Italy. Sam sang *Flossie from Aussie* in Austrailia with the submariners. Coyd took the place of Tokyo Rose on Radio Tokyo. Adam, a Marine, guarded President Roosevelt at the Little White House and a prisoner in the brig of a ship.

From the hearts of the World War II Veterans now retired in Sonoma, California come hundreds of war stories. They were told to the author in oral interviews. Notes, diaries and men's own books have added chapter and verse to this work. Bill and his publisher of *Milk Run* permitted his dynamic book to be summarized. The Pilot's bombing missions are described as well as a second look into Stalag 17. Other participants allowed the author's choice of material from their records and their personal books. The 300 pages of Kermit's autobiographies created the longest story. Childhood in an Indian Camp, raised as a boy in a Conestoga Wagon was impressive. But Kermit looked for adventure in his army life every day and he found it! Rising a step at a time, the Private retired as Colonel. Kermit's memories have provided a great deal of humor, knowledge and have brought forth again the concept that education is key to a worthy life.

Each oral narration transcribed by the author was given back to the participant for correction. Placing the historical events in chronological order was a burden to some individuals. Oral interviewing had some drawbacks. The author found that people do not tell events in order but jump around as thoughts occur which trigger still other thoughts. Expending time for changes and accuracy was sometimes a long and arduous task for both the Veteran and the author. Forging ahead to completion, let me assure all, checking background information, that the historical significance of his or her effort has been realized into more than the average book about World War II !

The author felt it was like dancing with the mind to bring full joy and measure of these memories into history on a written page. There are no holdbacks in information or language used by the Veteran. The work is considered by the author to be a composite picture of America from the end of the depression era to its people stretching forth with a renewal of new hope for world peace. Pearl Harbor bombed was catalyst for patriotism. The men and women came home with their country's freedom for the world !

Walter Hassel

United States Marines, 1933 - 1937

United States Navy, 1940 - 1947

In his book, *In My Country's Service*, Walter Hassel writes, "There have been countless books written of the terror, the battles and the heroes of World War II." Walter felt "There was need of a change of pace from that type of writing." His memories were focused on "...humorous sidelights of his experiences leading up to and including World War II." Walter's experiences were concentrated on the everyday challenges of military life between battles and the enjoyment of shore leave.

Joining the Marines during the Depression of 1933, receiving a Midshipman's base pay of $21.00 per month, Walter born in Buffalo, New York was treated to European ports of call three months of every year. There was plenty of food served the Marines including occasional steaks for dinner. Walter believed the civilians on the outside of the services were in more dire straits than he was experiencing. His encounters in Italy during 1934 occured when Hitler was just beginning his rise to power in Germany. Walter enjoyed England, France, Gibraltar and Portugal during those prewar years.

Examining pictures in his book proved that Walter was a handsome United States Marine. He had many amorous adventures including one standout event with a woman in the United States. While on shore duty during Mardi Gras in New Orleans, a new bride who literally lost her new husband in the press of the crowded streets ended up sampling an exciting night with Walter. When the Marine left the room they had shared the next morning, he noted, "the new bride wore expensive jewelry. She appeared to be a high born looking woman..." Walter believed, "She was lucky she was not robbed by some individual that might not have been so honest as to leave her with all that lovely jewelry..."

Finding the Marine Corps was not an especially meritorious channel for promotion, Walter returned to civilian life after four years. Another four years of being a placid-private-citizen-type influenced the young man to re-enlist so he could have more exciting adventures. This time he chose the United States Navy. Walter achieved the rank of Warrant Gunner described as one-half way between enlisted man and officer. The only way to obtain this rank was by a slow step-by-step process of study plus attention to detail. The difference in promotion strategy, as Walter judged it, was that in the Marines, you were assigned into small groups with little chance to be promoted while in the Navy within six months you could obtain rank as Seaman First Class. It was more economical to be in the Navy. The job title as Warrant Gunner meant taking over the care and maintenance of one of the five inch guns of the antiaircraft batteries. Six years after Walter served the Marines technology had drastically changed. The five inch broadside gun which he had taken care of on the USS Arkansas was completely different. Developed from an old gun having a separate projectile which used a silk bag of powder for a propellant and a complex loading procedure requiring two to three minutes between firings, the replacement was completely modernized. The new firearm used a one piece shell with a brass casing that could fire about once every five or ten seconds. The older guns described in Walter's book had been designed for ship-to-ship battle whereas the later ones were made for antiaircraft defense. Walter eventually earned the title as Aviation Ordnance Officer.

Hawaii was considered gateway to the Pacific wonderland. What young man would not enjoy the islands for their colorful sunsets, clean sandy beaches and beautiful girls? Long lazy days were enjoyed before the Pearl Harbor attack by Japanese Bomber Pilots. Only two hotels graced the shores of Waikiki Beach. They were the big pink Royal Hawaiian and the Moana. During idyllic prewar days, when Pilots were not practicing gunnery, they thought up daring aerial maneuvers in order to excite bystanders using their airplanes. One example was tying three planes together with a rope. Three Pilots would then take-off and perform aerobatics still tied together. This was probably part of the inspiration for what was to become known as Blue Angels precision flying. These dare-devil exploits took incredible flying skills but were also a release for breaking tension which was high in those days. Intense training programs for Pilots were in preparation for an expected war with the Japanese.

Two days before the December 7th, 1941 air attack on Pearl Harbor, Walter's assigned ship, USS Lexington was ordered to deliver a squadron of Marine scout planes to reinforce troops on Wake Island. While at sea on the following day a lookout spotted a strange airplane in the distance. The Officer of the Deck called the Aircraft Recognition Officer to the Bridge. He identified and reported, "It looked like a Japanese plane." The crew of USS Lexington, according to Walter, "was on the largest and most powerful fighting machine known to man." It was also referred to as a "floating airfield." With the uncertainty of the times, the noncommissioned men scuttlebutted and wondered, "why very little was made of a Japanese plane in that area?"

Next morning, the ship's personnel learned of the Pearl Harbor attack. It was, according to Franklin Delano Roosevelt, "...a day that will live in infamy." The USS Lexington, with one accompanying cruiser and four plane guard destroyers, was ordered to proceed back to Pearl Harbor. Missing the Japanese planes by eighty miles, the Lexington steamed into Pearl Harbor on the twelfth of December, 1941. The men witnessed the carnage that shook the world. The first scenes upon entering the channel were hulks of several American planes scattered on the beaches. The view of the destruction was unimaginable. The crew of the "Lex" was stunned! The aircraft carrier stayed but a short twelve hours to refuel and to resupply. New orders to the officers of the large ship were "to be prepared to hunt the Japanese Navy." This was quite a directive in what seemed like a limitless Pacific Ocean. After viewing Hawaii, however, the group dedicated their lives to the job that lay ahead of them. They would try to locate and engage the Japanese Fleet. Individuals on the Lexington also helped airplanes land on the decks of the carrier.

Pilots, in addition to concentrating on duties of flying their assigned planes were also trained as Bombardiers working their gun from the planes. The second man in those fighter planes was Radio Man, Observer and Tail Gunner all rolled into one. Pilots had to be their own accurate navigational plotters or they would not be able to find their way back to the carrier. They also had to know how to accurately calculate where their moving ship would be found from the time they left until they returned. Details of wind, weather and speed of the aircraft carrier had to be taken into account. During the war the radio could not used for guidance because the enemy would also hear and perhaps locate 'the floating city'. The landing area for the planes on the Lexington was the size of three football fields. The height of the ship was the equivalent of an eight story building! Rescue ships were always looking for Pilots who had run out of gas. Many were battle scarred with injuries. The majority of Pilots were successful in returning safely from the endless miles of vast seas, "perhaps with their navigational skills tattooed on the inside of their brains," according to the 'old salts'. The men on the Lexington were the hunters and the hunted. It was kill or be killed, a fact of war.

On the fateful day when the Lexington was sunk, radar had picked up enemy aircraft at about 65 miles away. The new instrument proved to be accurate. Even though the American Aircraft had shot down other approaching planes, a startling announcement was made that torpedo planes were sighted on the Port Beam.

One of the dive bombers overhead dropped an armor piercing bomb with a delayed action fuse. It detonated a deadly charge deep in the bowels of the ship mortally wounding the USS Lexington in the Coral Sea. The detonation penetrated the central electrical system causing short circuits and fires. The tremendous quantity of aviation gasoline fueled fires which were soon out of control on the hangar deck. Walter noted that men trapped below were given hope of being rescued. Those words were promised by a member of a gun crew. There was no hope... That day developed into a nightmare of fire, terror and death. Two hundred men were lost in the lower depths of the ship. Two thousand seven hundred others survived the ordeal.

Early on, before leaving ship, the survivors ate hats full of strawberry ice cream as the food storage lockers were opened for the last time. An orderly descent over the side of the "Lady Lex" was observed by Walter, who also noticed rows of shoes lined up with flashlights tucked inside one shoe. This was a custom that the men were taught to do each night before they went to bed. When the order to abandon ship was given, it was reported to Captain Sherman that the twenty four aerial torpedoes stored at the rear of the Hangar Deck were so hot that the messenger could not hold his hands on them. Walter hung on to a life raft full of men and swam in the Coral Sea for almost two hours before being picked up by the Cruiser New Orleans. His last view of the USS Lexington was her magnificent silhouette against a fast falling tropical night. Her flight deck was shrouded in smoke coming from every porthole and open doorway. White hot flames of gasoline consumed her. Word was received that the Admiral ordered the destroyer escort to sink the "Lex" with torpedoes to prevent the enemy from knowing that the American Fleet had one less aircraft carrier.

One interested in the art of gunnery would enjoy reading about the art of caretaking and expertise needed in the field of heavy armament including the task of loading 1000 pound shells as found in Walter's book full of memories.

Everyday stories, *In My Country's Service*, includes everything from bathing in salt water, using salt water soap for cleaning, and the care of a ship in dry-dock. Walter had a rolls royce shaver for his whiskers. He helped create a "jewel of a john" in the Philippines from oil drums. He fixed a steam laundry equipped to handle the clothes of perhaps a thousand men. The latter turned disasterous when white clothes turned bright rusty brown. Tropical jungle heat caused water to rust in the pipes during the two months the equipment had been abandoned before his repair! One of Walter's fun stories, follows. It is entitled:

Red Stripes.

"It was the summer of 1934. We on the USS Arkansas were on a midshipmen cruise to Europe and one of the most exciting ports of call was Nice on the French Riviera. I was a Marine Private assigned to the ship's guard.

One of my fellow Marines, a native of New Orleans and of French descent, spoke the language fluently. We teamed up for liberty ashore, he and three more of us. We cooked up a little scheme to have some fun. He taught us the French words *Oui mon ami*, which means 'yes, my friend,' and coached us until we had it down pat. We then went for a walk on the esplanade where most of the French girls did their promenading. When a group of them came within ear shot, he would start talking rapidly in perfect French. When he would pause, we other three would nod and reply, "*Oui, mon ami; Oui, mon ami,*" and those girls would stare open mouthed at four American Marines conversing so fluently in perfect French.

Then, we went to a cabaret on the waterfront, the Lido. Although it was out of our price range, we decided to at least have one drink. In those days enlisted servicemen were pretty low on the social scale and not welcomed in the "nicer" places, but our linguist shipmate convinced the maitre d' who was impressed by our Marine Corps dress blue uniforms that we were officers. During the time that we were there, two separate groups of Sailors in their bell bottom trousers and little white hats tried to get in, but the maitre d' refused them entry. When they pointed to us questioningly, he rattled off a string of French that no one understood but one of the words sounded an awful lot like "officers".

As our spending money was extremely limited, we decided to make our next stop at a simple barroom. We were disappointed to find several of the senior Marine NCOs there, resplendent in their dress blues with the two inch red stripe down the leg worn by all who were Sergeant and above. They had made quite a hit and were surrounded by a bevy of pretty French girls. Again our French speaking buddy came to our rescue. After ordering a round of beers and discussing the situation, he called the waitress over and they had a whispered conversation. She sauntered over to the group at the bar and quietly whispered a message into the ear of one of the other girls. Very shortly, one by one, the girls excused themselves and drifted away from the puzzled NCOs. With the female attraction gone, they soon left to find greener pastures. With the competition gone, we then received all the attention. When we finally got a chance to question 'our hero,' he told us that he had explained to the waitress that the United States government felt it only fair to warn people of certain hazards and the red stripe on the trousers was a sign the wearer had been afflicted with a contagious social disease."

Hassell, Walter., *In My Country's Service.* Vantage Press, Inc., 516 West 34th St., New York, N.Y., 10001. 116 pp.

Walter Farmer

United States Army, 1940 - 1945

Walter Farmer was born in Chatanooga, Tennessee. As a member of the 29th Reconnaissance Army Division he was on the big English steamship known as the famous Queen Mary. There were 11,000 service men on the super ship close to the end of the month of September, 1942. He remembers, "It was one of those beautiful days, the water was calm." They were cruising about 300 miles off Glascoe, Scotland. The Queen Mary traveling at 32 knots per hour was zigzagging every twelve minutes which was her usual procedure. When ships zigzagged, then an enemy submarine in those days couldn't line up the torpedos fast enough to do damage. This was because the big ships were too fast for the apparatus containing an explosive to be prepared and fired.

Technology was on the side of super Queen Mary. On this particular day in late September, a British destroyer was in approximately the same area as the supership. Destroyers accompanied big ships for extra protection in case of attack. The destroyer had 340 men on board. There was a submarine alert on the Portside of the steamship and the destroyer cut in front of Queen Mary. The supership caught the destroyer exactly in the middle cutting it like a loaf of bread folding it under the water. Walter recalled, "The Queen Mary traveling at its 32 knot speed when the accident happened only slowed to 17 knots and just kept on going!"

The American soldier was in the dining room of the Queen Mary before the incident. His plate started going back and forth on the table. When the submarine alert was sounded, Walter made it up to the Promenade Deck just in time to see a puff of smoke as the British Destroyer disappeared from sight and sank!

The explanation for the way the incident was handled was explained, "if the Queen Mary had hit the destroyer vessel by just a five inch margin in either direction, Queen Mary would have blown her bow and become the fatality."

When Walter's Company finished the exercise for which they had been assigned the super ship, they were evacuated onto barges in Glasgow. Walter looked back to see a hole of great magnitude in the front end of the Queen Mary. The greatness of the hole was estimated to be about fifty feet. The British Crew had closed off compartments in the center of the ship. No one was in that section of the ship when the accident happened.

In day to day soldiering, the 29th Division practiced a whole year in the British Isles before going to France to help with Operation: Overlord on D-Day. Walter states, "I think we invaded England about 100 times hitting the beaches from small yachts used for war practice games." After about six months of swimming and thrashing around in cold seas, LCIs (water crafts with no keels; the front drops down for landing) were brought for use instead. Walter jumped with a roll into the water, then waded ashore. The men of his company spent so much time in the icy seas, their bodies became used to being cold all the time. He does not remember any of them being sick from the constant wading or living in wet clothing.

It was ironic, then, that a man who spent so much time in water was delivered all the way up on Omaha

Beach on D-Day in Normandy. After all those 'wet' runs in England, he arrived high and dry with orders "to camp in some hedgerows." Somewhere, off a swamp or river bottom his company was dodging bullets from Italians and Czechoslovakians who had been forced-marched by gun point for over 100 miles by German Soldiers. Walter's Company took these men as prisoners almost immediately. The Czechslovakians and Italians started coming down the hedgerows and surrendering. The American 29th Recognizance Group turned them over to the infantry. The Americans learned that the German's choice by order was "if you don't shoot the enemy (the Americans and British) we'll shoot you!" By using the prisoners, the Germans did not have to do the shooting! However, the Italians and Czechoslovakians did not try to shoot with great marksmanship at the "enemy" but aimed over their heads. A break for Americans! They spent a whole day receiving prisoners who were co-operative and eager to be interrogated. Prisoners were a great source of intelligence regarding the Germans troop movements. D-Day+3, Walter was back on the Beach of Normandy to obtain the company's vehicles.

The German Army had been busy in their hedgerows before D-Day. They felled trees cutting them in half making long poles which were then erected in the air. These sharp ended poles were used against the Allies being flown in and dropped by gliders. If parachute or gliders came in contact with the poles, it tore them up causing men to hang on the poles often shot at or hurt in a brutal way. Once, Walter asked a paratrooper who had just landed, "what did you have to do to become a paratrooper?" The man was shaking like a leaf. He answered, "All you have to be is a dammed fool!"

After experiencing a rout by Germans who had five 88's opened up on Walter's division, the Company received word that a Colonel up the road was asking for help. It took many planes and lots of artillery to finally advance forward. On the 33rd day in France, Walter was standing near a Jeep that was blown up. He was never sure... was he hit by a mine, artillery or a bomb? He was paralyzed on the right side with injury to the groin. In an English Hospital, Walter was exercised, massaged and given water and heat therapy in a jacuzzi.

Behind the hospital building where he was recuperating some rookie soldiers were in training on how to plant mines. After the exercise, a truckful of mines had been picked up. The driver backed into a mine that was undetected and still in the ground. It was described as one of the biggest explosions that a person could ever experience in a lifetime! Still in England, sitting on a park bench enjoying some sunshine, all by himself, someone passed by Walter to exclaim, "the war is over!" As a Reconnaissance man, he likes to remember a song heard somewhere with words *"Only Uncle Sam's Heros go to Heaven!"*

In Sonoma since 1985, Walter, a Veteran of Foreign Wars Member for eighteen years, serves as Chaplin of Bear Flag Post 1943.

(In 1945, the story of the Queen Mary and her destroyer accident was printed in a British paper. For a long time Walter had a copy of the story but does not know now where it hides. He believes it was in a newspaper call the British Mirror. He has told the Queen Mary incident to approximately 100 persons, mostly Veterans of World War II. No one had ever heard the story before.)

Samuel James Robinson, Jr.

United States Navy, Captain Retired, 1942 - 1972

Sam Robinson, Jr., referred to by his Navy Colleagues as Robby wrote a very short history of his travels and employments as a Naval Officer during World War II. Sam, a Naval Academy Graduate made the Navy a career for thirty years, until he was feted at a very nice retirement party as a Staff Officer of the Fourth Naval District at Treasure Island, San Francisco in July of 1972.

Born in Seaford, Delaware in 1919, Sam remembers the days when the kids worked hard and played hard. He delivered telegrams for Western Union, newpapers for the Philadelphia Bulletin and sold strawberries that his Dad brought home from the produce block. He then delivered Kraft Cheese and other foodstuffs for his Cousin. He and his friends found an old boat along the Nanticoke River. Paying one dollar for a can of red paint, they fixed up the old boat and had great times for a whole summer, paddling, then sailing the boat with a handmade canvas sail up and down the river. Sam was a Boy Scout. He became manager of the baseball, basketball and football teams for four years in high school as he considered himself not a successful athlete at 128 pounds. In the band, he also considered himself as a pretty poor clarinet player.

After studying at Prep School for one year for the exams to Annapolis and being appointed by Congressman Allen to the Naval Academy, he entered his Plebe year in June of 1939. The summer was punctuated with battleship cruises to Panama, Venezuela and San Juan.

When Pearl Harbor was bombed most of the men at the academy did not know where Pearl Harbor was but it changed their lives. No more midshipman cruises for the students but more academics and speeded up graduation. The Class of '42 graduated in 3 1/2 years and Sam's class of '43 was the first three year class to graduate. Sam put down his first choice of service to his country as submarine duty. Since there were fewer volunteers for submarine duty, Sam was a "shoo in." Proceeding to Submarine School after graduation, Ensign Robinson was assigned to a World War I submarine the USS 0-7. It was a training sub for submarine school students which allowed them to make a great many training dives off New London.

Sam also married his wife Barbara Blair at this time and rented a furnished apartment in New London complete with a mouse!

Because Lt.(jg) Turk Kerstein attached to the USS 0-10 was on a weeks leave, Lt. (jg) Sam Robinson was next to go to a new submarine and so was summoned to take his place on the USS Pintado (SS-387). Since the sub was going to be stationed at Key West, Florida for a couple of weeks, Sam's wife, Barbara now three months pregnant followed her husband to Key West. She braved the long train trip sometimes sitting on her luggage in the aisles of the crowded trains.

The Pintado was engaged in a secret torpedo project during the day. In the evening, officers and their wives became acquainted at Hotel La Concha. All too soon the submariners were making way through Panama Canal. (It is interesting to note that the water of the Atlantic is saltier and heavier than that of the Pacific.) This fact brought forth into play the Archimedes principal that a body immersed in a liquid is bouyed up by the weight of the displaced liquid. Sam as diving officer made adjustments within the ship for the difference in buoyancy caused by the extra salt or the lack thereof. In the case of the Pintado, 10,000 pounds of water was pumped out to meet the Pacific Ocean's less dense factor.

Submarines in those days were named after a kind of fish. Pintado is a Spanish mackerel. Traveling the canal, Pintado was joined by USS Shark (SS-314) a new construction submarine from the Electric Boat Company. Appointed to Shark was Turk Kierstein back from his leave. He was the person for whom Sam had substituted for on the Pintado. USS Shark was lost by depth charges on her second war patrol. Sam was not appointed to the Shark but had opportunity for a gallant career receiving 20 medals including two silver stars and one bronze star medal. Sam was a success story on Pintado instead of enduring a watery death sentence on the Shark. Pintado's first patrol was that of flagship of a wolfpack known as Blair's Blasters and commanded by Captain Leon P. Blair (no relation to Barbara).

As Diving Officer during the first three patrols of United States Ship Pintado, Sam received citations in bravery and gallantry. The Pintado was first operating in areas West of the Mariana and South of Formosa. Second, she was in the East China and Yellow Seas Areas and thirdly in the South China Sea. The Presidential Unit Citation was presented to the Sub and its heroic and gallant officers. Pintado had by war's end, sunk thirteen Japanese ships including a 2,300-ton destroyer for a total of 98,600 tons. She damaged two additional vessels, one a 28,000 ton aircraft carrier. Pintado made six war patrols and was credited for destroying a Japanese Army Division and its equipment on their way to Saipan. The sub rescued twelve United States Army Air Corps B-29 crewmen (six officers and six sergeants).

In *Robinson's Chronicles*, entitled *"The Way it Was"* while the big invasion of Normandy in France was taking place, Pintado made some of her 'kills' shortly before noon on June 6th, 1944, D-Day. Victim Japanese ships sunk on this date were the Havre Maru and Kashimason Maru. Enemy aircraft and five escorts tried to box in Pintado dropping over 60 depth charges breaking light bulbs, high pressure air lines and some other damages. Pintado was forced deep but by pumping out some water the sub slowly eased up to 450 feet and finally lost the tenacious enemy. Pintado and two sister subs in the wolfpack had all but destroyed the convoy trying to re-inforce Japanese defenses in the Marianas.

A diary written by a Japanese sailor was found on the lone surviving cargo ship from the eight ship convoy that was destroyed in Saipan Harbor by bombardment. Interpreted tales of the diary stated, "that the Japanese were sinking three or four American Submarines every day!" The men of Pintado were delighted to prove that the diary was incorrect and merely a figment of the enemy's imagination. Of course, Sam also points out that Tokyo Rose claimed the Japanese forces sank an American Sub every day!

Perhaps Pintado was saved many times in the early part of the war due to the following "after thoughts" mentioned in the Robinson *Chronicles*." It seemed a Republican Congressman, Andrew Jackson May, Member of House Military Affairs Committee returned from a war zone junket and in a press interview stated " American submarine commanders weren't afraid of Jap depth charges because they were too light and not dropped deep enough." Reading papers too it was noted, the Japanese quickly remedied their defects. VADM Lockwood, COMSUBPAC considered that indiscretion cost the United States 10 submarines and 800 officers and men. The Admiral was furious and wrote, "I hear Congressman May said the Jap depth charges are not set deep enough ... he would be pleased to know the Japs set 'em deeper now."

One exciting event for the crew of the Pintado was activated by spotting an eleven ship Japanese convoy guarded by three destroyer escorts. *Robinson's Chronicle's* relate "After dark, on the surface the

Pintado moved into the center of the convoy (passing a scant 75 yards from an escort) to attack the largest ship of the formation the Tanan Maru No. 2, a former whale factory then converted tanker. Two spreads of torpedos left the monster ablaze and sinking." Two other oil tankers were also damaged. "The Tanan Maru was the largest merchant ship sunk by an American submarine in World War II. The escorts began dropping their depth charges but as yet had no idea the Pintado was on the surface." ... Pintado submerged and began reloading torpedos. Pintado carried 24 torpedos on patrol, and finally four miles away from the surface confusion "the entire crew had time to look through the periscope at the burning ships."

"As a torpedo was being loaded into a tube in the forward torpedo room the tripping latch on top of the torpedo hit the side of the opening and began running. Dense white smoke from the alcohol in the fish filled the room and forward battery compartment." Closing water tight doors and surfacing was all the crew could do. They had to clear the air in the boat. Even though the Skipper could still see the destroyers on the horizon they evidently did not see Pintado. Probably they were very busy picking up survivors. Later, search flashes appeared on the radar screen indicating a hunter killer group. Setting an escape course because Pintado's time in that patrol was up, she left East China Sea heading east toward Pearl Harbor.

Since submarines were incapable of staying submerged for long periods of time, it was recalled that the Pintado had to surface every evening for star sights. The crew had to recharge air banks and batteries. The sub generally dived at dawn. Clothes were washed by condensation from air conditioners! A cigarette smoker in late afternoon under the sea would have to puff harder trying to get enough oxygen to keep a cigarette burning.

At one dollar a day the submarine officers and crews could stay at the Royal Hawaiian between patrols. The Men from the Submarine Pilotfish were also at the hotel during one of the 'breaks' from the war zone of the South China Seas. At a party one night "officers of both subs were in Captain Closes's room with his parakeet happily drinking bourbon as usual." According to Sam, "the Captain's bird was an alcoholic. The bird would fall off his perch and one of the men would set him back up on his clothes hanger and warn him about the evils of alcohol. He just didn't care. Well, he overindulged, fell off his hanger again and died." The men found a box, formed a procession and had a midnight burial on the grounds of the Royal Hawaiian with the comment "He was a brave bird and survived two war patrols but he couldn't take the good life!"

In Austrailia, each officer was allowed a case of beer in liter bottles and a few bottles of bourbon or gin for their two weeks ashore. Parties were spent in telling sea stories, playing games like *Clear the Bridge,* "*Crash Dive,*" and "*ABA.*" The men also sang old war songs such as "*Roll Your Leg Over,*" "*Bell Bottom Trousers,*" "*Roll Me Over,*" "*Six Pense,*" and "*Depth Charges*" to keep up morale. One of the songs Sam relates fully in his book that was conceived in Austrailia is as follows:

Flossie, the Aussie

"Now — Stalin wasn't stallin' when he told that beast of Berlin, that he never would rest contented 'til he'd Driven him from the land. So he called the Yanks and English and proceeded to exTinguish the Fuehrer and his vermin — this is how it all Began —

Oh — Flossie was an Aussie way down south in Aussie Land; She had a face that was a picture and a figure That was grand. But her mind was like an angel's not a Woman of the World. 'Cos Flossie was no Floozie — but An honest working girl.

Then — She met a Yankee sailor, who was as cute as he Could be. He had time to woo our Flossie 'Cos he never Did go to sea. He worked down in a Tender way on Fremantle Dock. He had time to see our Flossie — and to Woo her round the clock.

Oh — he brought her cigarettes, he brought her whisky, brought her gin. He brought her ration coupons when her Shoes were wearing thin and Flossie loved this sailor And the things that he could buy For this seaman was a Demon in the service of Supply.

Then — she met a Yankee sailor off a Yankee submarine... He was rough, he was tough, he was durty, he was mean, But he wooed her and pursued her and he finally won the Day... "I just love those big torpedos"...is what Flossie Used to say.

Now — Flossie was an Aussie and she knew her way around. She knew the paths of happiness and where those paths Were found. So she took him to a churchyard and shortly They were wed. And retired for some service in a Flossie Aussie bed.

Now — She gets no silken stockings . She gets dammed few Cigarettes. But when Flossie wakes each morning she Never never has regrets. For she learned a simple moral Just the same as you and I, That a good supply of Service beats the Service of Supply."

Pintado sailed from Perth in the Indian Ocean around the southern Coast of Austrailia near Tasmania and into the Harbor of Wellington, New Zealand enroute to Pearl Harbor. The ship was now manned with a new skipper and sent back on patrol for lifeguard duty. B-29's were flying from Guam to drop fire bombs on Tokyo. On July 26, just south of the Japanese Empire, twelve parachutes blossomed toward Pintado's position. Pintado picked up all the twelve as the bomber hit the sea, exploded, burned and sank.

Years later, Sam now a Commander as First Fleet Operations Officer in San Diego was sent to Anchorage, Alaska, to discuss coordination of Carrier Operations with Air Force Practice Interceptions Personnel. It was brought to General Mundy's attention that when he, as Squadron Commander and a Colonel had been rescued in the Pacific that Sam had been the OOD (Officer of the Deck) of Submarine Pintado. A picture taken together for the Air Force Times was entitled "Robinson and Mundy Meet Again with Four Feet on the Ground." The officers and men of the Army Air Corps rescued were assigned a new bomber and named it USS Pintado. The officers exchanged gold dolphins for silver wings but Sam never wore the wings which are still in his dresser drawer.

The General and the Commander reminisced about the last time they had met in Guam. The Army Air Corp later became the United States Air Force. Later as Chief of Staff to the Amphibians Command off the Viet Nam Coast, Sam earned the Bronze Star.

After World War II, Sam was ordered to a new construction sub, USS Tusk and sailed to Rio de Janeiro for a shake down cruise. While in Rio, Lieutenant Sam received orders to post-graduate school at Lehigh University for a degree in chemical engineering. His next assignments were SUBDIV 82 Engineer, Executive Officer, USS Sea Owl and a year as a student at the Naval War College in Newport, Rhode Island. The Lieutenant Commander took command of USS Runner a snorkle submarine. After two years command of Runner, Sam and his family were transferred to the staff of COMCARIB SEA Frontier in San Juan, Puerto Rico. After one year on staff, Sam had his first Pentagon duty in the Office of the Secretary of Defense (International Security Affairs.) This job was integrated with State Department desk officers for political-military policy matters toward countries of

Norway, Sweden, Denmark, Iceland and Soviet Satellites. Then across country to San Diego (Coronado), he was Operations Officer SUBRON 5, then COMSUBDIV 32 with five modern submarines in the command. After that great year, Sam joined the Staff of Commander First Fleet in San Diego on the cruiser USS Helena as Fleet Operations Officer. He was responsible for scheduling the movements, fleet exercises and in-port times for the 100 ships of the First Fleet. Returning to the Pentagon, Captain Sam was the Executive Aide to the Vice Chief of Naval Operations, Admiral Rickets. Business trips down the Potomac on the Presidential Yacht Williamsburg, a trip with the Joint Chiefs of Staff to Norad Headquarters and to Elmindorf Air Force Base in Alaska, plus an educational trip to White Sands Army Installation were other exciting sojourns.

Admiral Rickets died suddenly of a heart attack. Sam was assigned Command of the USS Tulare with chores of delivering many goodies to Marines in Vietnam. He was made Chief of Staff of Amphibian Force, Vietnam. He wound down his Navy career at Treasure Island as Chief Administrator of the Schools Command. Sam's family, comprising his wife and two children were assigned to live in a beautiful old house, Quarters 4, built before 1903. It had six bedrooms, three baths, butler's pantry, a call box in the kitchen to each room but no maid, steward or butler!

Overqualified for current jobs in civilian employment market, Sam studied to become an enthusiastic Real Estate Salesman. From 1972 until 1990, he was referred to by his clients and co-workers as Captain Sam! The Captain has lived many great moments in his life such as bringing his Submarine USS Runner into New York Harbor, sailing past the Statue of Liberty greeted by water sprays from fire boats. He looked down upon Hong Kong Harbor from Hilton's Eagles's Nest to see his ship Tulare resting at anchor. Sam now rests in hills above Sonoma replete with a beautiful office room in his home with bookshelves holding the *Time Life Collection of World War II* and a set of books on submarines including one of German submarine history. Citations and awards of merit decorate the walls as well as a picture of Captain Sam and Admiral Bernard A. Clarey (Skipper of Pintado). On August 12, 1971 Captain Samuel J. Robinson, Jr. was awarded the Armed Forces Honor Medal, First Class from the Vietnamese Government. It reads, "Outstanding performance of duty, resourcefulness of staff works knowledge, training experience, persistence to heighten good will, true cooperation spirit..."

Robinson, Jr. Samuel, *"The Way it Was, Robinson's Chronicle."* Unpublished. 1990. 20 pp, 7 exhibits.

Vernon Dearing

United States Army, 1944 - 1946

Born in Jamestown, Missouri in the year 1923, Vernon was sent to Liverpool, England in January of 1945 with a minimum amount of training for war. By way of the English Channel, he arrived at a big tent city of service men located at La Harve, France. Traveling by train, he was headed directly to Metz, France which was near the German Border. Vernon became immediately disenchanted with war. He was traveling on this ardous train trip in box cars called 40's and 8's. The name of the cars were so designated as they would hold 40 men or eight horses per carload. As Vern traveled the great expanse of miles inward and over the Continent of Europe, he was appalled at the sight of dead bodies near the railroad tracks at Metz. Bodies were also laden on trucks to be given back to proper authorities. He found out, "if the bodies were not negotiated back to a proper place then they were buried."

Vernon's second shock of war was that of the destroyed cities viewed across France. The most pulverized town he viewed was Aachen, Germany. Vernon was assigned to the Third Army, Division 94, directly under General Patton near the German border at Metz.

Division 94th of the U. S. Third Army had assembled behind the lines entering the campaign after the First Army achieved a sharp penetration and after intensive aerial bombardment had taken place. Vern found out "that when a division was going to attack an area, the Allies would have aircraft bomb out the area the day before." He noted that "Americans were kind to important buildings. If the enemy was using a famous landmark, the Allies would give them an alert to move from the site. If they did not move, then the building would be blown up! If a German was observed even in a church steeple, then the edifice would have to go!"

After D-Day, armoured columns poured over the land from the direction of Brittany which had been necessary to the Allies for deep port facilities. This area was full of tank traps due to the nature of the "hedgerow " land. Each field could expose a little fortress of high-banked earth along with the antitank and antipersonal mines. Some of the infantry in which Vernon marched would go in advance of tanks. Mines found were blown up before the main battalion of tanks were ushered through.

"It was a funny thing," he surmised, "but the infantry foot soldiers were necessary for the tank's protection. If the tanks were shot inbetween the tracks then the tank would not work or run." Infantry men accompanying the tanks carried a new weapon called the bazooka. It was a portable weapon which discharged a rocket projectile. Vern was carrying a bazooka when he was shot in the left shoulder by a sniper...

On February 22nd, 1945 the United States Third Army was crossing the Saar River after the men had fought all day to get hardware (tanks) in behind them. Vern was ordered as squad leader on March 13, 1945 to knock out a pill box held by Germans. Busy calling in artillery and antiaircraft fire, Vern was shot in the left shoulder by a "guy up in a tree" who was not seen by him. The bullet hit Vern's left shoulder and came out through his back below the shoulder blade. One of Vernon's buddies shot the German from the tree and the men took the pill box as ordered. Remembering this incident, while using his bazooka, Vern was clear in describing that "the bazooka instrument of war was one which shot a projectile rather than a bullet. The projectile would hit a target and then explode again." The bazooka was the largest thing an infantry man could carry. It was commonly used to knock in the doors of the pillboxes and Vernon hastens to add "destroy tanks!"

In a magazine article written by Fred Warshofsky, unknown publication, entitled "Saga of the 94th Infantry Division," about 1961, (The only clue to the date of the article is an ad referring to 1961), Vernon found part of his experience related in the extensive story. It described the setting of Vernon's experience as the Saar-Moselle Triangle. "The apex pointed toward Germany's oldest city, Trier. It held the most vital railhead behind the Siegfried. Rivers, Saar and Moselle framed the base of the triangle. It was also known as the Siegfried Switch and was heavily fortified." It was here that Vernon and his assembled company watched about 10,000 casualties sap the strength of the brave 94th.

General Patton their leader, known as "General Blood and Guts" was pushing his army in spite of obstacles of major proportions. Often, Patton surprised the troops by appearing before the men toward the front lines. He wore highly polished boots, helmet and pearl handled revolvers. It was a known fact that he wanted his beloved Third through the Seigfried Line into Germany's heartland before the other armies advanced.

There was a period of bad winter weather. In late December it was described as plain nasty! The German border terrain was narrow and severely restricting. There were natural and man made obstacles like the Moselle River on the French and German borderline, Mass and Rhine Rivers, the Vosges Mountain Chain, the Huertgon Forest plus dense German fortifications. The battle of Remagen Bridge occurred on March 7th, 1945. This was near the town of Aachen that was reduced to absolute rubble and of which lives in Vern's memories "as a reason for not having wars."

The German General Wend von Wietersheim threw the armoured strength of his entire division at Tettingen and Butzbach. It was a murderous barrage. Geysers of dirt were described along with snow, mud and steel fragments. Roofs fell in Tettingen until it seemed nothing in the town would remain but rubble. The men of the 94th gave every bit of energy they had while managing bazookas, satchel charges and small arms fire. Some soldiers threw white sheets and tableclothes over their uniforms to blend in with the snow. The blood in the snow from the killings did not blend in. By the evening of the 19th, the 94th Division had advanced seven square miles of German held terrain. They had taken out five pillboxes and 23 bunkers, destroyed four enemy tanks and captured 827 German prisoners. It was noted that the 94th Division had been 39 days straight in combat. Bodies of dead Germans became a problem. The winter cold tended to refrigerate them. A month of hard fighting cost Americans some 75,000 casualties and the German casualties estimated at from 80,000 to 100,000.

However, Vern's injury sustained on the 13th was just before the U.S. Third army made their surprise crossing of the Rhine River in assault boats on the 22nd of March. Vern was thankfully back in England for recouperation at a hospital. When the German Government surrendered to Allies on May 7th at Reims, France, the next day was designated as V-E Day. Vernon was given an extra 10 days leave. The Red Cross gave the wounded men some extra money to spend and they had a very happy time amidst a big celebration at Picadelli Square in London.

After his bout of healing in England in late May of 1945, Vernon was sent back to German soil to the Army of Occupation which picked its way through rubble of German cities. President Truman was just settling in after the death of Franklin Roosevelt when political solutions to territory of Germany was one of major concern. Vernon's job with the Army of Occupation was three-fold.

First, he had responsibilities of interrogating persons and cataloging live rounds of ammunition found in caches, tank barriers and on great battlefields full of mines. Soldiers were to report any vehicles blown up or anything suspicious that might hold live ammunition. Thereafter, the ammunition was removed and disposed of by demolition crews.

Secondly, Vernon helped his officers, who were working to set up military governments in Germany and Czechoslovakia. He believes "the people already in charge of a town were used." In a small historical book by Mark Tinney, it was learned that "at first, a process of 'de-Nazification' was put into operation under which any German who wanted a position of importance had to show he was not, nor ever had been, an active supporter of the Nazi Party. Since during Hitler's time virtually every professional or trade organization was compelled to affiliate itself to the Nazis, this condition was scrapped." Mark and other historians surmise that since President Truman was new in office, since the British had elected a new Prime Minister, Clement Attlee instead of Winston Churchill, that Stalin (the old manipulator of the decision making group) was most influential in the division of German soil. Stalin was the only leader in power throughout the war and into the early post war days of which Vernon was a part.

Russia kept the 75,000 square miles of Poland, she had annexed in 1939, then compensated Poland by allowing them to annex 42,000 miles of Eastern Germany. These new governments that Vernon was involved with in Germany and Czechoslovakia were then turned over to the Communists of Russia. Vernon, a young man from the placid State of Missouri could not have known he was part of 'political maneuvering'.

Vernon's third interesting post war job with the First Division was that of guarding the facilities of the higher-up German prisoners at Nurnberg (Nuremburg). These were the men who were brought to judicial examination at the famous Nuremburg Trial regarding the Jewish tragedies wrought by them in the concentration camps of Hitler. While the prisoners were under guard "they were not made to do labor" according to Vern.

Historically, Warshotshy writes and it has been noted "that the 94th Infantry Division had been a long time in its 'blooding'." Once its troops reached the war zone they made a combat record that ranks them among the great fighting men of World War II. They rolled up 209 combat days, suffered 10,937 casualties and captured 26,638 German prisoners. When the 94th Division returned to the United States for demobilization in February of 1946, Vern was still in Germany guarding Nuremburg prisoners with the First Army. After visiting seven different countries including Switzerland, Luxembourg, Germany, France, England, Belgium and Czechoslovakia, Vernon was proud to return as a Sergeant to the United States of America and to the quiet state of Missouri. He was ready to become just a plain American citizen!

Vernon L. Dearing of the 94th Division, 301st. Infantry Regiment, Company C of World War II has held an intregal part of the leadership of the Veterans of Foreign Wars of Bear Flag Post, 1943. Moving to Sonoma, California in 1985, he has served as Post Commander for four years.

Unknown Magazine, article entitled, "*Saga of the 94th Infantry Division*," by Warshofsky, Fred, 8 pp.

Tinney, Mark; *Europe, Germany Switzerland,* Mark Tinney, Laxfield Suffolk, England, 1983, pp.9

Ernest J. Mangiantini

United States Army, 1941 - 1945

Ernest J. Mangiantini was born in Sonoma, California spending a great deal of time as a young boy on the Kunde Ranches near Glen Ellen, California. Tagging along beside his father who supervised the work on the beautiful lands, Ernie fished in the sparkling streams. As a young man with his dog by his side, he did a lot of deer and quail hunting. He knew the ruins of the "Wolf House" of the Jack London Beauty Ranch.

Ernie and his sister's parents were Italian immigrants. His Father, Narciso Mangiantini, age fifteen came to the United States in the year 1901. After a sojourn around the country, Ernest's father, from an invitation of an old boyhood friend, Julius Sorini, was invited in 1914 to work at the Sorini Winery in Sonoma. Ernest's father and Concetta, his mother moved to Clark Ranch on Sonoma Mountain in 1923. It had been purchased by the Kundes. Ernest was five years old and Louise, his sister was three. A second son, Ezio was born on the ranch in 1925.

Ernie led a pretty sheltered life. In nearby Glen Ellen, his biggest delight was the movement of trains carrying San Francisco tourists. The trains blew their whistles and made a complete turnaround with local sightseers watching from their horses and buckboards. Ernest did not have many children to play with as the family was tucked away up on the mountain. He did have fun finding Indian arrowheads which were plentiful amidst redwood trees and little forest streamlets.

Included in the Book, *Childhood Memories of Glen Ellen*, are recollections of Ernie Mangiantini along with those of his sister, Louise. These writings include one of Ernie's childhood experiences. Once, a herd of horses, numbering 30 or 40 was in the way of the wagon driven by Ernie's father. "They are being taken to slaughter for tallow," his Dad explained. The poor animals, tired, worn out, hungry and thirsty were still being pushed ahead by men in charge of the dusty exodus. Ernie remembers thinking "How cruel, how cruel!" It's still a scene he'd like to forget. However, he was to experience many scenes in his future life as a member of the United States Army of World War II that would make the above occurrence become small by comparison! The men of the 19th Combat Engineer Regiment also endured being pushed ahead, tired, worn out, cold, thirsty and more than a little hungry at times!

With a soft heart coupled with sheltered life, it was a shock for Ernie to be sent half way across the United States to Fort Leonard Wood in Missouri. Ernie was one of few Sonomans that was stationed so far away from family and friends. Most of the young men that he knew were stationed at nearby Fort Ord near Monterey. Until the Pearl Harbor bombing, Ernie had wanted to return to California's Fort Ord where his buddies were stationed. He put in a transfer from the 2nd Calvary of the 9th Engineers to the 19th infantry located at Fort Ord.

When Ernie arrived at Fort Ord, the group he had wanted to be with had just moved to Pasadena, California stationed in the Rose Bowl! Since the men of the 19th had moved out Ernie was put in replacement barracks for 21 days with only a two hour walk in Monterey for a break.

Upon arrival at Pasadena the Sergeant informed the young engineer that he was on the Most Wanted List by the FBI and all police in California. He learned early what the words SNAFU stood for as Ernie was being sought as AWOL! It became a big army surprise that they were searching for the young man as absence without leave, then finding Ernie was where he was supposed to be all the time! They should have been trying to find the group to which he had been assigned!

No sooner had Ernie bedded down in the Rose Bowl, when on an alert that the Japanese had shelled the city of Santa Barbara, the whole regiment was deployed to the coast of Santa Barbara to guard California's Coastline.

Finally, the 19th Combat Engineers were ordered to Camp Kelmer Demarcation Port and then "nobody knew where...". The Sonoman found himself on a twelve story ship out of New York. The soldiers took shifts sleeping six hours per person, four to a room on the Atlantic crossing. They sailed to Scotland aboard the Queen Mary. It was raining "cats and dogs". On a "little baby cattle boat" the men were taken to Belfast, Ireland. A Red Cross girl met the men and invited them for coffee and doughnuts up at a barn! Looking for a warm dry place that was welcome news. There was no roof to the barn!

Ernie's World War II campaigns included Algeria, French Morocco (with Arrowhead), Tunisia, Sicily, Naples-Foggia, Rome-Arno, North Appennines and Po Valley. From the toe of Sicily he traveled the war all the length of Italy. He was under the Generals, Patton, Fredendall, Bradley, Clark, and Keyes. Ernie was designated a "sharp shooter." He was ultimately in four different large battles.

To begin the sojourn toward ultimate war the men were ordered "to get ready to invade"... somewhere ... "they were to sew patches on their uniforms by themselves." The President of the United States the Commander in Chief of all United States Forces, Franklin Delano Roosevelt made a speech which Ernie remembers as "Our boys in North Africa are ready for the biggest conflict up to this date." The President was referring to Ernest's future! which began with a bout of seasickness on the ship.

Hitting Green Beach at Oran, Africa on the Mediterranean Sea from a northern course past the Rock of Gibraltar on the European Continent to Africa, Ernie got off the boat with orders to clean up mine fields. As a Combat Engineer, he was also to spearhead some machine gun problems. Raining as per usual, soaking wet, he dug himself a trench. Then, he was on guard duty. The Lieutenant's orders were explicit, "There was to be no walking around. Shoot first and ask questions later." His first taste of war gave him goose bumps. He was glad war was not in America when he heard the woeful screaming of women and little children.

Ernest looks back fondly at that first Christmastide recalling a Priest, Father Moran. The army erected a double tent with a beautiful altar. The tent was packed with the soldiers for Midnight Mass. They sang Christmas songs. The men had turkey for Christmas dinner.

The 19th Combat Engineers were told to march for 1500 miles! All their equipment was loaded on trucks taken to Tunisia. Their sojourn was to back up the 26th Infantry engaged with the famous and undefeated dangerous General Erwin Rommel. Known as the "Desert Fox," Rommel was soon to meet the offensive forces known as TORCH. With no experience, no armor except bazookas, most of the men with Ernie fought with fixed bayonets attached to their rifles. His 19th was now under Bradley, receiving orders "to hold the Germans at all costs. Hold Kassarene Pass at all costs." The Germans were reported to have the same orders to hold the Pass which at its narrowest point was less than a mile wide. "Rockets called Nebelwerfers (literally 'fog throwers, nicknamed 'Moaning Minnies by the British) were used by the Germans as the Axis troops screamed into the Pass."

General Patton took over with a new mandate to "take Kasserine Pass at all costs." At midnight, the 19th

Army took the hill. The men could not hold it. They had no big guns. Americans fell back until eleven British tanks arrived as reinforcements. These tanks were also lost but eventually the Americans broke through the line. With only their fixed bayonets available, they also ran out of ammunition. They murmered to each other "If we don't take the hill again we will be forced into the sea! Bodies were a mess. Mines were tricky. Some mines had a fuse cap on them. If you turned the cap the wrong way you were hit in the face with TNT. The TNT mines were built to destroy tanks. To take a fuse out you had to check all way around, carefully," stated Ernie. Each time the Germans advanced Rommel expected a counter attack. It was later reported that Rommel decided the Allies reinforcements were of too great a number for an encounter. The German Army moved so quietly out of Kasserine Pass that it was 24 hours before the Allies knew the troops were gone! Americans suffered many casualties, thousands wounded, and thousands captured.

Ernie was part of a team that cleaned out 1500 mines and built bridges and roads. While attending to these dangerous chores, Ernie took a rest in a trench that he had dug. The trench was so deep and narrow that a tank ran over the hole while he was in it! Dusting himself off, he reasoned he had learned a lesson. "If you dug the foxhole deep and narrow, even shells were deflected away from your position, *and* there was some protection from possible tank mishaps!" His second military battle ended when the Americans captured the seaport capital of a French protectorate in the Northwest called Tunis.

The afternoon after a hard fought battle, Americans won the prize. The people in the town of about 171,000 residents showered the soldiers with wine and flowers. The people were half French and half Italian. Speaking Italian with ease, Ernie found Italians did not want to fight Americans stating, "our hearts are not with the Germans. You blow up one tank of yours, you Americans come back with five tanks!" they exclaimed!

There was one particular road block when the Italian Army and the American Infantrymen were camped side by side. The orders were "don't shoot nobody unless attacked." No one did any shooting. Americans were getting food. The Italians didn't get any food. "Hey, Americano, I got wine. You got food. We trade you wine for food." The American Army Leaders were afraid to take their wine. "No deal!" The American Officers were wary of a chance that the wine could be poisoned! The next day the Germans took the Italian Army away. Ernie was always sad that happened. He often wondered what would have happened if the men exchanged food for wine and perhaps joined forces ...

Back to his chore of working with mines, Ernie found that the Germans had built three kinds of mines. They were the Teller I (a vehicular mine detonated by heavy pressure such as a tank rolling over it), Teller II (any part of mine might detonate by small amount of pressure) and Teller III (same as Teller II, except underneath the fuse was extremely tricky.) In warfare, mines were applied to a system of tunnels dug under a fortification ending in a chamber where explosives were programed to detonate at a chosen time or by a stimulous. Mines could be detonated by electrical impulse, magnetic proximity or by contact. Land mines with pressure sensors slightly below or above the ground were in wide use by the Germans. Antitank mines were rigged so that it took more pressure to cause them to explode. The second type of mine was called antipersonal. That kind of mine was also referred to as the ASS mine. The ASS mine had a shell within another shell causing an explosion spreading shrapnel 300 feet. It was necessary to dig around the mine to see if any fuses were on either side of the mine. Ernie stated, "War is to kill. Sometimes you would find two or three mines laid in layers on top of each other. Step on that mine, you activate the fuse. Puff, hit the ground! until it exploded as it spread over you if you were underneath." No completely safe way was known for removing land mines at that time. Mines not in the pathways were marked by red or white ribbons if thought to be alive. This was to warn others or to remove them if the Army became stationary. The British developed a mine sweeper for use on land. The apparatus was held three feet in front of a walking man. "It was not effective," according to Ernie, "if you hit a mine ahead, the mines went off behind."

Teller III mines had booby traps. A judgment call was made by one's Sergeant as to what to do. Blow up the mine or put a marker on it. The development of the mines is attributed to Edward Teller. Edward Teller, a scientist born in Hungary before the war, became a professor of physics at George Washington University in the United States. He became a naturalized citizen of the United States in 1941. He worked on atomic bomb research and development of use of thermonuclear devices. He was instrumental in making possible the first United States hydrogen bomb explosion.

When tanks were hit in World War II, the men were generally killed. The American tank's gun turret was stationary. If fired on from the back, you had to turn the tank all the way around to use the gun. The German tanks were equipped with guns that could rotate all the way around. Their tanks were riveted as well as welded. Made of stronger metal than the American tanks, the German tank was not as vulnerable as a death trap like the thin-skinned American Tank. When tanks came upon a mine field, men marched in front of them to clean a pathway with a mine detector. Ernie spent lots of time walking and cleaning up in front of tanks. While in this risky business, he met a person from his home town!

After Allies routed Rommel and were winning the war in Africa, Ernie and his company crossed the Mediterranean Sea once again arriving at the Island of Sicily. That campaign was over when his regiment arrived. Ernie talked it over with a Buddy. "Let's get all the rest we can get. If we are shelled let us continue sleeping." They dug a long narrow hole figuring "if they were down low a shell was not likely to go in it." Putting a tent over their heads his buddy said, "we'll not have to jump in a foxhole!" The men found a generator and some phone wires. They rigged up lights in their pup tent.

On May 11th, at 11 P.M. on the front line, fellows knowing not where, all guns were ordered to be fired at once! This was the call, "that the march for Rome was on!" From May 11th to June 4th the American Armies took Rome, Pisa and Lucca. The infantry marched straight up the center of Italy. Men were sometimes sent 'backward' on rotation.

Between Rome and Bologna, Ernie changed jobs from a marching soldier to a truck driver to get away from marching and mines. Then he discovered he was in a worse mess than before. While hauling dirt in a ten-wheeler, he could not hear the planes strafing. At least on the ground, he could hear! He had a lot of close calls.

Ernie's Major liked Italian cheese, bread and wine. Knowing the Italian American had no trouble with the Italian language, the Officer sent Ernie to find these diet delights. He gave Ernie his command car, money and a driver! It was the first time the young man experienced an irritable Captain saluting a command car carrying a Private! This made Ernie laugh.

Ernie's father had immigrated to the United States from the beautiful Italian City of Florence. The men were allowed rest camp in the Florence area. The relatives fed the young soldier from Sonoma "real good everytime he went to see them." Feigning a flat tire on his truck when he had no pass to do so, Ernest went to the relatives to eat because he found out what a great delight it was to be with them.

While in the service to build a road, after living in the same clothes for days in a bitter cold winter, these conditions made Ernie upset. In his way, in the middle of the road, was a British truck stuck in some mud. Since it was impossible to get around the offending truck, Ernie offered a wench and services to help take the vehicle out of the way. The offer was rudely refused. About this time an American Three Star General appeared in a Jeep with words, "Hey driver, pull over, git out of my way!" Ernie had no place to go. Without thinking, he replied, "You're no better than anyone else. Wait in line." Ernie knew he was in trouble. He heard the Officer's Jeep door open. The Officer jotted down the address of his truck on a piece of paper. Ernie knew that was all the Officer needed to turn in...

The British finally pulled themselves out of the hole. The ten-wheeler under Ernies expertise spun out of the way fast! He moved the vehicle so fast that mud was slung all over the three star General's Jeep! Looking out his rear view mirror, Ernie knew he was in deep trouble. A worried Ernie never heard from command about the incident...

Another cold dark night, Ernest was on guard duty near the front line. His primary duty was to make sure a huge 240 gun was secured from the enemy. The order again was "shoot, ask questions later." Climbing up a lonely hill "to see if there was anyone up there" it was the second time that Ernie felt the chill of being scared in war. All alone, what could he do if he met the enemy? It was another drizzly night... "Perfect night for murder," he thought. He went back down the hill. All of a sudden two figures were approaching... No one was supposed to be moving around from his camp. "I know this is it! Do I shoot or call out halt? !" He put his gun to his shoulder with the bayonet attached. Should he kill the approaching men? He wavered. Finally, he heard his own voice call out the words, "Halt! Who goes there?" It was the Officer of the Day and Sergeant at Arms. Ernie stated, "Take a left side and hands beside your heads. You know orders." Ernie dreams about this episode...

The day the Allies took Rome, Ernie worked all night on the mines. The day dawned bright and sunny and warm! Tanks were on the horizon as far as the eye could see. Italians were exclaiming, "You do something for the good of people!" The Citizens of Rome were hugging and kissing the boys while passing out wine and flowers celebrating their liberation.

After skirmishes at Florence, Ernest was sent back on rotation to the United States. When asked about rank, he stated, "Didn't want to send fellows in battle. Didn't want to be a Sergeant!" Promoted Corporal, he decided "the airforce did not know what to bomb anymore. That's why he was one of the early ones to come back home. He was one of few to come back home from the 19th! He received a big welcome with girls dancing on the boat.

When Ernest Magiantini became just plain citizen again, he lived in Sonoma. He resumed working at Mare Island Navy Yard where he had been employed before the draft. He and his brother opened a bakery on East Napa Street known as the Pioneer French Bakery. He is a proud Member of the Veterans of Foreign Wars, celebrating 50 years membership in Sonoma, Bear Flag Post 1943, the 16th District, wearing the 50 year pin. He also is a Member of the Disabled American Veterans Post 'Hap' Arnold, #62.

As to land in Africa near Oran and Tunisa, he recalls that at the time, the Coast was more modern than England. There were grapes and vegetables planted much like his beloved California. The people used two tractors plowing back and forth with steam and big discs planted wheat and hay. It was not sand Ernie had to endure but farm lands full of mines!

In Italy, the Sonoman who was first in line when the meal included spagetti, was called "Spagetti Bender." While fixing a road in Italy one night, his crew was delayed at a gravel pit. He was supposed to be over the one way road by 6 A.M. It was necessary to be out of the area as the Germans would shell the road at 6:30 each morning. Driving at full throttle the men in back yelled, "Our life is in your hands!" Another 10 wheeler truck was being driven at breakneck speed and force toward the men in Ernie's truck. The driver of the other vehicle screamed "Hey, Spagetti Bender, your life is in your own hands!" Ernie closed his eyes. He turned the steering wheel right, he turned it left! On each side was an eight foot drop! Shells were falling all around! His truck went right on through. "The Good Lord took care of both trucks..." he finished his words quietly... "that's when you believe!"

Glotzbach, Bob, Ed., *Childhood Memories of Glen Ellen*, Regeneration Resources, Pub., P. O. Box 181, Glen Ellen, California 95442, 1992. pps. 103.

Columbia University, *The New Illustrated Colombia Encyclopedia,* Columbia University Press, N. Y., 1975., pages reviewed 6689 and 6690.

The World at Arms, The Reader's Digest Illustrated History of World War II, Pub. by The Reader's Digest Association Lt., London, New York, Sydney, Montreal, Capetown, 479 pp., 1989. Pages reviewed 234, 235, 236.

William Frapwell

United States Infantry 1943 - 1946

William Frapwell, retired Sonoma Valley High School Teacher, born in Santa Cruz, California took basic training in Fort Benning, Georgia and at Paris, Texas before making his way through the routes of England and France to the Siegfried Line of Germany.

The 99th Division of which Bill was a part was the first Allied group to be allowed through Le Havre Port when it was opened up in France. Other than Le Harve, ports along the Belgium and French Coasts were considered too small to handle the enormous flow of troops and materials in the post-invasion build up. The important port of Le Havre had been put on the back burner by the invasion of Sicily. Use of artificial harbours which had been developed for the invasion continued until the Operation named Axehead was instituted to obtain and secure the Port of Le Harve. The 99th Division assigned to the First Army was the historic 'first' group of Allies to enter the port.

At this point in the war there were inadequate supplies to serve so many men. Gasoline was in short supply to support the many thrusts of the war. Patton was convinced that the fabled Siegfried Line would be an empty promise to end the war unless the Third Army was brought in and moved rapidly east. By the end of August the Third Army was camped outside the gates of Metz. After the Third Army was in position, then the 99th of the First Army in which Bill was a part, was added at California Road (Other names are used for this road.) The 106th of the 2nd Army was also moved into position for assault on Germany. These two new divisions were to help with the breakthrough of the German Fortified Line. Even though the men of the 99th were not under General Patton, he was influencial in their being where they were. Patton was once quoted as employing the 'rock soup' method of advancing an army. The men of the 99th were part of the ingredients for the German surrender of the War. They were part of Patton's recipe for Rock Soup which is described as follows:

It seemed a tramp went to a house and asked for some boiling water to make rock soup. The woman of the house was interested. She gave him the boiling water he requested and he put two polished stones, he held in his hand, in the water. He then asked if he might have some carrots and potatoes to flavor his rock soup with. Finally, he asked for and received a little meat. In Patton's pretext of masking ulterior design, he suggested, first you pretend, then reinforce the reconnaissance and finally you put on the attack - all depending upon the gasoline and ammunition you beg, borrow or divert to your troops.

Montgomery was disgusted! He complained about Patton to Eisenhower when the Third Army literally ran out of fuel in the autumn of 1944. Patton had reportedly diverted some supplies meant for other troops to his own. It was into this cauldron that Bill Frapwell was 'on line' in November 1944.

Men in Bill's 99th Division had no idea as to where they exactly were a great deal of the time. They were aware, that "on the North pivot were German Tank Divisions. They were facing East to Germany and a bastion of Germans were encamped on the South. His group was in a wedge between two enemy armies!" In a short time, after the "Bulge" breakthrough, their table of organization showed 187 was down to 57; many of these were killed or taken prisoner by the Germans. The company spent a great deal of time filling in the V gap. On VE Day the men were "releasing their own men from the German prison camps!" Bill remembers pontooning a river and staying for 90 days in the same area after the Battle of the Bulge. The soldiers were occasionally sent to small villages in Belgium "for rest and recreation." On one of those rest periods, the company worked cutting trees in the Andenner to be used as corduroy roads. Corduroy roads were formed from logs laid transversely usually over miry ground. The logs usually touched one another.

During a rest period in Belgium, Bill remembers being lodged in the back room of a little old house and keeping isolated. It was winter with lots of snow and mud. Bill and a small group of three decided they were ready for something besides rations. Of course, packages came in the mail. Bless Bill's Aunt Paula. He received tuna, olives, crackers. They always seemed to come at the right time and were an immediate hit with his buddies.

One of Bill's friends worked as a mail clerk. His friend sorted and organized the mail to reach the soldiers. When men were killed or captured, the food portion of their packages was not returned to the States with the personal items but was portioned out to Bill's group. The men reasoned "that the food was meant for nourishing the soldiers and it would probably be spoiled or ruined in return shipment anyway!" This food was considered as arriving from "Somebody's Aunt Matilda." Aunt Mitilda was therefore a regular donor and much admired. It was "Bless Aunt Mitilda" as "she was a great cook giving the men a break from rations."

While on the move after being in Belgium awhile, Bill's infantry division walked to the Rhine River area. "Never saw anything like Aachen, Germany," he stated, "it was absolute rubble!" After sweating over some hilly country the men found the landscape dropped off, sort of like plains. Looking over the land the men "saw towers of churches, five, six, seven steeples towering where they headed." The 99th was cleaning up territory. Very few German civilians were around. The men spent time digging up their own food. Bill's group of about eight was now independently moving around the landscape. They were officially called Runners. They ran messages back and forth to the Company from regimental officers. No one seemed to claim them. At nightime, they would end up in a German Village usually using an empty house or attic for protection from the weather.

In the game of hustling food, they discovered that Germans kept canned goods in the basement of houses. The men did not choose the canned food as often as other accoutrements, as they were wary of possible poisoning. In German attics there were large chimneys between which was usually found caches of naturally smoked meats. A smoke house was ingeniously built between the fireplace chimneys which added warmth to cure smoked meats.

Chickens were fair game to an army on the move. Bill was lucky to have a companion buddy from Tennessee. The man "was the fastest catcher of live chickens that you could imagine. He had the science of a true Tennessee Hillbilly to not only catch the chicken but he could wring its neck and then skin it!" The skinning of the chicken deleted the problem of feather picking! It was easy to prepare the poultry with two frying pans at the men's disposal and a case of margarine "liberated" from a car load of margarine on a freight train!

These Infantry 'Runners' usually had wine with their food. The Germans often stored grain in bins and often hid loaves of rye bread buried under the grain plus bottles of wine. Bill noted the men "found no whiskey or gin in German houses." He did not elaborate on the possibility of beer. This group of eight men usually carried a couple of cases of wine with them in a liberated trailer attached to a message center Jeep. It was noted while mopping up the town Geisen, one of the Officers wanted some wine.

The lowly Privates with food and the ability to fry chickens had some wine to give to their superior.

As an aside, Bill said, "If the men wanted fish, a half block of dynamite thrown in a stream would induce shock waves that killed fish and this caused them to surface as additional nutritional supplement."

Bill was one of the first men to cross the Remagen Bridge. The regiment had finally reached the Rhine. They were North of Cologne in the Cologne Plains. Men were in dire need of a bath. They trucked down to the hills above Remagen Bridge. It was dark. They knew not where they were headed. When they reached the bridgehead, they "ran like hell." It was the first time they had seen a German Jet. The jets were a revelation and German Pilots were trying to bomb the bridge and men. There were big holes on the bridge. The crossing was described as " a very long bridge. It was a railroad bridge." The men of the 99th Division made up part of the first bridgehead across the Rhine River. Their armour was only a short distance across the bridge when the bombing was taking place from the German Jets. The Infantry group of which Bill was a part was told "to cross the bridge and reassemble at the right of it, heading toward the south of Germany."

During occupation, Bill's immediate circle of buddies occupied a tiny village called Margotshocheim. They billeted in the school building of a Catholic Church. Very few men were known to be in the area. A male custodian of the church was very, very old.

Bill also enjoyed the little town, Wurzburg in Bavaria. It was described as a "beautiful Gothic town." There was a fortress up on the hill near Marianberg with exceptionally beautiful stone work. The Bishop of Bavaria had a palace in Wurtzburg. Division staff moved into the palace. The palace was a backdrop for USO shows. Bob Hope was an entertainer at this place. An interesting song heard by the troops was "Lily of Picadilli." Bill also heard this song in camp in England while waiting for embarcation back to the States. When Bill returned to the United States and was back at California State in 1946, he was walking along when he heard two girls singing "Lily of Picadilli." His baritone voice joined in the music much to the embarrassment of the girls...

Another musical rememberance enjoyed by Bill, who now sings in a church choir and with the Silver Foxes of Sonoma, California (a double male quartette of World War II patriots) was that of hearing the organ at Salisbury, England. He noted, everyday at noon in Salisbury, everything stopped for a short prayer followed by The Lord's Prayer. He happened along at one time to experience this tradition.

Another enjoyable adventure in the 'diary of Bill's mind' while in Germany was staying at a beautiful hunting lodge owned by a German named Flesh. The man was apparently a wealthy dairy owner. The milk was placed in cans. Then, put into huge cement troughs of cold water, it was swirled around the cans making the milk cool. Mr Flesh. was purported to have an office in Amsterdam and property in Florida of the United States. His German property was restored like a castle appearing very luxurious. The men were given certain limits that were "off" but that didn't mean much. This was where they also found it was enjoyable to drink fresh milk! They helped themselves to milk and cream all the time.

While back on the subject of food, it was noted by Bill, "that armies truly lived on their stomachs." The subject of chocolate bars being washed down by the milk was considered delightful! D bars of chocolate found in the issued rations were from the Companies of Hershey, Cadbury, Girardelli and Nestles. A certain dried fruit bar found in the C Rations was totally wasted by lots of soldiers but Bill loved it. From four feet of snow, the lemonade mix crammed into the rations made good snow cones.

In the German's barn belonging to Mr. Flesh was a real California type convertible! It was a bright yellow Buick! The Buick was converted to burn charcoal instead of gasoline. It was noted to be in absolute pristine condition.

Bill was impressed at how the German village people were so resourceful with left over materials and how they were so 'before their time' in regard to recycling. Little old ladies carried bags of animal droppings from concrete areas to their garden plots. Each householder in Germany had a garden. From the use of the fertilizer, it was noted that the citizens had great strawberries, cherries and rhubarb "as big as a man's arm." Rhubarb was 'corded' in bundles looking much like a cord of wood. The men were partakers of the wonderful fruit and were in awe of the very clean premises, particularly in Germany.

Eventually, men of the 99th were sent back to England for a homeward bound trip. First however, they went to Wales on a train with 300 other troops. Because of lack of space in the troop ship, the seventy five men of the 99th were returned back by train to the former temporary shelters in South Fry. In that camp, they were treated with German and Italian Prisoner of War cooking. Three weeks later they retraced their steps to Wales. The men were loaded on an old tramp steamer named the Jeremiah O'Brien for the trip home. The travelers were caught in a trans-Atlantic storm on the second day out that continued until the day before they sighted the New York harbor with its welcoming Statue of Liberty. During the storm, even the lashed down refrigerator tipped over and all the food was spoiled. At that point, the returning soldiers were invited to partake of all the ice cream they wanted. Ice cream was the only food available since it was in the permanent refrigerator on the ship. However, with seasickness being prevalent and with the continued rocking and rolling, it was not a big ice cream party!

Bill ends his remembrances with a statement: "battles are past and over with. I had a lot of line-time and our group experienced a lot of casualties. I prefer to remember the adventures of the landscape and the joy of finding food. I came home with no scratches."

James P. Duchscherer

United States Army, 1941 - 1946

James Duchscherer, drafted into the Army in 1941 spent the first whole year of army life giving tests to Service inductees at Camp Upton Long Island Reception Center. Tests were to classify men on their level of intelligence. Educational opportunies were diverse in the United States at that time. Basing a mans worth on intelligence tests which were standardized by higher educational opportunites classified many inductees as illiterate. Class V Tests (Mechanical Aptitude tests) for all men were particularly applicable when IQ tests were not a fair criterion or standard of judgment.

After the year of test giving came Pearl Harbor. "Heck," Jim thought, "this war is going to go on a while." After all those tests, James decided he would apply for OCS and attended Officer Engineer School located at Fort Belvoir, Virginia. In three months, he was one of those 90 day Wonders being commissioned a Second Lieutenant in the Corps of Engineers.

From a form letter signed by Dwight W. Eisenhower, Lieutenant James Duchscherer was notified "the eyes of the world are upon you. You will bring about the elimination of Nazi tyranny over the oppressed peoples of Europe. I have full confidence in your courage, devotion to duty and skill in battle." From his Colonel, Frank A. Pettit, Jim received a picture of a stern looking likeness with words, "The officers all think I am a son-of-a-bitch.... but they have to do what I tell them."......

Lieutenant James Duchscherer was assigned to a Black Regiment. At first all the Officers were White but later they did have some Black Officers. "Moving to Eastover Camp near Andover, Hampshire on 9th April, 1944, the men were in the center of the greatest staging area ever known. Everywhere, there were airstrips, row upon row of fighter planes, mile long ammunition dumps, tented camps and endless storage areas. The men of the 365th had work assignments of constructing air strip facilities, building temporary camps for paratroopers and conversion of hutted tents to general hospitals. Everyone participated in a training day at least one day per week in skills on Bailey bridge construction, design of timber trestle bridges, hasty bridge repair, camouflage, mines, and construction of roads, ditches and drainage structures and the art of road maintenance under heavy traffic conditions. The latter was to be especially useful when the regiment was given the task of maintaining the famed Red Ball Highway in France.

Morale was high. There was no doubt about success of the long awaited "Second Front." It meant the war would end and men could return home. While waiting for the invasion, the soldiers took a few interesting excursions to nearby cathedral towns of Salisbury, Winchester and to famous Stonehenge.

One day Joe Louis, world champ boxer came for lunch and that night he put on an exhibition bout in Andover attended by one third of the regiment.

In May, the regiment was alerted for overseas movement. At that time the drivers were taught to waterproof their vehicles which were tested in deep water. Anticipation dragged out. While waiting, one of the favorite radio programs tuned in by the troops was a German program entitled "When D-Day Calls." The station played a song by that name which ended with "We are waiting for you!" Many American songs were played and a man and a girl told Jewish jokes. Most of the program was corny. For example, they said they would be "sending Eisenhower a pair of woolen socks...for his cold feet!"

The regiment to which Jim was assigned was a "general service regiment." Duties encompassed all kinds of construction, bridge repair, road construction and repair, quarry operation, mine clearing and whatever else in labor that came along. Hundreds of recruits from reception centers in Georgia, Louisiana, Mississippi and Alabama had filled the 1800 quota of Black men. Other types of engineer units were added on the Continent including construction battalions, dump truck companies, forestry companies, heavy ship companies, maintenance companies, special brigades, utility detachments, water supply companies and similar specialized groups. In all, 34 general service regiments were assigned to the ADSEC Engineer Section on the Continent at one time or another.

Among the accomplishments between D-Day and VE-Day by this regiment were building vehicular and railroad bridges, construction of concrete slabs for tents for general hospitals, creating and installing power line poles, installing water systems, repairing wharves at Cherbourg and along beaches, POL installations for storage and transmission of gasoline and diesel for both aviation and motor transport, repair and maintenance of roads and highways, putting out fires, removing mines, drilling wells, mining coal, running printing presses and operating map depots.

James was Duty Officer at the Regimental Headquarters in Andover on the night of June 5th. When he retired to a cot after the evening's work was completed, he could hardly sleep. The roar of hundreds of overhead planes towing gliders with paratroopers caused his bed to vibrate. Thoughts were fairly certain that "D-Day would be on the morrow." Turning on the radio the next day, the only announcement was that of a German claim of Allied Landings. Hearing so many planes the night before, Jim believed the German broadcast and began his morning newspaper called "News Flashes." The radio finally interrupted with promise of "an important announcement in 13 minutes." While waiting for this major announcement the broadcaster proceeded by alerting all occupied countries: "Now we are going to alert the people of Norway...." now the people of Denmark....." It was one of the most thrilling and emotional moments Jim ever experienced. In the background the call to the people of those countries told of landings. The special announcement was Eisenhower's message to the occupied countries followed by speeches by the Prime Ministers of Holland, Belgium and other countries including King Haakon of Norway. All day Jim's telephone rang for calls from people hungry for news. It was one of Jim's main functions to spread the news. He put out the newspaper "News Flashes" every day. By afternoon, he had a map of France on the wall with the English Channel traced upon it. He also completed a special second newspaper that evening. King George VI of England spoke. Jim wrote stories from eyewitness accounts made by Pilots who had returned from France. The reaction of the Officers was one of great relief that D-Day had come.

One of the earliest pictures showing the ruin of war which was reproduced in Jim's newspaper was that of the Town of Isigny, France. It was referred to "as having taken a meat grinder treatment by Allied and later by German shells." It had been bombed by Allied warship salvos as well as by land guns. By the tenth of June bulldozers were clearing roads through great heaps of broken masonry and timbers in Isigny.

Jim was also in charge of the regiment's PX. He was responsible for terminating arrangements for merchandise before leaving England. One job was to return casks and equipment loaned to them by a brewery. While at camp, the PX served typically warm and non-carbonated beer. How to draw a canteen cupful of warm beer from a barrel and other tricks of the trade had been taught servers in a one day session at the brewery. Jim called it, "sending them to bartenders' school" and it was noted, "the chosen few who went to that school were very apt pupils!"

A lot of equipment had to be packed and Jim worked from reveille to retreat many days running. The soldiers closed down messhalls, abandoned sleeping quarters in tents and slept in pup tents. They dined on C-rations and tried to simulate field conditons. Trucks were loaded with everything not carried on the backs of the men.

On June 24th the men of the 365th Regiment were on six hour alert. Galvanized into action on the morning of June 27th, the troops began movement by rail and motor convoy toward the ports on the southern coast of England. This was perhaps the greatest mass movement over water of all time as the movement of troops was at its height. There was so much troop movement taking place, it took over 24 hours for the first units to reach the Channel which was but a few miles from Andover. Trains were shunted upon sidings and left as if forgotten in backwater yards. Truck convoys were similarly slow. Jim reasoned "he was just one of 3 1/2 million men who embarked from that point in World War II."

From the Liberty Ship transport crossing on June 30th which was "as peaceful as a pleasure cruise," they could make out Utah Beach studded with landing craft of all kinds including LCVS, LCTS. Slightly short of dry land Jim received his wish of having to wade through water the last few yards. As soon as the front end of the craft was lowered, the men rushed pell-mell for higher ground hoping to meet someone to tell them where they were going to next.

Moving inland from Utah Beach the men saw towns that were destroyed. They had seen printed pictures and newsreels of these very places! Coming to a tiny village called Huberville, they found a sign indicating "365th Engineers" and pulled into a small orchard bordered with hedgerows. Having no bedroll, not inclined to dig a foxhole late at night and without a blanket (these items being left behind and being shipped separately) Jim slept in the back seat of the command car. By piling gas masks and musette bags on the floor and stretching out as best he could on top of the gear, he simply was too exhausted to worry over the brilliant flashes and resounding booms from a neighboring anti-aircraft unit.

The size of the 365th grew every day as more men and equipment arrived. The men spent one week at the hedgerow location with no work assignments. Headquarters disbursed a few trucks around the field and used them for offices. On July 4th, Jim removed his truck from the Motor Pool and had a sort of office. He hung an American Flag from a tree. It did not take long for some enterprising Officers to go to Cherbourg and return with several truckloads of German furniture and equipment. Desks and folding tables were put right on the ground and used. One useful heavy iron grill became a grate for fire on which water and food was heated. All Jim got for his section was a wire wastebasket. Jim had an iron tea kettle from England which was used to heat water for coffee and for soup from tablets sent from home. The hot water was good for shaving and washing as well. He also had a large kettle and a frying pan and was complimented by staff officers that he had had the foresight to include these items in his "organizational equipment." Their food was called "10 in 1 Rations" which meant food for 10 men for one day. Groups of Officers teamed up to share one of these cartons which had the makings of various meals in small packages, cans and boxes. Cigarettes and lifesavers were in the packages. The Officers acquired a bottle or two of "Calvados" from a local farmer who distilled it from his own apples. It was potent stuff and not very pleasant to drink unless mixed with lemonade mix. Once in awhile the men splashed some of it onto the fire. Calvados was known to have been used to fill cigarette lighters.

Jim, who in civilian life was a food buff, carried his knowledge of food presentation learned at the

Statler Hotels in the United States with him. His Commanding Officer, Pettit was also a food connoisseur. From the very rudimentary conditions in the hedgerows to the fine dining rooms that the Officers would share as they made their journey across France, the two Officers would especially embellish the dinner meal. When there were French table cloths or beautiful dishes available they were used within beautiful old homes. A potpourri of different foods were purchased or bartered from the local citizenry.

Moving after most of the equipment arrived on the 6th of July, Jim was still missing his bedroll. Regimental headquarters was established in an ancient unoccupied farm house. In Jim's book *At War with the 365th, An Unorthodox View of World War II in France*, from which this narrative of his life in the service has been gleaned, Jim took a casual approach to the life and times. Without the bedroll, borrowing five blankets to keep warm, he curled up on a table top for sleeping. Other nights it was back in the command car! Appropriate for Jim at the time was a stanza from a ranger ballad by James Altieri published in Life Magazine of July 31, 1944.

> "With icy clothes, they slept in mud and water in their foxholes.
>
> More times than not, what sleep they got, It was without their bedrolls."

The men of the 365th were seldom out of sound of artillery fire which was described as as a steady ominous rumble similar to a thunderstorm brewing in the distance. Not to be outdone by warfare, they also endured a thunderous lightning storm-filled night sent from the Heavens.

Along with being Information and Education officer as well as Exchange Officer running a PX for 1800 men, Jim was ordered to also be Police and Prison Officer. This was in addition to putting out his newspaper, going into large cities at depots to get items for the PX, decorating the area of his workspace, teaching typewriting and shorthand skills, providing hundreds of books as a library source (many on the historical and beautiful cities they were near) and keeping his hand in creative cookery with presentation of the food for the evening meal. He argued hard and long to be relieved of the prisoner detail to no avail. The prisoners were to serve hard labor sentences requiring them to work every day. Jim assigned them jobs such as picking up debris, digging holes, and picking up cigarette butts. The prisoners were guarded by the regimental guard detail.

With all of these duties, Jim continued to set up his area of expertise, his classes, his books, a pot of geraniums, poppies, or Christmas Tree while living in sequences of being in lovely old homes, totally hopeless dwellings, old barns or in beautiful mansions. He hung his maps of the world, hauled out his typewriter equipment, cleaned out dirty places including use of doses of delice powder and set up book cases. He supervised installation of a 5 KW generator, framed bad walls with 'tomato-red' draperies which had been purchased from a chapel in Leicester, embellished another wall with a nine foot map showing every road and field of the area. This map was studied by men constantly. When Jim decorated the offices and areas he worked in, the men were always surprised and very appreciative.

It seemed odd that "while we were close enough to know what was happening and heard the gunfire all the time, that we had to pick up the news for the *News Flashes* paper that was issued every morning," according to Jim, "from the London Radio."

A group of Black war correspondents visited the 369th one day and they wrote about meeting such a progressive Commander, Colonel Frank Pettit. Jim says "he no doubt won a few points from the Colonel at the time." The news article written by Rudolph Dunbar, ANP War Correspondent stated "since being posted on the western front, I've never met a more progressive Commander than Col. Frank Pettit.....He is a West Pointer and is now commanding a Colored Engineer General Service Regiment just behind the German line. Colonel Pettit believes that mind, matter and application must be part and parcel of the Negro whether he may be working in a stone quarry or on a battery directing a fire mission with a 155 mm. Howitzer." The correspondent gave the Colonel credit for the library, the periodicals, the decorated atmosphere and general layout of the library, the evening classes and other subjects under the direction of Lt. James P. Duchscherer of Buffalo N.Y. who is a graduate of Cornell University."

Jim also took French lessons from a fifty year old lady he met at a local Civil Affairs Office in Trevieres. Seven Officers went to her home twice a week to talk and learn French. They learned much about life in France under the Germans. Her skirt was made of "ersatz" (wood fiber), the blouse was prewar, her shoes were paper (do not last at all). She had a sweater which she had unraveled and reknitted three times. It was full of knots on the inside. She had no stockings. She brought out a month's rations. The rations included about 30 coffee beans which she would stretch by adding roasted oats, barley or anything similar. There was one cup of sugar. Salt was made from gray lumps like asbestos, which you put in water and boiled it off to get pure salt. The men took the teacher, coffee, sugar, jam and a few oranges. "She seemed to think the milennium had arrived!" Mme. Delfoe was quite a linguist and was more than qualified for her full-time position as interpreter in the Civil Affairs Office.

Detail after detail of towns, room arrangements of mansions occupied by the Officers and the educational setup of Jim's work have been described to the nnth degree in Jim's book. The reason he could remember all the room arrangements was that he had drawn floor plans in his letters to his Mother. Jim's delights and excursions into the great cities of Brussels, Antwerp and Paris are chronicled. He visited the famous museums, the cathedrals, the stores. Most of his visits were for the PX with a few 'hurried hours' to see the historical, the enjoyable... He even planned ahead, ordering PX gifts in July for December.

When December did arrive he was questioned by his Commanding Officer. COLONEL PETTIT: "Lt. Duchscherer, do you know what I would like for Christmas?" Lt. DUCHSCHERER, "No Sir." COLONEL PETTIT: "Well, I would like to have a round pie. I do not like those pies or cobblers that they make in those square pans. I understand that you can buy ROUND pie tins in Namur. I would like you to go up there tomorrow and buy some so that we can have some round pies for Christmas." Lt. DUCHSCHERER: "Yes Sir."

Uncertain of the military operation, Jim set forth from their HQ., South of Bastogne on December 22nd with a driver in a Jeep headed for Namur. Holding his loaded carbine in his lap, he thought that this was the first time it was necessary. Assured by the Colonel and others he would not be in any danger, since he would be going west and north away from the fighting, and with words that "surely the bulge would be truncated and weakened," he headed into Belgium. Jim remembered "he and the driver were both scared silly all the way."

The two men had heard tales of Germans in GI clothing ambushing Americans, particularly those traveling in a single Jeep as these two men were. They also feared Americans might mistake them for Germans masquerading in American uniforms. Somewhere in a stretch of road toward Dinant, Belgium, they were stopped by a small group of men in American uniforms. These men sprung at the two travellers from a cluster of rocks. Jim surmised "they were probably as frightened as Jim and his driver were." Jim was asked the password. The two men knew the password but that did not satisfy the group standing on both sides of the Jeep. "Who won the World Series in 1943? Who is Orphan Annie?" After replying satisfactorily, Jim guessed they realized that his Black driver was an unlikely German and allowed the two to proceed.

From Dinant, Lt. Duchscherer and his driver continued along the road toward Namur. As they drove along, they wondered why every town or village had gun turrets on tanks pointed at them from around corners of buildings! and why the shoulder of the road was crowded with a steady stream of local inhabitants fleeing in their direction from SOMETHING! Families were pushing wheelbarrows, baby buggies and all kinds of carts loaded with household belongings. Livestock, children and pets were looking for some safer places in the direction from which the men had come.

Stopping at the command post in Namur, Jim requested information from a Colonel who escorted him behind a blanket hanging from the ceiling. Behind the blanket was a large scale map of the area. It seemed that Jim was the only source of information the Colonel had received that day and his observations were important. The Colonel suggested to Jim to complete his mission quickly and return home as soon as possible, if he wanted a chance of making it!

On the main street of the City of Namur, Jim located a store similar to a United States type Woolworth store. The bewildering contrast to realities outside was that inside the store there were artificial Christmas trees, red wreaths, tinsel and all the trappings of Christmas with a loudspeaker blaring out a Bing Crosby version of "Silent Night." Taking no time at all "to dawdle," he bought those ROUND PIE TINS as well as some other cooking paraphernalia and a few sundries.

By the time the teakettle with a whistle, some dippers and large aluminum kettles were loaded up with the ROUND PIE TINS in the back of the Jeep, it was getting late in the afternoon with darkness descending. Missing a turn in the dark and after many miles, Jim and his driver found themselves on a lonely deserted road. It seemed they were going due east directly toward the enemy spearheads.

"Once, upon entering a town, we came upon what must have been an armored division quietly waiting in the town square. Tanks, other vehicles and thousands of men were packed together," Jim said. "We blithly skirted them and kept on going." It was after this "that we began to realize that we were in 'no man's land,' ahead of the defending Americans and also ahead of the advancing Germans!"

Several times the two adventurers lost valuable time trying roads heading south, only to have the road end in a barnyard or gravel pit several miles from the road being traveled. After several false attempts to get out of Belgium, they finally made it! Feeling quite safe they headed in the dark with only blackout lights showing. Suddenly, they were stopped by a rag-tag bunch of individuals all brandishing weapons. Despite a language barrier, the men determined that they had met a group of French underground forces who suspected the two of being "some of those English speaking Germans in GI clothing whom they had heard about that were driving around in American Jeeps." By relaxing, the group on the road finally let Jim and his driver go.

The driver and Jim were so worn out from their hair-raising experience they were too exhausted to relate the story of their accomplished mission of obtaining ROUND PIE TINS for Colonel Pettit! The next morning Lt. Duchscherer learned that during the night, German Fifth Army Panzer Forces had occupied part of the territory through which they had driven.

After many hectic problems ranging from the company bugler accidentally killing himself while examining a German pistol, to receiving three medical shots a piece for typhus, typhoid and typhus, it was decreed that the regiment was moving before Christmas. Pulling out about noon of Christmas Eve with all the Christmas trappings packed, they arrived in the late afternoon and were guided to the magnificent CHATEAU MARBEAUMONT. Spirits immediately soared as the officers entered the great halls of the Chateau.

Jim, in the chronicles of his book described every area and home he had ever been privy to, but none like the Chateau Marbeaumont which was located in Bar Le Duc on the River Marne. He was overawed by the grandeur of the large rooms. His officer's third floor room was made cosy with a huge fire in the fireplace. Since it was Christmas Eve, a few friends shared a bottle of scotch, a can of lobster, a bottle of olives and some fruitcake. Since Jim had decorated three Christmas trees and set one outside the door, it was no surprise that they were suddenly shaken by sounds of gunfire from a German plane. There were so many windows in the place that blackout discipline was not perfected. On Christmas Day, after hors d'oeuvres, the Officers and men went to dinner in the great dining hall where a real Yule log blazed in the fireplace and red candles burned in clusters on the long table covered in a French tablecloth. Somehow the rations had come along with turkey, dressing and cranberry sauce. Jim did not remember what happened to the ROUND PIE TINS or if they had REAL PIE.

During dinner Christmas carols were played by "Skipper" Davis on the grand piano. The chateau was descibed as a palace including a grand entrance with steps, columns, canopies and light fixtures leading to a central rotunda. A colonnaded balcony on the second floor had a great dome over many rooms as well as the balcony. Rooms were compared as "grand as any Hollywood set ever was." Fifteen foot ceilings had double or sliding doors connecting all rooms with the court and with each other. Each room had a mammoth marble fireplace. Tall windows were framed in heavy rich red and gold satin draperies. Mirrors were everywhere and ceilings painted with clouds and cherubs embellished with crystal chandeliers. Sideboards, desks, tables all matching were built in the woodwork of each room. The concert grand piano was green and gold, There was a pool table and many leather high-backed chairs, each one like a throne. There was a telephone in each room with a buzzer system. Over beds were gold fixtures. Each room had adjoining dressing rooms with huge marble washbowls and tiled baths replete with iris designs around the walls matching the blue flowered porcelain. Parquet floors, red satin walls, an elevator, several dumbwaiters from basement to fourth floor and a tower containing a large clock with a carillon of 30 bells summarized a few more 'accouterments'.

The soldiers took great care of the house. They had no idea that they would stay there two months. From an envelope found in a drawer, the name of the dignitary in residence on May 11, 1938 was Monsieur Varin Bernier who received a letter from Prime Minister Neville Chamberlain at 10 Downing Street.

Jim's V-E day experience was also "a never to be forgotten day." With other Officers, he was present in Brussels, Antwerp and Mons all on the same day. Coins were pelted at the men in jubilation. Flags flew. People were dressed in their best clothes just promenading down the streets. The Officers were embarrassed to be treated like conquering heroes. Wildly cheering British and Canadian soldiers were in trucks tearing about the city of Antwerp. Having two ice cream sundaes in one afternoon was a treat. When it was dark the cities had their lights on again! Staring at neon lights and floodlighted buildings was exciting. All kinds of people jumped upon the Jeep's running board to shake hands. Amazingly, the celebration included fireworks of skyrockets that dived into the street among the crowds and cars. These seemed more dangerous than anything Jim had seen close to the front line. At the end of the day the British played *"Pomp and Circumstance"* finishing a program of music with *"The Hallelujah Chorus"* by Handel.

Receiving orders to go to Paris to return business equipment and make other business stops, as the men would soon be going back to the United States, Jim and another officer stopped at a bar not far from the Opera. An obvious prostitute amused the men with smiles and attempts to converse with them. She pointed to the other Officer, then at Bill's hair and said, "Him old, one bar, You young, two bars." Bill out of competition, treated the affair as a big joke laughing uproariously and not coming to Jim's rescue. When Jim refused her invitation for a trip upstairs, she suddenly reached over, grabbed his overseas cap and thrust it deep into her bosom. Efforts to retrieve the cap were unsuccessful. An Officer on the street without a head covering was unthinkable! The woman danced about waving the cap and then sequestering it out of sight eventually dashing up a stairway. Jim followed her up two flights of stairs, shot his right arm into her plunging neckline and grasped his property making a hasty descent to the street. After much laughter the men finished off the day with a little sight seeing followed by a sumptuous dinner and wines costing the two men about $170. American to cover the bills! They tumbled into bed with fuzzy heads knowing they had really experienced Paris!

A few days later Jim shook the mud and dust of LeHavre from his feet, boarded the victory ship, the Marine Angel for an eight day trip to New York.

After being a weekender in Sonoma, California in the sixties, Jim and his lovely wife 'Gerry' moved to the area in 1977. Jim and Gerry can usually be found at the Depot Museum where he was recently President of the Sonoma Valley Historical Society. (This editor served under him as Editor of the *Sonoma Valley Notes* the Society's newspaper.)

Jim and Gerry were enthusiastic travelers back to Utah Beach in 1994 for the 50th Aniversary of D-Day. He brought back a small bottle of Calvados especially brewed for souvenirs. They also brought back many thankful memories of rebuilt towns and beautifully kept graveyards. Sitting in the bleechers watching the pomp and ceremony of Presidents including his own, the Queen of England, Prime Ministers and especially meeting other returning Veterans was a great thrill. Watching other young men, now members of the United States Army, Navy, Marines and Airforce brought back memories of the World War II events. During Jim's second coming upon Utah Beach, he fell down on the sand arriving home with a wounded shoulder in a sling!

Duchscherer, James P., *At War with the 365th, An Unorthodox View of World War II in France*. Self-published. 1993. 233 pp.

Benjamin C. Jarvis

United States Navy, 1935 - 1968

Captain B. C. Jarvis retired to Sonoma Coastal Range Mountains with a view of the waters near Mare Island of the East Bay region of California. In his family room are beautiful mementos of a life spent as United States Navy Commissioned Officer involved in fourteen war patrols aboard four different submarines in the Western and South Pacific. Except for one assignment, Ben describes the patrols as "hair-raisers."

Calling forth memories of events, Ben's war stories include that of being shot at by two American Men-of-War. Submarines that he was assigned to were hit and bombed by Japanese war machines and planes. The Nautilus was run aground while running guns for MacArthur and attacked a task force including "Yomato" the largest battleship the Japanese owned.

From the Java Sea, Bergall was on a mission to the South China Sea Coast at the entrance to the Gulf of Siam. Ben was aboard as prospective commanding officer. Carrying a load of mines aft, Bergall was ordered to "go to the Royalist Bank and lay a mine field." Water in the seas in that part of the earth is very shallow, only 80 to 100 feet or less in depth. A submarine had to remain on surface killing time until darkness in order to lay mines. While on this particular mission, suddenly, there was an overriding sound of a radio transmission being broadcast by the Japanese. Information went to the C.O. "We have a Japanese ship very close with a lot of power." Men set additional lookouts and manned the high periscope. Nineteen feet above the "sheers" (the mast or tower housing the periscope and radar) men could see a faint smoky haze to the Southeast. In order to see more area, the commanding officer ordered the periscope to search ahead of the hazy smoke that marked position of the enemy ship. Ben made out a vertical stick. This was the Topmast of a Japanese warship. From bearings a course was obtained and it was decided to take the normal approach course as the shortest distance, that of taking a collision pursuit!

Water depth became shallower and shallower. The American Submarine would not be able to dive. It took 49 feet of water just to cover the periscope when a submarine went below surface. Ben knew they'd get by. He had experienced as many surface attacks during the war as periscope attacks. He figured the range. When the smoke appeared the enemy ship was 37,000 yards away. Then it was at 27,000 yards! Radar had registered the enemy vessel when it was about six miles away. With high powered glasses and with concentration on the target, the identification crew using their catalogue of features a ship is made of, matched booms, guns and bow... By comparing the Bridge structure and stacks as being larger than those of a destroyer, they were able to identify the warship ahead as, "one of the larger Japanese warships afloat in South East Asia!"

Ben recalled "It was a flat calm night. The sun had gone down. The Mast stood out from the Superstructure. The surface of the ocean was like plate glass. Moon and planets often leave streaks of light in the water. The waters were mirror beautiful... even the stars left streaks in the water that night."

The ship was definitely identified as a Tone Class Heavy Cruiser, Myoko. It had a second ship as escort which could barely be discerned in the haze and smoke. The second ship was identified as a similar class heavy cruiser.

With throttles wide open, all ballast tanks blown dry and all four engines full ahead, Bergall plowed to within 3,000 yards, firing six torpedos at eight second intervals. The submarine had had a run of from 32,000 to 35,000 yards. The first torpedo hit the enemy ship between the Aft end of the Bridge and the Stern. The second hit at midship went into the Engineer spaces. The first shot got a pretty good explosion tearing into the Magazines. The man-of-war Myoko blew in two and Ben watched a part of the ship sink. The enemy ship was on fire. Smoke columns 90 to 100 feet wide at the base and 600 to 800 feet high became a spectacular mushroom cloud not unlike a nuclear explosion. Ammunition exploded like rockets. The bottom of the ship was engulfed in red flames. The man of war was dead in the water!

After the torpedos, the submarine Bergall made a hard left turn to get out of harms way. While reloading with one torpedo in tube, two sticking out, Ben observed salvos heading toward the American sub. Having been shot at on surface before, Ben told the Captain, "that's gun fire." The Captain said, "No it's not!" The salvo arrived. Two eight inch shells caused a miss and a hit. A couple of high pressure air lines ruptured. The Port side of the forward torpedo room was hit! The loading hatch was torn out. A big jagged hole caused tremendous damage including part of the pressure hull. Several electrical lines were sheared along with water and hydraulic oil lines being cut.

During the attack a member of the crew was sitting in the small water-tight door of the forward torpedo room. The door was one of those squeeze-through-type-openings. A piece of shrapnel sheared off going between the man and door. The shrapnel became a splinter 10 inches long by 2 1/2" wide. It looked like it shaped itself to a needle point and was so hot! Traveling into the Forward Battery passageway, it ended in the Captain's cabin on the floor burning the only carpet in the submarine. It burned all the way through the underlayment to the steel beneath.

A Lieutenant five years junior to Ben stood next to him. He was one of the Captain's people. The Captain was Johnnie Hyde. "Captain, we have been hit." (The Captain was a short man needing a step stool to even look over the Bridge wind screen.) "Step up here, and look! See smoke and steam!" Water lines had been severed by the concentrated fire. The salvo caused five or six fires to dance around in the Torpedo room. Electric cables were severed. "I don't see anything!" the Captain replied. "Step on this platform!" By now a three by four foot hole had been knocked in the pressure hull. There were many more fires caused by electrical shorts.

Rather than easing around, the stern of the submarine was directed toward the target. The ship received two more salvos on Starboard side. A salvo was described by Ben "as a number of pieces of artillery in succession as a hostile broadside." Broadside meant "directly in the side of." One hundred fifty yards ahead, 25 yards off track, one of the salvos was directed Port side the Bergall. One shell hit abreast of the Bow and the other abreast the Bridge. The sea was hit 50 feet off the ship causing a spray of water 70 to 125 feet high. The water sprayed on Bridge. After that third salvo, no more armipotence was directed toward Bergall.

Bergall was left depleted. It could not dive with a hole in its side. It would have to hold a position at water line "get away full speed!" How was the crew to live? All water was forced out of Fore and Aft tanks of the sub; the submarine flooded so slowly....

Heading toward the Karimata Strait the crew had fires under control in less than an hour. The lube oil leaks were stopped. Decisions were hard to settle with consultations between Officers and Crew. Was the ship to run getting far enough into Java Sea to land? Maybe the men would end up in the hands of friendly guerrillas... or what was in store for the ship from the enemy?

There were long discussions of whether to transmit the submarine problems. The Karimata Strait was fairly wide from land to land but extremely shallow. Any message transmitted would give position of the ship to the enemy. The Captain prevailed to send a message with lead words "Busted Bergall!" The men were pretty well convinced that none of them would make it back to port. They were told that Bergall was unable to dive and so it would make a run for distance until daylight. There was a matter of classified equipment to dispose of. There were records, code books, radar, and sonar devices which had to be eliminated from possible enemy capture. Selectively, the transmitter to send messages was destroyed, the radio to receive messages retained.

Ben felt the officers could bring the ship back. It was a very new submarine having been commissioned on 12 June 1944. Eight Officers were convinced they could make a run for it. Eight Officers alone would stay with the ship. The Captain did not want to ditch the submarine. The men did save the surface radar; they destroyed the sonar, aircraft and periscope radar, then burned all classified material. The sub was smoked up, one hell of a mess!

About 6 1/2 hours after the transmission of Bergall's distress call, the Submarine Task Force Commander answered. The Admiral directed Bergall "to rendezvous with Angler at North Natoena Island. Transfer all officers and men. Scuttle Bergall." The American Submarine Angler approached the crew of Bergall. Ben had been on Angler as Relief Commanding Officer before being assigned to the present submarine.

The crew of Bergall was canvassed to see if anyone wanted to help bring the ship back. All Officers except one were willing to try the venture. Not a single crew member wished to stay with crippled Bergall. This meant it would be extremely difficult to man what was left of the submarine, let alone get any sleep between duties.

Three or four hours after the first request for staying with Bergall, a second call was made to enlist men. At that time, six enlisted men decided to stay. This meant that with no watch in the Control Room, using one or two officers on the Bridge, the men would be able to rotate in four hour sequences. This also made it easier down below for electrician and radio operation.

On a third vote, about one half of the men decided to stay. The rest were of opinion that "you can get a new boat but you can't get a new crew member!" By the time the Angler departed 54 men went with her and one officer who said, "My number is up!" Eight officers and twenty-one enlisted men remained on Bergall.

Preparation of demolition charges of TNT in foot square blocks were placed to blow the crippled ship up if caught in dire straights. The Angler was directed to follow Bergall. Should Bergall be attacked, then trailing Angler could pick up men remaining on board or in water. The two submarines made it through Karamata Strait and into Java Sea by daybreak.

Some drinking alcohol was on board. It was called the "depth charge allowance." It consisted of two to four ounces of Brandy to each man. That many ounces equated to one shot. Under severe stress conditions a shot was usually given of scotch, whisky or brandy.

Also, on board was alcohol used to run torpedos. That type alcohol comes in 65 gallon containers and is straight 200 proof strength. When high-powered torpedo alcohol is taken aboard, usually but not always, it is spiked with purple antidrink liquid. It is stored in thick steel built-in tanks under lock and key. If one tried to drink the purple substance straight, it would make you deathly sick. Sometimes under extended depth charge, straight alcohol was mixed with grapefruit juice. Each man got a dipperful from a galvanized water bucket. (Under one depth charge episode, Ben was subjected to 18 hours of attack!)

On this particular journey, it was discovered that many men had smuggled a bottle of liquor aboard. There were nine bottles of liquors brought forth most coming from the Forward Battery, the Chief Petty Officers and Officer's Quarters. The Captain ordered a bottle to be placed at each watch station. Two Officers were assigned to man the Bridge to sight any aircraft. One man was placed in the Maneuvering Room. Two more were assigned the Conning Tower and three men were assigned the Control Room. USS Bergall was still unable to dive.

While in the Java Sea, an airplane made a straight run for the ship. Everything was made ready for destruction. At about six miles out the plane made a turn. The Pilot apparently never saw the submarine. The men on the crippled sub experienced two more of the same kind of action. One plane came parallel by about eight miles. With no wake (track on the surface of water) and with the slow motion of the ship, it was apparently hard to discern the crippled submarine from the air.

The Java Sea was deep enough for big white rollers of waves. While Bergall made its way skies were overcast accompanied by black skirting cloud banks under which Bergall took cover. The submarine proceeded through the Lombok Straits. These waters are deep and narrow with a heavy current of approximately four to eight knots. The South China Sea empties into the Indian Ocean. Ben had been attacked many times previously in this area. Two more contacts were sighted but the offending enemy evidently did not sight the struggling Bergall. Near the Island of Bali, the ship was sheltered and went due south to Exmouth Gulf, Australia where the Americans kept a re-fueling station. At that point, having traversed over 2,000 miles of enemy controlled waters, they were then 800 miles out of Fremantle in West Austrailia.

In Exmouth Gulf, a 'bunch' of technicians sent from Perth attempted to weld close the hole in the Hull of the ship. When people were not on watch they stuffed the hole with mattresses to keep the deep spray out of the inward parts to the pressure Hull. There was not enough heat to make plate welding stick to the Hull. No satisfactory way of tying plates in place and shoring the gaping hole was found. Placing mattresses over the hole tied down with covers prevented water taken over the Bow from entering into the Torpedo Room.

On the 23rd of December after a 3,000 mile surface journey, USS Bergall moored at Fremantle. The Captain was decorated with the Navy Cross. Ben was recipient of a Silver Star. Humbly, he stated, "the Stars should have been given to the ships personnel." Admiral Cristie referred to the whole crew "as outstanding enlisted men."

In retrospect, Ben again stated "inventions were always at risk if a submarine was in trouble." When Nautilus went aground on Iuisan Shoal, Philippines, Ben helped burn secret things in the shower. Forced to lighten the load, her evacuees, mail, captured documents and cargo were sent ashore. Nautilus reserve tanks of fuel were blown dry and ammunition jettisoned over the side. By blowing her main ballast tanks, she was off the reef within three to 3 1/2 hours despite a receding tide.

Radar was developed by the British in the early days of World War II. A naval aide to Franklin D. Roosevelt entertained Ben with stories about the subject on several occasions. This aide was sent down to Dahlgren, Virginia by President Roosevelt to see a demonstration of radar. Lieutenant Commander

R. G. Voge was the brilliant Skipper of the Sailfish. The United States Navy would not allow men with patents to receive money for them. The invention of the disappearing hinge on the automobile was given to General Motors Corporation which gave the man called 'Voggie' a new Cadillac each year. He was allowed to sell the last year's model when he received the new model. That is how he got paid for his invention.

Voge laughed in a discussion of invention of "phosphorous luminations suspended from parachutes usually 20 in a line which illuminated the surface." A complaining Ben started with words, "the fools that invented those phosphorous luminations... Voge interrupted with, "I'm the one who developed those ..."

Since Ben was familiar with the word radar. He was appointed Radar Officer on the submarine carrying one of the first radars used on a ship in the Pacific Ocean. The radar arrived in ten foot long wooden crates to Sailfish located in King George Sound at the Southwest corner of Austrailia. Ben ordered a radio crewman to help him. "I'm the Radar Officer and you're going to help me." Ben boned up with the instruction book. He supervised.... the radar instrument was put together like a tinker kit. They received a few spare parts for it. In the beginning the radar antenna was fixed. Being stationary, it had no bearing but had a range. It had blind spots fore and aft. After two or three nearly disasterous aircraft attacks improved radars were developed. The manufacturers had conquered the problem of blind spots by working the radar in form of a loop. Radar was instrumental in protecting Ben four times from bombs and numerous times from enemy warships. Ben reiterated, "I have had almost every experience one could live through on a submarine." He stated, "historically, the Japanese were a little behind Americans in using radar. They did have it. Their latest 10 centimeter surface radar was the first to give Americans trouble. Development of better bearings and ranges helped radar to improve. Japanese people were ahead in development of the torpedo." One admonition by Ben, "If you destroy your ship destroy your radar."

In another Nautilus seagoing adventure, she slipped out of Pearl Harbor spending her sixth war patrol conducting photo-reconnaissance of the Gilbert Islands. Aboard the sub were 156 Marines and crew who entered into a bloody battle to secure an atoll, an island consisting of a ring of coral surrounding a central lagoon. The Marines' ultimate mission was to secure the island in order for SeaBees to build an airfield. When Nautilus pulled out to make a run, it was picked up by 'Friendly Forces.' At the same time there was no answer to the identification flare. Immediately, a first salvo hit Nautilus followed by two more. Ben knew the submarine was three times struck but only two hits were found. The first shell hit the ship in the conning tower. The third shell not yet detonated was wedged in the framing of the forward superstructure.

Red Porterfield put a rope around Ben, who carried a crowbar and red flashlight with him. He found the head of the unspent shell was cracked. Yellow cordite was dripping out. Ben figured the shell might go off any minute. Everytime the ship would get a wave, he wrestled the shell out of the superstructure. Men wanted to throw the dangerous thing over the side of the ship. No, the Captain wanted to see the shell. The Captain shook so hard that he couldn't look through the periscope but had the courage of a lion.

There was a big discussion as to the disposition of the dangerous explosive. It was identified as an American type. In Lowder's, *The Silent Service*, the United States destroyer Ringgold fired at Nautilus mistaking her as an enemy. The potentially alive 5" shell was kept tied to the deck and brought back to Pearl Harbor where it was defused as well as used to prove the hit had been one of 'friendly fire'.

The shell was screwed into the center of a table at the Pearl Harbor Submarine Officers Club for years. The top was squared off making it a very tall ash tray! Ben saw the displayed shell off and on for many years until 1966 when it disappeared. Ben's voice trailed off "it was always in the way..."

Regarding her mission after effecting temporary repairs, USS Nautilus was assigned her appointed task landing a 78 man scouting party on Abemama. Nautilus earned the Presidential Unit Citation in addition to fourteen battle stars for her World War II service.

As to the Bergall trip, it was discovered that all new electronic equipment would have to be installed. It took about a month to replace the gear back into the ship. In six weeks, Bergall was back on patrol thanks to the men who traveled about 3,000 miles in very precarious circumstances. USS Bergall earned four battle stars for her World War II service.

Ben has a picture given to him by his aunt. In his younger days, he was proud to refer to his birth in a beautiful old house called Chalmette Plantation which is located in Jefferson County Arkansas. The picture that his aunt gave him was one of a shiny black automobile with running boards. She told Ben, "You were born on the running board of this car in French Town Bottoms with two nurses, a doctor and your Dad in attendance. You were wrapped in your Dad's shirt on the way to the hospital."

The man wrapped in his Dad's shirt at birth has been cited 21 times by the United States of America for actions before the enemy. Ben's Navy experience would fill a book by itself! Ben has been awarded the Navy Cross, Silver Star with Gold Star, Bronze Star with Gold Star, Submarine Combat Insignia with two gold stars and two silver stars, and both Army and Navy Commendation Medals not to mention a plethora of other medals and insignias. Four of the battle stars were for World War II service for valor in the South China Sea, Gulf of Siam, Java Sea and Philippine Sea.

Captain Jarvis has a Navigational Star Finder from the U-3008, Class XXI German submarine, which was used by the vessel prior to surrender at the end of the War at Portmouth, New Hampshire in August of 1945. "The trick of using the instrument is knowing your position on the Earth. Setting the Globe of the Star Finder with the ship's latitude derived from sideral time, (time used by astronomers, measured by the stars) related to Greenwich mean time.." one could pick off the the Azimuth or Compass Bearing, and the Altitude or how many Degrees above the Horizon the Star was to be found in the Heavens." One felt comfortable listening to this learned man describe the use of the instrument and to hear the rhythm of poetry in the work of a seaman. Ben spoke of such things as "stars shot at twilight, weak stars, bright stars and planets making white streaks on a glassy still sea, the submarine rising in the evening to surface. Bring a star down to the horizon and write down the time." (For a layman's introduction to the mystery surrounding the work of the navigator and old principles guiding oceangoing vessels before the computer "push a button stage" the Editor would refer to a book by George W. Mixter, *Primer of Navigation*, particularly the chapter called "*Lighthouses in the Sky*.) Ben described the mystery of location of a ship on the waters of the earth's surface as clearly as Mixter.

Ben's officer sword on display at the Depot Museum in Sonoma was another adventure into unusual discussion. The weapon of offense and defense in personal combat historically "was developed from the dagger at the beginning of the Bronze Age." The sword, obsolete as a weapon is now used by Officers for ceremonial purposes. Officers have very precise regulations in the use of their swords. Ben's Officer sword has a genuine sharkskin handle and it is gold plated in the hilt with an engraved blade.

Since Ben commanded the Submarine named Baya for three patrols, we discussed fish. There is a fish called Baya and the Electric Boat Company had an artist's watercolored painting of each fish for which a submarine was named. The picture painted on wood was attached to the bulkhead of the ships as the company produced them. Ben has the painting of the Baya. Baya completed five war patrols sinking four Japanese vessels totalling 8855 tons. With Hawkbill, Baya sank an 8407 ton passenger cargo ship. After the war was over Baya received her four battle stars and went out of commission in reserve fleet at Mare Island Naval Ship Yard. The waters of this area are the same ones seen from Ben's house on the Hill.

Mixter, George W., *Primer of Navigation*, Sixth Edition, Litton Educational Publishing, Inc. by Van Nostrand Reinhold Company. 551 pp.

Hughston E. Lowder, *The Silent Service,* Silent Service Books, Baltimore, Maryland. 492 pps. (see pp. 23, 24,185-189).

James B. Alexander

United States Army 1942 - 1945

James Beauchamp Alexander, known as Beach by his friends, was a well-conducted, proper and handsome young freshman in college when he was inducted into the service of his country. Beach was born in the City of San Francisco, California to a family which could afford to send their son to Europe in the days of depression. Beach "found it easy to live in Europe as a young man on $400.00 per month during postwar days." His interest was in architecture. In his book, *Sonoma Valley Legacy,* he reviews the histories and sites of 70 historic adobes in and around Sonoma Valley, California. Alexander describes the qualities defining architecture as those of "beauty and permanence."

Believing "the world was his oyster" James embarked from Monterey on a train to Tyler, Texas for basic training. The train was so crowded "that he had to stand on the trip all the way to Texas with an occasional precarious perch on his dufflebag. In those days the trains were slow, so our intrepid traveler found the beginning of his army career was "no bed of roses." In fact, a San Franciscan used to the cooling breezes and the temperature of the Pacific Ocean-blessed-climate found Texas freezing in winter and humid the rest of the year.

Beach, the intrepid, decided if he was going to face the Nazis, he would become a sharpshooter. He would become an infantry rifleman! In fact, his first medal was that of a recognized "sharpshooter." To get to that level of marksmanship Beach started training for cadre. (Cadre being defined as a non-commissioned officer's school).

The young San Franciscan was assigned training with a tough old man. He can still hear the southern drawl of the teacher of marksmanship training. "Now, Honey, pull the trigger, breathe easy." Now that might have been easy for some but Beach had helmet trouble! As he tilted his head one way or another "the helmet slipped over his eyes." Out of his simulated foxhole "he just couldn't see!" When the group went on maneuvers, the candidate for Cadre would "get lost and left behind." The young man who educationally knew such things as "most of these military terms are French from Napoleon" was told to "get lost, take to another company!" Showing up late just because he put the top down on a half-track (armored vehicle, wheels in front, caterpillar tread on rear half), he found General Hartle waiting for him with words "Well, you certainly screwed up the whole maneuver!"

By the next summer, Beach found himself in a Naples replacement depot right after the Allied action at Anzio. In Naples under the command of Mark Clark, the men were given the once over by General Patton. Patton informed the young soldiers that "they were wearing their caps the wrong way" and stood over them until they "put their caps on right!" Jame's regiment forged straight towards Monte Cassino. Beach, whose talents were then being used as a Clerk of the 7th Army, declared: "I really became patriotic." He requested duty as a medic on the front lines. In the lofty heights of the Voges Mountains, he decided to transfer to the Medical Corps. In a very short while "he was yanked back to the 452nd Evacuation Hospital." This particular hospital was where wounded men were sent on their first transfer. Soldiers taken from the battlefields, if badly hurt, were then transported to a big general hospital. Some wounded men were actually sent back to the United States. Sometimes they were patched up at home or in England and then returned to the battlefield.

While in the Battle of the Bulge at Alsace Lorraine, James found himself encircled by Germans. The whole hospital was surrounded and all the personnel of the hospital became prisoners. It was just after Christmas. The Prisoners were sent to Bad Orb near Frankfurt, Germany. James does not remember a "hell of a lot" about the experience except he "was hungry most of the time." He recalls Allies were sent packages of food by the Red Cross and the German guards ate the food. American prisoners were given a bowl of gruel type cereal for their daily ration. "Like small children," Beach recalled "we tried to hide when we heard a lot of shooting by the German and American Armies."

The prisoners were taken to a German Hospital. Beach only weighed 90 pounds when he was released. The men were scared as they were being reviewed by a German doctor noted as having a reputation for "peculiar operations." James remembers the Germans as terrible soldiers. When German officers left beautiful chateaus, the soldiers "would defecate in each of the rooms, so that when the Allies arrived the stench would be overwhelming and practically impossible to rectify. This was the German soldiers "revenge on the advancing troops." To Beach, the war became "a nasty, dirty war." One of the prisoners also from San Francisco had boiling water thrown in his face which left permanent scars. James saw French children starving while the German children were strong and well fed.

Black soldiers were tossing bodies like cords of wood in trucks. The men assigned to that macabre task sang songs. Perhaps that singing was a way to keep them from thinking about their ghastly chore. Beach thanked God the prisoners were not left in the prison too long. When the war ended, he with his prison buddies were sensitized by an Army psychologist teaching them "to bury the memories of their forced degradation of the German prison along with the debasement endured from German guards."

Prior to the Battle of the Bulge, Beach spent time inside the Maginot Line. He described the underground fortress which the French built as protection against the Germans "as a maze of tunnels." The heavily fortified pillboxes and tank traps, named after Andre Maginot a French Minister of War, was considered impregnable. It failed to prevent the invasion of the Nazi Armies. For days, Beach never saw day light while in the manmade underground caves. Men used little candles for light. The soldiers only stayed where the guns were mounted and where food was prepared. One could become hopelessly lost in the artificial subterranean passageways. Those so-called 'defense tunnels' against the Germans were built after the First World War. According to Beach "The maze was built on the wrong side of France as it did not protect France from the Germans. As in the First World War the German Armies invaded by way of Belgium to the North." The area the men were encamped in was one of thick adobe like earth. The soil stuck to itself building layers of earth very thickly on the men's boots. The soldiers in a process of struggling and coping on a day to day basis, had to scrape their boots constantly! This same memory was shared by survivors of World War I, in Europe as well.

Beach and other surviving prisoners were rescued. Believing his was "an ailing experience" the young man was taken to a Chateau in Alsace Lorraine outside of Strasbourg. Since Beach had an education, he decided why not study the beautiful architecture all around him or what pieces of it that were still left standing! Whenever he was near any grand chateau, architectural building, or museum, he forged his way to study his interests even though he was once informed "you're walking across a minefield and you're going to get blown up doing it!"

He met a "guy on restoration of Arts and Monuments" with a long involved title. Beach was invited to go on an expedition. Having been in Europe in 1936, he was biting at the bit to partake an adventure with this acquaintance. Receiving a recreational leave, he had been to Nice. He had stayed at the Negresco Hotel which impressed our learned traveler with its solid marble bathtubs. He had visited

Saint Gore recognized as one of the largest monasteries and walled communites in France. Now, he was to see Mannheim, Germany which was in the German's Bulge. The Germans' had a bulge of their own which was near the Allied's version of the Bulge. At Mannheim, Beach could not find a single house left standing intact, just brownstone fronts which appeared like they were still intact. It was eerily like a movie set of destruction. There was rubble three stories high. It looked like there was nothing left, yet the Germans came out in the daytime in tidy hats and all dressed up. In Heidelberg, Jame's Colonel attended a hearing held by all the Allied Generals. James was apprised of the news that Montgomery "had wanted to retreat," Eisenhower "didn't know what to do" and Patton had taken off to "use the poor expendable soldiers."

When peace was declared James became a man of good fortune. As an ex-Prisoner of War, he was offered the option of staying on the continent. There were so many service men to send home that the ships were crowded. The army made way for Beach to spend the next six months at government expense at a school in Oxford, England. Beach opted for the School of Architecture at the University of Oxford where he could definitely turn his talents toward an educational opportunity.

Having viewed postwar Germany and France on the Restoration of Arts and Monuments jaunt, Beach was amazed to find postwar London looking amazingly intact. He thought, "how incredibly well the English survived the bombing!" One tale being told was that of an American Red Cross migrant who worried about being bombed. She kept saying she would not know what to do. When the time came for a hit from German planes upon the restaurant where she happened to be, she found out what she did. She puddled under a chair! "The crux of the story was that the English in their stoic Churchillian manner handled their war experience much like their food. They could live on brussel sprouts for years if they had to... they survived!"

Beach was knowledgeable that "Germans rebuilt like crazy." He felt "it took Paris fifteen years to get around to repair their one bombed out ruin." Beach knew these facts as he also knew the royal families of Germany and England after the war. He danced with Princess Margaret and became a friend of the Duchess of Kent. He knew Princess Hohenloe Langenborg of Germany. He visited the Prince of Darmstadt Hesse and he met the Bismarcks. (The little museum on the Bismarck Estate included a giant California redwood log sent to Bismark in 1890. The museum even had a picture of San Francisco and another of the famous redwood tree you could drive through.)

Beach remembers so many places...With timing not at best, after Oxford, he ended up in the Air Force assigned to the Korean/Japanese theatre of war. As a medical team member, he flew with a crew bringing back injured men to Japanese hospital areas. When he finally arrived back in the United States to muster out of the Service, he flew in all alone. His records were lost and true to the rest of his haphazard experiences in the war, he was considered AWOL for a period of time until the Air Force "found" and released him.

As civilian, Beach became a perennial scholar. He earned certificates from four universities: Washington and Lee in Lexington, Virginia; the National University of Mexico; the Ecole D'Architecture of Fountainbleau, France; and the Royal Academy at Copenhagen, Denmark. He has collaborated with the late Mr. John Bakewell, architect of the magnificent San Francisco City Hall on a published history of the classical tradition which dominated western building patterns for some 2000 years.

In the epilogue of his book, *Sonoma Valley Legacy*, last paragraph, Beach takes note of the fact that

"Washington sends out manuals on adobe construction to Third World Countries but in California the building codes do all that is possible to discourage its use. The makers of California's codes argue that adobe is unsafe in earthquake country. This is of course, to ignore the fact that California's oldest standing structures, the missions are of adobe."

Like his predecessor, Altimira, who migrated to a Valley called Sonoma, so did James. With his interest in architecture, he made a perfect candidate for the historical guide post at the Sonoma State Historical Park located in Sonoma. Finding the Valley a temptation, he built his Palladian styled home "Villa Demeter" in the Eastern Foothills. He has one of the most interesting architecturally styled homes in the entire area. His admiration of the classical tradition comes shining forth in this edifice. His 30 year old comfortable looking villa has tall doors framing the openings in a grand manner. Special niches hold a stone sculpture or some other bit of tradition. The brass bedecked fireplace, once in a house owned by Napoleon's Josephine, looks cozy. The view of a garden reflecting pool is at the front entrance and is centered with an arched central doorway to the inside of the house. A fabric covered chest is 'at home' with 18th Century Danish antiques as well as a Greek/Roman bench and fine framed drawings. A piece of old frieze is complimented by a leather topped game table. Beach showed his one and only "war loot." It was a fragment of a corinthian column, so small, you could hold it in the palm of your hand. It was from a smashed up museum of Germany.

Alexander, James B., *Sonoma Valley Legacy*, Sonoma Valley Historical Society, 270 First Street West, Sonoma, California 95476. 77 pps.

William H. Stalley

United States Navy 1939 - 1945

William H. Stalley, born in Jamestown, North Dakota volunteered for the United States Navy in Seattle, Washington for a six year hitch. An old farmer picked him up that afternoon and hearing what Bill had done, stated "well, young man, you want us to feed you now!"

Skipping over details of Navy training, Bill went direct to his experiences aboard the two ships of his life, that of USS Louisville and the spirited aircraft carrier, Essex. The first ship took him on adventures in South America and the second into the thick of battles in the South Pacific.

About the time Bill's military endeavors in 1939 were beginning, Britain declared war against Germany. A British liner Athenia heading toward Canada from Liverpool had been sunk by German Submarine U-30. The U-Boat Skipper, Lemp mistook the liner for a cruiser. 112 passengers including 28 American citizens were killed in the incident.

The British set about searching for U-Boats. Two more disasters were sustained by the British. British Ship Courageous was sunk with 518 lives lost. Then Battleship Royal Oak under two separate strikes was finally struck by three torpedoes causing 833 men to go to their watery graves. The grateful Fuhrer awarded Lt. Commander Prien the Knight's Cross for these actions against the British ships.

Reluctant to tackle the much stronger Royal Navy head-on, Hitler forbade Kriegsmarine (the German Navy) to attack British warships but to find Britain's merchant fleet. Orders included the words "to cut off trade the staff of life."

The Graf Spee, a German pocket battleship left for the South Atlantic about the time USS Louisville with Bill aboard headed in the same direction.

With Hitler's orders in hand, Captain Hans Langsdorff of the Graf Spee began attacking and sinking British merchant vessels in the South Atlantic and Indian Oceans. Langsdorff and his German crew had sunk nine vessels by early December. The "Royal Navy in retaliation organized several task forces to scour the Atlantic for the German menace." One British Cruiser under command of Commodore Henry Harwood was off River Plata near the South American Coastline.

On December 13th, a German Captain named Langsdorff approached and spotted smoke of British Ships. Believing the Cumberland, Exeter, Ajax and one ship from New Zealand named Achilles were convoy escorts for merchant vessels, Langsdorff attacked the group as if they were destroyers. He did not follow the strict instructions that he had received from the Fuhrer "not to tangle with enemy warships!" Exeter and Ajax were badly damaged. Commodore Harwood was about to withdraw from a burning battle when to his amazement, Lansdorff put up a heavy smokescreen and ran for port at Montevideo, Uruguay. Bill's assigned ship was headed for the same waterway in which the cities of Montevideo and Buenos Aires were located.

The German ship, Graf Spee had taken 17 shell hits from the four ships outside the port. The German Captain pessimistically believed his vessel could not make passage back home until it sustained some repairs. The English Commodore Harwood shadowed Graf Spee as the convoy remained anchored outside the Port of Montevideo. Because of neutrality terms of international law, the pocket battleship of the Germans was allowed sanctuary for 24 hours. The English Commodore put in a sham order for extra fuel oil. Information like this was deliberately leaked to the Germans. The German Captain was fooled that the fuel was for strong re-inforcements joining four ships lying in wait outside the waterway.

Huge crowds gathered in Montevideo on December 17th after radio contacts around the world stated Graf Spee would sail that day. The people expected to see a big sea battle between the British ships and Graf Spee. United States Navy men on the USS Louisville were arriving closer and closer to the scene. They were expecting a real live sea battle and wondered what they might be getting into... They were also human enough to have that uncertain anticipation of viewing a warship encounter. It could be the Americans' first chance to participate in a sea battle. If they arrived at the wrong time they might be a part of it!

At 5 km (3 miles) out of the Port of Rio de la Plata, the Graf Spee stopped. Suddenly a wall of smoke poured from Graf Spee. "With a blaze of light and earsplitting booms" the ship was blown up by orders of its own Captain! After the crew was evacuated off the ship, it was blown apart by its own torpedos in the ammunition magazines, The excuse for this destruction was to keep the early form of radar and other scientific equipment away from the British.

The USS Louisville and its crew were four days too late to hear and see the overwhelming explosion. The American ship passed the three English ships outside the Port of Rio de Plata before entering the mouth of the port. The crew of USS Louisville were spellbound to see the superstructure and other smaller floating pieces of the Graf Spee being tossed around by the quivering pulsation of the waves. The impact of this sight on a young man who had never been to sea before has caused Bill to bring up this vision for over fifty years. It is the first thing he talks about whenever anyone asks about his World War II experiences.

Three nights after orders to destroy his own Command ship, the German Captain Langdorff shot himself in Buenos Aires. His farewell letter stated, "I am quite happy to pay with my life for any possible reflection on the honour of the flag." He might have had to face a court-martial and the German firing line! The British greeted the captains and crews of their ships as heros! Bill and his buddies were left awestruck by the sight of a broken enemy supership followed by the suicide of its German Captain. They were also privy to conversations of people along the port who were filled with wonder about the German Captain Langdorff.

The USS Louisville made its way to Buenos Aires, Argentina on the other side of the Port of Rio de la Plata from Montevideo. Bill met another Navy man on ship who had been a polo trainer in Colorado before being drafted in the service. They went to a polo match in Buenos Aires. A young boy about age five approached the two Navy men while they were enjoying the games. While talking with the boy, his father approached the sailors to discover whether his son was annoying the young men. The five year old's mother had been a San Francisco Bay Area resident before she had married. The Argentines were Juan and Joan Raul and were very friendly.

Bill and his crewmate felt privileged. It was as if the two Navy men were "taken under their new found friend's wing when Juan invited the sailors to join himself and his son in their box seats." The Americans learned that the Rauls were also friends of Bing Crosby. In fact, Juan Raul had taught other famous movie stars how to play polo and ride horses. The sailors were invited to the Raul home for a drink. Their hosts were involved with the race horses that Bing Crosby had in Burlingame, California. In the house was a silver mounted hoof with an inscription from the singer. Juan Raul showed the men a gold watch he was wearing with inscription "to Juan from Bing." He then stated, "I'll take you anywhere you want to go." Bill and the other sailor were whisked away to a tennis match and Bill found they were in box seats above the American Ambassador's seating. Juan Raul talked about his family's ranch which was 20 miles up-country. He would take the young men there but Juan knew something Bill and his buddy did not even know. The sailors of USS Louisville did not have time to go to the ranch, he said "because you are leaving the port the day after tomorrow!"

Bill's next incredible adventure in the United States Navy was a trip to a naval yard 50 miles from Cape Town in South Africa. Still in the process of being an observer of unusual events, Bill helped load $150,000,000.00 of gold on the USS Louisville. Each gold brick was about 6" x 12" and was boxed. Each brick was reported to be worth $25,000.00. With a couple of riflemen watching, the ship's crew loaded the gold in about three hours. All the time the cargo was being stashed on the American ship, the conversation was about hurrying up and getting out of there! The gold was being sent by the British to the United States of America. Fearing a U-Boat attack, the ship began a record-pace toward the continent of North America and New York Harbor. On their second day there was a heavy sea storm that carried the ship "under one and over two waves in the Atlantic Ocean." The ship sustained a ruptured plate seam. This caused USS Louisville to be slowed down for the rest of the journey. When the shipment of gold was finally unloaded on the wharf in New York, police cars with armoured trucks stretched back one block long. The precious metal when unloaded was whisked away and the Navy men knew not where..... There was much scuttlebutt as to what each crew member could do with just one brick of that shiny metal!

For the first six months, after morning coffee, Bill's chore on board ship was to scrub decks. It took Bill two years and eight months to make First Class Gunners Mate. After another two years, he qualified as Chief Gunners Mate. His job was to clean, maintain and sometimes fire big eight inch guns. Bill continued to pass exams to complete six educational steps which eventually placed him over 30 trained men.

Men knew war was coming in the Pacific. Bill was out of Manilla when Pearl Harbor was bombed. His home away from home, the USS Louisville was ordered to rendezvous with two other ships. The Louisville was to join USS Coolidge and Scott and escort these two ships safely to Hawaii. There were women and children on the Coolidge and Scott along with a load of precious magnesium on one of the vessels. The USS Louisville and the other two ships headed for a 10 day cruise to Hawaii. They took a backward course past the Christmas Islands. Tokyo Rose, in her Japanese propaganda radio broadcasts sunk the three American ships every half hour. Rumors in the United States were "that all those women and children had been lost at sea." Uncertainty about the three ships whereabouts was caused by absolute radio silence. The priceless cargo of children, women and magnesium was delivered to the worried civilians of the United States. USS Louisville headed back toward Austrailia in the war zone.

After a few raids in the Marshall Islands where the Americans endured a shortage of ships, the Louisville eventually returned to native soil. Bill ended up in dry dock at Mare Island in 1942. He met his future wife, Maxine at a dance held at the Casa de Vallejo Hotel. Before the two married he went to the Aleutians. When he returned, they were married on Halloween in Las Vegas. Bill laughed, "it must have been trick or treat." The couple only saw each other for forty days out of the next three years, except for one eventful problem visit on the east coast by Maxine...

Bill was being transferred to the brand new Essex. Knowing her new husband would be in Newport

News, Virginia for a few days (while the Essex was being commissioned) Maxine decided to make the long journey to visit Bill from California. When his bride arrived it was Bill's luck to be on duty. He put out a distress call to some of his buddies. Another Gunner's Mate said he would be "stand-in." Checking with an Officer, Bill was informed he didn't have to change the duty roster. While Bill was dining with his wife, a false air raid was carried on at the duty station. The stand-in Gunner's Mate, Bill had depended upon had gone to sleep and did not show up for duty. Since no one showed up for the post, Bill was under the 'gun'. He was called in for summary courts marshal. Bill was restricted. Disappointed, Maxine headed on the 3,000 mile trip back to California.

Since the Essex was a brand new ship, a shakedown cruise was executed to make sure all the ship's components were in working order. The crew was expected to become acclimated to the ship. As preparations continued to be tested on the shiny new ship for war duty, word was whispered to Bill "that the Captain did not want anyone to go to sea with him that had a bad record." Bill went to trial. At the hearing, Bill did not tell about the stand-in sleeping. He did not mention the Officer nor the posting snafu. Men who liked Bill expressed good words about him. The Captain seemed real easy and that helped! The least fine one could receive from the incident was a fine of $8.00. That is what Bill was fined!

The Essex was a fleet carrier, 820 feet long at the waterline. She could steam at 33 knots and was able to carry 100 aircraft. The crew strength was that of 3,500 men. There was an elevator. Massive engines were able to deliver 150,000 horsepower to four propellers. A maze of working and living areas were found under the flight deck. Heavy elevators delivered aircraft to and from the uppermost Flight Deck. Further down the seven layers of working "city" were mess decks, bunk areas, giant turbine geared engines and finally oil fuel tanks which were located below the waterline on the lowest level of the ship. The ship even had its own Navy Band! Special fuel tankers, separate and apart from the carrier refueled the ship in the middle of the sea. This aircraft carrier and a few like her were considered the biggest, most complicated war machines ever devised by man. The 'floating city' was navigated and commanded from a Bridge perched high on an "Island." The Island was on the Starboard side of the Flight Deck which ran from bow to stern. Generators supplied electric power to all parts of the Essex. Seamen kept the carrier clean, mechanics serviced airplanes and crews directed the planes on deck. The everyday job description of the men on this 'floating city' " was to launch and recover the aircraft.

The carrier was equipped with three types of airplanes, the torpedo, dive bombers and fighters. Medical facilities included a fully staffed operating room. Frozen foods were introduced for more varied menus. Men had self-service meals which they chose from a central food counter. Lots of iced water and soft drinks were available. Latest movies from Hollywood were part of the provisions devised to remove strain and stress caused by prolonged journeys at sea.

One of the Navy's leading World War II aces was Capt. David McCampbell. Going on missions from the Essex, he shot down 34 Japanese planes, half of them Zero fighters. He was Commander of Air Group 15 aboard the USS Essex in the South Pacific. Nine of his "kills" were from a single sortie and he had an unmatched record. One of the Officers of the ship was Gene Tunney, the world's champion heavyweight boxer. (Gene Tunney an Officer, was in the gun room every morning working out his exercises). One of the fighter pilots was movie star, Wayne Morse. Chief Justice White had the same battle station as Bill for about six months. He was working in Naval Intelligence and as an Oxford Scholar "had little to say" according to Bill. One surgeon in the medical unit was from Mayo Clinic. Bill had attention from him on one occasion.

As First Class Gunner's Mate of the Essex, Bill spent thirty continous months in the Pacific. It was reported "that men of the Essex supported every major engagement from Tarawa to Tokyo Bay." The crew called the ship "the fightingest ship in the Navy!" Men were under extreme pressure all the time. Their most outstanding record was that of operating combat aircraft for 79 consecutive days in support of the Okinawa campaign. The Air Group 83 flew 36,841.2 combat hours up to the war's end, August 15, 1945. Commencing on the first day of service on the ship, Bill participated in 63 different operations entitling him to wear ten stars on the Asiatic-Pacific Ribbon and two stars on the Philippine Liberation Ribbon.

A few of the chronicled incidences reported by Essex's own history are locked in Bill's memory of "close calls!" In an area after Magazines, on the 5th deck, in the station of the flood valve, air was cut off. The men began sweating profusely. The ship was under attack by 15 Japanese in a diving run on the Essex. Their bomb missed the ship!

On another occasion, while on the deck of the ship, three shots were buffeted. Bill watched three shots fired from one five inch gun and two from another. A 250 pound bomb would have hit him had the Essex not turned at just the right angle to miss the bomb. Bill stated, "My number was not up on that day!"

In another battle, the Essex destroyed nine planes in the air and six on the ground. The Japanese, in a kamikaze suicidal move by two pilots which had already been hit, dove right into the Flight Deck just above a loaded deck of planes which had been fully gassed, armed and ready to take to the skies. The Japanese plane headed toward Bill's 40 mm gun located right below the Bridge. A parachute shrouded one of the dead pilots wrapped around the gun shield! A large gasoline explosion which killed 15 men and wounded 44 men took place. Fire fighters exhibiting superb damage control kept destruction to a minimum as the fires were in control in exactly 30 minutes.

Another time, in General Quarters, a bell warned that the ship was under attack. Bill went up to the Fantail for his station on the 40 milimeter gun. Three 'Bettys' (torpedo planes) were coming in fast. Bill had 10 seconds to reach his post. He had no shot off. He became utterly transfixed watching a torpedo that went right along side of the ship which did not strike it. If Essex had been hit, Stalley would have been one dead gunman. His associate gunner, who had already been on the deck and waiting for the attack said, "I got in eight shots."

Bill did not spend all of his time at the gun station. He also tended the Ordnance Store Room which automatically put him in charge of spare parts for guns. (Aviation Ordnance took care of their own guns on planes.) The Ordnance Store Room was for guns used on the ship's deck. It had been provisioned fairly well when the ship was prepared for its life on the ocean. If there was a part which was impossible to replace, an order was put in with no promises for its fullfillment. The men learned to create makeshift repairs. The store clerk job also included accounting.

From a USS Essex Plan of the Day (Bill still has one copy among his souvenirs) dated October 5th, 1943 sunrise is reported to be 0646 (Zone plus 12 time). Carry out Sea Routine. 0230 Reveille for Air Dept. (Will be sounded on bugle). 0245 Early breakfast for Air Dept. (100 officers, 850 men; use all mess lines). 0345 Flight Quarters. 0355 Reveille. 0415 Breakfast for all hands less Air Dept. Use all mess lines and form lines on 2nd deck to avoid planes turning up in Hangar. 0545 (About). General Quarters.   GENERAL PLAN:

To smash Wake.

Notes:(1) All hands will place the fire-retardant covers on their bedding at reveille this morning.

(2) All office and stateroom type non-watertight doors will be left unlocked commencing at reveille. This is essential in view of the possible necessity for repair parties to enter. Time may not be available to find man with the keys or to cut through doors.

(3) When "Condition Easy" is set Control Officers may:

(a) Permit up to 50% of men to sleep on station.

(b) Permit individuals to leave station for calls of nature, to obtain battle rations, etc.

All key stations and all telephone circuits must be manned continuously.

(4) The mid-day meal will be served in accordance with the Battle Ration Bill whether or not the ship is at General Quarters.

Two paragraphs in addition to the above was still about rations and permits, ending with examples of Ration Groups AIR, GUN, ENGINE, MEDICAL, NAVIGATOR, HULL, COMMISARY.

Notes on the orders also included that of the proper steps in taking a sea-going shower (refer to a poster), that a pair of sunglasses had been found and the fact that Lt. (jg) Guyon, # 498 had lost one brown wallet. Following names of the duty list for Tuesday and Wednesday the words HIROHITO HERE WE COME was centered across the bottom of the second page followed by an afterthought, that "There will be no movies tonight, (Monday).

Bill also has copies of small folders depicting the First Thanksgiving Day Prayer Service aboard the USS Essex on November 25, 1943 which was based on Psalm 106:1 "Oh, give thanks unto Jehovah for He is good, for His loving kindness endureth forever." The entire cover of the brocure, back and front, is made up of scriptural passages. The inside portion has readings and mentioned the tradition of the President of the United States having a usual Thanksgiving Proclamation which would be read throughout the world, but "Here in the mid-Pacific we do not have a copy of the President's words."

A second brocure, entitled FIRST ANNIVERSARY DINNER, December 1, 1944 was that of a menu served the "fightingest men" of Green Olives, Celery Hearts, Cream of Asparagus Soup, Crisp Saltines, Sweet Pickles, Roast Young Tom Turkey, Celery and Apple Dressing, Cranberry Sauce, Cream Whipped Potatoes, French Peas, Giblet Gravy, Plum Pudding, Hard Sauce, Pumpkin Chiffon Pie, Hard Candy, Tea Rolls, Bread, Butter, Coffee, Cigars and Cigarettes.

The "fightingest ship in the U.S. Navy" was described in a clipping from the New York Times "as having blasted a path for every Pacific invasion, sunk more of the Japanese Fleet than Tokyo has ever admitted and brought destruction to every major Japanese stronghold from Rabaul to Nansii Shote." Officers of the Essex were proud that their fighter planes, while shooting down a record number of enemy planes, had given such excellent cover to bombing missions.

Essex was considered a world traveler covering the World Map of the Pacific War Zones totalling 151,805 miles in 15 months. She participated in invasions of the Gilberts, Marshalls, Marianas, Palau and Philippines not to mention all the other islands receiving strikes and air attacks including two historic sea battles which completely destroyed Japanese Carrier air strength. On June 19th, in a Philippine Sea engagement, the air group created a new high for Naval Aviation by shooting down 68 and a half enemy aircraft in one day. A Pilot from another group helped down the 69th plane. On the same day of June 19th, the day of the first battle of the Philippine Sea, all planes were forward on the flight deck and two planes still were waiting to land from combat air patrol. Word was received that Jap planes were on the way. All of these planes, fighters, bombers and torpedo planes were targets for the enemy! The Hanger Deck was full too, so the planes could not be stowed away in the ship. The men with the flags landed the two planes that were late, got the others back Aft and sent them off. The hauling tractors were racing back and forth on the Flight Deck at speeds of 35 miles per hour!

The men of the Essex were so well trained and their work was so well co-ordinated, they could be contacted by field telephone from an island and in less than five minutes the Essex was known to have had divebombers silencing enemy fire.

Some Pacific Veterans relive their memories of World War II by revisiting some of those almost forgotton coastlines. Thinking of Mog Mog, Doug Hubbard of the Sun Times, brings back memories of Navy men standing shoulder to shoulder drinking warm beer, singing and playing in the surf. Today, there are rusted remains of a floating pier built in the hot humid sun by the American Navy Men. An old bulldozer is rusting away, where it used to push garbage including those mounds of beer cans into the sea. Life is now quiet in Mog Mog (and on other Pacific Islands.) Flowers bloom. Men fish. Women weave on their old fashioned looms. A 16 inch shell from the war serves as a trash barrel on a public street corner. Bill Stalley would notice that trash barrel and the metal powder cannisters from 12 and 16 inch naval guns catching rainwater at the the eaves of a metal roof...

In Sonoma, Bill tends his garden of flowers. His home on a quiet cul-de-sac affords views of a neighboring vineyard. He and Maxine are very busy with community activities. Maxine is presently the President of the Ladies Auxilliary for the Veterans of Foreign Wars. In a kitchen drawer are a few empty shell casings from a gun used in World War II airplanes. One other souvenir is a three-quarter inch bound book of pictures with stories of the heroic and dangerous battles along with activities of Bill's second ship called USS Essex.

The Reader's Digest Illustrated History of World War II, The World at Arms., 1989. 512 pps. p. 26, 27.

Humble, R., *World War Two Aircraft Carrier.*, Franklin Watts, London, New York Toronto, Sydney. 32 pp. p. 6,7.

Assembled by USS Essex, *Saga of the Essex.*, Army and Navy Publishing Co., Bldg., 234 Main St., Washington D.C., 1946.

Miscellaneous clippings and stories from William Stalley's private collection.

Jerold W. Tuller

United States Navy, 1944 - 1946
United States Naval Reserve until 1950

Jerold Tuller, born in San Bernadino, California by his senior year of high school was an Oregonian living in a small town called Yamhill, Oregon. He smiles, "I was a typical teenager. I knew the war was reaching out to take the young high school graduates to a place unknown. I really didn't want to be an infantryman. I was just a lazy teenager and didn't want to walk that much! That was the reason that I chose to be a Navy man."

Jerry's graduation night was traditional. The pomp and ceremony of the small town was in a celebration mood. There were nine boys graduating from Senior Class. As the diplomas were being handed out to each graduate in their right hand, five of the nine boys including Jerry received induction orders in their left hand! Soon after, a very beloved teacher drove the five graduates to Portland for their sufferance into the service of their choice.

Leaving Portland, Jerry enjoyed a train trip down the Columbia River to Seattle then over to Ferragut Naval Training Base close to Coeur d'Alene, Idaho. In boot camp, Jerry was sidetracked from the other young men of his graduation class as he had a foot problem. The young recruits were being readied to relieve men of overseas duty. Since Jerry had "joined the Navy to see the sea" he was now assigned to a SeaBees Construction Battalion. In a camp "somewhere back of Oakland over the hill from Berkeley" Jerry waited for a ship. His job description as a construction battalion recruit was "to dredge harbors, prepare docking facilities and develop harbors."

Aboard ship, the young teenagers were informed they were going toward the war zone. On the beautiful isles of Hawaii the only thing seen by the Navy recruits was what they saw on the bus ride. There were no shore leaves but a seven day wait period in the camp. Not only that news but once back on board a troop ship to Guam, Jerry was bunked as low as you can get on a ship. He believed there was only a hull of metal and then came the water! The tiers of bunks were so narrow, that Jerry being so very tall and lean, found it difficult making it into the bunks very well. Ventilation was like going into the Veteran's Memorial Building in Sonoma after a full complement of exercisers have been working out for an hour with the windows closed on a winter's morning. On one occasion the ventilator broke down when the man on duty had fallen asleep. The stagnant air became extremely nauseating. Managing to get out of the murky passageways to the deck of the ship, as the young men reached forward to breathe good air a cold wave washed across the ship. It was pretty rough but it actually felt pretty good and helped to restore life back into the recruits.

This troop ship carrying Jerry toward Guam in the Marianas was filled to capacity with replacement troops. There were so many men on the ship that in order to get a place on top side during the waking hours, you would have to stake out the place. The men ate standing up twice a day. The weather was fantastically hot! Besides the breathing-stale-air problems, there was a little gun to shoot at submarines which was located under the main deck. Young men were assigned all hours of the day and night to practice this artillery. The only trouble with that method of operation was the gun stationed one level above the bunks kept the beds shaking continously.

When the weather was 100 degrees and up which was most of the time and as food was being served sweat would roll off the servers into the food that they were serving. One time Jerry misplaced his ticket for lunch and he was hungry. When he requested another ticket from the troop transport commander he was informed that "You'll have to go without, then! I have a half a notion to put you in the brig." That "difficult man was responsible for making sure you were given food but he made me go without it all day!" recalled Jerry.

The ship, USS Cleveland, was extremely large to Jerry's young eyes. It was considered the largest of its type. A burly Marine would lead anyone who would follow into singing. A Chaplain lead some groups in Christian stories. Otherwise there was nothing for men to do but play a little cards below deck, be disciplined immediately and severely or stand in long lines to get a drink of water in the 100 degree heat. A lot of guys wanted to get home. "Let us rush into this battle and get done with it" was the general conversation of each day.

When he arrived at Guam, Jerry's confirmed assignment was to the 301st Construction Battalion. He was put aboard a tugboat with floating pipes and orders to "put the pipes together with a sledge hammer." (At this juncture, the Editor would point out that those who know Jerry would describe him as tall, lanky and lean. He had a most unlikely build to be wielding a sledge hammer for very long.) However, the camaraderie on this tug boat was one of his great remembrances of being at the right place at the right time. The boat was a tug to Mother ship USS City of Delhart which was originally an old banana boat which carried bananas to the United States. The boat had been converted as a place to live. The young Navy men moved lines around building a harbor with docks for ships to move in.

Jerry was assigned temporarily to remove planking from the battleship USS Oregon which had been converted to an ammunition barge. An officer asked if anyone was interested in communication school and Jerry's hand shot up. The young man thought "I'll take that. It's better than dirt and heavy equipment." The job description requested a person who could type. "After all," thought Jerry, "I've had two typing courses - one in middle school and one in high school. I think that's the kind of stuff I can handle." Navy training took place aboard a barge which included learning the Morse Code, the radio and knowledge of flag identification. A red flag for example, meant that explosive fuels were being put into another ship.

It was at this point that Jerry laughingly states "I took the place of a Wave!" This job was perfect for our very meticulous and methodical young Navy man. He served as a member of the Communication Center for Guam Harbor. No ship came in or out unless it was cleared by the Center. The radio traffic and Morse Code traffic was a large part of the work. Ships came to port for extra food and refueling.

Jerry's closest experience to a real battle, except target practice above the bunk on that first ship going to Guam was while "doing radio." During a major Japanese attack on Tinian, he was privy to on-going conversations being transmitted. There were comments of a buddy going down... there were explosions followed by comments of the Pilots.

At the Communication Center you sometimes had a few breezes from the waters. You had drinking water without standing in lines. Hours were great. Jerry's skills were needed and were beneficial. He felt in his life at that moment, he had a significant duty. Due to men that Jerry worked with, he became interested in college by taking correspondence courses. These men are given credit as causing a turning point and influencing his choices the rest of Jerry's life.

About a year and eight months later from arrival to Guam, Jerry was on a troopship headed for home via the Marshall Islands. The ship rendezvoused with a bunch of boats loaded with Marines who were also assigned to rotate home. Anywhere from 50 to 100 Marines took 45 minutes to load on the troopship. In the attitude of being 'super-human', the Marines cried out, "All you swabs, you're dismissed from all security duty. No more duty to Seattle!" The Marines took over all the glory of standing watches. The rest of the men were happy to learn the psychology of "its great that they have the responsibility and we'll let them have it!"

Stateside, taking advantage of the great educational opportunities offered by the United States to its World War II Veterans, Jerry entered college taking a business course of study. During the second year, he met his wife, Sally and they both were graduated from University of Southern California. Jerry's enlistment in the Naval Reserve ended days before the Korean War started. Jobs were scarce and contacts did not produce desirable employment. Jerry returned to college in Long Beach to get his teaching credential. Sally worked as a technical writer to support their family now with their first baby.

Jerry became a teacher in Orange County California for one year. Then, the family moved to Boonville, California where Jerry was teacher and principal for four years. Their two daughters were born there. These jobs were followed by a principalship in Sonoma Valley for 24 years dating from 1959 through 1983. Jerry was City Councilman for 16 years, on the Sonoma Valley Hospital Board for six years and is presently its Past President. He has served as Mayor for the City of Sonoma and was appointed Honorary Acalde. At the Methodist Church, he has served almost every job including that of Lay Leader. He chaired the building of the educational wing, has been Pastoral Relations Committee Chairman and is an usher.

Looking back on those two years in the service spent at the end of World War II, Jerry again believes that the goals of his life were changed by the experience. The Government of the United States of America had wisdom in providing the Retraining Act of 1946. That act showed faith in the young people who had returned from the war. It was time and money well spent for the country as well. Jerry has had an association with people who mean a lot to him. His favorite thing that happened due to his service in the community was when El Verano School named its Athletic Field in his name. "They knew my frailties and the rest of me," he stated.

Brice Pace

United States Army, 1938 - 1959

Brice Pace retiring from the United States Army in 1959 as a full Colonel, had been serving on the Department Army General Staff under General Maxwell Taylor as the comptroller of the Army data processing systems. Brice is a Life Member of the Retired Officers Association. At time of retirement, he had been awarded eight medals including a Bronze Star in Normandy, two Commendation medals for the Battle of Northern France as well as several service medals. In early retirement years, Brice worked briefly for Bank of America in San Francisco as a systems analyst. He left that position to accept an assignment for math teacher at San Rafael Military Academy. In 1966, he became Academic Dean of the Academy. During this period of employment he attended San Francisco State University to earn a General Secondary Teaching Credential and obtained a Master of Science Degree in Education from Dominican College. In 1977, he graduated from the Anthony School of Real Estate. Working for Marin Town and Country Real Estate until 1986 he was compelled to retire because of a life threatening illness which required a kidney machine. He lives in an immaculate home in an adult community with his second wife, Jane. All of the aforementioned activities of retirement followed a totally unexpected life career in the United States Army, Brice smiles "Life plays strange tricks on one."

Although, Brice spent his first whole career in the military, initially it was never anticipated. In college as a young man, he specialized in geology. Upon graduation he was associated with Chivor Emerald Company in New York. He served as an advisor and as a Member of the Corporation Board of Directors of the company. Emerald mines were operated in Bogota, Colombia. These were devastated by Colombian guerillas and virtually impossible to manage. "Strangely," Brice relates, "prime agitators seemingly were the earlier close relatives of the members of current drug cartels. Today, dealing in drugs is a more profitable business than trying to sell contraband emeralds. The Chivor Emerald Company bankrupted."

After all the excitement with the emerald company in the late 1930s, Brice's military career commenced. He served with the 26th Infantry at Plattsburg Barracks, New York as a 2nd Lietuenant Platoon leader. It was not a long time before he was recognized for leadership and managerial qualities, so he rose rather rapidly. In his late twenties he held the rank of a Lieutenant Colonel. Today, Brice is quick to emphasize, the educational back ground of the United States Army is incredible. Ninety percent of the officers hold Bachelor Degrees, over 40% have Master Degrees and close to 30% are PHDs. Opportunities for educational advancement in the services border on the phenomenal. For instance in 1948 and again in 1954, Brice was offered opportunities to earn an MBA at Harvard University which he declined for personal reasons. He did pursue extensive education on the G.I. Bill.

In 1942, Brice was a hand picked staff member of the then Army Chief of Staff, General George C. Marshall as the future designated European Theater Commander for the forthcoming invasion of Europe. President Roosevelt sensing the need to have Marshall remain in Washington, D. C., instead selected General Dwight D. Eisenhower to transfer from North Africa to assume the post. When this occurred Eisenhower brought his own staff with him. This event left the entire staff of George Marshall then located in England, in limbo and available for re-assignment. Just before the English Channel crossing Brice was designated as a liaison with front line elements and served in that capacity for the period of the invasion and for several months thereafter.

Brice's primary mission was to manage and control units which had the responsibility for personnel accounting and casualty reporting which served as a basis for troop replacement. This meant that the armies reported their loss statistics daily. Replacements were assigned based on this information. Brice also surpervised casualty reports for the Ground Forces. His personnel was kept busy in the accounting process. Every unit in the Army made out reports which were accumulated and processed by his unit. The accounting process not only kept track of losses but also included the numbers of wounded as well as the sick. From the numbers received, vacancies were filled in the First, Third and Ninth Armies. Illness was particularly rampant in Italy as anemic dysentry was a widespread problem. This illness would keep an individual sick for approximately a month requiring replacements on the battlefield.

He recalls, "England was so conjested with American troops, it was a wonder the ground simply did not sink beneath them. So, too, the perimeter of Normany. The American troops were under the misconception that an invasion of Europe was near. This idea continued for weeks and weeks and weeks. It was as if minds and bodies of troops wanted to break out!" As a high officer, Brice was cleared for top secret information but he was not privy to the exact date of the D-Day Invasion of France. He knew it would be imminent but also knew "the less something of that nature is discussed and to the fewest persons, it has a better chance of remaining a secret." The motto of the army was "Don't tell unless one had to know." That information was "for eyes only" of Omar Bradley, Patton and Eisenhower.

The big crack in the German defense came in the mid-summer of 1944 when the Allies were able to break through the German lines at St. Lo, France. Well does Brice recall that day "when literally thousands of planes of the 8th Air Force filled the sky to bomb the area, prior to the crushing onslaught of General George Patton's tanks of the Third Army." It was also on that day when Leslie McNair, the Commanding General of the U.S. Army Ground Forces, who was visiting from Washington, D.C. was accidently killed by a short drop of bombs from friendly planes. Brice was present watching it all happen! It was not unusual for incidents of this sort to occur during combat.

After D-Day, Brice was looking at the unbelievable sight of the Town of St. Lo. Destruction was so incredible that it was beyond belief. Large bull dozers tried to clear a path for vehicles so that food and ammunition could reach the thousands upon thousands of soldiers who were already on their way inland from the beaches. There were lots of bodies. The stench was unforgettable. Brice held his arm in front of his nose to get rid of the raw smell of dead bodies and animals. Piles of rubble unfortunately stayed in heaps for a long time to come and the bodies and pets that had been buried beneath continued to be a health problem. The army moved on...

When St. Lo fell, it paved the way for the tanks to fan out across France and it was not long before Paris was ready to be recaptured. Paris was declared an "open city" which meant that neither the Wehrmacht nor the Allies would bomb the city which according to Brice "was a blessing to spare such beauty."

Brice recalled "For awhile you collect things." He reviewed the coastal fortifications when they had recently been evacuated by the Germans at Omaha Beach. The personal possessions of German Soldiers were scattered all over the area including letters from family and friends. Brice knew how to read German. For one whole day he reviewed these letters, reading words that could also have been written to American soldiers by their parents. He thought "but for the will of God, these could be our soldiers. How stupid this whole thing is killing people you didn't know or should be concerned about."

For awhile Brice carried the letters with him to show friends and family but they became an impedimenta to slow him down. They got heavy...

Standing one day in chow line as a Major in Normandy, he remembers yellow jackets pouring out the sugared lemonaid. The stinging droves of yellow jackets swarmed over cups, on them and in them and by one's mouth. Besieged by these social wasps, he talked over his shoulder with another soldier standing in the line regarding the miserable phenomenon. The Officer turned out to be Omar Bradley whom Brice referred to as a "very down to earth sort of guy."

Brice was sent to Paris in 1944 on a mission to locate and commandeer a suitable building in that city for use of troops needed to implement his responsibility of managing the personnel accounting and casualty reporting. Since resources were only restricted to those premises previously occupied by Germans, locating something was not all that difficult. Germans had handpicked whatever real estate they wanted. Brice surmised "The Germans had all cleared out in a mad scramble to save their hides, except for Gestapo agents who had infiltrated the society in civilian clothes estimated to be 50,000 in number. Gestapo agents were everywhere but very undetectable. Great caution had to be taken." Brice continued, "These members were desperate and like cornered rats."

One of the potential premises inspected by Brice was a residence located at 54 Avenue D'Iena near the Etiole in the center of Paris. It just so happened, this same building had been the gathering point for stolen art treasures taken from Parisians and the French countryside. The building had been periodically visited by Field Marshall Hermann Goering, known as an avid art collector for his review of paintings. He directed selected shipments to Germany of known and valued artists such as those of the famous Rembrandt.

Upon Brice's initial reconnaisance of the premises at 54 Avenue D'Iena he was unexpectedly set upon by a Gestapo agent, who without any warning at point blank range fired a 25 Cal. Steyr automatic. The gun misfired. Brice quickly responded. The agent was carried out feet first.

Unwrapping a flannel cloth, the small black Austrian automatic used by the Gestapo agent was shown as Brice's only souvenir. The 25 CAL Steyr weapon used by German Officer was so small it barely passed ones fingertips. The gun has been kept with its faulty firing pin the same as it was on that fateful day. It has not been repaired, as that would distort the true nature of its historical value. It is of great attraction to Brice's six grandchildren. "Ultimately, it will be framed as a wall decoration" Brice speculates "but only after his demise as it is simply a sad reminder of an incident he would rather forget."

At the three story building, 54 Avenue D'Iena, Brice came upon all types of German possessions.There were open books they had been reading and cigarettes they had been smoking. In their haste to leave the edifice, cigarettes were left on edge of ashtrays to smoulder. Underwear was discarded on the floors, countless half-used wine glasses were strewn around with priceless bottles of wine filling rows upon rows of shelves. It was quite a spectacle of people who had lived lavishly but departing in haste. Asking, "When does an Army decide to get out?" Brice replied, "When the heat is on!"

The art work at 54 Avenue D'Iena was left in charge of a French concierge for the delicate task of sanctuary. Even after the Army Criminal Investigation Division had been advised of the presence of these valuable pieces of art, much disappeared. Brice feels that "in time of hostilities there is just too much to keep track of and much goes wrong but always hindsight seems to offer a radically different perspective." Ultimately the job of the Investigation Division was to identify from whom the paintings were stolen from and then have them returned.

As a Lieutenant Colonel, out for an everyday occurrence, Brice and his driver were on the way to Brittany Peninsula adjacent to the Cotentin Peninsula. Brice was checking out field conditions and verification of data regarding casualties. As Liason Officer, he could designate necessary orders for informal trips and investigations as need arose. As they crossed into France, the two men were caught in an assault by the Germans converging on two sides. The Jeep got blown over. They were caught in a cross fire! The driver of the vehicle was so scared, he hid under the conveyance in a fetal position. Brice pulled the driver out from under the Jeep by his legs demanding that they "turn the vehicle back over so they could get the hell out of there!"

Following VE-Day in May of 1945, Brice was transferred to the Mediterranean Theater of operations in Caserta, Italy. He was to continue in the same line of work but also to assist in demobilization of US Forces. This also included transfer of Forces to the still active area of operations in the Pacific. Things were definitely winding down during that period of time. However, there was still considerable guerilla activity in the northern part of Italy where the Germans were tenaciously resisting. (It was at this time, that Benito Mussilini was captured and strung up by his feet in the little town square of northern Italy.)

In Paris on VE-Day, Brice describes absolute bedlam! "People in the high buildings were throwing condoms filled with water on people in the street. There wasn't a dry stomach in Paris. P38 Fighter planes came flying over the center of the twelve lane arterial street, Champs-Elysees at roof level. The French populace were wild and uncontrolled."

Architecturally, Brice felt buildings not bombed, last a lot longer in European countries. Buildings are not torn down so much. Paris being an open city with not much shelling during World War II kept the historical, picturesque and fascinating Notre-Dame Cathedral with its mullioned windows and Gothic pinnacles intact.

Brice described the German Army as a very efficient machine. He deduced, "the war was ended by many situations. The numbers of expendable soldiers were torrential. The Russian's interference into the activity was a major help in subduing and keeping the German Army busy on many fronts. Adolf Hitler's ridiculous handing of the German Armies was a big factor in their ultimate defeat."

Brice was re-assigned to the United States at the end of 1945 having spent two full years in two theaters of operation. When he departed from the United States, he had been married less than one year and was looking forward to seeing his new daughter Pam for the first time. He landed at Newport Beach, Virginia after a very stormy crossing of the Atlantic on board the aircraft carrier, Corregidor. He was greeted by his former wife, Doris and some good friends.

He recalls reciting the familiar poem as he approached the shores of the United States of America, "Is there a man with soul so dead who never to himself hath said, This is my own, my native land."

Ernest F. Power

United States Army 1942 - 1962

Retired, Reserve

At age 61, called back to Vietnam, 1969

In Sonoma the very popular Ernie Power is a people person. Get in line if you want an appointment. You will finally be embraced by this affable man with the shock of lightning white hair and meet those eyes that hold lots of world memories and history. Born in Worchester, Massachusettes on the last day of December in 1908, he became one of the eight "army brats" (his brothers and sisters numbered seven) who accompanied his Father to Army camps.

Ernie's Dad was a Major in the cavalry transferred to Fort Bliss, Texas in 1916. Two years before the Power's arrival at Fort Bliss, there were a series of Mexican revolutions involving rebel leaders of Mexico and the Americans. The only Five Star General of the United States at that time, excepting George Washington was General John J. Pershing. He commanded the American Cavalry not only from a horse but from a Dodge touring car at Fort Bliss. One of the most colorful of the Mexican rebels causing trouble in the area was Pancho Villa described in the book, *Black Jack Pershing*. As a bandit chief and character degenerated with each success, Pancho Villa, jovial and expansive had a personality holding charm for the Americans. After Pancho Villa's capture of Juarez "he looted banks and storehouses, extorted money from American ranch and mine owners and began living high like a Chinese war lord." He bought five useless airplanes, Pierce-Arrow touring cars for himself and favorite officers, a luxurious special train with drawing room, barber and salon shops, a flush toilet which kept him marveling at, incessantly. The great mission of Villa was to divide up haciendas and give the land to the peons.

Pershing was vigilent and wary of Villa even though earlier he had entertained the guerrilla. Pancho was made an outlaw by the United States State Department. Villa had sworn vengence on the United States after losing 8,500 men in one battle to U. S. Forces. On January 10th, 1916, nineteen Americans taken from a train by the rebel were shot to death. On March 9th, Pancho Villa and what was left of his 1,000 troops raided the border town of Columbus, New Mexico. Columbus was a little desolate town, headquarters of the 13th Cavalry which had banks, storehouses, military supplies and machine guns. The early morning was very dark when Villa riders in an unwise move set fire to the village hotel causing flames to rise high in the sky. The light from the fire outlined the Mexican invaders making them easy target practice for the American riflemen. Two-hundred fifteen Villistas lay dead. Corpses piled high then soaked in oil were burned in the desert.

It was in this forsaken country in a hostile foreign environment, that Ernie Power age eight was impressed with Army life. Ernie decided "I will become a soldier just like Dad." After all, he was brought up around General Pershing and a young officer from West Point, George S. Patton, Jr. of the 8th Cavalry who was Pershing's Aide.

Ernie's family was too large to live at camp so the Army provided a house which was rented from the Flying Cordova Circus. While the kids were sleeping in pup tents one night, a bunch of Mexican Soldiers ran through the yard. When the children told their parents about the event, they were considered to have been using their imaginations. This could be just one more colorful tale in the fertile minds of the children. A week later, Mexican Soldiers were all over the house. Ernie's Mother started screaming when she saw these soldiers were carrying rifles! When the family had moved into the house, they had been warned not to go into the cellar. It was loaded with trunks of circus stuff and off limits! The soldiers made it to the cellar and stripped the trunks of guns! Rifles in the trunks had been brought in by a tunnel route from the Rio Grande River. From that excitement, the children were motivated to spend time on the roof tops watching for Pancho Villa. The first recollection Ernie has is sitting on the house top and watching Villa fire across from the vicinity of Jarez, Mexico. When Ernie was old enough for joining the Army, he became a part of the Signal Corps and was sent overseas with the 9th Air Force.

While Ernie was still a small child, his Mother reached over him to close a bedroom window during a storm. She was struck by lightning. Another time, Ernie living in Lawton, Oklahoma went to close a window over Ernie Jr., his son's bed and was also struck by lightning! He couldn't move a muscle! Other lightning strikes to Ernie were in a tent in ROTC and in a tent in CCC Camp. While overseas, lightning struck his hut and hit his phone. While driving a car near Decatur, Illinois lightning struck his car and melted the tail light! A few years ago during a storm in Sonoma, California his T.V. was knocked out of power.

Lightning of another kind struck when the Army man was introduced to an Army nurse at Fort Sill, Oklahoma. Ernie and Loyce were married but in secret. Army nurses were not supposed to marry. They met almost anywhere. When Ernie's wife heard some nurses were going to be sent to the Philippines from Fort Sill, she resigned and established a home in Oklahoma where Ernie enlisted in the Signal Corps in 1942, graduating from Officers Training as a Lieutenant.

As a recruit on the way to Europe, he was in a large convoy five or six ships in width. Two ships on each end were torpedoed and sunk. Ernie made it to Scotland at Hiwycomb. Following Patton, Ernie was given command of a Unit Airbase. Landing D-Day+6, Ernie was on Normandy Beach to maintain and operate the airbase "just like in a control room" for the 9th Air Force Signal Corps.

Glen Miller the famous band leader of the 40's occasionally visited the command post. After the landing on Normandy beaches, Miller operated from an airbase outside of Paris. His famous theme song "*Moonlight Serenade*" was played every night after taps bugle was summoned to the troops. One night a Corporal came running in shouting! "Captain, Captain, we lost him!" He was referring to Glen Miller who disappeared off the radar screen. Search teams never did find the band leader. His plane hit in the channel never to be recovered. (Interestingly while interviewing Ernie, he had a radio quietly playing "good old classics from the 1940's" in the background. While he told this story about his friend, the station played "*Moonlight Serenade*" by Miller's band.)

Ernie found out he had been promoted to Captain from a telegram sent by his wife. The telegram read, "Daughter born. You've been promoted to Captain." It was two years before the Captain saw his child. Colleen called everyone in uniform "You Daddy! You Soldier." It made Ernie's day when she finally came up to him, pointing to one of his buddies and said "You papa, he soldier."

Moving across France following Patton, Ernie established airbases with control towers in tents. Their radar was the early version which left out the complete circle. When Glen Miller was lost, it was monitored on the part of the scope that did not pick up the image.

While in the German area, Officers were required to take their companies and see the Holocaust, a scene never to be forgotten by any of them.

In the proximity of Battle of the Bulge, Ernie recalled quite a lot of Germans surrendered to the Americans. They "just gave up." After the war was declared over, Captain Powers went back to France awaiting new orders. Ernie and a few others were called to Eisenhower's Quarters. They were told that "You will be excused for 24 months from combat duty." On the day after the meeting while on ship, so no one would know where the men were headed, they were given amended orders to Okinawa! From that point until they came into Boston Harbor everyone was drunk!! After a brief leave to meet his new daughter and enjoy his wife's company, Ernie was sent to Ogden, Utah with a job classification as Supply Management Officer for Okinawa. His family followed him to that far distant shore in the Pacific. His son graduated from high school in Okinawa during 1947. A typhoon hit and almost wiped out the high school!

Returning to the United States to Decator, Illinois (where he met one of his lightning attacks) he then proceeded to Haneau, Germany near Frankfurt. Powers began to believe that everywhere he went a crisis erupted. This time the powers-that-be called the political problem the Berlin Crisis. The Army worked back and forth from East and West Germany. Ernie's Mother died. This was a catalyst for moving his family back home. His hope and dream to stay put for a little while was dashed. He was sent back to Okinawa as Special Advisor to Chiang Kai-shek on the subject of Supply and Accounting. He settled on the Formosa Island. Ernie supervised manual accounting.

The Army called their experienced Supply and Accountant man to Washington D.C., to meet with representives of the I.B.M. Corporation. There were representatives from the Navy, Air Force, Marines as well as those of the Army. A big screen was put up in front of the men. "This is the machine of the future!" they were informed. "It will be called the computer." A machine almost as big as a railroad box car was installed in Philadelphia for the Army. Having attended this conference, a woman employee came up to Ernie when he was Colonel and said, "something is wrong. I have an order for 400 Jeeps." After a little investigation and notification to Washington, he was ordered to the Pentagon. "Since you know about these things (computers) and you're responsible for all items going to the Pacific, you go to Vietnam and check on this!" At 61 years of age Ernie thought "Oh, no! not again!" He took a Sergeant along and the Sergeant discovered 'two discs' were not functioning which caused zeros to be shown on the machine. The computer was reporting incorrect information. When that problem was fixed, Ernie could go home.

It was while Ernie was in Tiawan to advise Chiang Kai-shek that he had a houseboy. When the Colonel was about to leave for home he received an unusual letter handwritten in purple ink. He still has the letter written exactly as follows: Dated 3rd May 1948. from a boy of yesterday. "Thank you very .much for the day befor day I was coming to see you like I promised but. last two days I was so bucy with our young school hood friends meeting so pleas for give me. I have been going every day to look for a job. but failed Mean time and not only failed fortunetly you got me one and was very glad to start but that failed too. so will you kindly help me out and find for me another. I will come up to see you to morrow morning will yuo feel to difficult read this letter but please let me Excuse for you I wish I am wishing your happy and your shinciely. Name Kyakaby (the Boy who had come to Here.)

Ernie really retired in 1973 to Agua Caliente and Sonoma. He mustered out at Fort Mason, San Francisco. With his wife Loyce and three children including his second son Jim, the family spent time at Crissey Field. He was even late in getting there... In Sonoma, Ernie and Loyce along with Jerry Casson helped establish a large Senior Center called Jerry Casson Vintage House. He and his wife also helped establish the Health Fair and Flu Clinics. In 1989, the busy couple obtained a condo in town. In 1990, the Powers were named Honorary Alcaldes by the city of Sonoma for outstanding volunteer work. In 1991, Loyce was called to her Heavenly life and Ernie moved to Westlake House continuing to be one of the busiest seniors of the area.

On Mondays, he has helped preschool children at the Methodist Church learn softball. On Tuesday and Thursdays, he assists the Council of Aging Senior Program. On Friday, he helps direct the Alzheimers Program. He helped organize NARF (Association Retired Federal Employees). He still enjoys a game of bowling. When he gets old enough (his eyes light up) "I'll take up the game of golf!"

Richard, O'connor, *Black Jack Pershing*, Doubleday & Company, Inc., Garden City, New York, 1961. 431 pp. See chapts. 5 and 6.

Jack T. Kimbrell

United States Navy, 1943 - 1946

Jack Kimbrell was a civilian on one day and an Ensign the next. He had the title of Ensign DVS, USNR. The DVS meant Deck Volunteer Specialist. He had been working in Chicago, Illinois with a Bachelor of Science degree in Mechanical Engineering. With a college degree in engineering, the Navy offered a direct officers commission.

Initially, the taste of Navy life included a 10 day indoctrination period at Hollywood Beach Hotel in Florida. Accommodations were considered to be first class. The indoctrination consisted mainly of Navy customs and traditions plus an introduction to the subject of navigation. For physical endurance, men were required to run in sand on the beach. If one realizes how hard it is to walk in sand, then make believe you were a Navy man along with Jack. You would find out, "it was not easy to run in sand, especially if you wear a raincoat, carry a pack on your back, and tote a rifle."

Jack's immediate orders were to report to Newport News, Virginia to become a navigator. He had been a mechanical engineer with skills to design and build things, generate electricity and build rockets. With little feeling of being scared the new Navy recruit decided the Captain would show him how to be a navigator. Jack had found a second-hand bookstore and purchased a book by Bowditch, called *Practical Navigator.* The Captain, that he naively believed was going to give him pointers about navigation techniques was not even aboard the first ship that Jack was to navigate! "The Captain was in New York running in sand learning to be a Captain!" Jack said. Some very helpful Petty Officers including a Quartermaster took him under their wings.

Jack's first sea journey to Greenland delivering materials was very cold. It was wintertime in the North Atlantic. Jack rummaged around for every piece of clothing he could muster, still remaining bodily chilled while on watch.

From one extreme to another the Navy rewarded the new recruit by sending his crew to sunny California, at Long Beach followed by a stint in Honolulu, Hawaii. They made these ports of call from aboard the Battleship USS New York. The New York BB34 had the distinction of being Flagship of the Fleet at the surrender of the Germans at the end of World War I. She was built about 1910 as a coal burning ship and later converted to an oil burning ship. From Hawaii, the ship went to the Islands of Saipan and Tinian. Saipan is the island where Inola Gay took off with the atom bomb which was dropped on the Japanese mainland. The United States Pacific Fleet had gathered at Saipan/Tinian for invasion of Iwo Jima.

Jack was assigned to an underwater demolition team with the task of removing underwater obstacles made of concrete, steel and wood. The Japanese had built these impediments to keep ships out and to detour invasion troops. The obstructions were great hindrances used by the Japanese soldiers so they could better practice their marksmanship on the unsuspecting Americans. Progress was very slow and extremely dangerous toward the beaches. Some clearing was done by setting charges of dynamite in and around those obstacles blowing them up and out of the way. Little yellow bouys were floated with an anchor about every 20 to 30 yards marking the cleared paths.

Jack's demolition detail on Red Beach was on the southwest shore of Iwo Jima. There were several teams working on demolition tasks and quite a few men were hurt or killed by the Japanese. As the workers struggled with the dangerous job of identifying and removing mines, the enemy picked the workers off one by one with their guns. This island was filled with thousands upon thousands of Jap soldiers who not only had an airport but also big guns and powerfully built pillboxes, some hid in caves.

The American Pacific Fleet surrounded the island with ships. There were destroyers, cruisers, battleships and aircraft carriers and maybe even some submarines. The orders were to take Iwo Jima. One reason for the importance of the island was to obtain the airstrip which would support other fields of operation in the Pacific. The beach of Iwo Jima was terrible. It was made up of volcanic ash. If you tried to dig a foxhole you could barely dig a dent. It was impossible to have straight up and down sides which were needed to deflect shrapnel and debris of gunfire.

The Pacific Fleet had encircled the island target. One of the problems that occurred was when the ships on the southwest side of the island fired, the shells would bounce and rebound off the strong pillboxes, then ricochet into the fleet on the northeast side of the island. So the entire fleet moved to one side of the island.

The Navy engaged in a lot of bombardment. Jack was then serving as a Gunnery Officer in the lower handling room of Turret Four on board the USS New York. The air force bombed and strafed the island. Soldiers landed and men were deployed on Red Beach. The landing strip was taken first, then Mount Surabachi. The battles were no fun. Japanese shot straight down from the mountain while soldiers were climbing the mountain and while Navy was providing bombardment support. Men were caught in the middle of this gunfire!

One memorable event was that the island was ham-shaped with Mount Surabachi at the small end and a large plateau at the big end of the ham. About 7:30 every night a six or an eight inch gun on the plateau opened up on the fleet. One evening, every gun battery of the ships fired back as one. That part of the island disappeared!

The USS New York had ten guns which fired fourteen inch diameter projectiles weighing 2,000 pounds each. Each salvo consisted of 20,000 pounds of projectiles, when New York expended her entire salvo of shells. To hoist one of those 2,000 pound shells, a chain fall on a track was used. The bottom of the shell was fitted with a pad eye to which the chain was attached. The shell was moved to an elevator, taken up one deck... then to another elevator, up to the gun room. The powder was delivered through another elevator system. There were 480 pounds of powder used to fire one of the 2,000 pound shells.

On other ships, levels were modified as to where you and the guns were located. You could be four decks away from the guns, if they were located on the Boat Deck below the Bridge. If guns were located on the Foremast, they might be located as high as 150 feet up in the air.

Jack knew the USS Guam was present with its heavy cruiser guns. After the heavy shelling, the foot soldiers captured the Island. This battle was one of the most intensly bloody, costing both sides of the conflict extreme loss of life.

After the invasion of Iwo Jima, Jack was sent to the Island of Ie Shima where he became a Shore Fire Control Officer It was then that Jack decided that DVS meant "any rotten detail becomes my mission!" The duty of a shore-fire-control-officer was to find a target. He would radio coordinates to the ship by directing the fire up or down, right or left, to more accurately hit targets. Abandoning the little boat they used to get to the shore on the beach, and while lying in some scrubby bushes, Jack was also considered expendable. From a radio which he carried on his back, he would send messages to Officers on the ship "as to where their last shot landed." He was also expected to discover new targets. These suggestions might be barracks of the enemy, radio or gun emplacements, enemy planes or tanks. This job could take place either night or day with close calls always at hand. On one life threatening call, Jack was approaching the shore in a small boat with seven men aboard. The boat (landing craft vehicular personnel, LCP) was destroyed by the enemy and only one person survived... It was not "friendly fire." He was not sure if the explosion was caused by a shell or a mine. Of the seven buddies on the detail, Jack was the only one left alive...

The motto of his ship was "run or fight." The USS New York could only travel at 15 knots top speed. Even the ship itself was considered "expendable." The next unforsaken destination in the Pacific they traveled to was the Island of Manus in the Admiralties. One blade was knocked off each of the ship's two propellers. When they are working properly, the propellers are moved by steam engines. Each of the two engines was capable of 76,000 horsepower. Each of the blades weighed in at 7 tons of brass. Each propeller on the New York weighed 21 tons not including the 9 tons for the propeller hub. The Admiralty Islands had a floating dry dock capable of lifting the 45,000 ton USS New York completely out of the water.

There were no opportunities for recreation, no shore leaves and no fun. All the men could do was repair the ship and prepare to go back to sea. Jack was transferred to the Engineering B Division which was responsible for generating the steam for steam engines and also for operating the evaporators to make fresh water from sea water. The fresh water was for the crew and for the steam boilers. The ship had six boilers and two evaporators. The evaporators provided about 100,000 gallons of fresh water each day. The water was stored in tanks along the sides of the ship.

There were also fuel tanks along the sides and bottom of the ship. When fully loaded with fuel, the ship held 1,575,000 gallons of fuel oil. The fuel was used to make steam and to supply other ships with fuel. With two ships moving close together, a line was thrown from the New York to another ship. The line was used to pull across another heavier line which was then used to pull the fuel hose aboard. The hose was held up by cranes on the New York. There were several loops in the hoses to allow slack, so if the ships moved farther apart the hoses would not break. With the hoses fastened to the piping system of the New York and the other ship, the New York pumped fuel oil into their tanks. If a ship started to list, water could be pumped from one side to another side of the ship for balance and to keep the ship in an upright position. The heavy liquid was kept moving as hoses were tossed through the air on a crane as it swung out to the receiving ship. The men on the other ship pulled the huge hoses over. With loops in the hoses for give or slack the men attached the hoses to the piping system of the second ship. Hoses remained in these big loops so as to allow for enough play, yet security of connection between the two moving ships.

While the fuel was being transferred, it was time to swap things. One constant item available for swapping was movies. After having a movie and showing it so many times, it became a bore. Movies were exchanged between ships to obtain a little variety. The only trouble with the New York's movie was that it was "Snow White and the Seven Dwarfs" and the other ships, in spite of being serviced with life blood of fuel, wouldn't trade their movie for Snow White!

At Admiralty Island Dock, two new propeller blades were scrounged up from somewhere. They were hoisted up and bolted on the hub that weighed an additional 9 tons. It took an 8 ton crane to lift the bolt. B Division reported to the Captain each morning as to how much fuel the ship carried and how much fresh water was available. Besides sharing fuel with other ships, the New York a 45,000 ton ship, used 275 gallons of fuel each mile traveled. At 15 knots, the top speed of the ship was 20 miles per hour. If the ship was traveling at full speed for a 24 hour day it could use up to 132,000 gallons of fuel oil per day!

Karama Retto Island "took it!" in one afternoon!! It was a little island. No messing around! It was important for use as an advance base for the invasion of Okinawa. After the Karama Retto Island rout, the invasion of Okinawa was dished up on the full plate of the men from the New York. The gunners bombarded Naha, Okinawa. The ship was anchored 500 yards off shore. The United States Pacific Fleet had three or four battleships, some aircraft carriers, crusiers, destroyers and corvets in attendance. For 86 days and nights, the island was bombarded and bombed. Boom! take down one row of buildings in the town. Boom! take down the second row of buildings in the town. One salvo after another in succession was expended. Ten guns holding 14 inch shells expelled them each time from the New York.

Naha, Okinawa had been a fairly modern city. Row after row of dwellings and shops were leveled. Japanese people were still around. Jack would have hated to have been one of them. Kamikazes were coming in every night numbering a hundred or so. One would have had to have been there to even imagine the carnage of equipment and the loss of the lives of men. The gunners contined to bomb Naha, Okinawa. The shells had 11 mile ranges. Their guns were hardly elevated.

Fifty to 150 to 200 planes were destroyed every night. Only two planes hit the New York. The ship had ten 5" antiaircraft guns, 10 quad 40 MM guns and many 50 caliber machine guns for air defense. Fourteen inch guns and 8" guns were no good for antiaircraft. Five inch antiaircraft guns were good. 40MM were deployed. At 144 shells per minute, four guns battering away used 4,000 rounds a minute. Not counting all the above, fifty calibre machine guns were sending their load through the air. The ship was nothing but guns "a floating guns ship."

The suicide attacks by the Japanese Pilots during the war (the Kamikazes) "sank many American ships!" The dare devil Japanese pilots that hit the New York destroyed two airplanes used for aerial spotting of gunfire. These planes were old 0S2U Kingfishers (biplanes) with open cockpit. Their top speed wide open would be 150 miles per hour, straight down! The planes had been used to see where shells were going in the daytime. The Kamikazes hit up front on the New York and very effectively killed themselves. They came in not particularly fast. Each carried one big bomb which exploded upon contact.

After 86 days and nights of gunfire, the Island of Okinawa was still with the Japanese. But, the USS New York moved away from the shore due to a typhoon. The typhoon was worse than the Japanese!! The ship had to get out and run! so as to not capsize or be pushed into the island ashore. New York was a 580 foot long ship. Jack saw the first 150 feet buried in water. The ship carried a 175 foot Foremast. Waves broke over the Foremast. One young sailor asked if "he could switch bunks." He was on the Third Deck and waves were breaking over his bunk. The sailor asked, "Where can I move to where it is dry?" Jack replied, "beats me, nothing is dry."

An inclinometer is a needle, free to swing in a verticle plane, used to indicate the horizontal plane. An airplane uses an inclinometer as a reference to the horizon, a turn and bank indicator. As the New York rolled in the Pacific waters during the typhoon, the needle on the ship's inclinometer moved over 22 degrees. Waves were estimated at 50 feet to 75 feet high. The sky was dark, day and night. Heavy rains swept men off their feet. Winds pushed at 120 to 140 miles per hour. A great wave would overcome the ship with a Wham! The men were 500 miles out to sea where there was no other land except Okinawa Island from where they had evacuated. The New York had tried to run away from the storm. Jack declares, "the Florida and Carolina storm of 1992 was mild to this storm. The men on LCI's couldn't make it. They sunk. LST's didn't make it, they sunk!

The typhoon lasted like a forever but it was four or five days in length. Men could hardly walk. They held on to every solitary thing to move around. All they could eat was sandwiches as liquid stuff would slop all over everything and everybody.

When the typhoon was over, there were two white streaks catapulting in the waters. These streaks were not exactly like star streaks reflected in calm waters. The streaks turned out to be the genus, Procaena, gorgeous beautiful porpoises with triangular shaped fins on their backs. What a welcome relief from a possible torpedo on the run. The porpoises were promises for a renewal of spiritual strength to the men. It was like a God given gift chosen from a calm and peaceful Pacific as a present to the men.

After the storm, the men of USS New York were spared from returning or shelling more of Okinawa. The Japanese homeland had been bombed by the Atomic bomb and the enemy gave up the fight and ended the war. The New York lingered at sea around Okinawa. There were no celebrations regarding VJ-Day except the crew eventually went back to Hawaii. With the signing of the peace treaty the ship became a troopship bound for New York. Transferred by request Jack went to Great Lakes Naval Training School near Chicago. He did not want to return on the New York's next mission bound for Bikini Atoll. That mission would include atomic bomb testing. Jack had read about those kind of tests and wanted no part of them!

Jack spent some temporary duty at the Great Lakes Naval Training Station. One afternoon he was given a choice of becoming a civilian. As swift as that suggestion was made, Jack was an ex-Navy man by merely saying the word "Yes."

A professor for 40 years at Washington State University, Jack's titles include being a Professional Engineer and Professor Emeritus. Upon retirement in 1986, he and his wife Maxine, moved to Albuquerque, New Mexico. As retirees they have had an enjoyable time helping the Habitat for Humanities build houses for the poor. Jack and Maxine have traded homes with a couple from Sonoma, California. The Sonomans are building the houses in the Habitat for Humanities program in 1994 in the place of Jack and his wife. The Kimbrells were residents in the Sonoma area for one-half year in exile.

Bill Barnes

United States Navy, 1931 - 1959

Bill Barnes, born in Milltown Indiana in 1914 was on duty. The USS Dale 353 was anchored near the Pacific Ocean in Pearl Harbor on December 7, 1941. Bill was a First Class Water Tender assigned to the Fire Room in the Dale as one of the "boiler men." His duty for Saturday and Sunday that week gave him authority to be in charge of the boiler rooms. He and a Chief Petty Officer enjoyed the early morning sunshine as it warmed the Deck of the ship. While balancing cups of coffee on their knees, Bill noticed a plane coming in. The sun's rays "caught" under the plane. This reflection caused an unusual shining under its wings. "Holy, cow!" Bill said, "Did you ever see anything like that?!" There were two suns on the wings, one on each wing tip.

Since September 1939, Bill was aware men stationed in and near the Pacific Ocean knew that a war with Japan was "just waiting to happen." It was common knowledge and a topic of conversation. Being a Naval man for ten years privy to all the scuttlebutt and, as if driven by a premonition on December 7th, 1941, Bill and the Chief Petty Officer charged to the bowels of their ship. They got a couple of firemen "to light off the boiler" and "bring steam pressure up." They ordered the Engine Room staff "get ready to go out to sea!" The first ship preceding USS Dale out of the Harbor was the USS Monihan. By 4:30 in the afternoon, Bill realized he had not even had time to go to the bathroom. Being short of hands there had been no relief in the fire room.

All executive officers of the Dale on December 7th, 1941 were not with the fledgling crew. The Officers were on liberty in Honolulu, or thereabouts. The highest ranking person in charge of USS Dale was Ensign Radell. He made the decision and would hold the responsiblity for leaving port. Out the narrow channel, following USS Monihan the two ships escaped. They rendezvoused by taking formation with other United States ships. At that point in time, the USS Dale came under the command of the highest ranking officer of the assembled fleet.

Bill spent the rest of the day in the bowels of USS Dale, He did not know that Commander of all air groups of the Japanese First Air Fleet had "an assignment beyond all of his dreams." When Fuchida, the Japanese Commander had been informed of a possible air attack on Pearl Harbor, he remembered "catching his breath" in awe. The more he heard about the event "the more astonishing it seemed." He knew the water depth in Pearl Harbor was only 12 meters and the harbor itself was only 500 meters in width. When he pointed this out, his good friend Minoru Genda kept urging and insisting torpedoes could be launched. Torpedoes would "add to the surprise of attack" and "multiply its effectiveness." According to an article written by Captain Mitsuo Fuchida "there was specific training and expansive preparations begun in September, 1941 which included torpedo launching for the ships of Pearl Harbor."

It took two months for Japanese Flyers to figure out how to solve torpedo launching in shallow water. The problem was solved by "fixing additional fins to the torpedoes." In November of 1941, First Air Fleet planes were taken on board six Japanese carriers, two battleships, one light cruiser, nine destroyers, three submarines and nine tankers that were assembled in isolated Tankan Bay. This was the second island from the southern end of a chain of islands extending from Hokkaido to the northeast.

The ships moved into the cold waters of the northern Pacific Ocean.

When Bill and Ensign Radell of USS Dale moved out of Pearl Harbor on December 7th, 1941 that early morning, they were unaware that Japanese Captain Fuchida had lots of worries, misgivings and ideas of strategy that were different from his orders. But when the time came he felt "keen enthusiasm and was reassured" realizing his duty was that of a warrior which was "to fight and win victory for his country." The Japanese Imperial Fleet had proceeded past the Aleutians and Midway Island to keep away from U. S. submarines and range of air patrols. Bill could not have known that Japanese intelligence knew identities of American ships in Pearl Harbor and exactly where they were anchored. (This was interesting as the United States itself, carried out a mock attack on Pearl Harbor as early as 7 February 1932 using the northerly approach for exercise with similar information gathered.)

Bill did not know to what extent the Japanese were aware of the activities of the Officers of the ships on week ends in Hawaii. But, Bill was aware that a campaign of letters had been written by American moms and dads to their Congressmen requesting weekend 'leavetaking' into Pearl Harbor. This action was instigated so that men stationed in the Pacific could have relaxation and recreation on the week ends. It was a known fact by even the Japanese that most of the Pacific Fleet making it into the port of Pearl Harbor stayed until Tuesday mornings.

Bill was not aware that the Japanese knew the general practices of the United States Pacific Fleet, such as their usual procedure of leaving Hawaii on certain days of the week and their coming in, so as to enjoy weekends. This practice was well known in the Pacific region, why not the Japanese? The men taking USS Dale out of port on 7 December 1941 could not have known the Japanese even kept tab on which ships were back on the U.S. shores under repair in San Diego and when those ships were expected to return to Hawaii.

Bill and the men busy in the bottom of USS Dale could not have known that on this particular Japanese mission, there was the sum of 183 fighters, bombers and torpedo planes. These planes had flown in, going due south from their carriers toward Oahu Island into Pearl Harbor that morning. There were forty nine level bombers, fifty one dive-bombers and forty-three fighters plus another forty-three fighters flying cover, according to the man who led the attack.

No one but Commander Fuchida knew that the Japanese planes were guided into Pearl Harbor by the morning radio cast at Honolulu. The Japanese Commander later wrote "flying through thick clouds we had drifted off course five degrees and corrected this course by turning the antenna in the exact direction of the lazy Sunday morning broadcast." The radio station even gave the Pilot the weather and conditions around Pearl Harbor that morning. The Commander changed his plan of attack based upon the radio station weather news.

In case Bill hadn't noticed, the first dive-bombers attacked Hickam and Wheeler at 7:55 a.m. At 7:57 torpedo planes were at battleships. At 8:00 a.m fighters were strafing air bases and at 8:05 level bombers were at the battleships. Bill and his shipmates were unaware that there was no indication of air combat from the Americans on the first attacks. Men on ships in the harbor still appeared to be sleeping. The radio station kept on playing the normal broadcast information. Directly from the Commander's plane the code for a successful surprise attack was sent to Hiroshima Bay. The words were "Tora, tora, tora." There is a Japanese saying "A tiger (tora) goes out 1,000 ri (2,000 miles) and returns without fail."

Bill and his shipmates were definitely not cognizant "of waterspouts rising alongside the battleships or of dark gray bursts of gunfire clouds." Being in the bowels of USS Dale, Bill could not have known the Commander's plane was headed for the USS Nevada flying at only 3,000 meters with a load of bombs. The "colossal explosion" of the USS Arizona in Battleship Row was mostly for the enemy's eyes during the attack. The USS Tennessee was on fire and then the lead Japanese Commander hit the USS Maryland. "Four bombs in perfect pattern" reached the ships like "devils of doom" according to Fuchida. When he reviewed the destruction he was "laying on the floor of his plane watching the fall of the bombs through a peephole." The Japanese Captain Fuchida knew the target ship USS Utah had already capsized. He knew both USS West Virginia and Oklahoma had sides almost blasted off and were sinking in a flood of heavy oil. The USS Arizona had apparently blown up when her magazine was hit. USS Maryland and Tennessee were also on fire. Other hits were made on USS Nevada, West Virginia, Oklahoma and California. Torpedo bombers also zeroed in on USS Helena and Oglala.

The Second Japanese air strike was not seen by Bill nor by his buddies. It was composed of thirty-six fighters with suns on their wings, fifty-four high level bombers to attack Hickamfield and naval air station Kaneohe and there were 81 more dive-bombers sent to hit warships. By then the sky was so covered with smoke that targets were very difficult to make out. By then the antiaircraft fire was also very heavy. The seaplane base at Ford Island was all in flames as was Wheeler Field. Mitsuo Fuchida was in the air over the area for over three hours and photographed results. He even rescued two of his own fighter planes that had gone astray. His was the last plane back on the Japanese Carrier, Akagi.

Bill was on USS Dale on December 7th, 1941 as he had not cared for weekends in Honolulu. There were "just too many sailors on shore." One had to stand in line for just about everything. Standing in line included: for sandwiches, ice cream, for the bus, to get a beer and if one believes in literature of the times, it included ten minute sessions with prostitutes while standing in line waiting for them, as well. Since there had been increasing problems of drunken sailors sleeping all over, orders were "that unless you had private quarters, you were expected to be aboard ship by 12 P.M." Bars were closed at midnight. Bill simply did not care much about going to shore. Except once, he was chosen to go with 10 other "White Hats" for two nights at the Royal Hawaiian Hotel. But that was before the war started.

In the 1939-1941 era, the armed forces had a hard time getting any money from Congress to fix up the ships. You couldn't get work done in the Navy yards. If you complained "that the pump needed work" the answer was "there was no more money." When men expended the time they had enlisted for, many did not re-enlist due to the hardships. In 1941 a lot of ships were on the East Coast of the United States because of the war in Europe. After December 7th, the United States Fleet in the Pacific received more ships.

Bill had planned on joining the Navy in high school but waited until he graduated. He went to the Navy Recruiting Station in 1931. He was only sixteen years old. The Naval Recruiting Officer stated "Come back again when you are seventeen." Bill took a test, passed the physical and then was told "we'll call you!" In September of that year, he received a letter stating "there is a special opening for a Navy man in the Navy Medical Corps. Go to school, go now. Let us know if you are interested, we'll send papers." Bill went to Portsmouth, Virginia to the Naval Hospital Corps School. He was assigned to a Veterans Hospital located in Philadelphia, Pennsylvania where he worked hard and conscientiously. The young man made good marks on the written tests. In fact, he had the highest marks. Men were paid $36.00 per month as Hospital Apprentice 2nd Class.

In 1933, Bill was called to the office. "We have bad news for you. We don't want you anymore. You can change your rate to Apprentice Seaman and go on a ship. You can go into engineering and go as a fireman or you can go home, no questions asked." The pay for the new job with new skills to be learned was the same pay as the old job at $36.00 per month. That was until President Roosevelt was elected, then the men received a 15% pay cut which changed the amount to $29.00 per month! What was Bill to do? He was too ashamed to go home. He had been away for two years. He was humiliated that he received a pay cut after two years from $36.00 to $29.00!

Bill took "being kicked out of the U.S. Naval Medical Hospital" very hard. The real reason for the action was the U.S. Naval Hospitals, traditionally taken care of by other Veterans, was changed by a very blunt Franklin D. Roosevelt to the civilian market. President Roosevelt had just been elected. He dictated that all Veteran Hospitals be transferred to the civilian job market for staffing. There were 555 Naval hospital apprentices in excess. Bill had been one of them. He was more than disappointed. He was utterly disgusted! After working very hard and out of a clear blue sky, he had only a week to make up his mind as to what he was going to do next.

Economically it was "depression times." Bill's Dad had three kids in college. Bill had an older brother and sister in college. There were three more children at home. With six siblings in the family, Bill felt sorry for his dad who had a black smith shop. The family worked hard all summer to make ends meet. His mother canned food. Three pigs were bought to raise and butcher each year. The family kept chickens and a cow. Sometimes, Bill's mother only had $2.00 a month to buy groceries. After being away a couple of years, it was embarrassing to add more weight to his family's shoulders by returning home.

Choosing to be an apprentice and learning the work of a Seaman in the Boiler Room within six months, Bill was surprised by a raise to $54.00 a month. After about six months he received a letter on the ship informing him "You can go back in the Hospital Corps, if you want at $29.00 a month!" After three years in the Navy, he was disgusted with that kind of ridiculousness and stayed put!

Never being a quitter, Bill stayed with the Navy and was assigned to the Engineering Department of USS Bainbridge DD246, a destroyer. He worked in the boiler room of eight different ships from that time until retirement. The ships were USS's Bainbridge, Essex, Dale, Shea, St. Paul, Worden, Cape Esperance and Helm. The ships were all types including aircraft carriers, destroyers, a cruiser, a mine layer and one, the Worden was sunk in Alaska.

It was during a four day visit to the States when the USS Dale received radar that Bill met his wife, Lorene. She was from Kansas visiting her brother in Oakland. Some friends wanted Bill to meet the girl up the street. He saw her two nights. One year later on Christmas day 1943, they married. It was a nice day, sun shining, clear, no problems. Bill described himself as being "just a sailor in a white hat, who knew very little."

Regarding a question by the Editor, about a published picture of men dressed up like women, in the publication, *Essex*, Bill told the following story: "I experienced crossing the equator in 1936. The Fleet was out in the Pacific having exercises in war games. The Admiral with the task force knew he was nearing the equator. The Admiral's Chief of Staff, a Captain had never been over the imaginary line before. "My God, the Admiral decided to take the whole fleet of ships over the equator one day and to initiate all the people that had not been across the center of the earth previously." Since no one, except six men (shellbacks) had been initiated before on the Admiral's ship, twenty guys were taken over the equator, initiated and then returned as "shellbacks." In that way, they could initiate the rest of the guys the very same day.

There were different things to do to be initiated. Men dressed up in all sorts of unusual costumes and colored paint. Dressing up like a woman was a perennial choice for lots of laughter, especially using mop heads for hair and oranges for bosoms. Most generally men were in their skivvys (underwear) as the activities were too dangerous for keeping their clothes in good condition. The uninitiated were beat up as they crawled through a tube made from cloth. When you raised up to move through the tube it was a wonder you were not maimed. You had to keep moving, as other uninitiated guys were behind you. The longer you were in the tube the more blows you received. Grudges were taken out. When it was all over, you were called 'shellback' and you were told "its the Navy."

On one ship there were 200 guys beating 50. Bill felt sorry for them. But, in the Navy it was historically significant and a normal practice. Bill's Captain had not crossed the equator before this time. When Bill reported to the man the next morning after his initiation, the Captain was still in bed in his skivvys. He was bruised from head to toe. He was barely able to rise up to take the morning report. Joining in this event were 50 to 75 ships crossing the equator at one time for this initiation rite. Certificates were given to the shellbacks and were usually decorated with pictures of mermaids.

While in the South Pacific on a task force with USS Dale 353, the Chief Engineer reported to the men that they "were" bombed last night. The information was not relayed to General Quarters as the bombs missed the ship completely. Bombs had been released from United States planes bombing their own force but from so high up the bombs missed the ship completely.

On another event while USS St. Paul was assigned as a cruiser on maneuvers, General Quarters was shaken out of bed in the middle of the night. It was "All attention! and be accounted for!" The Lieutenant (Jg) had the division get up, line up and report "as to all present and accounted for." The whole division aboard the ship seemed to be secured so the men went back to bed...

Soon, General Quarters was awakened and mustered again. Something weird! The Officers were to personally see that everyone was aboard the ship. The chiefs declared "something funny is going on. See that every man in your department is here. See him, touch him." All came back and everybody present was accounted for. The next morning, no one seemed to know what had happened the night before! It was a big story but no one seemed to be missing! "What was going on?" was the general topic of conversation.

It seemed, the Officer of the Deck reported to the Captain "I think a man fell over the side of the ship." The Captain had thought, "if a man went over the side of the ship then the crew would try to save him." But evidently "this guy was mistaken!" Later on the next day the Captain went to see the visiting Admiral. Generally, even a Captain does not muster an Admiral! The Admiral was given a special cabin. He was king! An ordinary seaman has to have permission even to speak to a Captain. The Captain was almost out of bounds to go to the Admiral's quarters. When the Captain arrived at the cabin the Admiral was missing! The quarters were empty! At this juncture the questions swirling around the ship included "Did he jump? Was he thrown? Did he commit suicide? Was he drunk and stumbled over?" With so much conjecture and questioning, the Captain ordered that "there would be no more conversation on the ship regarding the Admiral." The Captain issued a statement "The Admiral is lost at Sea." If one tried to say something about the incident, no one would talk or make a comment. It was common to say, "don't talk to me."

When the USS Dale returned to Pearl Harbor after the 7th in 1941, the ship was anchored at Pearl City. Bill felt nothing had physically changed in Honolulu. The whole damage and concentration by the

Japanese airstrikes had been in the Navy Yard. It was a blessing the oil depot had not been hit. When sailors visited the damaged areas for the first time the impact was of dry docks being beat up. The USS Arizona appeared to look like it had just sat down on the bottom of the port. Its magazine of ammunition had exploded wide open. The ship was under water and bodies were still buried within the ship. The Memorial at first, run by Navy ships was taken over by the National Park Service. Bill attended the thirtieth Pearl Harbor Survivors Association Anniversary. He belongs to a Napa, California group which has a meeting in Honolulu every fifth year. He is called a Pearl Harbor Survivor.

Bill and his shipmates believed "it was lucky that Americans did not lose more ships in the attack. If an aircraft carrier like USS Lexington had been there it would have been bombed. Had the Japanese planned differently, they probably could have taken Honolulu. After all, the United States was 2,000 miles away. At that time Japanese ships outnumbered the U.S. ships in all categories and by large numbers. It took the USS Dale four days to make a trip to the United States Mare Island Ship Yard near San Francisco to receive radar. Radar installed on USS Dale in 1942 was already obsolete!"

The attack on Pearl Harbor was historically caused "in retribution for an embargo placed on the Japanese." Japan was embargoed by the United States Government because she joined Germany and Italy in the War. Japan had been cut off from steel (scrap iron had been purchased by the Japanese from Americans to make gun casings) and they were cut off from sources of oil in the South Pacific. After war was declared on Japan by the United States, Congress gave money for services and equipment that the Navy had needed for years. According to Bill "Conditions then became very wasteful." The motto was "to knock out Japan early."

After the war started with Japan, Bill was at sea from then on. He remembers he was on duty every day except for twelve days from years 1939 to 1943. He began to wonder "Am I the only guy in this Navy?" It was during this time, he was promoted to Chief Petty Officer in 1942 followed by three more promotions eventually receiving a Commission as Ensign in 1944. By 1959 after 28 years of service, he retired as Lieutenant Commander. He earned eight battlestars from Okinawa to the Philippines.

During World War II two of Bill's bothers were also in the conflict. One Brother, Vincent made it out of Iwo Jima. He was four years younger than Bill. His other brother, Delmar was drafted as Private First Class in the U. S. Army. These two Barnes Brothers did not stay in the "Services" after the war. Nor, did the three brothers see each other during the war period. Once in a while, playing cards with Vincent and Delmar, they kidded Bill about Navy money. Their oldest brother, of course, had stayed in the Navy long enough to receive retirement pay. Bill's brothers egged him on "to bid higher on the hand" after all "it was just Navy money." To Bill retirement meant "having been a crew member on eight different ships with the U. S. Navy for twenty eight years under all kinds of conditions!" Pictures of all eight ships on which Bill was assigned hang in his garage on a special wall.

Not a weed shows in the 'shipshape' rock garden at the back of Bill's home. Located near permanent open space a few cows can be seen in the distance. This is a quiet spot where one can contemplate one's life career. It is also a great home for enjoying the present with wife, Lorene in a small historic town called Sonoma, California.

Stillwell, Paul, ed., *Air Raid, Pearl Harbor, Recollections of a Day of Infamy*, United States Naval Institute, Naval Institute Press, Annapolis, Maryland, 1981. pps. 299, (p. 1-17). *I Led the Air Attack on Pearl Harbor*, By Captain Mitsuo Fuchida, former Imperial Japanese Navy. Edited by Captain Roger Pineau, U.S. Naval Reserve, (Retired).

Bob Bohna

Army Air Corps, 1942 - 1945

During the early years of World War II Bob was attending the University of California and "just to dodge the draft" decided to enter a cadet program. Actually there was a 'deal' made with General 'Hap' Arnold and the students, that if you joined the Army Air Force ROTC Cadet Program you would be deferred from the war until you finished college. The young college student had joined the Air Corp based on the promised deferment and mainly because he had absolutely no interest in the military. Not reading the small print which modified the affirmation as to the country's need, in two months Bob discovered the 'deal' as he had interpreted it was not in force any more. Believing he had three years security from the war, Bob was soon surprised. In six months he was receiving basic training while marching in cold winds and snow near Lincoln, Nebraska.

Bob had a little trouble with hand-eye coordination, a condition that had given him stumbling blocks in high school baseball games. He just couldn't hit the ball! In order "to make the Air Corps" he cheated on the induction vision test by memorizing the 20-20 line. With a blur in his right eye, he really did not have "Air Corps eyes." He had not even been up in an airplane!

Bob was transferred to Cedar Rapids, Iowa where officials discovered there was no more room for cadets. Instructions were given "go back to college and wait for an opening in training." At the two cities COE College, Bob took five hours of Taylor Craft (Piper Cub Plane orientation) and for the rest of the time studied Red Cross, speech and history. While Bob was at COE College he met an optometrist, his teacher of the Red Cross Class. This man helped him with eye exercises on the left eye after school in his Cedar Rapids based office. Bob then read 20-20 throughout the war.

Moving fairly quickly, the Air Corps sent the new recruits to Santa Anna, California. Bob began preflight training. He looks back on the ages of the young men and states "we were all 19 and 20 years of age, just kids." Instruction at preflight school included military drill and Morse Code. Trying to make military people out of "the kids" was hard after some weekends on Balboa Beach. The military dress parades on Sunday on the airfield were risky. If a "guy" had celebrated with too much drink on Saturday night the other "guys" would try to squeeze their shoulders together, touching so as to hold the fellow up while in formation.

Even though Bob had read comic books that pictured dramatic dogfights on a horizon with smoking wrecked planes and distorted faces, the young college student did not have a passion for flight like some of his comrades. Having no real infatuation with flying he arrived at Rankin Aeronautic Academy in Tulare, California and met a pre-war stunt pilot Charles LeGault, his new French airplane instructor. LeGault, a real flambouyant character dressed as *roué* [Fr.] (a man of fashion), was full of *sans souci* [Fr.] (without care) and exhibited *savoir faire* [Fr.] (knowing how to act, with style). LeGault was tall and was known to drink and womanize all night in Tulare bars.

Bob in contrast was just a short, awkward, shy farm boy having trouble hitting a baseball! In high school, he had payed close attention to Sue Lang a well-proportioned brunette, who was one year ahead of him in geometry class. He had not generated enough courage to even say hello to her before she graduated!

He did not have slick black hair, confidence or stylish clothes including a long scarf for flowing in the wind like LeGault.

Between drinks one night, LeGault told Bob "you are a good stick and rudder man." He continued "you have that certain skill and knack not found in books but is instinctive for combat flying." LeGault warming up on the subject stated, "flying is an art. Hands, feet, eyes and even stomach work in combination." All of a sudden! Bob saw himself like his instructor, handsome, debonaire, jaunty, stylish, fearless, ready for good living! With these rewards in mind, Bob engaged in the rest of his training with enthusiasm.

In primary training bouts, the young man flew Stearmans for fifty hours. Stearmans were primary trainers. They were referred to as P-17s. Bob trained for the P-51, a Mustang. Primary training also included acrobatics and basic airmanship at Marana, Arizona (near Tucson). Advance training quickly followed in a two-seater Pursuit plane at Williams Field near Phoenix, Arizona with some P-38' s. He also trained on B-17s which carried a crew of eleven people. On the P-51s there were six 50 calibre guns on which to practice. On the P-38s there were four 50 calibre guns plus one cannon. A torpedo bomber carried two men. Each of the men was expected to shoot at an enemy plane and for this possibility, the Pilot trained on the guns.

Out of three hundred Army Air Force students at the Rankin Aeronautical Academy near Tulare, California in the autumn of 1943, Bob, aged 19, was picked first from the group to solo. He was confident, feeling good, excited, and happy. As he enjoyed the beautiful day, all alone in a plane for the first time, he said to himself "I'm all by myself. This whole thing is on my shoulders. I've got to get down by myself! Everybody probably feels like this! Where's my sense of accomplishment?" With fearless courage and fine thoughts between hope and fear, when the moment came to return to the airport, Bob made a perfect three-point landing on his first attempt! It was indeed a beautiful day! During the first month of 1944 after training in a twin-engine Lightning, the young farm boy traded earth for air by receiving his wings. He still looked like a shy farm boy, not dashing like LeGault but he was going to be a bold fighter pilot at age of twenty!

With an *au revoir* [Fr.] (good-bye until we meet again) and a promise toward a future filled with youthful exuberance Bob found himself listening to veteran flyers on a troop ship. Their advice including combat flying was "Keep altitude, don't try to climb away. Don't pursue in a dive and keep your speed up!"

Bob was flying cover after D-Day at Normandy in July, 1944. He flew inland for twenty miles from Normandy Beach to an airstrip named Le Veille. Just outside of St. Lo, he described the landscape as "smoking ruins." From an eagle's height, he watched German Panzer troops escaping east of the devastated town of St. Lo.

The Pilots of the 402nd Division flew about twenty-five P-38s. On the day Bob arrived and as he went to bed that night, he calculated that he had about two months to live. He based his calculations on the survival odds of the mission. Twelve fighters went out that day on a strafing mission. Half an hour later only ten returned. Bob's first glide-bomb and strafing attacks were on Panzer troops fleeing from St. Lo. He came in fast and low while watching the target closely to shoot it up. He was following instructions, pure textbook. There were no German planes in the air for interference.

The 402nd Division moved as the war moved east and settled on a concrete airstrip outside Florennes, Belgium. One of Bob's first missions from Belgium was ordered as a glide-bomb attack on some concealed German artillery in a forest near Aachen, Germany. Twelve P-38s lined up in single file, each dropping two 500 pound bombs. When it was Bob's turn, coming in at tree level, he released his bombs so close to the earth that "they skipped and backfired." The exploding bombs caused flak damage to one rudder of his plane. "The plane vibrated and waffled. The compass was spinning wildly. The plane's rudder flapped like a flag in the wind," stated Bob. The young man climbed to higher altitude and took an escape route heading toward the west. Immediately there came antiaircraft gun fire from the Germans. Small pieces of flying matter resembling black clusters were around the plane. When the plane stopped vibrating, Bob believed he had been hit by German antiaircraft fire. When he looked back, he saw the rudder had broken away. With the rudder gone, he had no more air disturbance and the plane continued along in a smooth flight pattern. His compass had also stopped spinning and pointed toward the East! Ever mindful of death, he realized with excitement he was heading in the wrong direction straight for the Ruhr Valley! Turning the plane sharply and trying to settle his mind, forty minutes later he executed a normal landing with controls of the airplane jammed after landing. This excitement took place in front of the entire squadron at Florennes. Surrounded by ambulances, a crowd of Pilots inspected damages. His plane had only half a tail and it had huge holes in the fuselage. The P-38 was towed up a hill where it was cannibalized for parts, until it finally disappeared... Bob joked to his buddies "I am claiming credit for one American kill."

In early winter Bob's squadron flew daily into the area of the Siegfried line. Their mission was to strafe convoys, cut rail lines, glide-bomb bridges and dive bomb over the cities of Koblenze, Koln, Frankfurt and Bonn. In December, believing the Third Reich would collapse, the 402nd Squadron was sent to the Ardennes Forest to investigate intelligence reports of a German tank buildup. Just across the German border over the town of Simmerath, thirty German Focke-Wulfe 190s caused a mass of entanglement with the American bombers. With flaming airplanes in all directions and trailing long plumes of black smoke, Bob was separated from his lead plane. Old comic book pictures of dogfights were crazily going through his mind.

Then, rules given at squadron briefings steadfastly followed "that it was impossible to out-climb the German Focke-Wulfe. It was better to take a turn, get space and speed!" To get the space and speed necessary Bob put his P-38 into a steep dive. He found he was heading for an American P-38 which was also trying to come out and away from a German plane. His buddy was doomed unless he braked his dive. Cutting the throttle, setting the prop in a flat pitch and jerking the stick back, he felt the pullout tugging at his body. Fifty feet away at a wrong angle, he was unable to successfully target his guns on the rising German plane. Swooping down on the Focke-Wulfe Pilot was all Bob could do to save the other American. The German Pilot was terrorized and rolled sharply to escape collision. Bob left the scene and fled west to Florennes. Five men and fighters were lost in the worst combat that the squadron endured. The Squadron Officer reviewing the gun camera film credited Bob with a kill. Bob only remembered the degree of horror on the face of the German fighter. He could only recall comic book pictures of a dogfight that was in the camera of his mind!

Hitler had secretly ordered a build-up of troops, tanks and artillery into the Ardennes as a last ditch effort to move the Allies back to the sea in the direction of Bob's squadron. In a blinding fog which covered an icy-cold winter landscape for most of December, the Pilots could hear the Panzer tanks a few miles from Florennes. On Christmas Eve the men were packing only essential clothes for evacuation from the airstrip. Planes were readied for take-off. Trucks were idled all night for Operation Retreat. As Christmas day dawned clear and bright, the 402nd met the German offensive flying three to four missions that day, returning to refuel and take off again. The weather continued clear into the new year and by aerial combat above and the wretched offensive taking place by ground troops in the Bulge, by February, Hitler's Panzer troops were vanquished. The young Pilots turned their planes toward Berlin.

The 402nd moved east to an airstrip near Zwartberg, Belgium. Five more Pilots were lost by the division on missions deep into Germany. Bob earned a seven day leave spending it in England. When he returned Major Barth informed him he had a new plane, a P-51. "Get your parachute. Go to the flight line. This is your bird" the Major said.

Having a lot of confidence in the P-38, knowing it would still take you home even when you lost one engine, Bob worried little about the sleek menacing looking new plane. Bob slide his hand along the belly of the fuselage. He walked around the plane slowly. Operations Officer Barth gave some negative opinions regarding the torque of the plane (a combination of forces which produce a twisting or rotating motion [called torsion] and a fuselage tank when full, would waffle and tuck [contract, pucker, draw together] due to a balance problem). With orders to "shoot three landings" Bob took off gently. Untroubled by an easy flowing rhythm, he brought the plane to rest three times in perfect three point landings.

Bob's real complaint about the plane was the forward vision was limited during taxi and mounting the cockpit was difficult as it was extremely high off the ground. After a fourth takeoff for an extended ride, he explained his observations and told the officer "That's all that is wrong with her!" That very afternoon, Bob located a squadron sergeant who painted cowling insignia on airplanes for veteran pilots. Beneath the left engine stack, he asked the sergeant to paint on Sierra Sue in blue script. Further back on the body of the plane, a beautiful brunette wearing a Stetson hat and a low cut blouse was portrayed. Not wishing to discuss the real Sue, that Bob had been too bashful to speak with in high school, he had a convenient substitute reason for painting the fuselage. It was a new cowboy ballad gaining popularity on the charts. Words of the song included: "Sierra Sue, I'm sad and lonely. The rocks and hills are lonely too. Sierra Sue, I want you only. No one but you, Sierra Sue." Actually, no one ever asked who she was or why he painted the picture.

Bob's first mission in Sierra Sue was a VIP escort for Winston Churchill who sojourned across the Rhine River to observe the Allied action. A week after that exciting prestigious adventure, Bob was made a Squadron Test Pilot which meant he would be checking out new Mustangs. Flying to targets in tight formations did not leave much time for aerial combat maneuvers. In his new position, Bob tested Mustangs to the very edge. He practiced high over the Alps in Switzerland, twisting, turning, and rolling, just like his old teacher. "If LeGault could see me now!" he thought, as he roared in front of skiers on ski runs. He practiced fake glide-bombing while skiers ducked, cheering him on. "Wouldn't LeGault drink to that!"

After weeks of practicing Sierra Sue over beautiful high mountain peaks, Bob was ready for the mission ordered "to glide-bomb a woods near Hanover, Germany." The mission was to bomb German tanks, trucks and artillery. Orders included methods "come in fast over the forest, drop your load of two 500 pound bombs and get out in a hurry!" From 3000 feet, Bob reached just a tad above the treetops. Sierra Sue flattened out and received a little gunfire. He considered his two bombs as wasted. At 2000 feet his Wing Man yelled on the radio "Something's leaking from your scoop!" Checking closer it was discovered to be coolant. That small amount of flak had damaged Sierra Sue! She had received a break in her coolant lines. Bob's cockpit temperature gauges were accelerating. Smoke was pouring from both stacks. Bob adjusted to a thousand rpms's and set the manifold pressure at 30 inches with an effect of the two settings keeping the overheated engine running. Still, he lost altitude. The Flight Leader and Bob's Wing Man stayed with him. At 2000 feet and dropping, they told him to bail out.

Checking the terrain, he was not sure if he was in enemy territory or not. Bailing out in Germany meant a probable kill for the enemy in retaliation against Allied bombings of innocent civilians. "Go on west." he told himself. A few minutes later, he was so low he would have been a fool to bail out. After some efforts to adjust rpm's and pressure again, with both smoke stacks pouring out even blacker smoke, he found an open field below. Knowing all was wrong with the field, it being too uneven, a power line at the end, a canal and a wall of woods not to mention it being too short, he squeezed under a power line which cut through Sierra Sue's rudder. He lifted the plane over the canal banks by jerking the stick. He slammed the plane on the ground and it bounced. He smashed his head against the gunsite. When Sierra Sue hit the ground again her scoop plowed the field. As the plane slid to an abrupt stop and dust was swirling, Bob saw an old German farmer with pitchfork in hand. The injured Pilot reached for his .45 believing he was still in farmlands of the Germans.

Washing over his body was a feeling of relief when he recognized green painted ambulances racing toward him. They were American ambulances. Face streaked with blood, he was lifted from the cockpit by two Corpsmen while he was being cursed by the German farmer for breaking the power line in his final pass over the field. "Well," he thought "chalk up another American airplane!" Bob had crash-landed just five hundred yards from the 100th American Evacuation Hospital located just behind the Allied lines near Gutersloh. He was kept for observation after having his forehead sewn up. Moving around he viewed the wreakage of Sierra Sue while having his picture taken. He removed her altimeter for a souvenir.

Returning to the 402nd squadron three days later, the Operation Officer complained "You wrecked not only a P-38 but now a Mustang." Rather than defend himself, Bob decided to joke "Three more and I'll be a reverse ace!" (When German pilots made five kills they were considered an ace!) "This is your new airplane" the Operation Officer didn't pick up on Bob's joke. "She came in new just this week." Bob slowly walked around the new plane. She looked the same as the wrecked Sierra Sue except for serial numbers. She had that same animal Mustang look as if poised to spring into battle. Since one-half of the Pilots of the 402nd had been lost from the Corps, Bob wondered again as he occasionally did, how long would he and the new plane last? Since he survived two crashes and 'totaling' two planes, perhaps he was just plain lucky! Maybe the planes were jinxed. Bob had the second Mustang painted with the same image of Sierra Sue except a II went after her name. Sierra Sue II was even more lifelike and colorful than Sierra Sue, the first had been.

Sierra Sue II was involved in strafing missions in support of the 3rd Allied Armored Division. No fighter opposition, hardly any antiaircraft flak but finding good targets was the main difficulty. Rubble was everywhere. Horses were seen pulling German artillery as destroyed targets. Only six barges on the Elbe River were counted as casualties. In Berlin, the flyers found only a civilian radio tower to bomb. For a week in April, Sierra Sue II with the 402nd Division escorted 8th Air Force B-17s on "milk runs" to bomb Berlin. Targets included apartment houses. These were bombed to demoralize the German citizens morale.

On April 22nd not far from the crash of Sierra Sue I, Bob spotted a German Me-262 jet afar on the horizon. Not breaking radio silence, he left the formation of B-17s and Mustangs hoping to get a shot at the jet. With the jet only a distant speck, he pressed his trigger switch. His camera clicked on, Sierra Sue II shuddered as six guns poured forth their load. After weeks of little action, Bob felt a rush!

When the flight squadron returned to base, two other pilots reported seeing 262s. One other pilot shot at the German jet for a joke. Reviewing film, the Squadron Gun Officer credited each man with 1/2 a kill. Three weeks later the Allies declared victory. It was the last time the 402nd encountered a German plane in combat.

Having lived in constant excitement since reaching the European Continent, life now became dullsville for the flyers. The psychology of being at nerve-end-combat-ready-status had become a part of their life. The men itched to go to Japan. They buzzed barges on the Rhine for practice. On one Sunday, Bob saw a couple all dressed up paddling their boat toward church. He swooped down on them. They dove in the water fully clothed in their Sunday best. Sitting in Germany, Pilots kibitzed how much fun it would be to shoot down a Jap Zero. The Pilots did have fun watching the masses of people celebrating down below while they were flying over the twelve lanes of Champs-Elyees at roof tops in Paris on V-E Day. They buzzed in town from over the top of Chaillot Hill.

The 402th Division Squadron received word "they would not be going to Japan" on the night of a big Bob Hope show. Entertainers included Jerry Colona, Billy Cann, and Gail Russel. The flat feeling of the men became "so low down" it caused the exuberance of the show to reach a "high of nil." Bob Hope just couldn't bring the men to laughter. He complained "I think I have lost my touch!"

After V-E Day, so many flyers were buzzing Paris for fun that a flying patrol was set up. A derelic drunk Colonel hung one on at 1 a.m. one night. He got up and could not find a place for coffee at 5 a.m. He put his plane on auto-pilot and flew under the Eiffel Tower. A flying police force was set in motion because he ended up having only stubs for legs. The Champs-Elysees, the Cathedral of Notre Dame and the Eiffel Tower had all been targets for action-oriented pilots. The city of Paris requested and would receive protection from a flying police force. With orders to get plane numbers, intercept and chase away Allied fighters for disturbing the peace, a flying police force was set in motion. Paris was divided into quarter sections and patrolled in three hour shifts. Sierra Sue II was assigned air space above the Eiffel Tower.

At 10,000 feet, Bob almost begged himself to consider the challenge of flying under the tower. Never being timid in an airplane, he almost dared himself to try it. After all, he was the guard... With a clear vision of a court-martial, he figured he'd be grounded. That would definitely make it proof-positive there would be no combat flying in the Pacific. He returned to base reporting "no problem over my section of Paris." (Bob's Wingman, Lincoln flew under the Eiffel Tower to look for low flying airplanes, however.)

At the end of June, 1945 moving to Sandhofen near Mannheim, Germany Bob spent some routinely dull days looking for friendly fighters to engage in playful sport. He was awarded the 7th Oak Leaf Cluster and the Distinguished Flying Cross for his combat performance in military actions during World War II. Japan's unconditional surrender on August 14, 1945 meant the men were definitely out of war combat. Feeling at age twenty-one his life had spent its most exciting years, Bob wondered "what will I accomplish now?"

In a plan for one more exciting adventure before leaving Europe, Bob Bohna, Jim Gillespie and Bob Blandin walked together to their planes. They secretly planned to meet over Heidelberg Woods at 12,000 feet and exercise a dogfight over Odenwald Forest. With his parachute dragging, Bob was disappointed that Sierra Sue II was out of commission that day. After Blandin and Gillespie left the airstrip, he talked the Operations Officer into a Mustang. He caught up with Blandin and Gillespie who were in a tight formation at 12,000 feet. The other two pilots were already diving and peeling off from each other. They had not yet realized Bob was closing fast inside their formation. All leaders moved at 7,000 feet into the sun. They crossed. Gillespie leveled and lowered the nose. Bob saw his propeller meet Blandin's plane. He knew they would crash. Life flashed by in Bob's brain. What should he have done? What had he done... ?

Meanwhile Blandin's plane dived and Blandin bailed out. His chute hardly opened as his plane smashed itself into a hill of Odenwald Forest. As the airplanes had ripped apart from their formation Bob also bailed out. As he pulled the ripcord on the parachute he realized he was still strapped to the seat which was floating about. He took off the seat. Just missing its barn, his flaming plane made it over the tall roof of an Odenwald farmhouse. The plane slopped into a huge compost mound and disappeared.

As the young man and his parachute drifted toward the earth, Bob was cognizant of lush green and peaceful farm lands which had been a battleground only a few days past. He remembered his joke about being a reverse ace. Two more planes left only one more for a "reverse ace." He reminded himself, "I am lucky, my planes are jinxed. Two Sierra Sues destroyed!" Then he remembered, Sierra Sue II was back at the field! That was not Sierra Sue II now burning in that smoking manure-heap wreakage! As he manuevered his parachute to land while flexing his knees, he stated "Sierra Sue II is as lucky as I am!" He squished onto the soft pasture.

Disciplinary action also came tumbling down on Bob. He was blamed for the mid-air collision. The loss of the two airplanes was considered Bob's fault. The Intelligence Officer recommended the 104th Article of War which was corporal punishment. The General took action and wrote a letter about Bob's excellent record before and after the war. Bob was restricted from the Officer's Club. His promotion was being denied. He refused to accept the punishment of the 104th verdict and demanded a court-marshal procedure to clear himself. Rotating pilots and decommissioning of airplanes were more important activities for the Officers than taking time to discipline three wayward Pilots. All charges were dropped. No one had energy or time for a court-marshal. Bob was promoted from 2nd Lieutenant to First Lieutenant. He retired as a Lieutenant Colonel from the reserves in 1972.

As Bob left his Sierra Sue II, in the autumn of 1945 she sat with about 1500 fighters waiting for disposal as scrap by the 10th Air Repair Squadron. The planes sat side by side in neat rows. Americans were copying Nazi jet planes. Fighters were considered obsolete and would probably just sit and rust in the weather.

After the war, Bob worked for commercial airlines for 29 years. He was pilot for South West Airways, Pacific West, Air West, and Republic now renamed Northwest. Most of the flights were to medium sized towns up and down the coast of California from San Francisco. Twenty-three years ago Bob opened a car sales business in Sonoma, moving to the area in 1984. He is affectionately called "cowboy" because he wears a cowboy hat!

In 1993, a book called *Sierra Sue II* was written by the brother of a midwest surgeon who now owns the Mustang, Sierra Sue II. Bob was contacted by the author and Bob said "the dramatic story of my adventures or misadventures are in that book." The plane, Sierra Sue II leads a very exciting life as a survivor of World War II. She and her latest owner prepare for air shows. She had been flown in Sweden in the early fifties when more than fifty Swedish pilots died in Mustang crashes. She went to Nicaragua where she was involved in Dictator Luis Samoza's military adventures. In the late fifties she came to California where Dave Allender modified her with intent for world speed record setting for piston aircraft. About 40 years after her combat missions with Bob in the war, Sierra Sue II was bought by a hard-flying air show circuit pilot/surgeon. Repainted in all her beautiful glory, Sierra Sue II's picture on the fuselage of the plane thrills millions of spectators each year. For a plane left standing in the sun after World War II, Sierra Sue II is now considered to be worth a half a million dollars!

Bob, looking back to the times with Sierra Sue II, remembers: "Briefings at 5 a.m. Lots of security. B-17s going up. Axis Sally's sweet words "one half of you pilots will be killed by evening. You will send out 200 planes. Only 100 will come back tonight." Lack of training was wasteful. Pilots were lost. Germans attacking an airfield and knocking out 35 airplanes. Battle of the Bulge. St. Lo and Mannheim rubble. Any target of opportunity, straif it! The whole thing was wasteful and expensive. A war to end all wars! In a few short months, it would be Korea, then Vietnam!"

Cristgau, John, *Sierra Sue II,* Great Planes Press, San Mateo, California, Minneapolis, Minnesota. 1993. pps. 188.

Frank Greengrass

United States Army Coast Artillery, 1942 - 1945
Reserve 1945; recalled to Korea, 1950, Discharged 1953

Frank tried to enlist in the Navy right after Pearl Harbor. He was too flat-footed. Eventually Frank was drafted into the Army at San Francisco, California. For basic training he was sent to Fort Ord, Monterey, California. The post was simply a reception center. The men were gathered together and "shot down to Camp Callan at La Jolla." Frank enjoyed basic training as he already had a background of all sorts of training by the ROTC and National Guard. He felt "sorry for some of the other guys that had a hard time."

After thirteen weeks, he was promoted to Sergeant and assigned to the Base Cadre to train new recruits. He took the place of another trainer who had been sent overseas. The men were bunked in a two story barracks with a different platoon on each floor. Frank's prime duty was being Platoon Sergeant.

In July of 1942, Frank married the girl he had been going with for one year. He and Odessa were married in the Chapel at Camp Callan "so that they could have something between them before Frank would be transferred overseas." He was born in Chicago, Illinois and Odessa was a California native.

Frank gave instructions on how to use the bayonet, a detachable daggerlike blade put on the muzzle end of a rifle used for hand-to-hand combat fighting. The men learned how to fix the bayonet in the pin of the gun. He showed new recruits how to hold the bayoneted gun, approach an enemy and to stab, prod or kill that target. These were techniques in the field and art of bayonet instruction. Large straw filled bags were standing up where trainees pushed in, then pulled out.

Since Frank conducted these bayonet courses hour after hour, he went to the hospital, shortly before Christmas of 1942 with an erupted hernia caused by the intense pushing and pulling demonstrations. Medical procedures were primitive. He felt a shot given in his back and was conscious while asking, "Hey Doc. What are you doing!" The doctor shot back, "I'm busy, leave me alone." Frank laid "in the sack" for fifteen days immobilized. Instead of moving muscles, he got to the point of not even being able to urinate.

Lying a few feet away was a Mexican fellow also enduring an operation that morning. He had an appendectomy. He was up and away immediately.

Frank resumed teaching again and remained in that same capacity until March, 1943. He was sent to OCS (Officers Candidate School) at Aberdeen, Maryland for 13 weeks and graduated "a 90 day wonder." Frank had a history of so much physical activity in day to day experiences, he did not feel insufficient in any way for his new assignment. The work-out at this school was tough but Frank thoroughly enjoyed it. He called OCS "a real cinch." He had never experienced any trouble when at school or with training in different subjects. A lot of the men were "washed out in two months time." Frank however, with his former military training found "it all a breeze." He graduated as a 2nd Lieutenant.

Frank's wife, Odessa arrived in New York where she visited her sister-in-law. Frank's sister bought a 1937 Plymouth sedan. Odessa picked up Frank with the automobile and some gas coupons given to the couple from friends and family. They drove across the country to Camp Young in the Mojave Desert.

Frank did most of the driving. He had to put air in the tires every morning. Water was a problem when the radiator became hot on mountainous roads. The auto courts didn't look too good. There were no running toilets on the inside. Guests of auto courts had to have a flashlight in the middle of the night to find the "john." It was most often a wooden one-holer. Due to blackouts there was curfew on driving at night.

Frank was assigned to the 283rd Ordnance Maintenance Co. His prime concern at Camp Young as a new Lieutenant was to act under his superior's orders as a specialist to help 160 men continue to be good soldiers. The First Lieutenant to whom Frank was assigned had been in the Army for twenty years with a background of 20 years in cutting hair! This fellow had been promoted to a direct field commission when "all he could do was cut hair!" The First Lieutenant could hardly read or write and could hardly speak English. His first name was Guster. There was practically no happiness or "prosperity of feeling" in the Ordnance. In this isolated and remote jumping-off-place, it became an extreme case of limiting ones's temperment to cope with the man. It made Frank sick just to hear him speak. Frank would have liked to court-martial him for the things he did to the men. Frank said, "they would have probably court-martialed me for the way I felt about him."

The men received no leave. They received no breaks from boredom or drill. Bad grades were meted out to the men. Because Frank stood up for the men, his ratings also drafted by Guster became very poor. The trainees had no enthusiasm because of the insensitivity of the First Lieutenant. Listlessness, doldrums, apathy and fatigue from the wearying conditions built-up layer upon layer. All this so-called-good-training was done at 140 degrees in the shade. Men were allowed one canteen of water, a pint for a whole day. Men would drop down and die of heat, right in this desert camp located in California! Nine full months of the year, clothes were white with salt. Woolen shirts were worn to protect bodies. Men would sweat, then cool. They took salt tablets.

After one and one-half years of this torture, the men were declared "ready for combat in deserts like Egypt. Orders directed for embarkment from San Francisco to the Pacific. While at San Francisco, Frank learned a top secret. Their mission was to go to Hawaii and then they would be prepared to push on to Saipan. He was now with the 27th Division. While at San Francisco, Frank got to visit his family twice. Then off to Oahu, Hawaii, Oahu:Ewa Plantation to Ewa (Eva) Plantation near Barber's Point.

At Ewa Plantation mud and red clayey soil was a mess but the tropical climate was a nice experience. A little Methodist Church was on the plantation where men were allowed to attend Sunday services. This little church helped the men. They still had their S.O.B. for a Commander, who was now a Captain.

While waiting for Saipan, the men did not know where they were going except for the Officers, who were not allowed to talk to their families or each other about the destination. Frank was "selected" by the C.O. as a "volunteer" to take 35 more enlisted volunteers as an advanced contingent detail to Saipan. As a "volunteer" Frank met with the men telling them, "You will be an advanced unit. You will not know where you will be going. There will be just 35 men and myself (18 couples paired off) to maintain, keep and repair antiaircraft armament. You will work primarily on instruments built in the shape of a boxlike designed apparatus. It is a two foot by two foot cube with a bunch of apertures (holes or openings, as in a telescope through which light passes). This little box has a mechanism to calculate the distance of an object to be hit. It is run by electricity which is stored each evening from a little generator. The mechanism is like a computer. It will site an enemy airplane. It will be your pipeline for information on direction and speed of a plane. As observers you will then translate to the Gunners the information calculated." Men in this volunteer group were informed, "None of you might come back!"

Thirty-five of the best men did not hesitate to volunteer. They knew the rest of the men would be following with the S.O.B. C.O. The men remaining were planning that the C.O. would not arrive alive with them. Before Frank left, he went to see the I.G. (Inspector General). He informed the inspector, "I don't want to see any of our men punished. Saipan, would be reached by a voyage by ship. It would be easy to get rid of someone like him. I'm going ahead. I don't care about him. I care about the men." Frank and his company of 35 men left the next day or two. He learned later, the I. G. had picked the S. O. B. C.O. for a garbage disposal officer on Oahu!

Before reaching the shore of Saipan, the men of the 27th Division were shot at in their LSTs (Landing Ship Transports). Their company followed along with some Marines, who were walking out of the transports to shore through the water. Before leaving Oahu, Frank had rolled a bottle of Canadian Club in his bedroll. He rolled it tightly, so that nothing could disturb the fine high grade whiskey. On the island, everywhere he walked were corpses. Tropical climate decomposes flesh quickly. The stench was horrible. It filtered the air. Frank was reminded of compost piles of cattle dung, only he multiplied the odor by 1,000 fold! The smell came from the burned and decomposed corpses of American troops and those of their dead enemies. He could have used a drink or two to deal with it all !

Day after day, Frank worked along side of his men. They set up their pup tents. His men checked and maintained the antiaircraft weapons. He used a 3/4 ton weapons carrier. The driver and Frank would travel together a great deal of the time. His driver was nervous. A bullet hit and grazed the driver's wrist. He fainted at the wheel. Frank had to rescue the wheel from beneath the driver and stop the moving vehicle. Conditions improved. There was not so much bombing in the daytime but "bed-check Charlie bombed the camps every night." After July, they were bombed just once in a while. It was like in a movie to run for cover whenever a bombing took place.

About the 2nd of August, Frank received word he had a son, Gilbert born in San Francisco on July 22nd. The cablegram sent by his Father-in-Law stated "that Mother and child were doing fine." Again, on that night the men were machine-gunned. Frank found his bottle of Canadian Club. Every man in his unit got a capful of whisky. It was like Jesus passing the loaves and fishes!

The men living in the little tents became individual Japanese targets. There were bugs galore in the tropical vegetation which was all around. When you took off your sweaty shoes to dry them and to get some air for your feet, by next morning they were usually full of bugs! Shoes would mold and turn green overnight. There was no bathing as there was very little water. Ocean water would make things worse. Just to live through the experience was a wonder. Very few of the Soldiers made it back home. The company captured some Japanese Soldiers. Frank learned a little Japanese language. He discovered Japanese tools were of better quality than American tools. To use their saw, you pulled to cut. You pulled a plane as well. He brought home some tools as souvenirs.

Like a lion, after the worst conditions were over, Frank re-assembled the tents to resemble a pyramid. Since they had not been bombed for a good period of time, the men could live a little more leisurely. They covered the floors with wood like in a home. As Commanding Officer, Frank visited Navy ships in the harbor where there were desaltification units for clean water. There were crates of fresh food (at least fresher than canned foods) on these ships. Men were issued two beers a week and small packs of tobacco which came in the rations. Frank became an experienced trader. By inducing the men to save up beer and tobacco, Frank would take these items to the ships and bargain for fresh eggs, a piece of ham, fresh bologna, bread or whatever else might be fresh to change the menu. He felt like a proverbial Indian trader in American history!

While preparing to leave Saipan, Frank looked at some cliffs that reminded him of ones on the windy side of Oahu. The area was much like Pali where the Hawaiians used to commit suicide. Frank saw an eerie unshapely form. In paralyzing amazement, he discerned a confused and twisted mass of Army equipment followed by something pushing it forward. This jumblement was being pushed by an American bulldozer. High on this cliff, the soldier driving the bulldozer methodically pushed thousands upon thousands of tons of good equipment and machines over the cliff. It was an irrevocable act making instant worthless scrap from good machinery. The tanks, guns, and vehicles paid for originally by public funds were now being destroyed by more public funds. This bordered on the concept of shameful as to the waste being generated. As so happened after many major battles were completed, the tools of battlement were considered too heavy or expensive to return to the lands from whence they had come. They were considered too good for use by any enemy that might return to claim and make use of them.

Men were placed on a point system to go home. Things had quieted down but Frank's hernia acted up again. In the rudimentary conditions of Saipan, Field Medics were doing the same operation he had previously endured, all over again! The operation was as bad as the other experience and again "he lay in the sack for another fifteen days." After that bout, he was granted rest and relaxation in Oahu. He had an easy time getting to Hickam Field Officers Quarters. At the hotel while having lunch, he met a Padre at one of the tables. "Hey Lieutenant, how are you doing?" It was Father Roy. The Father had a room at the quarters and befriended people. He had luaus for them. Men would sing with harmonicas. There was lots of wholesome respect for the Catholic Priest. The Priest had lots of compassion for the men.

Soon, Frank was mustered out of the service at Marysville, California as a Reservist. He was sent back to Europe in November, 1950 to help establish a line of communication from the Saar Basin of Germany to the southwest corner of the French Coast. Because Russia was a worrisome ingredient in the politics of the region, the United States believed it needed access to Germany for bringing in supplies and more men. $30,000,000.00 a month went down the tubes in France to maintain this line of communication. This money was spent by the United States government to feed men and to hire French civilians for laborers. The civilians receiving jobs were being paid, obtaining most of this money for their economy Yet, the Army personnel were not appreciated by the French civilians. Again, Frank was disgusted with his government's waste paying out all of this money. On the brighter side, the little depot at Fontenet in the Cognac area had a good Ordnance Unit to be proud of. Frank was a confidential Adjutant Aide to a very good Commanding Officer, a Major.

The Major at this Ordnance Depot was also a pretty friendly guy with his troops. He was honest and a hard worker. He wrote Frank quite a few good letters of recommendation. Nothing happened in regard to promotion. The French didn't want the Americans around so they sabotaged American vehicles. The men lived six months on French frugality. There were no toilets or running water in homes.

At Christmastime, Frank knew the pangs of how Americans felt, who were sentimental about home and tradition. He suggested to the Officers "Let's try a plan to get together with the French families for Christmas for better relationships. This would give the men something to do and to look forward to during the holiday." The reasoning behind the plan was "if the Frenchman was a cobbler, he might also speak a little Hungarian. Find among the G Is one of Hungarian descent and couple this man with a Cobbler's family." By ingeniously looking at backgounds in common with one another, come Christmas on the 24th in Saintes, France, American soldiers met their French counterparts, who might also have something in common to experience. In a big parking ground, prearranged for identification and with matching lists, the Officers got the men together with their hosts for a two day liberty in French homes. The whole idea worked out beautifully.

For example, Lucien and Suzette Pasquet had a coin laundry. Frank introduced himself to this couple who could speak no word of English. Frank was utterly forced to learn French, using exact pronounciation. Again, Frank lucked out. Languages came easily to him as he had received three years of German in school. At this couple's home, he met Henri and Simone Carlier close friends of the Pasquets. This French couple sold perfumes and luggage. What was beautiful about the experience, was with no word of English, the GI was given a cultural experience of high intensity. Frank bought a Studebaker. He spent many weekends with one couple. Sometimes, a group of five happy patriots were merrily driving on pleasure trips to Paris.

As usually happens when someone tries to do good for others, the good rubs off on the person who carries out the good deed. In Frank's case, he had better communication and better relationships with the French civilians while managing employees at the depot. He kept up his social relationship and communication with the two couples of the region.

Back from Europe in 1953, Frank was discharged. He attended Golden Gate University in San Francisco for one term towards a Masters in Business Education. He was trying to make a living, finding it difficult because his family was 50 miles away living in the town of Sonoma. Frank stayed at a boarding house in San Francisco from Monday to Friday night. He carried 16 units, did homework making top grades and then drove to Sonoma on weekends. He opened up his own Real Estate and Insurance Office in 1955. In 1972, he slowed down a bit. By selling his office to a conglomerate real estate company which is now a part of a large franchise, he figured he would not have to work so hard. As is the case in real estate, when you are good and have a wide client base, you simply do not slow down. Frank retired a second time from real estate sales. He works alone in a small building with no windows where he develops microfilming and purges old escrow files for a title company.

Daniel T. Ruggles, Sr.

United States Army Air Force 1943 - 1945

Daniel T. Ruggles, Sr., born in Wisconsin on April 20, 1911, is the son of Daniel Ruggles Jr., born 1866 in Wisconsin, the grandson of Daniel Ruggles, Sr. born, 1823 in Hardwick, Massachusetts great-grandson of Anson Ruggles born in 1785, Hardwick, Massachusetts, great-great-grandson of Daniel Ruggles born in 1755 in the town of Hardwick. Daniel T. Ruggles, Sr. of Sonoma has a son, Daniel T. Ruggles, Jr. and a daughter, Jane. His wife, Doroylene is a retired school teacher. Dan, referred affectionately as Mr. Music Man, still sings occasionally, plays the organ in church and is in the music business on the Plaza, in Sonoma.

As Dan traced his ancestory in the United States and into England, he found the Ruggele's lived in 1220 during the time of Henry III. In 1298, William de Ruggele was honored for faithful service to the King, Edward I, in the King's Army at Flanders. Captain Samuel Ruggles was prominent in Roxbury, Massachusetts as a Selectman and Representative, actively engaged in deposing Governor Sir Edmond Andros who was tyrannical and very unpopular; he was also Governor of Virginia and of Maryland in 1692 - 1698. Brigadier General Timothy Ruggles at Rochester, Massachusetts entered the British Army under Lord Amherst. He was a Captain. He came to the United States in 1634 from Dedham, England to Dedham, Massachusetts.

Following closely in family footsteps, Daniel T. Ruggles, Sr. of Sonoma, a life member of the Veterans of Foreign Wars, Bear Flag Post, 1943 came by his heritage naturally. Not only was he a singer in church services (one of his relatives was a minister) but he was with the 317th troop carrier group to Australia, New Guinea during World War II. Dan was drafted into the service from Sonoma, California. Before leaving the United States, he took a lot of tests at Monterey. He was at Duncan Airfield in San Antonio, Texas for two weeks just laying around. He states, with a twinkle in his eye "We were transients, waiting for assignment and didn't even have to do 'K P'."

Before going to Texas, he attended a clerical school at Fort Logan, Colorado on "how to run an office." On the last day of school, the men had a contest of 50 questions back and forth. The score reached 23 to 24, with answers to questions in favor of the other side. The next three questions were to be on baseball. One man had talked of nothing else since he had been there and he was on the other side. Dan wondered "if that fellow might not run away with the contest." The next three questions were to be on baseball.

The first of these last three questions was, "Who made an unassisted triple play in baseball, what year, and who was it? The chap who talked of nothing else but baseball missed the question. It was Dan's turn. He thought a moment, then stated "it was Bill Wambgans, short stop of the Cleveland, Indians. He caught a line drive, pursued the hitter on first, chased a player, stopped, and put the second man out on second base, threw the ball to home plate and caught the man who had dashed home!" The point went to Dan's side and the groups were even. Two more questions and Dan's side won a free dinner paid for by the other side! Dan's popularity rose by leaps and bounds due to the contest!

Heading over to Bowman Field near Louisville, Kentucky he also "got in like Flynn" as he met a

Chaplain. He was immediately enlisted as substitute organist and he joined chapel choir as a baritone. Dan was religious soloist all the time he was stationed there. For 13 weeks he broadcasted on a major radio station. "As he had to make rehearsals, it was a lovely diversion for getting out of a lot more KP!"

Jaunting to Lawson Field, Georgia there were rumors that men were preparing to go overseas "to chase the German General Rommel across the sands of the Sahara." Dan got chicken pox quite conveniently along with 49 other men. They were all bedded down in one room. Measles and chicken pox were quite common according to Dan, as mess hall dishes were not sterilized. Health practices were as yet, rudimentary.

After the 49 detainees got out of bed, they were shuttled on a train which "chugged along merrily" through Georgia, Alabama, Texas and other western states ending up just a few miles from Dan's home town of Sonoma. The troops were brought to the small overseas shipping point called Port Chicago, California and boarded the ship, USS Maui. Everyone believed they were headed in the direction and looked forward to seeing the beautiful Islands of Hawaii. Instead, the ship's course was south-southwest way down below Hawaii, above New Zealand close to the Great Barrier Reef near Brisbane. It seemed "the Japanese could not penetrate the Great Barrier Reef. The Allies wanted to keep them out!"

Dan operated his equipment for quite a while in Townsville, Austrailia. At this post, he became part of a double-quartet singing group. The men sang in Chapel. They were contacted by the one and only radio station where they were invited to sing sacred songs every Sunday morning. There was a radio contest for a name. Halcyon Singers was chosen. To be part of the group, you were called a Halcyon Singer. Halcyon meant "days of tranquility, season of relaxation, retrospection. It meant beautiful days in the South Seas and all's right with the world." The Halcyon Singers sang together for eight or nine months. Recordings from the Salt Lake Tabernacle Choir was the only other church program on the air each Sunday.

Then, a fascinating thing happened. Dan heard about a little Christian Church near the edge of Burauen Valley. The Japanese had taken the organ and burned all the equipment. A resident family, living near the church, had 5 little girls, ages 8, 7, 6, 5 and 4 years. They sang for Dan. He invited them to sing at chapel. They showed up the next Sunday dressed in five different colors of parachute material, red, yellow, blue, purple and ecru. Men were teary eyed; some recalled their own little daughters. Some men said, "I have not even seen my own little daughter born while I've been out in this jungle!" The five little girls sang gospel songs from little hymn books. Their daddy, Jose Pilpa was a lay leader in the United Church of the Philippines. Of course, they made repeat appearances.

It was at Garbutt Air Field near Townsville, Queensland, Australia, along the Eastern shores where it is so very beautiful, that Dan set up a ground office as Intelligence Section for the Army Air Force. The section had a C-47 transport plane, maps and secret information where the Japanese were located. New recruits were trained in practices expected of them, such as "what to do, if the enemy shot you down." There was information entitled *How to Deal with Natives.* At meetings with Pilots and staff, pamphlets for disbursement to Natives and to the American Paratroopers were discussed. Supplies were dropped to both Natives and American Paratroopers in the jungles. American Flyers regularly dropped food and supplies to inhabitants and replenished food and medicine to Paratroopers.

Natives had run away from the Japanese as extreme cruelty had been endured by them. Indiginous people were also deprived of a lot of food taken by Japanese including their staples. American Flyers dropped wheat, flour and other needed foods to aborigines. Each parachute had a different color identifying whether the contents floating down from the skies would be ammunition, rifles or food. C-47 transport planes also dropped Paratroopers into those jungles. There were still Japanese Soldiers isolated in the forests. Americans wanted to get rid of the enemy for many reasons, one reason being, the Japanese had money to bribe some indiginous persons against the Americans.

Dan moved to another airfield located near Port Moresby, New Guinea. His Intelligence Corps stayed there quite a few months. The men helped stem the Japanese invasion with fighter planes. Not having long flying range opportunities, due to a lack of gasoline within a manageable distance nor enough ammunition, the interior of New Guinea relied for help, upon ships along the coast. Dan was at Lae, New Britain for one month. He was sick again at Hollandie, Dutch New Guinea. It was scary to be sick in that region as there were so many deadly diseases from poor sanitation. He was in the area of Dutch New Guinea where people spoke both English and Dutch languages.

New Guinea had been pretty well liberated by others. General Douglas MacArthur built a mansion in the high mountains at Hollandia. "He wanted his luxury," Dan stated; "I saw him once. He had his perennial pipe in his mouth, a floppy jacket and a hat." Dan was at Hollandia Air Port on that occasion.

One of the American planes on its return to Australia went down in the jungles south of Hollandia. It was reported "the Natives had never seen a white man before." These people were big and burly and wore little. The men wore leather belts around their waists from which each attached a huge horn exhibition "likened to a pecker!" It was their proudest possession. Word filtered around " they practiced polygamy."

There was a Hottentot boy, who sang, *Praise the Lord and Pass the Ammunition!* The fliers used to give the boy a nickle or dime for a coke when he sang the song. They didn't know where he was found. He could hardly speak. Perhaps his parents were displaced from Africa as in the mid-17th century the Dutch colonials ousted Hottentots from farms, exterminated or dispossessed them in south-west Africa. The Khoikhois of Africa have been called Hottentots.

In order to escape from wild animals and their enemies the Japanese, the Natives built bamboo shacks on poles in water. Animals in those jungles included wild cats, snakes, leopards, and huge insects. In order to sleep, it was a requirement to place mosquito nets over beds. You could be eaten alive or get malaria from the pesky insects. It was slow moving for Paratroopers to find and kill Japanese in those jungles. There were no marching armies, just groups or individuals such as those depicted in the famous stage play musical, *South Pacific.*

Orders were to participate in Leyte. All desks and equipment were loaded in LSTs (landing ship transports). After setting sail, the small conveyances ran into a typhoon way up on the other side of New Guinea. The Intelligence Officers were delayed awhile. Several in one ship got ahead of the group. They landed early on dry land. Some of the party left items on the sand. It became dark. Before morning the "stuff got covered in sand." Dan's box of office materials, desk and miscellaneous items were sticking up about ten inches out of the sand. He worked awfully hard to uncover the stuff. All maps in the desk were dry and usable.

The typhoon had washed out the road to the Burauen Air Strip. For a while, the group operated in a protected area just a little way from the beach. The intelligence group simply could not get up to where the planes were on the airstrip.

A young fellow showed up from San Francisco. He was very disgruntled that he had been transferred to

317th Headquarters. He was assigned to Dan's tent. The Japanese retaliated for being pushed off the island. They were known for strafing the Americans each night. The young man was instructed on how important it was to dig his foxhole before dark. The hole was to be 18" wide, 18 inches deep and six feet long. The young fellow did not want to dig the trench. He dug around a little bit. He found a troubling root near the middle surface of the opening. This was the excuse he was waiting for, so stating he "couldn't finish" the young man went to bed. Three red lights went up. This meant, "go to fox holes because of an air raid." The young man was naked. He was of large stature, big, cussing. Entering the foxhole naked, he poked his head in one end and his feet in the other, face down. Dan said, "I never saw such a thing! His bright white rear-end stuck up toward the bright full white moonlight! The rear-end looked so funny just sticking up!"

Orders were received, "You are to go to Clark Field ninety miles north of Manila." There were real ancient peoples in the mountains of that area. They were very short in stature and identifiable with kinky hair. Males carried long black spears. When the Americans took Manila, the Japanese had fled north. Most did not have much. GIs gave them some hammocks which were strung between trees for sleeping. These peoples had also been mistreated by the Japanese invader. Dan wondered, "why were the Japanese so cruel to the Natives?" The Natives retaliated in vengeful retribution against the remaining Japanese. As stray Orientals were discovered, the ancient peoples waited stealthily until their marauders were asleep in their hammocks. Long spears were stabbed laterally through the bodies of the sleeping Japanese invaders, from their bottoms and out their mouths. It was reported "the natives of the jungle had great fun in doing that."

A pleasure trip enjoyed by Dan was to the Malacanan Palace, residence of the Governor of Manila. The palace was a gorgeous Spanish styled hacienda. Some furniture had been spared by the Japanese evacuees. Manila was in shambles. There were no shops to visit, only a few pillars of concrete were remaining. The area had been mercilessly shelled by the United States Army Pilots and the Navy personnel in the harbor. It was cruel business in those days. In what was the city of Manila, about all one could do was spend eight hours looking at debris or go sing at chapel.

At Clark Field, orders were received that certain people would be going home based upon length of service. Some people including Dan had overtime. His group flew to Tacloban the northeast corner of Leyte. The men were picked up by a Dutch liner, Bloemfontein which had been in the South Seas when the war started. When the Germans surrendered in Europe, the ship was berthed at Pearl Harbor. It did not take the men to California. When whistles went off on VE Day, the Dutch ship had a new order change. The Queen wanted her ships home. Going south-southeast in the middle of the night, the ship passed old Panama City through Panama Canal over to the Bahamas. The ship received 1200 British RAF fighters on board who had served the Allies since the war started. The whole ship load stopped at New York City where the RAF group caught the vessel Queen Elizabeth for England. The Americans were welcomed home by a huge banner over the New York Times Building "Welcome Home 5th Airforce!"

Dan crossed his country on a meandering train and had been assigned a railroad sleeper car. He enjoyed first class accommodations. All total, it was a 13,000 mile trip to get home! Like on Noah's Ark the returning veterans took forty days and nights to make it from Tacloban to San Francisco. When Dan arrived in Martinez, he hitchhiked about 20 miles to Napa, California, only 14 miles from Sonoma. He was rescued by his Dad who arrived to pick him up at the bus station in a big Packard automobile.

From the time Dan became a Citizen of Sonoma, he became a dynamic human historical landmark. His history is one of being a part of, starting, or participating in social musical events. He was City Councilman for 16 years, Honorary Alcalde in 1980, Sonoma Treasure in 1986. He loves to dress up in a Spanish broad brimmed sombero, black pants and cutaway coat for just about anything historical. From national to local Chamber of Commerces, Plaza Merchants, to numerous Plaza events, he has presented or participated in approximately 500 musical programs in the Grinstead Memorial Ampitheater. He is presently a member or has been a member of the Arts Alliance, Valley of the Moon Vintage Festival Association, Sonoma Film Festival, Friends of the Community Center, Friends of the Sebastiani Theatre, Veterans of Foreign War Organizations, Sons of American Revolution, Mayflower Descendants, Redwood Chapter of American Guild of Organists, Music Teacher Associations, Sonoma Valley Chorale, Sonoma Valley Chorus and Oratorio Singers, Silver Foxes double quartet, organist for over 50 years at one church and while in retirement, substitute organist for other churches. He has been Church Choir Director, Santa Rosa Symphony Board Member, Baritone soloist in numerous events, Leadership and past Moderator for the Congregational Church. He attended San Francisco Conservatory of Music, taught voice lessons, studied song cycles, actively supports the Sonoma City Opera. He continues to be part of Sonoma State Historical Park, General Vallejo Memorial Association, Sonoma Valley Historical and Depot Park Museum Associations. Many of the above associations were served by Dan as their president, founder, or vice president. He allowed his store to be used for ticket sales and the place to read advertisements for social events and musical events. It was also used by the Sonoma Valley Art Center as an art gallery. Dan belongs to, but is not active in California Retired Teachers Association, American Retired Persons Organizations and Independent Order of Foresters.

He finishes all of his resumes with the words "I am about three months younger than former President Reagan. So, I may have forgotten something!" (Oh, yes, the former President Reagan was in Sonoma many years ago for the premier of *Sea Wolf* at the Sebastiani Theatre. Dan was also in the audience for that occasion!)

William P. G. Chapin

United States Air Corps 1942 - 1946

Bill Chapin, as a young college student is one person that the average Joe on the street would have liked to emulate. He had it all! He was handsome, he could dash down ski slopes and he taught skiing classes to others which could earn him up to $50.00 a week. Bill had a side job as a cub reporter on the Rutland Herald the second largest newspaper in Vermont. The cub reporter job paid an additional $12.00 per week. With three hundred dollars burning a hole in his pocket, money his Dad gave him for a graduation present, he enjoyed Mexico City. Bill had just graduated from Dartmouth College. Born in Proctor, Vermont in 1918 he developed attributes that included a gift of making friends easily. He could play the violin. He could drink socially and get drunk on "rotgut" whisky. Bill was devoted to a Gamma Phi Beta sorority sister, "a pretty coed" at McGill University in Montreal. He married Eleanor O'Hara. She took the name O'Hara as her first name. Mr. and Mrs. Chapin were both twenty-two.

On 7 December 1941 the newlyweds were at a concert. Bill was acting as music critic for the Herald. Returning to his office there were banners on windows of the newspaper building. "Japs Bomb Pearl Harbor! Japs Bomb Pearl Harbor!" Bill's first thoughts were of pending draft in the service of his country. He did not want to be a foot soldier. He was wary of trenches and being a submariner was the last thing on his mind!

In less than two months from December 7th, Bill saw a list of draftees sent to the editor of the paper. His name was on the list! Bill hurriedly shopped around. There was a Meteorology program at MIT for the Air Force. Having lots of math in college, he elected to join the Cadet Detachment at Massachusetts Institute of Technology. After receiving a commission as Second Lieutenant in November of 1942, he attended a plethora of airfields toward a goal of finding that cushy, agreeable job.

At MIT he learned "it was absolutely impossible to make long range accurate weather forecasting." Bill was assigned duty as a Commanding Officer at Pope Field, North Carolina to sign "weather clearances" on Pilots flight plans. It made him squeamish. He was also ordered to teach mathematics. One of his students had a doctorate in the subject!

O'Hara joined Bill. The newly married couple shared a single room with another couple. Two squeaky beds were separated by a sheet suspended from the ceiling. In 1943 that cushy job description Bill was searching for was pinned to a bulletin board. The Army Air Force wanted a flying weather officer. During 1943 Bill went through flight training "not once climbing in an airplane." He and O'Hara hung around the Officers Club playing slot machines, drinking beer and swimming in the club's pool. Her claim to fame was retrieving a bottom half of a swim suit on the top of the water after a dive into the deep end of the pool. She demurely retrieved it while being cheered!

When Bill finally flew PT-17s (Stearman biplanes) his instructor yelled at him so much that O'Hara witnessed Bill complaining in his sleep. He soloed after eight hours of instruction. He did not win honor as "best flier in the class." There was a lot of partying and eating black market steaks at a roadhouse. Bill ended up "sitting in a tub of cold water one night, fully dressed replete with a kitten curled up on top of his head under his officer's cap!" One of Bill's good friends went to England to fly fighters and was killed on his first mission.

Bill flew BT-13s. He took the plane as high as it would go before spinning out. This caused "gray outs" for a few seconds. It was weird. His vision would return as he came out of the loop and blood returned to his brain. Bill flew AT-10s at Lawrenceville, Illinois. He felt they were hard to fly. He got lost up in the skies more than once. This occurred especially at night.

After a three-day search for housing, O'Hara and Bill got an apartment at a "good price." They found upon occupancy, it formerly "was rented by a whore named Rosie." Several men were disappointed. Bill and O'Hara were disappointed, too. Bill declared "cockroaches owned the kitchen." The cockroaches even joined the couple in their double bed!

Another of Bill's friends lost his life at the airfield in a fog. Soon after that Bill received his wings. His shock was to hear that he would be a Bomber Pilot. The flying weather officer was a figment of imagination. Bomber Pilots in Europe were inundated with heavy losses. Replacements were needed badly. Bill wondered "what was it going to be like to be shot at?"

Fliers were given a choice. They could train for two-engine or four-engine planes. Bill chose four-engine, considering it might lead to an advancement as a commercial pilot after the war. Bill learned to fly B-24 Liberators. The B-24 was unofficially called "The Flying Boxcar." It took a lot of powerful muscle to lift the plane off the ground when full of people, fuel and bombs. It caused sweat to pour off Bill's face upon each liftoff. He'd wait for altitude evaporation relief. One of Bill's instructors got so upset with him regarding instruments he took off his own headset and beat up his steering wheel with it. Breaking the headset, the instructor screamed at Bill who really did not understand what his teacher was saying due to all that engine noise. A crew was assembled for "staging" 516 training hours later. "Staging" included pactice for bombing missions, formation flying and target practice for the gunners. There were night air practices and an occasional cross-country trip. The crew included: pilot, co-pilot, bombardier, navigator, flight engineer, radio operator, nose gunner, tail gunner, ball-turret gunner, top-turret gunner. Generally the Flight Engineer and Radio Operator also used guns. At age 25, Bill was the oldest one in the plane and its Commander.

Bill first sighted German soldiers at Charleston, South Carolina before heading overseas. They were Prisoners-of-war from Rommel's Afrika Corps. The 'guys' in green uniforms looked content and well fed. They served Officers their meals in an Officers Club.

At Mitchel Field, Long Island "the 746th Squadron, 456th Bomb Group, 304th Bombardment wing of the Fifteenth Air Force was given a B-24 (a brand new plane from the Ford Motor Company) to fly across the Atlantic." The orders were "take the crew and deliver the plane to the 456th." Bill flew the new plane for one hour and signed a paper "it was okay." The next morning after briefing, the fledgling crew began a course of 180 miles to New Hampshire. After that stop, flight plans included pause at Newfoundland, the Azores, then to North Africa, with final destination Stornara, Italy.

While executing the first stop at Grenier in New Hampshire, Bill felt a slight bump during one of his smoother landings. The plane rolled along until it began to lean to the left. The left wing tip touched the ground and a "horrible clatter of propeller blades began chewing up concrete." He was landing north but when the plane came to a stop through much dust, it was facing south. Fire engines and sirens were followed by shouts of people to leave the airplane. No fire, no injuries, no scratches! "The left landing gear assembly had sheared off completely at the moment of impact." Returning to New York for reassignment, Bill and his crew said goodbyes all over again to their wives and friends. Upon further orders the crew was divided up and flown overseas by Air Transport Command.

Upon arrival in Italy, a grizzled master Sergeant asked Bill what type of plane would he be commanding. Bill said "B-24s." The burly Sergeant opined, "You poor sonsabitches." Assigned canvas tents to live in, the men practiced flying formations. "With one wing of Bill's plane he overlapped one wing of a lead plane." By boxing in seven airplanes together," they were informed; "when you hit targets, there will be greater concentration of gunfire against an enemy. Using four squadrons with 28 airplanes was also a method of attaining mutual protection."

August 3rd, 1944 was Bill's first combat mission. His very nervous Co-Pilot was experienced. He was on his last mission (No. 35). That was the magic number of missions to earn a homeward bound vacation. The Co-Pilot was excitable because his last mission was with a "green crew." Target: a factory in Friedrichshafen, the German side of Lake Constance on the other side of Switzerland. They dropped twelve 500-pound bombs. Bill saw 20 or so puffs of smoke. "How harmless they look," he thought. The formation did not encounter any German fighters. On the way back, the plane lost power in two engines. Bill made an emergency landing at 15th Air Force, one hundred miles north of his own field. "There had been a foul up in the way fuel was supposed to be transferred from one tank to another." The plane resumed to home base. As soon as the plane came to a stop, the Co-Pilot danced a little jig. He was alive! He was going home!

August 6, 1944: Combat mission was Lyon Vaise Oil Storage, France followed by August 10th bombing of Campina Oil Refinery, Rumania.

August 13th, while on a mission to bomb an orange railroad bridge in Orange, France with flak heavy and approaching the target Bill saw a B-24 blow up. It was not in Bill's box but very close. He exclaimed, "It just disappeared in a big ball of flame, then nothing, absolutely nothing! There was a void in the sky where ten human beings in a plane had been." Right after that Bill's plane was hit by flak. His Nose Gunner Corporal Shay received a sliver of metal in his ankle. Navigator Grundman, applied tourniquet and gave morphine. A large piece of flak smashed into the plane's four throttles as it came through the windshield. The bent throttles were difficult to manipulate. The cockpit became very windy with a hole in it. Back at base Bill knew "a new sense of vulnerability regarding the danger of flak. Corporal Shay had a big sleepy grin as he knew he was returning to the United States."

August 14th, the bombers were headed to South France to bomb gun positions of the Germans. It was routine. However, the men had increased their respect or fearfulness regarding German antiaircraft fire which caused flak. The German's accuracy was deadly. 88 millimeter guns hurled explosives six miles in the air, often directed by ground radar. Bill "wondered why he never observed fighters. There were no Messerschmitts or Focke Wulfs. Throughout his whole combat tour he did not see a single enemy fighter in the air."

August 17th, the orders were to bomb the Roman/America Oil Refinery, Ploesti, Rumania. Bill wondered about the people on the ground who died. Only for a second these thoughts would wander through his head. "He was simply too busy flying the airplane. People killed were thousands of feet below. Impossible to fly combat missions and feel guilty," he opined. Hundreds of miles from the morning target, as if by fluke probably from a single antiaircraft gun mounted on a railroad car, the plane lost the #2 engine. The officers "jettisoned the bombs" before returning to base. The mission would receive one credit for one raid anyway. The Radio Operator, the quietest man on the crew cracked up while in flight. The crew did not tell Bill until the plane reached base. The calmest guy was sent back to the United States.

August 20th, Smash Dubova Oil Refinery in Czechoslovakia. Now, this mission meant double points toward credits to go home. But rules had changed. It now took 50 credits to receive a leave to United States. Other double-point targets included Vienna and Munich as they were dangerous adventures. It seemed the men never had the same airplane twice. They flew by numbers found on the fuselage. They rose at 4 a.m, were briefed then driven in a Jeep to their numbered plane.

August 21, the briefing detailed their target Hadju Boszormeny Airdrome, Hungary. After that mission, one of the Waist Gunners absolutely refused to fly anymore. He was busted to a Private and put on guard duty to watch over B-24s at night. A West Point Officer with a tough manner told Bill "he better show some leadership!" Bill said, "Sir, I'll try to." Two days later that same squadron CO got shot down. Bill received excellent replacements for Nose Gunner, Radio Operator and the Waist Gunner who quit.

August 24, the B-24s were sent to Kolin Oil Refinery, Czechoslovakia, a double credit. August 25, it was Brno Kurin Oil Refinery in Czechoslovakia, a double credit. August 27th, another double credit mission this time to Blechhammer Synthetic Oil Factory, Germany. September 1, Debrecen Marshaling Yards, Hungary, September 2nd, Nis W. Marshaling Yards, Yugoslavia, September 3rd, Szeged Railroad Bridge, Hungary, September 5th, Szolnok Railroad Bridge, Hungary, September 6th, Novi Sad Marshaling Yards, Yugoslavia and on September 15th, Tatoi Airdrome, Athens, Greece.

After all missions the entire crew was de-briefed. An officer took pages of notes with as many details as each crew member remembered. "What was the weather like? What was the flak like? Was the flak light, heavy, accurate? Were there many fighters? Any special problems? After de-briefing, the group lined up at a little shed to receive "a generous shot of good bourbon."

The 18th mission was to Munich Airdrome, Germany another double. It was September 22nd, 1944. Munich was considered "a mean target." According to the briefing that morning "Munich was ringed by some 200 antiaircraft guns. These guns were 88s and they were very concentrated." Scuttlebutt of the bomber crews considered "Munich gunners elite, more accurate and dangerous."

Bill's squadron lead the "box" of planes at 21,800 feet. Flak was heavy! There were what seemed to the Pilot, thousands of grey-black puffs about the planes. Ribbons of tinfoil were thrown from planes to confuse radar of the enemy. (Grammar school children in the United States collected tinfoil from candy, food and gum wrappers and rolled it into balls for the war effort.) From one of the planes Bill noticed one gunner was so excited the fellow threw out the whole box. He forgot to take the tinfoil out of the container!

Bill's crew dropped their bombs on target. Seconds later, they were hit! The plane shuddered under Bill's hands but he saw no explosion. The smell of high-octane gas was strong as if the whole plane was drenched in gas. Huggins, monitoring the gauges "reached up and popped a button feathering the propeller of No. I engine. Then he feathered # 2. Two engines were out. Both were portside. No one but the plane was wounded." Nursed by another plane, the airship was down to 5,000 feet. Huggins and Bill "stood" on the right rudder pedals out of their safety belts to keep the port wing from dipping below the horizon. Bill explained "If the plane was allowed to sink further they would never be able to get it up again. The airplane flew the way a crab walks, a bit sideways. It was very sweaty work." With great luck, the crew made it safely over enemy territory of Austria and Northern Italy. To lighten the B-24, the crew threw over .50 caliber machine guns, all ammunition and flak suits, their heavy camera with its automatic bombsite and recorded bomb damage.

The Navigator found a British Fighter Field south of the front line near Ancona. "After a slow careful turn to the right, the plane was eased to 2,000 feet. The landing gear was lowered. Bill pulled throttles all the way to effect a glider in action. He would have only one landing attempt." With no radio contact, the British shot off red flares "don't land, don't land!" At 500 feet the plane had to land or crash. The landing strip was torn up and a steamroller was on it doing repair work! Bill nudged the left rudder pedal and the plane lurched left to touch down on some straggly grass. Bill gave instructions to the Co-Pilot. The Waist Gunners were radioed to pull parachute ripcords. Chutes opened. The plane rolled to a stop fifty feet from a thick line of trees. The 18th mission found nine crewmen hastily exiting the plane in relief. Bill just sat there numb and too tired to move. Someone counted. The airplane had a hundred ragged holes in it! The British gave supper and a lecture for ignoring the flares. Three American Jeeps picked up the crew.

On October 7th, Bill Chapin piloted the B-24 over the Vienna Winterhaven Oil Depot, a double credit mission. Five days later, on October 12th, his crew bombed Bologna Munitions Factory, Italy. October 14th mission was to Komarom Railroad Bridge, Hungary followed on October 17th by Vienna South Marshaling Yards, Austria another double credit. October 21, the crew was zeroing in over the Szombathely Marshaling Yards, Hungary.

From the 7th of October on the above five missions, Bill was promoted to fly "group lead." Bill believed his very accurate Bombardier, Dutch Deen "figured in the promotion." All other planes kept eyes on the Lead Bombardier. When bombs were seen leaving the lead plane the remainder of the aircraft in the box formation expended their load of bombs. It all happened at the touch of a toggle. Accuracy of the first Lead Bombardier was crucial to the success of an assignment.

The 24th mission of November 5, 1944 was to bomb troop concentrations, German soldiers retreating from Greece. The retreating Germans were in Mitrovica, Southern Yugoslavia. This easy minor target was considered a milk run. A milk run was a call for action which did not include heavily fortified cities such as Vienna, Berlin, Munich or Ploesti. Often, a milk run was just a lonely railroad bridge.

Actually, bombers had left early in the day. Bill was wandering around in the "everlasting yellow Italian dust" trying to think of something to do. It was about 10:30 in the morning on a sunny "piercingly bright" day. Bill felt good and comfortable. He believed he would not be flying that day. In fact, part of his crew were still on an earlier mission. Except Colonel Steed, 456th's Commanding Officer "very splendid in his white nylon scarf tossed carelessly around his neck" called a meeting.

He explained "troop concentrations were in the town of Mitrovica and ripe for blitzkrieging!" There was belief that there would be no flak at target. They might have one four-gun battery. If hit badly, Pilots were to go east to the town of Nis where Russians were in occupancy. "This was a rare gift; it was a milk run." To Bill, it meant his first raid on human beings as target. Somehow the civilians killed at all those other raids were so far away...

Bill's airplane was called "Jenny" No. 383. It was a new B-24 Liberator. There were not enough flak suits for all the occupants. Men were dressed in heavy flying boots and dark green coveralls. Bill wore his treasured light leather flying jacket and a Mae West life jacket (a life jacket that was also used in water) along with a British parachute. His backpack was hooked onto harness. He did not wear a helmet or hat which is standard dress. As per usual, Bill casually slid under bombs suspended in the bomb bay. Later he would put on a heavy flak suit. It was a front and back armor attire designed to keep shrapnel from flak or from rockets away from his body torso and from the groin. This modern flak suit would lay over his chest and lap during a battle run. He put on his radio headphones and attached the throat mike.

Major Stuck, an Intelligence Officer joined the milk run as his first mission. Bill never saw him again. Bill's superior took lead plane position. Air was bumpy with cumulous clouds. "Bill was sweating like he always did on takeoff. He was jerking around 80,000 pounds of loaded airplane at 10,000 feet." He did not like to wear the oxygen masks and waited until they crossed the Yugoslavia Coast. Masks, which got wet, slimy, full of drool and condensed air very soon upon use were miserable if worn too long. Reaching 19,500 feet, Bill saw the lead plane had its bomb bay opened. Bill felt a blast of cold air which proved his plane's bomb bay was also open. The bomb run seemed long. He saw "three bursts of flak off the left wing at 10 o'clock high." Three more bursts were closer with three black puffs even nearer.

Bill felt bombs leave the belly of the plane, Jenny. It was the "finest of jolts" to an experienced flier. The aircraft lifted just a bit, now that 15,000 pounds of bombs were heading toward target. After that, a piece of flak entered the plane with an evil force of its own. In the explosion that followed, Major Clark who was not wearing his seatbelt, was picked up by the force which "bounced" the Co-Pilot up and out of his seat, "shot the Co-Pilot straight up, turned him in midair and dropped the dead Co-Pilot between the seats." In that one breath, Bill sensed no soul was left in Major Clark.

That evil force that took away Major Clark's life caused Bill to moan. As he watched the lead airplane swerve to the right and slip below his plane. He realized his controls were shot away. "The steering wheel turned easily, the control column had no resistance." He pressed the throat mike with words "stand by to bail out." No answer, the mike was dead. No signals were followed from the auto pilot. The entire system was gone like Major Clark on the floor of the drumming airplane. "Not a single member of the plane communicated. The electrical system was destroyed, not yet on fire. Number three engine was dead too. Air speed was 280 miles per hour which on ground meant 400 miles per hour ground speed."

With horror on the face of the numbed Pilot, still wearing his heavy flak suit he climbed over Major Clark. Sergeant Brooks had left his top turret and was kneeling by the open bomb bay, snapping his parachute onto his harness. Bill motioned for him to go on out. He shook his head. Bill believed that meant he was not quite ready with his preparation for disembarking. Bill looked out the opening and saw the horizon upside down in a giant concave curve. That picture was not as shown in practices. Bill dropped his head out first; now that was standard procedure. With a terrible crack in his ears Bill was swiftly falling, falling... and then he went completely black...

Bill's leg hit the rapidly moving airplane. The pain in his brain numbed his leg. When the black of unconsciousness cleared, air was cold. "Bill floated on his back staring at his right flying boot." Body horizontal, right boot straight up, while whipping like a flag in a gale, blood spraying up in the air, not down, he surmised, "It was some one else's leg." Oh, no, not one of his skiing legs! He thought, "If I pull the ripcord of the parachute the shock will be so severe that my foot will tear away completely, so I better not pull the ripcord." What would happen if he did not pull the ripcord did not enter his head. Having no idea where ground was, he finally tried to turn over to see it and failed. Giving up he pulled the ripcord. When the parachute opened Bill blacked out again. He was perfectly motionless and grateful that his right foot was still attached and dangling.

The ripcord was gone as well as his flying gloves. The gloves had been heavy and designed to protectively reach over his forearms. Now his hands were getting cold. He moaned and babbled like a child. Then he swore incoherently. The earth was incredibly green and peaceful... The land was coming fast... faster. He was drifting into trees. Flight training drummed into his ears. "Cross your legs if you land in trees to save the family jewels!" Managing only to squeeze his legs together, crossing arms in front of his face, he felt he utterly slammed into branches of a tree! His right flying boot swung back and forth like a grandfather's clock pendulum. He heard a barking dog. He just hung in the parachute harness 30 feet up in the tree. He was now "just a used up Pilot!" He wondered about each of the other men positioned on the plane. The only one seen alive was Brooks.

Bill's cold hands bothered him more than the numbed-out-leg-injury. One hand to his mouth made a discovery of dribbling blood. He called for help. "He was answered by a spray of bullets through the leaves of the tree." Cursing and yelling again he thought a bullet hit the swinging boot. No feeling? registered in his brain. Shouts were followed by eight or nine German soldiers. This was his first meeting of Germans in the war since being waited upon by the German prisoners of war in the United States. Hanging in the tree, he was ordered to raise his hands. He tried to obey and couldn't. "Too weak, too weak" was all he could muster. As blood continued to drip from his mouth, he saw a blond boyish soldier shinny up the tree. Bill thought of him as a savior. Two more soldiers climbed up. Bill hugged his 'saviors' closer as one soldier cut the parachute shroud lines. When the last line was cut, the four men supported each other and half slipped, half climbed down from the tree.

Bill felt one testicle had been rammed up into his body. It hurt. Someone issued an order. Four Albanians picked up Bill's body. The fifth person cradled his right foot like one of those POWs at home might carry overflowing bowls of soup to a table. More soldiers met the group. Someone said, "we are going a small distance." That seemed to be miles! The men laughed "It was an extremely exciting day." Bill began to feel pain. A tall bleary-eyed soldier gave him a shot of morphine. Bill couldn't believe "any harm would come from an enemy to such a likeable character as he was."

Bill pointed to his interior pocket in his trousers where an escape kit was concealed. "We are all friends here, you know." He had never reviewed the kit before. It was of great interest to his captors. There was a rayon map which they peered at intently in the light of the sun. Some money, concentrated chocolate, water purification tablets, a tiny compass, fish hook and line were fondled by his rescuers. Hearing footsteps, it was George Geiger, the Bombardier from the plane, Jenny. His comrade had been captured immediately on ground. He told Bill, "Brooks, you and myself were the only ones out of the plane."

Geiger declared the devilish flak had torn off the entire right side of Jenny's nose section all the way to the wing. Lieutenant Miller took pieces of flak in his stomach. The Nose Gunner had been pinned inside his turret by debris and endured the horrible plunge to a mountainside. Later, Bill would learn the plane had taken three direct hits. That was the last time he saw Geiger or another American for days.

After a rotten ambulance ride to Mitrovica the town he had helped bomb, he was taken at night into a blacked-out hospital. It remained dark day and night. Ten Germans, the men he helped blitz were strewn upon the floor of an operating room waiting their turn. He saw enough blood on the floor for treacherous walking. Bill wondered "if the Officer's bars on his tunic gave him priority." Bill noticed "Rubber aprons on the physicians were covered with gore." He felt "the room reeked of deliberate butchery."A technician reached out and pinched his injured foot. The individual then shook his head negatively. A bulging-eyed German with white thin hair and thick horn-rimmed spectacles utterly beamed with joy. He leaned over and declared, "But this is war, Baby. Baby, we must amputate!"

"Are you sure?" Bill asked in a pleading voice. "But this is war, Baby. You are a soldier, Baby." He wished he'd quit calling him, "Baby!" There was something awful in the smile of that albino. It was like he enjoyed having wounded people all around him. It was as if he enjoyed wounding the people around him. The albino performed a "guillotine" operation and did it well. It was routinely a first, of two. Another operation would follow. American surgeons would perform the second operation on his right leg. To Bill, it was one of his important two skiing legs.

In this albino's hospital, Bill would end up urinating in the pocket of his coveralls because of need. He would use that same pocket to carry food. His wrist watch was gone. He could not eat the black bread which tasted like heavy cardboard. A man with coffee told him "the thermometer was to be placed under your armpit not in your mouth." He wondered how many other armpits the thermometer had been under before it reached his mouth. He knew how to read their thermometers by converting centigrade to fahrenheit. His temperature was normal. His second meal was black bread, margarine and cold boiled potatoes. He still could not eat.

He learned how people were on the run during an air raid. They were like birds gathering under branches before a storm. A scream was in his head. No sound like bombs falling. He slid out of bed and slithered his cut-off limb across the room from the piercing pain caused by winds of screeching bombers overhead. "Oh my God, oh my God! he wanted to melt into the wall!" One deafening clamor. A train whistled continously a lonely cry. On and on and on it continued. A town was being destroyed... From the hospital window, he peeked into pits holding flak guns. Germans in great long coats were running here and there. The guns were placed in sunken holes around the hospital. Bill tortured his mind "So this is what I have been doing for 24 missions." There was soup and more black bread for supper. Bill could not eat. Ten more injured Germans were brought into the room. "What did you think of the bombing, Baby?" the albino beamed with an evil sort of joy." The albino leaned over the bed. "I'm afraid all your comrades are dead."

On the second morning, a Serbian girl gave the Pilot a bag of mealy apples. It was the first food Bill had eaten in twenty-four hours. He stayed in Mitrovica for nine days. Bandages were changed, men died in the beds around him, a second air raid was heard. Conversation between the hospitalized men was "Who made war. It was shit." Germans blamed Jews. Bill kept saying "all men are equal." His worst moment, second to being bombed was seeing four P-38s in combat formation disappear into little white cumulous clouds. They swung and drifted so freely... This caused thoughts "of O'Hara, how sexy and perfect she was, wild strawberry ice cream, his Dad's Sunday steak barbecues, the smell of Ballantine Ale, skiing on Pico Peak." Skiing as easily as those planes drifted into the clouds...

As Bill traveled in open cold straw-bedded lice ridden box cars, once parked into a black tunnel for three days with other captives of the war, he moved from town to city and onward to his ultimate destination, that of Stalag 17-B. Stalag 17-B was located near Krems on the Danube River near Vienna. The prison camp was a huge establishment. (In William Chapin's book, *Milk Run*, copyrighted in 1992, and published by Windgate Press, Bill devoted 149 pages on day-to-day life of being a prisoner of war. The book is intense. It is considered a time capsule as Chapin wrote the book while recovering in the hospital immediately after World War II).

During his prisoner-of-war days in Stalag-17, Bill described the bathroom plumbing as backed up flush on the floor. In order to use the facility and in order to keep others' defecation from accumulating on his body, Bill would "perch like a stork on one leg." Walls and floors were wretched with brown streaks. The floors were not only wet but reeked of human waste to travel over.

In order to create that waste, the prisoners had fetishes over food. French prisoners were great traders and in the barter business each time a Red Cross package arrived. Red Cross packages weighing in at eleven pounds became high stakes in card games. Mostly, men ate ravenously in one swoop knowing they would be depriving themselves on the morrow. Then they would go hungry. They would play and toy with food watching it intently while squirreling it away in drawers. Placing a loaf of bread under one's head was common. This practice was to protect the bread for another hard cold morning which would dawn all too soon. Hunger would not go away from their wretched existence.

Bill did not describe cruelty of guards but cruelty of conditions. Wounded lie in their own pus, smell permeated sleeping quarters. Bodies lie unwashed, hair matted. Bill's gift of gab was a deterrent to crying and or insanity. He dared not think of home like he had when he saw those soft gliding airplanes disappear into the clouds.

During the saga of train trips to get to Stalag-17, Bill squashed lice and searched for more lice, making a home in the pubic and bandaged leg sections of his warm body. Men had squatted in an uncivilized mode out the door of the moving trains to defecate. He remembered a weird feeling coming from shots of morphine. At one stop, he was strangely moved by hearing some German Army singers. He remembered never being warm, especially while in boxcars. On one occasion slushy dirty water was dumped on his head adding more injurious cold. He whimpered. Black bread and soup, watery soup and black bread, smoking too many Dominoes cigarettes made him dizzy. A young Yugoslav girl cleaning his wound had an infant daughter killed in a raid. He remembered his face grimy with coal dust and when eventually washed in cold water, it was chalk white. An ambulance driver whispered "Munich was bombed last night." His matted hair was shaved off, completely! His head was round and bumpy.

At Stalag-17 in the winter, their room was so cold you could see your breath. Only one small blanket was at each cot. It was supposed to ward off the frigid temperature. The men burned a bench for fuel. It was a good thing the guards did not catch the men burning the bench. Cry babies were unpopular since they kept others from sleeping. Card games were punctuated by intricate bidding systems. High stakes included a Red Cross package. Bill started the book, Don Quixote, only read a few pages. Perhaps the book was too long to interest the young flyer. (The library version of this book is composed of about 900 pages of short stories.) He was busy talking, instead. Men talked, thought and dreamed food. Sex, an abstraction was not discussed much, too painful. There were bets on beetles and contests on flatulence.

Passersby told thousands of stories. The prisoners expected the Russians to come for them. Some groups boiled rotten potato peelings and dandelion greens for dinner. Before the war ended, the Germans cleared out leaving the sick and injured prisoners to fend for themselves. The SS troops formally marched away. They took the ambulatory Americans and a few other Allies. They marched out of the prison in one big huge forminable group. There was no food left by the time they cleared out. On VE-Day, no one came to take the place of the guards or the Allied prisoners that had left. Bill was put in charge of the wounded non-ambulatory patients in the hospital wing. There was no one to help the injured or limited ambulatory cases. Prisoners who could walk and left Stalag-17 carried what food they scraped together in their knapsacks. The badly wounded had no store of food to draw upon, except remnants of their Red Cross packages.

On May 8th, the men knew by radio, they were free. With the SS troops gone, the men did not know what to do with their new found freedom. On May 9th, their real liberation took place at 11 a.m. when five 2 ½ ton American-built trucks approached the tree-lined lane. Men on crutches hobbled toward the trucks driven by Red Army Soldiers. Now food was plentiful. The Russians brought lots of apples and roasted a cow.

On May 9th at 8 a.m., a magnificent thing! Third Army ambulances brought tears to Bill's eyes. A driver who saw the rooms got sick to his stomach. Bill was last man aboard. He forgot to take his dog tags which were left on his bedpost.

Bill weighed in at 135 pounds. Wolfing down lots of ice cream, he also got drunk, then vomited on a flight of stairs. He saw movies. He kidded Army nurses. German pistols and a big Nazi flag were given to him. He was "like a giddy child." Eventually, the men were taken to a most grand hospital in Versailles, France. On a lawn of soft green grass, at Versailles, he met his brother-in-law who informed him, his kid brother Taff had died in action a month or so earlier.

Bill did not know how to tell his wife about his leg, so he didn't. He did not know she had received a Western Union telegram, dated March 30th from the war department informing her that her husband was a prisoner of war. He did not know that on June 5th, 1945 she was informed Bill was making normal improvement on an amputated leg. When Bill arrived back in the United States, he was met by his wife in a long black limousine driven by a chauffeur. After Bill and O'Hara went to bed, Bill cried for hours. He felt rage "at all the old men of the world who made wars and sent young men to fight them."

Bill was wheeled into surgery August 1, 1945 followed by months of physical therapy, weight lifting and fittings for a new leg. He learned to walk through parallel bars. O'Hara got pregnant on purpose. Bill received his Captain rating. He wrote the experiences that now appear in his book, *Milk Run*. In 1948 he received his purple heart medal. In checking details of official Air Force records in Washington D.C., in 1992 before publishing his book, Chapin discovered he had been awarded the Distinguished Flying Cross in 1944 for his bombing missions, prior to capture.

After the war and the second surgery, Bill has played lots of tennis. He lived in Sausalito, California spending fifteen years as Chief Copy Editor for the San Francisco Chronicle. On a one year sabbatical he wrote some news, sports and military articles for Pacific Stars and Stripes, printed in Tokyo. He and his wife, O'Hara moved to Sonoma in 1982. Bill walks a great deal in the Adult Community where they live. He plays lots of poker and still does some writing. Recently, he wrote about his wife's heart surgery. Bill does editing and proof reading. He works on articles for Fireman's Fund Insurance. Bill dislikes air travel. He especially does not appreciate cramped airplanes!

The above story is gratefully acknowledged:

Selected from interviews with William Chapin and from the book MILK RUN, by William Chapin, published by Windgate Press, Sausalito, California.

Chapin, William, *Milk Run, Prisoner of War, 1944: An American Flier in Stalag 17-B.*, Windgate Press, P.O. Box 1715, Sausalito, California, 94966.

Newton Dal Poggetto

United States Naval Reserve 1942 - 1946
Honorary Naval Reserve 1994

Newton Dal Poggetto has had the privilege of being a Sonoman since birth. His grandfather settled the prominent family in Glen Ellen, near Sonoma, California in 1875. His father was born behind the Dal Poggetto Apartments located on East Napa Street in Sonoma. As a young man, Newton referred by his friends as Dal, obtained a job as lifeguard at the wonderfully big hot swim pool complex located in Boyes Hot Springs. Historically, Indians used the hot waters for sweat baths. Years ago the large buildings were burned and the absentee owners elected to close the facility. The property was sold as development land for homes. The 130 degree waters were covered over and forever lost to recreation. While Dal was lifeguard at the oversized pool. The resort became famous for massages, picnic grounds, baseball games, dance bands and leisurely summer living. Dal watched over San Franciscans seeking summertime recreation away from their city fog

During summertime college days, Dal also enjoyed working at Mare Island Ship Yard which lay south of Sonoma and north of San Francisco. He was cost accountant and time keeper for the government of the United States during the period. Dal kept records on a large San Francisco construction company which was awarded construction contracts. Costs plus 10% as per their contract with the government were monitored. The Mare Island Shipyard was rapidly expanding. Building projects included additions of shop and telephone buildings, barracks, Officers Club and construction of sewer and water mains. As a side issue, he also traced where equipment was being used and where it was on a given day. When his figuring was completed, Dal turned his computations over to a real accountant, Jerry Casson.

Dal got this fun job through an accountant named Bachelder, who had offices in the famous Barracks Building which is now part of the State of California Park System. The Barracks Building borders the Plaza known for the raising of the Bear Flag in 1846, with the ultimate raising of the Stars and Stripes a few days later leading to statehood of California.

Newton Dal Poggetto was allowed to attend the University of Colorado until his number was called by the Naval Reserve. To keep tabs on the young man, the Twelfth Naval District of San Francisco requested his phone number. He finished a whole year at Colorado University before being inducted into active duty. On 1 July 1943, a contingent of 45 University of Colorado men, 60 Brigham Young collegians and 40 Santa Clara students were assembled with some junior college Reservists at the University of New Mexico. A total of 500 college men were given the equivalence of two years training. Courses included engineering, physics, drawing and navigation. Upon graduation from these courses, the Reservists would be sent to one of three midshipment schools for four months Officers training. There the Reservists would graduate as "Four Month Wonders of the Navy" similar to "90 day wonders of the Army." Dal had enough credits to graduate from regular college but he could not graduate at Boulder, Colorado because he had not fullfilled the senior residence requirement.

In a surprise move, four thousand Reservists were sent to Norfolk Naval Yard, Virginia because there was no room in three existing midshipman's schools, namely, Northwestern in Chicago, Notre Dame and Columbia Universities in New York. The 'guys' just toured around toting wooden guns for three months as pre-midshipmen. Their life was a makeshift sort of existence. On the 20th of December, it was Dal's good fortune to go to Columbia University where he was commissioned on 13 April 1944.

Dal experienced a great social life while in New York. A nice little old lady on a Civilian Committee took care of social needs of the service personnel. Dal was on her preferred list. She arranged for free theatre tickets and invitations to dinner being held by upper fashionable prominent socialites. Many of these happy times took place in Manhatten on the Long Island Gold Coast or around Grenwich, Connecticut. On a given Saturday, Dal would take in three parties from afternoon until midnight. Once he went up an exclusive separate elevator to a fancy school to meet young debutantes. These girls ranged in schooling from senior high school through second year of college. Arriving at the floor level for the special private school, he faced a completely blank wall. The school area had been a former speakeasy which was then converted to the private debutant girls school.

Dal was overwhelmed by an Easter dinner held at the lovely eastside home of Chief Counsel of United Press. The lady from the social committee arranged tickets at Perry Como and Milton Berle shows. New musicals *Carousel* and *Oklahoma* were included in this dizzying whirlwind of social events. Dal rounded out his musical experience with *La Boheme* and *Madam Butterfly* performances at the Metropolitan Opera House. As a Midshipman, his uniform was snappy and life was just plain wonderful!

After all this activity on Saturday nights, the Sonoman sang in the Catholic Choir on Sunday morning. He met famous Harry Emerson Fosdick, Pastor and a well known intellectual, Monsignor Ford. As all good things come to an eventual end, Dal was sent to Miami Naval Training Center to become a Destroyer Gunner Officer. With a side trip to Ohio State University, he finished up Naval training with classes in Aircraft and Ship Recognition. He was ordered aboard USS Canfield V262 as Assistant Gunnery Officer and headed for Hawaii. The Canfield operated around the Gilberts, Marshalls, Saipan and Tinian Islands, the Philippines, Iwo Jima and off Japan.

The destroyer was an escort for larger ships. It was primarily used for an anti-submarine and antiaircraft screen. The USS Canfield was equipped with three inch guns, torpedo tubes, depth charges and antiaircraft batteries. Radar played a significant role in convoying ships. As an escort vessel the Canfield was considered a small destroyer in the Battle Fleet. It measured 260 feet carrying 240 men. The Gun Platform held 20 mm and 40 mm torpedo tubes. The most important job for the destroyer was to protect the aircraft carriers and to protect troop ship convoys.

The Canfield was out too far from shore to help with shore bombardment of Iwo Jima. Their mission primarily was for anti-submarine protection of the bigger ships. Japanese Air Force was shot up by then, so the work of the destroyer was uneventful as to airstrikes. Gunnery Officers of the ship were not privy to "what was going on." The general weather conditions were cold, windy and wet. It was tiresome being chilled most of the time. Dal said, "it was like going to a football game with no announcer. The men on destroyers were simply not privy to action taking place on the islands or on the ships they were guarding."

On one lovely summer's morning at Ulithi west of Guam, Dal had Deck Watch. A dozen transports filled with troops were going past them on their way to Japan. Then, Dal saw a large foreign cargo ship on the horizon all by itself. It had appearance of a bulk carrier being identified by its booms in the air. Dal mumbled, "Why the Hell is that cargoe ship going alone?" The Canfield made three separate runs on this vessel. In tropical waters the enemy ship's wake just wouldn't break up, so it was easy to follow. One day it just disappeared where it sank out of sight beyond the horizon...

The Canfield made another run on a submarine contact! The Captain took over and the submarine was sunk. It had been stalking a merchant ship from another country not a Navy Ship. The question of the day became "why was the sub all alone?"

Back at Ulithi Atoll there was a little more excitement. Orders were to pick up a half-dozen tankers. On the first three days of the journey there was a typhoon. In order to rendezvous with the main fleet three hundred miles away the destroyer went through mines. There were buoys set up for paths. 20mm ammunition was used to hit mine spurs outside the big round buoys.

While following one typhoon, another came up in another direction as indicated on air radar. Two Japanese spotter planes were also seen on the horizon. The destroyer was located between all these entities. It was windy and blowing. It was the first and last time that Tokyo Rose told the Japanese "the Canfield is coming" and it was the last time she broadcasted "the Americans will be dead and drowned by morning."

Dal repeated, "Can you imagine a more horrible situation? There were two Japanese spotter planes overhead, a typhoon aft, another typhoon behind and Tokyo Rose! The wind was picking up when we went to bed. We did not know if we would be wet or dry when we woke up. I looked out the porthole the next morning and was awe struck, I never saw so many ships in my life! There were massive amounts of ships as to be utterly amazing! Around us was Admiral Halsey's Fleet. Support fleet had another 200 to 300 ships. Sixty ships made a protective screen around six oilers which took frontal positions. Anti-submarine and antiaircraft screens were in place."

After this, USS Canfield was ordered on picket duty. A picket ship scouts the ocean area for enemy ships or other problems by sailing ahead in front of the fleet. It travels twenty to thirty miles ahead all by itself. Nobody on board cared for picket duty with radar extending knowledge to the enemy about ship movements. Dal stayed in general quarters all the time when that kind of duty was ordered. Their mission was to safely lead sixty empty ammunition ships back to the Philippines for re-supply of munitions and for refilling them with fuel. The Canfield was one of six ships used for picket duty as a team for that assignment.

Early June 1945 some training exercises for shore bombardment of Japan were ordered. Approaching the Island of Oahu, a wind sock would be towed behind a plane at 500 feet. This was someone's idea of target practice. The Navy gunners used 20 mm and 40 mm cannon to try to knock the sock down while a so-called fearless Pilot guided his plane towing the wind sock. While shooting at the windsock toward the sun, a triple tail was seen coming at the gunners. The Captain went crazy. Target practice was raising smoke. The tail belonged to an incoming plane! It was a Pan American Clipper full of passengers! The commercial plane made it through the smoke and shells. Everybody was relieved. The plane missed the shells. The Commercial Pilot was scared, so he had come in low. The Navy was happily relieved the plane had missed the shells.

When the crew of Canfield was in Mare Island for overhaul, the Captain chose a new Chef. The Captain was pleased as punch about the cooking and his wise choice as he believed all Black Stewards were pretty good Chefs! The Captain also had a fetish about cleanliness and was very germ conscious. The new Chef jumped in the ocean one nice calm day near Pearl Harbor. The ship had a little tower so the Captain locked his new Chef up in there. The Captain dropped the cook off in Eniwetok. The Black

Steward turned up with syphilis. The Captain found heat, grease, smell of diesel oil and butter coupled with refrigerator odors a bit contrary to his sense of cleanliness while checking the kitchen.

Dennis Day was a bunk mate for awhile. He was an Ensign and was liked. At Pearl Harbor, he was picked-off by Nimitz for the Admiral's staff. There were three ranks of Admirals consisting of Land Admirals, Fleet Admirals and Staff Planning Admirals. The Planning Admirals had a whole group of people divided into submarine, cruiser and destroyer planners. For example, Admiral Nimitz had 25 Admirals on ships. A Captain in the Navy was equivalent to a full Colonel in the Army. A group of six ships were run by Lieutenant Commanders. Approximately every 36 ships would have an Admiral. A flagship was usually nothing less than a cruiser with an Admiral in charge. An Air Craft Carrier would have another Captain. Three or four carriers with a dozen escorts would be considered a Battle group. Men were all over the Hawaiian Islands in August of 1944. DES PAC (Destroyer Pacific) was very discriminatory. They had their own Officers Club in Hawaii. There were exchange privileges with submariner and air wings. It was dynamite to be on submarine duty. Men practiced upon each other's skills. The Fleet Officers had a plushy General Officers Club located in Pearl City. For twenty cents you could buy a drink and eat Macadamia nuts. Cigarettes were a nickle a pack.

In Leyte Gulf on the first week of August, Dal saw another mega-collection of United States Pacific Fleet Ships. There were about 400 ships with an additional 300 more waiting near Japan. On one hour standby, men were ready for an invasion planned for September 10th. To soften up the beaches there were 400 to 500 older battleships equipped with old gun platforms. Jeep carriers looked very impressive. It was hot! On the third consecutive day, men were placed on 24 hour notice for invasion.

Dal asked to go ashore to an Officer's Club. There he found Dave Eraldi another Sonoman. Eraldi was a chum who went to grammar and high school with Dal. Dave's ship was in floating dry dock. Taking a ride in an old whale boat, Dave and Dal enjoyed an afternoon visit. Dal's Dad and Dave's Dad had also gone to school together. Needless to say, the two men had a wonderful time discussing the old home town and their lives as Navy men.

Shortly thereafter, USS Canfield sailed right into Tokyo Bay. The atomic bomb had been dropped on Hiroshima and Nagasaki. Seven hundred ships were anchored in the Bay. No one was allowed to go ashore for two days until the peace treaty was signed aboard the USS Missouri. In three weeks, Dal was smelling the air where bombs had been dropped. Yokohama had been firebombed and was flattened. It had been built on little hills like San Francisco. There was only one department store left and a row of buildings that had no back walls. There was the smell of dead bodies in the rubble. It was weird that there were 100,000 people standing around with no buildings or shopkeepers to service their needs. There was also a ridge about the town similar to Twin Peaks in San Francisco. Some houses were seen away off in the shadowy distance.

Tokyo was visited. Dal discovered the business district had been about one-third destroyed. Houses were obliterated. Many homes had been of bamboo and frame construction. The people had sustained enormous casualties having no fire protection.

After leaving the Japanese mainland Dal went to Eniwetok, then Hawaii and back to Mare Island, California. The San Francisco Bay was full of ships and service personnel. Mare Island was full of ships and people. Dal had a thirty day leave, a day or two before Christmas. Home was but a half-hour drive up the valley from Mare Island.

After the USS Canfield was decommissioned, Dal was ordered back to Japan as Navigator on a Sea

Plane. In 1950, the Navy tendered him to San Diego with words, "Where in the hell have you been?" Being single he had not qualified for release from active duty. As a Sea Plane Tender, Dal was aboard a big ship that repaired sea planes. It had a machine shop used by other ships for small repair jobs. Dal was acclaimed Movie Officer by his Captain. He had trouble even getting any new movies, let alone exchanging any! Then he learned one had to bribe the Officer of Supply with booze to get movies. When Dal found out how to barter, he managed to bring the ship extra foods to spice up the menu along with a big supply of movies.

Dal noted the USS Indianapolis was sunk while running on a submarine. It had been three days in the same waters. It had just delivered the atomic bomb. It was caught within a matter of hours before the bomb was dropped by Pilots of the Enola Gay on Hiroshima.

Recently, Newton Dal Poggetto, an attorney and former Judge wrote the Navy as to his receiving inactive Reserve Status. At a ripe age of about 70 years, he still had an active but non-paying Reserve Status! He merely wrote the letter asking for a new replacement of his Navy ID card. His letter of inquiry to Washington D.C. was answered in two days! Since Dal had not been formally discharged and had continued to be on the rolls as a Navy Reserve Officer, he was now considered by the Navy to be an Honorary Naval Reserve Officer. As Honorary Reserve Officer his I D card would not be re-issued. He asked, "what does Honorary Naval Reserve mean?" It meant, the Navy was not going to issue a new I.D. card and that the Navy had about 17,000 other persons like Newton Dal Poggetto. In the United States there were 17,000 other Naval Reservists that had served in World War II and were not formally dismissed from the Navy. They were all classified as "Honorary." Interestingly, Newton Dal Poggetto has been referred to as Your Honor while wearing judicial robes and he is now referred to as an Honorary Naval Reserve Officer of the United States Navy. The latter designation comes without pay!

Lee J. Tunkis

United States Army 1942 - 1946

Born in Chicago, Illinois, Lee was the sole support for his mother and dad as he neared a pending draft into service of his country. His classification was 3A. This was mostly a married man's status, but his support of his parents gave him that classification. Working as a salesman selling furniture, he decided to try for a Volunteer Officer Candidate Test. If Lee became an Officer his service pay would naturally be higher than that of a drafted Private.

After passing the test, the hardest three months of his life was spent at Elwood Arsenal, Maryland. Since World War I, the training at this facility was about use of Chemical Warfare. The poison gases he was introduced to included mustard gas, phosgene and CNS. Mustard gas is an oily amber liquid, dichlorethyl sulfide, $C4H8CL2S$ having an odor of mustard or garlic and used in warfare because of its powerful blistering effect. Phosgene and CNS are commonly known as tear gas. Through books, Lee made acquaintance with definal carcine (poisonous gas).

The men at this school were also trained in heavy 4.2 mortars. This preparation was for combat in the chemical branch of the United States Army. The 4.2 mortar shell was equivalent to a 105 artillery shell. It was the largest mortar shell the Allied Forces had at their disposal in 1942. While trained in the use of poisonous gases, Lee never had occasion to use them and he never even saw a poison gas shell. His training was for prevention or retaliation should the enemy be so unwise as to use poison gases. Allied Forces were not the only ones having chemical warfare knowledge. Historically, chemical warfare existed as far back as Greek Civilization. Poisonous gases were prohibited after World War I in the Geneva Pact. A soldier on the battlefield would absolutely make no decisions as to use of chemical warfare. That would have been a political choice made in Washington D.C.

Thousands of rounds of white phosphorous shells from the antipersonnel weapon were used as a smoke screen against the enemy. The Battle of Cassino in Italy was an important location for use of such shells. Puffs of white smoke sprayed upwards when phosphorus was exposed to the air. When it struck the body of a human it burned through one's skin. The only way to stop the dreadful burning was to roll in mud. Even this compound used extensively by both sides in battle disregarded the concerns for a fellow human being.

After graduating from Officer's Candidate School, Lee was shipped to England and was part of a nucleus for the 92nd Chemical Mortar Battalion. This body of troops (900 personnel) moved about on wheels. They were separate units used in various numbered armies. The Battalion was assigned to the 5th Army in Africa attached to the 36th Infantry Division. They supported the 2nd Corp in Italy as well as the British Army at Cassino in Italy.

As Lee arrived in Port of Casablanca, Morocco in Africa, he walked off the ship dryfooted. He had his first view of German Desert Corp Prisoners while waiting at a railhead. They were a sight to behold! They formally marched off the same trains that Lee's unit was about to board. Germans prepared to march on the ships bound for America as Lee's group left the transport. At the railhead approximately

2,000 German soldiers unloaded off the trains. An Officer in command shouted. In one click of the heels all the Germans were at attention. In the course of three steps, all 2,000 men were singing in four part harmony and formally marching onto the ship.

Asking why the prisoners of war were being shipped all the way to the United States instead of being kept in Africa, Lee's explanation was as follows: "There were thousands of prisoners. It would take many shiploads of food to feed them. The ship returning to the United States was emptied of service personnel and military cargoes brought to Africa. If the prisoners of war were shipped to the United States it would cut down on shipment of all those foodstuffs needed to feed them. Since prisoners of war could not be forced to do military labor, they were used as waiters in Officer's Clubs in the United States. The reason they could work in the Officers Clubs was due to a military convention ruling regarding prisoners. An agreement was reached to use prisoners of war for domestic chores. Lee said, "It was a sight to see German waiters clicking their heels together and asking, "How can I serve you, Sir!"

Lee's stay in Africa was brief and uneventful. He was in no battles. The invasion of Sicily was being readied by the Allied Forces. Lee smiled. "I knew Patton and Eisenhower very well but they did not know me!" he said.

The invasion of Sicily was another example of nonsense in war. The right hand making up the orders certainly did not know what the left hand was doing. The Mortar Battalion was assigned to the British. The Battalion was on the first available British landing craft to Sicily. The British were at Marsala on the Mediterranian Sea. The Americans had only a few big shells for their guns that were on the trucks. There were only 48 rounds per gun. After the first day the Americans had no ammunition. Their job to support the English Infantry with high explosives and with white phosphorus shells was limited. Without more ammunition they could not help in British battle operations. Within five days, the Mortar Battalion was ordered back on ship. This was not a bit like the popular song, *Praise the Lord and Pass the Ammunition*! Since the Americans couldn't get their special ammunition to the Battalion they sent their Battalion to the ammunition!

The Americans established a beachhead in the southern port of Sicily at Licata. The unit proceeded high up in the mountains where it was the rainy season. Sicily was the group's first exposure to full time combat. Being early in the Italian campaign, the men found themselves doubly at risk. Every area had been previously occupied by the Germans. The enemy knew the territory and its buildings intimately.

Lee's job as Platoon Leader was to act as Forward Observer. The well being of the troops was guarded like a plague. He would not allow any of the men to sleep in any building under any roof. Since Germans troops had been there before, they knew the terrain better than the fresh American troops. It was too risky to stay in permanent structures knowing that German Batteries would fire upon well plotted buildings.

The stench of bodies was horrible. For awhile the men could not make out where some of the bodies were located. Then they found the odor was emitting from fragments and slivers of human flesh actually stuck high in the trees. "It was difficult for the human mind to deal with this malignancy. "Thank God," Lee stated, "the human mind can shut out this kind of picture."

The bloodiest battle for the 36th Infantry Division was at Rapido River. There were tremendous casualties after crossing the stream. Port Battalions unloaded and filled gasoline tanks. There were Quartermaster Units supplying goods and ammunition. Favorite targets for the Germans were trucks of supplies and truck drivers.

At the Rapido River the battle was fought twice. The Germans in retreat turned around and came back to fight the battle all over again. Lee sympathized with anyone who might exhibit fear. There were many. Lee had bars on his collar. He was frightened too, but he could not show it. This battle cost thousands of casualties. Battle changes took place forcing Germans back in full retreat. At this point, as if to release tension of these memories and to change the subject, Lee sang his favorite raunchy war song.

I Don't Want to Be a Soldier.

I don't want to go to War.

I would rather hang around Piccadilly underground,

Living off the earnings of a high class lassie.

Monday, I kissed her on the ankle, Tuesday, I kissed her on her knee.

Wednesday, success, I took off her dress. Thursday, her chemise gor-bli-mee.

Friday, I put my hand upon it. Saturday, she gave the balls a tweek,

Sunday after supper I shoved the old boy upper,

and now she pays me 20 Bob a week, gor-bli-mee.

I don't want to be a Soldier. I don't want to go to War.

I just want to hang around, Picadilly underground

and live off the earnings of a Whore.

Lee continued on with the observation, ours was not a singing army like the Germans. We had no rousing marching songs like *Over There* of World War I. Over the very heavy radios with God awful batteries the most one heard was that old plaintive song *Lilli Marlene* and the words of Axis Sally. Her greeting to men arriving in Africa was "Hope you enjoy it in Africa like your wives and girl friends are enjoying themselves at home."

Part of Lee's work was training wire and radio men. Telephone wired walky-talkies were somewhat inefficient but were good for about 100 yards. Wires were all over the ground. Lee surmised "all of Europe could be mined for 1,000s of miles of copper wire used there." Wiring was done often. It took two persons to a roll of wire on a spindle to give support needed for communication. Wire was replaced constantly. Observers reported to the 80mm mortar firing centers which held the most dangerous mortars. There were any number of guns in the Battalion firing centers. At Cassino, fifty miles south of Rome the 4.2 mortar even helped Ghurka Troops from India (British Soldiers) as they supported Polish troops.

Every morning Observation Posts sent messages by wire to the direct firing area. Orders for the day might include firing missions along with objectives and maps. There were usually four large guns with about 50 men in the firing area. At 0600, squads would move out with preparation to give cover. At the Officer's discretion smoke covering phosphorous shells were used.

The situation at Cassino was a stalemate. The 36th Division moved into position discovering a German Tiger Tank was disabled below the Allies encampment. The tank was within 1,000 yards of Lee's position. The German Tiger Tank was about 13 feet tall. The men first saw it while marching from a distance. When they walked by it, it was frightening. In defense of our smaller tanks, Lee stated, "keep in mind a German tank was about 500 miles from it's homeland while we would have had to ship tanks across the ocean. The big Tiger Tank did not fit into U.S. statistics. While using materials to make one big tank, smaller tanks could be made and they had more maneuverability."

In order to keep the Germans from recovering the gigantic Tiger Tank, Lee assigned one gun to fire every 15 minutes. A phosphorous shell was also sent out by the tank. Sure enough, Lee saw a recovery unit. The Germans did not succeed in getting the tank back. The Americans stayed at this post for a God awful amount of time.

Basic training had a premise that you never stayed in one position. Some other group would soon be occupying the spot you were presently encamped upon. Lee restated, "The biggest advantage the Germans had was their knowledge of topographical and physical positons from where they retreated."

Mortars were used to fire over hills. The mortar had a relatively effective range at 1500 yards maximum. One did not really know exactly where the shell was going. Lee was eventually wounded at the Observation Post. He now wonders, "How in the hell do you find people to go to war?" Every morning the enemy had raked the hills with shells. They hit all the high points. "They were south of Mt. Cassino," Lee said, "never heard the round that got me. I woke up in a field hospital. I have tremendous admiration for the Army Medical Corp. I came into consciousness and then would pass in and out. I had tremendous pain in my head." Someone murmured, "Got to curl up more and get on your side." They gave a spinal tap to draw blood out of the brain. It was a tremendous sensation. Pain began disappearing. The nature of the injury was called subarchonoid hemmorage."

The wounded soldier had a glorious nurse. She explained that his "brain was floating in a waterproof bag. The concussion of the shell had caused the brain to contract. If the brain contracted too much it would burst blood vessels in the bag the brain was floating in. We have to get the blood out of the brain, otherwise you'll be gone. The main brain blood source comes from the spine." Lee was at the hospital for four days. In reality he began to feel great. He enjoyed the recouperative powers of his young body.

Orders directed him back to the United States on the first returning vessel. For Lee "That's when the fun started." It was glorious to sit at the Officer's Mess on the ship. Four men grouped around a table with table cloths. "We were served steak, duck and other great food. I centered my attention on steaks," Lee's eyes sparkled with those memories.

In the United States, Lee was assigned to the detatchment of patients at Walter Reed Hospital in Washington D.C. He felt awkward about being at the hospital as he felt perfectly well. There were fifty other young wounded men in the hospital ward. Men had had feet blown off, guts blown up and faces disfigured. Lee was impressed that the men did not sympathize or ask for sympathy regarding their injuries. One married chap at the end of the ward had stepped on a land mine. One leg had been blown off at the ankle and the other at the knee. His face was patched up and his genitalia was torn up. The medics were restoring his reproductive parts. As Lee refreshed his memory he recalled, "The Army was doing the right thing by this soldier." Every morning a beautiful nurse came to get the battered up soldier. She looked just like a Hollywood star. Everybody in the ward knew what she was working on when she announced, "let's go for physical therapy." The men would say to the young man, "I'll go in your place." His face would turn red. The nurse would enter the good natured banter with "Don't you guys wish you could go in his place? You don't have as much there as he has!"

Lee was transferred to rehab after using up a bed in the hospital for a week. He was given five glorious months in the service at Washington D.C. The young man felt he was in good shape. He was single. He had battle ribbons and he had the City of Washington D.C. to explore! The City was jampacked. He was reminded of the song, *They're either too Young or too Old* as the men in the City were generally older or younger than Lee. There were also many WACs and WAVEs. Like a kid in a candy store, Lee enjoyed his stay in the Capitol.

The Medical Board was an interesting situation. Lee was one of the first officers in chemical warfare back with combat experience. When the men were trained for war in the 4.2 mortar techniques, they had never had a training manual. Lee was assigned to develop a manual. His classification was designated as "limited service." Moving to Edgewood Arsenal, Maryland his old military training school, he was assigned a squad of mortar men. He chose a photographer and a male secretary to work on the 4.2 Chemical Mortar Manual. The photographer photographed various parts of the weapon for identification and labeling. Photographs taken included the weapon parts, care of the weapon, firing the big gun and motion of the squad. The work turned out to be a 2" reference manual, a first person "How to do it book." The project lasted three months.

Fate sent Lee to Camp Swift, Texas where his life really began! Lee met his wife to be, Marian. He was with a battalion of brand new ROTC Officers and new college students recruits from MIT. The favorite hunting ground for the single Officers was the University of Texas located in Austin. Introduced to that "candy store" Lee considered he got the most beautiful girl of all the young ladies from the Chi Omega House, his wife, Marian of 50 years!

The war ended. Lee went back to Edgewood, Texas because he was in love and married. The Tunkis's stayed at Corpus Christi near the Gulf of Mexico. With limited funds they manufactured furniture. They struggled for eight years. They had no money until they sold the business. Lee was interested in Japan. He and his brother Paul manufactured boats in Japan for export back to the United States.

Lee was for 30 years a retired Captain. He moved back to the mainland in 1960 when he opened a real estate office on the Plaza in Sonoma. He was very successful in selling new homes built by one particularly prolific developer. He always felt he deprived the educational system of Sonoma by stealing away his wife Marian because she had a teaching credential. She was a consistent top saleslady in this office. He and his wife became world travelers. They visited all of Europe. They went back to Japan many times. Lee believes he has had more interesting discussions with the Japanese than with any other peoples of the world. He liked Japanese traditions and architecture. To Lee, the Japanese were a contradiction. They were individualists, admirable and had an interesting culture. When he hears tales of atrocities committed by Japanese soldiers on other peoples during World War II, he finds it hard to take it in. Lee, the retired Real Estate Broker known for philosophizing states, "Who wins? Who loses? People have no conception how disorganized wars are. Who wins? Who loses? The army with the fewest mistakes."

He further noted, "We had the 50th Celebration of Normandy Landings. How many veterans go back again based upon their own experience? In 1975 or so, Lee and Marian hired a guide in Rome. The mission was to find the old battleground at Cassino. Driving south, they saw the Abbey was rebuilt and the town of Cassino was rebuilt overlooking the Liri Valley. Going further south, names of places that had never crossed Lee's mind since the war were right there on the road map. The couple traveled on until it became more and more uncomfortable. At the Rapido River, the town was on the west side of the highway instead of on the east side as Lee remembered. The old town had not been rebuilt. A new town was built on the west side instead. After a planned ride to Solarno and by the time the couple reached Amalfi, Lee had enough! He was no longer curious. He had too many unpleasant memories of this particular area. He philosophized again, "God in his wisdom has helped men not to try to remember too much...Take the color of chartreuse, that pale yellowish green color. I never liked the color. It reminds me of morning meals on the battlefield with those dammed dehydrated eggs..."

Mark D. Tuel

United States Air Corp., 1941 - 1948

United States Army, 1948 - 1963

Mark Tuel, born in Lehigh, Iowa hitchhiked into Des Moines on December 7th, 1941. He headed for his favorite hangout, the airport. Mark was into civilian air training at the facility, but more important, he hoped "to make out" before the night ended. There was a dance being held on the second floor of the facility to the music of Big Band radio. While kibitzing around and filling in time, an announcer cut through the simplicity of the American lifestyle and fun to announce that "Pearl Harbor had been bombed by the Japanese Air Command." The Franklin D. Roosevelt speech including the President's famous quote, "day of infamy," would interrupt another American life.

Mark, did not "make out" that night. His thoughts were on his a perfect 1A draft status. The thought of being in the infantry cried out, "definitely not!" His next consideration included thoughts about his two year junior college status and the possible role in the service of his country as an Air Force Cadet. He drove to Des Moines. At his own request he was administered a test by the Army Corp. Mark's mission was for a possible training course as an aviation cadet. He was sent home to await news.

Almost immediately, the young recruit went to Santa Anna, California for preflight training. He was given instructions "on how to be a soldier and live in a tent." He went to Santa Maria for instruction on bi-planes. At Taft, near Bakersfield, planes for training were more advanced. Mark graduated with wings (!) at Williams Air Field, Chandler, Arizona.

Cadets worked very hard at ground school. There were eleven other fellows along with Mark that soloed aircraft at night. They took orders from an Officer who controlled the maneuvers from Jeep radio messages. One night they kept circling so long they were almost dizzy. The planes' fuel tanks were getting very low. After a while Mark wondered "if the control radio was out." Mark radioed out "If your radio is not working then blink your lights as we do not have much gas left!" The Jeep blinked its lights. The twelve pilots broke for home base with so little gas that some planes ran out of gas while taxiing to their stations on the field.

Soon Mark was by himself flying a Lightning Fighter. He also made acquaintance with P-38s. At the Los Angeles Civilian Air Raid Warning Center controllers were required to have a Pilot there for emergencies. That Pilot became Mark. All air bases had P-38s. The Controller was responsible for directions in space 50 miles from the airfield. P-38s could take off quickly with high velocity and they could accelerate quickly. During the war many movie stars' wives spent time at the airfield to move planes around. There were huge maps for viewing and for placing unidentified targets into position. Mark met his wife in Los Angeles at Christmas. He then went to Texas to fly B-26s the medium sized bomber plane.

For the rest of the war and for the rest of Mark's flying career, he towed targets at 150 miles per hour. On steel cables a long box-like target made of chicken wire, which had a weight on the bottom and was wrapped in cloth, sailed along behind Mark's plane. Sometimes the practicing gunners would shoot so close the bullets would come in at 30 degrees and hit the plane. They were using 50 calibre bullets. If there was trouble, you'd break off and get down fast!

Mark readied for the 20th tow target while at Harding Field near Baton Rouge. This area was north of New Orleans. It was the only gunnery area which included flying over Lake Ponchartrain. While in the air with a target, there was a message that a P-38 was coming in from Washington D.C. and it was all alone. The flier of this airplane was the highest and most famous Ace in the United States. He had 40 kills. He had downed forty Japanese planes. He was an eight times Ace. The lonely flier was Richard Bong. Colonel Tiptin immediately ordered a ground parade in honor of the ace. With pomp and ceremony arranged for in a hurry, the Colonel appeared in full dress uniform standing in an open vehicle for the parade. So much was going on, the Colonel couldn't hear the screaming of the plane coming in low over a stand of trees. The plane sped full throttle over the foliage coming so close to Tiptin's head, the Colonel leaped head first into the dirt!

"Richard Bong turned out to be a short 5'7" little blonde guy," according to Mark. There was a big party scheduled for him at the Officer's Club. The Ace came to the air school for some extra gunnery practice. His fame allowed him freedom, independence and popularity all the while he took lessons there. After he returned to the Pacific it was reported that Richard Bong shot down another 12 more Japanese planes. After the war the Ace obtained a safe job in Burbank, California where he crashed and died in a flaming aircraft.

Mark was married at the Officers Club in Texas on Christmas Day, 1943. His wife traveled from Iowa. She arrived two days early in the worst snow storm since 1898. Mark's Brother, Dean was an 18 year old cadet. He was an enlisted man and was at another air base in Texas just a few miles away.

The Officers Club had explicit rules "that a service man could not come in the Officer's Club unless he was an Officer." This meant that Brother Dean was being left out of the wedding occasion. The groom's best man was Bill Bostwich, a highly decorated Engineer and Top Turf Gunner of Susie Q. He was most famous for his Pacific missions. Bostwich was at Delhart Air Base. Further more he was celebrating rather heavily two days in advance. He hauled off and hit the Commanding Officer over Brother Dean being left out of the wedding ceremonies. Bill was a military attache to Sweden but "now he was in deep doo doo," as he could be courts martialed for hitting a Commanding Officer. The Military Attache contacted Washington TWX. A teletyped massage received from 'Hap' Arnold directed the Commanding Officer to "Reprimand the Man and do nothing to him." Mark's brother was at the wedding, after all!

Mark towed a few more targets but was shot at so closely he decided to get out of the military in 1945. Mark worked for his father as a tailor. They formed a partnership. By 1947, Mark was back in the military as a Second Lieutenant. He was sent to Washington D.C. as student in the field of Special Agent of Counter Intelligence. The Counter Intelligence Corp (CIC) tendered his graduation by sending him to a Japanese language school in the Country of Japan.

Prime target for counter intelligence was the world wide communist movement. Mark did back ground investigations of persons at very sensitive sites. In Japan, the Communist Party was all over the place. "Prior to World War II all the big communists were in prison. After MacArthur, the Communists became a legal party and infiltrated coal mines, electrical unions, businesses, railways and anywhere else they could kick up trouble. My job was to counter what the Communists were doing by sabotaging their efforts. It was a game of disaffection," according to Mark.

In 1951, Mark was part of the Korean War as a special agent. His wife Dawn and son, Mark Eric stayed in Japan as they were not allowed to travel into the war zone. The United States Government did not want them subject to capture. They were returned to the United States.

Mark dressed as special agent in the same type of clothes that war correspondents used. It was a khaki civilian battle dress. Daily security checks were carried out, as were intense background investigations. Mark gave security lectures. He tried to break up black market operations and did criminal investigation of black markets.

After the Korean War, Mark attended a Language School in Monterey, California. He was then deployed to Salzburg, Austria looking like a regular tourist and having a passport as any ordinary man. Austria was occupied by four nations. Vienna was in the Russian Zone. Austria did not have an anti-esponage law, so it was not a crime to commit esponage there. The U.S. was neutral. The Hungarians had many intelligence agents employed in Vienna businesses.

In the American Quarter, there were many Iron Curtin Countries ostensibly running the spy business. The CIA was there as Mark's Big Brother. Often, each counter intelligent agent would be following everyone else in a line. On one occasion, Mark saw five different counter spies following each other like a daisy chain. As Mark's family arrived at Leghorn, Italy, their picture was taken by a scrungy looking guy.

When Occupation ended in Austria and it became a neutral nation. The Americans were the last to leave. They did extraordinary security checks to make sure all classified information was gone.

For four years Mark worked for the United States Government as Special Agent obtaining security clearances for Military men in sensitive positions. He then moved his operation to Kaiserslautern, Germany for another four years. Upon retirement in 1962, Mark was a highly trained special investigator. As he left the Army, he began working for the State of California. He made investigations for the Department of Motor Vehicles and the Department of Corporations regarding security and fraud. He examined and reported medical and welfare fraud as well.

Legislature in 1976 mandated a Special Investigator for each State Hospital. The work was to track standard care practices for the mentally ill and retarded. Mark was Sonoma Development Center's first investigator. The job description called for investigation of all deaths, abuse, theft or substance abuse.

As an uniformed cop, Mark retired in 1983 when his wife passed on. He was "filled up and overloaded." At this writing, he helps out 10 to 20 hours a month at the Development Center and gives lectures to all new employees there. (It's called "blowing them up.")

In 1985, Mark became interested in singing tenor and began exercises in vocal training. He joined practices and performances with the Silver Foxes (a double Quartet World War II men's group). He became a worthy member of the 140 voice Sonoma Valley Chorale. He helps put on two cabaret shows each year and has sung in six operas with the Sonoma Opera Company. Besides soloing at Protestant churches, he has even done a bit of music for a bar mitzvah. Mark can sing in eight languages. He enjoys classical music and Jazz.

While remembering World War II, he particularly remembers Nagasaki, Japan. Three years after the atomic bomb blast, Mark was sitting on a cannon in that city.

H. H. 'Hap' Arnold
Five Star General of the United States Army and
Army Air Force, 1907 - 1946
Born 1886 Gladwyne, Pennsylvania,
Died Sonoma, California, 1950.

Photo courtesy of Robert Bruce Arnold.

Ernest J. Mangiantini
19th Combat Engineers in Africa and Italy.
De-activated Mines
Helped build bridges and roads.

Photo Courtesy of Sonoma Index Tribune.
Bill Lynch, Editor.
Tom Noonan, Photographer.
(Originally in color, edited.)

Bob Bohna
Bomber Pilot
402nd Division
Squadron
of
Army Air Force.
over
Germany.
His plane
Sierra Sue II.

Photos from Bob Bohna

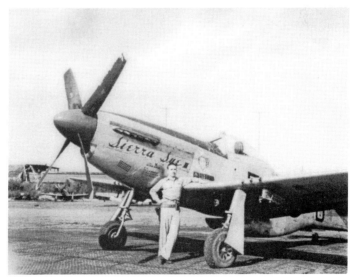

**Atomic Bomb
Hiroshima
August 1945**

Photo taken by buddy in
5th Reconnaissance
of 7th Air Force.
This photo developed
three hours after bomb
drop.

Frank S. Wedekind Collection.

Okinawa
on the night
of
recapitulation.
Gunfire
Celebration
that
Japan
had
Surrendered.

Frank Wedekind Photo

OKINAWA   AUGUST 10, 1945

Naha University
shows the extreme
shelling that took
place in Naha Harbor.

Private collection
of Pictures
developed by
Friend of Frank
Wedekind.

**Kermit Roosevelt
Parker**

United States Army
1937-1958

Air Force (13 Years)

Radio,
Telephone,
Radar Specialist.

Train
Enthusiast.

Picture
taken
by
Kermit,
himself.

Vincent Tuminello
Quartermaster, First Infantry, lst Division of l6th
Infantry. Omaha Beach on D-Day, 1944
Squad Leader with machine gun

Photos courtesy Vincent Tuminello.

Flags surrendered by the Prisoners of War

Japanese Flag held by Claude Gordon
Mars Task Force, Burma

Charles Stormont Photo.
****
German Flag held by Walter Farmer
D-Day Participant
Infantry, 29th Division

Walter Farmer Photo.

Captain Sam J. Robinson, Jr.
United States, USS Pintado.
Pacific Theatre

Photo Courtesy
Sam Robinson

James B. Alexander
Medic in U.S. Army
Prisoner of war
after hospital
surrounded.
Photo courtesy of
James Alexander.

USS Dale 353 in Pearl Harbor
on December 7th, 1941.

Bill Barnes
at
left.

Photos from
Bill Barnes
Collection.

Bill Stalley
at
right.

Photos from
Bill Stalley's
Collection.

USS Louisville Carried gold.
Escorted Children, Women and precious metals.

**Charles Stormont, Officer
in China, India, Burma.**

Kachin Girls near Camp Landis in Burma
Young Women favors were bartered for 1/2 a parachute.

Photo from Charles Stormont Collection.

Mules brought in 250-300 miles to Myitkyina, Burma

For the 612th Field Artillery Battalion (5332 Brigade)
Mars Task Force Mule Pack. Mules were worth $2,000.00 each.

Charles Stormont Photo.

Vernon Dearing
Infantryman of
U.S. Army.

Photo thanks to
Vernon Dearing.

Irving Mills
Tail Gunner in 8th
Airforce.

Photo from Irving Mills

William C. Johnson, United States Army Air Force
Bomber Pilot in the South Pacific with an A-20
Douglas Light Bomber at Wheeler Field, Hawaii.

Photo from William C. Johnson collection.

Picture taken at Santa Cruz Air Force Base in Rio, Brazil.
Rich Peterson on left, **Jack Reams,** 4th from left of the 347th Fighter Squadron
with **General Moura** (Center) and two **Brazilian Fighter Pilots.**

Served together in Italy during World War II.
Photo courtesy of Richard W. Peterson.

Richard W. Peterson
at
left.
Shoe shine in Italy.

Photo from Richard.

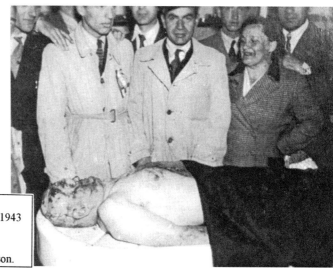

Benito Mussolini, 1883-1945
Italian Fascist Leader; premier 1922-1943
Executed during World War II.

Photo courtesy of Richard W. Peterson.

James and Marguerite Vanderbilt
Met and married in Hawaii.
Marguerite saw the bombing of Pearl Harbor.
James, United States Naval Reserve Signalman.

Photo courtesy of Mr. and Mrs. Vanderbilt.

Mr. and Mrs. John La Boyteaux
Married in Maria Novella Cathedral,
Florence, Italy.
John made all the wedding preparations.

Peggy La Boyteaux photo.

Mr. and Mrs. Morris Hoaglund
at United States Naval Training and Distribution
Center, Shoemaker, California.

Maxine Hoaglund photo.

Adam DiGennaro
Marine at Iwo Jima.

His photo to left.
Courtesy of Adam DiGennaro.

Photo below:

James P. Duchscherer
U.S. Army Engineer Corps.
in France,

Photo from James Duchscherer
Collection.

Frank D. Gregory, Jr.

**Sharpshooter,
Point Man
in
Infantry.**

Battle of Bulge.

General Whitehead's Aircrew C-54 # 4272569 (K. C. Headwind)
Haneda Air Base, Tokyo, Japan. February 1947

Front Row (L to R) Will Payne, Steward; Charley Glenn, Pilot; Chody Howard, Flight Engineer;
Back Row (L to R) George Kelly, Radio Operator; Dick Ingram, Radio Operator; Lloyd
Underbrink, Flight Engineer; Walt Purdy, Navigator and Charles A. Lindbergh, Passenger.

Not pictured: Griff Griffith, Crew Chief who took the picture and John Werner, Co-Pilot.

Photo courtesy of Walter Purdy.

LEAN DAYS

Irv J. Mills

United States Army Air Corps, 1942 - 1945

Irv J. Mills was destined to take part in what has been referred to as "the world's largest air battle in the history of the planet." As Tail Gunner in the 423rd Squadron of the 306th Bombardment Group with the Eighth Bomber Command, he would have a distinctive story in the history of World War II. His manner of evacuation from a 423rd airplane was extra-ordinary. It has been described by other airmen flying in other planes on the same mission. The sequence of events following Irv's ejection from the plane would try a man's soul. Not only would he be a part of the air battle known in history books as "Black Thursday" which took place on October 14, 1943 but he would also become a prisoner of war in the notorious Stalag 17. More importantly, he kept a secret log of the forced march that began April 8, 1945 and ended May 2nd, 1945.

The reader is privileged to look into this diary, a chronicle of American and Allied prisoners taken on an endurance march enforced by German prison guards. These men, numbering 3,500 to 4,000 Stalag 17 prisoners were exploited approximately 400 miles on an agonizing odyessy into the heart of Germany. The log actually written at the time of the march itself by Irv, contains no second thoughts or easy judgments. He wishes to impart "what you read in the log were my actual thoughts along with the exact spelling, as written during the time those thoughts occurred."

Born in Bridgeport, Connecticut, Irv was twenty-two years old when he entered the service. Before the war, he had graduated from high school and obtained employment in a factory beginning with manual labor. He eventually worked on drill presses as well as punch presses. Finally, Irv was Quality Control Inspector. This employment was at the General Electric Company in Bridgeport. The more interesting part of being a Quality Control Inspector was to examine toasters, waffle irons and sandwich grills to make sure they functioned properly. Irv placed two slices of white Wonder Bread in every tenth toaster to see if they browned properly, as toasters came down an assembly line. For lunch, he and fellow inspectors most often brought cheese sandwiches which they heated in sandwich grills. Later, Irv was inspector of very primitive bomb racks that G.E. was building. Unfortunately, a job shift was from four in the afternoon until four in the morning. Irv says, "I joined the Army Air Corps because I just wanted a little fresh air and had to be out in the sunshine."

In 1942, Irv was inducted into the service at Fort Devins, Massachusetts and was shipped to Miami, Florida for basic training. The duty was great. For two or three months the trainees were billeted in small apartments surrounded by orange trees. Daily chores included patrolling Florida beaches for German submarines and their likelihood of landing spies into the country. There was a great deal of paranoia.

True excitement came one evening while Irv was on patrol duty along Miami Beach. Service men were not allowed to carry real firearms, but they patrolled the beach carrying a wooden gun. For a couple hundred yards a soldier would move back and forth, then meet up with another soldier who would be patrolling the adjoining one hundred yards. The fellows were to meet every one-half to one hour. On one particular evening, the other soldier failed to show up at the predetermined location. This was very unsettling for Irv. The next morning a discovery was made. The other guard had been clobbered by a falling cocoanut and knocked out cold! While this duty seemed frivolous, with any likelihood of German spies appearing on the beach being remote, there were a few intruders who actually landed from submarines on the Atlantic Coast.

The good fresh air of the Florida sunshine along with fun and games came to an end. Irv was selected as a member for a flying crew. He was sent to Denver, Colorado to learn all about armament. The classes were at night which meant he was back sleeping again during daytime. He was then ordered to McCarren Field near Las Vegas, Nevada for actual gunnery practice. He learned from a world champion skeet shooter, "You are naturally left-handed and you are never going to be able to hit the side of a barn if you continue to shoot a gun from your right shoulder while closing your right eye."

It was the left-handed, right-eyed business that taught Irv "the big fallacy of benefits derived from the posture of conformity." He had been taught in school during the 1920s and 1930s, "that you write with your right hand even though you were left-handed." By not conforming to this rule "you received a whack on the knuckles from the Catholic Nun." However, this learned skill caused problems in using a gun. The champion skeet shooter explained, "If you hold a gun to your right shoulder and close your right eye, you can not line up a target if you are left-handed. Hold this gun to your left shoulder, close your right eye and you will be much more accurate." The real gunnery practice on a moving object took place over Death Valley near Las Vegas. A moving sleeve was towed in the air by another plane. The brave pilot of the other plane was the real target for what Irv called "a bunch of clowns in their airplanes who, for the first time were shooting guns with real bullets high in the sky!"

Being a part of the Air Force when it was in its early years of development gave the men a great sense of importance and drama. They wore leather jackets, leather helmets, goggles and silk scarfs. In an open aircraft, they appeared like Pilots straight out of World War I movies. It was glamorous! to be in the Air Force!! Public relations buildup and Hollywood influence were present. These young impressionable fellows adopted a heightened sense of importance. They were sent off to Dalhart, Texas. Irv was assigned to a B-17 crew. In the Texas Panhandle they were taken to some makeshift towers in the desert where four corners of the towers were lit up. The fashionable daring Flyers were then allowed to practice bombing targets with 100 pound sand bombs!

Two instances stand out in Irv's memory. In one circumstance everything went fine when the crew numbering nine went out with no Navigator. Halfway through training they were assigned a Navigator. On the first flight with him, they got lost! The second incident took place on a rare night bombing of the four corners of the light-illuminated-target. After just one pass the lights began to go out. Checking closer the group saw that they had bombed the City Hall of Texarcana, Texas with their 100 pound sand bombs! The Mayor of Dalhart countered the action by asking the Commanding Officer for a 4th of July demonstration. He suggested placing a barrel in the middle of the street. Then, the Bombers could drop some of those sand bombs. Afraid his crew might hit a whole town the Officer declined but declared, "the men could march in their parade..."

When this group of Air Force Gunners were being readied for overseas duty and using military logic, the B-17s they were using for practice were changed. The plane in which this group practiced had armor-plating. Preparing for overseas combat, the crew removed the armor plate and substituted plywood with the premise that the plane would then be able to carry a much heavier bomb payload. With fewer bombs the lighter planes should also be able to fly longer distances.

After flying the northerly route across Greenland and Iceland, their unit arrived in Ayr, Scotland. They had stopped first at Bangor, Maine where the Pilot had to bounce the plane off the runway to get it airborne. Over New Foundland the group's next major stop amounted to a 24 hour break. Being in the land of the midnight sun, windows were painted out, so one man guarded the plane while the other fellows slept in the darkened barracks. The poor guard almost froze to death while carrying out his duty on the runway! When the crew made it to Scotland the modified plane was promptly taken away from them because they were told, "it was so badly needed for combat duty." That was the last they ever saw their "own" aircraft. As the crew traveled by train to an old RAF air base called Thurleigh, the Americans were assigned different airplanes. They were taken on practice missions over "the wash" out over the English Coast. (The Wash, near St. Ives in Cornwall was where Irv's wife's family hailed from. Joan was the only member of the family born in the USA.)

The base at Thurleigh was a very busy place. It was operated with as much precision as possible. Many jobs were being done simultaneously. It was mighty uncomfortable because the weather was cold, damp, cloudy and foggy. All briefings were at 4 a.m. All too often the crews would go to their assigned aircraft, then the rest of the morning one just sat on the runway to watch the fog lift for takeoff. Many times missions were "scrubbed." Men went back to their barracks to await another day. The discipline and patience learned at this air base was a most valuable thing for Irv and his future.

The 306th Bombardment Group was the earliest squadron to target France, Germany, Belgium and Holland. This tactical unit had a history of men and airplanes meeting death and destruction over the skies of Nazi-occupied Europe. Out of the bomb group came eleven men who were promoted to command the entire 8th Air Force proving it was a well led disciplined organization. (The whole American Air Force was under the direct command of General 'Hap' Arnold, one of four men designated as Joint Chiefs of Staff named by President Roosevelt.)

A story of a conference hosted by Prime Minister Winston Churchill which included Lieutenant General Ira Eaker of the 8th Bomber Group made the rounds. It seemed "the Prime Minister rolled a ball bearing down a table. Eaker picked it up and by doing so "he committed the United States 8th Air force to bomb Schweinfurt, Germany." This target was one of the most dreaded targets. It was the location of a huge ball bearing plant. In August of 1943, the first Schweinfurt raid had taken place. As far as the Americans were concerned it had been a disaster. The Eighth Air Force lost a large number of planes and crews. The bombing had done a lot of damage to the German real estate but little or no damage to the factorie's inner workings nor to the machinery which created the ball bearings.

Germans worked around the clock making ball bearings. "Keep in mind," Irv points out, "Airplanes, tanks, submarines, warships, armored and motor vehicles, weapons, electrical equipment, plant machinery, precision instruments all depended upon the anti-friction bearings for rapidity of motion and efficient performance." It was calculated that in December 1943, German aircraft used about 2,400,000 anti-friction bearings in a single month. Each aircraft reportedly used 1,056 bearings. Its instruments and motors would require more bearings. An aircraft plant would be disabled by loss of anti-friction bearings. Tanks and trucks demanded six to seven hundred bearings, each, in construction. The anti-aircraft gun required 47 bearings. A single search light was quoted as taking 90 bearings.

Just about every mechanical device and weapon used in World War II had anti-friction bearings as a component. It was clearly pointed out to the fliers, "If you could put out of commission, even for a few weeks, the German plants making ball-bearings, you could put out of commission their war effort." 41% of the anti-friction bearings produced in Nazi Germany were reportedly developed in Schweinfurt. The prospects for success were not auspicious. Daylight bombing as a whole was taking a terrible toll on American crews and equipment. In just three days, October 8th, 9th and 10th, the Eighth Air Force lost 88 bombers and hundreds of other planes were damaged. Ground crews were cannibalizing damaged planes to get spare parts in order to get other planes back in the air. The wisdom of daylight bombing was being dogmatically questioned by the highest American Command of the Air Force and particularly by the British Prime Minister Churchill. It should also be recalled the British were flying at night. Their bombing might not have been as accurate as the daylight bombing but it did save men and equipment to fly another day...

Irv remembers "being dressed in big fur fleeced lined jackets and pants. The men wore strong heavy boots. I had a fancy leather jacket which was left at the base. I am sorry to report that after planes returned and some men did not come home, people left on the ground who were not flying would go into the barracks and help themselves to whatever was available. Personal belongings left would be G.I. underwear. I purchased a complete bolt of Harrison Tweed for a suit. Some ghoulish person took my valuables including the bolt of material when I did not return."

As Commanders opened their orders on October 14th, 1943 the words, "Schweinfurt, it is then..." leaped out at them! The orders were sent over the entire expanse of England. It would be the air battle of the century!

Irv remembered it as "one of my longest days. October 14th, 1943 proved to be another cold, damp foggy morning. Odds were bet that even if the planes were able to take off, they would not break into sunshine until 8,000 to 9,000 feet. The crews were still mindful of another foggy morning when ten planes piled up on the runway with full bomb loads. One hundred men died on the ground in front of their buddies. Heavy trucks moved parts and equipment through wet puddles of the streets. The commanding officers received copies of combat orders with takeoff scheduling and altitude mapping. Bomb loads and everything else was listed to effect the massed endeavor. Colonel Budd J. Peaslee was to lead the First Air Division in Battle."

The planes lumbered down the runway into the fog. The 423rd Squadron was designated high squadron. Irv's bomb group, the 306th was the highest group. This meant that they were flying at approximately 30,000 feet when they reached altitude. This position was considered "reasonably safe." The fighter escorts, mostly English, only had fuel capacity to fly about halfway over the English Channel before being forced to return to their respective bases. The Germans were known to wait for the fighters to leave and then they began to press their attacks against the American planes.

Irv began his personal unique war story. "The Germans came in with a lot of combat experience and on that day would continue practicing on us all the way to Holland. Early in the war Germans had a potent Air Force. Range of 50 caliber guns was at 1,000 yards. Germans for the first time in history used air-to-air rockets. They could stay out 1,500 yards beyond our guns. So, one of their rockets went into our bomb bay. We still had bombs in there but they did not go off. Our bomb bay door was still closed. We were not yet near our target. Then, in a few minutes we caught another hit in the right wing that took off the wing. An airplane does not fly too well without its wing. We started going down..."

In the book *Black Thursday*, Irv's plane, as seen by another, is described. "A few hundred feet in front of us a bomber has been hit by a rocket. I 'catch' sight of it just as the right wing starts to fold upward. The fuselage opens like an eggshell, and a man dressed in a flying suit spins clear out in front. I see the Pilots still at the controls, then the plane is swept with flame. The right wing breaks free and with the two engines still spinning, it drifts to the rear, flaming at the ragged end. The scattered mess disappears under our left wing and the sky is clean again. It all happens instantaneously but to me it is like a slow-motioned movie scene."

In the Book, *First Over Germany*, Irv's aircraft is described "as one of the earlier planes to leave the formation. It was flown by First Lieutenant Vernon K. Cole. Tagged by a rocket-firing JU-88 over the continent, the plane was hit in the bomb bay and caught on fire. T/Sgt. Robah C. Shields, Jr., radio, and S/Sgt. Donald Richardson, ball turret were both killed in the plane by rocket fragments. S/Sgt. Frederick W. Zumpf, waist, failed to bail out. T/Sgt. Robert D. Folk, engineer, went to the back of the plane to check damage and returned to the front where he passed out from lack of oxygen. He was pushed out the nose hatch by the bombardier, 2nd Lt. Joseph M. Columbus. Lt. Cole stayed with the plane as long as he could and was blown out when the aircraft exploded. His body was later found hanging in his parachute in a woods. S/Sgt. Irv J. Mills was able to extricate himself from the tail section after the plane came apart. 2nd Lt. Robert E. Partridge, copilot; 2nd Lt. Charles R. Kuehn, navigator, and S/Sgt Adrien H. Wright, waist, all successfully bailed out."

While being Tail Gunner, Irv was in the rear of the plane, by himself. The area was extremely small and confining. In case of emergency he was supposed to exit through a tiny door. The emergency handle was pulled. The door did not fall off as it was supposed to, possibly because the plane was somewhat warped from so many takeoffs and landings. In any event, he had to kick the door out!

That day was the first day that he had ever been issued a chest-type parachute. While he could fasten the harness, he could not wear the actual chute and still reach two 50 caliber guns that he was supposed to operate. So, he set the parachute off to the side by itself. He glanced around and he saw bullet holes in the fuselage. "I remember looking over at the parachute and during the German attack saw fur flying off and around my fleece lined jacket. Bits of material were flying around the plane which looked as if my chute had been shot up. The thought went through my mind, "Well I won't use that today." Suddenly! the rocket in his plane blew the aircraft up! When the plane started to go down, Irv totally forgot his earlier thought about the parachute. He had one side of his chute clipped on when the plane blew up. How he got the other side clipped on, he doesn't know. He also hasn't the foggiest idea what he did with the ripcord handle when he pulled the chute open. He thinks, "I may have thrown it all the way back to England!"

One of Irv's most vivid memories was that before each mission, crews were given a candy bar and either cigarettes, cigars or pipe tobacco. Most men took the candy bar, generally a Milky Way, and ate it on the trip home once they had dropped below 10,000 feet. By this time, the candy was frozen and a frozen Milky Way in the 1940s was a great favorite. Crazily, coming down in his parachute and badly burned, Irv's major thought was "my Milky Way is still up there!" On the way down, Irv also "remembered flying snow coming up at me. I was being bathed in snow swirling up hitting my face as I was gliding downwards. It was the first and last time, I was ever suspended in a parachute!"

Things Irv remembers fifty years later includes a little remark by a Staff Sergeant. "Staff today, stiff tomorrow." As mentioned previously, bombing was done by Americans in the daylight but the British preferred night bombing. Bombing was done as a blanket formation with the hope to hit something! In the fall and winter of 1943 the way losses of daylight bombing were piling up, the Americans would have to give up daylight bombing if the averages kept continuing. There were too many men and airplanes being lost. That was the real reason the mission on October 14th, 1943 would be called "Black Thursday." Keep in mind British Spitfires had limited range. They would escort the American planes for one half of the English Channel and then return home. Germans would wait until the British planes went back and then bomb American planes.

Irv landed in a small village near the Belgium border and tumbled from a tree. He was in the backyard of a police chief's home in Holland near the Belgium border. The nearest large town was Maastrich. Being eight months before D-Day, the Police Chief was cooperating with German occupying forces. Obviously, an American Flyer falling out of the sky in broad daylight doesn't go unnoticed. It took four to five hours for the German Officers to show up.

While Irv was in the policeman's house, he knew he was badly burned on his face, hands and feet. Mostly, his hands and face were scorched. He might be guessing but he believed the burns came from an oxygen fire. The German Officers took him to a hospital and he was placed in a private room. He was treated by Catholic Nuns for the burns and felt quite comfortable. Three or four days later, injured German soldiers came in from the Eastern Front and were packed into what once had been the hospital chapel. The American believes he received much better treatment than the Germans. Food, definitely different from American fare was eatable.

"Everything was down hill from then on," according to Irv. The airman was taken to Amsterdam and confined in what appeared to be a medieval prison with a moat around it. Its cells resembled those from an old Count of Monte Christo story. The building had thick dungeon stone walls and heavy doors with bars on the windows. (Many years later, Irv returned to Amsterdam and from the window of a very fine French Restaurant he spotted the building which was then deserted. What he thought of as a moat during the war was actually one of Amsterdam's famous canals.) Irv stated, "It gave me great pleasure to be drinking fine wine and eating marvelous food while viewing this old building from my past."

For the next twenty-five to thirty days Irv realized the Nazi's watched Hollywood movies, too. Two guards would come to the cell and practically grab him while his arms were still wrapped for burns. They would interrogate the American five or six times a day in a very dramatic setting. The jail had big rooms displaying an oversized Nazi Flag illuminated with bright glaring lights. The Nazi Officer sat behind an enormous desk, again like Hollywood. The building had stone floors so the clicking of the guards' hobnailed boots would echo throughout the rooms. The interrogator would sit at the opposite end of the room under another huge Nazi flag which had a glaring spotlight on it. It was all a wonderful touch, like in the movie when Jackie Oakie played Benito Mussolini and Charlie Chaplin played Adolf Hitler. The dominant person had to have a high chair so they put Irv in a chair that had been sawed off four or five inches. By setting it up that way the confined person was forced to look up at the German Officer and the Nazi Flag.

The whole scene without comedy was right out of the motion picture *The Great Dictator* starring Chaplin and Oakie. The interrogation always started simply enough. The officer requested name, rank and the prisoner's serial number. They interviewed and they interviewed. As trained, Irv would give name, rank and serial number. When they asked the name of the bomb group, the prisoner was not permitted to respond under standing instructions from United States Authorities. "I'm not allowed to tell that," Irv replied. The Nazi would blow up and yell at the guards. Eventually, he would calm down and offer a cigarette. Philosophical discussions about war took place. It was all very interesting. But Irv had been trained to keep his mouth shut. Dog tags in those days revealed your religion preference. The German would peer at Irv's dog tag and ask him "how can a good Catholic in all good conscience fly over Europe bombing other good Catholics on instructions of "that Jew President, Rosenfelt?!"

Realizing that this Nazi's military profession was one of interrogation, it was clear to Irv that it would be foolish to enter into such a discussion and so he therefore remained silent. Once again, the German would appear to lose his temper. He would start screaming in German. When the German Officer tired of the psychological chatter, he sent Irv back into the cold cell room with the big old fashioned decor. It became a little less scary after the same performance was repeated over and over again.

The cell room had twenty foot high ceilings with large crown moulding strips. One piece of moulding had fallen off. One day, a male who said he was a Red Cross Volunteer suddenly discovered the piece of moulding that was lying against the wall. He was about to blame Irv for tearing the moulding off the ceiling. Irv reminded him, "I have both arms in a sling!" Climbing a twenty foot ceiling height was not exactly something the prisoner could accomplish. The Volunteer spoke very good English.

Taken from this prison, Irv was put in an old 40 foot x 8 foot train box car and shipped to Krems, Austria. He was placed in Stalag 17 and pressed into the routine of German prison life. He was in the main compound along with 3,500 to 4,000 Americans. The main nationalities of the camp were Serbians, Russians, Polish, French and Italians. There were about 70,000 Prisoners in this group.

Stalag 17 was the largest and oldest permanent prisoner-of-war camp for Air Force non-commissioned officers. It was located in the German Alpine Mountains about fifty miles north-west of Vienna near the Danube Valley. The camp itself occupied about one square mile and was completely enclosed by barbed wire fencing. Smaller enclosures of barbed wire defined compounds within the fenced area. Prisoners were segregated into different nationalities. In October, 1943 the camp reportedly had 45,000 prisoners-of-war. Of these, 1,356 were Americans. As war progressed the population increased. It reached a peak in March of 1944 with roughly 75,000 men when four thousand two hundred thirty-five of these prisoners were Americans.

Americans in the prison camp represented a cross-section of the United States Army Air Forces. Backgrounds and personalities differed. There were men from every state in the union and from every walk of life. There were jockeys, gamblers, bankers and lawyers. Their educational backgrounds were as widely differentiated as were their occupations. Some men had only bare rudiments of a formal elementary education. Others had master's and doctoral degrees. Irv believes that all of these men, regardless of their former education, learned a great deal about their fellow men and how to get along with each other while suffering it out in Stalag 17.

The American compound consisted of 12 barracks at the east end of the camp. Each building was 197 feet long and 33 feet wide with accommodations for 420 men. Each barracks was divided into A and B sections that were separated by what had once been a washroom. The bunks were a curious mass of scaffolding having three platforms, one on top of the other. Each of these platforms became a bed for four men. Each section of scaffolding held twelve men. In all fairness to the Germans, although these bunks were made for twelve men, the Americans as commissioned and non-commissioned Officers were allowed the privilege of having only eight men in each bunk.

These bunks were the only furniture in the entire barracks in 1943. The building of benches, stools, chairs or even shelves was 'verboten'. One massive stove was located at each end of the building but unfortunately little coal and no wood was supplied. Resourcefulness of men provided some heat by the simple means of tearing down what were deemed to be surplus parts of the wooden structure. This same wood was also used to build some furniture and by 1944 the Germans became reconciled to the fact that the prisoners were going to have furniture.

Life began each morning at 7 a.m. with roll call. The prisoners were then allowed one cup of hot water per man. You, the prisoner supplied your own Nescafe or you drank weak German tea. There was no food for breakfast. If you had something in your Red Cross parcel, you might eat it or hoard it for some other time during the day. Some Red Cross parcels had razors. Often cigarettes were traded for razors. You could use your share of hot water in the morning for shaving instead of drinking. Running water was available twice a day. The midday meal consisted of one cup of horrible soup meted out at 11 a.m. During the afternoon, a daily bread ration was distributed. There would be one loaf of bread per six men during the early part of the war. The amount was constantly cut when the war turned for the worse for the Germans. Three boiled potatoes per man were distributed at 5 p.m. The potatoes were about the size of marbles or sometimes the size of golf balls. There could be watery soup with some horse meat in it. Eight men were expected to share a loaf of dark bread. There were many times when twenty men had to share one loaf of bread. In the afternoon, there would be another formal roll call. If the guards were upset for any reason, they might call two more roll calls. The guards were old men. They were not fit for front line duty. The Red Cross packages stopped after the attempt on Hitler's life. Following July 1944 being a prisoner was like being between a rock and a hard place. "Even with harsh times," Irv declared, "keep in mind the great bulk of American prisoners were not discouraged." When, regular German troops and the SS Troops were mixed in with the older guards they became more caught up with harsh discipline mixed with meanness toward the inmates.

Irv is quite adamant, "that if it had not been for the International Red Cross and the Red Cross parcels that the men would not have survived. If it were not for Red Cross packages, I would not be alive." One parcel was received almost every week up until the attempt on Hitler's life by his own staff in July of 1944. From then on Red Cross parcel delivery was very iffy. When packages were distributed German guards punched holes into the Spam cans so meat would not be hoarded for escapees to use.

The last roll call for each day was held at 5:30 p.m. every evening. Health conditions in these barracks were deplorable. Irv and his fellow prisoners spent many weeks trying in small ways to bring the living quarters within sanitary bounds with little aid from the detaining power.

The monotony of prison life can well be imagined. The men, the majority of whom were between 19 and 25 having been snatched out of their exalted position as Fliers where privileges were many, were thrown into this long, dull monotony of routine existence. The first reaction of a man newly shot down was that of depression. The period of intense discouragement varied with the man. Some men never did snap out of it. The average length of feeling sorry for one's self was usually two weeks to a month. Then, men began to plan for their livelihood after the war. Little thoughts might have been given to them while on combat duty. Now, they could take time to plan for a business. They could draw plans for a dream cottage. In general, the men just had to have some reason to become hopeful. Interestingly, during the darkest days of the war when only a little good news was forthcoming, no one lost faith in the ultimate outcome of the war.

Under the Geneva Convention, relative to treatment of prisoners of war, no commissioned or non-commissioned officers were compelled to work. The prisoners started a school in order to keep their minds and bodies active. Subjects included everything from physical education, auto mechanics, algebra and business law to American history. Irv taught American history using one text book that had been smuggled into camp. One fascinating event occurred when Irv reached the point of World War I victories. The Germans always seemed to know when this time arrived and would show up to listen to the lecture. When Irv pointed out that the Allies had won the war and the Germans had lost, the guards would get quite threatening, dismiss the class and yell, "the German Army had been betrayed by the Jews and Bolsheviks and the German Army had not lost the war!"

Among the approximate 4,000 Americans in the camp, it was estimated there were about 1,800 crystal radio sets. Some had been smuggled into camp; others had been traded for cigarettes with the German guards. The men certainly did keep up on news.

One of the things, the Prisoners of war did not like to hear was bombing of nearby towns and cities by the United States Air Force. Dropping bombs was one thing, being on the receiving end was another! The City of Krems and other areas close to the camp were being bombed. There were physical motions of bombs crashing to the ground on the order of vibrations coming from a heavy freight train going too fast! Men dove under anything they could find when the intensity of vibrations were close by. The air man now knew there was terror on the ground as well as there was terror being in those planes above.

As Irv tells it, "Stalag 17 was probably no better or worse than other POW camps in the European Theatre. Its notority came because of a Broadway play and later a popular movie called Stalag 17, starring William Holden. Some readers will also remember the TV series called Hogan's Heroes. While Stalag 17 wasn't quite the barrel of laughs of that comedy the prisoners did have their moments. Some atypical Americans played pranks on Germans just for fun. For example, at Christmas 1943, the Americans decorated a tree made from a European twig broom. They made the Christmas Tree sparkle with icicles made by using the metal off Spam cans. They twisted the little metal strips tightly so light would shine and glimmer on the metal. They shaved soap for snow and put it on the tree because the group had lots of soap, more soap than water. One prisoner had the brilliant idea to carve bars of soap into three tombstones. In front of the tombstones were three figurines. One image was inscribed Hitler, one depicted Mussolini and the third image was that of Hideki Tojo. (Tojo was the Japanese Prime Minister responsible for the attack on Pearl Harbor.) On Christmas Eve, German Officers came up to the rooms and admired the Christmas Tree. They lost their Christmas spirit when they figured out the images of the three figurines. They ordered the whole display demolished. That ended the Christmas spirit!

It was apparent that the war would be ending soon as the Russian Army was moving in on Vienna, Austria which was about fifty miles from Stalag 17. Under orders, the Germans and their prisoners began to make plans for evacuation of the camp. All American prisoners capable of walking were mobilized. They were marched out of Stalag 17 by the German Officers. For a while the walk was dreaded but it was also a type of freedom from the scourge of Stalag 17. A sort of commaderie which momentarily lifted the spirits of the men, soon became a trial for the men's very lives! Following is a full text of a secret LOG kept by Irv of this ordeal suffered by 3,500 to 4,000 Americans.

LOG

April, 8, 1945. Sunday 5:30 a.m. Got up at four o'clock to start for God knows where! Had barley and raisins for breakfast. Am already packed: two blankets, 5 pairs of soks, half Red Cross parcel, 1/6 of loaf of bread, overcoat, 1 pair long johns, 1 pair shorts, 8 packs of Camels, one of Prince Albert, Gym shoes, 6 bars of soap (5 for trading). Left camp at 8:15 (one hour 15 min. late) in the first five hundred men. We have 39 guards, Army, Luftwaffe, S.S., and Vollstrum.

8:00 p.m. Marched 28 km. (rough). Stopped four times. Weather fine. Came through 5 towns snuggled in mountains. This is the most beautiful part of the world I've seen yet. Army * S.S. have taken over 4 of the towns. People friendly (surprised). Some very beautiful (because of simplicity) shrines along the road. Fellows in fair condition considering little food and no exercise for about 2 years. 4 fellows passed out. Sleeping out in open with two other fellows to keep warm. (no food from Jerry yet). Leave at 8:00 a.m., rise at 6:30.

April 9. 7:00 a.m. Cold and damp last night, not much sleep.

8:00 a.m.   Leave at 9:00   (no food from Jerry yet).

Jerry Capt. so sorry.

12:00 Not bad so far today. 10 min. break every hour.

Walked about 6 km. Stop for lunch 1 ½ hr.

(No Jerry chow yet).   Mountains are beautiful but hard on feet.

April 10. 1:30 p.m.   Didn't have time to log last night. Yesterday we marched 13 km. at a slow pace. Most of the fellows were dead on their feet because of the 28 km. the first day. Had beautiful weather yesterday and passed thru only 3 small villages. S.S. has them all. Jerries did not feed us at all yesterday. We have stopped at a small town here (Sat. night) and have a 24 hr. rest which we need badly. Last night very damp but fairly warm. At 10 this morning fed barley, very good (because we're hungry). 18 men to a loaf of bread (all bread last 18 months black). We have had wonderful weather so far. I dread that rain that is bound to come. Wheels seem to be leaving too! Two ---R.I.P. None of us (yet). Got a chance to wash and shave today in mountain stream. Cold but refreshing.

April 11 7:15 p.m. First time I've had a chance to log because kept busy. Yesterday afternoon I had 2 fresh eggs (soft boiled), the first since Oct. 12, 1943. Slept warm last night for first time because I was in the middle. 18 men to a loaf of bread again in the afternoon. This morning up at six, had Jerry beans for breakfast, walked 9 km. to a small town where we had a hot soup. All in all, we walked 20 km. today. Two blisters on feet and sunburned but O.K. otherwise. 18 men to a loaf tonight and that is all. We are running out of G.I. chow don't know how we'll fair after! We are supposed to sleep in a barn tonight (ought to be great after outdoors). The soup we got today was gotten by Jerry Hollywood style! Much better treatment than I expected. Still walking in mountains. Weather perfect.

Been thinking of Cokes and ice cream for the first time in 18 months. Still no idea where we're going! (think we are walking until the end of the war).

April 12, 1945. 7:00 p.m. Am writing in a barn where we are to sleep. The weather is bad. Raining all day and we marked 20 km. Am soaked with no chance to dry out. Got 25 men to a loaf today and also a bowl of barley soup. Slept fine last night in another barn. Still going south and can now see snow-capped mountains. I would like to bring Joan back here as it is beautiful even though our condition is rough. People are still friendly and although I'm tired, I'm still much surprised at the conditions. I'll try to dry my blankets before turning in. We got up at 5:30 this morning.

April 13, 1945. 11:00.   Still raining. Am soaked through. Just starting to leave barn. 4 biscuits today, that is all. Hear from Jerry that Pres. Roosevelt died. He was a very good Pres. Don't think it will hurt prisoners-or-war. Looks like the right wing of Dem. knew what they were doing when they got rid of Wallace and put in Truman.

April 14, 1945 10:30 a.m. Am in another barn. Weather is clearing up but rained last night. Marched 18 km from 11 to 5. Hard marching in mud and rain. No food today and no more G.I. chow and am hungry. Staying here for 24 hrs. rest which we need badly. Trying to dry clothes. Shave and washed. Face is pealing from sunburn. Still going south and reached Danube River. Mountains are beautiful, well kept forests and streams with little waterfalls. Killed a cow. Guards (39) get half, G.I.'s (500) get other half. Hope we get something to eat soon. Came through one fairly big town yesterday, people didn't speak but no violence!

April 16, 1945. Didn't get a chance to write yesterday. Came down out of mountains. Easy walking going west. The people aren't as friendly here but last night the Jerries gave us a good hot meal and a bag of dog biscuits (biscuits last supper on the 15th). Breakfast and dinner the 16th. Walked 18 km. yesterday. Just as many shrines here as in mountains.

5:30 p.m. Walked 23 km. today. Still in valley and followed Danube for awhile. Today saw a sight I never will forget. There is much truth in our propaganda about the anti-semitic feeling here. The treatment is unbelieveable! City staying in tonight is 13 km. from Linz and has been bombed, as has Linz. Hope we get fed tonignt as I'm hungry. Weather hot. Sun hot and roads dusty.

April 17, 1945. Today I am 25 years old and growing older every hour. Am staying in town for 24 hour layover and rest but so far 6 (six) air raids. I feel like hell as my stomach is in an uproar. Last night 9 men to a loaf of bread, that is all. Ran out of G.I. chow about 4 days ago and am living (?) on Jerry chow which is edible but not much of it. Cold sleeping last night in shelter with roof and floor, no sides. Still don't know how far we have to go yet. I believe they intend to march us until end of war. Anyone of the Four Horsemen could get us. Happy Birthday!

April 18, 1945. 6:00 p.m. Walked 30 km. today on 1 cup of Jerry coffee! The past 24 hours were beauties. On the 17th, got up at 7:00 a.m., we got one thin cup of soup (very thin) and at this hour nothing more except 9 men to a loaf of bread. At 6:30 last night air raid started and ended at 3:00 a.m. this morning. Left at 6:00 a.m. and walked 22 km. before noon. Walked thru Linz and crossed Danube with air raid on. Roll call coming now and still nothing to eat. Still going S.W. but need food badly. Water was no problem in mountains but down here can't even get water and people not so friendly.

April 19, 1945. 5:00 p.m. Last night at 10:00 p.m. received some soup (not enough to cover a 6 in. dia. pan!) and 8 men to a loaf of bread. Left at 8:00 a.m., walked 17 km. until noon and then stopped for day! Reason - protecting power checking on conditions. So Jerry gave us 5 men to a small loaf, 7 1/2 men to a can of meat and we bought a few spuds. Jerry promised to give us a hot meal tonight but the stove broke down or some damn excuse. Jerry is very nice while a man from Geneva is around but as soon as he leaves, back we go again. This morning I almost dropped from hunger. All we get is excuses from Jerry but nothing to eat! R.C. man said we would have parcels in a few days. Let's hope so.

April 20, 1945 6:00 p.m. Marched about 33 km. from 7 to 4:30 in hot sun. Very hard marching as weak from hunger No food yet today. None of us can go on much longer marching 33 km. a day on a cup of Jerry coffee. The energy we are burning is our youth. We are like a lighter with no fluid, just burning the wick. Country is getting hilly again. The people are more friendly. Still going west. Have seen at least two old women with tears in their eyes as we went by. I think some of the people would like to trade with us. We use soap and cig. to trade which we have left from R.C. parcels (the only things we have left). 1 cig. is worth 8 marks so if the guards with us would let us trade we could eat. A loaf of bread is worth 80 marks or ten cig. The last town we came thru was as near on a peace time basis as I have seen. Kids eating ice cream and cookies. Every day we pass hundreds of roadside shrines and, strange as it seems, with bombs knocking down everything, I haven't seen a shrine hit yet.

April 21, 1945. 1:00 p.m. staying here for 24 hr. rest. 2 R.C. parcels for 5 men came to us in G.I. trucks and jeeps driven by Swiss. We have not received them yet but expect to late today. At 11 last night Jerry gave us some warm soup (very weak and very little and no bread.) For today I have eaten nothing but boiled turnips. Still have some oats but am going to save them. Shave and washed today. My right heal has been giving me trouble for 5 days but can do nothing for it. Men are stealing from farms, from Jerry, and from G.I.s. (Nature in the raw is seldom mild).   Just heard chow came in.-----

April 22, 1945. 5:00 p.m. Up at 5:00, off at 7:00 and walked 25 km. Rain, sleet, hail and snow were the combination for today. Soaked through and frozen. More hills and can see Swiss Alps. Jerry says we should reach camp in 3 more days. Let's hope so. Yesterday we got a thin soup (very little) and no bread. But we did get Red Cross parcels. So this morning I have oatmeal and Ovaltine (very good). I received a British invalid parcel (not bad.) Today the people are much more friendly. When we arrived here we have a good soup (best by Jerry yet) and five men to a small loaf of bread. Am very tired and shall go to bed.

April 23, 1945. Up at 4, off at 7, marched 26 km. in rain most of way. Rumor has it that we layover here 24 hr, then march 16 km. and layover for awhile. I sure hope so. Very tired again, ankle and foot still up like a balloon. Just figured roughly we have walked 251 km. up to today, the 16th day on the road.

April 24, 1945 4:30 p.m. Rest day today. Too cold and damp to do much, didn't even shave! Last night Jerry gave us uncooked barley, horse meat and potatoes, plus 12 men to a loaf. Today he gave us a very thin barley soup. Have rested most of day. Understand we don't reach camp tomorrow as per rumor. Oh well!

April 25, 1945. On this Wed., the 18th day on the road, we arrived at our "camp"! We marched 25 km. to about 15 km. southwest of Branau, to a forest where we were told, this is it. There is nothing here. No barracks, no hospital, no water within a km - just forest. We arrived at 3:00 p.m. It is now 7:00 p.m. and we have built a shelter for 5 men out of pines. Jerry gave us 7 men to a small loaf of bread last night, that is all. There is a field kitchen here but not set up. There are roughly 4,000 men (Americans) who arrived here with me. We walked 18 days and 276 hrs. according to my guess. The Red Cross arrived with 3,200 French parcels.

April 26, 1945. 5:30 p.m. Had to break off last night to get water then it was too dark. The 3,200 parcels were given out today - 3 to 4 men. The parcel is O.K., lots of sweets and cake, but also bulk food to be cooked and biscuits. Jerry gave us our first food in two days, barley (very, very little), soup (water) and 18 men to a loaf. Tonight we get sugar (spoonful), coffee (one cup) and potatoes (3 per man). Slept a little cold last night! Nice weather today. We rebuilt our home. It is about 12 ft. by 18 ft. about 2/3 of which we have been able to put on a roof of pine needles. We worked all day and I'm tired as hell but feel good to be off the road and know the Red Cross (thank God for the R.C.) is feeding us and knows where we are. The Jerries would have killed us all long ago by starvation! I have a feeling the end of the war is near and we won't be moved from here. We Americans are getting organized for the first time since I've been a prisoner and I hope on a military basis. We need it and we need it bad. I have seen men at their worst and although I lost my temper at least I didn't resort to stealing. I'm still amazed at the punishment the human body can take and still survive. I got a chance for the first time in three days to wash and brush my teeth. Tomorrow, I hope to shave.

April 27, 1945. 5:30 p.m. Today some more R.C. parcels came in here. Don't know how many or when we will get them. Today I shave and looked in a mirror, have lost some weight but if R.C. parcels keep coming in and the weather stays like it is or gets warmer, I'll be O.K. Got up at 8:00 a.m. Jerry had a roll call at 10 after not missing a day, built a fireplace, put more roof on shack. No bread from Jerry today, did get raw barley and a little butter. We are almost free here, we can wander in the woods, go to the river and, in general, a week or two in the open with good food such as we have now (I'm eating better than I have in 18 months) and nice weather, it is a little cool at night but I have a Jerry and a G.I. blanket plus an overcoat. I am told we marched in all 330 km. Some walking for the Air Corps!

April 28, 1945. Rain!

April 29, 1945. Still working hard drying out. More rain!

April 30, 1945   3:00 p.m. What a life! Haven't had time to log for two days. Started to rain 8 p.m. the 27th and rained continually until 4 a.m the 29th. Didn't sleep until last night. The hut didn't leak too much but getting drinking water, fire wood and cooking, we got soaked to the skin. So with that and the blankets being so damp, we didn't dare go to sleep or even lay down on the ground as resistance is lower when asleep. The weather is still cool and damp and always trying to rain even yet. Sitting by the fire did dry us out but the smoke ruined my eyes and yesterday I could hardly see but that is a small price to pay, so near the end, for not catching a helluva cold. We have a new place to get water and it is twice as hard to get, a 100 ft. sheer drop to a natural spring. At 4:00 today I go to help build our hosp. We cut the trees, saw them, and put them in place for a log hut. We got 1/4 of a French and 1/4 of American Red Cross parcel yesterday and as Jerry has given us nothing but a little raw barley, salt and a few potatoes and no bread at all, the parcels come in damn handy. Munich fell yesterday so that cuts us off from the Swiss so no more parcels but in another week we should be free.

May 1, 1945. Rained last night. Slept damp and cold, still cold today. Nothing new. Jerry gave us 20 men to a small loaf and a little raw barley.

May 2, 1945. 4:00 p.m. What a life! Last night it snowed and rained and our roof leaked like hell! I didn't get much sleep and was soaked to the skin and chilled to the bone. At this hour the sun is trying to shine. I have spent most of the day trying to dry out myself, clothes and blankets. Jerry gave us a little more raw barley, that is all. I understand that is the last of Jerry chow. American troops took Branau last night so by Saturday (this is Wed.) at the latest we expect to be recaptured.

    5:20 p.m. Just arrived American Officers here and Jerry Officers have surrendered camp to our forces at 3:00 p.m. today! Troops 3 km. down road and expected any minute. Roll Call (American) to read Articles of War! And so it looks as if this unholy life that started Oct. 14, 1943 will end May 2, 1945.

This log only includes road trip and time spent in woods. It's been rough but I'm alive and feel fine. <u>It could have been worse!</u>

    6:25 p.m. American tanks arrived in camp! End of long, hard journey!   Irv J. Mills.

A copy of the log is held in the History of Warfare
Library at Yale University in New Haven, Connecticut

Thirty five years after the forced march, Irv and his wife Joan whom he had married before he went overseas, did visit the Bavarian Alps and the general route of the march itself. (See log entry of April 12, 1945.)

Irv states that the words "our propaganda" recorded on April 16, 1945 refers to the hundreds of Jewish civilians he and his fellow prisoners met on the road. The Jewish prisoners were marching in the opposite direction and consisted primarily of older men and women, all forced to wear the Star of David on their ragged, torn and dirty clothing. Even under these conditions Irv felt from the cut of the clothing and the material as well as the appearance, that these people had once been important and prosperous in whatever country they originated.

Returning to civilian life as a veteran, Irv attended college in Washington, D. C. earning a Bachelor of Science degree. The largest part of his business career was spent in and around the foodservice-hospitality industry. He has served as President of a china manufacturing company, President of a Food Service Design and Engineering firm, Senior Vice President of a distribution arm of Holiday Inn and has owned restaurants and been a consultant.

In addition, Irv served on numerous Boards of Directors and is a Life Fellow of Foodservice Research and prior to retiring in Sonoma, spent a number of years as a lobbyist in Washington D.C. He represented commercial manufacturers of chinaware for hotels and restaurants. In 1989, he had a book published entitled *Tabletop Presentations: A Guide for the Foodservice Professional.*

The appreciation for fine food and great wine which Irv developed over the years sprang, he believes, from being deprived of even the simplest rations while a POW. Irv's philosopy from that time forward has recognized that the only true freedom is to want "nothin' from nobody nohow!"

Before Irv arrived in the United States he ended up in Branau where Hitler had a castle retreat. It was General Patton's Son-in-Law who liberated the American prisoners. Patton wanted to reach the camp early, before VE-Day, as Germans had talked of killing the Americans. Rumors had always circulated in the camp. Many of the stories were started by the prisoners themselves. There was no sense to break out of camp, since the end of the war was considered to be ending very soon. When rescued, the men were taken to a series of American camps to build up their emaciated bodies. They made their exodus toward home by G.I. trucks to DC-3s into the Port of La Harve, France.

One of the first things Irv enjoyed as to unlimited food was a multitude of cans of G.I. milk shakes. He does not remember other food choices or how much he ate at the time. On the ship heading for America there were briefings preparing the men to go to the Pacific war in the Far East!

Back in the United States, Irv was taken to Atlantic City, New Jersey for physical exams plus rest and recreation. Joan and Irv were guests at the Ambassador Hotel for $1.00 per night. Irv was having medical and dental work. He shuffled papers. Their mail boy was Donald O'Conner. There was a Miss America Pageant in progress and Beth Meyerson won the honor of being Miss America. The former POWs were asked to be escorts and ride in the parade with beautiful girls. They had lots of medals and "it would give honor to be part of the parade," according to the Parade Sponsors. All the Veterans declined by saying, "No thank you."

One night in Atlantic City, Irv and Joan went night clubbing. There was a roller skating act. The performers started searching for a volunteer. The spotlight fell on all of Irv's wings and ribbons. After all! the United States invested millions of dollars for their Flyers! The girl and fellow started swinging

Irv back and forth in a silly manner for laughs. When they put him down, he was extremely dizzy!

On VJ-Day, Irv and Joan were in Times Square, New York where there was such a wild celebration that the couple decided to get out of there and head for the quiet rural country of their childhood in the State of Connecticut.

Joan and Irv purchased a condominium in Sonoma, California in 1976 near the northeast mountains just a short walk from town. Irv can gaze out at the homeowners' pool and see his wife, Joan sun bathe. Often the couple enjoy a visit with their daughter, Susan. In the town of Sonoma, Irv is best known as the one lay person in the community who has spent the most time as watch dog of Sonoma City Council Meetings. Irv exudes a feeling for what's right in America.

Asking Irv, "Why did the Germans take the prisoners out of the camp before the war ended?" He answered, "The Russians were coming in from the East. The Germans were more afraid of the Russians than Americans. Guards wanted to get away from the Russians. They figured if they took the Americans, they might be able to use the men in some way for advantage. By moving into the depths of Germany near where Hitler had been, older guards might receive more sympathy from Americans." Irv saw German villagers in the mountains who had no radios. They were not full of hate. He remembers the old women with tears in their eyes... The beautiful little villages that were not bombed...

On October 18th four days after Mission 115, Henry H. Arnold, Commander General of the Army Air Forces stated to the press, "Regardless of our losses, I'm ready to send replacements of planes and crews and continue building up our strength. The opposition is not nearly what it was, and we are wearing them down. The loss of 60 American bombers in the Schweinfurt raid was incidental."

The total from the successive raids was really incalcuable. In four missions alone, 148 planes were lost along with 1,048 fliers lost, injured or maimed. This price to pay for destroying the German bearings factories was like the whole war, one of excesses. The losses were so high that future bombing raids were on a very light schedule for months. The factories bombed on "Black Thursday" were found to be more in the nature of real estate and not much in the realm of factory equipment destroyed. While the lull in bombing raids was evidenced, the Germans had moved many of their drill presses to other cities. Records show 12,000 tons of bombs were unleashed upon the bearings industry, but that endeavor did not stop the recouperative powers of the tenacious German people in their production. No matter how cruel the test of the men, those American Air Corps Men left from this "Black Thursday" and other bombing raids followed the same spirit as that of the Revolutionary Soldier, the Confederate Officers, and the brave World War I Veterans by never giving up the cause of liberty.

Caidin, Martin, *Black Thursday,* Ballantine Books, 101 Fifth Avenue, New York, N.Y., 1960. pp. 280. pps, 4,5,40,42,157.

Strong, Russell A., *First Over Germany, A History of the 306th Bombardment Group,* 1982, Printed by Hunter Publishing Company, Winston-Salem, North Carolina. Copies available from Russell A. Strong, 2041 Hillsdale, Kalamazoo, MI 49007. pps. 325. pps. 149, 171

Kermit Roosevelt Parker

United States Army 1937 - 1958

United States Army Air Corps (13 years.)

It was four o'clock on a cold December morning, 1919. Electricity had not been invented as far as Lame Deer, Montana was concerned. On a knoll, overlooking a frozen creek, fresh tracks in knee deep snow led directly to a little cabin. On this cold shivery morning, no lights were showing in the small Indian village except for one dim kerosene lamp. That light flickered in the Parkers' one room cabin. This little shelter from winter storms was located in a remote region of south central Montana near what's now Yellowstone National Park. It was on a Cheyenne Indian Reservation.

Several people were rushing around. Excitement was high. If you paused just a moment on the frozen landscape, you might have heard the piercing cry of a new born baby, Kermit. Who wouldn't scream when whacked on the bottom that hard? Kermit would personally recognize that cry anywhere, because he got the whack and he let out the scream! It was his birthday! The birth was a family affair. There was no doctor or midwife. Half-sister Mildred was there; at seventeen years of age her contribution was staying out of the way. There were no telephones to summon the doctor who lived fifty miles north of Lame Deer. Even had there been telephones, snow was too deep. Twenty degree below zero temperature registered outside. The poor old doctor could not have traveled that distance by horseback in that much snow and bitter cold.

It is an Indian custom to name a child after the first thing seen by the father following birth. This baby was named "High Wolf" by members of the Cheyenne Tribe. Kermit's father, Charles Parker was the first government agent for the Northern Cheyenne Reservation in 1884, and later he operated a relay telegraph at a railroad station. This type of telegraph system put the pony express out of business. At the time Kermit Roosevelt Parker was born, Theodore Roosevelt's son, Kermit was well known. Maybe Kermit's dad voted for Teddy. In any case, with a first name chosen as Kermit for the new baby and a middle name tagged on as Roosevelt, Parker was certainly well endowed with names!

Kermit's dad was reported to have had some kind of a fascinating life. It was filled with high adventure around the area and the time of the Battle of Little Big Horn, Custer's Last Stand. He was very secretive about his past. When Kermit was born, his dad was sixty-four years old; Kermit's mother, Mauda, was forty four. It was a second marriage for his dad who had married a full-blooded Indian maiden in his youth. Kermit's father had nine children. Kermit's mother had ten children. This was a second marriage for the couple. The family remained at the reservation for the next three years. Kermit does not remember much until at age three his mother decided she and the boy would move to "the city." Mauda believed, "there were more opportunites to earn a living in Billings, Montana." Kermit's dad visited the boy and his mother when Kermit was five years old. That was the last time he ever saw his dad.

It was Kermit's good fortune that the landlord of the little apartment took a liking to him. Landlord took the boy to the city park and the two always managed to go by an old fashioned drug store on the way home. The drug store had a soda fountain for ice cream!

When two barnstorming, World War I pilots brought airplanes to town and were taking passengers for rides, Landlord grasped Kermit by the hand and said, "Young man, we are going for an airplane ride." Kermit skipped happily across the field ready for a wonderful adventure. But the Pilot refused to take a four year old kid in his plane. That wonderful adventure ended on the ground! But there were many other good times with Landlord along the nearby Yellowstone River. Fish that were caught, flopped upon the grass. Swims in sun-warmed-water inside a big old tub were a big part of summer fun. Swinging high while pumping hard on the park swings was exhiliarating. Picking up fruit and vegetables and helping his mother sell popcorn balls brought other exciting adventures to the impressionable young man. Culinary operation of producing popcorn balls by Kermit's mother became a way of life!

In 1925, Kermit's mother decided it was time to move on. She busied herself for a month or more, preparing a wagon for journeying in the springtime weather. She had never traveled by any other mode than behind a team of horses in a covered wagon. She had crossed the prairie states as a young woman in a "Prairie Schooner." It was that same faithful covered wagon that she filled to the brim and packed so tightly.

In an unpublished book, from which this information was given, called *Kermit's Story: (His Childhood, an Autobiography)*, Kermit in 1991, describes sights and sounds he experienced as a child traveling around the western United States in that covered wagon. On this strange wonderment odyessy which took place from 1924 until 1934, mother and son sojourned from town to town. They traveled in the lumbering Conestoga wagon through mountains of Colorado, Montana, Idaho, Utah, Oregon and Washington. Kermit at fourteen years, began wondering about being on the roads in 1934. Where once dusty roads were lonely and full of potholes, cars whizzed by impatiently. These roads were being maintained as highways for popular new automobiles! Perhaps Kermit's mother was getting tired of looking for that perfect place to live. In any case, she decided to settle in Walla Walla, Washington so that her son, Kermit could attend school for a higher education.

Up to this time the boy went to one room schoolhouses located mostly in Colorado and Provo, Utah. The class had three graduates when he graduated from the eighth grade in Provo. There were cultural activities in Provo as well. At North Park, where Kermit lived in a tent, a local family would stage impromptu musical concerts. Some members played instruments, some would sing. They attracted quite a crowd. Their name was Osmond. One time the House of David played a local team on the baseball diamond. The House of David was an all male member religious order wearing long beards. After that to Kermit, anyone with a beard was either a House of David Baseball Player or a tramp! But this is getting ahead of a fascinating story!

During that wondrous period of life lived in the covered wagon, Kermit was always looking for "an adventure every day of his life." He noticed how equipment worked. He picked the right time to be more curious than the average person. It was the decade of new inventions. Changes from old ways of doing things were taking place. Many new and faster techniques were being used. A huge gasoline pump with glass cylinder pumped pink colored gas which sold for 12 ½ cents per gallon. The boy watched diligently as a newspaper man using a keyboard with slugs of metal popping out of a machine, caused them to fall in lines. This endeavor made a newspaper at the printshop. Eight men pushed a funny looking wagon, then pumped up and down on long bars squirting water from a hose on a fire. Kermit paid attention to water boiling out of radiators of cars and how tires were fixed and changed.

An adventure in the mountains included a couple of young adults practice-shooting a pistol at a mountain cliff. The side of the mountain to broke loose at the very spot they were shooting. The appreciation of the power of gunfire was respected, when with a deafening roar, the family's screaming horses took off for safer ground. Mauda did recover her horses the next morning. Some trees as large as three feet in diameter were cast in the rubble of the mountainside that had broken loose!

While a blacksmith shoed horses, Kermit watched the smithy's skill very closely. He learned about the rasp, anvil, forge, tongs and the operation of shoeing horses. The boy studied dams, streams, and camping techniques. He reviewed workings of a two burner kerosene stove. Riding in a Model T Ford was fun, especially if you asked questions regarding details of such things as the pressure in the tires and how the wheels stayed on the car. Who could be interested in how the flat tire was being fixed? Not only was there an innertube and rubber cement but sometimes an old boot was added to the rubber tire. The boy wanted answers as to how all these things worked including the hand brake. (After all, his method of holding back his mother's covered wagon with a small log or heavy stick, as they went down steep mountain roads had been risky and dangerous! They also experienced flat tires, continually!) Kermit saw large cities such as Denver and Salt Lake City when they were little towns. He investigated water spouts, wild animals and red barrel cactus that had jelly inside that tasted like red raspberry jam. But the most fascinating and exciting thing that Kermit saw was a "narrow gauge" train running from Mount Rose to Salida through Gunnison, Colorado. He was also filled with joy one night as mother and son camped at Soldiers Summit, a very steep pass over the mountains. The Denver and Rio Grande Western main line railroad used three monstrous engines under full throttle to push loaded coal cars through the winding and steep mountains. Kermit would stand on the tracks feeling the hot metal and smelling the super heated oil. The earth would shake as 300 tons of thundering power surged forward. The fascination of trains would stay with Kermit for the rest of his life and in his future work with small gauge trains. On and on, this boy took in educational opportunities around his every day life. This education included spraying techniques, potato planting, and even historic events in the news, such as Lindberg's flight across the Atlantic Ocean.

Back in Provo, mother and son had to move from North Park. A new library was being built by the W.P.A. They ended up pitching their tent in a vacant area near a coal yard. Of course, a branch of the Union Pacific Railroad ran from Provo to Heber, Utah right near that coal yard. The train was known as the Heber Creeper. One day Kermit's friend, Jack and he talked their way into a ride to Heber and a return on the "Creeper."

Kermit read about crystal radios but he did not own one. That type radio did not require power to operate it. Since the family had no electricity, Kermit decided to build a crystal radio! He started to collect things like a cardboard cylinder, enough magnet wire to wrap around the cyclinder for about four inches, a crystal and a pair of earphones. The crystal was hard to come by. It was a small chip of galena embedded in about a half thimbleful of lead. But the earphones proved to be the most difficult part to acquire. An old cast iron water main was being replaced and the salvaged pipe was piled in one of the vacant lots near the family tent. The joints of the water pipe had been made watertight by pounding lead around a lip of each joint. The workmen had not removed the lead when they dug up the pipe. Kermit was told he could have the lead if he could get it out of the joints. Working long hours, it came out a chunk at a time. He finally had a hundred pounds! Selling the lead for a penny a pound netted him one dollar for a second-hand pair of earphones on sale for the same amount. The round cyclinder for the radio was an oatmeal box. An old transformer had all the magnet wire needed and more. To his amazement after assembling the materials as instructed, the boy heard music loud and clear! Kermit could get several stations by sliding a bent piece of tin along the coil. The crystal set went through many revisions but sparked a lifelong interest in the mysterious world of electronics.

Departure from Provo for the last time was a bit of a picture. A team of horses pulled their wagon equipped with rubber tires, overhead bows and a canvas top. A cage which stuck out on the back carried two goats. A fifty-six year old woman and a fourteen year old boy perched high on the seat in the front end of the Conestoga wagon. It wasn't an everyday sight in 1934 but rather a view of the 1860's.

By now, the boy born on the Indian Reservation reached fifteen. Mother and son saw an ad in the paper that indicated "you could attend school in Chicago all summer and learn about electricity! Just send in an amount of $25.00." This great promise stirred the pair to action. Securing the money somehow and sending it to Chicago, Kermit automatically qualified for the ninety day course. With no money for transportation but $5.00 for food, the young promising student settled upon taking a freight train to the far off distant destination of Chicago, Illinois. With a small suitcase, savings of $5.00 and with lots of enthusiasm, Kermit set out to gain an 'exciter' skill. Hitch hiking was common in the great depression. In the maze of railroad cars and tracks, the intrepid adventurer took advice from other "passengers" awaiting to catch the Union Pacific mainline, "the hobos." A hobo-self-appointed-teacher showed the wayfarer how to tell when the locomotive was ready for departure, where to go to get on and what part of the train to board. He explained about sealed railroad cars and that it was a federal offence to break a seal. After many adventuresome trials as a vagabond on various trains, Kermit made it to Chicago in three weeks time, only to discover he needed another $100.00 a month for tuition, room and board. Finding no way to work out the money problems, the company sent $20.00 back to Mauda and gave the young man the other $5.00 for his trip back to Washington state. Before Kermit left the Coyne Electrical Company, he was impressed by the latest telephone device known to the commerce world as a circular dial telephone!

By seventeen, Kermit was working at farm jobs across Washington, Oregon and California. There wasn't much employment to make money. After traveling up California's Central Valley, spending weeks in Marysville and Yuba City, Kermit finally returned to Seattle, Washington. Headlines in the local newspaper declared President Roosevelt was going to visit the city. Kermit went to the barber shop and got a 25 cent hair cut so he would look presentable. "FDR was due to make an appearance at 6:00 p.m." according to the newspaper. Kermit stood on that street corner until 11:00 p.m. The President of the United States and his entourage made their appearance five hours late. The wait was worth it! Franklin Delano Roosevelt came within a few feet of the young man. He looked right at him and waved. Kermit was sure he waved at him because who else was standing there to wave at?

Soon after that night, Kermit read the famous sign with a hand on it, that said, "Uncle Sam Needs You!" Kermit's mother had conditions before she would sign a consent form for his admission into the Army. She was dogmatic, "that a church member would not join the Army that was in the business to kill people!" So Kermit had to resign from the church. He sold his ailing car for $10.00. He said goodbye to his mother. As Kermit was leaving to join the Army, his mother's parting words were, "Son, I hope I never see you again!"

The clatter, rattle and squeaking of tanks as they slowly advanced through dense pine forest, disappearing in undergrowth, then reappearing as brush and small trees came crashing down, was history in the making. This was a final assault by those clanking monsters of destruction first seen by German soldiers in World War I.

On an early January morning, Whippet Tanks came charging from ideal cover of the forest into a clearing heading directly toward the new recruits. The men had no choice. They could stand ground or scatter to avoid onslaught. The row of neatly dressed men held ground just as the tanks were almost upon them. The tanks made a sharp flanking movement and passed the reviewing stand directly in front of the group. Kermit was watching the review of the last company of Whippet Tanks left in the Army before their next assault on a junk yard. The time was 1938. Having joined the Army one month before and not yet aquainted with basic training, the recruits had been placed in the reviewing stand to see the last parade of the old relics of World War I. This type of tank was very small. It amounted to being a suspended oblong steel box between two tractor type track treads. If two men were skinny, three could squeeze into the apparatus. This product of war was engineered by the British. The tanks came too late to see much action in the other war and now they were being replaced by the (then) Modern MIA2 American designed tank.

The name tank also came from the British. Parts shipped in wooden boxes were labeled TANK so the casual viewer wouldn't know the crate was shipping war equipment. The old Whippets had a speed of four and one half miles per hour. These 'new' MIA2 replacements could do sixty miles per hour, jump over ditches and crawl over other obstacles at that speed.

Kermit was not in a tank company as matter of choice. It was the only game the Army offered when he joined in Wenatchee, Washington. Kermit was in the Third Tank Company of the Third Infantry Division located at Fort Lewis, Washington. Kermit was not thrilled about his choice of that branch of service after watching the old Whippets clatter around the field that morning. However, everything possible was done the next six months to keep the newly enlisted man from being bored. Put through the "school of the soldier" (bootcamp) for standard infantry, he was introduced to close order drill, military courtesy, articles of war and of course rifle training.

Rifle training, being of utmost importance included "to field strip a rifle, clean it, and reasssemble it within a period of five minutes, blindfolded!" Two numbers were to be on the tip of the tongue for instant release upon request. They were the Army serial number of the individual and his rifle serial number. KP was just plain flunky duty to most everyone but they did get quite a bit of police duty called "policing up" which included peeling potatoes, washing dishes, sweeping and mopping floors. Another popular sport was guard duty. One day there was a formal ceremony of "mounting the guard." The new recruits were called Soldiers now, instead of some other names tagged on them as recruits. A truck drove the Soldiers to posts with numbers. On guard post twelve, Private Parker was given instructions. "This is guard post number twelve, you will walk your post in a military manner." And so, the new Soldier walked his post for four hours in a military manner in the boonies of the Fort Lewis Reservation. That pile of lumber that was guarded was used to build the building that housed the Construction Quartermaster that built McChord Field. In a sense, he was the first military man to do duty at McChord Field, now an air base of the same name.

Kermit's interest in communications was almost nil in the Tank Company. The company did have one radio something akin to a relic. Left over from the First World War, it looked like a box contraption and required two men to carry it. Set up on four short legs, a foot off the ground, with a diamond shaped antenna attached to the top, the front of the box opened along the top, hinged along the bottom. It folded out to form an operating table which gave the operator access to dials and switches contained in the box. The operator could sit on the ground with legs under the box to send or receive messages. There was a telegraph key attached to the lid for sending and earphones to be placed over both ears for receiving messages. The operator needed an assistant. The assistant did not have to learn Morse Code. Oh, yes, there was a little more to the radio equipment. There was a three legged stool with a smaller metal box and a seat attached. A crank stuck out of each side of the box that resembled pedals on a bicycle. This was the generator that supplied power for the radio to work. Now you know what Kermit the Assistant Operator did. He had to turn the generator when the radio was operated. It was easy when the operator was receiving a message, but when the operator used the telegraph key to send a message it was like someone put a brake on the generator.

Tanks were an Infantry weapon. Training was basically the same as received by all Infantry troops except tank crews received specialized instructions in the tank's use. Rifle training was number one. There were rewards for high level skills depending upon how many "bulls eyes" or "maggies drawers" (completely missing the target) you acquired. Lowest score was "Qualifying." This score was mandatory. A soldier could repeat the course as many times as needed to obtain it. In sequence, scores were named "Qualifying, Marksman, Expert and Sharpshooter." The reward for Expert Sharpshooter was an additional five dollars a month at the pay table. Kermit really applied himself to come up as "Expert." His pay of twenty-one dollars a month was increased to twenty-six dollars.

The young man kept an eye on the bulletin board. The 8th Signal Corp Detachment needed a telephone operator for post switchboard. After an interview, Kermit was transferred within the week. He did lose his "Expert Rifleman" pay. "Oh well," the new Signalman surmised, "easy come, easy go." He didn't make switchboarding his career but the Signal Corps was Kermit's branch of service for the next twenty years.

The telephone switchboard was a thousand line six position manual system. Each position had access to all lines appearing on a vertical panel in front of the operator as a small light with a jack underneath it. There were twelve pairs of three foot long cords with a plug attached to one end. In front of each pair of cords were two keys and two lights. When a telephone was removed from it's cradle, (called off the hook) the light corresponding to their number would light into the associated jack. The light would go out, so another operator wouldn't answer the same line. The key by the cord would be opened and the operator would say "Operator." The military did not use "number please." When the desired number was given, the "calling cord" was inserted into the jack of the called number. The key associated with that cord was operated and that rang the called telephone number. The lights beside the cord keys told the operator when each telephone was "on the hook." An operator might have any number of cords all in operation at any time. Lights blinked by the dozens, coming on and going off. With both hands busy plugging cords, pushing keys, and at the same time talking with as many as three people, without time for a breath, it was a mad house! Rarely was a mistake made. Did Kermit jump out of a tank into a fire? Actually he did learn all about those tangled cords and how to do the operation. He gained speed and worked during busy periods of the day. It was called Post Telephone System. It was in operation twenty-four hours a day, seven days a week. There was little time for soldiering and no duties except for operation of the switchboard and a fixed radio station.

Kermit felt useful. He knew most of the Officers by name. He had conversations with important and interesting people such as Major Mark Clark. If you couldn't find the Major's party in the time that he thought you should, he would be back on the line making uncomplimentary remarks about your competence. You can understand then, that Major Mark Clark was not one of the telephone operator's favorite personalities.

Fortunately, there were few like that. For example, there was a Lieutenant Colonel on post who had just arrived from the Philippines. He was assigned Executive Officer of the 15th Infantry Division. He found that the telephone operator was the best and fastest way to locate personnel and activities. He became well known for asking all kinds of information in a pleasant undemanding way. He would thank the telephone operators for helping him locate a party. Few high ranking officers ever did that. His name? It was Lieutenant Colonel Dwight D. Eisenhower!

Colonel Eisenhower called one day asking, "Is there anyone who could repair a washing machine?" Kermit was chosen as the one most likely to succeed with such a task. He went to the Colonel's quarters on post and met Mrs. Eisenhower (who became known to the world as Mamie). The washing machine problem turned out to be minor. After that, Kermit became Mamie's handyman. At the slightest problem, he got a call. He received a check for $5.00 from Mamie's husband one time. (He wishes now he had never cashed it!)

Receiving a promotion to Specialist Third Class put the Signalman back to twenty-six dollars a month. Out of that pay came a deduction for Old Soldiers Home. At the tender age of nineteen it was difficult for the soldier to see any use for an old soldiers home. So far he was right, he hasn't needed one, yet!

Kermit went roller skating where he learned to dance on skates. He never did get the hang of regular dancing. He met Helen Richmond, his wife for forty years. They met casually as a call was made to change partners. They skated as partners, often. It was almost a year before they started dating.

As Hitler invaded one small country after another, there was definite increase of activity in the military. In 1939, almost the whole garrison went on maneuvers in California at Fort Ord. While troops were away, Fort Lewis felt like it was deserted. Lots of furloughs, three day passes and relaxation took place. Things got busy in a hurry when the troops returned. The Army was expanding! Kermit got promoted to Private First Class. This gave him another five dollars a month and a single chevron on his sleeve. In February, 1940, Signal Officer Lieutenant Kelsey detailed that McChord Field was almost completed and it was time to install a telephone plant. It would be a dial system. He asked, "would you like to go with me and help with the installation?" "Yes Sir!" was Kermit's answer without a single hesitation on his part.

The role of helper on the telephone construction installation was that of aiding in the laying of telephone distribution cables and the installation of the dial system itself. As the Private First Class took on the project with great enthusiasm, his pay was increased by promotion to Specialist First Class. One chevron up and one rocker down was sewn on the uniform. This promotion was almost equal to Staff Sergeant but without the rank. With more money, there were more friends and functions. Boat trips, swimming, picnics and other recreational events became commonplace.

Kermit attended night school while stationed at McChord Field. The Detachment was notified of an opening at Automatic Electric's Dial Telephone School for one student from the unit. The lucky student was Kermit and he got to go back to Chicago! However, there was one stipulation. One could not go to the school with less than two years left on the enlistment. So one would have to re-enlist to qualify. Also, army regulations stated a married man could not re-enlist without permission. If he married Helen before re-enlistment, he could not re-enlist. He was not to be discharged for re-enlistment until the orders were received assigning the Signalman to the school. The couple decided that a wedding would have to take place between re-enlistment and departure for school to meet all regulations. Young and inexperienced in the ways of the military, the two set the wedding date four times before the arrival of orders. Kermit was discharged, re-enlisted, married in a church and boarded a train for Chicago all in a three day time period. Of course, the newly married couple took the North Coast Limited Train heading for Chicago as a honeymoon. This time Kermit was riding in a plush seat on the train instead of cramped-down in a big pipe on an open flat railroad car, such as he rode as a hobo. He was on the fastest train of its time requiring three days and two nights to make the trip.

It was winter of 1940. The Automatic Electric Company manufactured all of their own equipment in their Chicago factory. They made everything that was a part of their telephone equipment such as magnet wire that went into relays, transformers, bells and like items. Automatic Electric Company was known world wide for quality products such as the central office dial system. That was the machinery used in a central office to make connections when a rotary dial telephone was operated. Kermit's course started with manufacturing techniques of each item along with the engineering principals behind the production. He learned about the heart of the entire dial exchange, the "Stroger Switch." That mechanical device working on dial pulses came over the telephone line making the connection to the dialed number. Here, Kermit who was but five years from seeing a dial telephone the first time, right in the same city of Chicago, was studying the complexities of machines and what made them work. He was in paradise. In a months time, he was appointed student instructor.

To understand the Stroger switch one had to work with a bank of one hundred contacts in a half circle around a vertical shaft. There were ten rows of ten contacts. The first digit received by the switch stepped the shaft vertically corresponding to the number of pulses received. The second digit would rotate the shaft horizontally. For example: if the number 56 was received, the first digit would step the shaft and its contacts up to the fifth level. The second digit would rotate it to the sixth contact. The switch would be connected to number fifty six. Kermit made good grades with a final of 97% for the course.

The novel and interesting final exam consisted of each student receiving a wooden box full of parts. There were relays, shafts, cams, gears and all kinds of paraphernalia. The student was expected to build an individual item indicated on a slip of paper. He had to construct the indicated piece of equipment by use of diagrams, mechanical specifications and adjustment information from the equipment in his box. In the box, there were about ten times more parts than the student needed. When all students completed their devices, their assembled work was put together into a mockup of a telephone exchange! If the mockup worked, a phone rang and everybody would pass the course. If the phone did not ring, an icy chill ran through the group. Whose switch didn't work? The telephone rang the first time for the group Kermit was in. The group could breathe again...

Chicago itself was exciting to the newly married couple during Christmastime. They looked at grand sights in windows. Attending live radio shows and visiting museums for free was fun. The tinkle of Santa Claus bells, honking of horns, din of elevated railroad trains, traffic stop signs, clop, clop of mounted police horses, whistles of traffic cops became a homogenized din that surely did not make a boy from the wilds of Montana or a girl from the plains of North Dakota homesick.

The couple finally hit the road to go home in a 1939 Plymouth four door sedan. The car was only one year old and cost $475. Gasoline was less than 20 cents a gallon, motel rooms $2.00 per night and a good hot dinner cost less than a dollar. Arriving back at McChord Field, the supervisor of the telephone system, Master Sergeant Jack Hopkins was transferred to another station. Kermit was appointed Wire Chief. Accelerated at an unbelievable rate, McCord Field became a training base, maintenance facility and an aircraft storage base for the Boeing Aircraft Factory in Seattle. Kermit was promoted to Staff Sergeant by midsummer, skipping over grades of Corporal and Sergeant. He was put in charge of all telephone system activities. This work included crash and fire alarms, teletypes and anything that utilized telephone wire for transmission. He installed new equipment, modified existing facilities or designed new devices to fulfill a particular requirement.

Cable was buried underground with a series of manholes required to install telephone facilities between McChord Field and Fort Lewis.

On 7 December, 1941 all resemblance of normality went down the drain. At noon, the radio announced Imperial Japanese bombed Pearl Harbor. By nightfall the base was surrounded by armed Soldiers. All passes and leaves were cancelled. All military personnel were restricted to base. Kermit spent the afternoon and evening securing cable manholes by welding the covers on. Upon arrival at home about midnight, having a delayed dinner and getting into bed, wearily relaxing, the telephone began ringing. The operator informed the intrepid Signalman turned Telephone Specialist, that all communication with Fort Lewis was lost! An incident of sabotage? This could be a serious devastating blow by an enemy cutting off communication between two major military installations in the Pacific Northwest. A test of the cable showed it was badly damaged. Circuits were dead. Cables within the forts seemed to be okay. An emergency call to the Tacoma wire chief put an emergency plan into operation by commercial cable. Service was limited. After great effort on the cold rainy night, checking manhole to manhole and having to identify themselves every few minutes to guards on roving patrols, the men finally found a big footprint on a cable inside a manhole. The lead covered cable was muddy where it was spliced. With Kermit held upside down, hanging from his very heels, he fixed the problem! In study at Automatic Electric Company, it had been an unbreakable rule "that one does not use a lead covered cable as a step to get in and out of a vault." Someone had! By so doing, that individual had cracked the lead sheath allowing moisture to enter the cable and shorting it out. The Army never found out who broke the cable but it was speculated that some Soldier fancying he had found a ready made foxhole, tried the manhole on for size and this individual did not know what trouble he caused! It took more time to get somewhere, with guards now posted everywhere, than it did to do the operation at hand.

The second day after Pearl Harbor's bombing, a siren atop the water tank broke into a screaming wail. Everybody and everything went into overdrive on the base. All dependents and civilians vacated their living quarters, got into cars and evacuated the base just as practiced. Within ten minutes all auto traffic had cleared the base and all systems were ready to repulse the air raid whenever the enemy arrived...

After much howling by the siren, the Base Commander's nerves were frayed. Calling everyone in a position of control to find where the air raid warning originated and who was the operator, the unanimous answer was, "I don't know, Sir."

This was the beginning of "If-you-can't-fix-it, call-Kermit-syndrome." Asked, "Can you fix the siren?" by the Base Commander, Kermit assured him, "I will start immediately to ascertain the reason the machine is wailing and how it can be stopped!" Checking the control cable, it was okay. That meant the problem was at the siren and not the remote control. Going to a control box which contained all wiring for clearance lights and siren, Kermit disconnected the power. Upon opening the box, he discovered an override switch had failed that allowed the alarm to be operated from the base of the tower. Fifteen minutes had elasped by the time the earsplitting noise stopped. The community, Mc Chord Field and half the city of Tacoma was in panic.

The Base Commander with the Provost Marshal (the Chief of Military Police) soon arrived at the water tower's base. A high level command decision was made. In order to control panic, everyone would be notified "the enemy had been repulsed!" The only way to sound "all clear" was by using the siren and sending a series of short blasts. The control switch was inoperative! "Is there any way the siren can be operated without the switch?" Kermit was asked. "Only if I connect a jumper wire around the switch," he declared. "Do it!" came the command. "Yes Sir," Kermit responded and proceded to sound the "all clear" signal that returned the base and surrounding community back to high gear from overdrive!

Events moved at dizzying speed on the base. The war, two days old, caused work in all departments. Frameworks were constructed to guard the telephone exchange. Sand bags were piled to protect sensitive operations. Windows were covered. Antiaircraft guns were established. Roofs of hangers and buildings were painted for camouflage. An entire highway was painted to look like fields, pastures, yards and countryside objects. This deception was to fool Japanese Bomber Pilots as radar did not yet exist. Even a new turn in the highway was created to fool someone in the air who might be searching for the base. It was a serious concern, since Japanese Pilots were already attacking the Aleutian Islands. It was conceivable they might attempt to destroy the defense bases in the area. Intensity of activity was further increased as equipment and supplies were being rushed north through Canada to build a highway to Alaska. This highway was to be vital to America's northern territory just in case the Japanese Fleet denied Americans access by sea. Finding manpower to build new barracks was a problem. Men were either in the military or in war production.

Kermit was paid a dollar an hour on off duty hours to help an electrical contractor wire furnaces in about one hundred buildings. That actually paid almost three times as much as he was getting as Staff Sergeant. Lieutenant Kelsey was replaced by Major Weil, who had been an engineer on Coulee Dam. A fine relationship developed between the two men. Kermit was promoted to Technical Sergeant. He attached three chevrons up and two rockers down upon his sleeve.

With hardly any time off for vacation, Kermit was always glad he and Helen took two weeks off in the Spring of 1941 to camp at the base of Mount St. Helens on beautiful Spirit Lake. They camped a quarter of a mile from Spirit Lake Lodge, owned by Harry Truman. (He was the man buried about four hundred feet deep when he refused to leave the eruption of Mount St. Helens in 1980. The other Harry Truman was not his relative).

Routine was not the norm in those early war days. A good example was re-assignment of a new P-55 fighter aircraft squadron from March Field in southern California to McChord Field. The P-55 experimental fighter looked identical to a P-47 (Thunderbolt) but was two-thirds its size. The squadron left in formation. Only three planes arrived at destination. The remainder were scattered along route, some never found. Needless to say, few people ever heard of a P-55.

In 1942, the base telephone system's maintenance was contracted to the local Bell System. With days numbered as to Kermit's stay at McChord, Major Weil called the talented man into his office and asked, "Why don't you apply for OCS?" "What is OCS?" the Signalman man asked. "Officer Candidate School," the Major replied. Major Weil already had necessary papers and arranged an interview. Three Officers would have to make recommendation with the application form. In a few short weeks Kermit was at Signal Corps Officer Candidate School in Fort Monmouth, New Jersey. You guessed it! The army provided Kermit with a railroad ticket on the North Coast Limited from Tacoma, Washington to Red Bank, New Jersey.

From the train, the serviceman watched America go flashing by. It was still the same America he was familiar with. The little towns and their thoroughfares looked like scenes from silent movies. Only a slight click could be heard when the train moved over a switch. The clickety-click of wheels on rail joints were useful to Kermit in judging the speed of the train. For five days, the endless panorama was neither tiring nor boring. There was something to see each passing mile. Arrival at Pennsylvania Station in New York City was an experience of a lifetime. The steam locomotive was replaced by an electric one because of early environmental concern of smoke from steam engines. Passengers from the two trains merged and for one block it would have been almost impossible to have walked in a different direction due to the spectacle of people going toward the grand turnstyle gates. The Pennsylvania Station which covered twenty-eight acres was patterned after the Caracalla Baths in Rome. The inside of the building had cathedral ceilings almost a hundred feet over the marble floors. Grand pillars supported overhead arches. A taxi ride from the Pennsylvania to Grand Central Station was another new experience for the dauntless traveler. At Grand Central, souvenir shops outnumbered everything except newspaper stands.

Upon arrival at Fort Monmouth, Kermit was assigned to Company L, 802nd Signal Training Battalion. Orders of the day included "You will remove all unit and branch insignia, including shoulder patches. All rank designation will be removed. You will no longer respond to or address each other by rank. From now on, you will be known only as MISTER." So, the officer candidate was now to be just plain Mister Parker! At first, when his name was called, Kermit would look around to see who Mr. Parker was.

The OCS (Officer Candidate School) was a screening process to evaluate individual capabilities to perform officer's duties. West Point Officers taught a student to become a gentleman Officer and required four years of intensive study. OCS was deliberately designed as a provoking, intimidating, maddening and miserable set of conditions as possible. The objective was to find out if an individual would come unglued. An entire day might be spent by the students trying to outsmart a Tact Officer who used "gigs" to harass students. A "gig" was any infraction of rules, real or imaginary, that the Tact Officer might impose upon your bed, shoes, or demeanor. The belief was if you collected ten gigs your school days were over. Kermit collected more than ten gigs, so he disproved the conception. The graduates were handed Commissions instead of diplomas. Within a couple of hours, there was no such thing as Company L, 802nd Signal Training Battalion. A nice gesture on part of the Army was to enclose travel orders for the newly Commissioned Officers. Kermit was directed to an Aircraft Control and Warning Training Battalion at Drew Field, Tampa, Florida. He had ten days to get there.

After five days and nights taking in New York City delights, the newly commissioned Officer and his wife headed by train to Drew Field. It turned out to be a large tent city. Kermit was assigned to a training battalion composed entirely of Second Lieutenants. The group attended classes on the new science called Radar. Company Commander Lieutenant Colonel George Kilpatrick reviewed Kermit's past experience and appointed him Communication Officer to the newly activated 684th Signal Aircraft and Warning Company. His first duty was to train all communication personnel in their individual skills which was a monumental task considering he did not even know what his own were.

Kermit stood on the street corner at six o'clock in the morning during January and February trying to keep his teeth from rattling while experiencing 40 degree temperature. He had to catch a bus, whether he wanted to or not, as it was the only vehicle allowed to enter the base. Within a few hours, the thermometer would rise to 80 degrees and everyone would start shedding clothes. By noon, people were hunting for shade! Buses were the only vehicles allowed on the base. After the war, facts became known. The Colonel, in command of the base, leased the land to the government and owned the bus line! He had a racket going and got away with it during the war.

Alerted for overseas assignment, a train backed onto the base and sat there. It consisted of five chair cars and a baggage car. The baggage car also became a kitchen on wheels. After, the curious men were packed on the train, it would move for an hour and then go onto a siding and sit for fifteen minutes. Sometimes, something would interrupt it for a few hours. The chair cars had no toilets so the men soon learned some of those pauses were rest stops. Kermit said, "It was a good thing this trip was before woman's lib!" The battalion arrived at temporary quarters near New Orleans Port of Embarkation. Where it was exactly located, no one in the group seemed to know. Their train was tucked onto a siding, much like the one in Tampa. The group was near one end of Huey Long Bridge. Taking advantage of visiting the historical atmosphere found in New Orleans was right up Kermit's alley. Walking the French Quarters, seeing picturesque cast iron balcony railings, strolling up and down Canal Street was enjoyable.

After a stay of several days, they were on the train again with stopping, standing, backing and going forward in jolts and jump starts that kept even the most intrepid sleeper awake. Doors were finally unlatched and the group fell into company formation. No talking. No smoking. No flashlights were allowed. A little after 4 a.m. in a very dark residential area on unpaved streets the group hiked for about an hour to a long warehouse. Men laid down on long rows of army cots set up in an extra large room at the remote location. Most of the men hadn't bothered to remove their clothes, so a couple of hours later when chow was called, they found the latreen and were ready for whatever was on the menu.

The group found the old warehouse they were in had mesh fencing, like one would experience in a jail. They were at a ship loading dock on the Mississippi River called Chalmette Slip. This place was less than twenty miles from where they started! From all the time and messing around they had done to get there, they could have gone to Chicago and back! The name of the ship, tied up on the dock unloading bananas, was Algonquian owned by United Fruit Company. The men parked at this location for over two weeks. Helen and Kermit missed seeing each other by two hours as the men were finally loaded on the ship and headed towards South America. Helen arriving from Florida obtained a job and stayed in New Orleans until Kermit came back to the United States.

Officers were housed in the only stateroom of the Algonquian. Twelve men occupied the room with space at a premium. In places packed like this with Army men, Kermit always said, "I kept my lifejacket handy in case we were going to drown in each others sweat!" By next morning the clanging ship's bell caused by rolling of the sea announced to the men that they were no longer in the calm waters of the Mississippi River. Always the curious traveler, Kermit was awed by the experience of seeing one thing in every direction, water. He told himself, "After all, three quarters of the earth's surface was water. If it had to be put somewhere, the ocean was good as anyplace to keep it." The men were informed they were going to the Island of Trinidad. Before the Andrews Sisters sang the hit song *Rum and Coca Cola* very few ever heard of it. However, before they would reach this British Colony located off the north coast of Venezuela to establish radar stations as defense for the Panama Canal, they would be going to the American Naval Base at Guantanamo Bay, Cuba. The voyage taken by the ship was close enough to the Coast of Florida that men could see Key West. That seemed somewhat out of the way to get to the southeast Coast of Cuba but "so far the entire adventure did not add up to anything resembling logic," according to Kermit.

Soon, men learned what the stalling freight trains and waiting at Chalmette Slip was all about. A pack of German Submarines were operating in the Gulf of Mexico sinking merchant ships. Their spies were getting information regarding sailing dates, routes and destinations of American ships. The Algonquian waited while a submarine net was cleared from Guantanamo Harbor. A dozen Great White Sharks kept the company on the boat entertained during more delays. Sharks were after garbage dumped from the fantail of the ship by the kitchen crew.

The group was navigated across the balmy Caribbean Sea on the fourth day. All was calm and the water was as blue as the sky above. Phosphorous in the sea water glowed. Flying fish, birds, and dolphins played in the waves. No submarines were sighted by the "watch" assigned to scan the sea. Upon arrival, the ship entered a narrow passageway called "the Dragons Mouth." Lush green foliage was everywhere. The only break in lines of palm trees were docks for loading and unloading ships. Two ships tied up at the shore were smoldering, the result of being torpedoed.

You guessed it! The transportation provided for the rest of the journey to the base was by narrow gauge steam locomotive with five passenger coaches. The Army base was half way across the island. Being train buff that he was, Kermit was delighted to be introduced to a new country by railway. Everything was done in this island as English tradition, including afternoon tea before departure on the little train. The new encampment was reached with pauses at many gates through dense tropical foliage. It was called Waller Field. The American Air Base had operational runways and one C-47 aircraft used for administration purposes. The radar equipment to be installed on the forested hilltops had not yet arrived.

Wildlife was everywhere. A book, *Snake Hunters Holiday* by Ditmar and Bridges, came into possession for reference and caution. Snakes were Trinidad's speciality. There were dozens. Most of them were poisonous. The largest captured was an eighteen feet long Anacondas, weighing in at one hundred thirty eight pounds. The Bushmaster was largest poisonous and Fer-de-lance was a tree climbing rattlesnake. The tiny, beautiful but deadly Coral snake made its home in the jungle as well. Bats came in thirty two varieties. There were flying foxes with a five foot wing spread, toads were ten inches wide, centipedes a foot long, cockroaches as large as humming birds and grasshoppers measured many inches in length. Oysters grew on trees and there were bird eating spiders. On the beautiful Caribbean Sea there were sharks. On the Atlantic side of the island, jelly fish tangled up with and stung swimmers. On the beach the poisonous Manzinetta tree grew in great numbers. Within a few minutes of getting its juice on the skin blisters would appear. Kermit could tell right away that he was not going to be bored in such an interesting place. He wanted to explore, study and just plain sight see...

Opening crates labled "central office equipment" reminded Kermit of his tests in Chicago. The equipment had been used. It was a jumblement of articles akin to a pile of junk. Cables were cut close to terminals. Telephone head sets with cords wrapped around them were stuffed in boxes with lids nailed on. Nowhere in this pile of mainframes, relays, rolls of cable, hand sets, jacks, plugs and panels was there any trace of plans or diagrams. Colonel Kilpatrick was filled with anger that the United States Army would ship such a pile of junk for such a vital defense operation. "What do you think we should do with this pile of scrap?" he asked Kermit. "We are going to construct a fine operating Information Center out of it, Sir." Kermit replied. So as Kermit stated "the department set to work to make silk purses out of that pile of sows ears." First, searching every man's records, one man was found that had been a telephone installer repairman before the war. The rest of the crew had to be trained from information received and remembered from Automatic Electric Company training Kermit had received two and one-half years previously.

The whole Information Center System was approached from classes in basic electricity to designing the entire control system. Before long, the first operational information system manned entirely by the American Army was scanning the surface of the ocean for enemy submarines. When a submarine was discerned, the Aircraft Controller would dispatch a heavy bomber to deal with the submarine. The string of radar stations placed on hillocks were throughout the Lesser Antilles. There were three stations on Trinidad and one on each of the Islands of Tobago, Grenada, St. Vincent, Barbados and Martinique. All reported to the Information Center on Trinidad. Plots were moved on a map while men in stocking feet walked around on top of the table wearing a head set while carrying a stick six feet long to move colored discs. The movable discs indicated such things as aircraft, friendly ships or enemy movement in the waters. A Radar Operator was tied directly to one of eight plotters on the board at all times.

Besides going on a crazy trip into one of the densest rain forests of South America with six men, something akin to the dangers of a Tarzan movie and dropping into a forty foot cave, Lieutenant Parker chronicles all sorts of ideas tried by the Army to discourage Germans from intruding into the American hemisphere.

Before Thanksgiving of 1943 the same little train that took the men to the base took them back to the beach. The same little boat, the Algonquin took them through the Bermuda Triangle heading home. With a big storm at sea, the little boat of men pitched forward and blowed onward! After the storm, Kermit saw another sight he could hardly believe. The ship's rigging was covered with ice. By noon, the motley crew sailed into New York Harbor. Ice remained on the ship due to five degree below zero weather in the harbor. The little boat had just weathered a hundred mile an hour storm off the coast of Cape Hatteras. All agreed "it was a fine trip just to be home!"

As Commanding Officer of Group C3-13, which consisted of nine enlisted men and Kermit, they were shuttled to Fort Lewis, Washington. After a telephone call to Helen, the two met in Chicago between trains. Helen went along on the train ride with the troops. The army issued ten vouchers for meal tickets at 75 cents per meal to each man. Meals were $1.00 in the dining car. Helen didn't have a voucher. But the dining room steward told Kermit to bring her along for each meal as he wasn't good at counting.

After several weeks at Fort Lewis, the next stop was Santa Monica, California. At the Beach Front Hotel there were two indoor swimming pools. Free tickets were made available to almost any show in town. Movie studios, live radio broadcasts and gobs of movies were attended. A nightly show at the hotel included many of Hollywood's golden era stars.

Next assignment, read Tampa, Florida. With a heavy heart, Kermit was back on another train to Chicago. This was a Santa Fe Chief. Why back to Chicago? Because in 1943 all trains went to Chicago! "A pig could change trains somewhere else in the United States, a human could not," according to the intrepid traveler. It took over a week to make it back to Tampa. The group was not glad to be there. Kermit became a trainer instead of a trainee. In the Inspector General's Department and assigned as Communication Inspector for the training center, he seriously inspected the handling of equipment and submitted long detailed reports. Woops! he goofed! He was assigned to the first unit activated for overseas duty. That did not hurt Kermit's feelings one bit! From Fort Lawton, Seattle he was soon in sight of Diamond Head near the city of Honolulu. After loading in a tent city at Hickamfield, the men saw much of the damage from the recent Pearl Harbor bombing. For four months, Bellows Field was home. In the middle of July, the 598th Signal Aircraft Warning Battalion was loaded aboard a specially built ship called a Landing Ship Vehicle. This ship was called the USS Catskill (LSV-1). The mission was to make an assault landing on the Island of Yap. The island was off the southern most tip of the Mariana Islands about six hundred miles south of the Island of Guam.

Spending hours studying the map of the island, men learned where the coral reefs were, what beaches were purportedly mined and how deep water was at high and low tides. They were warned "to be as careful as possible" regarding activity on this premise "as the large stone monoliths were historic like the huge statues found on Easter Island in the South Pacific."

For days and weeks on end, the LSV plowed along with several hundred other ships without seeing anything except the same ships in the same locations. Every few days an airplane would fly over and drop mail to the fleet but no one Kermit knew ever got any. It must have been all official business. For forty-nine days they milled around in the Pacific, only to break the monotony with an occasional fly-by from a fighter dragging a sleeve. Then, the gunners could get in a little target practice. They endured the ridiculous Navy custom (Kermit's words) of the initiation ceremony "making them shellbacks out of pollywogs when crossing the equator." Men's hair was whacked in gruesome patterns and they endured extreme displeasure of crawling through tubs filled with garbage from the mess hall.

The mission of Yap was changed to another place on the way to Austrailia. The group steamed into Leyte Gulf in the Philippines with a fleet so vast one could not have believed a Jap in the world could stop it. Everything was so quiet as to be almost frightening. The smallest sized boats were LSTs and there were hundreds! Kermit's boat was due east of Catman Hill. Suddenly bright flashes roared as large caliber navel guns fired on various targets along the shore. Hundreds of guns blended into a continous roar! Where the town of Dulag had been was just columns of smoke and dust so dense that everything was obscured. After each broadside, Kermit would feel his teeth to see if they were all there. After the naval bombardment with continous explosions from thousands of guns, the air quieted and an airplane dipped toward the earth and released a stream of white fog that settled over the beach. The shore became covered with a heavy smoke screen. Hundreds of assault boats left streaks of white foam behind them as they raced for assigned beachheads.. With use of his binoculars, Kermit could see soldiers pouring out of LCVPs (Landing Craft Vehicle and Personnel) and LCMs (Landing Craft Material). Amtracks (Amphibious tanks) churned the water to a foam around their mother ships. "Ducks, Buffalo and Alligator Amphibious vehicles were seen disappearing into debris and into cocoanut groves. For the rest of the day, little boats continued to stream from transports to shore, then return for more cargo. Big LSTs (Landing Ship Tanks) were dropping large ramps into the sand of the beach to unload tanks, armored cars, and half-tracks. Mountains of ammunition and supplies poured forth.

During a small attack on the USS Honolulu by a Jap Fighter, the fleet put out a smoke screen. Dense white smoke poured from every ship in the harbor and from hundreds of smoke pots carried by landing craft. From smoke stacks of battleships, cruisers, and destroyers came great rolling billows of black oily looking smoke. By the time the novices of battle recovered from the excitement of their first air attack, the smoke was so dense the men on the ship had to feel their way around deck. It was better to just retire to the bunks, below.

On the second day, orders were received to leave the ship. Wounded men had been arriving to take the place of ones being disembarked. The ship was scheduled to be unloaded by midnight as the Japanese Battle Fleet was seen coming in from the North. The Marine Battalion of Artillery were the first to leave the ship. Trying Blue Beach, Kermit's boat was sent elsewhere as Japanese soldiers occupied the island straight in front of them. The same news was received further down the beach. The little boat the men were in sprung a leak. Not exactly like an army training, the motley group were brought to the beach by a tiny light waving back and forth. No one was in the right place. The Colonel came over where some of the group were playing mole and stated, "we're either in the wrong place or the guide has the wrong group."

Thirty men did not know where they were or had the slightest idea of where to go. The guide from K Company of the 102nd Infantry was a couple of miles away. Someone suggested,"Let's go inland and dig in for the night." Thinking it was a good idea, the Colonel suggested a 'looksee' first. Two officers with Kermit stumbled into a tank trap. These traps were constructed by tying three cocoanut tree trunks together and burying them in ground with about four feet above and ten feet below ground. The men made way around the barriers. Bodies lay all over the ground. One of the companions leaned over and said, "are all of these guys dead?" Just then, one of the bodies raised his head and said, "Hell no!, but if you two stay there jabbering, we'll have a couple." Dropping down, the scout asked if anyone knew what was out in front of them. "Sure, Japs, lots and lots of them. Don't try to go over to 'em because the area between here and there is full of GIs. You wouldn't get ten yards before you'd either get shot or you'd break your neck by falling in foxholes."

Taking the informant at his word, the two men went back to their own group behind the tanks. The decision was unanimous, "Let us stay the night, here." Scooping out a shallow hole in the sand was all one could do for a foxhole as there was an oversupply of water in the sand. Kermit rolled up in his "poncho" (a South American cloak like a blanket with a hole in the middle for the head) and was sound asleep in no time. Sharp cracks of mortar shells nor chatter of small arms fire disturbed him in the least. At four o'clock in the morning a landing craft nosed up on the beach and had to be unloaded. 155 millimeter projectiles were handed from man to man like a bucket brigade. The man nearest the boat was in water to his waist.

After that a searchlight came on with a beam lighting the beach up as bright as day. Rows and rows of LSTs with bows opened were disgorging loads of equipment, food, ammunition and vehicles. Before that night was over, Kermit equated it as "the longest in recorded history." When daylight arrived, the bay that had been full of ships the night before was almost empty, except for a few LSTs still unloading. There were a few freighters away out in the harbor. The vast armada of American ships had gone to sea like phantoms of the night. They were out of harms way from the Japanese Fleet steaming towards the Philippines at full speed. Future looked doubtful. The men watched their first Kamikaze attack made by three aircraft in the direction of the Island of Samar. Kamikazes continued their death dives through antiaircraft fire. The lead Kamikaze was successful in going through an open hatch amid ship on one of the freighters. A huge fire ball cleared to display the ship was listing very heavily to one side. It took only ten minutes for the last hull of the ship to disappear below surface of the water. Small craft sped to the rescue.

Searching for the other three companies of the group's battalion was necessary. The group astray had no idea where their equipment was. They had not been trained to go into combat with an enemy. They had been sent to establish radar stations to warn of approaching enemy aircraft. About all the men could do was stay out of the way of the fighting battalions. With antiaircraft guns firing, what seemed straight up, Kermit knew a rain of steel had to come back down in a free falling reaction. A large track laying machine with armored sides was standing on the wet sand. It made ideal shelter. Five men plus Kermit crowded under. Once flat on their backs, they could hear the motor idling. "I sure hope the driver doesn't decide to drive away," Kermit said to the soldier next to him. "Don't worry, he won't," came a comment from one of the other men. "How do you know?" Kermit asked. "Because, I'm the driver," he replied. Everybody got a chuckle out of that remark. Soon the GIs were all engrossed in friendly conversation.

Finding some evacuated Japanese pillboxes, the men rested and watched while mass graves were being dug by a large bulldozer. Civilian and enemy soldier's bodies were released into trenches. Individual graves were prepared for the American dead. As American bodies were brought to the site, dog tags were removed and enclosed with a document showing the time and place of death with other pertinent information. The second dog tag was tied to the victims right big toe and the body was wrapped in a GI blanket. There were two Chaplains in attendance, one Catholic, one Protestant. The position and number of each grave was recorded, then the bulldozer covered them up. The entire operation was a duty of the Graves Registration Unit. It was an absolute necessity, due to tropical sun decompositon and the matter of health, to get the bodies taken care of as quickly as possible. After the American graves were covered, a sniper hit one of the clergymen with a bullet. It was pointed out the civilian and enemy dead did not have identification, so processing time was quicker and in mass graves.

The Colonel had been unable to contact the headquarters of the 24th Infantry Division for instructions, so the group continued to stay where they were. Armament activity kept up day and night. Ammunition was stacked by cranes piling boxes upon boxes of explosives on top of each other. After a gourmet dinner of K rations, the men talked themselves into darkness. Suddenly a huge fireball exploded on the beach! The heaviest piece of equipment working in the ammunition dump was flying through the air as if it were a large tin can. One D-8 bulldozer was going skyward end over end. The concussion wave lifted Kermit from his observation position on the pill box and deposited him in a trench some twenty five feet away. The entire area was on fire from continous explosions as artillery shells and burning fuel drums were added to the holocaust on the beach. Having no sensation of fear, more of wonderment, it did cross Kermit's mind he had to go urinate every few minutes. The inferno burned and exploded all night. The area was a tangled mass of twisted steel, smouldering debris and human body parts. Still concerned as to the whereabouts of the other three companies of the Battalion, a search party was finally appointed to go straight through the devastated area. Being some of the first people to enter the ammunition debarkation area, what met the men's eyes could never be described nor believed! Finding none of their units they started along the beach, south of what had been the town of Dulag.

A mile or so down the beach the rest of the outfit was found along with most of the equipment of Company A. On the way, they dodged shell holes twenty feet in diameter. These craters were half full of water. Cobra snakes floated in almost every one. After setting up a rudimentary communication center, the men dreamed up an old fashioned infallible alarm system. It was a cord strung about twenty feet from the tent walls to which was tied empty tin cans every few feet along the cord. After that, the men lay down their weary bodies on their bunks that felt so good they utterly forgot these beds were good old Army cots. Awakened by the rattling of cans and loud snickering, the soldiers found two small girls laughing and two huge water buffalo prowling around. Each buffalo looked to be about a ton of blubber each. Having invaded the perimeter of the secured area, both buffalo and children were very friendly. The little girls became camp mascots and the buffalo took up residence in a nearby stream spending most of the day submerged with only their heads above water.

Looking at maps, it appeared there was a good radar site eastward. That would be toward the center of the Island of Leyte, near the town of Baybay. The only road on the out of date maps showed a single track wagon trail winding over a few hills. The men thought it was strange that they met no one. Later, they found that everyone in the forest was trained to disappear when they heard a strange sound. A little village was found deserted. No one was in sight to talk to. Over the mountain, a beach stretched out to the west on Mindanao Sea. The Island of Camoles was the only land visible. A large boat was beached near a village. It had a large hole completely through it. Suddenly, a voice from an unnoticed old man asked, "Are you Americans?"

Declaring the affirmitive, a new response was, "Thank God, thank God." He threw his arms around the Americans. The damaged vessel was a Japanese supply boat. Local gorilla bands had just received weapons from an American Submarine and among the guns were rocket launchers known as bazookas. With no training or experience, the locals by reading instructions used them to eliminate the Japanese supply boat. The only trouble with their adventure was the antitank weapon needed something solid to hit in order to detonate its charge. After the natives had waited a whole day to take careful aim, the rocket passed completely through the wooden boat. The bazooka crew escaped while Japanese occupants abandoned the boat.

As the communication scouts moved south, people stood along both sides of the road waving and calling "Mabohi,"which was the warmest greeting in Tagalog. They also exclaimed, "Hi, Joe" in English. Americans were offered "tuba" a powerful two hundred proof alcoholic drink by tribal chieftains. The drink was made from blossoms of the cocoanut tree. The liquor was declined. It was against Army regulations to eat or drink anything not G.I. Arriving at Baybay, the group was met by an impressive delegation. The disappearing natives had received information about the travelers and were now out in full force. The information was sent by Philippino telegraph executed by large conk shells heard for great distances while a skilled operator blew into the shell. The group was treated to a two room hotel with a bell girl to wait upon them. The natives also made ready a celebration held in their honor. They were treated to native dances including a lively bamboo pole dance which required perfect synchronization or a dancers foot could be injured. Music was by guitar, trumpet and several local percussion instruments.

A long search for a radio crystal for one of the radar stations was the next event. Kermit took a Jeep with driver to a designated airstrip to receive the crystal. On the trip to the airfield, a Jap fighter was coming down the road with machine guns blazing. Kermit's truck headed for a ditch. His head crashed through a windshield and as a result, blood ran down his face from a smashed nose. The plane had not arrived at the airstrip. It did not make an appearance before dark. So Kermit occupied the bunk of the Pilot who had gone after the crystal. Later the tent gave a violent jerk and crashed down winding mosquito netting around Kermit like a spider's net preparing a victim for storage. He could not figure out how to free himself in the dark. The tent had collapsed due to a high altitude bomber attack. Next morning's light showed a crater fifty feet across which was already full of water.

Even the Navy asked for help from the busy Communication Officer. After a harrowing plane ride on his next adventure, the Air Corp sent a sea rescue boat to take Kermit across the gulf to the Island of Samar. He sensed the boat was akin to the sensation of flying. A second trip by a real plane ended up on a side trip to a sand bar. That plane had water in the fuel line. After that problem was corrected the Pilot resumed their flight to the final destination. Arriving back at the airstrip, while climbing out of the plane, a person yelled, "look out." A P-47 Thunderbolt fighter was skidding down the runway on its belly directly for Kermit. Landing face down, the Signalman in harm's way sensed the tip of the fighter's wing as it swished over him.

Back at headquarters there was quiet, until Japanese passed overhead stringing Paratroopers out an open door as they went over. The altitude was too low for the parachute to open before the Soldiers hit the ground. So few survived. The Americans saw no living Japanese Paratroopers after the raid. Two

Japanese assaults had happened that day. It was surmised that someone in the Japanese High Command of the Japanese troops mixed up the timing of the Japanese assaults on the Americans. Part of their activity was at 6:30 a.m and part at 6:30 p.m. Kermit felt if they had been coordinated correctly the Americans would have been in big trouble! During the 6:30 p.m. raid, the Colonel put in an appearance and asked Kermit, "Can I share your shelter?" "Sure," he replied, "Yours full of water?" "No, nothing like that. There is a Cobra in it," he replied. Kermit had company for the duration of the raid.

After a Christmas dinner of turkey from a can, the weather continually rained. It was the monsoon season. Thirty-two inches of rain fell in a twenty-four hour period. Trucks were in quagmires. Cocoanut log roads were made to get in and out of an area. This really brought the war to a halt. Major Wilson and Kermit were sent to the Island of Saipan to observe the latest radar equipment known as microwave radar. Long, wide, hard, smooth runways had been developed from coral. The B-29s took off with heavy bomb loads, returning empty after visits to Japanese islands on a twenty-four hour basis.

From that time, the unit was ordered aboard a ship for landing on Okinawa. Then, jubilation! The ship for Okinawa was canceled and the order came to go to Hawaii! On Hawaii an inner island telephone system was undergoing a major upgrade. One of Automatic Electric Company's civilian employees now headed this operation. He asked Kermit. "Will you help in engineering studies necessary for the actual modifications to be accomplished?" After temporary duty, the Base Signal Officer asked for Kermit to transfer to the local unit. That was accomplished and Kermit was promoted to Captain. He now outranked the Lieutenant of the company. By army regulations, the Company Commander is the highest ranking Officer. Kermit had to transfer to another unit. Due to his promotion, he now became surplus baggage to the Pacific Ocean Area Command. He was assigned Base Commander to a small air base on the far northern tip of Oahu near Kahuku.

Before he had time to take up new duties, news of the atomic bomb drop came over the radio. Everything was in suspended animation until the surrender of Japan was announced. Then, like someone cut a string holding up suspenders, everything became unglued.

Kermit paints the picture of downtown Honolulu as a celebration of sudden release of pent up human emotions. The war, that had started on that very island was equaled by combined energy of happy souls totalling something like an erupting volcano. The sound level was an ear deafening roar along with automobile horns, people screaming and yelling. All manner of pots, pans and steel drums were beaten by hammers, sticks of wood and even stones. Everybody was dancing with each other, by themselves and many with imaginary partners. Humanity in the mass was tearing up newspapers, magazines, anything of paper and covering the streets in shredded debris.

The one big bottleneck to going home, stateside, was transportation. There were several million people scattered throughout the Pacific. Points were used for lists. Kermit only had ninety points. Eventually, he received orders for the fifteen hour flight back to the Bay Area and a thirty day leave. His orders made the following changes over a period of time. To Fairfield-Suisun Air Base to Fort Lewis, Washington to Santa Anna, California to Hamilton Field, California to March Field at Riverside, California, to the Atomic bomb test in the Pacific (cancelled), to Greenville Army Air Base, South Carolina to Bergstrom Field, Austin, Texas to Mitchell Field, Long Island, New York to Hamilton Field, California. The last order allowed the married couple to settle in for five years. While assigned to the Fourth Air Force he watched test flights of both new propeller driven and jet model planes at Mojave Test Center, later renamed Edwards Air Force Base. "Don't let anyone tell you that it's not true, that you can join the Army and see the world!" stated Kermit.

While at Hamilton Field the couple lived in El Verano near Sonoma with their son, Keith, who had been born in Texas in 1948. They enjoyed the Valley of the Moon known in Jack London's books. The second year of the couple's stay, the family was increased by one little girl. Linda Louise Parker was her name. Her father, who could not spell very well, put Louse on her birth notices. She forgave him in later years and they have always been on loving terms!

Among duties of peacetime, Kermit was appointed First Command Director of the Air Force Mars Program, (Military Amateur Radio System). He applied himself and passed tests for an Amateur Radio License. In 1948, the Army Air Force decided they should become a separate branch of the service and persuaded Congress to go along with the idea. Many of the names of fields changed. Fairfield-Suisun became Travis Air Force Base. Mojave Test Center, Edwards Air Force Base and Moses Lake became Larson Air Force Base in California. The Army Air Force became the United States Air Force.

Kermit had a choice of staying with the Army or going Air Force. He stayed with the Army. However, the Air Force needed communication people so a new class was created, "Special Category Army Remaining with Air Force" (SCARWAF). The very busy Army man was sent to install radar stations along the United States and Canadian border. Operation FENCE extended from Oregon, north Washington Coast across Washington, Montana and North Dakota. The work stations were isolated places, off the beaten path. The project mission was installing radar equipment along the Canadian Border to warn of any Soviet aircraft attack over the North Pole. It was a high priority project. During assignment with the heavy construction company, Kermit was promoted to Major from a former project. The promotion put him in the same situation as the one in Hawaii. This time he did not outrank the Company Commander but had the same place on the table of organization. There were now two Majors in the company. So guess what? Kermit was ordered to Korea. He served his year in that war. Kermit retired as Lieutenant Colonel of the United States Army at the tender age of 38. He moved the family back to the beautiful Valley of the Moon on a two acre ranch.

Kermit was one of the first 16 employees of the Optical Coating Laboratories, Inc. of Santa Rosa, California which now employs over a thousand people. But he is known on television as the man dressed up like a railroad engineer and he speaks about "the over-sophisticated and the under-sophisticated are the people who appreciate Train Town the most." In his striped engineer overalls and red bandana he is well known to countless families that visit Sonoma's second most popular tourist attraction. Wineries are the first attraction.

When he noticed bulldozers rearranging a cow pasture on the outskirts of Sonoma, he paused to find out what was up. It was owner Stanley Frank and he stated he was building a model railroad. Kermit shook his hand and said, "Congratulations, you've just met your best friend."

Kermit has been vital in the continuing success of Train Town which features a mile of track on ten acres, three tunnels, two bridges, a lilliputian village and a petting farm. He's helped lay track, build the bridges and plan the town of Lakeview. One of the miniature structures in the park bears his name: "The Parker Palace Hotel."

In 1980, his first wife Helen died of cancer. In December 1981 Kermit married Janet Wilcox, a long time neighbor and mother-in-law to Kermit's daughter who had married Janet's son. Janet brought three sons into the Parker family, namely David, Donald and John Wilcox. Her spouse died in 1967. Since the couple's two children married in 1970 and one of Kermit's half-brothers had long ago married one of his half-sisters, the branches of the Parker family tree were tangled ever more confusedly. Speaking of family, Kermit also visited his mother, Mauda from time to time in Washington State until her death.

Kermit's homestead is crammed with evidence of the couple's many diverse interests. These paraphenalia include books, motors, antennae, video screens, wood burning stove, computer keyboards and a radio room with map of the world and framed photographs of Train Town not excepting a few Kermit the Frog dolls. Kermit Roosevelt Parker recently took a class on how to write an autobiography. The basis of this narrative came from over 125 pages of his memories and the *Autobiography of His Childhood* encompassing another 98 pages. Kermit still has the crinkly manila sheets on which he kept a handwritten journal about the first day of the invasion, October 20th, 1944 of the Philippines. It begins, "This is a very special morning in my life and in the history of the world." He was there when MacArthur fullfilled his promise, "I shall return."

Parker, Kermit Roosevelt, *Kermit's Story, (His Childhood)*,pages 98, Zeroxed 1991.

Parker, Kermit Roosevelt, *Kermit's Story, Adulthood.* Miscellaneous pages 125.

Wheeler, Dennis, The Press Democrat, Section Profiles, *Whether in trains or planes, Parker's always on the go;* November 12, 1989, pages D and D2.

Cecil S. Atwood

United States Army Air Force 1940 - 1964

Born to a family working the orchard and lumber business in the State of Maine, present day retired Lieutenant Colonel Atwood with a smile stated, "I was replacement for the United States Army's first reject of the draft." Entering the Army in the state of Maine, Cecil was soon a part of the military establishment of World War II. First, he was sent to Camp Lee, Virginia to the cook and bakers school. He attended Officers Candidate School and was commissioned a Second Lieutenant in September of 1942. Cecil graduated as an Ordnance Officer rather than a chef for Quartermaster.

The Army Air Corps needed Ordnance Officers at that time and Lieutenant Atwood was assigned to an Ordnance Maintenance Squadron attached to the 15th Air Depot Group at Kelly Field (as it was referred to then) located in San Antonio, Texas. He was responsible for maintenance and repair of all vehicles and equipment used in the Air Depot Group. Particularly, the young recruit worked to become a specialist in the fine tuning of engines for such vehicles as trucks, Jeeps and other vehicular devices used for carrying persons or objects. Special work included the art of fine tuning gears.

After several months, the 15th Air Depot Group at Kelly Air Force Base and the Ordnance Maintenance Squadron completed training. They were ordered to get their equipment packed for a trip overseas. The men were not told that they were in for a long ride! They boarded a train traveling through the Midwestern states into Canada, and then in an easterly direction to New Hampshire south to Camp Shanks, New York. The Air Depot Group boarded what was a Luxury Liner of Uruguay that was in a United States port when war was declared. It had been impounded and it became a converted troop ship called the SS Uruguay. The ship was one of thirty on a convoy. The squadron was not informed of their destination until they were several days at sea. They became a bit knowledgeable that they were headed toward the Pacific region as they waited for the thirty ships, one by one, and one after the other, to pass through the locks of the Panama Canal. Finally, to their surprise they found Australia would be their destination. The group landed at Brisbane, Australia where they boarded a narrow gauge railroad for Townsville near Queensland. The 15th Depot Group then combined with three air depot groups for the job of maintenance of airplanes.

Maintenance was super-important since war in the Pacific Theatre was not only dependent upon men, but upon airplanes, submarines and ships. It was imperative to see that vehicles and equipment were ready for operation at all times. The ordnance groups worked in garages and tents. In the Philippines, the group even worked in a church. During the Battle of the Coral Sea, the squadron had to be on alert seven days a week. Many days were twelve hour ones. The Ordnance Squadron was not subject to the harassment of being in the general area of bombings. They did maintain the guns and ammunition scheduled for large battles.

After being in Australia for about one and a half years, Cecil took a short leave into Sydney. There he met a blue eyed blond on a blind date. She was the first woman to enlist in the (WAAF) Women in Austrailian Air Force. Cecil's buddy who had a date with another girl from the Air Force station arranged a foursome. The blue eyed blond Rita, nicknamed 'Mickie' was stationed with the WAAF Squadron in Townsville. Their group had taken over the Convent. Women were all assigned to that building. Needless to say, it was a very popular place with American servicemen. Rita and Cecil found out that they both had entered the military on the same day, April 1, 1940 (April Fools Day!). It was not long before the couple decided to get married. Rita was of Catholic faith and Cecil was not. That meant the marriage had to take place in a sacristy which was a room for the sacred vessels and vestments in the Catholic Church. Mickie's mother joined the wedding party in the old brick church. The couple was married thirty-five years and had four children, Sandra, Nadine, Carey, and Kevin.

In years since that time, Cecil went back to see the old sacristy and found it had become a dirty old storage shed. When the couple was directed to use the room for their wedding, people looked upon mixed-faith marriages with a jaundiced eye. To begin with, Cecil had to get permission for marrying an Australian from an American First General Officer. He was a bird Colonel. (A bird Colonel is an Air Force Colonel.) Then, the young man had to deal with a Brigadier General. The couple were given individual background checks and character investigations. It was suggested that American service personnel were not prone to telling the truth. Both sides of this anticipated union were traced as to their family. The pretty blond Australian had to endure her Commanding Officer's intense interrogation as to her morality and integrity. To some extent, the whole system of tedium checking was to discourage marriages. Foreign countries were interested in the possibility that G.I.s would leave pregnant girls behind them when they traveled back to America. Occupied country's leaders did not want the expense of supporting women left with children when G.I. fathers blithely headed back to the United States.

As the war moved, so did the men who maintained the equipment. The 15th Air Depot Group transferred to Tacloban, Leyte. The Air Force had just completed an important landing strip. Most of the surveying of the area had been by plane. The spot picked from the sky for the Air Depot was a grassy place. It turned out to be a rice paddy! A lot of the buildings had to be built on stilts to keep out water from the paddy. Logs were hued for roads. Canvas materials were thrown over equipment for rust retention and general protection. Cecil remembers lots of canned spam and cold black coffee at this location. He does not like either, to this day.

The Leyte region turned out to be one of the major American Naval victories during the war. To live in that area of the earth at that time was very dangerous. Americans were trying to neutralize enemy air power. The largest amphibious assault yet encountered in the Pacific was when four Army divisions went ashore at Leyte Gulf. They endured slow and difficult progress. Supplies were unloaded on 21 October 1944 for a Naval-Air battle for Leyte. It took until late December that year to secure parts of Leyte necessary for the air bases. Japanese sorties dropped bombs as they were fighting to hold the air and ground space. There were really bad nights of strafing. Double guards were posted around the very large ordnance base.

The men took Atabrine (quinacrine) for malaria. You could get schistomiasis which invaded the intestines and bladder by drinking unclean water or swimming in the rivers. Taking the polluted water into the mouth or nose while swimming was one way to invite disaster. Larve could enter the skin causing blood flukes in the bowels of the human. The parasite came from fresh water snails who in the cycle of the ecosystem took in the eggs from human waste products. When the parasite rehatched, it then re-infected the water supply due to poor sanitation. When one became sick of that plague, they were never heard of again.

The men built a system of arrangement for the tents on the scheme of a pyramid, using twelve square feet per frame per man. The pyramid housing had screen doors and circulation devices. They were also sheltered under nets for sleeping. The men also built wooden floors inside the units which helped during the rainy seasons and kept the huge bugs to a minimum.

Cecil learned from the Red Cross that he had a daughter several months old and that she had jaundice. He applied and was assigned to the Far East Air Force. He was transferred to an evaluation team known as Air Evaluations Board. This group was formed to make a study of ordnance equipment and other materiel used during the war. Their mission statement was focused upon "a determination to find out the effectiveness of materiel used." Was there a way to improve the equipment? Should they accept the materiels as were presently used? Should the Army scuttle some of the materiel? The team was committed to a study of these questions. The team commuted back and forth from the Philippines to Sydney, Australia. Part of the committee's job was interviewing Air Force Squadron Commanders of all installations as to their needs, criticisms and recommendations for special equipment. Other areas visited were to Manila, many small islands in the Pacific and to Guadalcanal. These particular areas included fueling stations. The work of interviewing and compiling results lasted until the end of the war.

When VJ day was announced, having a child was a plus for points counted toward re-embarkation to the United States. Cecil gained twelve extra points toward being sent home just for having a daughter. Cecil was transferred to a ship bound for San Francisco, California and then boarded a train to New York for release from active duty. 'Mickie' came to the United States nine months later. War brides of G.I.s came over on the luxury liner USS Lurline. 1,000 war brides came over on the ship. Several women went to San Jose, California. Rita took a train to Maine. In six months, the Atwoods were heading back to San Jose to live. Their tour by car lasted for a month. Sandra, their daughter was a good traveler but her mother was discomforted, as she was again pregnant. The family journied over 10,000 miles. They stayed at fairly good auto courts (the forerunner of motels) usually stopping around 3 o'clock p.m. in the afternoon. Cecil joined an Air Reserve Squadron of about 60,000 people when the couple settled in San Jose.

As a member of the Air Corps Reserves, Cecil effected some thirty years of off-and-on-duty in the service of his country. He was active in Viet Nam, Korea and other related military actions. He retired after 24 years from this phase of service due to a mortal illness of his wife. He kept his hand into Air Force Academy Recruitment by making presentations to high school students. He described what the academy was like and how to get to Officer's schools by making application requests through United States Congressmen and Senators. He also did a bit of singing in church services in the Philippines and was known as a 'baritone or below' at the local Officers Club. Cecil became a sales manager for a title company working in their public relations department. Leaving the title company, he became an associate real estate salesman for a number of years. Adding a new layer to his Army education, Cecil took 14 units in the subject of real estate related courses for civilian life. He sold properties in the Lake Tahoe region of California.

It was at Lake Tahoe where he helped start a Retired Officers Association that he met Frances his present wife. They met in 1983 at a colorful Christmas party. Actually, Cecil's date to the party was his sister-in-law who was visiting from Australia. Cecil had been a widower for seven years. After being introduced to Frances and after the party was over, Cecil was asked by this lovely lady to attend an after-the-party-group for a brandy at her residence. Asking, "May I call again?" She said, "Yes." Frances, from Omaha, Nebraska had been a widow for over five years. Her husband had been a retired Colonel from the Infantry Tank Corps. She had three children, Harry 'Bud,' Marilyn and Andrew. Cecil and Frances seemed to be perfectly matched. They celebrated their tenth wedding anniversary on a cruise line. They have seven sons and daughters between them and twelve grandchildren.

The Atwoods moved to Sonoma because they were attracted by the golf courses. Since moving and purchasing a condominium on the East Side, Frances has had difficulty in breathing. She hasn't played a game of golf in two years. Cecil is an avid golfer. He is difficult to find standing still for such things as interviews! They both miss South Lake Tahoe. Frances had bought and built her home there in 1965.

As a member of the very active SIRs Club, Cecil believes in the dignity of retirement. That concept is an on-going theme expressed by the SIRs group. Members play cards, golf in Sonoma and at Oakmont, go to baseball games at Candlestick and cruise on steam ships from the Caribbean Sea to the Port of Acapulco. Otherwise, the Atwood family enjoys the large pool behind their condo or a short walk to many events held in Sonoma's Plaza.

Department of the Army, *American Military History, 1607-1953, ROTCM 145-20. Department of the Army ROTC Manual.*, Washington D.C., July 1956., pps. 510., p.437, 438.

Kenneth J. Moore

United States Army, 1942 - 1946

Airborne Division

Kenneth J. Moore, born in Los Angeles, California went to high school in Redding. Right after his eighteenth birthday, Ken had an ambition to be in the service. He was received into the reception center at San Francisco and then sent to the Presidio in Monterey.

Standing in line, during induction procedure, a soldier in front of him said, "an army man should ask to be in the Paratroopers. There is an extra jump in pay of $50.00 a month for jumping out of airplanes as a paratrooper!" Ken said, "Sounds good to me!"

The young men were asked preferences for the type of service they would like to volunteer for. There was a new branch of paratroopers being organized. Upon choosing that unknown quantity with enthusiasm, Ken was sent to Toccoa, Georgia. He went through eight weeks of the most violent basic training one could ever imagine. There was running. The forced marches were from two to twenty five miles. It was constant movement for eight long weeks. When the men were not keeping warm by moving, they were chilled to the bone from living in tarpaper barracks in the wintertime. There were many fellows sick with pnemonia. Little round stoves were just plain inadequate!

Cadre men, who were already qualified parachuters were violent, bullied the recruits and were generally unpleasant. Men were told the training was similar to Marine Division instruction. There were mock-up towers thirty feet high on which to practice jumping. The soldier climbed a ladder with a parachute strapped on his shoulders. The tower had a little shack on the top where a cable was attached that ran down to a sawdust pit. The wary soul was hooked up to the cable which was employed to hold a man while he trusted it, falling about 20 feet. The fall was completed by taking a finishing slide into the pit. It was a claustrophobic frightening experience.

On the first venture of jumping down the tower, the training instructor stated, "you must count 1,000, 2,000, 3,000 then pull the parachute cord." When Ken jumped out he yelled, "Jesus Christ!" He was scared stiff. The instructor said, "Jesus Christ won't help you! You better learn to count!" If the parachute did not open in the course of saying, one thousand, two thousand, three thousand, then you pulled the reserve chute.

There were no accidents until the men arrived at Fort Benning for actual parachute jumping. They had to learn to pack their own parachutes. They had a four week course with an additional three more weeks of physical conditioning. That was followed by one week of jumping from 250 foot towers with the parachute on. Ken guessed the $50.00 per week was worth it... Along with parachute practice men were required to execute full infantry training. This included close order drill, marching, maintenance, practice of weapons and classes on sanitation. There was no time at all to sit around and feel sorry for yourself!

Everything was done on a triangular based concept. There were groups of 20 persons in the one story barracks. There were three squadrons to a platoon and 12 men to a squad. There were three platoons to a company. There were three companies to a battalion, three battalions to a regiment, and three regiments to a divis˙ ˙ The division was the largest organization part of a corps that was then allied with an Army. Auxiliary units that made up their division included artillery, engineers, graves registration, military police, medics, signals, quartermaster, and ordnances. Ken believes the structure used then is now changed. However, the squad of 12 men was a basic unit when it came to initial training.

The premise of being a Paratrooper was one of being an Infantryman who accomplished work of the Army by airborne assault. A Paratrooper was a member of highly trained shock troops to seize an objective behind enemy lines. The men were not as heavily armed as a regular Infantryman. Being airborne, they were not able to carry large guns by parachute. The regular Infantry carried water cooled machine guns of the 30 and 50 caliber variety which were too heavy for the Paratrooper.

Only five men qualified for wings after the last week jump phase in training of the first twelve men who were part of Ken's initial squad. Five Parachuters graduated which made Ken one proud jaunty fellow! He received a leave, came home and as he stated, "I strutted a little, wearing my patch which showed a parachute and a glider upon its embroidered surface." During training the men packed their parachutes for the first five jumps. After that, the Paratrooper was reasonably sure the gizmo would work and then paid little attention to it as a mechanism.

Graduate Paratroopers joined others in North Carolina for advanced infantry training as to field problems. A regular lesson was to leave base camp on Monday, march into the woods, set up a bivouac area (an encampment usually without shelter) and conduct exercises all week until Friday. Sometimes the men had pup tents if they were not sleeping out. Ken said, "this training spoiled camping for me for the rest of my life."

On a slow small ship to England the men thought they were going to starve to death. Eventually off the coast of Glasgow, Scotland they saw the Irish Navy passing in review in two local little boats. The American men were shuttled upon a train to Newbury, England. Newbury was twenty five miles south west of London. The unit was stationed at a large estate. The woman who owned the property referred to the Paratroopers as "uncouth Americans on her property." Some 'uncouth' men dynamited her fish pond for some fresh fish. Three practice jumps were carried out in England before D-Day. The practicing was done at night.

In the month of June, 1944 the men were moved to a marshaling area and sealed up inside it, so that individuals could not talk to anybody! The group was briefed at an airfield on objectives of the Normandy invasion which was also referred to as Project:Overlord. They were scheduled to go on the 4th of June. Wind and heavy rains delayed the big invasion movement until D-Day, the 6th of June.

Paratroopers actually went the night before D-Day. Some troopers blackened their faces for camouflage. They shaved their heads. Some looked like weird Indians or modern kids in high school with weird hairdos. They strapped 125 pounds of weapons, ammunition and equipment to their bodies. The airplane also had extra munitions and equipment strapped to its underbelly. This equipment would be jettisoned over the drop zones. The Paratroopers loaded in the airplanes at sundown. It was quite late as it was summertime. They needed a bright moon for their night drop. The flight took two hours which included the 'land fall' by the men. Over the English Channel and before the troopers got to France, they understood the Germans had somehow been alerted and were waiting for them.

There was a lot of antiaircraft fire. The Pilots, at the controls of the planes, carrying troops had never been shot at before. They were what has been called "goosey." The formation and armada that was formed when they headed for the Normandy Coast was broken up which exposed them to heavy losses. Pilots taking evasive action scattered men all over the Normandy Pennisula and the men were not together as a group, as planned.

Ken had taken extra training in how to give aid to wounded men. He was attached to the Medic Detatchment with a special Red Cross type patch on his sleeve. The Major had the option of picking out the Medic Detatchment. As such, the men could help the surgical technician by giving first aid, giving blood plasma and bandaging wounds.

The drop pattern of the 501st regiment was to be Drop Zone D. Their mission was one of capturing the locks at La Barquette, destroying a railroad bridge and securing four highway bridges northwest of Carentan. The mission of destroying the bridges was vital for keeping out German Army reinforcements from entering Utah Beach Area. The idea was to seize and hold some flood locks until the men of the 4th made it over some causeways. This was important so Germans would not open locks and flood the area as well.

The great armada of the 101st Airborne, of which the 501st regiment was a part, flew in darkness skimming over water at 500 feet. All did not go well with the men programmed to be dropped over Carentan. There was fog and German antiaircraft fire. By planes breaking formation, the Pilots lost their bearings and dropped men miles from intended drop zones. At 12:15 a.m. a fellow named Captain Frank L Lillyman became the first Paratrooper to tumble into space and drop onto French occupied lands. For identification, the men were supplied toy crickets on which to recognize a signal by a fellow Paratrooper.

It was not dark for long. Once Germans realized the invasion was really happening they played huge searchlights upon the sky picking out transport planes and pinning them like moths to a big display, the sky. Death to men and the aircraft was like some eerie play of fireworks. It was unreal. It was real to the men crying out in pain from flak and bullets. Many slumped quietly to breathe no more.

Ken was one of those men in a maneuvering plane forced out of the protection of formation and scattered on the countryside in a swamp! He jumped out of a plane flying at 150 miles per hour. It was reported the group lost 60 airplanes going in. Ken jumped At 500 feet. There was a two minute warning light. "Check your equipment!" came an interjection from the Jumpmaster. Each man doublechecked his hookup on his chute to a cable running overhead on the aircraft ceiling. When each man jumped, this 15 foot long static line would pull the chute from its pack in an automatic way. When the Jumpmaster screamed "Let's go!" he pushed a bag of equipment through the door following it by himself. Men then took turns through the same doorway. In order, they stepped out the doorway quickly turning left, or they stepped out the door and quickly turned to the right. Down the line of jumpers men followed each other alternately, as to direction of turn. By alternating left and right, they stayed out of the way of each other's parachute. Once outside, when the parachute opened it jerked the trooper's body as it caught cold freezing air.

A man had orders to jump unless he had been wounded. "Many wounded men jumped. Some who shouldn't have, jumped." The drop on to French soil was chaotic. Some of the unfortunate ones dropped into the channel. With so much equipment upon their backs, they drowned by the weight of materiel and extra added water weight. German soldiers picked off some of the Paratroopers by filling their bodies with shrapnel before their chutes even opened. Some Americans dropped right into German encampments. Many landed in trees, gardens and on rooftops. During the June 5th jump, 213 men died by gunfire, 490 were wounded and 195 were missing (captured). Of the 1800 men of the 101st Airborne who were scattered in Normandy, every other person was wounded, captured or killed. Ken expressed a feeling, "that the effectiveness of aerial warfare was overrated."

Before Ken had taken off in the plane his Sergeant asked, "where is your gun?" Ken replied, "I don't have one. I have a Red Cross band." The Sergeant replied, "here, put this in your pocket." It was a hand grenade. After Ken made his landing into a swamp and as he was wading out, he heard a noise approaching. He pulled the pin on the grenade. It was not a German in front of him but a cow! He then carried the grenade around with him for two solid hours with the pin out of it. He hoped he would not fall down! For using toy crickets he remembered: one crick was a challenge and two cricks were a response. By using the crickets the men were trying to get together with other men that had safely dropped.

Wading through three feet of water in the swamp was not exactly easy. Ken worked his way carefully through the rushes toward a little cluster of buildings with a church in the midst of some closely grouped buildings. Another Medic showed up and so the two men used the church as an aid station. All day long, on June 6th, they gathered up wounded injured men and put them into the church. They used a little farm cart to haul the men back and forth and up and down roads. By nightfall, the two weary men had seventy-five wounded Paratroopers in the edifice.

Two Germans visited the little aid station inside the church. They chased American soldiers away and said, "We will return with a doctor." Ken and his helper identified themselves as just lowly Privates and stated, "we will appreciate a doctor helping with this case load." During the night, two of their injured bled to death. Next morning an American tank came up from the beach and chased the German Soldiers away from the area. They were unaware that two German Soldiers were hiding up in the Church's attic for two days until the Soldiers gave themselves up for prisoners! Bob Wright and Ken got silver stars for their first days' work.

On the morning of June 7th an advance led by Colonel Sink was sent to flush out the enemy. Inch by inch the soldiers cleaned out homes, hedgerows and made it through the little town of Carentan until they were at St. Come-du-Mont. Grenades, rifles and knives were used in house by house, room by room battles with the Germans. The little town was torn to pieces. Germans hid in seven foot deep ditches to blast soldiers as they passed on the roads. Americans jumped headlong in the same ditches with bullets slamming into them. Tanks were brought into the battle. Machine gun and cannon fire helped the belaguered troops. "At St. Come-du-Mont an armor piercing shell from an 88 caught a tank right through its turret. The little tank exploded and began to burn. The crew was killed instantly. The tank Commander's body draped out of the open turret." The little tank and its dead crew remained in that burnt out hull for many days as battles raged around the crossroads. The place was called "Dead Man's Corner." Taking this area was key to uniting the Normandy Invasion Forces. The town of Carentan was considered by the Germans as one town to be held to the last man. On June 8th, artillery attack of the 101st lasted more than an hour. The advance of fighting men passed Dead Man's Corner. Americans were attacked by Germans not only in front of them but from behind. In the afternoon the Americans outflanked the German position and Germans were leaving their dead behind. Six times that day the Germans countered and six times they were driven off. They blew up the bridge across the causeway into Carentan. Battles raged continuously. Fields seem to blow up in the faces of men. After some of the bloodiest battles of the entire war, a short truce was declared to clean up the dead bodies on each side. Then, the awful battle resumed.

The troopers found that when they won one of those thick thorny hedgerows they were then faced with an open field with no cover between themselves and the next row of prickly hedge. They would run at unseen guns and face more mortar fire. Wounded men crawled back. Often they were shot again. They moved no more. Both armies lost so many men they became exhausted from combat. A barrage of American artillery fire caught the Germans out in the open and pounded them for five minutes. The German troops were ordered by Hitler to die to the last man. In that particular German regiment, they did die to the last one. Then, all was quiet. According to German Army records that were captured, the Commandment of the Carentan Garrison reported to Seventh Army headquarters, "that Carentan had fallen."

Hitler was consumed with rage! He sent in re-inforcements. For two more days tenacious German SS Panzergrenadiers were leading another attack. In the two days of quiet, the 101st reorganized their own strength and now they also had some armoured units and fresh infantry. By the 15th of June all was secured from the new German re-inforcements, who were also beaten. Thereafter, the 101st division moved towards Cherbourg. On July 7th, General Taylor complimented the men by saying, "You proved the German soldier is no superman...You can beat him on any ground."

During the battles some Medical Officers showed up at the little church and evacuated some of the men that Bob and Ken had nursed. Taking wounded back to the beach, those men were provided transportation back to England. During the battles mortar had hit the roof of the church. A big chunk of the roof fell in. Ken and his medic buddy just kept on bandaging men day after day and hour after hour. For thirty-two days, foot soldiers were in and out of the town of Carentan. It was a major holding sector. The Allies were building up the beach. Armies were advancing to St. Lo and Cherbourg. In the midst of all the raging battles, a big storm tore up harbors and beaches. This set the invasion back somewhat. Lots of patroling was needed.

After his work as a Medic in this very trying location, Ken received the Combat Medic Badge. His parachute badge could now be decorated with a star. He had the 101st Airborne patch and the regiment patch. Later, he would receive the Presidential Unit Citation for Normandy and Bastogne, the Silver and Bronze Stars. He received the Purple heart for being wounded in the church when his head was split open. After thirty days, Ken went back to England for rest.

On September 17th, the 101st Airborne was sent to Holland on an operation referred to as Market Garden. Commander Maxwell D. Taylor, who had led the men in Normandy was the leader in Holland. He also commanded the group in Bastogne, Alsace and made the trip to Berchtesgaden. On the Sunday drop into Holland, some of the same Pilots used in the Normandy drop were at the controls of the aircraft. This time, they were great, even when a few of the planes caught fire. The planes were flown where they were supposed to go as the Pilots held a steady course. Taking off in the morning, planes were flown across the Channel with a lot of fighter escorts in attendance. When the planes reached the front lines they received a great deal of antiaircraft fire. Fighter pilots would dive their planes and attack the German antiaircraft guns.

British Troops were given instructions to secure a corridor that ran from Holland, turn a corner and get to the Ruhr Valley. Their plans did not work out that way. This time Ken carried a gun. He had a carbine. The objective was to obtain a bridge that crossed the canal. He could see the bridge as he floated down in his parachute. He took off for the bridge as fast as he could and was the first one to arrive there. A group of real Dutch people were extremely excited. They appeared to be readying a barbecue. They had lots of fresh fruits including apples and pears with them. They offered the

Paratroopers bowls of fresh fruit and mugs of beer. At one time, eight of the Americans were talking to the Dutch people. A car drove up 50 yards away. Two Germans got out of the car carrying guns. An American Colonel was there. He yelled, "Hande Hoch" which meant put your hands up. The Germans decided to run. All of the Americans shot them. Ken took his first souvenir. He got a real impressive Luger automatic pistol with a shoulder holster. He does not have it any more.

The task of the 101st Airborne was to take sixteen miles of road behind the German front line. This sixteen miles was soon called "Hell's Highway." All the men could really do was hold bridges and major towns. There were many weak links along the roads. Actually all of the different divisions in this Market phase of Market-Garden were to hold sixty-four miles of roads! During one of the briefings, a Lieutenant General Frederick Browning was quoted as saying to Field Marshall Montgomery, "Sir I think we might be going a bridge too far." The famous book and movie, *A Bridge Too Far* was named after the quote.

Three bridges were taken immediately as well as the Aa River Railroad Bridge. Colonel Sink of the 506th regiment commented, "We enjoyed a picture drop." A memorable quote of the war was made by Melvin C. Davis, a Company Commander hit by fire. As he was receiving first aid, the Commander was fired upon again. He said, "You better hurry up Medics, they're gaining on you."

The 101st was back into a tanglement of machine gun and rifle fire. They were not prepared to face a thousand enemy troops in the town of Best. The Best Bridge was blown by a time-fuse right in front of their faces. The troopers were soon out of ammunition. Only three men were left without wounds as Germans kept coming. Medical supplies were stolen by the enemy. With no artillery, hayfields became a slaughterhouse. Casualties were running 20%. Thirty-six hours behind schedule, Operation Market-Garden got going again. Then, they had to keep the road open. 159 German prisoners were taken first along with one American Major Elkins who was freed from being a German prisoner! By nightfall 600 Germans lay dead and 1100 surrendered. The American Division lost 373 killed, 1436 wounded and 547 missing. The new German multi-barreled "Screaming Meemies" were used on the troopers. Dangerous days went on and on along with living in dampness and cold. Men cursed the weather, the Germans and patrols.

Someone found a Thanksgiving goose. The men hid the goose in a cellar for two weeks. They were all looking forward to a good dinner. The goose was the toughest old thing and the dinner was a bust! About all one could say was "he really looked good!" By the end of November, relief came. The men who were still alive were allowed some rest and refit at a camp near Reims, France.

The "Screaming Eagles" were sent into the Battle of the Bulge, their third campaign. Germans secretly lined up 700 tanks and 250,000 men in the Ardennes Forest on express orders by Hitler. The overall purpose of the blitzkrieg was to destroy the three American Allied Armies. The American strength was some 83,000 men and 242 tanks. Ken was in the thick of it, in Bastogne. A lot of men did not have weapons, overcoats or overshoes. The Germans surrounded Bastogne. The group called themselves "the hole in the donut." Food was scarce. Soldiers suffered trench foot and had frozen feet. Men lost toes and still kept going. People left were found hiding or living in cellars. It was a dreadful situation. Ken said, "I became an observer. I was there when momentous events took place. I wasn't a terrific fighting man or a hero, just happened to be there." He was amazed at the amount of resistance that was put up by the enemy. It was an uneasy feeling being surrounded. Paratroopers had been surrounded before...The Germans sent in a request for surrender. General McAuliffe answered, "Nuts." Eventually, the Fourth Army under Patton broke through and relieved the men. For a day by day description of the

Battle of the Bulge at Bastogne see the Books, *The Screaming Eagles* by Milton J. Shapiro which Ken has added to his library.

As soon as the fog lifted aerial supply brought in a long column of aircraft with medicine, and food. Gasoline was replenished. After two months of fighting in the Bulge, German tanks were shot up. German bombers had been bombarded from the skies. "The Germans were pretty much on their last gasp and winding it up," according to Ken. He went back to Reims only to find the men were going to jump into the Prisoner-of-war camp in Germany!

Berchtesgaden was Hitler's Eagles Nest. It was on top of a mountain in the Bavarian Alps. In the Eagles Nest there were exotic souvenirs. The mountains were covered with beautiful white deep snow. Hitler's chateau was up on top of the mountain. One had to ride an elevator inside the mountain to reach the big enormous patio. The view was utterly spectacular. One could see Austria from there. (Hitler was reported to have committed suicide inside the Eagles Nest).

The area was a popular ski resort setting with hairpin roads whipping around the mountainsides. American men got killed while driving drunk. They dove off the roads in 6 x 6 trucks at high speeds. Lots of booze and off the cliffs they went! Sometimes, there would be eight or ten men carousing together while barreling around the winding roads.

There were many displaced refugees in the area. Slave laborers for the Germans had been brought in to run factories so that their own men could be used on the battlefields. When the Russians arrived, they were sent to Austria to the big DP camp to booze and party with women. "It was remarkable" to Ken "how the Russians were gallant heros and then in a short time they were people we were going to shoot." To Ken "It was startling to the troopers how from one day to the next, that Stalin was a ruthless man, an absolute bastard as far as human rights were concerned. How our government reversed itself on the matter of policy was amazing. He had heard the Russians carried the load during the war and the Russians took a beating. He believes with all his heart that our country wasted forty-five years. Our country spent our treasure to defend the world. Germany and Japan are now in fat city. Americans have spent billions for defending what?"

Ken remembers the European cemeteries are full of his friends. During Operation: Overlord he was an 18 year old kid and so were many of them. He watched guys blown up and blown apart. It was real tramatic. He took an emotional sojourn across Europe in 1994 to pay his respects to those fellows. He found the graves of some of his buddies in those beautifully kept graveyards in France.

Ken married Genevieve in 1946. They have three children, Stephanie, Christopher and Francis. They also have five grandchildren. Ken worked with Standard Oil Company after the war. He had the Chevron Gas Station behind the Valley Mart in Sonoma for twelve years after previously having another station in San Francico. The family lived in Fairfax, California at first. Ken had a little airplane for fun. He parked it at the small airport on Eighth Street. Now, he lives on a country acre where a very small creeklet that rises from the Eastern foothills meanders to San Francisco Bay. Ken retired in 1986. He saw a lot of World War II, he'd rather forget.

Shapiro, Milton J., *The Screaming Eagles, The 101st Airborne Division in World War II,* Julian Messner, New York, 1976, pps. 191. pps 20,23,52.

Lauren Carl Peterson

United States Navy, 1943 - 1946

L. C. "Pete" Peterson, born in Worthington, Minnesota joined the United States Navy in Denver Colorado. At an early stage in his Navy career Pete was stationed at the Glen L. Martin Plant in Middle River, Maryland. Along with thirty other Machinist Mates he was made privy to the huge Martin Mars Flying Boat. The plant was not set up for classroom training as yet, so the men were turned loose in the plant to ask questions. Interestingly, at least half of the workers in the plant were young women. Pete remembers with a grin on his face, "What a place for a bunch of sailors!"

Pete was born on a farm. His favorite expression was, "Our family is so poor that I have a tumbleweed for a pet." The family lived the best way they could. With two brothers, Pete believed he had an incentive to try and build a better life than the one his struggling parents had lived. Due to the health of one of his brothers suffering asthma, the family moved to Colorado where the mile high mountain air was pure and clear. The boys rode bicycles, enjoyed mountain stream fishing and hunted jack rabbits on prairie lands. The mile high city seemed to have a mild climate as snow did not last as long as it did in Minnesota.

Pete graduated from high school. His best buddy, Edward was Margaret's brother. Margaret caught Pete's eye and would become his bride when he returned from the war. One summer Pete and Edward drove to California in a 1936 Ford. They made it past all those filling station bathrooms where scrawlers defaced the walls with grafiti, Kilroy was here! Attending the Hawthorne School of Aeronautics in Englewood, California**Error! Bookmark not defined.** the young men took a short course on aircraft sheetmetal work. Pete, a high school graduate, was recruited to work at Consolidated Aircraft Corporation in San Diego to build B-24 bombers. It was 1941. The young fellows worked along side of all those Rosie the Riveters credited with working long hard hours in the American factories. Pete's interesting job was joining soft metal firmly together to create the skin on the wings and bodies of aircraft. After working at the plant for about a year, Pete sensed the draft was about to catch up with him. He decided he would travel back to Denver, see the family and then join the service.

After working with the motor pool at Buckley Air Field, Pete volunteered for the Navy. He was sent to the Marines. After one-half hour with the Marines, he begged the recruiter "to please let me go back to the Navy! After all, that's the thing to do, to see the world..." The recruiter was in a good mood, so Pete was given new papers with changes directing him to the service of his choice. There was a 'ditty' of a song going around which amounted to a couple of phrases. *"If you have a daughter, spank her on the butt, and if it is a son, send him up to Farragut, singing bell bottom trousers..., But never Lake Pondoree."* Farragut was the place Pete was exhaustingly paced for all those Navy bootcamp experiences.

Pete was sent to the Alameda Naval Air Facility at Alameda, California. The assemblage he was joining was initialed CASU meaning Carrier Aircraft Service Unit which was to be land based. His unit #15 was aborted to Monterey Auxilliary Naval Air Base awaiting overseas orders. But that was just a ploy to set any enemy intelligence off base, should any information been leaked about troop movements. The men were informed privately, "This is it." Unit # 15 troops were trucked into a grove of trees and impatiently waited for a train. The train moved them inside a dark warehouse in Oakland. From that warehouse the 450 men of the 15th traveled through a tunnel and boarded directly into the lower level areas of the waiting ship. There were other troops on the vessel along with those brought in by the train.

Sailing out the Golden Gate on the SS Bloemfontein in the dark of the night, the men were somewhat disappointed. They did not get to see the famous Golden Gate Bridge nor for that matter did they see the coast of their country while leaving it's shores. Orders were dispatched for the entire group. "Stay below decks and out of sight until the ship is well out of the harbor and beyond scrutiny of an enemy's eyes." This order was to minimize knowledge of troop movements. The SS Bloemfontein was under contract to the United States Government from Holland. It was referred to as "the Dutch ship."

The food was really bad. It was so bad at one point, a buddy with Pete stole below decks and found the galley. The two guys entered the storage room and proceeded to acquire some food. The intruders found a partial sack of carrots, some of which were rotten. They removed the rotten ones and had a feast on the remaining good carrots. The next night, feeling a little like two Peter Rabbits in Mr. MacGregor's Cabbage Patch, they went again to the galley. This time, like Peter Rabbit the two were caught by an enterprising cook. Rather than punish the two 'scavengers' the cook asked, "would you like to work for some sandwiches?" Answering in the affirmative, the two bold and venturesome recruits ended up swabbing the deck. From then on, the advantageous galley cook and the two reciprocating Navy men continually shared good times and good food. Pete believes the food they enjoyed was reserved for the Dutch Crew.

There were a host of other experiences aboard that Dutch Merchantman Ship which had to do with bathing in salt water, an almost impossible feat. Fellows cut most of their hair to the scalp, so it would not become a tangled mess after using the special salt water soap. There were the usual sea sicknesses and the abandon ship drills. Drills went very slowly, until one exciting day the ship started a zig zag course. An announcement was made "This is not a drill!" You should have seen the men move to the rail in no time! An enemy submarine was sighted. The group was able to avoid it or it decided to avoid confronting the ship.

After thirty-one days on the Bloemfontein, Air Craft Service Unit # 15 of the Navy was disembarked at Guadalcanal. The island was semi-secured but some of the stubborn Japanese fighters were dug into the hills of the island. All of a sudden Pete came to the realization that "the Japanese were there in those hideouts to kill the Americans." Marines and Army Artillery Units had Japanese corralled but detonated bombs as needed to keep them in check. In return, Wash-machine Charlie (Japanese aircraft on strafing missions) were everyday occurrences. Spools of wire strung with coke bottles made weird noises and was enough to "scare the hell out of you," if you happened to run into one of those weird booby traps.

Everything felt damp on the Island of Guadalcanal. The moist army cots had mosquito netting strung over them to keep out mosquitos. In order to keep out other critters that loved to crawl in one's shoes while sleeping, men took their smelly shoes to bed with them. If you got up in the night, you might squash a few land crabs. The next morning, whether you got up or not, you could see where they walked through the tent leaving their draggy telltale trails behind them.

Devoted to advancing the welfare of their group, men erected funny looking square tanks which were taken from ships that had been run aground. These tanks were hung up in trees to catch rain water. With a pipe and shower head, men were able to take soft rainwater showers out in the open. On one occasion, while Pete was showering, along came an Army Jeep with two nurses riding in the vehicle.

Well, they were out to see the sights!

While operating in his unit, yet not quite settled, Pete contracted bronchial pnemonia. He was flown in a DC-3 to New Hebrides Hospital, then transferred to New Caledonia. For 105 days Pete had bouts of Dengue fever, akin to Malaria. Transmitted by the mosquito bite, it was characterized by fever, eruptions and severe pains of the joints. It is also referred to as "breakbone dandy." While Pete was bedridden, Marines were all around him on life support devices. Most of them did not make it. There was constant movement of taking out one injured soul and bringing in another. Two Marines named Ledbetter and Boyle came in off Bougainville Islands. Pete asked them, "What were you doing there?" Boyle replied, "Shining up my mess kit." When asked why he replied, "To hold it back of me like a mirror to see if I still had my ass!" Ledbetter stated he had been fighting in the jungles. He had a BAR, a piece of equipment similar to a machine gun. Both, Ledbetter and his ammo-bearer had sided up to a tree trunk. He whispered to his 'bearer.' He received no answer. The ammo-bearer on the opposite side of the tree was dead! Ledbetter and Boil were now in the hospital with a few hundred more of those Marines who might be lucky enough to make it home with their injuries.

When Pete went back to duty, he weighed in at 117 pounds. He re-joined his unit on the island of Efate. Actually, the doctor had advised him to do nothing for thirty days. Go to the beach. Due to censoring, Pete had not been able to describe to his family the nature of his hospital visit. His Mother worried as to why he was in the hospital for such a long period.

Pete recalls that one of the worst environmental oil spills in world history had taken place during the Coral Sea Battle. The Allies had sunk 24 Japanese ships. Likewise, the Japanese had sunk 24 American and Allied ships. Talk about an oil spill! Diesel oil from all of those sunken vessels covered the shallow seas with sticky 'goo' which lapped at reefs, islets, islands and gulfs. It moved along the shores of the capes dissipating shore life as it was also being swallowed up in the waves of the Pacific.

Pete had now been in the service for 32 months. A homebound troop ship came by. Pete was scheduled by the doctor to make the trip back to the States. There were 400 men waiting to be shipped home. One hundred twenty made it to the ship. It was as if the officials pulled every other name, then skipped a few for the transition home. Pete was in San Francisco when the war ended.

Margaret (Mickey) from Denver, Pete's wife to be had entered nurses training. Margaret contacted Pete to be a pallbearer at her Father's funeral in 1947. After meeting once again, Pete and Margaret were married in 1947. They had two children, Lauren Carl, Jr. of Loveland, Colorado and Cathy Lou, who lives in the Bay Area. When Pete's son was three months old, his dad began employment as an aircraft mechanic with the United Air Lines in San Francisco, California. He worked for 4 1/2 years before returning to a farm in Colorado. Pete decided, he liked aircraft work best. It had an alluring built-in retirement system, so he made it back to United Air Lines.

When it was time for retirement, Pete and Margaret looked towards northern California for a quiet place in the country. They checked out Oakmont, the golfing community near Santa Rosa. They bought one unit in a triplex. Deciding they did not care for a wholly adult community, they sold the Oakmont property and found a condo in Sonoma. Furnishing it with Early American garage sale, the couple rented it out while ultimately moving into another condo for their own abode. Trading both condos, in a rapid rising real estate market the couple finally settled on a beautiful new single story duplex.

As an energetic retiree, Pete went right to work to enlarge the Sonoma Valley Chamber of Commerce. He became volunteer Membership Director of the organization. With the help of the Director,

Ambassadors, Board Members and Staff, the membership rose from 338 to approximately 630 in a four year period.

The chamber cooks an annual ox roast in the Plaza each June. Pete also helped with the annual Kiwanis Club turkey barbecue every summer. One other feature of the Chamber instituted by Pete and his staff was the monthly "Business after Hours." Held at various businesses, usually accompanied by wines and foods, the monthly meet was eagerly looked forward to and attended by many members and guests. There were small gifts given to attendees by drawing their business cards.

Pete Peterson, presently volunteering at the Community Center commands his own schedule. He is a member of the Disabled American Veterans, belonging to the Veterans of Foreign Wars in Greeley, Colorado. He received a leg injury in Guadalcanal from which has developed some arthritus of the knee joints. Ending his Navy career as Aviation Machinist Mate Second Class, Pete received the usual medals for the Pacific Theater of War. He believes his ribbons are lost or misplaced.

Besides all those other activities, Pete managed to spend eight years working on the Public Utilities Commission for the City of Sonoma. His recognition came when Valeric Brown, Mayor, present State Representative gave him a beautiful gold key to the City of Sonoma. He believes this 'reward' was due to his building up the membership of the Chamber of Commerce for a wine-country-tourist-town. He loves to wear the key to the city. "May I have your attention?" he asks, then, flashing the ornate key on the chain worn proudly around his neck and with a twinkle in his eye, he states "I love Sonoma!"

Donald A. Mellen

United States Army, 1948 - 1950

United States Navy, 1950 - 1971

In this special chapter, the reader is given a glimpse into the subject matter of the atomic bomb used on Hiroshima and Nagasaki, Japan to end World War II. This story is of one American Naval Man's experience. Not only were atomic bombs tested but also hydrogen thermonuclear bombs. These tests took place after World War II.

At the tender age of fourteen years, three months and twenty-two days, Don Mellen and his friend Tommy Coty both of Worchester, Massassachusetts broke into the town hall. Their mission was to confiscate two blank birth certificates. Finding exactly what they were looking for, and with youthful exhuberance, the rascals each took pen in hand and inscribed a fake certificate. Each boy filled in the other one's document. New birth dates were filled in so each young boy could join the Army!

Don was the baby of boot camp at Fort Devins, Massachusetts. He spent his time "being scared to death someone would catch him" until he reasoned; "Actually when called out to muster at least one-half the company was underage." Guys wanted to get off farms. Their dads were poor dirt farmers. In Massachusetts the rainy weather was fine all year around for growing vegetables. Their dads ran a few dairy cattle for milk along with flocks of chickens which were the main staples for the family diet. The boys wanted something better for a living and they couldn't wait to grow up to find it.

At Fort Devins which became Camp Edwards (known as Cape Kennedy) where missiles are presently sent skyward, the always hungry-adolescent-Army-boys would steal food in the middle of the night. They moved about quietly not only for adventure but to keep their constant growing pains satisfied. The fellows were introduced to the BAR. It was a Brownie Automatic Repeater weapon developed for and carried by foot soldiers. This gun was akin to a portable machine gun. They were informed, "The first persons to ever feel its power will be your enemy targets!" Besides marching, marching, marching and going to class, the youngsters along with their eighteen year old peers spent a lot of time on the firing range. Those vigorous young bloods learned how to care for the weapon. If one of them dropped a BAR, too bad! Punishment was taking that big gun to bed with you as a reminder "never to drop it again!"

Don became his Captain's Orderly. This was not exactly his ideal picture of Army life. He spent a lot of time driving the Captain whensoever and wheresoever the Officer wanted to go. Often it was to run the CO out to dinner. Always hungry, Don had the 'privilege' of loitering outside, taking in some tantalizing restaurant odors while waiting for his slow-moving boss to return. As Captain's Orderly, it was clearly understood that Don was to wear a clean, pressed, and sharp-looking uniform at all times. Whatever the Captain wanted, whether it was picking up an item at Quartermaster or keeping the vehicle clean, Don was the 'gofer or doer' as his Captain's Assistant.

Don's dad found out his run-away-son was in the service after about three years. The run-away had come home on leave in civilian clothes. His dad was about to turn his son in but Don made it clear "If you ever tell on me I'll never see you again!" Don took a discharge when his enlistment was up while still under age for the service. Three days after discharge from the Army, as a seventeen year old with absolutely no plans for the future, he joined the Navy! In his words, "I went out to see the world!" Still being underage he used the false birth certificate for the second time. This was also the second time that he entered the service in his home State of Massachusetts.

Navy bootcamp was taken at Great Lakes, Illinois near Chicago. Back through the orientation and exercise paces he went! His new superiors were not cognizant that Don previously lived an Army life. He couldn't produce his former discharge due to his age. Enlistments were not accepted in the Navy if it was known one had prior Army service. Don waited until he re-enlisted in the Navy the second time before divulging his pesky and risky little secret.

Don became a Seaman's Apprentice on the World War II Battleship Missouri. (This was the same ship used for signing the peace treaty between the Japanese and Americans at the end of World War II). From Norfolk, Virginia the ship sailed for Korea immediately. It did not take a long time for Don to begin to see a part of the world! They went through the Panama Canal through many locks. Don said, "It was a surprise to find fresh water in the center lock." The USS Missouri's hulk was so very wide, there was only eight inches of space remaining on either side. Maneuvering the ship was tedious and at the same time exciting while trying to keep from hitting abutment walls of the locks. As the ship moved through the Canal it had a difficult time reacting from water bouyancy which tended to keep the ship bouncing and rubbing its hull on each side of the walls.

The USS Missouri berthed at Pearl Harbor for two days in order to replentish food and fuel. Then, the Navy recruits were steaming toward South Korea. At the port city Inch'on, located on the Yellow Sea the crew joined the Inch'on Invasion. Inch'on had a population of over 300,000 people. Someone exclaimed, "This is where the fight originated!" Don did not know the political ramifications involved. He could have cared less. The USS Missouri worked its way up to the 38th Parallel bombarding shorelines of the coast. The Army and Marines landed on shore. They called the Navy for munitions support. Projectiles as tall as a man were sent over hills from 16" guns. The USS Missouri had carried its own spotting plane in World War II. The plane was gone by the time of the Korean battles.

The men figured they were not really winning or losing any war. They played a game of hide and seek with beach Koreans at Wonsan Harbor. Ranges for fire power were marked by sticks in the waters. The Navy would bombard the shore targets and then move on. Day in, day out, they spent a whole year shelling the Island of Inch'on to above the 38th parallel. The only souvenir Don wished for and received was a big map of Korea.

Don was transferred to USS Renshaw DDE499, a destroyer escort. He left Korea. He had an emergency home leave and then he was transferred to Eniwetok Atoll for H Bomb and A Bomb testing.

Tests for the atom and hydrogen bombs were set up with a central core of 'dead' ships taken from moth ball fleets. Ships for the epicenter of the bombs impact test were grouped a few miles out in the ocean away from Eniwetok. At 25 miles from a given epicenter, a ring of manned ships were circled about the dead ships. Ten miles out from the first ring another group of manned ships were clustered. At zero hour, each bomb tested was dropped in the center of the dead ships. Damage assessment would be carried out as to any effect the bombs had on the rings of manned ships and as to what distances there was any impact. It was from the mushroom clouds that fallout falls. The descent of minute particles of radioactive material from the explosion of an atomic or thermonuclear device was its bi-product. Monitoring was necessary to check effects of the huge wind that almost capsized the ring of ships at their twenty-five mile and 35 mile posts. Monitoring continued to take place for twenty-four hours following the blast of an explosion. Geiger counters were employed to check the fallout particle dust, also known as nuclear waste.

The only safe way to look at the detonation when a bomb was being dropped was by especially developed colored glasses to protect one's eyes from blindness. However, if one put an arm over their eyes that person could look through their own blood and bone as if peering at an X-ray. Don watched quite a few explosions this way. He could make out the heavy smoke mushroom cloud as it formed with its distinct shape and he could see the eerie imagery of the gigantic explosion and destruction of the graveyard ships. To actually see the spectacle of one of the bomb experiences, one wore a special pair of glasses described as being designed almost like and similar to welding glasses.

Before any nuclear bomb was unleashed, a beeper sounded on the manned ships alerting the crews to the event. There were actually a series of three beeps, two short ones and one long one. The men had time to get into their crouched positions. Some people on each deck of each ship were being monitored. After the blast, a geiger counter was used to go over everything and everybody. The geiger counter was an instrument used for detecting any ionizing radiation by means of a sealed tube containing a gas that when struck by ionizing particles conducted an electrical impulse between two electrodes connected to a suitable counting device. Leaking energy from the bombs could cause death. A person's hair could fall out. Looking directly at the blast could cause blindness.

Any contaminated area was washed with a lye solution soap should any particles be found by the geiger counter. Persons were washed down and their clothes were destroyed inside a decontamination station. Don said, "You were ordered to strip down in one area, shower in a different area and receive a new set of clothes for every item you wore." The ship upon which Don was a crew member had a small amount of contamination in reduced dosage. One of the jobs they inherited was evacuating a whole island. This was necessary because a bomb being tested was 20 megatons stronger than anticipated.

Eniwetok Atoll, located close to Bikini near the Marshall Islands was a nothing island in Don's eyes. He could see why it was chosen for bomb testing. From the ship he could see waves of the ocean on the other side of it. The island was pancake flat. Barren looking quonset huts and lonely appearing sandy beaches were the other dreary things one viewed. The Marines and the Army were dug in. After transporting the contaminated souls from the Island was accomplished, the ships used for transportation were considered wasted and had to be destroyed. The act of squandering ships for the purpose of tests was considered a necessary expenditure for all the life of Planet Earth. The actual laying of waste and devastation was considered "just another ravage and cost of war prevention." Ships with contamination might be anchored for a while and then used for destruction in another test. Often, the atomic and hydrogen bombs were hitting the same ships over again.

Just to show what one of these type bombs could do in 1954, Don was sent to view what a 20 megaton or higher bomb was capable of. Asking Don, "Are Atomic bombs really as bad as they are made out to be?" His comments were, "Atomic bombs are very dangerous. They could wipe out a whole country. A very large area of the earth could be devastated. On the test site in 1954 a whole island was sunk into the Pacific waters. If one dropped a fusion type bomb on San Francisco, an area as large as Cities of Sausalito, San Francisco and San Rafael would be wiped out. You would feel the fallout through the sloughs as far as the Sonoma wetlands."

When a radioactive bomb explodes and forms the big mushroom cloud pressure extends out for miles and miles. The wind that is formed by the explosion carries debris out. Debris is the dangerous part. Should fallout come by a tree everything on both sides of the tree is gone akin to a forest fire that rages out of control and doesn't stop. Don, with nuclear top secret clearance was twenty-five miles away from a blast when he could feel wind whip past his body. "Natural wind currents of an area also influence and push that fallout stuff around," he declared; "Navy men were not allowed to carry any photographic equipment or radios on missions of the Eniwetok experience. They were highly monitored."

Operation:Castle at the Atomic Test Proving Grounds of the Marshall Islands near Eniwetok was conducted by the Army, Navy, Air Force and Atomic Energy Commission. Important officers included: Major General, United States Army Commander of the Joint Task Force Seven; Scientific Director, Brigadier General of the United States Army Chief of Staff; Colonel of the United States Army Commander of Army Task Group; Rear Admiral of the United States Navy, Commander of the Navy Task Group; Commander of the Scientific Task Group; Brigadier General of the United States Air Force, Commander of the Air Force task group; and Commander of the Base Facilities Task Group. These nuclear veterans were written up in a story around the time of the testing.

In 1972, Don came to Sonoma because of his wife, Wauna. Living in Hawaii, he had traveled back and forth on weekends to see her. He also helped his father build single family dwellings. The two men also accomplished a lot of remodeling of existing dwellings in the Sonoma area. Father and son enjoyed fishing and camping. Don is one of those persons with a camper who really uses it. He and Wauna have three children, Donald, Raymond and Bonnie. After retiring from the Navy where he did receive credit for his early years of service in the Army, Don has continued his unretirement years in the construction business. Wauna was formerly a real estate saleslady and loan broker. She rather likes the employment she has now working at a title company. The Mellens live on a country place in one of the area's serene and quiet locations.

If one of those big bombs dropped on nearby San Francisco, the area where they live would probably "feel a bit of the wind!" In spite of all his past exposure to atomic testing, Don looks robust and appears to enjoy life!

Marguerite Vanderbilt

This is a very special story about an Hawaiian Lady during the bombing of Pearl Harbor and her life during the war.

Born in Hana, Maui she married a United States Naval Lieutenant, James Vanderbilt whose story follows hers.

"It all happened on Sunday morning. The United States Fleet that had been out for two weeks came in on Saturday night. Most of the Officers were off their ships. My father finished breakfast then retired to the Den to turn on the radio." He came in to tell us, "This is the real McCoy. The radio announcer says to stay off the streets. We're being attacked by the Japanese!" Marguerite got up and went to the window. Planes were over Diamond Head and headed toward Pearl. She could see smoke and all those planes. She thoughtfully continued her memories of that historic day, "I lived on hills in Monoa Valley. I had a good view of the Japanese Planes heading for Pearl."

Her father had admonished, the radio had said, "Don't go out, stay at home." But Marguerite had a close acquaintance nearby and she went to the top of the hill to see her friend and more of the Pearl Harbor area. A guard was already posted there. The guard said, "If you see any plane directly overhead drop to the ground." Marguerite's eyes were fascinated and drawn toward Pearl Harbor. The sky was filling with black smoke in that direction from all those destroyed ships. In the evening the family heard a plane overhead. There was an awful explosion near them in the Punahau School grounds. Later someone told the neighbors "the explosion had been a stranded Japanese Plane going home jettisoning its bombs."

Marguerite's family had Japanese house servants. Their nice little Japanese girl was so scared with all the bombing. She was crocheting a bedspread. The interlacing thread to form the fancy work was being used at breakneck speed as the little fingers of the girl were moving so very quickly. She was so frightened she kept crocheting faster and faster. Marguerite could hardly believe anyone could move their fingers so rapidly.

Honolulu was under curfew from December 7th, 1941 until the Battle of Midway was over in early summer of 1942. Hawaii was darkened at night until that turning point in the hostilities. After Midway, the Island's lights went on again even at night. From December 7, 1941 until the end of the war not one Japanese person on the Hawaiian Islands was known to have sabotaged anything. The government was surveying quite a few suspicious persons but no trouble was reported. The faithful Japanese were embarrassed by the attack. Marguerite's maid's husband enlisted in the Army. Many Japanese men who wanted to help the Allies in the war were sent from Hawaii to Italy.

Hawaii, was officially known as a Territory of the United States during the war, not yet a State of the Union. (The Islands were ratified as a state in 1959.) The Hawaiian geological group consists of eight major islands with many islets in the central Pacific Ocean. Generally fertile with a mild climate, this paradise of the Pacific has miles of green plants and beautifully colored flowers. Coastal waters abound with fish. Sugar cane and pineapples were the major exports during wartime as they are today. Other locally grown products included coffee, cattle, and dairy bi-products. The military defense installations of the United States at Pearl Harbor and elsewhere in the territory were important to Hawaii's economy. A variety of food was rationed during the war. Many foods were imported from the United States. Marguerite remembers how people stood in line for foods such as butter, flour and imported meats such as lamb.

Restaurants and hotels grew at a quick pace. If you went into a restaurant after the Pearl Harbor attack you found the owners and their employees on extremely busy work schedules. There were so many ships being supplied and refueled in the harbor. American Officers and enlisted men were known to stand in long lines for beer, sandwiches and coffee. In order to help with the crowded situated and to express their gratitude to the service personnel, women from different churches worked every day at the Episcopal Church to provide lunches for the servicemen. Their effort was called the Hawaiian USO and was an interdenominational city-wide woman's church project held at the St. Andrews Episcopal Cathedral.

The Cathedral was designed under the rule of King Kamhama IV and Queen Emma. It consisted of a nave or main body of the church, several buildings, offices, and landscaped grounds. Historically, St. Andrews Episcopal Cathedral was the first Episcopal Cathedral completed in the western hemisphere.

Marguerite was born in Hana, Maui. Tourists know this area as the very little town at the end of the one way road going toward the seven pools. Many tourists traveling the slow meandering road have worn tee shirts that stated, "I made it to Hana!" Lush forest growth encloses the Walt Whitman *'road less traveled.'* The one lane road, through the thick forest of many beautiful trees, ferns and flowers, is completely void of commercialism. This part of the world is a beauteous vision of untouched nature.

The Greenwell Family were English. Marguerite's grandfather, a graduate of Sandhurst Military Academy in England came to California in 1850. He found the San Francisco Harbor filled with deserted sailing ships, their Crews deserting to the gold fields. Captain Henry Nicholas Greenwell, unfortunately fell and sustained an injury to his back. The British Counsel visited him and agreed that he needed a warm climate and rest. Hawaii was suggested, so after replacing the Crew he sailed to Hawaii. British Citizens were much in favor at this time with the Monarchy. The Royal family had been guests of Queen Victoria. Mr. Greenwell was so impressed with the Islands, arrangements were made for him to purchase his first large land holdings, including the home ranch that grew to over one hundred thousand acres. The land was mostly, fee simple. He became the Harbormaster, Postmaster and owned the general store in the Kona area of Hawaii. Instead of finding gold in California, he amassed two more beautiful ranches in Hawaii. Several generations of ranch hands that cared for the ranches came from the tropical islands. Some families worked on the Greenwell Ranches for five generations and there are still faithful 'puolos' (ranch hands) on the land now. These 'puolos' could be described as cowboys.

Marguerite's Grandfather Greenwell was born at an ancient home near Durham, Northern England. The setting is beautiful around the old English manor. Notably, its walls were once the stones from Adrian's Wall between England and Scotland. Marguerite's family is one of the 75 families in all England who have owned and maintained their lands since the Middle Ages. She is listed in Burkes, A Genealogical and Heraldic Dictionary of the Peerage and Baronetage of the United Kingdom. It is an annual guide commonly called Burke's Peerage first published in 1826.

Marguerite was educated at St. Margaret School in Victoria, British Columbia. She was a sheltered young lady. She loved working for the USO. It was considered social work. From St. Andrews Cathedral she was directed all over the city. The ladies took sandwiches down to Pearl. They prepared meals for the Red Cross. The boys at the USO asked all sorts of questions about the Islands. Marguerite knew the answers to their questions as a Kamaaina (native born on the Islands). During the war the Hawaiian Islands were the chief Pacific base for U.S. forces and the islands were under martial law from December 7, 1941 until March of 1943. One question invariably asked Marguerite was "Where were you born?" She answered, "I was born here on the Island." "No, you weren't, you sound like a Bostonian." During this type of conversation, she met and fell in love with Lieutenant James Vanderbilt.

James C. Vanderbilt

United States Naval Reserve, 1942 - 1960

On the morning of December 7th, 1941 Jim was expected to join a group for (riding in the ring) at a ranch in San Fernando Valley. He tied a string to his big toe and passed it out the key hole of his apartment to be awakened by 10: a.m. A neighbor had agreed to pull the string at the appointed time. Instead, at 9 a.m. he was surprised by a group outside his door shouting, "Get up and go to war. The Japanese have attacked Pearl Harbor." The string broke when they almost pulled his toe off! He did go to war.

James Vanderbilt, a dashing Hollywoodite drove his Rolls Royce up and down the California Coast. He spent about one year with the Western Sea Frontier Group on seaworthy yachts. He was a Member of the United States Naval Reserve. Jim had been assigned John Ford's beautiful eighty foot yacht called The Arner, an Alden design. James was chosen to board this beautiful craft during wartime in order to report on enemy airplane or submarine activity along the California Coastline. Immediately upon Commandeering The Arner, the Navy scuttled the elaborate four poster beds, the fireplace in the salon and the extravagant yards and yards of elegant white carpet. Stripping ship also included all combustible materials which were simply thrown over the side of the vessel into the ocean depths. Furniture was stored. A very large Koa round table was missing from storage with not a trace of it after the war.

Some sixty larger yachts were commandeered along with The Arner. The largest yacht was The Pioneer, a three masted sailing ship, property of George Vanderbilt. James reported, "I had one terrific year fishing." But, instead of a fish story, Jim tells a mammal story. An astounding event was that of watching a great blue whale. While off the California Coast, the Crew noticed thousands of birds feeding on something. Closing in on the sight the Crew made out an immense whale about twenty feet smaller than the Arner. The mammal was estimated to be 60 feet long. The men wondered why it was out of its natural habitat from the cold Northern waters and why it was in such a state of existence. Birds were pecking all over the top of the whale's body and there appeared to be about one-hundred sharks feasting on the underside beneath the water. The whale appeared to be in pain and was quivering as it was slowly being eaten alive! Feeling sorry for this great blue whale, the men shot it in the head to put it out of its misery.

While at sea, James kept his land baby, his first Rolls Royce in San Diego. He had an art studio at #27 Olvero Street, Los Angeles. Later this area was restored as an historical area becoming a part of the State of California Park System. Before World War II, Jim studied art at various Los Angeles studios and had been in and through many art studios of Hollywood. In the field of Fine Art, he studied at universities in the United States and Mexico. His most technical expertise was credited to the year spent under the tutelage of Helmet Rhuemann, Chief Conservator for the National Gallery of London. James contributed his expertise to restoring a piece that turned out to be a preliminary sketch of the Mona Lisa. This experience highlighted his adventures during the year with the National Gallery. Jim sketched, painted and continued his endeavor in the arts during the war. He was commissioned to create posters for the Navy on wartime subjects.

James' proud father was a Texan! His grandfather was a member of the First Republic of Texas. As a conservator of paintings and an artist, James credits his early love of history to his upbringing in the Deep South. He has stated, "Nearly every classic painting or sculpture that appears rich, crisp or vivid has passed through the hands of an art restorer." James has restored several thousand canvases. The paintings have become his friends. A single painting can take over two years of full time labor to restore it. He was drawn to art because of his fascination for family portraits that graced his boyhood home in Louisiana. Appointed by his father as a sort of impromptu conservator of the family gallery, Jim began exploring methods of restoration. Studying painting and drawing he found "conservatism required artistic versatility with the ability to mimic the characteristic style of the artist whose canvas was being worked on. This included such styles as impressionism to cubism, Old Master styles and Colonial American."

Jim was assigned to a mine sweeper for a stint in the South Pacific. His ship was last to arrive in California for its maiden embarkation to the Pacific regions. He passed Hawaii via convoy after joining the fleet to the New Hebrides Islands. He was in several major sea battles for which he was awarded battle ribbons. Commissioned at sea as an Ensign the young man became a member of the Pacific Fleet. One time, he was transferred back to the States for a series of training exercises and then sent back to the South Seas. On the trip back and forth stopping at Pearl Harbor, he met and became great friends with Marguerite Bryant. James had Christmas dinner in Pearl Harbor aboard his vessel in 1943. Then he went to church. He was dressed in his brown kaiki uniform according to Marguerite. After he met Marguerite, they saw each other every time Jim anchored at Pearl.

Jim was classified as a Signalman in the Naval Reserve before he was commissioned and transferred to a minesweeper. A minesweeping operational ship was equipped with detectors for use in several ways. It could disarm or explode acoustical mine equipment. The acoustical apparatus that sent out pulses to set a mine off was called the hammer. The Crew sent out a small vibration or pulse to rend an explosion to set off a mine before reaching it. Mines suspended under water about twenty feet were exploded. "When the blast happened the ship would bounce out of the water and often your feet would fly out from under you," Jim said. The job of mine sweeping was to keep shipping lanes open. Their all wooden ship was depurmed against magnetism and all kinds of mines. The men were at New Hebrides Islands (Vanuatu) and they spent a great deal of time near Ile Efate' near the Port Vila Airbase and at Espereto Santos. One of the roommates at BOQ (Bachelor Officer's Quarters) was Tyrone Power. He was flying for the United States Air Force as Fighter Pilot.

There was firing still going on while at Guadalcanal. Six major Naval engagements were fought off the island while air battles were almost daily occurrences. Planes, ships and men were unmercifully sacrificed to secure local air and naval superiority. Before the island of Guadalcanal was finally won in January 1943, two Marine divisions, two Army divisions plus an addition Army regiment were committed to battle. Success for an amphibious attack was considered essential. Jim spent four days on base, waiting for transportation to San Francisco and Soloman, Maryland. James had spent four years at sea with a bit of service in the Caribbean. He had traveled thirteen times through the Panama Canal. He laughed, by that time, "I'd seen the same old certain alligators!"

Getting ready for the invasion of Japan, orders were received to mass at Mariannas Islands. From that huge armada, thousands of ships ended up in Tokyo Bay. James forgets what day it was but he'll never forget the sight of those ships! Another thing he forgot during those hectic early days of peacetime was his beautiful dog that looked like a seal. After Jim left the ship, his dog was kept and cared for by the Crew. (His company had a monkey too.) When the boat to take Jim to the States came along, he was so excited he forgot his dog! In about eight months, he was called by a faithful Crew Member and drove down to the wharf in San Diego to pick up his dog.

Marguerite and James were married at her family church in Kona, Hawaii. Christ Church, Kona is the oldest continously used Episcopal Church in the Islands. After forty-one years, James is still enamored with his wife whom he calls "a distinguished Kamaaina." He loves her wonderful family of ten uncles and aunts. All of the descendants developed into fine people. At a recent family reunion of 186 descendants, James and Marguerite were the only ones not present for the festivities due to health.

After the Vanderbilt's exquisite church wedding the newly weds came to Pasadena, California to settle some affairs and then left for Mexico. They drove to New Orleans to be with the Vanderbilt Family for Christmas. James describes his life with Marguerite as an interesting vivacious life. After the war, the newly-weds took off for a tour of the world. At Greenbrea Gallery in London, England at St. John's Woods, Jim worked in conservation of paintings with the head conservator. James went back to the portrait gallery. The talented husband and wife spent time traveling and viewing great houses in out of way places. Most of these architectural treasures are on the National Register of England.

It was easy to remain with the Naval Reserve after the war in Pearl Harbor. Jim and Marguerite came to Sonoma in 1968. James had seen the area in the 1930's while on leave from a ship being overhauled in Vallejo, California. He enjoyed a drive into the coastal mountains north of San Francisco. Sonoma roads at that time were gravel. Most of the buildings around the Plaza were closed. The Plaza itself was deteriorated and in very poor looking condition. From that day, James always had a strange feeling he would return to Sonoma.

James retired as a Lieutenant Commander of 36 LCTs (Landing Craft Tank Carriers). The whole Crew of 75 on each ship could move tanks on and off the transport. The LCTs were self-contained and were 75 feet long. Most Officers were inexperienced as to seamanship. There were a lot of ninety day wonders sent for replacement.

Flags were at half-mast. Jim could signal with his hands to find out why the flags were flying that way, so he did. (He had learned hand signaling as a Boy Scout.) The answer to his question, "What happened?" was "FDR had died." Ironically, the first message he had ever sent that way was to Franklin Delano Roosevelt. His toes were run over in a parade which was honoring Franklin Delano Roosevelt.

Not only have James and Marguerite experienced a great deal of history, they have sustained history. They have given their time and substance to three museums. They have helped with the Kona Museum under care of the Kona Historical Society. The museum is on the big Island of Hawaii and is valued at $2,000,000.00. Marguerite's whole family are Patrons of the Museum. Most of the Hawaiian memorabilia that the Sonoma couple owned or inherited has been returned to the Museum. The artifacts include calabashas (Hawaiian Urns) early Hawaiian clothing and a Calabash Cousin (one big pot). Some items donated were made in England, some American. Others were from the Summer

Palace Era. The latter items were from a time when English children played at the Hawaiian Palace with the children of the Royal line.

Jim has created a world quality museum in Sonoma at the Depot Museum. He has worked continously and very diligently for the Sonoma Valley Historical Society. He has devoted time to one of California's greatest needs, that of art conservation of the Early California history. James consults regularly with curators and conservators from National Gallaries around the world. The main room of the Sonoma Depot Museum was dedicated in 1992 as the Vanderbilt Room. Both Marguerite and James were honored and were presented with a large bronze placque sculpted by Anthony Stellon. The placque is hung in the Vanderbilt Room at the museum. Jim was honored as Sonoma Treasure in 1985. He was further honored by being named Alcalde (Honorary Mayor) in 1993.

James even fought for and sustained the hanging rope and graffeti in the Hemphill, Texas Museum. It was from Hemphill, that he was awarded the beautiful Honorary Citizenship of the Republic of Texas. His great grandfather freed slaves and gave them land. Jim and Marguerite have helped to honor his great grandfather Joshua Speights an early Judge there.

When Marguerite had left the room during these interviews, James again told how delighted he was with his beautiful wife. "How did she escape marriage until I came along," he wondered. He feels like, "I'm the luckiest guy! Here she was a graduate in music, a very fine pianist."

He again recalled his very glamourous life. He had three Rolls Royce Automobiles and still owns one. He knew many of the Hollywood greats. He created illustrations for *My Sister, Eileen* and color work in *Gone with the Wind*. As an art center student with a studio on Olvero Street he worked with the enchanting Casa Spedulvada. In Sonoma, James restores great paintings that other persons would be afraid to even touch. He conceived the permanent Bear Flag Exhibit at the museum called *Manifest Destiny*. His architecturally designed home is most unusual. The Vanderbilts have great wall space for artistic medium in many forms, broad gardens filled with exotic Hawaiian flora and one great big restored door. When the City Hall in Sonoma was remodeled, one of the dirtiest ugliest, tallest oak doors lay in the mud in a hole on the ground inside the building. Jim was asked if he would like to have the door. From the old oak door, Jim created a masterpiece. Its beauty fills a very tall opening near his kitchen. This little piece of history of the Sonoma's past shines brightly. Nearby, an American beauty colored bougainvillea is seen on the patio and the Hawaiian ginger plant fills the air with high perfume. Everything is peaceful and calm.

The night before Pearl Harbor, Jim tied a string on his big toe. His friends said, "Get up and go to war!" He volunteered. He believes his greatest achievement was meeting his wife.

Some references for Jim's article were through the Courtesy of the City of Sonoma for access to the displays of the Treasures hung in the Court Chambers at 177 First Street West, Sonoma, California. Some references were also from an article in the Sonoma Index Tribune as part of the above referenced display, entitled *Bringing Beauty Back to Life,* written by Olivia Casey in the LIVING section of the Sonoma Index, dated March 11, 1986.

Milano C. Rispoli

United States Army, 1942 - 1945

Milano Rispoli, nicknamed early on, as 'Rip' was born in Milford, Massachusettes. Rip was son of a granite layer and cutter. Should one visit the Capitol Building of the State of Utah in Salt Lake City, that person could view the floors and walls laid down by Rip's father between the years, 1915-1920. By the year 1921, Rip was a student in an elementary school in San Francisco, California followed by high school attendance at Mission High in the same city. He took general economic courses at St. Mary's College, graduating in 1931. Only 450 students comprised the roster at Moraga, California. The school did have the best football team that year beating University of Southern California and Stanford.

Rip ended up working at odd jobs until he landed employment with the State Relief Administration. It was in the depression and Franklin Delano Roosevelt was President of the United States when Rip found this job. It was under the auspices of the WPA which was really a welfare program. In short, Rip was a social worker. His case load was probably around two-hundred single men in San Francisco. They lived south of Market Street and North Beach. He was paid $19.75 a month for board and room. He used $8.00 for the room and the rest for food for thirty days.

Wonderful things happened during the Works Progress Administration under Roosevelt. Doctors received a fee of $100.00 a month. Lawyers and professional people also received $100.00 a month to service the ailments and problems of these poor people. The professionals were very happy with their $100.00 a month stipend and made a big contribution to the country. These federal funds were used with the San Francisco unemployed for five or six years.

Rip was promoted to the Italian Welfare Agency. He was the new director for about four years. He met such notable people as A.P. Giannini of the Bank of America and Ghiradelli of the famous Chocolate Factory. These men were advisors and helped with ideas. The agency had a private social service agenda taking care of problems in the Italian community such as illness, employment for the unemployed and especially aiding indigents in State Hospitals. Rip also assisted people for getting help from State and Federal government agencies.

After leaving Italian welfare, resigning to represent Naval Intelligence, Rip monitored ship building companies and their employees regarding war production lines. Along with former San Francisco Chief of Police Quinn, he investigated possiblity of crime, sabotage and infiltration into defense manufacturing factories.

Eventually, the Marina Draft Board directed Milano (Rip) to Monterey. He was assigned to the Medical Administration Corps after which he attended Officers training in Abilene, Texas. In ninety days, Rip was wearing insignia designating status of Second Lieutenant. He was then sent to Oregon. As a 96th Infantryman Division Member he went on maneuvers and training never carrying a gun. He wore an arm band designating he was a Medic.

Rip was one of the hundreds of American soldiers who stormed the beachhead of Normandy. His group made it on D-DAY+5. During training in the United States he had noticed a sign on the bulletin board regarding classes at Stanford University on Military Government. In three or four months he had graduated and was transferred to England. While in England waiting for embarkation and the invasion of Normandy he became connected with tour guidemanship to Shakespeare's Hometown of Stratford-on-Avon. He took service men to the area to commemorate the English dramatist and poet considered to be the greatest playwright who ever lived. On D-Day+5, Rip was just like any other soldier doing his duty. It was the Battle of Brest, from August 5th to September 20th, 1944 that he became designated a hero. He earned the French Legion of Honor award - that nation's highest award for heroism. Rip Rispoli helped evacuate 180 to 230 French civilians from the submarine pits (covered docks in Brest, France) while under attack from the Germans. The rescue was deemed distinctive because he was only a Captain in the Medical Administrative Corps attached to the 8th Corps and was the lowest ranking Officer to get the Legion of Honor medal. "I was surprised to receive an award, I wasn't even allowed to carry a gun," he said matter-of-factly.

Rip prefers to speak about what he did following that fateful event. After the honor ceremony held in Frankfurt, Germany where he was decorated by Deputy Commander to De Gaulle, he was privileged to lunch with General Dwight Eisenhower. General Eisenhower could have had the noonday meal with fourteen American Generals but instead he came to sit and eat with Rip. "You earned yours," General Eisenhower introduced himself to their private luncheon.

After that exciting event, Rip Rispoli was transferred to General Simpson's 9th Army Unit with headquarters in Holland. Because of his heroism in Brest, he was assigned for twenty-eight weeks to control movements of refugees in the Ruhr Valley in Northern Germany. He was now a Staff Officer and helped move 3,000,000 people as refugees back to their respective homelands. He served in co-ordination with Head of Supply and Transportation Headquarters of the 9th Army. As such, decisions were made on movement and transportation by trucks and trains (40's and 8's) to ship loads of displaced persons back to their native countries from all over the continent.

In this position, Milano was not to interfere in any country's personal problems. He was not to bother or interfere with the war in any way nor to help overthrow Hitler. However, following orders was a great big change from using gut feelings as he did to save the persons at Brest. General Charles DeGaulle of France complained that Rip and his command were working too fast. DeGaulle, according to Rip was trying to be elected PRESIDENT by contacting the French refugees to vote for him. He gave the refugees clothes and food and sent them back to their homes in France. DeGaulle protested that the great numbers of people being sent were difficult to handle but Rip knew combat conditions made it necessary. General Bradley, according to Rip declared, "Keep it up, boy! Keep it up!" By then, Rispoli increased his original number from 2,000 to 3,000 refugees handled per day to 5,000 refugees moved per day. DeGaulle continued complaining about it all. Much of this movement was to keep these displaced peoples out of the way of the Allied Armies finishing up the last months of the war.

Rip lived in Masstricht, Netherlands during this time waiting for the invasion of the Rhine. The Military had a strong foundation up and down France, Belgium, Holland and the crossing of the Rhine River. Getting started with the refugee project was touchy at first. One had to handle the refugee problem for all Northern Germany. Rip was actually just verbally appointed from the time he took on the job until the war ended. He moved 260,000 Italians from slave labor under Hitler. He repatriated Latvians, Estonians and Lithuanians into Russia. These three nations' refugees had superior intelligence. They had culture and religious refinements. But as soon as Russia received them, Allied intelligence reported that Stalin kept those peoples captives of the Russian Government. Therefore, no more groups were sent to the Russian government.

Refugees were Dutch, French, Danish, Polish and a few Belgium and English people. Most of the displaced persons were in Germany as slave laborers. Two hundred sixty thousand Italians were used as civilian labor on docks. The largest collection of people came from Poland. The French also made up a large group. Belgium and Holland natives were a fair-sized assemblage.

Usually, the Transportation Department of the Army would hear of problems impeding the military movement of food, ammunition or equipment. Masses of people were in the way. Rip was ordered, "Get those people the hell out of there!"

Actually only two people controlled the movement of these masses of people. Rip consulted once with General Simpson, 9th Army Commander at Rhur River when 1,200,000 people were uncovered working German steel mills and production. The 30th Division Infantry of 30,000 men were assigned and took control of this set of refugees. The war was still going on. It was like a vacation for the military to receive the job of caring for those peoples. Food for so many refugees was a big drain from military supplies. The biggest problem continued to be General DeGaulle. In order to appease DeGaulle, the British, French, American and Canadian Generals had to let DeGaulle ride in pomp and ceremony into Paris first, as a political maneuver. This gave DeGaulle precedence over General Marshall and over Eisenhower. NOTE: This applied to DeGaulle's entry into Paris, only.

When people were moved in masses across the various countries, they were taken to the borders of their own respective countries. The 260,000 special Italian slave workers hated the Germans. Where to send them out of harms way? Where to put them out of the way from causing trouble? Refugees were blocking the ports. This impeded the American Armies receipt of important supplies for the front lines. Lives were at risk.

"Where's General Patton?" one Officer asked; "I got an idea." "He's south of Munich," was the answer. After a few more comments about how Patton "got things done" Rip called the head of transportation and sent a group of 260,000 refugees a little south of Munich. Later on, a fellow heard Patton lecture and reported back, "He, Patton made a decision to get rid of all those people that arrived near his battle zone." In Rip's eyes, "General Patton was quite a guy!" Patton could make a decision following through to make it happen! Within a week those people were back in Italy, their homeland and the Armies did not have to deal with them again. Rip felt, "Patton was killed by the Russians." Rip believes, "Patton was right and we should not have trusted the Russians. Because, 41,000,000 men had been killed under Stalin's Armies."

Rip was sent to see the the infamous Buchenwald Concentration Camp in Germany. He was assigned to accompany the then, Congressman Dirksen. Rip viewed 2,000 bodies covered by canvas sheets and an additional 6,000 to 8,000 souls in the infirmary. Most of these emaciated people weighed less than sixty pounds and lived under terrible conditions. Patients in those sections had their eyes bulging out due to malnutrition. They were placed on crude wooden shelves like one would stack sacks of groceries, three or four to a shelf. There were twelve patients to a group. It was one of the worse prisons kept by Hitler. The macabre sight has haunted Rip the rest of his life.

Milano was a little angry towards Congressman Dirkson. The man spent his visit there getting drunk with a Russian Captain. The two men drank all day long. When Dirkson did talk to Rip, he kept asking him to get in touch with all the GI's from Illinois. Then, extremely drunk, he made a speech to the Illinois recruits, telling the soldiers who hailed from that fair state, "You'll be going home soon. Tell your parents to be sure and vote for me when I run for Congress." Sure enough, they did. Dirksen was there to visit one of the worse concentration camps of the German regime. Rip couldn't even get him to look at one of the concentration camp's incinderators. Rip felt, "DeGaulle and Dirkson were both alike." He scornfully branded them "cheap politicians."

Milano back in the United States worked as a salesman for canned food. He started his own company as a food broker. He represents canneries or manufacturing companies with olive oil, pasta from Nestles Foods and anchovies. Users of his products include shoppers of Safeway or Lucky Stores from 1948 until 1994. He is still involved in the business in limited capacity. Rip sells Sasso Olive Oil which he claims, "is the number one olive oil of Italy." He still goes to Italy to reminiscent. He met his wife, Faye about twenty-five years ago at the Ahwahanee Hotel in Yosemite National Park. She was an 'Ansel Adams Model' and a hairdresser at the hotel. She was an excellent gardener and he proudly pointed at an acrylic picture she had painted. About 1983, they decided to avoid the increasing traffic of city life in Marin County. They saw some new houses being constructed near Sonoma. They enjoyed their last years together in that quiet adult community until the end of her life. Rip misses Faye. He has a housekeeper to keep things in order and continues on living a busy existence.

His French Legion of Honor award reads as follows:

1945, 12th of December.   Registered 52751

Highest Award. Republique Francaise

Order Nat'l De La Legion D'Honneur

M. le-Captain Milano C. Rispoli

First United States Army

est Nomme' Chevalier de la Legion d' Honneur

12th September 1945

Registered 10th December 1946.

Charles J. Stormont

United States Army, 1942 - 1946

Charles J. Stormont when a young man became a member of the Army Field Artillery in the China-Burma-India Theater of World War II. He began his life in the little town of Viola, Wisconsin born in 1914. Charles' father was a doctor administering to patients in the influenza epidemic of 1918. He caught the plague himself and died when Charles was but four years old. Charles had a brother, age two and another on the way. His pregnant mother had to get a job to raise her young family. She became a telephone operator. The boy's grandfather, a druggist helped. On the maternal side his grandmother was there for the fellows when they arrived home each night from school.

At that time, Viola had about 800 numbered population. The town had three doctors for years, then none. After high school graduation in Viola, Charles attended the University of Wisconsin at Madison. He started out as a premed student but graduated in Zoology. He decided not to be a doctor. What he did start was a mink farm.

He visited a mink farm while out partying one night. Making a big U-turn in the road, Charles decided to visit this place displaying such a big sign welcoming visitors. The young man was given a big hearty greeting. In the process of being hospitable the owners of the farm sold Charles two soft cuddly mink. They were bred females. By the time these mink babies grew up they were worth about $20.00 per skin. Very soon, Charles was taking care of thirty-five mink. The critters were taking more and more of his time.

Charles worked as a Chief Clerk in a County Agriculture Adjustment Act [AAA] Office. He could either stay with that type of job or experiment becoming a real full-time mink farmer. He chose the minks. The mink ranch industry as a farming concept was about twenty years old when Charles bought those first two mink. Established mink farmers were in the states of Washington, Oregon and Minnesota. Climate had a great deal to do with such an operation and was influential as to whether a mink farm would flourish.

One particular aspect of mink farming was difficult for a person who liked animals. Charles actually hated the process of killing and skinning his brood. After all, he had nurtured and cared for the furry little critters from birth until the preparation for market. It was inevitable to actually be a mink farmer one had to sell the mink in order to make a living and to make room for more mink! The mink were sold to two major outlets, Hudson Bay Company and New York Auction Company. He sold to both. The companies supplied their own cartons which the mink farmer filled with skins. The pelts were prepared by taking off the fat and then skins were allowed to dry. Sixty pelts were considered a full box. Eventually, some mink skins brought as much as $200.00 each. One expensive cost of doing business was insurance. Sending the boxes of fur pelts by air freight, insurance was costly but necessary. It was a valuable cargo.

After four or five years of being a mink rancher in Wisconsin, Charles step-father (his mother had remarried) said he'd hire and manage people to do the work for the mink operation if Charles volunteered for the service. Charles knew his draft number would be coming up. He said, "I felt that I should volunteer." He jokingly laughed, "I waved the flag, grabbed a knapsack and was off to Richland Center, Wisconsin and was advised by a recruiter, "if you want to become a survey and instrument man, you can learn to survey and point large guns and shoot them!" Charles was promptly sent by train to Fort Sheridan, Illinois for two days and from there to Fort Sill, Oklahoma. He was promoted from Private to Corporal right away while in basic training. Charles said, "I had a hell of a good time at Fort Sill. We marched, did exercises, drank beer and went out with girls on dates. I was asked if I would be interested in attending the Officers Candidate School at Fort Sill. Naturally, I said, "Yes!" He jumped at the chance and after graduating was commissioned as a Second Lieutenant.

While in OCS, Charles noticed on the Officers Bulletin Board that anyone interested in animals should report to a certain Colonel's Office. Thinking it might be a chance to work with hogs, he reported and found he was assigned to a Mule Pack Artillery Division. He learned how to shoe mules, pack mules and care for them in general. At the conclusion of this preliminary class at Fort Sill, he was shipped to Camp Hale, Colorado at an altitude of 11,000 feet. He trained there for two weeks and then was shipped to Camp Carson, Colorado just outside the city of Colorado Springs. Here at an altitude of roughly 7,000 feet he was additionally schooled in the art of Mule Pack Artillery. (1) He Learned how to pack the seven sections or pieces of a 75 millimeter pack artillery Howitzer aboard the Phillips saddles which the mules would wear upon their backs. (2) He would learn the fine points in how to saddle the mules. (3) The men were given suggestions as to traveling techniques on long single file marches with the mules packed. (4) They added the four Howitzers which comprised a battery of Pack Artillery. (5) Other mules were packed with with ammunition loads. (6) They Pretended the unit was in contact with an enemy in certain areas. (7) They learned to quickly unload and assemble the Howitzers. (8) They practiced unpacking the 75 millimeter shells and after a quick survey would start bringing designated targets under fire. The mule, as far as Charles was concerned was not stubborn, as generally referred to but was a wonderful animal. He watched over the mules as they ate bailed hay and grain. He spoke to them and patted them on the rump. It was not his job but he did hang around and helped feed them.

One incident of training was a bit unnerving, however. On a side trip to Camp Carson, Colorado for a training expedition, the men were introduced to sheer rock climbing. The men were ordered to climb Chimney Rock. Going up this rock you would move your feet a little then back up a little. The climb was up 150 feet of granite. It was raining and there was moss growing on the walls. Charles got so terrified he couldn't move. The rock got slick. He almost gave up and dropped. He desperately clung to the rock. Regaining his composure and with words of encouragement from a couple of friends who had already made it, he safely made it to the top. His friend, a Second Lieutenant from Minneapolis fell off the precipice to his death passing over two climbing comrades on the way. The friend was killed instantly.

The Army recruits were schooled as a mountain outfit. Most of the men had been cadred from other Pack Artillery Battalions to form the 612 Field Artillery Battalion (Pack.) Some had made the long march from Camp Hale to Camp Carson and most had bivouaced up and over the 14,110 foot Pikes Peak Summit in Central Colorado. They became privy to trials, tribulations and sheer exhaustion which accompanied long arduous mountainous marches but few realized what was in store for them in their very near future... They just tried to act like tough mean men, some who were heavy drinkers.

The Battalion sailed from Camp Anza, California on July 25th, 1944. They had spent two weeks in a healthy exhilarating environment at that camp. Each night, one found most of these brawny guys in Hollywood. The next morning, the same fellows were wearing off a hangover on a short fast road march.

Being on the Pacific Coast was just a paradox. The men found themselves sailing from the Atlantic Coast on the USS General Butner. The ship was a large speedy vessel considered to be well-armed. Built as a troop carrier, it was capable of traveling alone. In addition to the burly mountain men known as the 612th Field Artillery Battalion, a Black troop known as the 124th Cavalry Regiment was aboard along with a few special service troops, a handful of Red Cross Girls and a U.S.O Show. Before long, the group organized their own band.

While on the trip, there were a couple of submarine scares. At Melbourne, Austrailia the men managed to sneak a little liquor aboard. In the 8 by 14 foot compartment, number 218, where twelve Officer's luggage and miscellaneous furniture was packed ever so tightly, the group had quite a party! The 612th Battalion had another wild party after landing at Bombay, India on the 25th of August, 1944. After about two days in Bombay most were ready to move on. Their short time there was considered "a fair glance of seeing India and her teeming millions of people." The troops were then herded aboard a stinky English narrow gauge train which began a lengthy and tortuous journey. Food consisted of "C" and "K" rations which one grew tired of in a hurry but desirous of when about to starve. The troops did not know it at the time but the same rations were to provide substance for months to come. At first, the men supplemented the canned diet with bananas and cocoanuts purchased from the Indians who gathered in huge crowds to beg for "Baksheesh Sahib" (money) every place one stopped. Indians at the train stops were a dirty, motley lot and some men stated, "We will be glad to see the last of India before we ever get into those jungles!"

After one of the worst journeys imaginable, the group arrived at Rhamgarrh in northeastern India which was called General Stillwell's rear-echelon. It was a training center for Chinese Troops that had escaped with him from Burma when Japanese soldiers had overrun the area. The 612th Battalion spent another three weeks of training at this location by means of improvising tactics but mostly sweltering in a torrid sun. The troops were given atabrine because of the danger of malaria from mosquitos. They learned of diseases familiar to the country but foreign to the United States of America. They wondered why they had not already taken enough shots and vaccinations to protect them from anything and everything!

The men were given a lecture by General Boetner which did not set a stage the men wanted to hear. He told them, "You are going to Burma which is a Hell of a Place. You are going to drive the Japanese out who are 'dammed good fighters' and they are as treacherous as any group you will ever meet. You will drive them out of Northern Burma."

The 612th Battalion left the 124th Cavalry who had accompanied each other so far since meeting on the ship. The men of the 612th were crowded into filthy cattle cars and some men did sleep standing up. After creeping along in this uncomfortable smelly condition at about ten miles an hour clip, the group arrived at DinJan in the evening. They were tired out, filthy dirty, stinking and ready for the sack. DinJan was only a short way from Ledo where the Stillwell Road begins. At the time of their arrival, it was the campsite for most of the Marauders. They, with the help of the Chinese Army were just back from driving the Japanese from Myitkyina. The Maurauders were miscellaneous characters and were a slaphappy bunch being tipsy most of the time. Like most of the places the Americans stopped, the other Army groups would not be aware of their coming. So, no preparations had been made. As a result the new arrivals slogged around in knee deep mud until midnight. The new arrivals also had barracks bags loaded with clothing and equipment to sort through in order to finally find something on which to lay down. Hardly anyone had a mosquito net. Many men caught a wink or two lying in mud holes. For Charles part, he was darned disgusted! With a few other Officers of the 612th and a smattering of

Marauders they got acquainted sharing some putrid Indian gin. At reveille, about one tenth of the Battalion was present, half dressed and without headgear. Many were still tight because the Marauders had been very free with their liquor.

At DinJan, the group piled their excess equipment on the ground without much in the line of accountability. The pile grew with almost all the items that Battalion Commander Major Reed had been so darned careful to see that the men should take with them. "None of the group," Charles stated; "would ever forget the clothing and equipment checks that we had endured every day, day after day, at both Camp Carson, Camp Anza and again several times in India. All of that preparation proved to be pretty stupid when we arrived in Dinjan. We flung everything in huge piles on the muddy ground and walked off, wondering what would become of it all?" If you needed a rifle, all you had to do was pick one up, anyplace, it was yours. If you needed jungle boots or any other article of clothing, you could walk into supply and help yourself to as much as you cared to carry."

The troops noticed the American Cemetery going to supply. There were quite a number of graves in it. Not all men were killed from bullets but from scrub typhus, which made its appearance with the Japanese. Scrub typhus was a disease confined to a few river valleys of Japan before the war. It was a disease few Western Doctors knew anything about. It was known to burn the victim to death with very high temperatures. Those who had scrub typhus usually had malaria and amoebic dysentery as well.

The group made the last part of their difficult journey by plane arriving at Myitkyina. They saw ravages of a very recent war. There were pieces of buildings hanging in the trees like a spiders web from the approaching airplanes. Very little materiality was left standing. Rotting flesh of Japanese was unburied. Stubbles of trees were uncannily jammed with cawing crows. Magpies ambled here and there along the ground. The men saw Budda temples. Some were blown to bits, others were quite intact.

Weeks were spent clearing a patch of jungle for a campsite. Tents had to be lined up. A corral was prepared for the mules which were to arrive later. Bamboo was cut and fashioned into a framework for kitchens, recreation rooms, class rooms and latrines. All of these facilities were covered with tarpaulins and burlap. Mornings, the men practiced jungle fighting in a thicket of high grasses, vines, trees and undergrowth. They fired their artillery pieces. They had been issued a worn-out battery of pack Howitzers and a battery of field Howitzers. These, they pushed to and fro from gun positions in tropical downpours of rain and sweltering heat as the mules had not yet arrived. Afternoons, the fellows washed their clothes, which was an almost "have to" every day. They bathed in the mighty waters of the Irrawaddy River which swirled past the camp at a frightful speed. The jungle was so dense it reminded one of a river bottom tangle of swamplands where immense trees stood. One such tree close to camp caused Charles to take 26 paces, approximately 78 feet to pass beside it in a straight line. Everyone was armed with machettes. Vines were so thick, you could only go a few yards in a day, if off the trail, just hacking yourself away. The men stuck pretty much to established game trails and pretty close to camp. At night, it was often difficult to sleep because of the terrific racket played out by the insects. As to beautiful things, Charles felt, "it was safe to say that hardly anything rivals the Burma moon for splendor." The men could play cards and read until 11 o'clock at night by nothing but moonlight.

The men received a beer ration which consisted of one case per man for a month. In addition, the Officers received a quart of Schenleys Whiskey, just out the vat but still held in high esteem. The camp was in a rather good mood for a couple of nights after receiving the ration. Charles and a First Lieutenant Johnson from the State of Minnesota sipped their drinks while sitting on an old teak wooden log of immense proportions. By moonlight, they argued philosophy and politics until the wee hours of the morning. When the ration was consumed the A Battery Cook brewed a concoction which should have borne the name 'Jungle pate' instead of whiskey.

Troop activities included writing letters to home by men who spent utterly hours at the task. As an Officer, Charles found plenty of mail had to be censored by the Battery Officers. Some men fished the Irrawaddy and the fish which included two main types was excellent. One looked like a catfish and the other like a carp. The meat on the second type fish reminded Charles of Walleye Pike right out of a cold Wisconsin lake. Some men constructed fishing poles from bamboo. Others fished lazily with hand grenades. Many men hunted squirrels, deer, and chicken. Carbines were constantly cracking. All of this meat was a delicious supplement to army rations. "We read in an old newspaper once we were eating ice cream!" Charles exclaimed; "We did get one spoonful of ice cream once and many turned it down in scorn."

As to coldness, one only had to try to stand in the swirling Irrawaddy River. It was ice cold for it had not flowed too far from its source in the Himalayas Mountains. Clothes were washed in its clear waters and the men dove in for a cold swim from a Kachin dugout canoe which was firmly anchored to the bank. Uniforms were dipped sort of haphazardly in the swift waters with the hope the current of the stream would do the washing.

Part of the unit was sent back up to Ledo to help herd the mules down the road to Myitkyina and they finally arrived after a very tough journey of from 250 to 300 miles. Equipment also came as expected. The mules were then shod and then everything was shipshaped for the jumping off place they knew was in the offing. The 124th arrived and the Merrill Marauders were still in the area. "Historically, on the morning of November 17, 1944, under command of Lieutenant General Severn T. Wallis, the 612th Field Artillery Battalion marched from Camp Landis near Myitkyina, Burma on its first combat mission." Attached to the 475th Infantry Regiment, it constituted the artillery element of one of the two Combat Teams which together formed the 5332 Brigade, known proudly as the Mars Task Force. Their mission was to open up the Burma Road so that oil, gas, ammunition and food could be brought from India to China. The Mars Task Force was one of two American Long Range Penetration Units circling around and behind Japanese lines. Their only outside communication was by radio. This included air drops of supplies and liason with small planes regarding the troops. John Randolph, in the introduction of his book, *Marsmen in Burma,* in his book written primarily for Marsmen, stated, "this Task Force might well have been marching as a band of warriors out of ancient history books --better still, from fairy tales or comic strips." In another place, he describes the same territory as "going through country few white men had ever seen but country steeped in a background as ancient as the ages."

Randolph states the mule-pack 612th and 613th arrived by September 16th, and he attempted to get information on the 612th with no success. Charles' written notes, generously shared in this book fills in gaps of information sought regarding the 612th Field Artillery Battalion. Here and there throughout Charles' copy of that book was inscribed "This is where I was." Most of these notes are where the 2nd Battalion activites were described.

China's supply route from India was important to the United States of America in order to keep China's Nationalist Government alive, well and active in the war. At one time the Japanese occupied all of Burma and even east of the Burma Road into China. The Allies wanted the Japanese stopped. It took men of high physical stamina to climb a day's march that might start at 500 feet and reach close to 5,000 feet before dark. The usual walking schedule around trails so narrow that "mules could not be turned sideways" was fifty minutes walking and 10 minutes resting.

Twice, while located at Camp Landis, the Japanese bombed Myitkyina in good style. The men were all deep in their foxholes which had been built for such an occasion. They watched the antiaircraft cross the sky. The Japanese were after the airport and did do some damage. Two zeros were brought down in one attack by the antiaircraft. That was the last raid.

The men of Battery A were to support the First Battalion of the 475th Infantry and were to separate from the rest of the regiment near Bhamo to go on a separate mission of their own. A couple of days before leaving, they were again issued clothing and equipment. They chose what they wanted, only. They took a march down the Irawaddy as a test to see how everything would work. Thousands more dollars worth of clothing was discarded that day to balance the packs. The local Katchins must have had a regular 'once in a lifetime picnic' when they came across all that loot.

Katchins were short-statured people like India people. Charles feels sure that no foreigners ever respected them or enjoyed them as much as the Americans did. After the Battle of Myitkyina, MI rifles and even carbines were easy to get from so many soldiers that would not be shooting them anymore. Many local Katchins were packing MIs as big as themselves. Each battalion in the Regiment had its own group of Katchin Rangers for guides. These guides also acted as spies. Everyone in the battalion learned a few native words and occasionally traded with them for vegetables, rice and saki. They in turn, loved American rations "C" and "D" as well as American cigarettes. (It was noted here, as in other South Pacific regions, that the Japanese soldier had treated the Natives with brutality.)

After a one day trip down a trail close to the Irrawaddy, the group crossed the river on flat barges powered with outboard motors. There was one casualty in the hazardous crossing. A mule badly trampled one of the fellows in "A" Battery. The fellow had to be evacuated to the hospital.

From that point, Charles believes he was part of a journey that could well be described as "the most difficult march ever taken by troops, in strength, in modern history." The march was a long range penetration into enemy territory. The movement was hoped to be hidden as long as possible from the enemy. The group stuck pretty much to game trails and cart trails. The British called these trails "tracks." The men marched single file into heavy jungle. Contact to the rear was maintained by radio and messenger. Contact was made by radio in code. The I and R Platoon was usually about a day ahead and marked the trail as well as picked the bivouacs. The group was utterly strung out for miles on these trails. The marchers wound back and forth in irregular bends and up and down in devious twists over snake coiled tortuous trails. Men were subjected to extreme physical pain. The thicket was like it was never ending. Evidence of game was everywhere. Elephant paths were followed in many places. Paths were shown on the best army maps of Burma but often the routes taken were known only to Katchin guides and sometimes, even they were not certain where they terminated. The group forded river after river in ice water up to their belts. They trudged on the opposite side soaking wet until the hot Burma sun sifting through the thicket dried their clothing. Often, they crossed an icy river by wading just prior to bivouac. They went to sleep soaked. Up each morning before dawn, bivouacking in the dark, they took their first rest two days out of Bhamo. They remained in that camp for three days. After crossing another small river the men hacked their way through almost impenetrable jungle to gain their bivouac.

Several Katchin settlements found near them allowed a bazaar for trading. At first a chicken was traded for a pack of cigarettes. Soon, it was impossible to get one for a carton of cigarettes.

Supply was carried on for the entire campaign by C-47 airdrop from the Combat Cargo Command. In some places it was necessary to clear a space to receive the drop. Panels of white parachute strips were laid out in rice paddies. Radio communication was established with the plane and then came the drop. The airplane might circle from four to eight times to dump all its cargo. Three days of rations were carried on the jungle march. On the fourth day, an airdrop was received. The Thanksgiving drop allowed a big feed with canned turkey and cranberries. A few fellows got well 'crocked' on saki which they had bartered from the natives. For the most part, men were satisfied to just rest. Mules took some care every day. On Thanksgiving, they were in nearby rice paddies and with guards out at all times. Nothing eventful happened during the group's stay at this point except a Japanese radio station on a nearby mountain was knocked out along with the occupants.

"A" Battery, for which Charles was Recognaissance Officer was slated to be the supporting artillery for the First Battalion of the 475th which was parting company for a mission of its own. They crossed a swift wide mountain stream at Myothit on barges and outboard motors operated by an engineering group. The Japs had established an elaborate defense system there but abandoned it prior to their crossing. Large air holes led down to underground tunnels and defenses. Some of these holes were thirty feet deep and all of this overlooked the spot on the river being crossed. A couple of dead Japanese lay half in the water which marked the only resemblance of a battle. It was believed these enemy were killed sometime before the Americans arrival either by Katchins or by Chinese who were beseiging the Japanese garrison at Bhamo. That garrison was a short way ahead.

As the group went around Bhano, they could hear the Chinese artillery firing and watch P-47s dive, strafe and bomb the town. Charles' group traveled west as the mission of the First Battalion was to go to Swegu and set up headquarters. Swegu was about two-thirds the way from Bhano to Cathay where the British were engaged with the Japanese in the railroad corridore. The First Battalion was to hold Swegu, supposedly unoccupied and patrol the region on over to the Irrawaddy where the river turned back south again. Then they were to meet up with British patrols.

Charles was one of the first to cross the top of Pikes Peak in Colorado but this march onward had Pikes Peak beat every day for the entire journey. Heading off into the wildest game country in all Burma, they made their own path in places that required hacking jungle growth all day long. They climbed mountains that Charles swore they would never rise to the top of. Looking ahead one day through a clearing, he saw a temple. By nightfall, they had reached it. Each night, the men complained they would not be able to take another step. Every morning they did.

Swegu was a fine town. A few of the natives talked a bit of English. People were clean and the best dressed seen so far. There was a large temple in town. The group spent two weeks resting and repairing equipment while camped around the perimeter of the village. The mules were in the bad shape, the worst Charles had ever seen. How the men or their pack mules ever stood the physically-ill-punishment of the jungle was beyond imagination. The men worked hard treating the mules' sores, graining and grazing them. They also had to take care of their own scratches, blisters and abrasions.

An even less favorable march was ahead. As Reconnaisance Officer, Charles surveyed near the village so that should an attack be waged, the artillery could lay down a barrage of fire designed to protect the troops. Infantry troops did on one occasion ambush 30 Japanese near the native village. The group suffered one wounded and lost one man in the jungle. He later returned.

Charles had to identify or know by previous knowledge how to make surveys and positions for the guns. The men ran copper wires to connect the radios in the field. In the 612th Battalion, Battery A. of which Charles was an Officer there were four large guns, 75 MM Pack Howitzers. Each of these guns broke down into seven pieces. Each mule could only carry one gun piece. Each piece fitted on a cargo saddle on the back of a mule. The heaviest piece was the gun barrel which weighed 220 pounds. Coupled with the saddle which weighed 60 pounds the whole weight would be secured upon the back of a 1,200 pound mule. The tenacious animal carried on its back that 280 pound burden all day! It took a group of 28 mules to carry four guns for Battery A.

It was the duty of the Battery Commander to pick a position and order the guns to be set up. The seven pieces would have to be fitted together. For example, as Reconnaissance Officer using binoculars, Charles would spot Japanese calvary or tanks. He would then call for fire on these targets. The 75MM pack Howitzer would shoot 15 pound shells. The shells had a twelve mile range. These battles in Burma were taking place at the same time as those battles of France, Germany and Netherlands were taking place in Europe.

Some of the men would occasionally bag a squirrel or two for dinner. In the evening, it was custom to sit around a five gallon can of warm coffee and kibitz for a couple of hours. The men bathed daily in the Irrawaddy which at this location was broad, deep and slow as compared to the Camp Landis location. Across the way was a long sand bar reaching out from an island. In mid-stream lay a dead Japanese or Chinese partly in and partly out of the water. Crows picked at him on a daily basis. It was speculated, he floated down from Bhamo. Japanese and Chinese were still firing at each other in the Bhamo region. Natives from Swegu came to camp daily. They traded vegetables and rice. They also traded their women. The price for a woman was half of a silk parachute. There were no prophylactics such as a condom in the outfit. In spite of that condition, no one ever contracted a venereal disease which was surprising, in view of the fact that the Japanese had been in Swegu prior to the Americans arrival. It was a rumor that Burmese people had a high rate of venereal infections. These rumors were purposely circulated to frighten GIs in order to keep sex at a minimum.

The next move back to Tonkwa, a two week journey was over a different route. Much of the pilgrimage did not even follow a game trail. The group received their Christmas drop on this trek back. They took a half day off to cram themselves with canned turkey. They finally reached Tonkwa and joined the rest of the group just as the enemy withdrew leaving a considerable sum of dead Japanese behind. There were enough Americans lost that there is now a little American Cemetery there.

Wild elephants were in abundance. They seemed to have very good scent and hearing. A herd of unrestrained elephants might take off and come crashing through the jungle. There were also little tiny deer, wild cats and of course snakes in the thickets. When 2,000 men went single file in the forest it would scare the animals, especially the monkeys. Where mules had trouble walking was where bamboo had fallen across the trail. The elephants would easily move the bamboo up in the air with their trunks from left to right and walk under the poles as the bamboo fell over their backs. The bamboo would fall back across the trail behind them. The men on Point had to cut bamboo with machettes. Elephants just took care of the problem, so easily...

Charles was known to occasionally remark, "Isn't it beautiful out here?" Another Lieutenant from Minneapolis would say, "Keep your mouth shut, all I want to do is go home." When in a bivouac area, Charles loved to take his submachine gun, take off to see the scenery and on a couple of occasions wander into a native village. There he might trade "C" rations for rice and chicken. Nine-tenths of the fellows thought Charles was crazy. He always walked ahead even when they were close to the Burma Road and Hosi Valley. If the group got pinned down or had to go forward, he'd use the radio and tell the men where to fire. He could hear the staccato of the 475th Infantry and fire break out. When that happened, training went out the back door. When the group made it all the way to Mount Hosi Ridge, the Japanese controlled one side of the ridge and GIs the other. They had two weeks of fighting with them with no relief. The American forces dug into foxholes. They could see the Burma Road 2,000 feet down. The Japanese fired 150 MM shells and they looked as big as a person coming through the air. You'd hear a sound, look up and see the big shells approaching as men were blown out of fox holes. One man got killed by an airdrop. The C-47 cargo planes dropped heavily bound sacks of grain free falling for the mules. One of these sacks hit the soldier. There were huge quantities of supplies wasted. One drop included 2,000 pairs of all leather boots. Charles does not believe one-fifth of the troops took any boots. Hundreds and hundreds of pairs of leather boots were left abandoned where they lay. The Natives would find them...

In a foxhole with two others, a Lieutenant and a Captain, a 150MM shell came in with a fuse delay. That kind of shell would detonate after burying itself several feet in the ground. It caved in their foxhole on detonation with 150 feet of shrapnel and debris. The Captain went "beserk" and they had to fly him back to India in an LC-5 Liason Plane. Now, Charles knew what shell shocked really meant. Some men received hunks of metal in their leg, another had schrapnel in his hand. Bonsai charges in the dark came from hyped-up Japanese who smoked marihuana cigarettes. They would work themselves up into a frenzy and then holler their screaming greeting, "Banzai," along with a charge of gunfire. That cigarette in many cases would be the last they ever smoked.

Between the 12th and 24th of December there were many targets of opportunity and approximately 2500 rounds were fired by B and C Batteries. Battery A was the first Battery to open fire on Japanese motor traffic on the road. Intensive fire took place. B and C Batteries followed and supported. Mule pack casualties were light. One artillery man died and two were wounded.

December 24th, 1944 Japanese forces retreated southward. On January 1, 1945 the Mars Task Force started on the first leg of the arduous march to the Burma Road leading eastward to Mong-Wi, the terrain became so difficult, the narrow trails plus steps cut in the mud for the mules, did not keep the mules from falling with their loads on a few occasions deep into ravines. Each mule loss was purported to be $2,000.00 not counting losses from its pack. The only thing one could say was, "now the poor mule is out of his misery." In order to arrive at the line of departure on D-Day, 17th January, the Battalion on two previous days marched thirty-six hours with only one two hour halt. Much of this march was taken along beds of rock-bottomed streams with men and mules chest deep in water for hours. It was a fact that had the 475th Combat Team failed to secure the Hosi Valley for use in receiving supplies by air, it could not long have sustained itself. Rations were exhausted on the 17th and ammunition supplies were very limited. Gun parts were lost as the mules fell into the ravines. The objective for this endurance march was three hills grouped around the Hosi Valley overlooking the Burma Road. One night, Charles climbed into a Japanese tank which had been fired upon. He took a Japanese blanket and a tube of tooth paste and went back up the hill.

From January 24th through February 5th all three firing Batteries and Headquarters received intensive and very accurate fire from well camouflaged Japanese artillery positions along Burma Road to the North. By the 5th of Februar with the help of the Tenth Air Force P-47s, the 612th and 613th Battalions forced a cessation of all enemy artillery action. There were many casualties and four men were killed. Many were wounded. Twelve Howitizers were hit and unfit for firing. The Battalion had about seven guns in action and fired about 9500 rounds.

On the 6th of February, the Chinese First Army including medium and light tanks hove into sight on the Burma Road and the Mars Task Force was considered to have been relieved. Previous action at Tonkwa enabled the 22nd Chinese Division to be safely flown from the airstrip at Nansin without fear of enemy forces deployed in that area. When General Stillwell and the Chinese Army, under dark went past positions to Rangoon and Mandalay that was when the battles were over.

The above few descriptions do not include the many battles fought in that dense rain forest of Burma. The men were commended by Lieutenant General Dan I. Sultan who arrived by air. Two days later, Admiral Lord Louis Mountbatten also praised their bravery and fortitude. The Officers praised the men highly for their part in reopening the Ledo-Burma Road to China.

One last long grueling march would be taken from March 5th down the Burma Road to Lashio. Intense heat and humidity of early spring was grueling even though the march was conducted for the most part during hours of darkness. When Lashio was retrieved by the American troops, the Battery was flown to Kunming, China. The number of days the group was engaged in combat missions was 152. 12,000 of the 76MM shells had been fired against the enemy. Four hundred twelve miles had been covered. Forty-eight men were evacuatuated for wounds in action, another 46 evacuated for disease or illness and five men were killed in action.

Charles met his first wife, Margaret, at Fort Sill. She was visiting a girlfriend at the camp while he was there. She was from Viola, Wisconsin, his home town. When he returned from the war they were married. They had two children, John Paul and Jean Anne who grew up in Sonoma, California. The Stormonts also welcomed a girl named Judy Ford in their home. She was like another daughter. She was actually a daughter to the Viola Town Marshall who had lost his wife. He had other children to care for as a widower, so the Stormonts agreed to raise Judy.

Tired of wading snow in 45 degree below zero weather in Wisconsin and having read a story in the *National Geographic* written about General 'Hap' Arnold, who lived in Sonoma, California. Charles wondered about raising mink in the beautiful Valley of the Moon described by the article. Contacting his brother, a professor at Davis in the Genetic Department of the University of California Agricultural School, Charles found the North Bay Area might be feasible for a mink farm. He took a real quick vacation to the area including a drive to the Sonoma area. With Margaret and his two children, they met a real estate salesman, the late Harry Crouse. The family considered purchasing five acres of land with a little cottage for $8,000. "Jesus!" Charles told Harry; "I can buy 275 acres, an eight room house, silos and barn for less than that in Wisconsin!" Charles finally did buy that property in Sonoma in 1954 and began mink farming in the area. The location of the ranch was in the windier area of the valley. The family cooled the mink off in the summertime by running a sprinkler system. Using a combination of wind and water kept the mink cooler in the summertime. Charles had 2,400 mink in Sonoma under family care and 5,000 mink in Wisconsin under a foreman. It was cheaper to raise the mink in Sonoma. The family sold the place in Wisconsin after a few years.

After the war, Charles built a bomb shelter on the Sonoma property because the United States Government recommended it for all who could do so. In later years, he believed the hydrogen bomb would make the bomb shelter obsolete. The family had stocked the shelter with water, some food, and bedding in those earlier years. That shelter has long been plowed under.

After his first wife, Margaret died Charles missed her and was restless. He used to travel a great deal on planned bus trips around America. He thought he might meet someone interesting on these trips. He met Dorothy Dow, his second wife back in St. Paul Minnesota. Actually, he had bounced her on his knee when she was about four or five years old. He was about twenty-five years old at the time. Dorothy's mother had taken care of 'Charlie' when he was four years old. She probably bounced him on her knee as well. Anyway. Charles found the companion he was searching for and has settled back down in Sonoma.

At the Sonoma property, the mink ranch has been shut down for quite a few years. At least one outbuilding became a remodeled rental. Driving into the very neat property one is met by a slow motioned dog. Wind still blows through the area in the afternoons, which was the big prerequisite for the mink farm.

There are a couple of interesting paintings in the cottage. One is inscribed "To Lieutenant Stormont from Colonel Hu Ka Shang. Regiment Commander of the 10th Field Artillery Regiment of the Chinese Army." It is dated: September 30th, 1945 at Kunming, China. The picture on cloth is known as a fine silk thread painting. It portrays a house, a quiet stream and a bluish-purple mountain with puffs of white clouds in the far horizon. The color of the distant Himilayas remind Charles of those mountain peaks where he once fought the Japanese soldiers.

A second silk thread painting in the house is an image of a lion. When Charles' mother received it, she cut off the edge of the material to fit into the frame. It was the edge of the second painting that was historically important. That was where inscriptions in Chinese to Charles were also inscribed. The Captain who gave the paintings to Charles was a real good friend out there in that Burmese jungle. Charles' friend became a full General in command of missile sites in Formosa. Now, the fellow lives in San Jose, California.

Charles has not dwelled on thoughts of the hard ardous marches through the dense jungles. These thoughts were gleaned from written notes which he logged on the nightmarish journies through the Burmese Forests while the Americans were there. Rather, Charles talks of the beauty of the Himilaya Range of Mountains as portrayed on the silk thread painting. He thinks of the crystal cold mountain streams but not of days when the men were soaking wet from those streams. Charles' eyes light up remembering his very special friends, the sure-footed hard working mules and the fact they carried so much weight upon their backs all day long. He does not like the fact that many of the mules were destroyed because of their condition from the very grueling work they were put through for the men. He speaks well of the Native people known as Kachins. He does not hold any emnity toward the Japanese people. Instead Charles admires their intellect. He enjoys correspondence with his Chinese friend in San Jose.

The descriptions of the area and the material in this story are from Charles own notes taken down at the time he was serving his country in that far off jungle. The history of 612 F.A. Battalion was to be written sometime by him at the suggestion of his Commanding Officer. A few other notes are from a three page *Combat History* entitled *Men of Mars*, 612 F.A. Bn. Pack of the 612th Field Artillery Battalion (Pack) in the North and Central Burma Campaigns. 18 November 1944 through 18 April, 1945. This little memento has an interesting cover and three pages of notes. For more intense stories of the period written in great style along with whimsical drawings, a full section of pictures and a few great mule stories, enjoy *Marsmen in Burma*.

Randolph, John. *Marsmen in Burma.*, Mrs. John Randolph, Publisher, 1977. 24035 Kuykendahl Road, Tomball, Texas, 77375. pps. 229 plus pictures. pp. intro, 34, 111.

Frank S. Wedekind

United States Army, 1942 - 1946

Seventy-eight years ago, Frank F. Wedekind was born in San Francisco, California. His mother before him, was born in San Francisco and his father came from Santa Barbara, California. The family business was surgical appliances. Frank's father wanted to work with growing plants. He wanted to be a farmer.

When Frank was very young, Sonoma Valley was considered an agricultural valley. Farmers sent produce to San Francisco daily by boat from the Schellville embarcadero. Quarries were located back of town at Shocken Hill. Cobblestone streets in San Francisco and in many other cities were paved with stone from those quarries. In the Valley there were many orchards producing apples, cherries, prunes, apricots, peaches and the biggest quince in California. There was an abundance of eggs and milk. Everyone had some chickens and about fifty dairy ranches in the area provided gallons upon gallons of milk.

When the Wedekind family came to Sonoma, they built a cottage about 40 feet from the home that Frank and Lorraine, his wife live in today. The second Wedekind home is an imposing victorian house, circa 1886, with gigantic screened porch and high lofty ceilings. The home was built on 50 plus acres which were to be used for horse breeding. Horses have always been an important part of Sonoma. In the early days there was racing and in the 20's and 30's the annual rodeo was a big event. There were organized rides to view the seven moons which could be seen from horseback. (It was told, "that if you rode a horse from the north end of the Valley of the Moon toward Sonoma, the moon would rise seven times from behind the mountains.") During World War II, buses were taken to Skaggs and Mare Islands to pick up service men on shore leave. They were brought to Sonoma for the annual rodeo, for picnics, skating or rest and relaxation at the Sonoma Mission Inn. There was also a USO type hospitality center. The farmers and business people of the area donated produce and time for the outreach events.

The Wedekind family farmed their property for thirty years. There were prunes, pears and grapes. Frank's dad planted additional acreage in peaches and pears. The victorian home was offered to the Wedekinds by Colonel and Mrs. Alfane and the Wedekind family has enjoyed it for thirty-five years.

Frank moved to Sonoma when he was four years old. It was 1920. He attended the big brick Sonoma Grammar School known in the nineties as the Community Center. He was a 1920 graduate from Sonoma High School. From farmer to an enlisted Army man was one transition Frank will never forget. Along with 'Rich' Peterson and Bob Andrieux of Sonoma, Frank enlisted in San Francisco in 1942. The fellows asked for training at Mather Field, Sacramento. The enlistment officer in charge said, "Come back in two weeks and check your status." When Frank returned, Mather Field had been scratched out and La Junta, Colorado penned upon his enlistment papers. Frank spoke up, "I enlisted for Mather Field, California." "That's tough," the enlistment Officer said; "You are in the Army as of tomorrow and will be sent elsewhere."

On the next day, Halloween, the new recruits were sent to Monterey, California for shots and some odds and ends of uniforms. Five days later the group of young California men were loaded on a troop train in Oakland. It was one of those perfect Indian summer days as the suntanned Californians left their golden state. At destination, La Juanta, Colorado, it was four degrees below zero! It was a week later, that the group was issued overcoats, oversized shoes and long underwear. By that time many of the California boys were in the camp infirmary suffering pnemonia.

Instead of seeing lush valleys and fields of trees at La Jaunta, Frank saw a most desolate place. There was little vegetation and there were no trees. No wild life was seen. This base was adjacent to Division Headquarters for the Santa Fe Railroad. The facility was newly opened; there was just a Cadre there. Frank recalled, "the rest of the inmates were from the Bay Area, mostly guys from San Francisco and Northern California. In the mess hall, we were served cold scrambled powdered eggs, which I equated with the whole dismal scene..."

The Californians were given three weeks of basic training which included marching in snow. The good Sergeant was smart enough to keep them fifteen minutes extra at the latrine location where they could get thawed out. The recruits called the busy ambulance hauling the sick out and away, the "meat wagon." They were all thankfully back on the line working by Thanksgiving. At that point, a special and unique solicitation for twenty-five persons was requested. The 26th MOS posted a notice directed towards anyone interested to see the Engineering Chief "for work in supply and handling repair parts for airplanes." This employment opportunity, away from the usual Army fare, was to work with twin-engined airplanes at the Western Flying Training Command. It turned out to be a job that actually busied men around the clock. There were three shifts of workers in winter enduring 28 degree below zero weather. The men struggled to return to the barracks from the line after their shifts. There were three pot-bellied stoves in each long tar-papered-shack barracks. The bunk next to a stove was too hot while three bunks down from the stove was in the 'freezing zone.' When any G I opened the door to the barracks, cold winds roared and rattled through the non-insulated building.

When the unpaved areas of the post were not frozen these yards melted into sticky mud. Frank spent the next two and one-half years out there in those cold, windy, frozen, snowy fields except for one twenty-four hour period which was deemed unsafe for flying. On that occasion, the base officials had a large amount of snow bulldozed out. By noon, they were again directing planes to take-off or come in. At this Western Flying Training Command one was "frozen to their jobs and their ranks." Frank really wanted to go to Officers School, but he was just plain stuck in La Jaunta. He said, "I was frozen in all categories until released." Officers Candidate School just didn't materialize.

Frank's dad was getting old. His mother called, "I need you to visit your dad." Frank went to Colonel Garrells office requesting a leave for home. The good Colonel said, "I don't know how I can let you go, you are an important cog in this organization." Frank pointed to his sleeve with the PFC embroidered insignia upon it and said to the Colonel, "I'm not too important with only one stripe." Frank got the five day emergency home leave. He found some Corporal stripes waiting for him when he got back to camp!

Active all his life in athletics, Frank had coached, managed and played basketball and baseball. He was lucky to acquire a baseball team at La Juanta. The Second Lieutenant in charge of conditioning the men was in charge of the baseball team for the base. Frank went to his office about the time the practice was going to start. The Second Lieutenant did not know much about baseball. After that visit, Frank became the manager and catcher of the team for two years. The Commanding Officer was not athletically inclined and not very interested in ideas about travel with the team. The team rode in 6 x 6 trucks to compete with the nearest air bases in the sporting events. Fortunately, that part of the world was full of air bases. They played teams in Colorado, Texas and Kansas.

There were many impressive professional baseball players from mid-western states. They came from minor league teams. Generally, the players from La Juanta ran into a lot of ball players who were good! "It was a challenging respite from everyday Army work activities. The games were something to look forward to on weekends," according to Frank.

After three to six months in the first season of the camp baseball team, a new Colonel became Commanding Officer of the field. He was athletically-minded. From thereon, the team was assigned two planes to shuttle the men back and forth to the games. Frank entered wholeheartedly into his new world of baseball as soon as he was relieved on Friday afternoons. It was the best thing that happened to him at the Air Force as far as he was concerned.

Frank finally graduated off the graveyard shift at the work station. Since he had been raised on a farm, he had a lot of mechanical 'know how' which translated into mechanical ability. Each squadron at the base had a parts supply room. Frank built shelves, sorted parts and labeled them. In a visit with the Colonel, Frank suggested a management plan that would relieve 16 men from duplicated jobs. He told the Colonel, "it is ridiculous to have four stations of supplies. I suggest that we have a Base Supply, a consolidation warehouse set up. With four men assigned to an 8 a.m. to 5 p.m. job, it would be something to be proud of." (Each squadron had its own shed and station of supplies.) The Colonel accepted Frank's ideas and he had an eight to five job. He became a Corporal.

Frank worked with an old-time Sergeant who was well-liked. Under Sergeant Murphy the men quickly accomplished a great deal. The act of consolidation of parts made the field the leading air base for squadron flying hours. Airplanes had less time off. One of the reasons was the salvage yard that was created. When there was a wreck or a problem plane, the Ordnance men tore the aircraft apart and room was made in the warehouse for more and more stock. The base particularly needed generators and starter motors in sub-zero weather conditions. The warehouse tried to keep from fifteen to twenty extra starter motors available at all times for replacing anywhere from ten to fifteen burned up motors that occurred in the winter.

The Colonel in charge of the flying operation was tough. He wanted a report from Frank every night with an inventory of airplane parts. Why was a part needed or used? Where were parts ordered from? When would a part be there? Submit paper work on any plane, down. He was to confirm information on sub-depo supplies warehoused in other states. This kind of attention to detail was right up Frank's alley and akin to his own philosophy.

The intrepid worker got his first real furlough for Christmas in 1944. In twenty-four hours, he was ordered to report back immediately for overseas duty. In was January! Lorraine, Frank's wife had lived off base in G I housing. It was the day before the couple's anniversary when Lorraine and their first daughter, Joanne and baby Francine came to say, "Goodbye." The girls' dad was then the recipient of a three day ride on a train from Colorado to Salt Lake City...

At Salt Lake City, Utah the men received additional training. This time it was called "weapons training." Lying upon the snow, while on their stomachs in four to ten below zero weather, they had to locate and dodge firepower. Paradoxically, Frank trained in the snow all this time was then sent to Fort Lewis, Washington for a trip to the tropics! Being what Frank now believed was an efficiency expert, due to his very successful Ordnance supply service at La Juanta, he found it hard to hurry up and wait for shipment to the Pacific. In Seattle, there were more exercises especially designed for the tropics. This training lasted for a week. It rained every day during the exercises.

On a day before the men shipped from port, the Captain got up before the whole group and told the men, "You are very fortunate. You should consider this trip, you are about to embark upon, as a pure pleasure excursion to the tropics. You are even going to Hawaii! You are going on the Dutch Ship known as the Blomfontein."

This miserable ship meandered through the Juan de Fuca Straits on the way out to the great Pacific Ocean. A storm came up as soon as the crew steered into the broad waters of the Pacific Ocean. The hatches were kept closed for three days. There were 400 men in each hold. Frank was assigned a deep rack # 11 bunk. There was no water to wash your face, except in a salt water fountain. While in his bunk, the anchor would hit the hull constantly on the metal hull near his head. It seemed like all but two men were throwing up inside the sealed hatch. Two men were taken out of the area, dead. The rest wanted the hatch open for fresh air.

The galley was four decks below. One had to use the outside rail to go three decks to get to the fourth deck. Long tables set up for eating were very greasy on the tops. One couldn't keep a mess tray from sliding about in the goo. If you wanted to eat, first get in line then stand in line, twice. Some very short men that worked on the ship as stewards had come from the Andaman Islands off India. They climbed around like proverbial monkeys. They stole spam and with big onions made sandwiches that they sold for $1.00 a piece.

The Blomfontein anchored in Hawaii. The men were taken off to some temporary barracks. Fresh water was the first thought of the men. Hawaii's weather was cold! The barracks they moved into had chicken-wire-walls. Condensation of moisture dropped off the ceilings on the bedding. The men shivered. One cotton blanket had been issued for warding off the cold and damp environment.

Newspaper hackers came through. For insulation, they sold newspapers to line the bunks. It was interesting to be in beautiful sunny Hawaii and needing insulation for sleeping. Hickamfield had been bombed so the men were transported on a narrow gauge railway to an Infantry Depot. All Officers were assigned to an Infantry Battery. The first morning out on roll call, all non-commissioned Officers were ordered to take two steps forward. All the men stepped forward. The Officer put all the men back in formation and told them, "You will all be on K P." The men were outraged! They were Air Corps Technicians and they didn't pull that kind of duty! Somehow, that whole idea hit the fan. Eventually, they did not have to pull that roster duty.

Frank's papers were lost by the staff. All the other men shipped out. Frank was the only one left behind. He spent a week at the base. Then, there was a roll call for non-commissioned Officers. The Officer asked Frank, "What happened to your face? Where have you been to get spots? What part of town have you been in???" "Sir," Frank replied; "We're frozen here. I can't get out the front gate." So, the Officer sent Frank off to Tripler General Hospital.

The hospital was the largest in Hawaii and was considered top-choice. Doctors put Frank in a contagion ward for chicken pox and with all other kinds of contagious diseases. The-bed-check-Lieutenant came in. "Are you alergic to bug bites?" he asked. Then, Frank remembered the heavy mosquito raid he had gone through. He lucked out and did not catch any contagious disease present in that ward.

Frank lost no time getting to the Sergeant and asking to be re-assigned. "We need you. We're loading G.I.s for the Philippines," was the answer. The youngsters he joined were so young... They looked like they could hardly struggle under their backpacks. Frank went over to Pearl Harbor and was put aboard a Landing Ship Medium. They stashed a load of pontoons and water containers. These containers were piled three rows high on the decks. Pontoons were flat bottomed boat air-tight metal cyclinders used for construction of temporary bridges over rivers. On this boat they were also designed to carry extra water. The water was used not only for drinking purposes but for shifting weight around on the small vessel. On the day President Roosevelt died, the small craft moved out of Pearl with twelve Non-Coms aboard. Destination was Guam.

The twelve Non-Coms lived in quarters the size of a 14 foot by 14 foot room. The hole had no airconditioning. Some men started sleeping upon the pontoons. The small craft moved about 8 knots and sailed west towards the South Pacific. The group thought they were going to Guam. Near Eniwetok, they suffered a burned out main drive shaft. It was 100 degrees temperature and no one was allowed off the ship. They were held standstill in the water for a week. Then, they started out alone in that endless ocean.

The intercom blasted on, "Now hear this, all personnel move up to Pontoon Deck and bring your life preservers." They had had drills daily on this deck. During the drills crew members also practiced shooting exercises. The twin guns on the Bow were the largest of the vessel and there were a few fellows with machine guns. When the men practiced shooting these guns, by aiming at balloons sent up in the air, Frank had yet to see one balloon hit. The intercom rattled on again, "now hear this, spotted planes are heading this way." When the final announcement was made, it droned, "They weren't Jap planes, but our own."

The Ordnance group finally arrived at Harmon Field, Guam. North Field was not yet completed. The new field was being built especially for B-29s. Bamboo had grown fourteen feet high. There were pup tents set up in the middle of the bamboo thicket. Frank was assigned guard duty. As soon as it grew dark, Japanese shells whistled weirdly through the bamboo. At Harmon Field there were damaged airplanes from all over the Pacific needing repair and maintenance. It was a daily occurrence to watch landings of B-24s having but one engine and a prayer for landing. The Ordnance group was then made ready for one big push toward the Island of Okinawa. They loaded up and, when leaving, unloaded down on the famous moving rope ladders. Packs bounced along the side of the ships and upon their tightly strapped shoulders.

The group spent a five day stay about twenty miles off Saipan. Next stop was Ulithe. Frank never saw so many ships massed in one place in his whole life! It was a great armada sailing to Japan. It reminded him of a dense forest of ships. The ships moved into Okinawa about 11:30 p.m. Naha Harbor was all lit up by giant portable lights. Their small craft weaved down to a front end position through the water to get on the beach. All of a sudden, there was an air raid! All lights simultaneously went out causing a pitch black sky at midnight that was so dark as to be incredulous!

The men from Frank's boat marched down a canyon. The put up pup tents in that total black darkness. Two men were to use one tent. There were ten raids that night. All the raids were high. The next morning, they viewed the Okinawa area. It was the month of July. It was the beginning of the capitulation of the Japanese.

Frank had a buddy in the 5th Reconnaissance of the 7th Air Force. Frank had been assigned 613th Army Air Corps Engineering Squadron. Frank's friend had extra cameras on his P-38 aircraft in place of some guns. He was part of the Air Force Squadrons assigned the Hiroshima atomic bombing. Three hours after the holocaust, Frank was holding developed pictures in his hand. He was with a group in the photo section, developing the pictures taken of the first atomic bombing of a major city in the world!

Word was received by short wave radio on the day of the surrender of Japan. It was just a little after dark about 7:30 at night. Frank's buddy and one other were the only ones in the area from California. A fellow named, Pfieffer from Chico and Don Poole of Marysville had been assigned the same tent.

On the night of the capitulation, Frank was holding a deck of cards in his right hand. Word of the surrender was passed like wild fire from man to man. "It looked like ten thousand 4th of July's in New York City," according to Frank. There were four Army Air Forces in the area, many Marines, Navy men and the Army Infantry. Men shot off their guns. The men got out of the tents as bullets went flying through them. A bullet went through the cards in Frank's right hand and into his big toe. Tents were shredded like shredded wheat from the gunfire. Everything was in a state of pandemonium. There were hundreds of ships in the harbor. It is hard to explain how things ever straightened out.

One month later, on September 15th, the men endured a typhoon. Don Poole and Frank were in the open, in a Jeep. They started to go to the plane ramps. Eight foot by four foot by four foot deep propeller boxes were spinning off the ground. A plane looked like a toy being tossed and turned around. The wind was whipping at 135 miles per hour. The two men were in fox holes before the next blow. Wind and water in sheets of rain put two feet of water in the fox holes in about five minutes. On the 16th, when the storm eased up a bit, it was discovered the tents and mess hall were gone. Not a plane was able to fly in Okinawa. Planes had turned upside down. If one spun the engines, they found the instrument boards were broken.

It was a two day wait for K rations before there was anything to eat. At Yonton, a B-25 Airfield, there had been miles of equipment which was now practically useless. The equipment had been lined up for pushing toward Japan before the bomb was used. Don and Frank took a ride to Buckner Bay. They had heard about devastation over there. Ships called Martin Mariners were all blown into trees way up in the hills. Not one ship was left on the water. At the Yonton area, a tanker was seen one quarter mile up from the ocean. Hangers to hold two B-24s were quonset-hut-type-buildings which had girders 12 inches by 14 inches deep. These girders were twisted like a paper straw might be flattened and turned in a coil while sipping an ice cream soda. The men at that destination had no tents. When it rained, their shelter amounted to a half of a pup tent held over their heads.

Awaiting discharge, Frank planned to work. He pushed the keys in the Jeep's starter. He was going to get some parts. The Sergeant said, "Sit down. That airplane will be there today, tomorrow and after." The 7th Air Corps were all over the Pacific. With no more flying missions to carry out, some members were reportedly talking to the gooney birds. The Sergeant finished his words, "Let that plane sit there. I have had it!"

Eventually, they found a Coleman stove and someone stole some bacon and eggs from somewhere. Somehow, the men survived with their tents full of holes and no mess hall. Three months later, on December 15th morale was so bad that for a month or so, the men would not even bother to move around. They just laid about in their battered tents. They had been promised discharges and return to the United States and were so often disappointed. Finally, a ship came in. It took the Military Police to urge the group out to the ship. That was how dejectedly and deeply the men had declined. The victors of the battle of the Pacific moved to the shore toward the ship that was to take them home!

The transport took the returning troops to Vancouver, Washington. Frank calculated he had been on board ships for 144 days. He never received an airplane ride after being on the baseball team. His brother, Warren in the Navy, never got on a boat. When Frank's group made it to the Vancouver barracks and mess hall, the most welcome sight of all was rows of quarts of milk lined up and down the tables. Frank was reminded of a poor comparison, but it looked like hogs going for whey. Ten to fifteen men at a time grabbed for the quarts of milk.

The irony, thank God, was that Frank headed for Camp Beale for discharge. Don and Frank were assigned a ship from Portland. At sunrise, they enjoyed the beautiful sights of the Golden Gate Bridge and San Francisco. Frank felt grateful to be back in the United States of America and the town where he was born!

After a bus ride to Camp Beale near Marysville, the men were herded into a hall while going through discharge. A Second Lieutenant on duty tried to re-enlist the men and offered them reserve status. Frank told him, "You can take your dammed Air Corp and keep it. I'm going back to farming where I can live with my wife." Janet, his third daughter was born in Sonoma in 1949.

One hot July day while farming, Frank pulled up under a prune tree on his tractor. While cooling off and wiping his brow in the shade, he counted the traffic on Highway 12. He thought, "I have tried to get prices changed for our fruits." He basically had prunes and pears and 17 varieties of peaches. He sent some of his crops to what was referred to as "the 40 thieves in San Francisco. If, instead of hauling our own produce and fooling around with all that paper work," Frank calculated; "by selling our own crops at home, we could give the differential to the Sonomans." After taking a second traffic count, he found in a day's time the incoming vehicles numbered about 250. Frank thought, "if I can just stop 5% of the total passengers going by my property, I could have a flowing business." Wedekind's Fruit Stand was the result.

The fledgling entrepeneur erected a little eight foot shack. In 1951, he enlarged the building. He quit farming full time and built a new building with a plant nursery in mind. He spent the next thirty-five years in the nursery business. His original fruit stand was one of the early ones in California. He became a Master Nurseryman selling quality nursery products under label. By the time of his retirement he had grown to over ninety products under label. Frank held pruning and plant care training sessions as a Master nurseryman. He retired in 1990.

In all the places he has visited, Frank has yet to find anything comparable to Sonoma for living and raising a family. He loves the proximity of the Pacific Ocean, the high Sierra Mountains, the Bay Area cultural activites and the incredible weather. In New England, he has seen the beautiful flaming red and yellow forests of October. He has visited purple mountains and orange rock formations in scenic Arizona in February and the cool green Northwest in summer. But in twelve months of the year, Sonoma comes out ahead in Frank's mind as having ideal living conditions. There were only two periods that were changeable from the norm. In 1932, it snowed in Glen Ellen in December. The kids from school took garbage bucket tops and slid around in the white stuff. In 1972, almost to the day, it was 14 degrees at Frank's store. All citrus trees were lost including a big ranch of lemon trees in the valley. The hottest day, he ever remembered was 111 degrees. In 74 years, he guesses only 50 nights being uncomfortably warm.

While in the Air Force, the closest event for being injured was his big toe on VJ Day. He brought home the bullet. He also brought home to his wife and daughters some interesting necklaces made of ignition wire off Japanese fighters interwoven with shells. On the night of capitulation, the armament being shot off willy-nilly by the American troops was collected. There were absolutely beautiful carbines turned in. Marines collected the armaments, including hand guns and stockpiled them.

Japanese stray soldiers were being collected all the time. When the men left, live Japanese warriors were still hidden in the island ceremonial burying caves. The islands were left to the Natives who were Japanese derivatives, the same peoples which populated the islands before the war. Those captured and placed in prison camps were left there in December, 1945.

Today, there are beautiful barracks and bases developed in the same area where once the tents stood.

William J. Lowenberg

United States Army, (Korean War) 1953 - 1955

Born in a small town in Germany in 1926, William J. Lowenberg lived but fifteen to twenty miles from the Dutch Border. He attended a Catholic School which had an enrollment of eight hundred boys. He was the only Jewish boy in the school. He was directed to sit in the back of the room all by himself. He was never called on to join or participate with the rest of the class. He was never allowed to recite verbally with the group. He was a very good student but his report card always showed that "William was an unsatisfactory student."

The Lowenberg family had lived in the Providence of Visphalia, since before the Inquisition of the 15th Century. William checked out the family tree in archives and on tombstones. His Mother's Family, his Father and Brother were all veterans of various German wars. William's Grandfather Abraham and his Father's Brother William were killed in the First World War I. They served the Germans for Germany.

In 1936, the family lost their family business, their bikes, motorcycles and cars. These conveyances were also being confiscated by the German Nazis from peoples they called "undesirables" in other areas of Germany. William's father was in the textile business. He had maintained a small store in a farm area. His dad told his family, "We are going to Holland." The place they moved to was about 1 1/2 hours from where William was born. William was accepted for the first time as a human being in school. He learned the Dutch language.

In 1940, the German Army overran and took four countries, Norway, Belgium, Denmark, and Holland. The citizens were left alone for about a year after these countries were under the German imperialism machine. However, as German Jews, the family had to purchase and wear Shields of David (8 by 10 centimeters in diameter). The shield, also known as Star of David emblem having a six pointed star shape, was to be attached permanently to their outer garments. The emblems were to be worn on the left side and also on the back of all coats. Any Jew not wearing such a badge would be arrested.

Movement of Jewish people in public streets was restricted from 6 a.m to 8 p.m. If a Jewish person broke curfew during other hours, he or she would be arrested. All arms and wireless receivers were demanded to be handed in to authorities. Many items of personal property were confisgated by the Nazis including bicycles and cars in Holland. The Lowenberg family knew these same type items had been taken from Jews in Germany. Demands came one after another including, "turn in all watercraft, horses and carts." William's father had to go back into business for the Germans.

In 1942, the Lowenbergs were arrested along with William and his sister. The family was sent to Westerbork Concentration Camp established in northeast Holland. From July 1942, when the Germans took command of the camp to December 1943, more than ninety trains left Westerbork for Auschwitz, Sabibor, Bergen-Belsen and Theresienstadt. These trains carried 88,363 Dutch and German Jews and approximately 500 Dutch Gypsies to their deaths. The Lowenberg family stayed at Westerbork for about four or five months. At age fifteen, William was taken away from his parents because he had passed the fifteenth birthday. He was taken to Auschwitz Prison near Cracow, (also known as Krakow), an historic city in southern Poland. Auschwitz was a complex, consisting of concentration, extermination and labor camps in Upper Silesia. It was established in 1940 as a concentration camp and included a killing center in 1942. Auschwitz I was the main camp. Auschwitz II was known as Birkenau: the extermination center. Birkenau Concentration Camp had 7 gas chambers or creamatoria. There were beatings for everything in Cracow. Guards with machine guns mowed down inmates for any excuse.

Birkenau was made up of four or five camps. Within those compounds, Germans worked around the clock to kill people. The dazed humans were transported in cattle cars which were contaminated with lice. When the new arrivals reached the camps, they were stripped of clothing as if to be deloused and showered but were really prepared for the creamatorium. For the first six months that William was at Auschwitz, he watched lines of people killed. The trains left Holland every Tuesday. About 150 to 200 men including William were kept for slave labor jobs. All the rest of the people brought in were killed. The Germans thought William was about eighteen and so he was pressed into the working crews which included digging up massed graves. This was done to hide the atrocious German behavior from the Allies that were winning the war. The slave labor prisoners were charged with the task of obliterating all traces of mass murder by digging up these graves and spreading the killings around.

Inside Birkenau Concentration Camp there were large rooms and halls. Shower heads came out of the ceilings. A herd of people including women and children would be whipped faster and faster into the gas chambers. The blows would fall upon their heads which seemed to be paralyzed with terror and pain. These herds of people were sealed inside when the slippery cells were filled and closed off. Steam was forced through apertures and suffocation began. (In Birkenau, they received a cyclone of B gas. Zyklon B gas was hydrogen cyanide, a pesticide used in crystalline form.) It took about fifteen minutes before the creamatorium was opened to view bodies massed and stuck together from heat and steam. Cold water was then sprayed upon the intertangled massed scene and gravediggers piled corpses on platforms.

Hair was cut off the bodies. It was subsequently cleaned, peroxided and dried carefully. A whole room was filled of hair which was constantly being prepared for mattresses. Gold fillings were taken out of teeth. All the naked bodies were checked for fat which was cut off for making into soap. Clothing pieces thrown in heaps were restacked for use somewhere and elsewhere, while peoples were humiliated and bodily stripped before entering the death chambers. Jewelry was taken from the dead. "This was a most orchestrated genocide," William stated; "It was organized in Berlin."

All of William's family members, about forty in number, including his Mother's sister, his uncles, and on through third generations were annihilated. The family was extinct except for William's Uncle who lived in San Francisco.

Jewish people were ordered to be registered. All their property had to be recorded. If they concealed anything, they were severely punished or killed. They were required to turn over all money exceeding 100 rubles per family. All valuables such as gold, silver, precious stones, paintings, furs, pianos, typewriters, good materials for making coats or suits and even stamp collections were confisgated. They had to hand over all black-out materials. In one area, the Germans boarded up their hospital and burned it down with the people inside.

Abstinance from work assigned was punishable by death. In 1942, a collection of all metal was directed toward the weary souls. Every type of metal was listed from copper to gold. This included such items as ashtrays, decorative pieces, table tops, kettles, utensils, door signs, fixtures, door and window handles, coins, brass weights, musical instruments, lead pipes clear down to birdcages. Always these demands were expected to be adhered to on a certain date. If not done timely heinous actions would take place or instant death. Any minor disobedience or offense would be used as an excuse for extermination.

William was sent out to work every day without much to eat until late Spring of 1943. Four people would be required to eat from only one enamel bowl in prison camps. Food consisted of one piece of bread and some watery soup. If you did not eat the bread, in the evening, it was taken away. If you slept with your bread, someone might kill you for the morsel. If you put bread under your head, you probably would be visited by one of the hungry rats eating it for you. You received a cup of weak tea for breakfast. In Cracow, when the prisoners arrived, they saw a town destroyed. The prisoners found some grains in some buildings. They would grab a handful and eat it quickly and greedily.

William volunteered to go to Warsaw, Poland to get out of where he was. He was taken to a ghetto in Warsaw. A ghetto was a section of a city, often run-down or overcrowded. It was inhabited chiefly by a minority group that was effectively barred from living in other communities because of racial prejudice or for other social reasons. Ghetto was an archaic title dating back to the Middle ages when a German prince would appoint an agent in the area of a town to which Jews were confined. The Ghetto would establish a Jewish Council of Elders to exercise authority within the Ghetto walls. In those days, a Prince might summon the Council or Elders and inform them that they must make a gift of a thousand guilders to finance his partition in the Crusades. Money would be raised as taxes on fellow Jews. This principal was the same principal carried on by the Nazi's domination of the Jewish people. The ghetto was used not only for a confining place where German officials gave controlling orders but for the inhabitants to carry out any demands made.

Usually Ghettos were operated by communications delivered from authorities. The idea of communication in the centuries past was focused by the Germans as a persecution. The communications from the German 'politizia' covered everything from prohibition to use the paved walks or the park benches to men not being allowed to put their hands in their pockets while walking. Edicts were received demanding them to stay away from river banks. Bibles, money, vegetables were taken. The Jewish people were even told to turn in the medicines from their medicine cabinets. Jewish artisans or craftsmen were forced to make contributions for the personal gain of individual Germans. Items to be made for enterprising Germans in the Ghetto, without payment, would include suits, shoes, rings and jewelry. In some areas, leaving ones place of employment carried a penalty of six months imprisonment. Jewish people were cooped up in cellars and hideouts.

William found out he was sent to Auschwitz to burn bodies and dynamite the ghetto in Warsaw. There were many children and old people in Auschwitz. William was given orders to salvage everything the Germans could use for their war machine. This action was in retaliation to a ghetto uprising of the Jews in Warsaw.

Early in June 1944, there was a death march referred to as Warsaw West March. There were thirty-six men in William's category included in the march along with 3,000 other people. They marched for about ten days. At one point, they were herded into boxcars for a second time and taken to Dachau, Germany. Three thousand people began the march. Some were deliberately left to drown in rivers as they crossed them. Some fell and were instantly shot. Only 240 survived to make it to Dachau. The only way to stay alive was to aim to appease and please the German guards. Ra r .om shootings, arrests, and incidents provoked daily torments.

The survivors were set up to build an underground camp for a V2 rocket factory.

In April, 1945 there was another death march which lasted five days into Dachau. The Guards killed a lot of young boys on this gruesome journey. William was liberated by the American Army on April 30th, 1945! He went back to Holland to trace his parents and sister. He had seen them marched into Auschwitz. He had seen them herded toward the gas chamber. Until he checked out their complete journey, his mind would not let him believe they had met their fate with the others in the holocaust.

William stayed a year in Holland. He lived three years in Switzerland and Northern Italy working for a chemical firm. He had one uncle in the world. His mother's brother lived in San Francisco. William received necessary papers to immigrate to the United States. He bought his own ticket to come to America by boat. His uncle had to sign an affidavit guaranteeing that William would not become an economic burden to the country. He found a job immediately in real estate. He became a rent collector and a handyman to put up signs for a real estate company. He made $100.00 a month. He lived in a rooming house paying $70.00 a month for the basement and use of a garage. He was "happy as a lark to be in America." In 1953, while not yet a citizen of the United States, he was drafted in the United States Army. William became a United States Citizen while in the American Army.

William entered the United States Army at Fort Ord, California and spent a one year reprieve in Fort Lewis, Washington. He stated, "The Americans liberated me and I felt I owed the country something." On his way to Korea, he stayed in training as a Supply Sergeant of Division II called the Indian Head Division.

Discharged from the service in 1955, William went back to work for the firm in San Francisco where he had been previously employed. The young American citizen was working as a civilian or was in the country's armed forces constantly from 1949 without a vacation until 1968. He then started his own real estate company specializing in development of warehousing and commercial buildings, not shopping centers.

Up until 1970, William was not involved in any community activities. Then, an incident took place in San Francisco which dramatically changed his life. Some Nazi skinheads came to town and burned a Jewish Bookstore. William that year had become President of the Jewish Community in San Francisco. He was called in by professionals to be on a committee to build a Remembrance Memorial across from the Legion of Honor in San Francisco. Surviving the German concentration camps, he was considered a perfect committee member by the group. William became known nationally and in Israel, from that assignment. President Carter, in the 1970s appointed him to a committee which was to prepare a memorial regarding the holocaust. It would be called the United States Holocaust Memorial Museum. This project was to keep William busy until 1993. He made two trips a month to Washington D. C. and became Vice Chairman of the project to build this important memorial in the United States. He was active on the committee during Reagan's campaign. He was appointed by Reagan to be on a committee that became a commission. Elie Wiezel, also a survivor of the prison camps became the founding Chairman until he won the Nobel Peace Prize for Literature, which created its own demands. Elie Wiezel was replaced by Harvey M. Meyerhoff, as Chairman.

When William went to Washington all the Commission Members were Democrats. He was the first Republican appointed. President Reagan made him Vice Chairman of the committee after a year on the council. The name of the group formed was called the United Holocaust Memorial Council. He spent the next twelve years flying to Washington and through the Bush, he Administration, picked out architects, studied building plans and supported the project.

The Committee went to the government and Congress gave them some beautiful land and the old Bureau of Printing and Engraving Building. The property was 1,000 feet from the Washington Monument. Privately, the group raised the money to build the museum building. They believed they needed $150,000,000.00 The new Chairman, Harvey Meyerhoff and William took on an accellerating business for the Commission. They were proud of the unusual building being built. Everything, including the rooms were planned differently. There was 300,000 feet built, including offices. The cost of the project came to $185,000,000.00 Actually the committee raised all the money from private individuals, Jewish and non-Jewish. Individual doners came from the business and private sectors. In 1993, the memorial was opened under extraordinary planning by the United States Department of Defense. The program delivered was conceived in minute detail. The museum is a huge success. Two and one-half million people visited the museum in the first eighteen months.

About a year before the official ceremonies were completed there was an event at the Capitol of the United States Rotunda. The Vice Chairman, William J. Lowenberg was the official speaker for a candle lite ceremony. His address follows:

"At 7:30 this morning, most of you were sleepily thinking about your day, anticipating this inspiring ceremony or perhaps even contemplating more mundane things. I was not. 7:30 a.m., April 30, 1945, was the moment of my liberation.

Forty-seven years ago today, I stood in the early morning sun at Dachau and stared in amazement as American tanks barreled over a hill, heading toward us. Today, I stand before members of those liberating forces, in this magnificent rotunda, a world away from Dachau, and together, we remember.

Forty-seven years ago today, I stood in bewilderment watching as Nazis continued killing innocent victims even after American forces had entered the camp. Today, I stand before the German president, and together, painfully, we remember.

Many details are now forgotten, but some striking moments remain in my mind. I remember that I was weak, dazed and sick - but overwhelmed by a kaleidoscope of conflicting emotions. I remember relief tinged by sorrow, happiness tempered by fear. I remember an American who gave me a cigarette, and then I fainted. I remember young soldiers who brought us much needed food. I remember realizing that I was one of the very few to survive. But most important, I remember standing on my native soil, vowing to myself that all I saw, all I heard, all I experienced would never be forgotten.

Those sacred vows - repeated by anguished survivors all over Europe - provided a small measure of consolation; but who could have imagined then that they would eventually result in the creation of a magnificent memorial museum in America's national capitol?

In one year we will stand together in a museum destined to become a historic and, more significantly, a moral landmark for all who cherish freedom. In one year, we will remember together the flames of hatred and fanaticism that once consumed a people as we now light a single candle to preserve their memory. We engage in this solemn tradition today for the millions who entered the depths of darkness never to return" ... The ceremony continued with participants from Congress and from all over the world.

Three weeks before the opening of the museum, the Chairman who had given 85% of his time and over $6,000,000.00 to the memorial project, along with William J. Lowenberg, the Vice Chairman, who had traveled twice a month to Washington D.C. for all of those years was being replaced by President

Clinton. All Republicans on Commissions were being replaced by Democrats. (The Chairman had also built a symphony hall for Baltimore.) It was but three weeks before the opening of the museum, which they had devoted so much love and time creating, and they were being replaced in a bad political move. The two men decided not to leave their posts until the opening of the museum. William was replaced by an active Democratic Black woman.

From this quiet man who showed the Editor the eight numbers tattooed under his skin on his left arm were some more remembrances as portrayed in the museum. As to the Red Cross packages as received in Stalag 17, the Jewish prison camps had no access for such foods and help. At Stalag 17 where the Red Cross did deliver packages, there were no beatings and gas chambers.

"In camps like Auschwitz and Birkenau, the people executed were not all Jews. The victims included Catholic nuns, Protestant ministers, Homosexuals, political Jews from various countries, Gypsies, Jehovah Witnesses, and Masons. The obsession to destroy all of these people was a fetish of Hitler and no one really knows the why of his manifest genocide cleansing operation in those killing centers," according to William.

When William arrived the first day in the prison camp, he saw a guard with a long black whip. The German Soldier would snap the whip hard on the ground directing persons to go one way or another. William saw others were boarding a truck after he was sent in one direction. He wished he had been able to go in the other direction, until he discovered those on the truck were taken on their last ride in the world to the gas chamber.

One of the jobs, William had to do to stay alive, was to help set up wooden forms where 100 or more people were burned at one time. For fun and games, German officers made people squat for hours. After a few minutes it hurts a human being to squat. The German officers would also make the prisoners stand in one place all day in cold rain. Those who could not keep squatting or standing would be shot.

There were 2,000 volts of electricity strung around the compound of the camps. Many strings of wire were grouped together. When the American Army approached the fence, the inmates cried out, "Don't touch the fence!" The Americans had to go somewhere to get electricians to disarm the fence before they could enter. Guards shot prisoners by the thousands before the Americans came back.

William Lowenberg had been through three death marches by that day of liberation and was found to weigh 60 pounds.

The young man who lost his family was sorrowed that the people of the village of Dachau knew what was happening in the camps and did not help. In the camps were political refugees from Italy, Greece, the Balkans, France and Belgium. William stated, "Six million Jews were killed. I have no good feelings for the Germans. They were a party of people who did not resist the few at the top of a political system. I don't think that America could develop that way." He was indignant that "even my Mother's family fought for Germany. My father was a Mayor of the town and he fought in the hinterland. Loyal countrymen were humiliated in the camps. I don't like to visit Germany."

When a German dignitary came to see the Museum before it opened, the official had a man with a camera accompanying him. William was showing the group around. The fellow with the camera stated, "I forgot to bring film." William felt it was done on purpose. They came to request a place at the end of the Memorial building to show Germany as it is today. The Committee would not hear of it.

William married in 1957 and the Lowenbergs have two children. Son, David is an orthopedic surgeon and Susan works in the family firm. William and his wife enjoy two grandchildren who come to their weekender home located in Sonoma's mountains which was purchased in 1968. The family liked Sonoma because the town had ambiance. It was like old town living. It had sunshine. William made a lot of friends in the area. The home in Sonoma is a very quiet gated estate lying to the north having direct views of Sonoma mountain and the town of Sonoma. The Lowenberg's main residence is in San Francisco, 45 miles to the south.

William blotted out his experiences for forty years. His wife protected him. One day, all of a sudden he stopped to tell his children about his life in the prison camps. His children stopped him. They said, "We know Dad, we found out for ourselves. You don't need to tell us." His children had researched William's path all on their own. William has remained in the field of real estate. He builds commercial buildings and warehouses.

Remembering for William J. Lowenberg, encompasses the spectrum of extreme lows and highs of human sorrow and joy. The little boy ignored and ostracized by his German teachers, used up in the Nazi prison camps until he weighed but sixty pounds, the only one left out of forty individuals comprising his family that lived in Germany, rescued from the extermination camps by the American Army, an American soldier in Korea, he presently enjoys being an honored citizen of the United States. William became speaker to a world assemblage. He helped to create one of the major modern museums of the world which carries a theme that could now, also be indicative of the quality of William's life. The theme of the museum: *Days of Remembrance.*

United States Holocaust Memorial Council, *Fifty Years Ago, Revolt Amid the Darkness,* 100 Raoul Wallenberg Place, S.W., Washington, D.C., April 18-25th, 1993., pps. 412, p. 303.

Richard W. Peterson

United States Air Corps 1942 - 1945

Bobby Andrieux, Lloyd Tracy, Donald Weise, Frank Wedekind, Richard W. Peterson with a couple of other fellows from Sonoma, California met at the Army induction center in San Francisco at the same time. The officers in charge did not induct that night. Some guys stayed over in the City.. They went to Lorraine's house, slept on the floor and acted like they didn't have a care in the world... Lorraine was the girl who had married Frank Wedekind.

By candlelight, at 440 Market Street, the seven Sonomans were sworn into the service for World War II at 7:p.m on Halloween! Rich Peterson took tests for flight school along with physicals from his tonsils and throat on down. Rich enlisted in the Army Air Corps while waiting for a call from the cadet program.

At La Junta, Colorado along with Frank Wedekind, he found it was colder than imaginable. Everyone was sick. Rich was in the hospital, too. They took out Rich's tonsils while almost everyone else was under influenza problems and the pneumonia bug. The base was not yet fully operational. Men receiving basic training spent much of the time tramping in the snow without proper warm clothing. The facility was generally a training base for B-25 pilots. Rich received classification in the Base Intelligence Office. There were 4,800 troops in the camp.

Rich ended up interrogating everyone with a German background including one of the men who went into the service with him from Sonoma, California. The biggest job for Rich was checking base security. He checked backgrounds and case files on any suspect of the war. There were some division Blacks who were always having fights. They were mostly from the Chicago area. They seemed to have a difficult time in getting along. Rich was at La Juanta until May 1944. Then, he was assigned to go overseas. "The assignment," he remembers; "triggered a time of apprehension as to the future."

Rich also recalls going back and forth across the country by train five times. He did not have much money after he left from Richmond, California on his fifth turnaround to Greensboro, North Carolina. At Albuquerque, New Mexico on the last trip before going overseas, he ran into money problems. He couldn't get a ticket at the lowest fare. He had to be back at a specific time in camp or be AWOL. The express fare only cost $19.00 more than the usual fare. He didn't have a penny left over from his original estimate. He wired collect to a buddy at post barracks for help. His buddy went up and down the barracks and collected the money Rich needed to complete the trip. Rich rode in the back of the bar car in the express. There he met a Senator of Colorado who bought him several drinks.

Arriving back to North Carolina on time, overseas training was more than just a promise. The men accomplished survival training at a lake. They jumped off heights as high as a ship. Their barracks bag was used like a parachute to ease the fall of the jump. They took lengthy marches and carried full packs. Aircraft swooped down over them as if they were under attack. Rich was loaded upon Liberty ship, USS Hawaiian Skipper. He was unassigned heading for Oran, Africa. Originally, the 350th was formed in Baton Rouge, Louisiana. Some of the 350th group went to England first, some went direct to Casablanca. From Oran, Africa, Rich was sent to Bari, Italy where he was assigned to a Group

Intelligence with the 350th Fighter Group of the Twelfth Air Force. Shortly thereafter, he was sent to the 349th Fighter Squadron which was a part of the 350th Group.

The 347th became a bit famous throughout the Mediterranean Theatre originally built around a cadre of enlisted men selected from the 54th Fighter Group. The unit activated at Hamilton Field, California and was sent to Washington. The 54th Fighter Group was dissolved and the 350th Fighter Group was activated in its place. The 347th Fighter Squadron operated as a member of the Northwest African Coastal Air Force. For 18 months the entire Mediterranean sector was covered by planes. Support was given to operations at Malta, Pantelbaria, Sicily, Sardinia, Corsica, Elba, Southern France and Eastern and Western Coasts of Italy.

In Africa, the staging area became known as "Mud Hill." Diet additions more than welcomed were oranges and wine purchased in great quantities. The wine helped change cranky attitudes about sleeping on the ground and in pup tents. The 347th unloaded gasoline brought to them in five gallon flimsy tin cans which often burst apart. There were no regular fueling facilities. Hundreds of barrels of fuel were used in one day. The men supervised Arab labor gangs, serviced, guarded and maintained the post. A grass field, little more than a pasture, served as runway. Heavy high desert winds caused suffocating dust storms requiring goggles and dust respirators being worn day and night. The entire 350th Fighter Group came together at the same time in Oujda, North Africa. Men were strictly confined in Oran due to a measles epidemic. A rowdy party did not make them very popular with the parents of girls in the area.

At Corsica, the Squadron was far above the fighting lines in Italy. The men could look across the Tyrrhenian Sea and see the firing from the ships toward Rome. The distance was covered in ten minutes by air from the post. Hundreds of missions were flown each month. During the Tunisian Campaign alone, the 347th flew 335 sorties on fighter sweeps flying against veteran German Pilots. The P-47s were new planes being flown after the Squadron had been flying P-39s since Africa. In Corsica, Pilots flew their planes off a converted race track. Pilots were informed they were at the place where Napoleon was born in Ajaccio, Corsica.

Parts for the planes were hard to come by. Due to malfunctions of the aircraft in flight, many Pilots were lost. Electrical systems of the planes deteriorated from dampness. Aircraft parts were hard to procure. Parts not obtainable were swiped from each other at night. Maintenance became a headache. It was stated, "A 21 year old Pilot NEVER became bossy with his 36 year old Crew Chief!" The group put out a call for a logo or name. They selected a loud-open-mouthed-picture and dubbed themselves, *The Screaming Red Ass.*

When they were in Algero, Sardina, the 12th Air Force was supporting the 5th Army under General Mark Clark. The 347th Tactical Fighter Squadron carried bombs and rockets in their P-47s. Besides German planes, the Squadron targeted German positions and equipment throughout the Po Valley and Northern Italy. The Squadron lost 48 Pilots out of 230. They received a new compliment of Pilots about every two or three months. The total Pilots at any one time ranged from 40 to 45 fellows flying around the clock. They flew out of Sardinia, Italy and after that moved to Tarquina, Italy. That was in November and December of 1944. It was rainy and muddy in Italy during that time of the year. Pilots flew off steel mats. Tent conditions were horrible.

Starting in Tunisia, Africa in order to lighten moods, a newspaper called the *De-Nuss-ance* was born by Staff Sergeant, Charles "Schifty" Schiffman. Originally having one page, the paper grew. Sometimes, it had from 14 to 16 pages. The paper enjoyed a life of interest, smiles, liberty, free speech and a verbal license beyond measure. Descriptions bordered on the derelict. In that narrow world where the men were confined, nothing was trivial. There were columns for corrections, text for the day, our creed, flash, short short stories, rumors, sports, the local scene, public opinion, The Brass, poetry, testimonials, vital statistics, the home front, so long (to buddies), society, the German radio, economics and ad extremum topics as to subject matter. In their little world where men were confined, nothing was kept secret and everything trivial was blown up out of proportion. To safeguard military operation, a limited number of copies were typed for the day. They were posted on the bulletin boards then, collected and destroyed.

The First Brazilian Fighter Squadron operated with the 350th Fighter Group in Italy combat operations. Eight of the Brazilian pilots were killed. Eight more were shot down, three made it back to camp and five became prisoners of war. After their arrival in Italy the South Americans, quick to follow American military traditions, had their P-47s decorated with their own squadron insignia. Pictures painted on their aircraft depicted a brightly colored fighting ostrich on long legs standing guard over a motto meaning "without fear." The Americans found the Brazilians to be good friends despite language barriers. They were efficient soldiers. They were referred to as "fine comrades to have in the struggle against tyranny."

Rich recalls a night to remember. It was a rainy, pitch black night in December, 1944. (Rich believes, "anyone who was in Tarquina on a rainy, moonless and muddy night can appreciate this story.") Rich, Sergeant of Guards for the evening, stationed four men to watch over each of four points surrounding a piece of ground which held from 25 to 30 P-47 airplanes. The guards were all armed with their trusty carbines. The planes were off the steel-matted air strip. Rich took needed shelter under a wing of one of the P-47s. Not being able to see his hand before his face, realizing the importance of his responsibility, he decided to tromp through the mud and check the guard. Approaching the northwest corner where he had stationed the group's newest recruit from the States, several shots were fired. Not knowing if the shots were at him or perhaps the Germans were invading, Rich hit the ground, mud! He thought, "Oh, my Golly, being on the sea coast, this will be my first battle to encounter." He waited for an invasion but nothing happened. Rich finally got up enough nerve to crawl closer to where the northwestern guard should be. In pitch darkness, he could hear someone moving. Rich quietly took a chance to call out, "Is it you, Joe Martinez? This is Peterson." "Thank the Lord," Joe answered; "It's me." Rich worried but he was relieved the man didn't shoot! As Rich crawled up next to Martinez, he asked, "What did you shoot at?" The burly fellow pointed out some bushes in the distance that were flowing in the breeze. The new recruit was sure the movement was caused by the enemy. Rich later learned that Joe had been in over 300 professional fights. He was so punched out that he was not really adapted for that type of duty nor qualified to handle a gun.

Another punchy fellow was a rowdy disorderly Greek cook who threw tantrums. He would deliberately smell diesel fumes. He also made Kadota Figs into liquor. Inhalation or drinking could set the fellow off enough to drive him into a crazy state. During those times, the men learned to stay out of the galley. The cook was apt to 'pluck' up a cleaver and throw it at the guys.

Rich was one of four men in the Intelligence Section that carried on administrative duties. There were administrative forms to fill out, interrogations, combat reports and daily briefings. Pilots were given their targets and destinations at four a.m. early hour briefings. This was part of the 12th Air Force. Information received and dispensed included antiaircraft activities and intelligence regarding the movements of German Planes as well as ground forces. Information came from Headquarters by radio for three squadrons. Codes were deciphered. If the Fifth Army needed help the 12th Air Force would give the needed support. Rich kept all sorts and kinds of maps on the walls. Many cities of Italy became totally bombed out, including houses and factories. Rich assisted in collection, evaluation, interpretation and distribution of knowledge of enemy and counterintelligence activities and the safeguarding of military information.

One night in Naples, all hell broke loose as to a bombing raid. The Americans were on a hillside in an open air type castle. There were large pillars all around but no windows left in the building. The men were sleeping on a tile floor. Several antiaircraft batteries caused unbearable noise. German planes bombed the harbor that night in Naples. A couple of times, Germans used flares at night to check on airplanes. This was before the Americans became superior in the air. Americans were lucky there were no German jets in the area.

Italy was used in a holding position (Operation: Strangle) to keep German troops busy and tied up in the area. By keeping eight to twelve divisions of Germans in combat (and they were pesky to hold back) they would not be available to join in fighting against Allied troops (Operation: Overlord) in France, which began on D-Day. Plans were designed to keep the Germans so busy in Italy they could not join the battles in France. After Tarquinia was in Allied hands, the Fifth Army took Piza. The Air Force spent six months in Italy supporting troops about 19 miles in advance. One day, at Piza, in a nicer building off the air strip, General Arnold came for a visit. Everyone dressed in the best clothes they had. After landing on the strip and receiving a welcome, Arnold sat down in front of the maps on the wall. In Arnold's own funny way, he said, "Colonel Neilson, tell me how's the war going?" The Colonel was surprised. He knew 'Hap' was aware of how the war was going.

Above the Arno River, Blacks had been integrated into the infantry. They were made soldiers instead of heavy equipment slavers. The Black division was nicknamed Eleanor Roosevelt's Division as she insisted upon integration of troops. Brazilians sent their air force to fly with the 347th. The Brazilians were trained in the United States to fly with this one group. They were trained on the P-47s. They were sent over to show loyalty to the cause. These two groups were chosen for the Italian Campaign.

Piza was a most unlikely spot to send in new inexperienced troops. For one thing, they were opposite the 10th Mountain boys who lost 1,000 men to crack Germans troops. Germans knew the territory well and dug in. In April 1945, all were alerted. After a stagnet line and many bloody affairs, the German push was deliberately pointed toward the area where the Blacks were. At that point, the Hawaiian Japanese joined the battle. They came right on through and wiped out the Germans. They saved all the American lives. The Japanese soldiers saved not only the Blacks but troops of all colors and nationalities! The Brazilians flying with the Air force did their excellent job, as well in this area.

Several pilots were shot down in Northern Italy. Clifton, being one of them escaped the Germans by way of the Italian Partisans. To make it back to base, it took him seventeen days to go from village to village under the Partisans direction. They took good care of him. He knew their life as well as his own was at risk by their rescuing attempts. A lot of the Italians hated the Germans. Several other Pilots who were shot down made their way back through the German lines.

In Piza, a girl name Lisa had been born and reared there. Johnny Laspina brought her home to the United States by marrying her. One of the biggest events in her life was when she anticipated the Americans coming! She just knew "the Americans would get the Germans out of the mountains around

Piza." This was a big event! Tanks were coming. She was waiting to see her first American! She had never seen a Black person in her life. She couldn't believe what she saw. All the persons in the tanks were Black. Could they be the Americans? At the end of the war and after the Germans were pushed out, Mussolini and his girl friend were hung in the square from a service station in Northern Italy.

Before leaving Italy in World War II, the entire 350th Fighter Group was requisitioned by United States General, Chennault for China. The Group being a tactical outfit flying P-47s was ideal for the war being fought there. All were loaded on a ship in Naples, battle-equipped to carry on the fight in China. They received word that an atom bomb had been dropped on Japan, three days out from the Panama Canal. Upon arriving at Panama City orders were reversed and the group was turned around. After twenty-one days at sea, the Fighter Group arrived in New York Harbor ready for discharge.

In Sonoma, General Arnold retired to a ranch after the war. Rich met him the second time while working for his uncle. Arnold appeared dressed in striped overalls. There were bins of fittings at the family store on Napa Street. "Can I help you, Sir," Rich inquired. Then Air Force retiree, Rich recognized the Five Star General he had seen in Italy. He described Arnold as being a very nice gentleman. Rich has bought some wines from Robert Bruce Arnold, the General's Grandson. The bottles have pictures of P-47s on them. The 347th have a Last Man Trophy which includes a bottle of the Arnold Wine with the P-47 picture. Frank Albro of Westminister, Colorado made a beautifully finished wine container as nice as a hand rubbed piece of furniture. The wine inside is being circulated from one person to the next. The wine in its encasement goes from re-union to re-union. The plaque is inscribed for the last man who will survive all the others of the 347th.

Rich with his wife Gloria have been active in attending and promoting anniversaries and gatherings of the men from the 347th. An unofficial Pictorial and Historical History of the 347th Fighter Squadron of the 350th Fighter Group of the 12th Air Force was edited and published by Charles Schiffman of Stockton, California. A special memorial dedication of the 350th Fighter Group was made at a reunion at the Wright-Patterson Air Force Base in Dayton, Ohio. Rich and his wife, Gloria were in attendance when a black polished marble bench and map of the Mediterranean theatre etched in detail was set in Dayton, Ohio. Tribute and recognition of the Brazilian Comrades in Arms was acknowledged. Sixty Brazilians were at the reunion in the United States. Subsequently, the Petersons joined other members of the 347th in Rio de Janeiro, Brazil at the invitation of the First Brazilian Air Force Members. Their hosts for this once in a lifetime experience were General Lima, General Moura, Colonel Lima, Major Kauffmann, Lieutenant De marco and Lieutenant Pellegrino. The attending members at Rio de Janerio were presented with velvet cases containing handsome beautifully designed medals. In 1989, the Petersons, along with the Seymour Cohns and Eleanor Edberg became instrumental in sending several items to the Brazilians for their "Museum Aerospacial" including pictures, plaques and group pictures taken in Dayton, Ohio.

Rich's Grandparents on the Peterson side came to Sonoma in the 1870s. They immigrated from southern Sweden. They came to Northern California because a recruiter was sent to Sweden to bring people over to help settle America. They became interested "in this land of plenty where you could grow fruit in warm sunshine." The grandparents came to America on a schooner which landed near San Jose, California. They were employed to work in fields by people who wanted or needed them tending fruit trees. Rich's grandmother was also employed as a maid. The grandparents had six sons and daughters. His dad was the third child, born in 1893. Rich's dad worked for a livery stable known as the Feed Store on the corner of First Street West and Napa Streets in Sonoma. It was called the Joe Ryan

Proprietary. There was a race track further down on First Street West. Rich's dad was a jockey while working for Joe Ryan. He raced horses on lower First Street West. Race tracks were also maintained in Napa and Santa Rosa as well as Sonoma. Joe Ryan was the County Sheriff.

Rich had an Uncle Ed, his Dad's oldest brother who was a bachelor. The uncle had a little shop, just a hole in the wall on Broadway. Then, he moved across from the Sonoma Index Tribune Office in 1949. The Petersons built a new building. It became a furniture store with hardware in front and mechanical operation in back. Rich and Gloria had a Buy/Sale Agreement with Ed and upon his death in 1961 went in debt and acquired the business. Rich founded the present location where once Acme Leather Company was housed. Rich and Gloria went into debt to buy the property and established Peterson Mechanical Inc. This company offers quality, full service in mechanical contracting for residential, commercial and industrial services. The company has grown to provide a legacy of experience in the field of heating, cooling and plumbing. The expertise and dependability has been passed down through three generations. Peterson Inc., serves both light and heavy commercial clients with complete service of boilers, chillers, cooling towers and rooftop HVAC units. A fleet of trucks stand ready to react to all situations from routine to emergency. Rich and Sons employ sixty to eighty people. Recent jobs included three at Travis Air Base, one in Bodega Bay, one at University of California at Davis and the huge new jails in Sonoma and Marin Counties. Rich believes his is probably the largest mechanical operation North of San Francisco. His two sons, Les and Kris do most of the work according to Rich. That may be hard to believe when you meet this vibrant man who claims he tries to play more golf. Wes is the President and Kris the Vice-President.

Above his desk and beyond the computer is an original picture. It is a drawing by a 12th Air Force Pilot, Dave Hammond. It shows a P-47 of the 12th Air Force ready to take off on a sortie in World War II. Rich purchased the original painting from the artist. The picture portrays shadows and graphics from special drawing pencils. It includes a P-47 Razorback, one of the planes of the 347th. Rich and Gloria's daughter, Nedra works in the hotel business in San Francisco. The family home is next to the mountains in northern Sonoma with a view of the town. Rich could actually walk to work.

Gloria and Rich have vacationed back to Italy twice since the war. The Squadron organized one trip and are re-doing another in 1995. The couple found it was hard to find places where Rich was stationed and where he crawled in the mud on that moonless night. They did find one bombed out building in Piza. In reviewing Rich's mementos and in the book by Schiffman, there are a couple of poems which probably show the commardarie of the men in those days of battle. The first one was written by the Men in Engineering Section who put in so many long hours fixing planes. They ganged up to write this poem.

The Sleeping Watchman.

I am a pilot, my name is Joe Fitch.
Take heed you fledglings and stay out of the ditch.
I came in for a landing, hit on all three.
Bounced a few times and just missed a tree.
I heaved a big sigh, wiped sweat from my brow.
And thought, "My God - what do I do now?"
Reaching for the flap switch, I retracted my gear.
Came down on my belly, ending up on my ear.
The moral of my story is plain you can see.
Keep your mind on your business or you'll wind up like me!

One morning a flight of five aircraft left Orleansville. Losing their course, they ran out of gas and made emergency landings in the desert. This incident became immortal in the history of the 347th. It was referred to as the Derelict Desert Airforce. To commemorate the event the enlisted men in the Engineering Section composed this poem.

The Lost Navigator.

I am a Flight Leader; my name is Joe Fitch.
At map reading and navigation, boy am I a bitch!
This is my story, and I swear it is true.
We took off one morning, out into the blue.
I checked all my bearings and plotted my course;
My engine was humming — pulling 1200 horse!
We flew a few hours, over mountains and waste.
When suddenly I discovered we were getting no place!
I looked at my gas gauge — it gave me a fright.
Where was the needle? It was clear out of sight!
I looked down below — where could we land?
All I could see was rock, cactus and sand!
I let down my flaps, kept up my gear.
Came in on my belly — said, "Lafayette, we are here!"
The moral of my story is plain, you can see,
Keep your mind on your business — or you'll wind up like me!

It could be stated many people would like the enviable position to wind up like Richard W. Peterson who must have kept his mind on his business! After a lifetime of work, he probably does deserve to play a bit more golf. But, one meeting Rich for the first time feels an energy and a kindness of spirit which probably relates to his business success. He is an epitome of an American success story.

Schiffman, Charles, *Pictoral and Historical History of the 347th Fighter Squadron of the 350th Fighter Group of the 12th Air Force,* Pub., Charles Schiffman, Stockton, Ca. no date, probably 1979. pps.152.

Frank D. Gregory, Jr.

United States Army Army, 1941 - 1945
Air Force and Signal Corp

Native Californian, Frank Jr. is son of another native Californian, Frank Delano Gregory, Sr. His father was born in the rolling countryside near Rocklin, California off old Highway 40 later named Interstate 80. Frank, Sr. and his wife, Edna built a home in Roseville, California, an important railroad town where Frank, Jr. was born. Rocklin and Roseville are northeast of the State Capitol, Sacramento, California. Frank, Sr. lived for more than a century. At age 103, he had seen California change from one way gravel roads for the horse and buggy to fancy eight lane highways for automobiles. Frank Jr.'s father was an Engineer on the Southern Pacific Railroad.

Frank Jr.'s mother, Edna came from Iowa. At an early age, she was in the Sacramento area. The family has a post card collection which was evidently the means of communication to and from her many friends and relatives during the early 1900's. (The cards were mailed for one cent each.) Her father delivered mail from Reno to Sacramento in an old buckboard. Edna also saw a century of change. At this writing, she is 102 years old.

Frank Jr. was struggling at Chico State College to become a school teacher in the early forties. Along with study of psychology and English, required to obtain a teaching credential in California, he ran a weekend dance hall. He never danced but booked some of the Big Dance Bands of the 40s. He saw band leaders before they became famous as a struggling bunch trying to make a living. They were on their way to fame and were very popular.

Frank like other young men of the times had this welling up in the breast known as patriotism. Bombs fell on Pearl Harbor and war was declared. He heard the news when he and a friend were coming out of a movie theater. He wanted to get away from worrying about spelling, his one big problem in keeping grade levels up at college. Frank made the statement many times, "I'll join the Army, I don't care if they shoot at me or not." With that attitude, he enlisted at Chico, California much to his family's dismay that he had done it so quickly!

He and Pal, Bruce Kimsey entered the Army Air Corps on the same day. This friend would become a topic of conversation for years after the war as Frank recalled the fun that they had at college. Joining the Army Air Corps at first, Frank was stationed near New Orleans. At Harding Field, in the Texas panhandle, he became part of the Signal Corps. Near DeRitter, Tennessee, he was defined as a sharpshooter for the Infantry before going to the European Theatre of War.

Before leaving for Europe and while yet stationed in Texas, Frank was home in Roseville on leave. It was not very risky to hitchhike during those days. Frank decided to "catch rides" across the western states back to base at Wichita Falls. At Kremling, Colorado with his thumb up in the air for another ride, he noticed a couple of young girls engaged in a water fight. Being a friendly guy, always ready to strike-up a conversation with anyone he met, the young soldier talked to the girls as he waited for another driver and "a lift." One of the girls, Neva Gosling asked Frank, Jr. for his address because she and her sister enjoyed a hobby of writing letters to service men. Neva would move to a little southeastern border town in Missouri, called Elsinore. She was moving there to stay with her aunt.

Before this time, in Macomb, Illinois a young girl, born in 1930 was singing popular songs as early as eight years of age. She strung a rope from the front door knob to the back door knob across the kitchen dining room. This was a busy place as these doors were the only ones in and out of the "little red house" near the tracks of the C, B and Q Railroad. Her father, Joe Kidd kept the steam engines heated by shoveling coal into their iron fire-boxes during the night. When this busy family of six was not entering or exiting the house to check for daddy or the big engines, this rope tied between the two doors became the edge of an imaginary stage. The first song, the little girl remembered imitating was *Elmer's Tune*. She learned to sing everything from *Mairsy Doats* to *Sentimental Journey* and all those wonderful love songs which came along each week on the Hit Parade. War songs included *This is the Army, Mr. Jones* to song *They're Either Too Young or Too Old* not to mention *Let's Remember Pearl Harbor* and *When the Lights Go on Again*. Gladys, the girl's mother, let her little girl at age ten move from Illinois to stay with the girl's Aunt Nettie in the little town of Hunter, Missouri near Elsinore, where Neva would come to live.

Evelyn attended the grammar school upon the hill. Teachers (there were three) marched the students down to the old Hunter Country Store below the knoll to hear President Franklin Delano Roosevelt's fireside chats on a radio. The teachers thought this was important as many "Arkie" students coming from large families did not have battery radios in their homes like Aunt Nettie had in hers. The store was the central meeting place for a few groceries and lots of people. You could not buy ice cream, frozen or prepared foods. The store was equipped with a potbelly stove and an old brass spitoon. Ozark Mountain Men seemed to loiter around the store. If they were not in the store around the potbelly stove, they congregated to gossip on a wooden bench in front the store.

In the country neighborhood where Aunt Nettie lived was the home of a German family. Evelyn, the budding singer played with the little German girl named Pansy, who was Hattie's daughter. Hattie was daughter of an old German farmer who's name to fame as far as Evelyn was concerned was that of growing huge strawberries in springtime. Evelyn's Aunt Nettie had a huge victory garden about a block long by a block wide. It was on her side of the gravel road. The German family lived on the other side of the road. For about three quarters of the year, Aunt Nettie weeded that huge victory garden every day. On terribly hot days and nights, with perspiration pouring off her body, she canned hundreds of quarts of vegetables in the two room cabin which had no airconditioning. She also milked a cow and raised chickens and goats. She taught the little girl how to cook, clean, cipher, spell and study.

Aunt Nettie and her friends also whispered intensely about a fear they seemed to have. "Did that German across the way have a radio hooked up to Germany?" With all these goings on, with wartime romances in the movies, reading pulp love stories in magazines similar in size to comic books, and with incessant love songs going through the young girl's head was it any wonder that Evelyn felt left out of World War II? She had a longing that she was not old enough to be a part of all that excitement that was broadcasted on radio, recited in music, in neighbor's conversations and pictured in the school's subscription of the students' "The Weekly Reader."

While Frank was still in the United States, the girl Neva to whom Frank Jr. had given his name and address moved to the Ozarks and became a friend of Evelyn. By now, the two girls were in their first year of high school in Elsinore, Missouri. Neva, the girl from Colorado could think of nothing to write to Frank, Jr. who was still in Texas. The two high school freshman having finished their homework in study hall, spent the remainder of time whispering back and forth. Evelyn asked Neva to let her "write a line" to that pen pal that Neva wrote to in the Army. Evelyn wrote an unusual letter in the form of a circle to the G.I. and he returned an answer. Ironically, he also had a hobby of writing letters to many people. "In that way," he stated; "I always got lots of mail during Army mail call."

Eventually, Frank, Jr. was deployed out of New York Harbor and was shipped to England. His transportation was by way of one of the largest American ships of the time, USS United States. He remembers only intense rocking and rolling on that Atlantic Ocean crossing. The big ship was supposedly dodging German submarines. Men were not allowed to go up on deck. Windows were kept tightly shuttered on the ship. The soldiers did not see where they were going. Frank has forgotten where he landed in England. He thinks his group landed on the west side of England and traveled across the country embarking right away for Omaha Beach from the English Channel.

Frank was deposited at Normandy by LST (Landing Ship Transport). He waded in the ocean through cold waves with his rifle over his head. It was so dark, it would be hours before dawn would break. He believes, he was in the second company of men to arrive on or about Omaha Beachhead on D-Day. It was cold. It was confusing and it was horrifying! He did not like falling against dead bodies on the beach while it was yet dark. He did not like the intermittant bright flashes of gunfire because there was no hiding place for cover. He did not like stumbling and brushing against so many men who lie all around him as lifeless shapes. The idea of "I don't care if I get shot at" was a little less boldly stated than in the protected environment of school or when at boot camp in the United States. However, Frank was a "sharpshooter." He had been a Boy Scout with all badges (except one) and so he forged his way toward bombed out little towns. He went "as the Army Officials directed that he go." Those little towns all bombed to rubble were the fourth thing, he found distasteful. He hated to see ruination and destruction. All those nameless people that had lived in those homes... Many were under that rubble and rock and the men knew it! The smell was incredible." He thought of his own mother and dad and was glad they were in America. He refused to talk about the stench of bodies in those devastated villages that accompanied the soldiers' march across France into Germany.

As Frank, Jr. moved through France, sometimes on foot and at other times was carried forward toward Germany by lumbering trucks or on the 40 and 8 train, he was always lucky at mail call. That girl Evelyn, he was writing to from Missouri wrote him many letters. In fact, she wrote him almost every day. She told him such trifles as, "I am sitting here among the goats on this grassy hillside thinking of you." She penned him fanciful letters just like the love stories she had been reading in pulp magazines. Frank wrote her back one hundred sixty-five letters while the Army moved across France. She kept his letters which also began to be about love. The girl was only fourteen when she started correspondence with this Soldier. She had never had a date and never would. Her very strict Aunt Nettie "kept her protected." Frank, nine years older than the girl, thought she was seventeen or eighteen years of age. Her pictures looked like she was older than fourteen years. She sent him one picture taken in a grass skirt and another in a nylon chenille spaghetti decorated pillbox hat! Those pictures were composed in a photo center booth in what was an early franchised drug store.

Frank was a point man in the Infantry. He would go in front of his company and try to locate the position of the enemy. He did tell one story over and over, "if no crickets were heard in those hedgerows chirping at night, then you did not creep forward. Crickets did not sing when there was something strange in their area." He traveled quietly in the darkness by way of singing crickets (which he quieted) to find the German encampments. Sometimes he carried a bulky radio on his back. It was the type of radio you had to crank, in order to send important messages back to camp. Often, he just stealthily moved back and forth between the American and German Armies. He declared, "Armies do not shoot all the time. They change positions when it is quiet. You know, that's when it is the most dangerous time for a point man. The enemy Army has their point men scouting, too."

Frank, Jr. was a man who could sleep even if bombs were falling. Many men did not sleep well in the war and were tired and weary from worry. A few were jealous of men who could sleep. Some, who had trouble sleeping were nervous wrecks. Some were envious of others who could sleep. In order to get even with Frank for sleeping, he endured being a victim of pranks including being left where he was sleeping while his company moved on. Often, he searched diligently before locating his platoon. On many occasions, as he wandered through a small town, he befriended little children. He found out the children studied English in the third grade and could communicate a bit with him. He shared chocolate bars with them from his rations and their little faces would light up in pleasure. Once, a little boy that had received chocolate from him, shook him to waken him. He told Frank Jr. in broken English and with motions "that the building he was sleeping in was going to be destroyed in a very short time!" Frank rolled up his sleeping gear while asking the little boy, "Which way did my Army go?"

Frank recently described his first German Soldier killed. He saw a group of German Soldiers through a small thicket while peering through dense branches of trees. The group appeared in conversation. They were less than a hundred feet away. Frank drew up his rifle and carefully sighted the chest of one of the Soldiers. He squeezed the trigger of the gun and saw the German fall. He confiscated a big round stainless steel watch from the dead German that he wore for about twenty years. When the watch quit ticking it went the way of the Soldier. Frank does not remember what happened to the rest of the German Soldiers that were standing with his prey. He only knows, "that was the first one." He does not want to talk about any others. He does not want to talk about the the 80,000 American bodies or the 80,000 to 100,000 German bodies that he and his buddies saw lying in pools of red blood on the frozen white snow during the Battle of the Bulge. These were prices paid by both opposing armies as the Allied Soldiers marched forward and forded cold European rivers. The German Soldiers of the German war machine were expended by the American Air Force, the paratroopers and the massed Allied Armies. (The above body count figures have been set in history books as losses in the last month's activity along the German line during the war.) The above losses do not account for those between the Germans and Russians or in other areas.

Frank viewed the Siegfried Line. He likened it to the long old fortresses that are north of San Francisco in the Marine Headlands. He agreed with other men in this book that American tanks were inferior to the heavier German tanks. German tanks had swiveled guns while the American gun turrets were stationary. Should a tank be disabled, American tanks had no trap doors out the back-side for evacuation. He eagerly remembered, however, "when we crossed the Rhine River, all German guns from their fortified walls were pointing toward France. The turrets on those guns in the border fortresses were all pointing one way with fixed turrets. That was why the American Army went in behind the German's big guns. The enemy could not turn their gun turrets around!"

Once Frank Jr. saw a man leaning over a part of a fence rail looking down at a pile of rubble. This was in Germany. Frank stopped to say, "hello." He asked, "why have you got tears in your eyes?" The German replied, "this was once my home..."

Frank was in the 'Bulge' when other American Soldiers were shivering from the cold. He had always been warm-blooded, so he did not feel the cold as others did. He attributes some warmth from drinking potato peeling brewed beer. When the platoon was not moving, someone started a batch of 'brew' usually in a bath tub. After the potato peelings were fermented in yeast, the guys strained the potent drink through nylons stretched over screens to remove the 'head' or goo on the top of the mixture. The Soldiers dipped their aluminum drinking cups into the smelly stuff for their alcoholic drink. (The cup could be anything handy. It might be a fancy cup found in a bashed building or even one's helmet.) No matter what it was drunk from, the brew tended to make one feel a bit uncomfortable and the alcohol helped to raise the body temperature!

Frank was still there when American Fighter Planes bombed Germany as men hurriedly crossed the famous rivers, Meuse and Rhine. He was in the thick of battle. He does not want to talk about it... Every day on his troop ship while coming home the men were deprogrammed. They were told not to speak about their experiences of this war on this battlefield.

When Frank, Jr. was discharged, he thought about that girl in Missouri whom he had written to and who then had a new address change in Illinois. After discharge from New York and back home in California, the ex-soldier still wrote love letters to the girl, Evelyn. He decided to hitchhike to Illinois to see the girl. He found out she was but sixteen and was a sophomore at East St. Louis High. He was nine years older than she.

For days, Frank and Evelyn's Aunt Nettie sequestered in conversation about letting Evelyn marry this stranger. Disappointed, the ex-Soldier returned to California. A few days later, after constant begging to go to Denver, Colorado, Evelyn, traveling with a cousin, left her aunt in tears. Evelyn boarded a bus for Denver and sent Frank a wire, "I'll be in Denver, meet me." A deal had been struck with Aunt Nettie. Both young people promised, "if we marry, we will see that Evelyn finishes school." Before the young girl boarded the bus for Colorado, her wandering father showed up to say goodbye. Acting upon his own suggestion, he signed a note giving his daughter permission to cross state lines and get married. This piece of paper came in handy when the couple roused a sleeping Methodist minister out of bed in Lovelock, Nevada for a 9 p.m. wedding. The Minister demanded permission of some sort before he would perform the marriage ceremony. The note sufficed. Evelyn even changed into a long white wedding dress complete with veil for the impromptu affair.

In 1946, the promise to finish high school was not as easy as one imagined. Married girls were not allowed to mix in high schools. They might 'taint' other students. Frank's brother, Elwyn was County Superintendent of Schools at Auburn, California. He made arrangements for the high school junior to keep up her studies at Auburn High. To make matters a little difficult, the couple started out their married life in a tent! For three months there was no housing to be found in the little foothill village of Forest Hill, California. Evelyn caught a bus each morning for the eighteen mile ride down the beautiful American River Canyon to Auburn. Frank was sixth grade teacher in Forest Hill. They purchased their first home to obtain housing and moved in before the first snowfall. It was a three room victorian cottage complete with porches and a wooden outside two-holer toilet. The house was substantial and was purchased for $500.00 from borrowed money loaned by Frank's parents.

The next three years the couple moved to small cities in California. Concord, California, now highly populated, had only one grammar school. Frank was sixth grade teacher. Two women running the high school were very "skeptical about letting a married woman in their high school." Evelyn was finally admitted as a senior after a lengthy meeting with those women. Evelyn graduated from Mount Diablo High with high scores and rendered *Now is the Hour* at the 1948 graduating party. She was congratulated by one of the older ladies running the school "as paying attention to education and not educating the girl students about married life!" Evelyn hadn't even thought of it!

The couple moved to the small town of Calistoga, California where Frank was teacher and Evelyn began classes at Santa Rosa Junior College. She graduated as A.A. in Music and Aunt Nettie attended. This was the highest level anyone in Evelyn's family had ever attained in schooling. The couple began a family after being married for five years. Four boys were born in Sonoma, California

In the late afternoon and evening over a period of the next fourteen years, Evelyn went to San Francisco State College and Sonoma State College, finishing with a Master's degree in Education. She accomplished this education while cooking, sewing and caring for the family in the daytime, her husband Frank cared for the family during the evening hours. She also helped her husband pass all those written papers and a theisis for his Masters Degree. Frank taught at Sonoma, California from 1949 until 1983. One of Frank's major achievements was telling stories to his classes that would be quite similar to a show called *Hillbillies* that subsequently appeared on television. He was beloved by his students, teaching some of their children as well. He was known as a champion for childrens' concerns, taking his classes on field trips and for his story telling.

Evelyn became a soloist in many Gilbert and Sullivan productions. Handel's *Messiah* and many religious cantatas became a part of her life. She played characters in historical pageants and sang professionally for twenty-four years as soloist for a Christian Science Church. She was soprano soloist in the 140 voice Sonoma Valley Chorale as well as the new Cantata Choir. After graduation from Sonoma State College, Evelyn taught college education courses at night and was involved in special education program with the college at a CYA facility. Those activities were through the same junior college from which she had graduated. When the special classes closed, Evelyn decided to earn a real estate broker's license from the State of California. She opened her own real estate company at the age of forty-three and sold a great deal of property in the growing wine country community known as Sonoma, California. Her success was due to her husband's assistance on time-consuming details and her Charter Membership as CRS (Certified Residential Specialist with the National Association of Realtors®.) The CRS designation was awarded because of a great deal of directed education in such fields as exchanges, counseling, legal updates, tax knowledge and ethical behavioral courses, plus the closing of 100 escrows verified by the local Multiple Listing Services. She became a professional in her work before franchises taught the concept. (This information has been added to show how one couple can achieve the American dream by education should one wish to apply determinination, study for professionalism and work hard together for success!")

As late in time as the 1960s, Frank used to have nightmares regarding the war. It would be as if someone would be chasing him during a battle. He would sit straight up in bed asleep while talking to the party that was doing the chasing. Then, he would bolt out of bed as if to take off. Once, he almost jumped out an open second story bedroom window! Evelyn would talk him out of his episodes and back into bed. Many times he did not even wake up. He evidently could still sleep under any circumstance. However, in later years, when the family's house caught fire, it was he who woke up to see the consuming flames from an outside patio glass door to the adjoining garage. It was after problems of the house fire with a major insurance company, that Evelyn wrote her first book, "Autobiography of a Fire." She conceived a cookbook for the Methodist Church combining three previous cookbooks and current recipes with history, chairing "A Century of Favorite Recipes."

This third book was prompted after a community program, organized by the Evelyn through church called "Shine Your Light on the Desert." Sonoma citizens, through their overwhelming generosity, sent over four tons of personal items, books and foods to their service sons and daughters during Operation: Desert Storm of the Gulf War. The Gregory's son, Mark helped pack the many boxes of items with his dad. Son, Robert was in Saudi Arabia in Desert Storm. Son, John had served a stint in the Navy. Evelyn sang for the Veterans of Foreign Wars of Sonoma. The Veterans of Foreign Wars Bear Flag Post 1943 were enthusiastic that she write a book about World War II Veterans and gave their enthusiastic support. Evelyn discovered through many months of interviewing and a great amount of time in proof-reading, checking and researching background materials regarding the war, that developing stories from oral interviews was an all-encompassing and time consuming task. She felt she truly became a part of World War II!

Evelyn is presently a member of a Commission ordered by the City of Sonoma to plan a large celebration, calendared for June of 1996, the Sesquicentennial of the raising of the Bear Flag. When the City of Sonoma celebrated its 150 year anniversary in 1987, Evelyn conceived, wrote and narrated a forty still-picture pageant entitled *"Pictures of the Past."* She is also a life member of the Sonoma Valley Historical Society and was Editor of *The Sonoma Notes*, the group's monthly newspaper. This organization is an important group in such a historically based environment. Sonoma, California is a retirement mecca for retired veterans. Historically, the town was the birthplace for California Statehood. In June of 1846, frontiersmen raised the first Bear Flag over the State of California in the little Spanish Pueblo after replacing the flag of the Spanish Conquistadore. A few days after the Bear Flag was raised, the Stars and Stripes took its place.

In this environment, it seems, every other grey-haired person is a Veteran of World War II. The population includes Army Privates to Colonels, Navy Captains, a few Marines and many Air Corps Pilots. GIs had found their way to Sonoma, while visiting Sonoma Mission Inn, used during the war as a rest and recouperation facility. This is true particularly for Pacific War Veterans. Many men were visitors from Mare Island Shipyard about twenty miles to the south. While their ships were in drydock and while many were on leave, Navy personnel drove into the Coastal Range for a quiet picnic. They stopped in at the Hospitality House provided by women of the American Women Voluntary Services. When they saw the beautiful valley, they remembered, and it lured them back.

Stories of the veterans have had such diverse backgounds that the writer has had tremendous variety of subject matter. To the writer, her effort has truly been considered a phenomenal experience of a life time! Oldest son, Donald programmed short cuts on the computer for his mother. Frank, Jr. with help of the Sonoma Valley Library Staff has been catalyst for information filling Evelyn's wish list for information regarding planes, tanks, mines, Pearl Harbor, aircraft carriers, records of submariners and even helped with spelling some of those far-away locations!

When the couple were planning to get married, a friend of Aunt Netties said, "that marriage will not last six months." Frank Gregory Sr. asked the couple with a laugh, "How do you get twenty-five into sixteen?" The couple recently celebrated their forty-eighth wedding anniversary. They live in a beautiful home by Nathanson Creek. The area where they live is the only place where a little spring keeps a stream of water flowing all year long in the meandering creek. It has been reported that Native Indians lived on the property. The couple can walk to the largest Plaza built in the State of California by its founder, General Guadalupe Vallejo. The last mission on a 300 year mission trail is located but two short blocks away.

According to the local historian, Robert D. Parmelee, in his book *Pioneer Sonoma*, about noon on July 9th, 1846, without warning, U.S. Navy, Lieutenant Joseph W. Revere (a grandson of Paul Revere) appeared on the Plaza and calmly walked to the Bear Flag pole, lowered the flag, and raised the American ensign, boldly pocketing the Bear Flag as he did so." Between 1849 and 1852, Union Officers were stationed in Sonoma. They included Major Generals: Sherman, Hooker, Stoneman, Gibbs, Smith, Pleasonton, Steele, Davidson, and Kearny. They also included Brigadier Generals Stone and Lyon. The heritage of Sonoma now is mingled with the Veterans of World War II and veterans of the later wars in the Pacific and that of Operation: Desert Storm. Evelyn points out, "taking just one small area, one small town in America, I found incredible wonderful biographies of this country's World War II defenders. These men hailed from all over the country; they retired to this one little town. The men remember adventures being happy or sad, exciting or boring, trifling or major events in their lives. Fifty years later many men speak from their own experiences for the very first time. For them, those memories are painful. Many wept as they remembered their fallen buddies and retraced their lives during those days and nights of World War II. One of those veterans is Frank D. Gregory, Jr. Just like Lieutenant Revere, who calmly raised the American flag in Sonoma's Plaza, Frank Jr. just calmly entered into enemy territory as a World War II point man. He cannot bear nor does he discuss the Battle of the Bulge. He is not alone. Others have the same trouble talking about that area of battle. From those days in the Army, he has two patches from his old uniform and a few brass buttons off a woolen Army jacket. He carries within his body a warm heart for the German people." To Frank during the war, "only young German men dressed up and trained as Soldiers were known as his country's enemy!"

(The Editor-Author of this book has included her autobiography in this story along with her husband's war experiences rather than as a formal separate addition to the book. As the reader will note, the couple has worked together in all areas of endeavor.)

Parmelee, Robert D., *Pioneer Sonoma,* Published by the Sonoma Valley Historical Society.,Depot Park Museum, 270 First Street West, Sonoma, California 95476, 1972, pp. 124. ps. 38, 39, 84.

Robert W. Best

United States Navy, 1945 - 1947
Reservist, Korean War, 1950 - 1952

On the night that Bob was to graduate from High School he was to be at Pennsylvania Station as an enlisted man for the Navy. His sister collected his diploma. The war with Germany had ended but the Japanese conflict was still raging in the Pacific. Bob enlisted in New Brunswick, New Jersey where he had been born. He was in boot camp when the war with Japan ended. The men were all elated. They were on a base at Sampson, New York near Lake Geneva and saw no celebrations. It was for sure the men breathed a sigh of relief that they were not going to Europe!

Bob had been inducted as a Hospital Corpsman with a Seaman First Class rating at $59.00 a month which reminded him of the song, *Twenty one dollars a day, once a month.* The Hospital Corpsman was like a Medic, in other words, a male nurse. After a while he found himself on an old smelly troop train for five days and four nights. The train made connections in Chicago for Wyoming and on to a training hospital in San Diego, California. He had never before this time seen any of these places in the United States of America.

Journeying back to the Atlantic Coast, this time down south across the southern states, Bob was given more training in a convalescent hospital. The medical facility was set up in an old converted building having once been a Biltmore Hotel in West Palm Beach, Florida. This time, the novice traveler enjoyed the train ride in an attractive comfortable Pullman car. A bout of rheumatic fever was raging at the convalescent hospital. The young medic was there for a couple of months taking temperatures, pulses and respirations of many patients. He also made the rounds handing out patients' medications including new penicillin tablets. He never worried or thought about catching any of the illnesses.

Soon, Bob was sent to Brooklyn, New York and was introduced to his new home, USS Kearsarge, a brand new aircraft carrier which was put into commission on March 5, 1946. Anyone assigned to the ship the day before the commissioning was dubbed a "Plank Owner" and received a certificate. Bob missed the designation by one day. The new residents were taken on several shake down cruises to Guantanamo Bay, Cuba. There were planes flying off the carrier by the Flights Operation Command. For two weeks men were allowed leave and recreation in Panama. The ship tied up at Christoble. Bob thought, "this is a dirty place to be stuck in." It reportedly had the fastest railroad in the world at that time. The train took one hour and forty-five minutes to reach the Pacific shore from the Atlantic shore. It was a regular-sized train which used both steam and coal. The riders saw some unspoiled jungles and some of the locks of the canal as they crossed Panama. Then, the Kearsarge sailed right back to Brooklyn.

During flight operations on and off the Kearsarge, planes crashed on deck. One plane hit a 5 inch gun mount and caught fire. The Pilot tried to get out on the right side. The right wing of the plane was sticking out over the ocean so he was caught over the ocean in this position. Since he finally realized he couldn't get out that way, he ended up climbing through the plane and into the fire to get out on the other side. He ended up as one of Bob's patients with 75% of his body burned. The Medics treated him as best they could and then took him to the hospital at Guantanamo Bay. He did survive.

Some Pilots would fly in too low. They cut their power too soon and ended up smashing the plane in the ocean. The Kearsarge, of course, was always moving. The carrier was built with had cables across the flight deck. Planes had hooks to catch the cables. One Officer in flight caught the cable all right but struck an Officer on deck and broke the fellow's leg. Pilots in those planes often missed the restraining hooks, then ran into other barriers. They crashed! Bob did not know many Pilots. He only met the ones in sick bay. Most of them were easy to get along with and were not problematic.

One incident in Norfolk, Virginia happened while the men were at liberty. A uniformed fellow on the beach was knifed in the leg and thigh. He was brought into sick bay and was so furious. He did not want treatment. He picked up sissors and wanted to fight with anyone while waving the sissors around. The Medics finally did get him calmed and bedded down.

While on the Atlantic Coast the recruits took several cruises on the Kearsarge. They were eventually assigned to go on a good-will tour to Mediterranean Countries. Bob never found out what went on with Navy men as friendly ambassadors as he did not get to go. Instead, he was sent to Quonset Point, Rhode Island and then bivouaced with a group of Marines at Camp Le Jeune, North Carolina. He was enjoined with the 2nd Battalion of the 2nd Marine Division. Marines, he found out, did not have their own Medics.

Corpsmen could go out with the Marines on their tanks and give sick pills. A Marine Lieutenant let Bob ride in a tank. He asked, "Can you drive a tank?" "No," was the answer. Bob found out "it was akin to driving a tractor. There were two levers for braking. One track slowed up or stopped and the other brake allowed the tank tracks to turn. The only way to get in or out of the tank was through the hatches. There were no trap doors out the back. Turrets had been manufactured like the German's tanks. They were improved to swivel round and around. One straddled very cold hard metal bucket seats." The Medic decided, "there was nothing plush about a tank." When he was finally allowed to drive, Bob did not care for the experience. He was only allowed to drive the tank in cases of emergency.

The Medics' services were used for tank spills, hangovers, cuts, bruises, and veneral diseases. Basically, food service plates were still dipped in hot water for cleaning, as practiced in the areas of Italy and Africa. There had been no streamlining in sterilization of utensils with the groups, so bacterial infections were still communicated.

When Bob paraded around, he wore clothes from both the Navy and Marines. He used Khaki mostly in fields. He used Navy clothes in evening social events as they were a little more impressive. Bob was discharged from the Marine Corps on November, 1947. He was surprised he was let out of the service two months early.

A girl who worked at an Electric company interested Bob. He obtained the job of testing and changing electric meters on houses working in the electric meter department. Bob worked for eleven years in his hometown for this firm. In 1950, he was called back into service for the Korean War. He had just bought a home. He was still not married. His brother sold his home to Bob. It was for his mother, sister and himself. He was in a play, *Showboat*. It was the first time he attempted to sing in music groups. In the chorus, his section sang the famous song *Old Man River*. By that time, Bob figured a lot of water had gone over the dam. He was always singing in church choirs from then on.

The Korean War call interrupted all good feelings about being settled down. In no time, Bob was back in St. Albans Hospital in New York working around tuberculosis patients. Then, he was sent to Beaufort, South Carolina Naval Hospital outside Parris Island near the boot camp for Marine Corps.

Rather than stay with medical duties, Bob now learned how to type and was assigned as a Chaplain's Assistant. He played golf at Parris Island and tennis in the afternoon. He wrote a lot of letters to parents for the Chaplain. He put out a weekly news letter. The typewriter and mimeograph machine were of the primitive type. It was a one man show to put out documents of any kind. Actually, Bob hated being called back in the Naval Reserve. He put up with it, one day at a time, until eighteen months passed. He was then discharged for the second time. Bob went back to work with the electric company and went back to singing in the Methodist Choir.

While singing in the choir, he met a girl named Margie Harrison from Wales. She was a student of Rutgers University when Bob started dating her. Meanwhile, his future wife worked at the commercial office where he was employed. She was a home economist at the utility company. When the girl, Margie, went back to Wales, she invited Bob to visit with her and her family. She used an event for a reason. The International Music Festival of Choirs and Instrumental Groups from all over the world met at Acrefair, Wales and England. There was a huge tent which held an audience of 10,000 people. The spectators were mostly Welch people. Bob was impressed! The choirs knew their parts by heart and sang without music in their hands. If a fellow was a tenor, he knew his melody and words by memory. It was the same for the other voices in the choirs. The month and year was July, 1958. Bob spent a whole month on European shores. Two months later Lois, Bob's future wife went to Germany to visit a girl friend. The girl friend had a husband in the service stationed in Germany. Lois was also going to see a fellow whom she was corresponding with in Europe.

Bob and Lois met again when they were both back in the States and spent time comparing notes on their trips. Bob asked Lois for a date. He changed jobs and the new company sent him to California. Bob found he was a bit lonely driving to California all by himself. The night before he left, he gave Lois an engagement ring. Three months of correspondence just didn't do it. They finally married in 1960. They lived first in Larkspur, then moved to Tiburon and Walnut Creek, California. Bob serviced precision balances for chemical laboratories. He traveled from El Paso, Texas to Seattle, Washington and from Seattle to Hawaii. Lois became a traveler on these jaunts.

They traveled to a lot of other places including back to New Jersey for a seven year period, changing jobs once again to Rosemead, California near Los Angeles. Lois became a Food Service Director for the School District. Bob invested in a Vending Machine Service with 43 machines in Northern California. He and a partner split up the business. Bob took Sonoma and Santa Rosa. The couple had four children, Pamela Jane, Randall Warren, Janet and Raymond. Notwithstanding all the traveling and change the couple managed to provide good schools, travel experiences and a good home in each of these locations for their sons and daughters.

Bob lives in Sonoma and sings in five different musical groups! Every week, he practices with the 140 voice Chorale, a 30 voice Cantata Choir, a 20 voice Vintage House Singers group, a 15 voice Church Choir and with the Silver Foxes, a World War II mens' double quartet. He takes a singing class. He also belongs to Sons in Retiremen (SIRS) which offers a lot of activities. Bob likes golf and bowling tournaments. He lives in a retirement community and enjoys everything about it, including the fact that the California Quail have the right of way! His wife, Lois travels back and forth from Los Angeles when possible. It is a 400 mile trip. She is finishing up her Food Directorship and a near retirement date. Both Bob and Lois are eagerly awaiting for her retirement to commence.

'Peggy' La Boyteaux

United States Army Nurse Corps, 1942 - 1945

Ida May, known as Peggy was born in Wilmington, Delaware. There were eight children in the family. America was in "the depth of the depression." Peggy's Dad was a Jack-of-All-Trades including talents in such activities as an awning maker, an upholsterer and even a plumber. When she was sixteen during a tonsilectomy, Peggy decided to make a career of nursing. After she graduated from high school, from 1937 until 1941, she attended classes at the Delaware Hospital School of Nursing.

Each afternoon after instruction, practicum rehearsal skills were carried out working along side the Registered Nurses. Activities for obtaining a nursing career were not expensive. The fee for entering the training was $100.00 initially. There was an additional payment of $8.00 per month for room, board and a uniform. The time was pre-war. The United States was experiencing the end of the depression when Peggy entered the nursing field.

The young girl lived in the hospital at the nurse's dormitory. When she was not in training, she worked nights in an emergency room. She felt a patriotic need to help in the war. The feeling increased when she saw a notice posted on the bulletin board by the Red Cross. Doctor and nurse recruits were being solicited for the war effort. Most everyone Peggy knew answered the call including herself and another inductee. The Red Cross actually had something to do with the Nurse Corps of the Army at that time. Peggy and her friend, Eleanor left Wilmington for Charleston, South Carolina. They were given no more formal schooling for their anticipated experience in the Nurse Corps. They marched and marched and drilled and drilled. At first, they wore white uniforms with caps, white socks and shoes. In 1942, they were issued new blue dress uniforms. The uniforms were very attractive in two shades of blue with a little red pin-stripe piping. Later. dress uniforms were exactly the same color and made with the same tailoring as the mens' uniforms.

The young ladies were at an Army WAC unit for nine months. They carried out regular ward duties waiting on patients sick from ordinary everyday illnesses. The work was in long halls. There were many cases of veneral disease which was not yet considered curable. There were many circumcisions performed on young soldiers as the Army decreed "it was a necessary thing-in-itself to keep young men from getting syphilis." Syphilis, caused by a spirochete was transmissible by direct contact and was worrisome as it could develop into three stages. The third and final stage was characterized as involving every system of the body, including the brain: also called pox. Many died of syphilis. Then, considering the lack of sterilization techniques in regard to eating utensils and the close contact of bunking together in small rooms and tents, childhood diseases ran rampant. Commonplace illnesses included measles, chickenpox and appendicitis. The nurses cared for newly enlisted men, older men from the service and a few German prisoners of war brought back to the United States.

It was a habit for Peggy to watch notices posted on the bulletin board. She saw there was a new group going from the 32nd Field Hospital to the European Theatre. The group was due to leave in September. Eleanor Hazewski, her friend from the beginning of nurse training, went with Peggy. The two signed up for European detail. It took awhile for the organization of eighteen nurses, 25 to 35 Officers and several Surgeons (a doctor for different fields of medicine) to be completed. The finalized group gathered at a staging ground in Louisiana near New Orleans. They were assigned to the 32nd Field Hospital which was not exactly the general nursing practice they had expected. For another month they marched and were issued more new clothes. The newest WAC uniform was an attractive dress with a dark green top and a tan necktie. There were also pinkish-tan slacks or skirt to match the top.

A Quartermaster Corps delivered all the supplies considered needed for their overseas 'hospital'. The supplies were chosen by one head nurse and one Commanding Officer. Materials were anticipated for operating procedures as well as the usual everyday type medications.

After a train ride from New Orleans to New York Harbor in September of 1943, Peggy glimpsed the Statue of Liberty from a distance. She was heading in the opposite direction aboard a converted civilian ship called the USS Wakefield. For two weeks the ship zigzagged through waters, unseen by the passengers, as no one was allowed to go out on deck. There was no smoking. The ship had complete blackout conditions. At times, Peggy was so sea sick. They were bunked three or four levels down. Both sexes were on the same level of the ship with separate quarters.

In the evening, the group put on their own entertainment in the form of variety shows. A friend with Peggy sang, "*I'm Going Back to Where I Come From...Where the mocking birds are singing in the lilac bush...*" (Sometimes they did not allow their minds to think about where they came from or what lay ahead or what they were getting into.) For that reason, skits were usually outrageously funny. Soldiers played the piano. Peggy tap-danced. There were many different talented groups and it was great zany fun to be one of the performers.

The Medics disembarked at Oran, Africa. It was dirty, sandy, hot and such a dry place. They were loaded on large canvas covered trucks almost reminiscent of covered wagons. These trucks had support bars for the canvas. The Medics were driven about ten to fifteen miles out of Oran where tents were set up in dirty sandy soil. The landscape was lonely looking and apprehensive. Peggy did get back to Oran once in a while, where she could buy some leather goods and handmade things. African Women did not uncover their faces. They hardly looked at Americans.

The Medical Crew ate in a mess hall from metal plates. You would pass through a line for cooked meals served under tents. After eating, you dipped your plate and silverware up and down in some real hot soapy water. Putting the plate and silverware in hot rinse water for a second dipping, you then carried your utensils back to the tent waving them in the air. By the time one reached their tent everything was air dried. This process was not exactly a sterile way to do dishes and diseases were transmitted from the practice. You kept your own two-sectioned plates together. Soldiers went to their own meal tents with Corpsmen and Orderlies," Peggy related.

There was no formal hospital set up at Oran. The group was merely being staged, waiting and on alert for traveling to Italy. They 'leap-frogged' to Sicily where other units had a field hospital. Then, the persevering group entered a ship for Naples, Italy. The ship's crew sailed ever-so-carefully through the waters as they knew the Port had been mined. Buildings had been blown apart in Naples. Little children, (waifs) were sleeping in doorways with no underpants, no home, no place to go, no families to care for them. Peggy wondered what they ate. She passed out candies to the homeless children. Naples was such a battered city. Germans had demolitioned the water conduits, destroyed electrical plants and placed time bombs in buildings. Allied bombing had bashed the harbor installations. The group just passed through Naples at first, then, meandered down to the southern part of Italy to Battipaglia. The 32nd set up their own field hospital tents for the first time since leaving the United States. The hospital unit was erected in a wide open field with no visible protection from trees, buildings or the enemy! On a map it was shown they were a little south of the famous ancient City of Pompeii which was destroyed by an eruption of Mount Vesuvius, A.D., 79.

Mount Vesuvius erupted again while Peggy was stationed at this post. The group awakened to a pink-dust-morning. The pink ash from the volcano was all over their tents. There was no smoke rising from the mountain, just volcanic ash for a few days. With a little time off for a visit, Peggy got into the active volcanic region a little closer. She walked up to the destroyed town of Pompeii and kept a piece of lava she found in the area for a few years. There were streams of hot lava rolls. Italian opportunists created paper weights from the new soft lava by pressing American pennies into their creations. Inside the ruins of the City of Pompeii there were many statues of nude men. In those days of innocence, it was even embarrassing for the nurses to see male statues with no modesty or fig leaf.

Patients brought into this medical unit were generally sick people having ordinary ailments or injuries caused by sniper attacks. No civilians were solicited nor were they treated. The hospital was just for people in uniform. The uniformed person could be a member of any Allied group or any prisoner of war from the Axis Armies.

The detachment crept up closer to the active war near Naples. One eighteen years old patient died because the medics had no penicillin. He would not have died had penicillin been available. That powerful antibiotic found in the mold fungus *Penicillium* was available about six months later. Penicillin was developed for treatment of a wide variety of bacterial infections. Even in six months time, it was only available in small quantities and was not distributed to the emergency tent hospital level.

The Medics were set up in a partly bombed out building and in tents while at Naples. The staff was split into three groups instead of one, so they could better serve the patients on shifts at different times. The units would 'leap-frog' again to follow the battles and Allied troops. Should there be time enough, a latreen with a door and two holes was erected in most places. A shower would be rigged outside designed with a canvas stall around a pole. Other times, one would bathe in their helmet top, using it like a basin. Orders were given limiting use of soap and water. One memorable event was when Peggy was in the latreen. All of a sudden, American antiaircraft began shooting over the tents and the latreen began shaking. Peggy barely dove out the door before the facility collapsed. The Germans were on one side of the hospital tents and the American Army on the other side during that shelling. Anyone able to walk, dove into foxholes which were shaped like a trench. Everyone was in great danger.

The wounded soldiers were given aid at the front line. Often, surgery was necessary, immediately! The patient would stay a day or two in the field tent and then the wounded would be shipped back to a more fully equipped hospital. This 32nd Field Hospital Station moved with the Armies and was right on the front lines from Naples until after the end of the war. Often, the nurses found themselves between the two fighting armies. They worked the hardest just south of Rome. There they administered to a large string of casualties. During the Battle of Cassino between Naples and Rome, the group was near a major highway, carrying out their duties in a building not unlike a monastery. Wounded Infantry Soldiers from the Rome conflict were being brought to the hospital in greater and greater numbers. Celebrating took place when the Infantry and Medics joyfully entered Rome. It was cold by the time Rome was liberated. The nurses wore green fatigues in order to keep warm. Their brown and white seersucker uniforms used in the desert heat had long before been stored away.

Peggy met a soldier, named John at a party while in the area of Battipaglia, Italy. She had attended the get-together held in a tent. She went to the party with another date. The fellow she went with got drunk. John took her back to her location. John and Peggy decided to go out to dinner on another date. They, also, went to an Italian civilian's home for an extremely nice dinner one night. They attended an Italian Opera in the town of Naples.

John's job classification was Ordnance Supply Officer in the Quartermaster. He worked with large groups handling materials for the 12th Airforce Corps as well as large items including crates of C Rations. John traveled back and forth from Naples to Corsica and even to France. He'd come to see her when Peggy's group was above Florence, Italy. "It was like right out of the movies." said Peggy; "John had enlisted right out of college to Fort Ord in California and took Officer's training. Here, I was in Italy dating an Officer and I got to go into the Officer's Clubs. I felt like hugging someone from just pure delight!" The couple found there was always music and dances in Naples Officer Club. John was a smooth ballroom dancer and the two even learned tango to the rhythm of *Jealousie*. They loved dancing to the music of Italian songs as those melodies were so very smooth and ultra-romantic. The two perfected their ballroom dancing. In the Italian clubs there was rarely a meal, just drinking and dancing.

The Americans had a feeling of pride when the armies liberated Rome on June 4th, 1944. The Allies had done something no other Army in the annals of that ancient city had ever done. All other armies in world's records had never been able to capture or liberate the 'eternal city'. It had taken the Allied Armies nine months with great losses of life to celebrate that day. Long lines of tanks stretched as far as one could see and past the horizon. Weary soldiers feeling fatigued were also covered with battle grime. They met a city full of joyful Italian faces. Congratulations were received by General Clark from all over the world. President Roosevelt: cabled: "You have made the American people very happy. It is a grand job well done. Congratulations to you and the men of the Fifth Army."

While Peggy was in liberated Rome she visited the Catacombs. Germans had stored a lot of their prisoners of war in the catacombs. They had not fed the prisoners. The prisoners died in their own body stench and were piled one on top of another on the shelves. Peggy still shudders when thinking of the sight of those bodies. The catacombs consisted of small passages and excavated rooms used by the early Christians. They were tunnel-like and dug out the side of the mountains. Peggy, having only one day to roam around in the Capitol City of Italy did see the Colosseum. She was in the Vatican near the Sistine Chapel when the Pope came out and shook hands with her. While in the corridor, it was clearly evident when he made his wish to leave. He came out a door on the right and shook hands with only those near the door. By way of his manner, Peggy knew when the interview was finished.

After Rome was taken, more intensive battles were fought. It was that cold winter of 1944. Campaigns in Northern Europe overshadowed all else to the Germans, but from the Vincenty of Rome on, this was not a forgotten front. The Allies needed to hold on to what they had already deeply suffered to obtain. The task for the Allied Armies in Italy was that of harassing, deceiving and keeping busy two first-rate German Armies and an Italian Fascist Army. Strategy was to keep the Axis Armies away from the Western and Eastern Fronts in France.

It has been chronicled "that the grounds were so saturated by winter storms that General Mark W. Clark and his staff pored over details and maps making ready for a spring movement, when the flooding rivers and the wet ground was dry enough to bear the weight of armor." The tired troops were of many nationalities, the Brazilian, Palestinian, Polish, Italian, New Zealander, South African and British Indian, British, Hawaiian-Japanese and American." Nothing was left undone. John saw more and more supplies being transported in behind the lines including clothing, cartridges, mortar shells, artillery shells, C-Rations, food, metal planks for Bailey Bridges, plus medical supplies. "Great coordination existed between the Air Forces and the Army. Problems involved in administering to different racial and religious groups with peculiar needs was solved. The roads into Rome and further northward were measured not only by miles but also by scenes of German defeat."

The medics and their patients were up to their elbows in mud in the tents. Men were brought into field hospitals in ambulances with axles deep in mud. Nurses were half-dead from weariness because there were so many injured receiving care. Everyone, including patients and nurses were dirty from the mud. It was wet, shivery cold and an overwhelming rain fell most of the time.

The hospital group moved to the area of Via Reggio. Then, they followed Allied Armies to Bologna and Lake Colma. You could hardly hear anyone talking for the deafening noise of artillery. Night and day artillery pounded enemy positions. It illuminated the surrounding country with flashes of bursting shells. Pictures were taken showing utterly mountains of shell cases stretching upon the land as far as a camera lens could document. Mines blew up continously. Frequent German air raids called for reciprocal antiaircraft fire. Picturesque villages in Italy were left a mass of rubble and the tanks rolled on... Abandoned equipment marked lines of German retreats.

The nurses in hospital tents had newly injured soldiers to care for taken from ambulances that arrived about every fifteen minutes. Intervenous injections were given by the hundreds and many blood transfusions were necessary. If patients could not mentally hold on, they simply died of shock. There were never enough syringes. By the use of only one needle the nurses administered doses of penicillin to many patients. They would go up and back down rows of injured soldiers with that one needle, using it over and over again but in various arms.

One little German soldier was brought in. Peggy offered help to him. She felt, he thought, "she'll give me a shot to kill me." There was nothing but fright in his eyes. She believed, he wondered, "what will the Americans do to harm me?" He did become well enough to be moved to a larger hospital. Another soul, she tried to save so diligently, slipped away due to too many internal injuries.

At Bologna, the hospital was a busy, busy place. A constant stream of patients with injuries were brought in. Men were full of shrapnel. Many had their legs blown off. Peggy did not know how the Surgeons could take such punishment. Some worked over twelve hours at a time to care for the wounded. After fierce battles at Bologna, "where the Air Forces twisted the enemy's rail lines into pretzels of steel," the armies overcame a maze of flooded fields, ditches, dikes, precipitous cliffs and German machine gun nests. The invasion of Normandy greatly influenced and sapped the strength of the German troops south of France. Strangulation caused by needed supplies to carry on the war, began to take effect on all fronts.

Also, during this time, Peggy viewed the body of Benito Mussolini, Italian Dictator and leader of the Fascist movement. After the German collapse in April, 1945, Mussolini was captured, tried in summary-courts martial and shot with his mistress, Clara Petacci. Their bodies were hung from poles in the town square of Milan, Italy. He had been hanging there a couple of days before Peggy happened by. Two or three pedestrians were looking up at his limp body.

Peggy received a proposal for marriage from John in Naples and the couple made preparation to be married in Florence. Known as the art capitol of the world, there was little damage in that renouned city. Both sets of parents objected vigorously to the marriage due to differences in religious faith. It was April of 1944 when John proposed. The betrothed went about their daily business. "We can't get married today," they told each other. John was head of his unit. His duties were demanding and he just couldn't take off any old time. Once in a while, when he was traveling north, he managed a few minutes visit. Sometimes, he had to drive a long way for the short time they had together. Conditions of the roads were very bad and it took a lot of time to travel anywhere in the region. John drove a Jeep.

"After Bologna," Peggy said; "You could tell the war was slowing down. Troops were being moved elsewhere and Germans were moving out. The hospital work was slower and there was not as much to do." The Medics moved into a villa for two or three weeks.

John, still stationed in Florence planned their whole wedding. It was held in the magnificent Santa Maria Novella Cathedral. The Church was inaugurated in 1287. Architecturally, it is an inspired Gothic Cistercian design with splendid central portal and grave niches. Three story mullioned windows rise above the roof of the church. The ceiling is vaulted. Arches and windows point skyward. Church walls are covered by frescoes. Its base is a black and white marble floor. Michelangelo loved Santa Maria Novella so much that he referred to her as "my beautiful bride."

John's beautiful bride tried to obtain a white wedding dress but had to settle for her dress blue uniform. The two were dressed alike in their matching dark blue uniforms which made a lovely picture. John had all his Officers in attendance in their dress uniforms. Peggy was accompanied by John's Commanding Officer. As Peggy and the Officer moved up the long central nave of the church to meet the groom, they ducked behind the huge pillars on their way to the altar. The service was short. Italian people put on a very beautiful reception which included a three-tiered decorated wedding cake. There was even a combo dance orchestra made up of Soldiers from John's unit. The newly married couple stayed overnight in Florence. The next day they went to Lake Como, a well known resort located near the Swiss Border. John and Peggy enjoyed a week's leave.

Military units began to break up and leave for America after that time. Peggy's hospital personnel unit consolidated with another detatchment located at Brenner Pass. Gradually the 32nd Field Hospital moved back through parts of Italy to other staging areas and then home. The hospital had become a "goof off place" after the war ended. After June 15th, 1945 it seemed everyone felt they had done the job they had come for and wanted to go home. One had a choice of remaining in the United States or going to Japan while on the Liberty Ship as it headed toward the United States. Peggy, newly married, opted to stay in the United States and wait for her new husband, John.

Peggy learned to play bridge with two other nurses while on ship. The ladies played cards, day in and day out, as they cruised the Atlantic. The ship anchored in Boston, Massachusetts. Peggy had lived in Delaware. It was a short ride to Fort Dix, New Jersey for disembaration. Peggy went to her family's home for six weeks. After Thanksgiving she boarded a train alone for California. Somewhere in Utah, she got off at a whistle stop and stood in the dark. She wondered, "what will life be like in the near future." John was waiting for her in San Francisco... The couple settled in San Anselmo, California for thirty-six years. John, as a civilian, was a Marine Insurance Underwriter for cargo and ocean going vessels. The insurance covered cargoes of flour, sugar, plywood and automobiles out of San Francisco to all parts of the world.

Motivation for moving to sunny Sonoma was one of simply leaving the fog bound area of San Anselmo. John had suffered a stroke. Peggy left her part-time job at University of California Hospital and the couple came to the area where their daughter, Peggy was living. Because of John's stroke, the couple bought a house on one floor and it had a swim pool for water therapy. Their daughter lived in a house around the corner. John and Peggy's son, John Jr. was in Garberville, north of Sonoma.

Peggy has had to move John into a convalescent hospital for the past three years and she visits him everyday. She enjoys sewing, bridge parties and particularly likes going to restaurants for lunch. She is not a heavy reader but likes to peruse lighter shorter articles. She was Treasurer of the United Methodist Woman's group in Sonoma. Historically, the church is the first Protestant Church built north of San Francisco in the State of California. The pool sparkles, the garden is beautifully maintained and Peggy reflects a busy life which is enjoyed by this effervesant woman.

By Field Press Censor, Headquarters of the Fifth Army, *Road to Rome*, a small phamplet, 56 pp. 1944. pps. 40,49.

Field Press Censor, *The Po Valley Campaign*, Small booklet. 62 pps. pps. 6,7.

P. Stefano Orlandi, O.P., Revised by P. Isnardo P. Grossi O.P., *Santa Maria Novella and her Monumental Cloisters*, Edition S. Becocci- Florence.

Dr. Robert L. Mollenhauer

United States Army Medical Corp, 1942 - 1946
In Reserves before 1942

Robert L. Mollenhauer received that joyous feeling that he had accomplished something by finishing his internship at the City and County Hospitals of San Francisco to become a Doctor of Medicine. Immediately, on August 1, 1942, he received orders in the mail to report to Fort Ord, California and to the First Medical Regiment of the United States Army! Robert, San Francisco born, found himself on his belly crawling under machine gun fire as one of his basic training exercises. He received no rifle practice for countering an enemy. He called the whole set of maneuvers "a hell of a basic training!" For three months, he helped with a field hospital set-up at La Mesa, California.

Following activities in California, Robert was sent to Camp White, Oregon near Medford. Having no experience whatsoever regarding snowy conditions, he almost froze to death as clothing was poorly designed for cold weather. The supposedly white stuff was not beautiful, clean or exhilarating as one pictured snow on calendars or ski lifts. In a busy Army camp, it was grey, dirty, cold and not exactly pleasant. For the first six months the doctor hated Army life! Maneuvers from Camp White were held near Bend, Oregon. The group camped at 5,000 feet elevation in a high desert type terrain. It was hot during the day and very cold at night. The campsite seemed to be located directly within a thunder and lightning zone. Men were killed by lightning. There were tank incidents. Bob took care of people from lightning strikes. It was just a matter of pronouncing the men dead from electrical shock! He had a few routine sick calls.

The Doctor was assigned the 412th Medical "Collecting" Company at Yakima, Washington on an artillery range. The collecting company consisted of about 100 men, about 10 ambulances, several jeeps, mid-sized vehicles and about five 2 1\2 ton trucks. Its function was to have men (litter bearers) go out to the battlefield or front line collecting stations and pick up sick and wounded men and transport them back to hospitals quite far back from the front lines. Along with the other events in his life, Robert was given the task to operate a Sherman Tank. The tank was a two-person affair and was not only an extremely noisy hot dirty ride but a real thrill. It chugged along and was not exactly outfitted for comfortable seating or riding. The armoured vehicle was considered a 'big range' piece of equipment. There were two things Robert did enjoy near the base at Yakima. One was that the people accepted the soldiers with open arms. The second pleasant part of the stint was the great trout fishing in nearby clear, swift and beautiful streams near Yakima.

The Doctor's Army experience as a whole was not getting any more cheerful. On March, 1944 he was in California, Oakland Port with orders to board what he referred to as "a most horrible ship." Its name? The Sea Scamp! There was an extremely rotten smell that permeated everything and everywhere. The second day out of port, the Officers of the vessel threw off all the meat which had been designated for the troops. The meat was so full of stench it was beyond putrid. "Even after the meat had been thrown off to corrupt the ocean," the men complained; "the ship never lost its bad smell." From that point on the Army men, except for the ship's crew, ate oatmeal and semi-rotten eggs. One man stole K-Rations for just one meal. The ship's Commander wanted the man courts-martialed, but Doctor Mollenhauer refused to accommodate that suggestion and stated, "He should receive a medal!" Before long, the Army Medic Personnel could count their ribs which were sticking out their sides.

The Sea Scamp was traveling all alone on the Pacific Ocean as far as the wary passengers could figure out. There were no convoy ships about. In their life jackets and wearing fatigues, the men held on to the rails of the ship. They were very leery of big enemy submarines which they believed might be undulating under the shadows of the water's surface such as they had seen in movies.

The Sea Scamp was a Merchant Marine Ship. The Merchant Marines Crew was enjoying good food including vegetables and meat. It seemed to be their own food and from a different supply than that given to the passengers. The Merchant Marines were privileged to eat in a very different place than the Army recruits. It appeared attractive. Furthermore, as Robert peered into their portholes, they were enjoying their food and they were often licking up spoonsful of ice cream! For thirty-one days, the men of his division endured hunger. They were taken to Milne Bay on the South tip of New Guinea. As the group disembarked, a person designating she was a Red Cross Representative was waving donuts at the men and asking them to pay $1.00 per donut. The fact that the woman wanted so much money for one donut did not bide well with the hungry malnutritioned men. The doctor was so disgusted, he turned away. Instead, he bought some cocoanut, bananas and some candy further down on the wharf.

The 412th Medical Collective Company was moved to Finschhafen on the eastern coast of New Guinea into a steamy jungle environment where they set up camp. There were many 'big' pesky bugs. It was a hot, wet, sticky climate as it rained a great deal of the time.

The men of the 412th were an industrious team. They hailed from Minnesota, the Dakotas and Florida. Previously being farmers, they knew how to improvise and developed beautiful camps. It was hard to get supplies but the men erected a very nice mess hall. Dr. Mollenhauer was the Commanding Officer of the group. One time he was offered a higher promotion accompanied with a change of location. He turned down the promotion to stay with this group because he appreciated their loyalty and workmanship as well as their high principles.

The doctor was responsible for five gallons of alcohol to be used as an antiseptic medical supply. He kept it under his bunk. It was 190 proof, 95% alcohol. No one tried to bother the stuff. A steel water tank was rigged up to take showers. The Medics received assistance from a welding Ordnance Company to build the shower. Nice soft rain water was caught in the tank for enjoyable bathing. However, it took a quart of the precious alcohol in trade for services of the welding group to build the tank...

Men's shoes would mold on the inside overnight. Big lizards and or big bugs would use them for explorations while you slept. If you forgot to shake your shoes out before sticking your feet in them any morning your toes could be in for one big surprise! A leather watch band would rot in no time.

After three months in the jungle, Robert had noticed some of the natives had what was called "native teeth." Their teeth were dark reddish brown. The brown color came from chewing betel nuts which were a type nut to give (a high) like cocaine to the one who was stimulated by the potent kernel. The doctor decided to photograph "the perfect picture of what could happen to your teeth, if you chewed the betel nut." The sun was in the wrong place behind the native participant being photographed. The native evidently had had his picture taken many times. He straightened Robert out, "that the sun was shining in the wrong direction for a good picture!"

One man in the area caused a big bang! He had tried to connect some charges together and the fast lit fuses caused an explosion. His chest caved in, his arms were blown off and face messed up. He died.

The doctor also got a speeding ticket while driving a Jeep. An MP issued the ticket. To this day, Robert can't understand how he could be speeding on a road that was just a very bumpy, deep, mud-filled rut! On this same road, he ran over a great huge snake. The old juicy snake just kept right on going across the road. Being squashed a little did not seem to phase him.

On the beach, Robert discovered a beautiful and perfect two-foot scalloped clam shell which he still exhibits in his home. He obtained a crate that was made of solid mahogany and packed his find in it. He sent the extraordinary package to his wife, Dorothy. The crate weighed fifty pounds. He'll never forget that it only cost 65 cents to send it to the United States! His wife could not lift the crate.

Referring to his diary that he kept during the war, Robert discovered they had only been at Finchaven for three months, "but it seemed longer than that when he was sent to Biak Island, New Guinea." The Island of Biak was located on the Equator. Americans had invaded the little island on April 27th. Dr. Mollenhauer was privileged to ride in General Krueger's plane to Hollandia. Then, he boarded and rode a PT boat for a day or so to get near to the main part of the narrow beachhead. Americans were pinned down. Six doctors had been killed on this unforsaken place. Americans were not doing well because the Japanese were foxholed in limestone caves. Japanese hid in the caves which had railroad tracks. They would roll out their guns on these tracks, stick out their gun barrels and kill everybody. Then, they pulled the mobilized guns back into the caves. In this way, the guns were practically impossible to see because they were so well hidden. The final landing on the beach was made at night in a Water Buffalo, a kind of amphibious tank. Landing was to be made where a flash light was blinking but there were several blinking lights. After circling for an hour or so, and getting very seasick, the correct light was located. They dashed into caves near the beach which were filled with wounded men and much blood. The stench was horrible due to hot humid air, rotten blood and wounded soldiers.

The following day after being deposited on the beach, the Infantry marched to an airstrip and received a beating from the Japanese cave guns. The Medics were caught in the midst of all manner of battles. Their services were needed all over the territory. Men were maimed and killed all around them. A Jeep lay rolled over where it was overturned by sniper fire. Robert was standing next to a Sergeant. A mortar shell fragment slammed into the Sergeant's heart. Standing next to him, there were so many dead Japanese and Americans that blue flies began to congregate. The tropical hot air was conducive to immediate decay accompanied by extreme health problems for those left living. Due to so much smoke from gunfire, it was very hard to breathe in. Men lived on K-rations. They could hardly bear to eat because of the smell in the area and fear of opening one's mouth because of all the flies. The forest was bombed until only tree stumps remained as splinters. Bob was standing by a very large crater. He decided to go in and rest awhile. As soon as he went inside, a bullet hit the rim of the crater exactly where he had been standing.

There was a particular cave which had a big verticle cavity about 200 feet deep with little horizontal caves at the bottom. Most caves of the area went off sideways. The Japanese made a practice of coming out of those caves at night. American Bomber Pilots and Gunners tried time and time again to get those enemy snipers. Over and over, several tons of T & T was exploded into the cave. Finally, the Americans sent two truck loads of gasoline over the edge of a cliff, accompanied by some big explosives into the cave. That finally got rid of the main Japanese stronghold. Two days later the doctor said, "there were stinking Japanese bodies everywhere. Americans were lost in great numbers as well."

Dr. Mollenhauer directed his Medics, "to give first aid and patch up injuries as possible." They had no field hospital. They put the injured on another little island out of danger. The reason for the battle was that the Americans wanted Biak for an airstrip to be called Mokmer Airstrip. Robert never thought he would get out alive. Big artillery shells swished over the Medic's heads and they were bombed continously. After this very strenuous battle, Robert was relieved to go back to his own unit at Finschhafen.

While Bob had been gone, his group had built a beautiful mess hall including the installation of wooden floors. Later, a tree fell over and wrecked the building. They had developed fairly good sanitation at the post. The troops were given Atabrine to prevent malaria. It was served with meals. It turned one's skin yellow. The Medics used syringes which were made of glass for injections. The needles had to be sharpened continously as the same needles were used over and over again. Larger base hospitals were behind the field operation where Robert was commanding. If he was near the base hospitals, he would tarry awhile to watch a little surgery. Robert was particularly interested in parasitology. This study included the scientific study of parasites and parasitism. In biology, a parasite is described as an animal or plant that lives in or on another organism, the host, at whose expense it obtains nourishment and shelter. In the relationship, the usually injurious parasite caused injury to its host. A diseased condition was then caused by infestation of the parasite. Near the Philippines, Robert studied some parasitology of tropical diseases. At that hospital visit, he took care of a ward of persons with tropical diseases caused by parasites.

The Collecting Company was sent to Tacloban on the third day of the Philippine Invasion. They boarded a big Navy ship and like the Last Supper, the men finally enjoyed some good food!! They had to leave the ship by a big cargo net into an LST landing craft. They jumped out of the LST on the beach into water estimated to be four feet deep. There were lots of bombings and scares from more Japanese fighters coming toward the ship. At Tacloban, Kamikazes in suicidal attacks would spiral in on the landing ships, one barely missed the Medic's ship.

After two weeks at Tacloban, Robert's Company was sent on to the invasion of Mindoro Island which was very close to the Jap stronghold in Manila and a long way from the Allied foothold at Tacloban. The men were told that it was suicide mission. One day at sunset, it appeared a whole Navy surrounded their ship. The USS Nashville was on their flank. All of a sudden a big ball of smoke came between the sun and the observer. You could not see the Nashville for a while. It had been hit by a Kamikaze (interpreted by the Japanese as "divine wind") but the ship didn't sink.

They were attacked by many kamikazes on the next day as the Medics were coming to the shore. Again one Japanese flyer on a suicide mission just missed the landing ship. A big Black Gunner that hit the Kamikaze and saved the men was glued to his gun as if mesmerized. He kept firing until pulled away. The Navy left the men on the island with only a PT Squadron and a few planes not equipped to fly at night. Every night the men were heavily bombed. One plane with bombs would come over every night. The men could hear him coming in their sleep. They called him Washing-Machine-Charlie. One night he unloaded dozens of small antipersonal bombs on the 412th. The tents were shredded and the company cook got a piece of shrapnel in his heart. Most of the men had good fox holes to duck into. One night, the Jap Navy came down and shelled them heavily. As Medics, the men were not armed. They got pinned down for one period by a machine gun. After that, Robert obtained a 45 pistol and a carbine rifle and he practiced how to shoot them. The Japs did not follow Geneva Laws of sparing Medical personnel. He believed being armed was necessary for survival.

The doctors were sent back to Biak again. Duds named washing-machine-charlies sounded like washing machine swishes as they came nearer and nearer. You could hear the sound coming even if you were dead asleep. When he had the chance Bob slept pretty well. He used his steel helmet as a pillow. The Japanese would yell, "Bonsai" (which meant surprise greeting!) and on the perimeter would trip hand granades into their midst. Then, machine guns would go off in a never stopping manner. Then, the group zigzagged back to Mindoro. It seemed everything they did at that time was haywire, all wrong. They set up camp and stacked their stuff around. They had no arms with them. Company 'A' yelled back and forth to Company 'C'. The trouble with that was Company 'C' was a Japanese camp! The sugar mill where they camped at Mindoro had a four or five story metal steel building. One of the American planes slammed right through the building. The Pilot was killed. The plane came out of the building on the other side. The load of bombs were still left in the plane unexploded. The Japanese finally left the island but there was still lots of bombing activity.

The field hospital was set up in a big sugar cane field which had a little railroad. Litter-bearers brought the injured guys back on the railroad. There were few roads and lots of sugar plants. The group had a short wave radio which they carried. But many times the tropical air ruined its parts by decomposition. They were alerted the Japanese were coming down with some naval guns. The men were by a coral airstrip which had very good paving but was not good for trying to make even a dent of a foxhole. Great big naval flares appeared making the dark night eerie, then the shells came...

The order came after the shelling, "Take to the hills!" The men took off as directed. The Japanese Navy left. Had they come on in, they could have taken the island. There was still lots of bombing, however. It seemed like a never ending cycle of ships, planes, kamikazes, artillery and bloody battles.

Dr. Mollenhauer heard about the leper colony which was named Cullion. He conned a PT Commander to take him there to see the island. He wanted to see what was going on at that place. An old caucasion man met him at the gate named Bert Parmelee. The doctor and crew were greeted very cordially. The individuals were a caretaking-kind-of-people. The visitors were invited to dinner.

Asking the doctor, "How do you become leperous?" he answered; "The malady is caused by a bug, a bacteria. You have to be around the bacteria a long time before you get it. Usually it runs through families." Many of the lepers had died, some from starvation as the Japs cut off their food supplies. Also, many had escaped. The doctor was shown through their hospital laboratory and examined some tissues and the bacteria through their microscope. He also toured the living area of the lepers and talked to some of them.

At the dinner table prepared by the care-takers, Robert thought, "I'm not going to eat anything uncooked as I know they use feces to fertilize gardens." The visitors were brought some beautiful glasses of liquor in order to celebrate a toast. The Medic's chemist had just made it. The Doctor held the glass up and downed it in one swoop. He almost died it was so strong. In those kind of places, the Doctor warned, "one should not touch the water, even though it was tempting." He had left the big tempting glass of water placed before his plate. That night the Doctor had to sleep in an area of three big Packard engines on the PT boat. There was a small catwalk to service the engines. There was no other place to sleep. Then, he felt he couldn't sleep after all.

On the Island of Cuyo off the coast of Leyte, the Captain of a PT Boat heard that a group of natives 100 miles away were starving to death. When a group with Dr. Mollenhauer arrived there to check out conditions they found a beautiful island with lots of tropical fruit. The Natives had no rice. The doctor asked them, "what do you want the most?" The answer was, "worm medicine." The people had an intestinal epidemic which was caused by three kinds of worms, at once. While being there, an old Catholic Priest showed the Doctor a big kidney stone a surgeon had removed from him a year before.

Officers hung around the Philippines quite a bit. Bob had good friends in Manila. He was Captain in command of his group. He had lots of paper work. He was attached to his Corps and believed he had a very liberal company. About this time, he also decided to 'hitchhike' by ordering himself to MacArthur's Headquarters in Manila. To tell the truth, he felt he did a little AWOL traveling. (He had been in Manila with his parents when he was nine years old). At MacArthur's Headquarters there was a friend, Colonel Overpeck, a consulting orthopedist. Charlie Mayo of Mayo Clinic asked Bob, "if he would like a drink." All of a sudden, all hell broke loose. Guns went off everywhere!!! It turned out, the pandemonium was just the men celebrating. All planes were grounded. Officers received word about the Atomic Bomb and the war was ending. Bob was not exactly sure how he was going to make it back those three hundred miles where he should have been with his own company. He found an Army Transport Plane which dropped him back where he belonged. There were millions of men in the Pacific that would now have to be moved around and back home. He had given himself orders to go back from where he had come. "Thank God," he heaved a sigh of relief, "I got back!"

During the eternal waiting period to officially go home, Doctor Mollenhauer studied shistosmaisis the denge tropical virus and other tropical diseases such as typhus, jaundice and hepatitis. There were some treatments for these maladies. He wrote about the three kinds of intestinal worms which infested the natives. He spent a lot of time in the laboratories of the areas around him. He was honored by offers to go to work at these hospitals. He said, "No, thank you, I'm attached to my men who are like brothers." Except for the cook felled by shrapnel in his heart, none of his men were killed. They were ingenious farmers.

Doctor Mollenhauer left Manila on the 12th of August and felt the Atomic Bomb saved his and his buddies lives. Eventually his men headed for Osaka, Japan. They landed at the wrong port. They got off the ship. No one was looking after them or directing them as to where they were to go. They managed to get some good food and bedding. They were supposed to have been on the other side of the island. All unloaded, the men did not want to reload. Using some Japanese language, they were told they could get to the other side of the island by going on a road over the mountains. The men fixed up a convoy with all their belongings which included ambulances and trucks. They started up the unknown road. The journey would be 120 miles. They had no idea what they were doing or how the Japanese people would receive them along the way. They carried all their semi-automatic machine guns hidden. These were known as 45 'Burp' guns.

As they moved over the mountain range in the daylight, at one intersection, the passage was 'not much of a road'. They really did not know which way to go. They kept asking for O SAK' A. The real problem in identifying where they were going was they were pronouncing the name of the city wrong. They should have been asking for O' Sak A! After the men learned how to pronounce their destination they began to relax and enjoy some absolutely beautiful mountain scenery. The road became extremely narrow. They had to saw off the eaves of a building to get their big truck past it. They moved into a bombed out hospital. The Japanese treated them very cordially. The company had no mission except to wait to go home, so they tried to enjoy themselves. Roll call was taken every morning. The recruits would take off during the day and look at Japan. Orders well taken were "be here in the morning." Robert went on a drive to Nara, the beautiful shrine city, which the American Pilots had not bombed.

Osaka, (O' SAK A!) was in shambles of twisted steel and ruins. The doctor enjoyed a High-Japanese-tea-ceremony while on this journey.

On the trip over the mountains, the men met a Belgium woman with three daughters near Kobi who all spoke English. They spent Christmas with them. The woman had a Christmas tree lighted dangerously with real candles burning on it. Dr. Mollenhauer wanted to buy a string of real pearls for his wife. He paid $90.00 for an irridescent 'temporarily strung' set. He was not gypped by the merchant. In America estimations were made that it would cost $900.00 to replace the same quality set of pearls in the United States.

Robert hitchhiked by plane to Tokyo. He had long admired General MacArthur. He saw the General come out of one of the buildings.

The Doctor was promoted to Major and received combat medic badges and ribbons. He qualified for a purple heart. A cow had walked in the tent. He picked up a metal can to throw and cut his thumb. Although the wound qualified as a war wound, he was too embarrassed to apply for the Purple Heart. He got a terribly stiff neck. By Jeep, he made it to a hospital with an X-ray machine. The X-ray films showed he had a fracture of the 4th cervical vertebra. He recalled that he had had a full pack on his back when a Jap sniper started shooting. He had rolled out of his Jeep into a ditch for a while. It had not hurt at the time. He said, "I didn't have sense but went home with a cracked vertebra. After weeks, the pain stopped."

Robert enjoyed remembering an incident regarding his dose of medicine for a big hefty Kentucky boy. It took place in the Philippines. The liquor in that area was inferior, like rotgut. This particular fellow was causing trouble by continually getting smashingly drunk! Doctor Mollenhauer told him, "this has to stop. Look, I have some medicine to give you if you come back in this condition again." The man came back drunk again! The Doctor gave him a shot to cause vomiting. The man vomited until they thought he would never stop. The Doctor never had any more trouble with the Kentuckian or any others of his company.

By re-reading his daily log, which had been kept during these very trying days, Robert shared the information regarding the terrible combats those men went through. People shot. Rotting bodies. He saw some Americans kicking out Japanese soldier's teeth for the gold. Philippinos were caught in the act of being thieves, also.

The Doctor finally caught up with the point system to come back home. He had offers to go to work at the Palo Alto Clinic and he took a Residency in the Sacramento County Hospital. He really felt he wanted to solo practice in a small town. His wife was from Santa Rosa, California. He was asked to go in practice with another doctor in New Orleans. Then, he met Dr. Andrews, called the Dean of Medical Doctors of the little town of Sonoma. For some time that doctor had been recruiting excellent doctors for the area. Doctor Mollenhauer spent five years with Dr. Andrews' group and then designed a building to be built by August Sebastiani on a piece of property near the Catholic Church in Sonoma. After a ten year lease, the Doctor negotiated the sale of the building and purchased it. He had met Dorothy, his wife when she was a student nurse and he was an intern. They were married before the war. She worked with a dermatologist in the U.C. Hospital at San Francisco during the war until she broke her back and ankle falling off a horse, while on a vacation. The couple had two children, Sally and Linda. Dorothy was the office nurse for the Doctor through some of the Doctor's 24 years in private practice. They lived in the beautiful exclusive area called Sobre Vista. The Doctor remembered when he paid $4,750.00 for his 6 1/3 acres; that price would be one hundred times that amount on today's market!

In these same beautiful mountains General 'Hap' Arnold made his home. He became one of Dr. Mollenhauer's patients. The General did not act like one would expect America's only permanent Five-Star General would. He was very friendly and had a good sense of humor. He complained that "he lived in a gold-fish bowl" since people were frequently invading his property looking for a glimpse of him or an autograph. As protectors, he had a flock of big noisy, generally angry geese. When Doctor Mollenhauer made home visits on the General, he was afraid to get out of his car until someone came out and called off the geese!

Henry Harley Arnold

United States Army and Army Air Force, 1907 - 1946*

Grateful acknowlegement is made to Robert Bruce Arnold
for this first story 'from his collection of anecdotes'
and the Autobiography of General 'Hap' Arnold.

May 27, 1949, President of the United States, Harry S. Truman, wrote Henry Harley Arnold, living in Sonoma, California that he had just signed a bill making 'Hap' the first permanent Five Star General of the Air Force of the United States. On that day, Henry Harley Arnold became one of only four permanent Five-Star Generals in the History of America.

General 'Hap' Arnold was the Commanding General of the United States Army Air Forces during World War II. Under his command, the force grew to over 2.3 million men and women and more than 80,000 aircraft in just three short years.

'Hap' Arnold was the principal architect of American Air Power and as such was a key player at many Allied Conferences during the war. These meetings often got heated as the strong wills of the players interacted and contested for the resources available. One such conference was code-named Quadrant and was held in Quebec in August 1943. Attending were President Roosevelt, Prime Minister Churchill and the Combined Chiefs of Staff of both countries.

Many important topics were on the agenda including operations in Burma, the supply of China by air over the "hump," and the rush to base the new B-29s in China for operations against Japan. Also, on the horizon were preparations for the D-Day Invasion in June of 1944.

To help with the air support of the invasion of France, someone had sold Churchill on the idea of building floating air bases made out of a combination of sawdust and sea water. The plan was to force ammonia through pipes surrounded by sea water and sawdust much as was done in a commercial ice plant forming large cakes of ice. With enough of these cakes, it might be possible to hitch them together to create "landing fields" where the fighter planes supporting the invasion might land and refuel.

The plan was code-named Habakkuk. At the conference the idea was presented to the Chiefs by Lord Louis Mountbatten. It was considered very top secret at the time. Only the top planners were supposed to know anything about it.

Now, these meetings between the Chiefs could be pretty rough behind closed doors. Angry words were frequently thrown back and forth. The Americans and British did not always have the same ideas about future plans. The Americans were eager to get on with the invasion of France and the British had a tendency to hold back. Many meetings were so hot that lower level Officers were not allowed to attend.

During one lunch break, Lord Mountbatten brought in a sample of the "landing field" ice. When the Chiefs re-assembled behind closed doors, Mountbatten gave them a briefing about construction and characteristics. To demonstrate the strength of the material, he invited 'Hap' Arnold to take a fire ax and strike the ice with it as hard as he could. General Arnold wound up and hit the block as hard as he could. There was a loud smash and he let out a loud "eyow" as he hit the solid substance. Then, Mountbatten suddenly pulled out a pistol and fired several shots into it. The sample Habakkuk piece was then put back on a wheeled litter and covered with a sheet. After that, Lord Mountbatten rolled it out the door. It was several feet long and the waiting staff outside after hearing all the angry voices were shocked. One officer, Air Marshall Walsh said, "My God! They've started shooting one another!"

* * * * * * * * * *

Henry Harley Arnold, General, ('Hap' Arnold), Commander of the Army Air Forces was born June 25, 1886 at Gladwyne, Montgomery County, Pennsylvania. He was son of Herbert Alonzo and Anna Louise (Harley) Arnold. His earliest paternal American ancestor, John Arnold, came from England in 1740 and settled in Philadelphia. A Peter Arnold served as a soldier in the Revolutionary War and his grandfather, Thomas Griffith served in the Federal Army in the Civil War. General Arnold's father fought in the Spanish-American War and was a physician by profession. General Arnold was graduated and commissioned a 2nd Lieutenant in 1907 and was subsequently promoted through the various grades to a General of the Army on December 21, 1944. After serving two years in the Philippines, he was stationed at Governor's Island and became interested in aviation. In 1911, he had instruction at the Wright School of Aviation, Dayton, Ohio graduating with military aviator's license, No. 2. The next year he was an instructor at the Signal Corps Aviation College, College Park, Maryland and Augusta, Georgia. He carried the first air mail in the United States on a flight of five miles, established an altitude record of 6,540 feet, and won the Mackay Trophy the first year (1912), it was offered. He served in Washington, the Philippines again and in San Diego. In the First World War, he was in Washington as head of Information Services of the Aviation Division of the Signal Corps and in the office of the Director of Military Aeronautics. He saw the reconnaissance value of planes and wanted them mounted with guns and wireless. He commanded several army airfields throughout the country. In 1934, he commanded a flight of 10 army bombers from Washington, D.C. to Juneau, Alaska, and was again awarded the Mackay Trophy. He was Assistant Chief and then Chief of the Army Air Forces. In March, 1942, he became Commanding General of these forces. He had the task of building a force capable of conducting global war in which control of the air was a prerequisite to Vincenty. 262,000 planes were produced during 1940-44. By July, 1940 some 8,300 students had been trained and graduated. By the end of 1942 this number was increased to over 125,000. The personnel of the forces was by 1944 increased to 2,000,000! He transformed airpower into an offensive, seizing control of the air from both Germany and Japan and destroyed their capacity to wage technological warfare. In June 1946, General Arnold was retired as one of the four permanent Generals of the Army and the first General of the Air Force. In 1949, he was the first permanent Five-Star General. He enjoyed being a gentleman farmer on his Rancho Feliz property near Sonoma, California. He was awarded the Distinguished Flying Cross, the Distinguished Service Medal with two oak leaf clusters and the Air Medal. Foreign decorations he received were: the French Croix de Guerre with Palm and the Grand Cross of the Legion of Honor, British Order of the Bath, Brazilian Orders of the Southern Cross and Aeronautical Merit, Ouissam Alaouite of Morocco, Yugoslavian Honoris Causo, Order of Aldon Calderon of Ecuador, Peruvian Order of the Sun and Aviation Cross, Swedish Royal Order of the

Sword, and the Mexican Order of Military Merit and Aztec Eagle. In 1945, he was awarded the Hubbard Medal of the National Geographic Society. Honorary degrees he has received are: Doctor of Aeronautical Sciences from Pennsylvania Military College (1941); Doctorate of Science from the University of Southern California (1941); Science Doctorate also from the University of Pennsylvania (1946); L.L.D. from Iowa State Wesleyan College (1942) from Hahnemann College of Philadelphia (1943) and from Harvard University (1946); Doctorate of English from the South Dakota School of Mines and Technology (1946). He was the author of the *Bill Bruce* series of boys stories and *Airmen and Aircraft* (1929) and co-author with General Eaker of *This Flying Game* (1936), *Winged Warfare* (1940) and *Army Flyer* (1942) and *Global Missions* (1949). He was a Mason and a Member of the Army and Navy and Bohemian Country Clubs of Washington, D.C. Hobbies included golf, fishing, hunting and woodwork. In religion, he was a Baptist. He was married September 10, 1913 at Philadelphia to Eleanor A., daughter of Sidney H. Pool of Ardmore, Pennsylvania. They had five children; Lois E., who married Commander Ernest Snowden; Colonel Henry Harley Jr., Captain William Bruce, and Lieutenant David L. Arnold. The General and Mrs. Arnold had a two year old son, John, who died of appendicitis, in (1923). General Arnold died, January 15, 1950 at his Sonoma ranch home in California. He is buried in Arlington National Cemetery.

The General Arnold said, "More than anyone I have ever known or read about, the Wright Brothers gave me the sense that nothing is impossible." Orville and Wilber Wright, 'Hap's Sunday dinner hosts were trying to launch the age of flight when the automobile had not yet replaced the horse and buggy. 'Hap' had not even noticed when the Wright Brothers got their airplane in the air at Kitty Hawk, North Carolina in December of 1903. 'Hap' was wearing his first year Plebes uniform at West Point. He was busy finding out rules and discipline at West Point were more lenient than his Father's authority. 'Hap' had observed a balloon gliding over the skies at the Academy in 1906. He wrote his Mom "I don't take this event very serious. I don't know why (the balloonist) selected this place for his ascension but he did. The balloon was about 25 feet in diameter, almost a sphere. He inflated it with illuminating gas. After going up he went due north and was still going north the last I saw of him."

Arnold's joy while at West Point was that of riding horses. He wanted to be an Army Cavalry Officer just like those "blood and guts" Pershing and Patton types. He dreamed of being in the glamorous cavalry. First-hand stories of older cavalrymen were still being told. Great gruesome tales, living cavalrymen expounded on included Indian battle cries. Military engagements with Mexican bandits on battalions of beautiful horses galloped along in the dust of far off places. Arnold's thoughts were absorbed by cavalry heros. He tried to beat riding stunts that were probably exaggerated along with the exciting stories. He rode in pyramid groups, jumped over two horses to a third and became an expert high jumper on horses. He swaggered to classes, cussed, chewed tobacco and tried to emulate cavalry troopers. One day in a race, he swallowed a wad of chewing tobacco the wrong way and ended up on the ground in a spasm. Because he did not tell the doctor what had happened, he was diagnosed for an apparent heart attack.

At the academy, Arnold seemed to be so full of adolescent energy. He caused trouble for himself. He was involved in mischievous activities during the nightime. This stealthy cadet society was called the "black hand." Arnold was one of its founders. The fun at the beginning was just being out of bunks without permission. The Cadets soaped windows, overturned buggies and garbage cans. They became more aggressive when lugging the reveille cannon up the barracks stairs all the way to the roof. They left it fully displayed and chuckled in satisfaction over its silence the next morning. The prank that backfired on Arnold was when he put a match to a whole roof of fireworks that "silhouetted him against the light of his own handiwork in view of the whole corps." This episode earned him a stint of several weeks in solitary confinement up near the 'hot' roof where he had set off the fireworks. From that point on, until graduation, he was only allowed to attend classes and walk miles of rounds on a quadrangle in full uniform in front of his classmates carrying a rifle on his shoulder.

It was while he was under disciplinary restriction that his sister visited him bringing along with her a girl from his hometown. Arnold being shy around women folk had no girl friends. The girl, Eleanor Pool lived in a large Tudor styled home in the best part of his home town. The family even had a tennis court. The girl was a pretty blue-eyed blond. All the two could do was wave at each other...

Despite all of his disciplinary problems, Hap was allowed to order his Cavalry uniform and since he had achieved so many skills in horsemanship, he was "named to the graduation riding exhibition team." But, on leave at home following graduation, his letter from the War Department assigned him as an Infantryman in the Army. His nocternal activities had hurt his grades and placed him in the sixties out of a class of 110. When he did not receive placement in the high class cavalry riding elite, he was outraged to the point that his father tried to intercede at the War Department. His father, along with Senators, Penrose and Wanger found out "only the Secretary of War, William Howard Taft had power to change assignments." The Secretary was on a trip to the Philippines. Whereupon, impatient Arnold, who had not accepted his commission yet, blurted out, "I would like to go to the Philippines."

One did not exactly "fly" to the Philippines in those days to catch up with important personalities. 'Hap' found himself in San Francisco, California at the Presidio in September of 1907. He was given orders by the Commanding Officer, "Your duties will consist of having a good time in San Francisco and letting me know your address, Goodday, Gentlemen!" There were no transports until November of 1907 to Manila of the Philippines. San Francisco was rebuilding from the earthquake of 1906. In the beautiful mild-weather hills and cool valleys around San Francisco there were many ranches with equestrian activities. Eventually, however, entering an old refurbished cattleboat called Beuford, the inductees spent their first six days heading for the Philippines in an ocean storm. Arnold wrote in his diary, "...on the briny deep. Can't even get sick to vary the monotony."

His job on this tiresome jaunt to the Philippines was to protect a cache of money. He did not have uniforms for the tropics. He spent all his time, while the boat refurbished its supplies in Hawaii, guarding the precious cargo which amounted to millions of dollars. He was responsible for these sums belonging to the host country, the Philippines. In Hawaii, he sweated heavily in his woolen uniform. It was 80 degrees while the boat languished in the port. He was not only 'hot' in his winter clothing which had serviced him very well in the San Francisco Bay Region, he was almost 'broke'. He had spent most of his money while he had been in the Bay Area on equestrian activities and eating in famous San Francisco restaurants.

Everything worked out with his assignment until he reached the Philippines. He was overwhelmed on the decks by big burly men, each pushing a "carabao cart" pulled by water buffalo. One group of swarthy brown complected men grabbed ten of his boxes and darted away in all directions. Other Philippino drivers took the rest of the millions of dollars and fled in different direction from the first group. He was in such a quandry now, he sweated and soaked his uniform which was now being worn in steamy tropical weather. The humidity was higher and the weather even hotter than that of Hawaii. This had been his first assignment of the Army. Unarmed, a gang of thieves had made off with millions of dollars! He was so distraught that he did not arrive at headquarters to report the incident until several hours had passed. Lo, and behold, officers were smiling. Every box had been delivered! They gave him a receipt for a job well done and thanked him! With that problem solved, he now noticed the humid weather inundating him through his scratchy sticky woolen clothing.

There were no screens on the windows of their assigned quarters. Armies of mosquitos searched for blood. By placing bed posts into cans of kerosene, men kept red ants out of their bedding. Cockroaches, mold and inundated by rain for two months at a time were other nuisances. As far as 'Hap' was concerned, it was also a nuisance to perform social graces regarding courtesy calls. Furthermore, his visit with his father and Senators to the Office of the Adjutant General in Washington had been spread around by some Army and Navy Journals. It was a source of jollity to others and an embarrassment to him, that "he could influence such an august group as an Army Headquarters in Washington D.C. What nerve to think he could choose his own choice of service to his country!" Infantry Officers had scorned those snobbish horsemen for years and were not happy over the "mounted pay stipend." They were just as unforgiving to a young man who wanted out of the Infantry to be one of those cavalry showoffs!

'Hap' was one disappointed Officer! This would not be the first time in his life to feel that way. One great characteristic that stands out in Arnold's life is that he did not let his disappointments get in the way of his road to success. Final fame came to him from hard work and his great imagination. During war years in Washington D.C., his work schedule started at 7:30 a.m. stretching to 9 p.m. and he took phone calls after hours! His imagination tended to get him in trouble... While in the Philippines, he saw a notice regarding a military mapping detail with the Signal Corps. He applied and was soon energetically charting some of the earth's surfaces on Islands of Luzon and Correigidore. This rugged detail included slashing away at jungle growth.

Captain Cowen, whom he had served with in the jungle was sent to Washington on a new assignment. He was ordered to recruit two Second Lieutenants to take up a new experience, that of flying. It was thought that airplanes might be a good way to deliver messages to an Army in the field. Arnold had worked so enthusiastically in the jungle camps that he was asked by the Captain, "Would you care to learn about flying?" He accepted the invitation to study with Orville and Wilbur Wright. Actually, Arnold had never seen an airplane and didn't care if he ever viewed one. His real motivation was to get out of the Infantry.

Henry Harley Arnold was ordered to report to New York on a specified date. Before he arrived at Governors Island, which is now one of the two major airports of the city, he spent his accumulated money saved while being on the mapping detail on a long trip around the world. The tour included Hong Kong, Singapore, Suez Canal, Alexandria, Egypt, Casio and Genoa, Italy, Lucerne, Switzerland and Paris, France. He had heard the blue eyed blond, Eleanor Pool was with her mother in Lucerne. He deliberately traveled to that area with hopes to make her acquaintance. She had often flitted through his thoughts. The closest he had been near her was while waving at her when serving solitary confinement at West Point. He found out that she was engaged to someone else and was finishing schooling in Europe. They did enjoy some sightseeing before he traveled onward.

Arnold took in an event of a flying machine flown from Calais across the English Channel to Dover. Monsieur Louis Blercort was piloting a very flimsey looking contraption. It raised a thought in Arnold's mind, "What if in the future a lot of men did that together in formation at the same time?"

Seven years after the invention of the airplane, the contraption was causing public excitement. It was beginning to work on Arnold's mind who wrote home, "I have little else to occupy my mind." He and some friends went to Belmont Park on Long Island, New York for a first international air meet. It was now inspirational for him to follow exploits of aviators. Companies, Wright Brothers and Curtiss had daredevil teams flying figure eights, tight turns and some dives at the meet. The Ordnance Department of the Army announced some vacancies. Lowest rank in Ordnance was that of a First Lieutenant. Arnold wrote the Adjutant General in Washington, "Sir: I have the honor to request that I be detailed for aeronautical work with the Signal Corps. It is believed that my experience in topographical work will prove to be of value in that work..." He received a letter inviting him to volunteer for training under the Wright Brothers at Dayton, Ohio as an airplane Pilot. His Commanding Officer reacted to the letter, "Young man, I know of no better way for a person to commit suicide." Upon advising the War Department, "I am ready..." he received the following Special Order 95, dated April 21, 1911.

The following named Officers are detailed for aeronautical duty with the Signal Corps, and will proceed to Dayton, Ohio for the purpose of undergoing a course of instruction in operating the Wright airplane:

2nd Lt. Henry H. Arnold, 29th Infantry

2nd Lt. Thomas DeW. Milling, 15th Cavalry."

Two aircraft were being manufactured in the Wright Factory for the Army. Twenty-five men were employed in the plant. These were the second and third planes being purchased by the Army. From $125,000 appropriated Congressional funds for an experiment in military aviation, part of the money was to be spent for planes and part for complete training of the two men in how to fly them. It was noted that most Army Officers were certain, "they did not need any help from airplanes."

Arnold and Milling's training in ground instruction at the factory began with long twelve hour days. They learned how the Wright Airplane was maintained, constructed and flown. Arnold's first flight in a light cypress framed concoction which had tightly-stretched canvas stiffened by chemical paint (known as dope and fabric) and with seats and engine exposed to the weather, made him nervous. He was aloft seven minutes and did not touch any controls. For the next eleven days he and his teacher, Welsh flew together. For twenty-eight times they accumulated three hours and 48 minutes flying time which averaged about 8 minutes per flight. On his third flight he put his hand on the the elevator. By his eleventh flight he handled levers nearly all the time. On his nineteenth flight he landed without assistance. From that time on he was in charge of the aircraft. "I could fly! I was an aviator!" he exclaimed. After his first solo flight, Arnold continued to practice almost daily. Like his acrobatics with horses, he now tried tight turns, figure eights, climbs and dives with the airplane. One day he tried racing a train. The train won. With fifteen hours in the air and newly qualified Pilots and with certificate #2 of the Aviation Service, Arnold was ready to instruct others.

The first Army Flying School and Airbase was near College Park, Maryland seven miles NE of Washington. Recruits lived in tents while four wooden hangers were built. Officers had to find their own quarters in Washington D.C. and perform administrative duties. Captain Chandler and Roy Kirtland were their first students. "Without radio air to ground communication," Arnold recalled; "the rapid delivery of intelligence still depended largely on horsemen." The pilots wrote down what they saw from the air on brightly colored paper which was weighted down before thrown to the ground. A Cavalryman picked up the rock borne message and delivered it to the Command Post. The fliers decided to define the airplane's role as a military weapon. They kept flying higher and farther each day and kept mounting new gadgets on the machine.

Arnold and Chandler became two heros because they made a "long military flight of 42 miles." On the way home, they got lost in heavy headwinds. They finally landed in a farmer's field and requested some directions. The instructors labled all parts of the airplane and photographed them for their mechanics. A "bomb dropper" was invented by a former Army Officer named Scott. It was a first bombsight complete with telescope and a table to calculate corrections for wind direction and altitude. It was heavy and the plane would not get off the ground until Milling weighing only 125 pounds took the controls and Arnold was left on the ground. The bombsight was considered by the men as worthy of development. The War Department was not interested. The inventor, Scott took the invention to France and won the Michelin prize of $5,000. by hitting a 60 foot square 12 times out of 15 at 650 feet. He hit a larger target eight times out of 15 at 2,600 feet. Six years later, during World War I, the United States had no bombsight. Arnold learned the Germans were using their version of Scott's invention against American troops.

In 1911, Arnold was the first Pilot to carry United States mail. In 1912, he broke his own altitude record in a Burgess-Wright Plane gaining nationwide publicity. In a sea mishap, he was rescued with Kirkland and brought to shore where the monument stated "the Pilgrims had landed." He was envisioning bigger faster planes to carry passengers. He wanted planes to dominate battlefields with bombs and machine guns. The war department rejected the experimental famous aerial machine gun invented by Colonel Isaac N. Lewis. Arnold felt such weapons would soon have to be mounted on planes. In 1912, Arnold experienced fear of flying and said, "That's it." he exclaimed; "A man should not have to face death twice." For four years he would not even look at an airplane in the air. It was during this period that Eleanor Pool returned home from her European studies. Arnold was depressed with the phobia of the airplane and was assigned a desk in Washington as an aid to Brigidier General Geo P. Scriven. Arnold was now a recognized aviation expert and afraid to get into an airplane! Eleanor paid attention to Arnold and rekindled his affectionate feelings for her.

In 1913, there were 600 aviators in France and only thirty or so fliers in the United States. The Army added a stipend of 35% of base pay for American aviators in the services. Arnold had made more than 1,000 flights before grounding himself. The Air Service began to create more flying schools. They bought planes with European engines. He was promoted to First Lieutenant and proposed to Eleanor. She accepted his proposal. He gave her his West Point class ring. The following Sunday he was asking for her hand in marriage at her home in Philadelphia. In Arnold's book *Global Mission,* he wrote, "I verified I was about to be relieved from aviation duty at my own request. Eleanor Pool and I intended to be married in September and in those days you didn't plan to keep on flying after married unless you were an optimist."

With his new bride, he drew a stint in Manila. Cockroaches were so bad his wife attacked one with a broom and failed to kill it. They were next door to senior First Lieutenant, George C. Marshall who invited them to dinner. Watching George Marshall on maneuvers, Arnold said, "That man will one day be Army Chief of Staff." In 1915-16, Arnold was approached to become a Captain if he would apply for detail in the Aviation Section of the Signal Corps. In May of 1916, he reported to the Aviation Section of Rockwell Field North Island, San Diego as Supply Officer for the new school. The sound of engines, smell of cockpit and Pilot enthusiasm made him want to fly again. The new planes had weight, power and speed. They were not like the flimsey kites in which he had learned to fly. After his first eight flights as a passenger over San Diego, he went up alone. In less than a month he was trying snap rolls, slow rolls, loops, stalling, spinning, flying upside down, diving and buzzing the ground. He conquered his phobia redeeming his self-respect and renewed his courage by sheer will.

Arnold was sent to Panama because he refused to lie about a permit for flight left blank. In 1917, he was called to Washington D.C. as the Aviation Section was desparate for Officers. He was put in charge of the Information Division. On August 5, 1917 he became temporary full colonel making him the youngest full Colonel in the Army at that time. He and his wife were so happy. He was 31 years old and a Colonel! In 1917, the total strength of the Air Section of the Signal Corps was 52 officers, 1100 men, 200 civilian mechanics, 55 planes. Arnold believed 51 of those planes as obsolete. The United States did not own a single bomber, bombsight or usuable machine guns for planes. Mitchell got the French Government to exert pressure on the United States regarding airplanes, pilots and mechanics. Congress passed a bill to develop 16 airplanes and sixteen balloons but no bombers and fighters. After a War Department plea by Baker, Congress passed a proposal to spend more money for planes. Arnold was intricately involved to convert money into effective warfare from that day.

Arnold's impatience caused him to visit auto factories, to train more Pilots and maintenance personnel. On May 21, 1918, Arnold was named Assistant Director of Military Aeronautics which made him #2 in the Air Service's Washington Headquarters. On November 11th, he visited the 103rd United States Infantry and he was on the front line, at last! Guns were exploding all around him. But they were being fired in celebration. It was 11 a.m. ceasefire of World War I.

James H. Doolittle was in trouble because he climbed out of a plane and climbed onto the cross bars between the landing wheels. Arnold grounded Doolittle for a month. Later, Doolittle would serve on a special committee of Arnold's that included Charles Lindbergh.

Forest fires were patrolled aerially. Border patrols regarding immigration with Mexico were organized. In 1923, the first non-stop transcontinental flight took place in 26 hours and 50 minutes. In September, Mitchell sank obsolete American battleships Virginia and New Jersey by airplanes. Refueling in flight took place. Both Mitchell and Arnold kept saying, "Airpower is coming."

In Washington, as Air Service Information Chief in General Patricks office, Arnold was ready to go all the way in this struggle for airpower. A German Airline called SCADTA wanted to lengthen a South American route over the Panama Canal to Cuba and to the United States. Arnold decided it was not good militarily for foreign powers to have air rights over the canal. In order to keep the postmaster from granting a franchise "unless there was some other line, preferably American to perform the service," the Pan American Airline was stretched by miles to block the mail franchise application of the Germans.

When Arnold sent a thunderous roar over a fact finding group in session, he announced, "You just heard the noise of the entire United States Air Force, thirty-five planes." The event annoyed a sick president, failed to help the air force, embarrassed General Patrick and caused Arnold to be in the doghouse again! Transferred to Kansas, he was asked "would you like to be President of Pan-American Airways? He was ill and he turned them down. In order to help his son with reading, he read the child's book his son was bored with. He felt the book was trite and not interesting. He wrote a series of books based upon a pioneer airman named *Bill Bruce.*

In 1927, he was demanded to supervise and fly mail to President Coolidge to the Black Hills, South Dakota. The President Coolidge wanted his mail every Tuesday and Thursday mornings. Rain, wind or snow was not a factor in his demand nor was danger to Pilots. The mail was packaged in two separate bundles. Arnold ordered ground crews "to hold back one bundle on each run so they would have something to deliver when there was inclimate weather." The President Coolidge received half of his mail late but Arnold saved lives.

In 1930, Arnold took charge of logistics for 250 planes in a mass maneuver at Sacramento, California. He believed Charles Lindbergh's flight in 1927 did more to help aviation than all other events. On and on, inventions were installed such as brakes on the aircraft wheels. Jimmy Doolittle made the first blind takeoff and landing with sophisticated instruments. In 1929, there were 1,000 commercial airports in the United States. Arnold was absorbed in research and development work. He was always impatient with his country's leaders. He kept asking Congress for faster progress and more appropriations.

During the depression he commanded March Field near Riverside. Both banks back East, where he had money, failed. The Arnold family lost their children's education fund held in Mrs. Arnold's Father's Bank. Her father had a stroke after the bank failure. Arnold made friends with Donald Doughlas, the airplane manufacturer. Foods were dropped to Indians in the storms of 1932 and 33. Dead drops were simulated as if they were a war tactic. Mail was flown when President Roosevelt cancelled airmail contracts. Arnold established command at Salt Lake City after dire results were experienced with pilots killed and planes lost over the Rockies. The planes could only fit fifty pounds of mail into each fighter plane. There were only 10 planes. The first run had 1,400 pounds of mail to carry. The reason for so much mail was a philatelist run on stamped envelopes for that day. Roosevelt was embarrassed when there was a total of 66 crashes and 12 fatalities. This hurried up the negotiations with the airlines. 'Hap' Arnold emerged with a good reputation as having handled the most mountainous section of the country with the fewest casualties on the mail run.

Arnold lead the flight into Alaska to help map the area and he gained even more popularity. There were no air routes North. The group made the first flight non-stop to the country's most isolated territory. The team photographed 20,800 miles of Alaskan wilderness including the highest peak of Mount McKinley. By flying 950 miles non stop from Juneau to Seattle, they linked the Territory of Alaska with United States by air without a stop on foreign lands for the first time in history. Arnold won the Mackay Trophy for the second time and the Distinguished Flying Cross for this event.

Roosevelt, after hearing Hitler speak in 1938, told Harry Hopkins to get a new aircraft factory on the West Coast. The President was sure air power would win a war. Arnold began to preach production line methods. On September 29th, 1938, Arnold was named Chief of Air Corps by Roosevelt. Arnold preached production power, pilots, mechanics, bases and replacements. Marshall and Arnold worked out an entire air plan to help win the war. They put on three shifts a day in factories. The ultimate production of 40,000 airplanes per year was instituted. Arnold believed the day would come that the country needed 100,000 pilots. When the French came to buy planes, Arnold had all secret equipment removed in case they lost the war. He had private schools borrow money to train Pilots until he got appropriations from Congress. He also began ordering planes to keep in the United States instead of selling them all to England and France. He met with Lindbergh to learn about Germany's planes. He learned about their equipment, leaders, plans, training methods and present defects. He asked Lindbergh to serve on a board to determine kinds of planes needed. Scientists were contacted for development of gadgets and devices. He built a wind tunnel at Wright Field.

In 1941, the Army Air Forces replaced the Air Corps with a staff of their own. Arnold was the official in control Their objectives were to defend the air over the Western Hemisphere, support strategy in the Pacific Region and protect America from Japanese invasions. In August, he attended the Newfoundland Conference where Roosevelt and Churchill signed the Atlantic Charter. The B-29 super bomber was okayed. Doolittle was on his staff. He made Spaatz overall Commander of the 8th Air Force. Eaker was over the 8th Air Force Bomber Command. There were life and death occasions all over the world. One thing, it was dangerous to tell Arnold was that something couldn't be done. "Maybe you can't do it, but I can. You're fired!"

When he wanted a training center for non-flying Officers, Arnold was told to wait nine months to set it up. His answer, "Hitler won't wait that long," Arnold said to Congress, "Neither will I." Instead of building facilities, Arnold adopted Universities for training schools. He solicited their students to be Pilots. He got hotels at Miami Beach and pressed 500 hotels into training programs. He cut P-38 accident rates by 200%. He took his place as a Chief of Staff Member of four men. Admirals Leathy and King and Generals Marshall and Arnold constituted the High Command of President Roosevelt.

Arnold launched a new Air Force proving ground under his direct control to try out new ideas. He developed an Artic, Tropic, Desert Information Center and permanent Air Force School. They developed permanent steel planks to land planes on in sloshy fields. April 18th, Doolittle begged for and got the assignment to lead B-25s over Tokyo. All B-25s were lost. Nine men were lost out of eighty.

In 1941, Arnold created the largest airline in the world known as the Air Transport Command for military transport. He appointed his wife to head an Air Forces Relief Society of 40,000 women to help injured airmen. He was instrumental in the invasion of North Africa known as Torch and that called Bolero in Guadalcanal. He was impatient with some people who developed inferior life boats and made them climb into the ones they developed to prove a point and to correct the deficiencies, before he would requisition their product.

Arnold had celebrated "impatience" and everybody knew it. He began having heart attacks, one on a trip to Asia and one before a conference with Churchill and Roosevelt.

He preached about fighter escorts needed to accompany planes on bombing missions, This was after the great loss of planes regarding the German Ball Bearing Plants known as "Black Thursday." He was "permanently never satisfied" when it came to aviation and the United States Government's lackadaisical attitude toward development.

He read 20 to 50 cables a day. He digested and answered several requests. He attended meetings with the Joint Chiefs of Staff. He counseled with Marshall. He wrote dozens of letters a day. He discussed a massive variety of projects per day. He worked directly with the men he assigned jobs. He could read a new letter and talk about something different. He never tried to win popularity contests. He could not tolerate incompetence or laziness.

When a group came to his office regarding the poor prosthesis being put on the amputated legs of injured air men, he ranted. "I spend all my time trying to get them the best airplanes, the best gasoline, the best clothes, the best food and best of everything... By God, they're going to have the best legs!"

Arnold was considered a genius as a builder and motivator. Before World War II was ended, he had 2.4 million men and women in the Air Force. There were 105,00 pilots trained per year. 4,000 airplanes were build per month, many of them sold to other countries.

He was there when a man named Giles raised his hand to take an oath about the atomic bomb. That operation was referred to as the Manhattan Project. You could hold the atomic bomb in your hand but the second half of the bomb would weigh 6 to 7 thousand pounds. Most of the weight went into the exploding mechanism. Only the B-29 could deliver such a bomb. Arnold was at the Riviera when Roosevelt died.

His old enemy Henry Morgantheau wrote, "I thank you and congratulate you for your great part in getting the machines and men and training directing our glorious army in the air." The Air Transport Command became the largest airline the world ever saw in 1944. It carried 1,200,000 passengers, 400,000 tons of cargo all over the world and had 3,000 planes over worldwide routes. The Age of Flight became a reality in Arnold's lifetime. He realized his own dream. He was architect of the Age of Flight building the United States Army Air Forces.

Bea, his wife, bought a ranch with an old house and barn in the beautiful Valley of the Moon near Sonoma. He bought feed for animals and hired an architect to draw plans for a new home. He had just watched 520 of his superfortresses take off for Osaka. They carried 3,000 tons of bombs each. The capture of Iwo Jima had helped 1,299 different sets of planes make it to other islands. He was informed when the first Atomic Bomb was detonated in the New Mexico Desert. President Truman met with Stimson, Marshall and Arnold privately regarding possible targets for the bomb. Hiroshima was bombed on August 5th, at 7:15 Washington time. Also, 2,333,000 homes in Japan had been leveled by the 20th Airforce. Most businesses and industry in sixty cities were gone. 240,000 people were killed, 300,000 reported wounded. On August 9th another bomb fell on Nagasaki. On the 11th of August, leaflets were dropped to the people of Japan describing these statistics. On August 14th, the Japanese Government surrendered unconditionally.

The end of World War II ended 'Hap' Arnold's active career. By then, he had had four heart attacks. He wrote a futuristic article, *"Our Power to Destroy War."* In 1945, only an airplane could deliver the atomic bomb. His message to all was "Get ready world, anticipate changes, discard obsolete methods and examine new ideas."

A doctor would fly to Sonoma and the Five Star General would guide him down the field with hand signals. The doctor was an amateur Pilot. Arnold puttered in his woodworking shop making redwood furniture. He watched his livestock grow and had a flock of chickens and geese. He worked on his memoirs. Watching a mock dogfight in the sky above his property, he saw the planes collide and one almost hit his new house. In 1948, he had his fifth heart attack. He wrote an article for the National Geographic entitled, *"My life in the Valley of the Moon."* He describes a family of unafraid deer a few hundred feet from his back door, coveys of quail about the house begging for feed and water, dozens of hummingbirds and many other species of birds. He described expansive horizons of "softly rolling wooded hills stretching away to blue-misted mountains." He liked the history and devotion to gracious living. He appreciated the romance of yesteryear.

Arnold never really learned how to accept the joys of leisure. On the 15th of January, 1946 he was dead. The town of Sonoma had changed the names of a few of its streets during the war. One street was changed from Germany to MacArthur. Others, were changed to names of those Sonoman's lost during the war. On the beautiful side of the Valley on the way to Arnold's 40 acres, a road was re-named Arnold Drive. As found on the book cover of his book, *Global Mission,* it states, "Hap Arnold's Five Stars never dimmed the lively curiosity of a Pennsylvania country boy."

H.H.Arnold, *Global Mission,* 1949, Pub. Harper and Row, 1949, copyright renewed 1977 by Eleanor P. Arnold. pps. 626. p. 7, 9, 15, 19, 31, 43 and book cover quote.

Coffey, Thomas M., *Hap,* Viking Press, 1982, 625 Madison Avenue, New York, N.Y. 10022., pps. p. 19, 52, 63, 80, 114, 141, 256 and 320.

Betty A. Castonguay

United States Navy (Wave), 1943 - 1945

Betty Castonguay was born in Oak Park, Illnois which is located a bit south of the O'Hare Airport and a bit west of Lake Michigan near downtown Chicago. Her father died while Betty was in Junior High. While she was in High School, her mother met a sailor who became her mother's boyfriend for a short period of time. Betty's mother did not marry the Navy man but he had influence upon Betty's life. The young girl decided she liked people from the Navy and was attracted to that branch of the service due to the sailor that had visited her mother.

Betty went to Beloit, Wisconsin to college and was a Sister of the Tri-Delta Sorority. This sorority was not a snobbish group. The members of Delta, Delta, Delta did not live in one place. In fact, Betty's roommates were not in the sorority group. "I didn't want to add to the burden of more expense upon my mother. I could save her additional costs for college by living in a co-ed group and by being independent," said Betty.

Betty graduated from Beloit College after the usual four year requirements were met. She had studied a little Spanish and some business courses. However, she found her shorthand was not acceptable for the Freeman Shoe Company and was fired in one day because of it. She did land a very interesting job as a report writer for Dunn and Bradstreet in a sweat shop atmosphere. The job taking place before wide-spread use of computers and copy machines was located in a huge edifice called W. Adams Building. All reports were done by hand on old typewriters and time consuming mimeograph machines.

Every working morning was given over to reviewing stacks of reports prepared much like a credit report is composed. Information for the reports was developed by men 'in the field' who searched out information about businesses and people in the suburbs. Clients of Dunn and Bradstreet had to pay for their reports being included on the famous list the company printed. Financial brackets and credit history were included in the reports. There was a certain format with information being rated. Reports were constantly updated. Celophane liquid carbon paper was used to make copies. There was a line count girl who spent all day counting the lines written by an individual employee. As motivation for fast work and accuracy, the typist that put in the most lines for the week was rewarded a bonus of $18.00 that week.

Betty chose to become a Wave when she decided to help with World War II. She discovered she could qualify for an Ensign, Lieutenant J.G. with her type of background. There was one catch for her admission into the service. She had to weigh 100 pounds, but she only weighed 95 pounds. Secondly, her teeth were in bad shape. She was advised to report back to the recruiting office when she gained five pounds and had her teeth fixed. She was 5 foot 2" and barely made the one-hundred pound limit from Spring to Fall of 1943. She had spent all those months drinking chocolate milk shakes and eating bananas resulting in still being a light-weight. Reaching those Navy set goals for admission, Peggy was ordered to OCS for training at Smith College, North Hampton, Massachusettes.

Just like the Navy men shown in pictures of their training ordeals, Waves were given arduous physical obstacle courses to endure. The women had two to three hours of calisthenics per day in an old gymnasium. Their instructor told them the exercises were for "promoting grace and health." The young ladies absailed on ropes to the main floor from a second story balcony. It was an exhausting eight weeks. Their muscles and bones were stiff and sore all the time. Waves were not allowed to work on ships at that time, even though a Wave was identified by pictures alongside ships and airplanes. Waves however, fell under Navy rules and regulations. The best part of the experience was that the Platoons marched down to North Hampton to a restaurant called the Wiggins Tavern. They did this three times a day for the most marvelous food!

After North Hampton OCS was but a memory, Peggy was one of two young women sent to the Mount Holyoke, Massachusetts Communication Center. At this post, the two Wave Officers studied secret warfare codes, cyphers, and an enigma code machine. According to Peggy, "The enigma machine had to do with anything that puzzled or baffled. It could be described as a machine that helped to clear up something obscure or like a riddle. Using this machine was like never having a real thing. All one could do was describe something. Strips of cyphers then came tumbling out of the machine on papers." The enigma machine was the top mechanical unit of its time for decoding secret messages. Its expertise was not a bit like computer mapping on software that one could minutely trace information. A little place such as Two Rock, Sonoma County California, used in the 1950s as an early warning station and intercontinental shield to keep Russia from coming over the Polar Cap, would not be on the early machine. But the Submarine Naval Facility at Hunters Point, near Candlestick Recreational Park, San Francisco would have been within the machine's retrieval capabilities.

Peggy was assigned at Hunters Point which was one of the drydocks for the Navy on San Francisco Bay. Hunters Point was a submarine base for repairs. The base employees also repaired and serviced aircraft carriers, destroyers and mine sweeps. The USS Essex came in for service on the day that Peggy arrived. The huge awe inspiring ship stayed quite a while. The nearby Mare Island on the other side of the Bay took in battleships and cruisers.

Peggy was very impressed by the Essex. It was so big. She was invited aboard for dinner. The Waves were more likely to be invited on board destroyers. It was extremely important to secure coding rooms when ships were in port. Many officers came up to the Wave offices. This was the Twelfth Naval District Headquarters for decoding messages. The facility had a huge room with a vault which was full of storage lockers. All publications were stowed in the locker room. Many papers had to be brought up to date on a daily basis, as codes were changed every day. There were sheets and sheets of keys for each day of the week. One other Wave along with Peggy made designations as Assistant Communications Officers. The two women Assistants were in charge of all publications and were held responsible to make an inventory each and every morning.

For example, Navy call signs for ships trying to get out of port were changed on a daily basis. Changes could be Morse Code or flags. These changes would be visual. The Navy 'call sign' was also changed every day. Once a month, Peggy with another Wave Officer had to carry all obsolete sheets of data to a regular round drum where they started a fire and used the tin barrel as an incinerator. Often, they were out in a brisk wind. Their job was to burn all of the information which included strip cyphers and word substitutions. This material was essential to the life blood of all ships and Naval vessels. Sometimes, the strip cyphers would get caught in mischievious winds that were prevalent in the area. These papers would start to blow down the steep hill. The neatly dressed women would chase these little cypher strips down the hillside. There was no doubt about it, every little strip was considered important and had to be retrieved and destroyed. These ladies felt extremely responsible for the war effort. They never spoke about their experiences.

When the Waves were invited aboard ships, they had to walk up and salute the Officer of the Deck just like a Navy male would. The women would have to be cognizant of and call each ship's part the same name the men did. They had to be privy to the Navy lingo.

Messages were encoded (convert a message or document from plain text to code) or decoded (to convert a message from code to plain language). Messages received or sent might be about such things as restrictions, repairs on ships, confidential officer messages or movements of ships in the ocean. A secret message meant it was a more serious communication. If a message was labeled "TOP SECRET" it was extremely secret. For a top secret message, the Wave had to stop and obtain a partner for decoding. That second person would have to help the Communication Officer or Assistant. Betty was an Assistant capable of breaking highly secret codes. Codes were locked up at midnight and guarded by a Marine.

Peggy could be called in at midnight regarding a round-robin-letter. That kind of letter had to be seen by her administrator. Then, she had to locate the top Officer. If she couldn't find him, she had to dress and go in the middle of the night to break the important coded message. Twice, she was put into this quandry.

One of the messages received in the dead of the night was quite long. It similarly stated, "There is going to be arriving at the commercial airport an Army Officer and a Navy Officer. They will be accompanying two boxes. One box will be small. The other box will weigh tons. The smaller box shall be met by Security Officers from Hunters Point. These Army and Navy men along with their boxes shall be isolated overnight and guarded in the Administration Building at Hunters Point. The boxes and the men are to be loaded aboard the U.S. Indianapolis". (The Indianapolis had been a curiosity for a few days. It was a cruiser and was not exactly the kind of ship usually moored at Hunters Point.)

The first message regarding this unusual request was received by Morse Code. There was a guy "all pushed out of shape" who accompanied the boxes. He wore big black galoshes above his ankles and they were not fastened down and would flap as he walked. He was all over the place because of the two boxes. One box was a problem, weighing so many tons. (When assembled, the contents of the box would be a bit shorter than a small car, about ten feet in length. It weighed about nine thousand pounds which would be about three times as much as that size car.) The man with the galoshes just knew "it was something serious because of the tons of weight." (In the future this box he was accompanying would be referred to as the "fat boy".) On display at the Travis Air Museum in Fairfield, California is a "fat boy." The bomb is shaped like a huge round ball. The "fat boy" was the type of bomb dropped on Nagasaki.

Peggy's coding room was her sanctuary. The man with galoshes tried to press into it. He was booted out of the coding room. The Commanding Officer of the Indianapolis accompanied the man into the coding room and was overheard trying to worm information from his guest, "what was in the boxes?" The man's answer was "Just keep track of time. In two weeks the war will be over!"

The Cruiser Indianapolis left port. Everyone went about their own business forgetting about the time and about the secret message... The Indianapolis went to Tinian. The Atomic Bomb (in its two pieces) was taken off the cruiser and put in the Enola Gay a modified B-29 airplane, at 2:45 a.m. On the same day, August 6, 1945, the Enola Gay's Gunner Officers released the bomb over Hiroshima, Japan at 9:14 a.m. It was reported, a brilliant flash of light was seen by Pilot and Crew. Shock waves from the explosion jolted the plane. Dark gray dust rolled out of the explosion and there were brilliant flashes of fire. A lava-like appearance crossed the city and a mushroom cloud of purple smoke rose forty thousand feet in the air. Estimates of death caused by the bomb are set at two hundred thousand souls. Sixty thousand buildings were destroyed. From the book entitled, *Oppenheimer and the Atomic Bomb* a full description of this "fate of Hiroshima" is described. The book refers to John Hersey's book, *Hiroshima*. The Indianapolis left Tinian. It was bombed and sunk two days after delivery of the bomb. A documentary of this event, filmed on Hunters Point, included the loss of life of the man wearing the galoshes that Peggy instructed to leave her decoding room.

The Captain of the ship was courts-marshaled. The verdict was rescinded. It was speculated the Captain committed suicide because of his intense grief over his men and ship. It was a year or so, before the famed Journalist Walter Winchell broke the silence that the Indianapolis had carried the Atomic bomb. Peggy never talked about her top secret code breaking assignment. Actually, she did not know at the time it was the bomb. She knew something was being delivered in two pieces, one piece you could hold in your hand, the other box quite large and with Army and Navy representatives in charge of the shipment. Peggy said, "I haven't even told my daughter of this historic event. You are the first one to know."

Peggy stated, "The Waves wore uniforms. They worked hard from 7 a.m. to midnight." There were only two Waves on assignment when Peggy came to Hunters Point. The staff grew and then there were eight. Waves discovered "there was a great bonding of patriotic people." The staff worked round-robin-shifts."

Peggy was one of the first two women allowed on a submarine while it was carrying out a duty. The USS Sunfish was making a trial run shake down cruise out to the Farallon Islands. These islands are located about thirty to forty miles from the Golden Gate Bridge. This visit was actually breaking a superstition, "that it was bad luck for women to be on a submarine while it was on duty." Early on, Peggy had a lady friend who was going with a Gunnery Officer now assigned to the Sunfish. She wrapped the Officer around her little finger and by begging constantly she wrangled this historic event. Peggy felt "it was a very dangerous duty to be a submariner! The submarine group appeared elitist in nature and seemed very much apart from the other Naval personnel. The Waves noticed the Officers from submarines were tired a lot of the time. The Wave that was Peggy's friend worked in the Office of Supply.

The ladies wore Navy slacks on the day of the submarine adventure. (The introduction of slacks to the women of the services was the forerunner of pant suits which became a fashion rage for women of the Forties.) It was 6 a.m. when the submarine made ready to leave port. Part of the mission included shooting some torpedos.

When the Waves were brought down to the ward room for coffee, the first thing Peggy noticed was a Christmas tree in the room. The Up periscope was up above water before the Sunfish was even submerged. It was very thrilling during that first dive. The passengers were submerged 250 feet toward noon. The girls were continually plied with coffee. With all of this liquid to drink, Peggy needed to go to the Head. There was supposed to be one Head fore and one Head aft. The crew and their guests had lunch. She knew the Head operated with a difficult mechanism. One had to regulate valves for flushing or the waters would flow back into the ship. She did not know how to operate these valves and was scared that if she tried to use the Head and flush, that the host's bathroom would end up flooded. She kept refusing more coffee. She could hardly pay attention to what was happening. She thought, "I am going to die if I don't find relief soon!"

The ladies had to obtain required clearance orders from Washington in order to be on the USS Sunfish. In the late afternoon, a ship called the Halibut was detatched from duty with new orders received at Hunters Point. Washington was "edgy" about Peggy being aboard the submarine. She was too important a person to be out there in the ocean. She was needed for her very special job on shore. The Halibut sent a tugboat out to get her. It was not quite 6 p.m. The tugboat came steaming up and made "all those waves." Two men lifted Peggy under her arms and into the tugboat. The motions were synchronized with the waves between the ships. Down she went with the feeling she might be using a sailor's head for a Head! She was so paralyzed, she did not even ask for a bathroom on the tug. She couldn't even make good conversation. The base sent a command car for her at the dock. After she arrived at the office, she was barely able to function. What she remembers the most about this adventure is that it was so thrilling and then how it became so awful. She had been too embarrased to ask for help in using the Head on the submarine. Here, she was one of the first two Waves to go out on a sub and she was in so much discomfort!

The USS Salmon was badly damaged by mines and torpedos in the Philippines. The crew brought the submarine back to Hunters Point for repair. Was it worth it? or should the sub be scuttled? Another Wave with Peggy had the afternoon off. They decided to tour the submarine. The public had been invited aboard. It was a very grey day, foggy and cold. The women wanted to see where the bombs had hit the sub. A young Torpedoman had on a long coat. He showed the two Waves the periscope. There appeared to be a jumble of hits on the top of the sub. It was the first time ladies were wearing purses over their shoulders. It was not yet a common thing to have a shoulder bag. The strap on Peggy's shoulder bag broke and Peggy's purse went into the brink. "You don't want it back," the Torpedoman said. "Oh, I have to have it back," Peggy replied; "My Navy I.D. card is in the purse and so is my pay check." The Navy man took off his coat and jumped in the Bay. He was sputtering, "It's colder than hell." He had nothing to hang onto to help him get back up on the ship. "You better get help," he yelled; "I'm getting cramps." Peggy ran to the top of the gangplank and yelled to the Officer, "Man overboard!" Men came running out of everywhere on the vessel. They looked at the young man holding up the bag. They laughed, "That'll teach you a lesson," as they hoisted up the wet and dirty looking fellow. After they hoisted him up, "Wait for me," he said as he disappeared; "I'll take you back."

About this time, the Waves noticed an Army Officer and his wife who had also arrived to view the submarine's damages. They took the route at the Hatch and went to where the periscope disappeared from view. The cleaned up Torpedoman now re-appeared that had rescued Peggy's purse. "I don't know what happened today," he said; "an Army wife just dropped her purse in the periscope well! Another Torpedoman came along from the USS Salmon with a long fishing pole to fish the purse out of the well! He sat with a bamboo fishing pole and eventually retrieved the second woman's purse. When final assessment was made regarding the damaged submarine, it was scuttled afterall.

There was a publication at the office referred to as *RPS for Baker*. This publication was loaded with information about everything Navy. It contained instructions on how to stow things and how to secure property. It was used as a guide with orders regarding burning of documents. This publication was used many times by the staff. Then, along came a Lieutenant Cox. He was allowed to use the office copy of the book in the big room inside the coding room. When a ship was being repaired, Officers came to their own room to work in the vault area. Lieutenant Cox was in there many hours. His destroyer left port. The next day, the *RPS and Baker book* was gone. He had last used it in the vault. Peggy surmised, "He must have it." Peggy sent a plain teletype message to San Diego regarding the missing book. There was absolutely no answer. She lived in fear her top commissioned Officer would ask for "the book."

The USS Morse came in port. The Commander was dating one of the Waves on the commission. He knew, if he played his cards right, the Morse would be scuttled. It was very scary to lose publications and his girl friend told him about the loss of the book in the department. When his ship was scuttled, in order to help the girls, he let the Waves have his publication of the manual permanently. The women inked out the name USS Morse on the cover of the book. The copy was dog-eared, dirty and reeked of diesel smell but now they had an *RPS for Baker Manual*.

When wartime experiences for Peggy ended, she also ended her World War II marriage. She went to San Francisco State College and obtained an elementary teaching credential. She did not really use the credential in a classroom but instead, obtained a job at San Francisco State College as Admissions Officer. She worked upward in the position until she was the third highest paid employee in the department. A good many years she hung onto this job, so that she could support her child, Nancy. She eventually found that she ran the office and kept breaking in men for the Directorship. In other words, she was passed over each time and the highest job was given to a man with little or no experience. She applied and obtained the Registrar position for the College of Marin. That job was enjoyed for five years until Peggy took a similar position at the University of Alaska Community College at Anchorage, Alaska.

Peggy liked living in Alaska. Due to weather conditions she discovered there were no snakes. In May and June, mosquitos were around but no bugs to speak of. In the summer, she could lie in the sun or go fishing. She would ride out to see beautiful Alaskan vistas with some civilians in an old coupe equipped with a mattress. At first, the little family of two had a bit of a cultural shock coming from the posh community of Marin County, California. Anchorage at the time was actually a frontier tacky town. It began to fill up with people. About 150,000 newcomers showed up when there was an oil strike on the slope.

Peggy got married again and moved to Oakpark, Illinois. Two years later, she divorced her second husband. During this period of her life, she dabbled in the decorating business for awhile. This was kind of a 'sophisticated idea' left over from her Marin County, California experience. , From her first divorce, the assets had been split between the two parties under California law. Marin County had become outrageously expensive for a divorced woman to live economically. She couldn't manage the rentals and wouldn't pay $950.00 a month for a dilapidated duplex apartment. She questioned herself, "Where shall I go? I don't know anyone here in Marin." She chose a newer spacious mobile home in one of the best adult parks on the edge of Sonoma, California. She decorated the home all in white for a light airy feeling. This was really her signature from the home decorating stint. The house she had had in Marin was a large one located in Pacheco Valley. That house was one of the ones lost in a storm, attributed to developer mistakes. The house made news on television when with fallen trees and erosion, it began to slide off it's foundation.

Larsen, Rebecca *Oppenheimer and the Atomic Bomb*, Franklin Watts, New York, London, Toronto, Sydney. 1988. pps. 192., p.111.

Charles A. Gill

United States Army, Infantry and Armor 1941 - 1961

Charles A. Gill, was born in New Middleton, Tennessee in 1915. The next night after Charles was born his mother died. His Aunt Jennie cared for the baby and kept Charles until he was ten years old. At that time, his Father remarried and the boy moved in with his dad and step-mother until he graduated from high school. During World War I, Charles knew people who had fought in the conflict. He had listened to, and highly respected the stories he had heard of the World War I Army adventures. All the people he had talked to had been Infantrymen. In 1941, even before Pearl Harbor, the young graduate felt like a draft notice would be coming his way. He volunteered ahead of the call and had a number issued him. He chose the Army as all the people whom he knew had been in the Army. He had no connection with the Navy, nor was Tennessee near any large bodies of water. It did not even enter Charles' mind to join that branch of the service.

Charles was inducted in the Army at Fort Oglethorpe, Georgia. He was assigned to a unit at Camp Wheeler, near Macon, Georgia. The physically-active recruit found the weather was a little warmer than Tennessee for basic Infantry training, especially when dressed in khaki woven uniforms and participating in strenuous physical exercises. From Camp Wheeler the young man was assigned to an Infantry unit which was sent to Panama to guard the Canal. Charles did not like Panama. Living accommodations on the Canal premises were very old. Duty was tough. Guard duty was strung out for 6 to 7 hours at a time. Ships came up and went back in the opposite direction without a break. There was no time to rest.

When assigned as transit-guard on ships, a vigilant watch was to maintain cautious control over any strategic places of the ship which might be sabotaged. The watch was to safeguard and protect the defense of the ship from any device, contrivance or attachment which might cause injury such as might sink a ship in the Lake between the locks or in any way sabotage the Canal. Captains were required to let guards on their ships whether they liked it or not while they used the Canal. No matter how Allied friendly a transport company was, they were to cooperate, so no incidents would surface.

Right after Charles went to Panama, he was a Guard Detail which accompanied some subversives back to New York for the Immigration and FBI. The United States Government had rounded up some German and Italian persons who were considered to be dangerous to the war effort. They were picked up in diplomatic offices in South America. The Navy brought these persons to the strategic area by a Grace Line Ship. The guards had to take a defensive posture over those people so they would not let any of them effect any damage. The unwanted guests were not allowed to ride a ship over the Canal. They were held by sentries in a gymnasium, then put on a train. It was not the fastest train at that time. The group was taken from the West to the East Coast by rail so the passengers would not learn any perceptions about the Canal. There was one place that if a ship was sunk it would block other ships. Some of the possible traitors taken to New York were locked up and put out of circulation for a long time.

Charles wanted to attend Officer Candidate School. He was finally accepted at Fort Benning, Georgia and found it was truly an experience to see how much irritation a person could handle! The idea behind passing the Officers Candidate School was to see if you could maintain your sweet calm attitude under the most trying circumstances. From Corporal, Charles was promoted to Staff Sergeant. But, best of all he was promoted from working at the Panama Canal. The men were given rifles, machine guns, bayonets and instruction on the use of these weapons. Men were also taught infantry tactics such as how to set up an attack and how to set up defensive positions. Asking "how would you set up an infantry defense in the City of Sonoma?" Charles stated, "Get on high ground. Use a covered approach on all roads. Put the troops up in the hills. Try to get higher than the enemy. Have observation points."

Charles was assigned to the 98th Infantry Division at Breckenridge, Kentucky after being commissioned a 2nd Lieutenant. He trained recruits. He worked together with other Officers and NCO's (non-Commissioned officers.) There would be four Platoons in a company. A Lieutenant would serve as Platoon leader. Giving orders to four Platoons and four Lieutenants would be a Captain. As in civilian life, one person was needed to manage. Sergeants, under the direction of Lieutenants took the men on maneuvers in Tennessee very close to Charles' home area. After maneuvers, orders came to go overseas to the China, Burma, India theatre of war. Charles felt like the perverbial step-child being sent there. He felt there were not as many Americans sent over there as in the other places of the War.

A whole group of Officers and advisors were sent by the United States Government to help the Chinese Army. Fighting had already been taking its toll before Charles was sent to Burma. Japanese soldiers were already entrenched over the territory. The Chinese had a unit in Burma. An interpreter was used between the Chinese Battalion of about 1,000 soldiers and the one American First Lieutenant, Charles. There were actually three Chinese Infantry regiments in the area with artillery Battalian, Supplies and Ordnance. The aim of the war in this part of the world was to push the Japanese out and re-open the Burma Road to China. Supplies needed were available to China from the Far East by that one road. Items forthcoming included food, ammunition and fuel. Ledo was in the most northern part. An air drop method was used to send in American supplies including ammunition which made it down from the plane without exploding. The kind of parachutes used for air-dropping had flaws and irregularities in their materials or construction and were not fit for human use by Paratroopers. Parachutes opened in different colors which reminded one of colored balloons in which people take rides. The color of the balloon indicated what was being dropped. Rice was dropped in toe sacks (gunny sacks). Rice was placed into two bags to keep the bundle from splitting open. Airdrops also included needed medicine and lots of corn beef in cans. Corn beef was about all one had to eat with the Chinese two times a day. Rice and corn beef was a pretty good combination but after a while it became more than tiresome.

Charles managed his tactical operations with only two radio operators. He made suggestions to the Chinese Army as to battle strategies. The troops were all on foot. Having no vehicles for a dense jungle environment did not favor one group over the other. Many a path led to a dead end up on the steep hillsides; roads were scarce.

Charles received the scar above his eye while heading into town on a late afternoon. Japanese soldiers with artillery had been threatening the group near Bhamo. After the shrapnel hit, Charles was taken to a field hospital set-up similar to the Mash-type variety as depicted on Television. It could be termed a collective hospital with tents located in the jungles. In Burma, Charles was evacuated through Dr. Seagraves missionary hospital. The noted doctor had hospital and Officer designations. Charles had been there for approximately two months before being evacuated by airlift to a General Hospital in India.

After the two month healing process, Charles was transferred to the United States Chinese Combat

Command in China. He saw and met Chiang kai Shek. The introduction took place in a receiving line after a speech. By this time, Charles knew and felt it was very necessary to be in the China, Burma, India theatre of war. The Allies were fighting the enemy that bombed Pearl Harbor! That same enemy was trying to take over much of Asia and the Pacific island groups. Charles served Headquarters in the Personnel Section. He was cognizant of where the individual Americans in the China Burma Area were and where their assignments and locations were located. His unit could find persons "like in the perverbial haystack." They were advisory on training and fighting the war. Under a General, they were the Personnel Section making assignments and re-assignments on an individual basis. When a new Officer came to the area, he was sent where needed. Charles, as a First Lieutenant made recommendations to his superior and that Officer would then assign persons to the jobs.

Charles had a new and different job in the latter days of the war. There were no Chinese units in the South. Therefore, the Chinese Units had to be co-ordinated and moved across a river. Outboard motors were supplied to take men across the river on rafts. The big job was to schedule activities so as not to jam up groups ready to go home to America.

At a French-Catholic Mission, Charles and his two operators stayed there to help them rebuild. Two missionaries came out with Chinese rice wine and drank a toast to Vincenty. The Japanese never did get into that particular area.

Charles was most impressed seeing elephants and colorful birds in the Burma jungles. In China, the lasting impression was that there were a lot of people. China was a more developed nation. The jungles were dangerous for amoebic dysentry. Boiled water was a necessity as well as halozone tablets. Hob-nailed shoes were worn by the British because of moist ground conditions. Some British made no bones about it, they were there "to get back at the Japanese!" The idea of the Japanese taking Burma would have been one of taking a great big bite out of Southern China and decreasing major British influence in the Pacific. China is a big country according to Charles, the Japanese were strung out all over it.

When World War II ended, Charles stopped at Fort McClellan, Alabama for a while, carrying out a stint in Supply. Soldiers at the base were there for training in weaponry not unlike a boot camp. But, this camp was a placement training center. Charles assisted in handling requests for training materials. The items issued for use were expected to be turned back in. The materials also included a weapon pool issued to individual units. They were to use certain weapons on one day, turn them back in, then receive a different weapon on another day.

Charles went to Germany for the Army. The year, 1947 found a cold war had taken the place of the World War II hot war. Charles was in another Headquarters Company, this time to help run the Army of Occupation. whose reason for existence was to make a "presence" in the area. Headquarters was made up of clerks, supply people, staff sections, and a Military Police Unit. The headquarters for the unit was stationed at Weisbaden, Germany on the west side of the German wall. The Russians were occupying the East Side. Throughout 1948 to 1951, Charles served the Constabulary Squadron, (a police force organized in a military fashion) that patrolled American-Russian-Zone borders. Alphabetized were the A B C D Troops with Charles as Commander of the D Troop. The guards moved in vehicles around the clock patrolling the border with a mission that they not let persons cross over the lines. The Americans were the eyes and ears for the European Allied Command. The Allieds were notified, if the Russians came by or gave an alert. Privates on up in grade specifications, were the guards of the border.

The area patrolled amounted to a little under 500 miles and was also known as the Iron Curtain. The term coined by Winston Churchill, designated an impenetrable barrier of censorship and secrecy. In essence it was a demarcation imposed by the Soviet Union between its sphere of influence and the rest of the world. The East zone was considered the Iron Curtain. Some Germans came through once in a while. There were not too many. Rain or shine, Americans patrolled the lines. The Russians never tried to cross the border. The groups from either side did not mingle or might not see each other patrolling. Squadron Headquarters, a training and operation section supervising the actions of the squadron, was in Herstfeld, Germany. Each Company had a level of supervision.

It was at Herstfeld, in 1951, that Charles met and married his wife, Madelle. She was one of the clerical staff. Madelle was from the state of Oregon. The couple was transferred back to the United States when Charles received a new assignment to Fort Mead, Maryland. Assigned to a light tank armored division, he had little to do with how tanks worked in this new undertaking. He was shifted to the Armor Training Center at Camp Irwin California, about 30 miles from Barstow where his tactical expertise was used once more, this time in strategic war games. The purpose of the war games was to group tank battalions from all over the United States in tactical situations in simulated battles and maneuvers with weapons. There were firing exercises in the desert. The area was windy and hot but Charles enjoyed the desert because it felt good. There was no humidity. Wide open spaces fringed with purple mountain peaks in the distance was a refreshing change.

All too soon, Charles left for overseas again, this time to Korea. The Korean War was over because it was now 1954. He became advisor to a Korean Tank Battalion. Again, he was assisting in training as well as making a "presence" felt in the area. If the Americans had not been there, it was felt the North Koreans would have gone back. Charles believes, "we needed to be there." In Japan, he gave instruction in Air Ground Operations. Various officers in the Oriental areas were taught how air ground operations worked. In the air, a forward observation person would tell what target to hit and where the bomb would go down. Charles taught these concepts to a few high ranking Japanese Officers acquainting them with air and ground reconnaisance. Cities were looking good, right out of Tokyo!

Johnson Air Base near Tokyo was used by both Army Personnel and Air Force Personnel for training in event of war. As a Ground Commander giving instructions, air support reacted to required strategic targets and this was known as close air support. The main objective was how to request an air strike. This request would move forward to an Air Force Officer who would call the Joint Operation Center and request airplanes. They actually did not use the airplanes in the week-long simulated courses.

Near the end of twenty years in service to his country, Charles became a National Guard Advisor at Fort Worth, Texas. The National Guard was composed of civilians who were in uniform like the Army during training. The Guard met once a week at the armory for drill. Each company was organized just like the Army with Platoons and Companies. The drills were Army oriented. This group was similar to Reserves in attending drills, making corrections and taking advice on how to do things. There were classes on use of weaponry, their care, cleaning of artillery pieces and updated field tactics. There were hundreds of subjects you could choose from including a little first aid. Both, Air National Guard and Army National Guard were under Charles control.

Charles retired in May of 1961, a few days beyond twenty years in the Army. He spent most of those twenty years in the service of the United States with the Fourth Army. At Fort Lawton, Washington Charles retired as a Reserve Officer. During those years at Fort Benning, Georgia, he attended Officer Candidate School after originally receiving one year of college by correspondence courses. In-between, he was an Officer Candidate at Infantry School, attending Army Information School, Troop Information & Education School, the Armored School as Associate Officer for advance courses and the Air Ground Operations School as Specialist. There were other educational endeavors.

Charles carries wounds from the gunshot on his face, thigh and forearm received in Bhamo, Burma on the 5th of December, 1944. His medals span from Purple Heart through Combat Infantryman Badge, Asiatic Pacific Camp Medal, American Defense Service Medal, WW II Vincenty Medal, American Campaign Medal, Army Occupation Medal (Germany), Armed Forces Reserve Medal and National Defense. His group of medals, filling a folder, also include Korean Service Medal, United Nations Service Medal, Bronze Star, 5 Bars, and the Oak Leaf Cluster Army Commendation Medal. He retired overseas, as Lieutenant Colonel.

Charles and his wife, Madell wanted to live on the West Coast and visited Sonoma as tourists. Charles tried selling real estate with Auberlin Real Estate. Interested in polishing colorful stones, he tried lapidary work. He and his wife ran the Sonoma Valley Art Center next to Marioni's Restaurant. They built a house in Agua Caliente and lived there until 1988 when they bought a condominium within walking distance of the Plaza in Sonoma.

Madelle volunteered work for the Chamber of Commerce for a few years. She was stricken with Parkinson's disease followed by Alzheimer's disease. He visits her at London House everyday. Every afternoon, when able, Charles works at the Boys and Girls Club helping the children with their homework. At St. Francis Catholic School, he made himself present on the playground in a security role. He also works at the Visitor's Center.

Charles used to hunt stones in the desert for polishing. Now, he cooks, cleans for himself and extends his knowledge to his fellow man. He likes the work of polishing minds of the children at the Boys and Girls club, the best.

Edward F. Kenny

United States Navy, 1944 - 1946

Born in San Francisco in 1927, Edward Kenny became a Navy man at the age of sixteen. His father had been a Motorman on the Market Street Railway. As a very young child, Edward got to ride the streetcar and watch the Japanese at Tanforan Field. Tanforan, El Camino and San Bruno were names of places he knew. That was where the action was in regard to horseracing. Tanforan was also the original airport for the San Francisco area. Due to family problems, the young man was separated from his mother and father at a very early age and was placed in care of his Uncle John who lived in Petaluma, California. Uncle John Donahue and his wife, Helen worked for Edward Long, a long-standing dairy man in Petaluma area. Petaluma was known as the egg basket of the world. Japanese farmers raised chickens and bedded them down at night in long low redwood sheds which dotted the Petaluma countryscape. Edward remembers the boys at St. Vincents School as being rambunctious. He and other fellows in the middle grades spent a lot of time throwing rocks at the little guys, (Japanese boys). Ed used to give them the finger.

When the Japanese Air Command bombed Pearl Harbor, Japanese Citizens in California were taken away to Tanforan, enclosed, then dispersed to detention camps. Ed liked a Japanese farmer named Jim Tamakaut, "who was such a nice man and who carried no animosity about the United States actions regarding the Japanese people." Ed did not like to see Jim included in the sweep of undesirables but he derived a certain sense of pleasure in taunting the Japanese boys behind those wires at Tanforan.

For recreation, Ed was a regular participant in swimming at the popular Hot Mineral Springs Bath House where he enjoyed other events held at the adjoining picnic and softball field in Boyes Hot Springs near Sonoma. After graduating from St. Vincents, Edward finished high school at Sacred Heart Catholic School in San Francisco.

Edward had a cousin who lived in nearby Martinez, California. Timothy Walsh was at Pearl Harbor during the December 7th, 1941 bombing. Timmy had been on watch aboard Destroyer, USS Mc Donough, DD 351. Timmy visited his cousin Edward. Either going to church or on a walk, Timothy spoke about and his cousin, Ed agreed, "What a hellva time it was in Pearl on that Sunday." Timothy declared, "this action of the Japanese was impossible to believe!" Timmy had seen the Arizona in Pearl Harbor capsize and he talked in great detail about the rest of the damaged ships. Edward could hardly believe that men had been buried inside some of the ships which had been turned upside down. Timmy's own ship had been bombed that day but it had not sunk. According to Timmy, the USS Mc Donough DD351 "didn't even have a chance to get out of that bombing action at Pearl." Timmy's influence over Ed, a sophomore in high school at the time was measurably strong. Both of the boys had wanted to join the Navy together. But Timmy being older was already in war battles before Edward had even graduated! Timmy also stated, "Food was better in the Navy." In those days, at age fourteen, anywhere with the promise of "better food" was alluring. Edward felt pretty hungry sometimes.

Two years after their conversation about Pearl Harbor, words spoken by Timmy still burned in Ed's mind. Edward absolutely wanted to be in the Navy. What if somebody hit his home? What if someone scorched him? Or buried him alive? He enlisted. He went to Shoemaker near Pleasanton, California and was sent to the San Diego Naval Training Station. He decided, "that was the training center where all the 'yokels' went." He did however, get to meet the famous tap dancer Gene Kelly, which he described as "a regular guy like the rest of us."

When the young Navy man left San Diego and arrived back at Bethlehem Steel at 16th and Illinois Streets in San Francisco for introduction into 'sweat labor', a ship that had been hit in the Philippines by a kamikaze came into port. That battered ship made another strong impression on the new Navy recruit. That ship took a hit down in the Flight Deck and further down into the Hanger Deck. Edward's crew at Bethlehem Steel replaced parts and repaired the ship. It headed back to sea.

The Ships Company then assigned the young man as electrician on the "Old Sal." The Sal was really named USS Salamaua. She was a Baby Attack Carrier. The Naval recruits boarded 'Old Sal" at Sand Point Naval Base in Seattle, Washington. The Salamaua carried antiaircraft guns; 20 and 40 MM guns were installed. The Salamaua carried supplies and additional airplanes which were supposed to stay well behind any enemy lines.

Edward was assigned duty in a basic Engineering Section of the Sal. His crew was known as "the Black Gang". They worked on the boilers and engines of the ship which tended to blacken their hands and faces. On the ship's company, Edward was busily learning skills from veteran engineers in the boiler room. The "Black Gang" referred to each other as "snipes" because they considered they did 'sweat labor' like the Blacks. Only difference was the 'snipes' were over the main fuel and oil procedures when the ship was in progress. They noted the Black people worked very hard and did their 'sweat labor' over hot stoves in the kitchens. There was a San Francisco real Black guy named Kelly who made friends with Edward. He lived opposite the ship on Portside. Kelly was the Mess Cook. By watching Kelly, Ed discovered "San Francisco (Northern) Blacks and Blacks from the Southern states did not mingle. Blacks were not treated too well by the Southern not-too-genteel Officers, either. Blacks, like Kelly, simply did not mingle but stayed close to General Quarters."

Edward finally got to see what was left of the ships in Pearl Harbor as the Salamaua dropped anchor into port for a couple of weeks. Edward was not too interested in standing still in port; he just mostly "wanted to go at it!" He was now out in the vast Pacific Ocean where Timmy was located. (He just didn't realize the ocean would be so big!) He was impatient for a first encounter with the enemy! Edward saw all kinds of islands and ships in the Pacific waters. The men in the boiler room section were anxious to hear what went on with the war. They spent a lot of time kibitzing about what they heard. Having no big battles or incidents experienced themselves, the attitude of most of the 'snipes' was, "So what! Really?" The Salamaua crew had only very minor scrapes until coming to the end of their journey toward the Philippines. They headed straight toward Okinawa. What still rang in Edward's ears were the words of Timmy, "the USS Mc Donough DD351 didn't even get a chance to get out of that bombing at Pearl!"

The Baby Attack Carrier with an accompanying two destroyers forged straight ahead into a typhoon! The intense storm split the carrier in half. Edward Kenny, a Catholic and his friend electrician, a Greek Orthodox found their split ship, hit in the middle of the bulkhead was worse than the one they worked on that had been hit by the kamikaze. The typhoon was calendared on June 6, 1945. General Quarters was at a 30 degree angle. The Salamaua, submarine hunting at the time, had launched some of their aircraft.

The typhoon was described by Ed as "feeling like an earthquake, or like somebody dropped dynamite...

Or, going like this." He moved his hands like an epileptic. The Navy men went through a shock period of unbelief. The crew had to use a concept called "aftersteering." Like two props in the back of a bus or caboose, aftersteering was used to somewhat control tons of water which sloshed around inside the ship caused by the action of the rolling winds and waves. The men on the Salamaua were in the typhoon for four days. It was considered the worst typhoon of the Pacific Ocean. It lasted, and lasted and lasted. The general consensus was everybody wanted to go back home. Everyone, many having different religions, was praying. In between times, the Whities would yell to the Blacks, "Hey, Nigger, bring me a sandwich." The crew ate bologna sandwiches wet. Ed asked, "Did you ever try to eat a wet bologna sandwich mixed with salt water?" Louie Montana, his Greek Orthodox friend and Edward promised each other, "if we ever get out of this mess, we will visit each other's churches..." Which they actually did.

The clean-up of the ship after the typhoon was a job beyond belief. The flight deck was not flat anymore as the broad surface looked wrinkled and twisted. Airplanes that had remained tied down on the ship were busted and broken. The planes supposedly secured, tied on top and bottom, were splattered around the deck like long strings of spaghetti. Planes leaving the deck that morning must have gone somewhere else or got lost in the storm as they never returned. The crew lost two fellows who had been whacked up against the bulkheads. They were put in a sheet, slid across and over the overhanging Fantail for burial in the throbbing grey sea. The service was for the men. It was not pleasant to see the bodies disappear into the ocean.

When the men viewed the Beach at Okinawa it was just too much! LSD's and other naval vessels were torn apart and ripped up. Humans were standing around in a state of shock and they kept repeating, "Nothing you can do, nothing you can do." Meanwhile, Ed's Cousin, Timmy had been at Coral Sea in the thick of battle where 96 ships were sunk. Forty-eight of those were Allied ships and 48 were from the Japanese Fleet. Oil was floating from all those sunken vessels all over the beautifully clear seas and sandy beaches. Timmy later reported to Ed, "I even got through another second bombing after that experience!"

Added to the incredible sight of the destruction viewed at Okinawa, men of Salamaua heard that the Indianapolis which had carried the atomic bomb from Hunters Point, San Francisco had been torpedoed and sunk. Scuttlebutt followed that only twelve or thirteen guys on the Indianapolis were reported exonerated. Gossip further continued that the Captain was in trouble. (The Captain was later depicted as a man driven crazy who committed suicide.) According to Edward, "He had wanted to get his name clean. The Captain came from a family of great Navy men." Edward's anticipation for being in the thick of battle or 'something' was not further enhanced by these rumors nor by the fate of persons aboard USS Indianapolis.

On September 2nd, 1945, Edward just eighteen years old was an onlooking participant of history. All available ships of the United States Pacific Fleet were congregated in Tokyo Harbor for the signing of the peace treaty by Japanese Officials on the USS Missouri. The Baby Attack Carrier, Salamaua, was directly astern the Fantail of the huge Battleship USS Missouri. Ed was on the Salamaua Flight Deck where men took turns watching the signing of the peace documents as well as close-up viewing with binoculars. Ed got to watch the Japanese Officials sign the documents ending the war. They were directed by Five Star General Douglas MacArthur, the controlling Commander in Chief of the Pacific Region. According to Ed, "It appeared, MacArthur moved and directed the ceremony like a God."

For a couple of hours before leaving Tokyo Bay, the men from the Salamaua were allowed visits to

Nagasaki and Hiroshima. They came away from those scenes in reverential fear and dread. "The towns were charcoal. Looking around what had been reported to be towns were scenes "like viewing a black flat desert," Ed recalled.

Then. like a magic carpet, an aircraft carrier came to deliver 1200 to 1300 fellows home. To Edward "this was very accommodating." As per usual, a stop at Pearl called "for a last Cat House visit for many of the snipes." Then, it was to San Francisco like an everyday shuttle run. Those discharged from the Salamaua were told they could visit their parents, so Edward went straight to Sausalito in a little boat called USS Randall APA 224. The very next day, he was with a group being shipped right back to the Pacific. Edward did not get to see his relatives even though he was very close to where they all lived. The newly selected Naval group were heading for the Marshall Islands and a little atoll. Bikini, was only two miles in length. Their job description was to continue to help evacute the area around the Island of Bikini where a bomb having more megatons than the atomic bomb had been detonated. The men were instructed to put on blinders designed as masks and to minister to the peoples evacuated from the atoll. One-hundred miles before their arrival to Bikini, the Sailors watched a mushroom cloud which appeared as a big mass of smoke. It was truly weird, high up and spread out. The men were advised to turn opposite and away from the spectacle for their own protection. This was a very strange phenonomen as one usually viewed the horizon at 32 miles. "To see this sphecter arising away from the earth, yet over the horizon "was akin to the world being dammed," according to Edward.

When the Navy men saw the big mushroom cloud everything else in the world seemed small in comparison. Before their arrival, the government had cleaned the island ahead of the bomb drop. People, pigs, the other domestic animals seemed so very small and insignificant now. The crew moved displaced and contaminated people onto their ship. As the ship moved back away from Bikini, people being moved could then see the bomb's evidence. Ed repeated, "Japan was charcoal six days prior to the treaty. While watching the peace treaty being signed aft the Missouri, his ship felt like a very small ship and the Missouri a very large battleship. Now, the Island of Bikini seemed so small and the bomb's evidence so big!"

The atomic bomb remained an influence in Edward's life. Timmie, his cousin worked on the bomb after his service in the Navy was terminated. He made it through Pearl Harbor and the Coral Sea. He died of cancer from his employment on nuclear devices.

Back at Puget Sound, Ed became a Reservist after World War II. He was called into Korea. His assigned ship, now the USS Ramora, a United States submarine 524 was readied for sailing Edward across the Pacific once more. The Captain called everybody on ship, except for two electricians. The two electricians did not have to go! Edward was one of those two electricians!

Ed became a sheetmetalist and airconditioning apprentice in San Francisco after his service experiences. He re-visited the Tanforan Race Track. Edward retired in an adult community near Sonoma, California because of the warm weather. His first wife, Henriette died of Alzheimer's disease. He met his second wife, Lorraine at a Golf Course in Marin. Lorraine was blessed with ten grandchildren. She had five children, three girls, Denise, Margie and Darlene and two boys, Peter and Melvin. All of her children and grandchildren live close by. Edward's daughter, Jacqueline, who lives in San Francisco, blessed the family with two more grandchildren. Twelve grandchildren keep the Kenny family a busy one. In Sonoma, Edward tends bar at Moose Lodge and is Starter at Adobe Golf Course. He enjoys raising vegetables, apples and flowers in his enclosed yard and he takes care of vineyards belonging to Raffini. A little side life of making vineyard wines corked in tall dark bottles is definitely the right activity in the famous Wine Country of California. He's definitely in the right area for this kind of activity.

The National Geographic Magazine, January 1995, reported that the March 1, 1954 blast of a 15 megaton hydrogen bomb, code-named Bravo was the most powerful bomb ever set off by the United States government. It was reported to have had a thousand times more force than the "fat boy" atomic bomb which fell on Hiroshima. The bomb that Ed saw on the horizon that day was detonated on Bikini. It opened a "mile-wide crater," vaporized a small island and part of another one. Fifty years later, "the soil on Bikini contains too much radioactive cesium to permit the 2,025 Bikinians to return." Even though the Lagoon has healed somewhat by the larger ocean waters and fish are seen "eclipsing in the sun," some reef areas have nothing but pulverized sand and coral where invertebrates such as clams and other marine life classifications are unable to catch hold in the still undesirable ecosystem.

National Geographic Society, *National Geographic,* January 1995, pps. 149. Article entitled, *At Nuclear Ground Zero,* Text in a group of stories with photographs by Bill Curtsinger. pp. 63.

Vincent Tuminello

United States Army, 1942 - 1945

As a boy, Vincent wanted to fly a plane. Born in Brooklyn, New York in 1916, Vincent Tuminello was son of a Sicilian immigrant. His dad, a stone mason chiseled cemetary vaults and memorial stones while his youngest son wandered off to watch sea and land planes fly into Jamaica Bay. It always fascinated the boy to see the wheels go up in a plane as it rose high in the sky.

While yet an impressionable youth, Vincent saw a good looking flier at Floyd Bennett Field. The brownbearded man was Italo Balbo with an acclaimed great Italian Air-Armada. The flier, Balboa had 24 fliers with him who had made trans-Atlantic flights. Balboa commandeered his armada from Rome to Rio de Janeiro and this time from Rome to Chicago. He and the flight group stopped in New York in an event which was carnival in nature. Sadie, Vincent's wife has a keepsake chiffon handkerchief with the flier's picture on it. She has kept the souvenir for over sixty years. Actually, this famous aviator, Balboa became an Italian Fascist Leader and Aviator in 1922 and he helped to bring Mussolini to power.

When Vincent was not watching planes come and go, he was home with five brothers and his father. His mother had died in 1937. When World War II happened, Vincent was kept at home, even by draft board members disqualifying him for service as they knew the situation in the Tuminello household. Vincent helped take care of one of his brothers who was crippled. His only embarrassment was with the general population. When Vincent went up and down the streets of Brooklyn, he was asked, "Why aren't you in the service?" Without waiting for an answer the neighbors chattered on, "You look old enough to go to war. What are you doing here?" One day at age 26, Vincent begged the draft board, " take me. Do me a favor," he stated; "Take me!"

Before this time his father was hurt by a hit and run driver. He kept crying out, "Oh my leg, oh my leg!" After much anguish and pain the doctor finally opened up his cast. Gangerine was found inside it. Everything seemed to be moving into difficult circumstances for the family as many of the brothers were working on defense projects and were not available for the household. His father went to the hospital and to bed. Brother Pete was left to take care of his ailing dad and brother when Vincent went to bootcamp.

Vincent had a friend named Sal. During childhood, kids met on vacant lots to play kickball or when walking down the street, they played kick the can. Vincent noticed a young girl who lived on the avenue where city trolley cars traveled. This girl stood within the shadows of curtained windows in a big two story house as she watched trolley cars filled with colorful people moving back and forth. Her home was in the heart of (Flatbush) Brooklyn. Vincent noticed the girl and told his friend Sal, "See that girl watching traffic going by? See her? God darn it! I'm going to marry that girl!" The girl turned out to be Sal's sister Sadie!

Sadie was not sure about her brother's friend. When that impetous fellow did ask her for a date, often the rascal did not show up. Sadie's mother would ask, "Why would you want to go with a guy like that?" Before Sadie's mother died, she whispered to Vincent, "You are my best son-in-law."

On the day that Vincent was drafted, he asked Sadie to wait for him. She said, "No." But being an enterprising young man, he delivered to her a diamond ring and that made all the difference! Sadie waited for Vincent for three whole years.

When the powers-that-be decided upon Vincent's assignment, they took into consideration that in civilian life he had been a heavy duty truck driver. So, after bootcamp at Camp Upton, New York the young recruit was sent to Fort Custer, Michigan to learn about Quartermastering. He was assigned to the 513th Quartermaster Regiment. He was also given basic training at Camp Phillips, Kansas where he was promoted to Corporal and became a 50 caliber antiaircraft machine gunner. When Vincent was shipped overseas, he became a part of the 3892nd QM Truck Company and was assigned to the 1st Division of the 16th Infantry preparing for the D-Day invasion of Normandy. He was among those actively engaged in the first assault on Omaha Beach.

Vincent was stationed in England for about seven months. He became violently ill. His diagnosis read Enteritis, acute catarrh. In layman's terms, that meant he was striken with ptomaine food poisoning. Guys were falling like flies. There were 82 men stricken down from the 1st, 2nd and 5th Rangers. Up and down the rows the sick were questioned in depth, "What did you eat? Did you have beans? Did you eat pork chops?" It was strange, but when leaving the hospital area, Vincent noticed many MPs stationed about the field hospital quonset building. Another strange thing happened when Vincent left. A hospital nurse ran up to him and apologized to him as to the way he had been treated. This action was a little strange and a bit remarkable. He had no idea what she was talking about...

Before Vincent had been taken to the hospital for food poisoning, his Division had been billeted near Sherborne Dorset in the southwestern corner of England. While Vincent was in the hospital absent from camp, orders had been given for the men of the 1st Division 96th Infantry to prepare for an exercise along with the 4th Division in an amphibious landing at Slapton Sands. The action was planned to take place between Dartmouth and Plymouth.

On the 27th of April, skies were clear and the sea was calm. American small craft heading for Lyme Bay off Devon were supposed to be accompanied by a network of British Destroyers. Devon was on the southwest coast of England. The area had been evacuated for Allied exercises. If he had not been lying in a hospital bed, Vincent believes he would have been on one of the LSTs along with his truck as part of the amphibious forces.

Vincent was #11 of his squad and that was his truck bumper number. He was in charge of a group of seven men. He visualizes he would have experienced the same confusion as his comrades when torpedos from German E-Boats (Enemy Boats) passed under and then hit a couple of landing ship tanks. In 1944, Vincent was unaware that his food poisoning malady would keep him in the dark about this operation turned traumatic for a period of 43 years. This practice mission at Slapton Sands was kept so secret, it was as if the event never happened. Even after the successful Normandy Invasion this practice was not made public.

Actually, Vincent's illness may have saved his life. The United States Government kept an official silence on what has been referred to as the "the least known and most disastrous single incident of World War II." The secret was a rehearsal for the D-Day invasion of Normandy. The Devon incident, Operation:Tiger ended up with final estimations of anywhere from 749 to 800 deaths and missing Americans. Bodies are believed to have been disposed of so quickly in a meadow bulldozed for a mass grave. The casualties at Utah Beach for which Tiger's participants had been training turned out to be only a fraction of those from the incident on Slapton Sands of April 28th.

General Dwight D. Eisenhower ordered the botched-up ill-planned rehearsal maneuvers to be hushed up for the duration of the war. When Operation:Tiger was exposed it was discovered poor planning, inexperience and plain old bad luck, partly caused by incompetent persons on shore had caused the horrendous disaster. New life vests had been issued with no instructions for wearing them. Hundreds of soldiers were drowned wearing their lifebelts around their waists when they should have been wearing them under their arms. Clericals on shore gave Americans in LSTs the wrong radio frequency. The one English Ship, Azalea that accompanied the group for protection of the convoy had the right radio frequency. They did not give Americans notice of the approaching German E-Boats believing that all the Allieds had the correct radio frequency. The English Government later issued apologies to the Americans for problems related to SNFUs regarding ships that did not show up to protect the small craft. German torpedo boats slipped through the poorly guarded convoy. Undetected, the Germans sank two of the American landing craft. Confusion added to mayhem. Americans died from direct gunfire spent upon the LSTs by the Germans. It was reported that the Azalea stayed away from the attack zone and zigzagged the ship as was custom in 1942 to miss torpedo shells from the submarines. Nor did the Azalea pick up or help Americans with drowning survivors. Another British ship appeared after 3 AM in the morning to help with that grizzly chore.

Before this bungled mess was over, a very bizarre and unusual scene took place on shore at the hospital where Vincent was in recovery. Described by one of the then-attending-Medics, in an article entitled *What Happened off Devon* by Ralph C. Greene and Oliver E. Allen, published in 1984, forty Medics were under stern orders from Colonel James Kendall. His message was "We're in the war at last. In less than an hour, we'll receive hundreds of emergency cases of shock due to immersion, compounded by explosion wounds." He went on to say that SHAEF, the Supreme Headquarters, Allied Expeditionary Force had demanded that he speak to them. Colonel Kendall demanded the Medics "to treat the soldiers as veterans. Ask no questions of your patients, take no personal histories, ask nothing about their injuries no matter how terrible in severity. Have no discussions about casualties or reasons for these injuries during your treatment of the men." These commands were subject to courts-martial for disobedience and subject to further orders.

Adding to the strategy for silence were threats made to the victims of the mishap. Conversation revealing or detailing the event would lead to court-martial. Counter-intelligence troops with bayoneted rifles surrounded the hospital compound, then ambulances and trucks came to the facility with "wet shivering, blue-skinned, blanketed and bandaged young Army and Navy men." According to Ralph C. Greene, M.D., one of the attending physicians, "Except for Medics calling out to each other for materials or help, there was no talking." Sighs and groans of the soldiers and sailors were the only sounds audible. Doctors found it odd working in such a strange vacuum. Some men died. Others were sent back to their units or whereever the Commanders ordered. When the survivors of Operation:Tiger returned to the 1st Division after their mis-adventure at Slapton Sands there was no usual scuttlebutt. Not a word filtered down to Vincent about their activities at the exercise.

Years after the Devon Invasion, a woman, Dorothy Seekings who in 1944 was a young eleven year old daughter of a baker in Stoke Fleming declared she had seen several dozen wet uniformed bodies stacked in the back of a truck. Another account declares she saw wet soldiers piled on top of each other in a mass grave while delivering bread on April 29th. A local fisherman who returned to his exiled home after the war entangled his fishing nets in the turret of a sunken tank in about 70 feet of water. This tank may have been lost earlier in the day, being referred to in the Butcher account. Butcher, an aide to Eisenhower acknowledges he was at the ill-fated practice in a boat along with General Bradley. His account does not appear to take place at the time of the torpodeo run by the Germans on the Allieds. Harry C. Butcher's book, *My Three Years with Eisenhower* was sketchy and described Operation:Tiger with other happenings of that day in a somewhat unimportant manner.

In the 1985, February/March Issue of American Heritage Magazine, Dr. Ralph C. Greene, a Chicago pathologist reconstructs the story from his participation and research. By happen-stance, in 1980, Doctor Greene was in Washington D.C. researching information for a book about outbreaks of malaria and hepatitus during the war. He ran across the remaining secrets of World War II which had been released in 1974 under the Freedom of Information Act. Excitment and successes of D-Day landings had long overshadowed the "cloak of secrecy" lifted in 1974 of the Devon disaster. Dr. Greene, one of those Medics in the 228th Station Hospital (the same hospital that treated Vincent for food poisoning) being ordered on that April day in 1944 to join the other Medics in the mysterious silence had long wondered about the men they had treated on April 28th, 1944. Why had they come? Where did the patients go? Excitement was high as the doctor set out to learn what was referred to in documents as Operation:Tiger. Doctor Greene wanted to know more because he stated in the article, "that curious day is just as clear to me now as if it were yesterday."

The doctor was evidently so excited about finding the material regarding April 27th, 1944 that he immediately shelved his research on diseases and began researching Operation:Tiger. He discovered the Schnellboot (German fast boat) Commander Gunther Rabe of Germany's Navy was in the service of NATO. Commander Rabe also remembered and described to him the German version of what happened on that night. The Germans had not been touched by all the firing that came their way from the American LSTs. The Germans obtained no prisoners. Doctor Greene talked to English people including the woman who was the eleven year old girl who saw the wet fully clothed bodies stacked in a mass grave.

In the newspaper article *Little Known Disaster of WWII* on this same subject, Ken Small an innkeeper at Torcross was noted as having found coins and military cartridge shells sparkling in the sun and sand. Through the years, he began to collect U.S. brass insignia and even men's gold signet rings that kept washing up on the beach at Slapton Sands. Ken Small found out that people living along the beach had been evacuated by British authorities. The natives declared tens of thousands of American troops had been housed in deserted farmhouses for D-Day preparation. When local people returned to their homes, some farmers found blood on floors of their buildings. Through the work of Small, it was discovered the American military had not exactly kept the exercise secret beyond the war but the military never went out of its way to disclose this unfavorable aspect of the war to the public. Nor, had the country given honor to those who lost their lives there. The innkeeper has been given full credit for needling the United States Government for a permanent memorial established in honor of the approximate 800 dead. It has been reported, the Pentagon states they moved the mass-grave-bodies to other European cemeteries. The locals say they have never seen any activity in this regard. The last casualty of the exercise was reported as Rear Admiral Don P. Moon who was overall command of the Naval part of the operation. He was given a lesser command and received a verbal reprimand by his superior in the presence of his Officers of lesser command. A few months later, he reportedly took his own life, being the only high-ranking officer to commit suicide during World War II.

For more information on Operation:Tiger including the 1st and 4th Infantry, an article occurred in

Newsday European Bureau by Adrian Peracchio. The article describes the innkeepers activities, the baker's daughter and it refers to the 1946 book entitled *My Three Years with Eisenhower*, written by Captain, Harry C. Butcher, a naval aide to 'Ike'. Vincent has lived with this strange phenomenon in the shadows of his life knowing at the same time, he's glad his guardian angel had other missions for him in life. He's glad he missed the secret invasion of Devon. At the same time, he has collected the information referred to in the above paragraphs.

Vincent was riding high as an Army trooper on a Rhino (landing barge) toward Omaha Beach at 1900 hours on June 6th, 1944. (He has received the medal for being on Normandy Beach on D-Day). Night was approaching at 1900 hours when his vehicle was one of the first three off the ship. The first vehicle went straight ahead to see if there were any shell holes or mines that might be unseen under the waters. The second vehicle went to the left, the third vehicle splashed down to the right. As the men guided their trucks on this last lap towards the shoreline with the First Infantry attached to the 1st Division of the 16th Infantry, there were two men to a truck. There were seven men assigned one squad leader and Vincent was leader of his squad. All total, there were three machine guns for antiaircraft with his particular group. There were six vehicles on each side, twelve trucks, four squads. The machinery did not carry the big guns. The small materials could be lost in the four feet of water without as much damage as the loss of the big guns. These smaller trucks were carrying ammunition, TNT and a load of grave markers. In all, there were fifty-two trucks carrying a bit of everything on the ship. The men referred to the whole convoy of trucks as a "fruit cocktail." Every fourth truck had a machine gun. Not all of the trucks were sent in to the beach at one time. They were carrying lifeblood materials and it would have been foolhardy to send in all the materials and trucks at one time. The 29th landing was off course about 1/2 mile. Vincent reminded himself "the whole invasion was 1/4 to 1/2 mile off course from where they were supposed to have come in."

Comrades in the waters had run into obstacles made of rails or heavy angle iron and logs driven into the tidal flats all along Normandy Beach. Most of the obstacles were mined with Teller mines and set within 250 yards out from the big-water line. These materials would blow or stave in the bottoms of landing craft. For months, Germans had intensively fortified this area. There were fortifications connected by underground tunnels. At the entrance of draws, the enemy had constructed concrete blockhouses and pill-boxes. Flat areas between the high-water line and bases of cliffs were heavily mined with antipersonnel and tank mines. Barbed wire entanglements had been barriers to the first wave of troops that disenbarked from their boats in these waters. They had waded ashore in water up to their waists or deeper. Those poor souls were the ones who first met death within these obstacles.

A great deal of equipment was lost to the high seas. Capsized boats had hit mined obstacles. Engineers had braved the circumstances and slowly opened up gaps with whatever equipment was retained. Minefields and other wire entanglements were blown up by Engineers and Infantry during the day while enemy fire rained down directly onto the troops. By 1400 hours the enemy fortifications along the cliffs were destroyed or reduced to a point of little resistence or value. As Vincent bobbed in the water toward the Beach, he recognized Seebeas in assualt boats with wounded and tagged people being brought out to the ship. Vincent exclaimed, "Oh, my God! these poor guys are dead!" Tankers were seen drowned and bodies were floating in the red blooded water as the Quartermasters landed on the beach. An LST was burning further down on the beach in the distance...

Vincent was riding on his gun mount. He was briefed what to do for support of troops already on land. He was directed what access road to move onto. There were more bodies along the route, this time it was German dead. The men were told to dig in up on a hill. It was now dusk. Vincent kept digging and digging with a pick and shovel. He kept sputtering, "I'm hitting, I'm hitting!" He was getting no where in the process of digging a foxhole so he crawled under his truck. A Lieutenant came over and stated, "You were battering a land mine. Are you trying to blow yourself up?!" Then, a Captain came out of somewhere and ordered everybody out, "go higher up on the hill." Then, they were ordered, "get out of here, now!" Later a Colonel told Vincent, "you should get off that gun, you are a target." Vincent told the Colonel his orders were to "stay on the gun." Unaccustomed to war, the young man was not sure what to do... As the trucks moved toward some hedgerows, gunfire was coming toward them from German artillery guns. Driving was extremely hazardous as there were holes all over the land. For one thing, just prior to the invasion during the month of May, the Air Forces reportedly dropped more than 37,000 tons of bombs in the area. Guarding equipment was also very difficult. Even some of the other divisions already needed some of your equipment! As the Quartermasters moved away from the mines, Vincent was the last man out.

The next day was D-Day+1 and Vincent was still riding high up on the gun. He could see French houses up against one another on the right. He saw dead children lying in front of demolished French houses. A Sergeant was screaming, "Stop! Stop! Get out of the vehicle. Germans in the Village!" Two 29th G Is remarked to Vincent, "How did you get over that gun mount so fast?" The young soldier from Brooklyn did not know he could move that fast himself! Vincent climbed down in a ready-made foxhole with the two other guys. Everything was under control until it was safe to go again. Another G I. was hit. He didn't make it at this stop. Trucks and tanks came to rest behind some hedgerows the second day and camouflage materials made of nets were placed over them. The First Division was now all back together to itself. The trucks were all lined up when 88s started coming in. It was the first time the group would hear the sound of those blood-curdling screaming meemies. Vincent said, "Our Captain, the Second Lieutenant and Lieutenants were greenhorns." Things were being thrown on top of Tuminello's truck as men were yelling "let's get the hell out of here!"

Each individual trooper carried one canteen of water along with five magazines of ammunition. One magazine of ammunition was already in the chamber of the gun. Vincent had a personal carbine gun. Every fourth truck had an extra 50 calibre barrel machine gun (not air cooled) and a bazooka plus seven pounds of TNT. Other trucks carried between three and four tons of K-Rations. Oh yes, and there was a ramrod to clean the guns.

On the third day, the men were becoming slimy inside their impregnated clothing. The soldiers were wearing special invasion clothing made of some kind of material that did not breathe. The material was chemicalized to protect the soldier against use of mustard gas. Their machine gun gloves were made of asbestos just in case their guns got too hot. These gloves were also treated like the rest of the clothing. The invasion forces were dressed in fatigues which included pants, shirt and makinaw coat. Shoes were pregnated. After about three days on shore another Quartermaster unit collected the chemicalized clothing and issued new clean clothes to the troops. A Laundry Quartermaster unit picked up and returned the dirty clothing back to the ships off the beach. A lot of Polish soldiers (not Germans) were marching in droves to the beach area. These were prisoners-of-war being taken back to England. Rather than having to deal with prisoners in stockades on the battle front, the prisoners were being shipped out of the way. As Quartermaster truckers passed the Polish Soldiers, they were being warmly greeted. Polish marchers took off their hats, waved them and greeted the Americans in a congratulatory manner.

A combat truck company was prepared for tanks. It had ammunition that could blow through hedges with white phosperous shells. Each truck leader was issued a grey grenade to throw into the engine of his vehicle if being overtaken by the enemy.

After D-Day +3, the Quartermaster Corps of the 3892nd were on the move. Their route included Isigny, through Dorset France to Burnesq, Balleroy, Annebecq, Sees, Gif, and many more small towns to St. Dennis. Again, Vincent rode high and proudly on his equipment in the famous Victory parade through Paris. He was surprised that buildings were intact. Paris was unlike other French cities of destruction which they had just passed through. The young Brooklynite was surprised the famous city was so beautiful. People were smiling and greeting troops down the broad Champs-Elyse'es Boulevard while throwing flowers. Drinks were handed to the men. The Quartermaster fellows raised their drinks high but their trucks did not stop.

The 3892nd QM Truck Company attached to the First Division of the 16th Infantry just kept on traveling. They spent a lot of time moving back and forth between Bastogne and other cities of Belgium. It was in these forest-covered lands with snow accompanied by bitter low temperatures that the enemy breakthrough occurred in the Battle of the Bulge. The Quartermaster units were alerted and moved into the city of Eupen to defend it. Parties searched for Paratroopers that had been dropped behind Allied lines. During the Battle of the Bulge passwords were changed every three days. Vincent's most vivid memory took place when his Captain ordered him to set up four machine guns in the Eupen Woods. When pass words were used counter signs were made if challenged. One time, Vincent was challenged by a Colonel. He pulled out his dog tags and even referred to the number 11 on the bumper of his truck. One thing was certain. Vincent's side had the guns. He said to the Colonel, "If we are the enemy, you are gone. Let me show you. Turn your head to the right. If I go, you go with me." There were four machine guns pointed in the Colonel's direction. 100 feet away there were 50 calibre guns pointed at him. "Looks good," the Colonel said as he smartly saluted and walked away. Vincent had a lot of fun over this episode. The Quartermaster did not have time to make booze. They made some homes of logs, tarps and miscellaneous materials to keep out the cold of that hard winter weather. In fact, they were laying low when the German's broke through their lines.

In Hofen, they were privileged to occupy houses (some were partial facades thereof) since first invading the continent.

Early in the invasion as he was standing on the seat behind his 50 calibre gun, Vincent learned that his group was one of the "Bastard Units." What Vincent meant by that expression was that he was ordered to work with all divisions in whatever direction needed. One of his bastardized special jobs was to meet the 606th Grave Yard Registration Unit and drive a load of bodies to their final resting place. The bodies were first taken out of the battlefield and were processed before shipping day. On shipping day, bodies were given Identification numbers and then thrown into his truck. Helmets and shoes were removed from the fallen soldiers and then they were wrapped in a mattress cover. There were four companies included in this detail. German SS Troops had slaughtered 250 G Is in a front line combat unit. These fallen soldiers were laid end-for-end in a long trench about 1/4 mile in length.

On a happier occasion at Wetzlar, the Quartermaster ended up in a German Army Camp but the Germans had hastily exiled. Food was still cooking. Foodstuffs and wines were on the tables. Vincent declared, "we ate hot food, liberated cases of foodstuffs, casks of wine and beer. Our stay was very short. We left the next day for Allendorf and were billeted in a slave labor house used by Germans."

During the Battle of the Bulge, the 28th Division was sent somewhere. The Lieutenant had the trucks lined up. He admitted they did not have much ammunition. Shells were going all around. Gas masks were in use. They went here, they went there. "You name it," Vincent says; "I was there carrying troops and ammunition." I saw men were short on golashes which were promised but never came. Bodies laying on the ground were frozen. For three years past the war after the Battle of the Bulge, Central Intelligence was still combing the whole area for bodies left behind in the rubble."

Other troops tell of crossing the Remagen Bridge while it was still intact. Vincent's squad crossed the river on pontoons (steel runners hooked together like big rafts) after the bridge fell.

On Allied grounds an individual which looked like a Corporal of the Guard was trying to keep warm while standing behind the exhaust of the car pool of the squad. After being halted the stranger was discovered to be a deserted German hiding his uniform under a long overcoat. He said he had come home. A Jewish Soldier wanted to kill the intruder on the spot. The Quartermaster took the prisoner to G2 Intelligence. No one knew if he was a spy or not or what became of him.

In Stavlot, Vincent dropped down into a 20 foot deep hole. He was in the middle of an ammunition dump which had a large assortment of ammunition. There were 105 MM for artillery all around the field. A Black Labor Battalion worked the dump. They heard an explosion down the road. Everybody, including Vincent jumped in the hole. There were steps in this deep underground bunker on which to exit. After everything quieted down the Quartermasters proceeded to pick up the artillery shells they had come for and they started on their return trip down the road.

A woman was screaming near an old farmhouse. She kept saying, "American Aviator, American Aviator!" Vincent decided to check out the circumstances. "Cover me," Vincent sang out as he approached the house and the woman. He saw a nice looking guy about 25 years old. "Put your hands on your head and come out," Vincent declared; "Give the pass word." The young man did not even challenge. The guy took his hands off his head and enthusiastically hugged Vincent. He was an American Aviator from Lie'ge, Belgium who had been pummeted from the skies by German fire. When Vincent took the man back to the Command Post, the Captain declared, "What in the hell do you want me to do with him?" The Aviator wanted to go back to the Ninth Airforce in Lie'ge. Vincent said, "Don't worry, Captain I'll take care of him." Vincent took the American to Stablot and asked an MP directing traffic to get the fellow a ride back to Belgium. As Vincent and the Pilot traveled toward the town, the Pilot stated he had been a fighter escort. He was from Cincinatti, Ohio. The squadron of fliers had seen a German train and peeled off to straif it. How he got hit, he did not know. Someone on the radio yelled "climb to 7,000 feet and bail out! That was what he did. He was thrown into a ditch. He saw entanglements of wire and thought he was in a booby trap. His smashed plane was described as two wings left lying on the ground. Vincent forgot to ask the aviator's name.

Then, his company was assigned the task of emptying the American gasoline dump in anticipation of a German attack. Of the fifty-two trucks assigned this job only eight got through. Four of the trucks that made it were from his own squad of twelve vehicles. The five gallon cans of gasoline were shuttled back from behind enemy lines under fire. (The Company was awarded the Meritorious Service Medal for Valor.) Vincent returned to the empty dumpsite in enemy fire to rescue Captain Wilson's stranded labor company.

Equipment was wearing out, tanks, guns and radios needed repair. G Is who had been cold, tired, hungry and scared in 6 inches of snow for most of the winter held on. Some waded freezing rivers at night, shoulder deep in the waters. Sometimes, they found raw turnips and potatoes which were foraged from the fields. Americans were holding on and the war was coming to an end.

After battle with Germans near Brundesen, Germany where SS Troops surrendered to U.S. Forces the 3892nd Quartermaster Truck Company moved on through Germany. On the day before VE day they moved into Pilsen, Czechslovakia. They were privy to the disorganization and political re-organization activity which took place after the war. The men of the 3892nd felt like they were stuck in Czechslovakia while displaced people were being shipped back to their homelands.

When Vincent came home to Brooklyn, he found Sadie was still wearing his diamond ring. She had planned and made ready a formal wedding held at the Hotel Granada Ballroom. The couple invited 100 people. They had a dance band and lots of food. Sadie found the cost of the liquors was the most expensive part of having a big wedding party.

It took the newly-marrieds three months to find a proper (cellar) apartment in Brooklyn because Vincent refused to take his new bride into some rat infested mouldy barracks made available for G Is as civilians. During this time, Vincent was a Teamster driving freight to five New York Boroughs. He picked up freight from large truck terminals and delivered the merchandise to such prestigious stores as New York's Macys. Everything was received and delivered in big cartons.

According to the relatives, good construction jobs paid higher salaries then truckers, so Vincent spent most of the rest of his working career laying bricks in buildings as high as thirty stories up in the air. One day, when he grew older, he took a job as Maintenance Mechanic for Burns Park at Massapequa, New York. In 1988, Sadie and Vincent moved to Sonoma, California to be near their two sons, Vincent, Jr. and Joseph. About forty family members live in California all the way from Pacific Grove to Chico. The relatives meet each year at the Tuminello home for a big family re-union. Vincent has plenty of room for all on the one and one-half acres that he keeps looking like a park. Once, the editor saw Vincent trying to push his 14 horsepower tractor out of a rain soaked grass lined ditch. He was not acting his age. He reminded one of a man about fifty.

Two big oak trees shade part of the parklike grounds around the large home. "Rainbows often come up behind the big new house," Sadie remarks as we converse together and see one. Vincent enjoys going to 'Vegas' once in a while. The couple attended the 50th Anniversary in 1994 at Normandy France. Vincent shook hands with President Clinton at that event. Vincent has met Bob Hope twice, once as a soldier and once as a veteran. He shook his hand on both occasions. When the couple visits Europe, they especially like Rome, Italy. Vincent proudly holds five Bronze Stars and the Indian Arrowhead.

Combat Diary, 3892 QM TruckCo., Attached 1st Division 16th Infantry. First page.

Newsday Europe Bureau, Little Known Disaster of WWII, U.S. to mark loss of 749 lives in bungled D-Day Rehearsal; by Adrian Peracchio. (one page refers to continued on Page 13. No time or date on material submitted.

American Heritage, April/May 1984 issue. pps 26-33. Article entitled What Happened off Devon., by Ralph C. Greene and Oliver E. Allen. p. 27,29,32, 34.

The American Battle Monuments Commission, Normandy American Cemetery and Memorial, 1994. pps. 6 and l picture. p. 4, 5.

Turner Publishing Co., Editor Scott Garrett. Veterans of Battle of the Bulge (Ardennes). Turner Publishing Company, Editor Scott Garrett. Article about Vincent Tuminello.

Robert H. Cannard

United States Army Air Force, 1943 - 1946

Robert Cannard was born in Danville, a rural Pennsylvania town with strong agricultural ties. His earliest memory was watching baby chicks running around in a box near the wood stove in a farm kitchen. He must have been about two years old when he became fascinated with that first little flock. Robert has been associated with chickens ever since and would not live where he could not keep this important part of his life. His family had been market gardeners for many generations leading back to the American Revolution.

One of eight siblings, Robert joined the service in 1943 at seventeen years and six months. Robert had five brothers and two sisters. The four older brothers were in the Medical, Navy, Infantry and Army Air Force services. (His brother, Jim, a Pilot was shot down during the war.) Bob joined the Army Air Force at Indiantown Gap, Pennsylvania and took basic training at Kessler Field, Biloxi, Mississippi. During basic training, he never worked with airplanes because he had taken examinations for work as an Air Force Cryptographer. Sent to University of Illinois to cryptographers school, he completed this training and was sent overseas just after his 18th birthday.

Bob was assigned as a cryptographer courier in the China, Burma, India theater. He spent the rest of the war travelling from base to base changing the code machines so that a clerk could type in clear messages, have it transmitted in secret code, and then have the message come out clear again at its destination. Bob travelled from Cairo, Egypt to Kunming, China on a regular cycle. A round trip sometimes took two weeks or longer. Being a courier was a difficult position held in the Far East as Robert's job was to change code machines from base to base to base on a timely schedule. That meant flying in all kinds of weather and under all sorts of conditions.

Robert was on a priority operations permit which allowed him to be dropped one day on one base and another day on another base. There were seven or eight air bases reaching from Calcutta to Karachie, and seven more air bases from Karachi to Cairo. For a period of fifteen months back he'd go again, on the same loop doing the same thing, changing codes. Bases were divided equally between CBI (China, Burma, India) and the Mediterranean. As Robert went from point to point, by land line telegraph or radio, he received messages. His primary job was to change the codes within the code machine on a weekly or less basis. Using a message received from a land line telegraph, he would type in a clear message into the machine. The message was transmitted in updated secret code and out would come a clear updated message. The machine would work automatically after set up with exact code instructions. Robert's job was to syncronize the encoding and decoding.

Time was often the catalyst in winning battles at sea, in the air or on land. Operational messages from the theatre of war had to come in clear. All was classified information which had no value whatsoever, if there was no way to decode the messages. "Japanese are reported as massing at a certain point" or "Japanese Air Power will strike at such and such place" would be a typical message received. There could be as many as 50 messages a day of that type. Most messages were between ten and fifteen words. Robert had access to top secret material such as the movement of troops in Burma and he was privy as to where the ships were at sea. He found the machines used could take intercepted Japanese codes and break the secret information within an hour of a message being sent. One event that triggered very high security was in August when the atomic bomb was used to decimate Japan's cities.

When Yamamoto was shot down, the Cryptographer knew exactly when the Admiral was flying down the Coast and where he intended going. Isorohu Yamamoto had four fighters covering his flight. (He was the Japanese Official that masterminded Pearl Harbor. He built an integrated Air surface arm for the Japanese Navy.) The joy of shooting him down was not only due to the great Pilots in the area but also due to an intelligence break. Robert believes "without the Allies in Burma, the Japanese would have run over the area. The Allies would have lost the Middle East Oil Fields which were critical during Allies and Russian Campaigns. The barrier for Western expansion was considered to be Austrailia. The China, Burma, India Theatre did allow a little breathing room."

In such an isolated terrain as CBI with transportation limited by gasoline, big artillery sweeps or airplane strikes were figured out many miles from the actual front lines. In the theatre of CBI there were twelve or fourteen men who had the same job as Robert. Everyone of the cryptographers came out of the war except for one man killed in an airplane crash. Robert was in one bad storm in an airplane. He lost the hearing in his left ear which probably came from a huge explosion immediately after landing.

The Burma Road was the supply through the back door for Chaing Kai shek's China. Supply for American troops was accomplished mostly by air. There were too many high mountains for vehicular transport of goods and ammunition. The Himalaya Mountains were 19,000 feet over the Hump. It became the graveyard for many heavily laden supply planes. "The Hump," was a name used by Airmen in World War II. It referred to the Himalaya Mountains between China, India or Burma and held an important supply depot.

After the atomic bombing, there was a lessening of pressure on the troops. There were Japanese skirmishes for a week or two after peace was declared. The Americans tended to pull back out of the way as there was no need to lose more lives in a war that was won. When the war was finally over, the Japanese in the jungles and fields of operation did not believe the news. It was at least a week before most of them believed that the Japanese Government had surrendered. Some isolated individuals in those heavily forested places were hid out for years before they finally comprehended the war was over. (Military Police Battalions of Marines were sent in many months after the war with interpreters and bull horns to flush these Japanese soldiers out of caves and forests. Messages, "the war is over, we'll send you home" were resounded in areas of Tinian, Okinawa, Guam and China., Ed.)

Robert recalls a truly recycled town made out of cans. All buildings were made out of cans including the barracks, movie theatre, fences and even the hospital. These cans were square fuel cans filled with sand. According to Robert, "One-hundred percent of all gasoline supplied in Burma was parachuted in these square cans. Air supply to the field troops was truly perfected. Delivery of gasoline by planes was risky. The square cans of gas rolled out of the planes into a lake in big sweeps. After the gas was used by the planes and land vehicles, the cans filled with sand then became building blocks for the Natives. There were plenty of gas cans as there were no filling stations out there in those forests. Air Transport Command Planes flew into and out of the area whenever the weather would allow. They traveled back and forth constantly, so thousands of cans of fuel were consumed and the cans recycled."

Next to letters from home, food was the most important ingredient for stability and a good state of mind for a man away from his country fighting a war. In regard to food, Robert could always tell a new-comer when he came into the field kitchens for his meals. All the bread the troops received had weevils in it. "There were more weevils in a slice of bread," according to Bob; "than a page of numbers. During the first week, the new recruit would not touch the bread. The second week the fellow would pick weevils out of the bread. Some of these weevils picked out would be alive and some dead. The third week the new-comer would go after them. If they tried to get away he would grab them back!" There were recruits who would eat snails and snakes while others couldn't touch 'em!"

When it came time to leave for home, Bob was pretty low on the point system. He did not make it back to the States until April of 1946, six months after the war. In June, he was discharged. Since he did not join the Reserves, he was 'treated' to a lecture every day. He took a book with him to the lectures and "just let them lecture."

Robert's mother died when the young man was twelve. His father died while he was at CBI. He had a sense of urgency now to get back to college after returning to the United States. He had joined the service as a teen. He was discharged 2 1/2 years later as a teen. He attended Pennsylvania State University obtaining a degree in Landscape Architecture.

While at the University, he made a comprehensive private study on all the cities and counties of California. He decided from the facts received that the area stretching from Sebastopol to Napa was a place to raise children. His study was composed of every environmental factor he could think of. At first, there were seven places of interest which he reduced to three and then down to one. The three interesting localities were the Palo Alto area, the Cupertino environ and then from Santa Rosa to Napa. He ultimately chose Sonoma, as it was not as developed as the other priority areas at the time, being more rural in character. He has been fighting ever since he came to Sonoma to keep it pristinely natural, rural and hospitable for chickens...

Bob met his wife, Edna in a swimming pool where he was serving as lifeguard. Both of them were in high school at the time. "Edna was a terrific swimmer, like a fish." according to Robert. They wrote letters to each other while Bob was in CBI. They were married in 1947 in Pennsylvania, while in college. Bob and Edna came to Sonoma area in 1957. Robert had written the State Agricultural College at Davis and was recommended to visit a Seed Farm located at Rohnert Park. At that time, Rohnert Park was looked upon by officials as a swamp. The builders of the area put in trapezoidal ditches to drain the area for housebuilding. It was then, the Cannards chose Kenwood as their first home.

When Bob was asked to be President of the Chamber of Commerce in Sonoma the organization was $13,000.00 in the red. As manager and with the help of many members, he got the organization out of the hole. The Vintage Festival Association also had $7,000.00 worth of deficits. Both organizations had voted to go into bankrupcy. Bob founded the first Sonoma Ox Roast which helped the Chamber out of debt. From that point, Bob became an industrious citizen serving as Board Member of the Community Center. He became President of the Historical Society, Vice President of the General Vallejo Memorial Association, an activist for the Sonoma Ecology Center, a member of the Kenwood Improvement Club, founder of the Kenwood Firemans' Association and was involved with putting on the Fourth of July community celebration in Kenwood of the National Pillow Fights. He has served on numerous committees of the Valley of the Moon in city and county capacities. He worked on general plans, community affairs, the Kenwood Boys and Girls Club and lately proved to be a colorful outspoken member of the Sonoma City Council. He believes one of his greatest achievements was saving the Eucalyptus trees after the big freeze of 1973. Bob showed the community why the trees would not have to be cut down and that they would return to leaf after the freeze. Bob has also been instrumental in raising funds for the local hospital. The private Cannard Fund of the General Vallejo Association has given $100,000.00 away.

The philosophy of the Cannards is to learn 1/3 of your life; work 1/3 of your life and give 1/3 of your life to the community. The last two-thirds of the concept work simultaneously. The Cannards apply the same concept on finances as to their energies.

Bob, taking a stance along with the admirable General Vallejo who founded the City of Sonoma and provided large homesites for chickens and cows, believes he will never live any place without chickens. He calls them, "the greatest recyclers in the world." He has taught thousands of students about chickens through an Agricultural Department which he started at Santa Rosa Junior College in 1966. The students instructed by him received the following philosophy:

(1) Everybody should plant a garden. Grow something, even if it is only a small amount.

(2) Everyone should keep four chickens as they are the greatest recyclers known to mankind.

(3) Never buy anything new you can't obtain second hand since Americans have become a throw-away society.

(4) Never vote for an incumbent politician. (He did not run for re-election to the Council.)

(5) Live these rules and you will change the country overnight.

Bob and Edna have six children. Timothy, Robert, Edward, James, Tom and Jack. All the boys live in the area. "Edna," described by Bob; "is a highly talented artist, especially in the water color medium. She has given balance to our family life." He admires her devotion and attention to the home and children. On a cold night in March, 1992 celebrating St. Patricks day, Edna and Bob became instant successes at the Sonoma Historical Society by serving her famous home-baked Irish Soda Bread accompanied by steaming mugs of Broccoli soup made from the vegetables grown in the Cannard yard. Their large flower garden is spectacular in all seasons. The Cannards are also instrumental in developing a community organic garden for homeowners who want to grow their own fresh vegetables. Bob often opens his General Vallejo Wine and makes toasts to the membership of the museum over just about anything that deserves celebration!

Maxine Y. Hoaglund

United States Navy W.A.V.E.S, 1944 - 1946

As a future W.A.V.E. (Women Accepted for Voluntary Emergency Service) Maxine was born in Beresford, South Dakota about thirty five miles from Sioux Falls. Maxine's mother went to South Dakota from San Francisco as her father thought she should be home with her mother for the birth. During the three months time waiting for birth, the babies' father started a tailor shop in Vancouver, Washington.

Yes, there was more than one baby! Maxine was one of a set of fraternal twins. Maxine said, "the nice thing about being a twin was you always had someone the same age to play games with." The twins being fraternal had different personalities. Soon, the family increased to six children. The twins were oldest. Marjorie was outgoing; Maxine was shy and a proverbial bookworm. Her first memorable book was the *Girl of the Limberlost* which was read in two intervals. She found and liked other Gene Stratton Porter books and then began reading some of the famous series of the period such as *Patty went to College* and *Just Patty*.

Maxine attended schools in Vancouver including that of a business college. Her first job was at a radio station. She worked for a reporter part-time and used many boxes of the old type carbon paper in her tedious work as a secretary. Of course, layman did not have computers for easy changes of typographical errors on their typewriters. So, when a graphic error was made, it was a job to change all copies with that messy carbon paper. Maxine pedaled her bicycle over to City Hall to obtain news. She made notes on marriage license information and called mortuaries for obituaries. The reporter she worked for sent the statistics to the Oregonian Newspaper by way of Greyhound Bus across the Columbia River to Portland. Most of her hours were spent being a receptionist and typist.

When Maxine joined the WAVES she was inducted over the air on radio station KVAN. She was sworn into the WAVES on a Monday evening in a special induction ceremony. Lieutenant Lucia Brown of Portland, Oregon administered the oath and assisted First Class Petty Officer Pipes in charge of local recruiting. A newspaper clipping of the event states, "Miss Wilson leaves February 1st for Hunters College, New York for training as a WAVE."

Maxine answered the frequently asked question, "Why did you join the WAVES?" She answered; "People were much more patriotic in the 1940s. If more women volunteered for the WAVES, they were told that desk jobs in the services would be filled by women instead of men. WAVES allowed more men to be released for overseas duty. This could also help the war effort and the civilian population by not having to call fathers into the service." In those days, the general population would ask Maxine, "How is it a nice girl like you wants to go in the Navy?" It was a time when people were outraged about the war and determined to win it! The general population wanted all able-bodied persons in the services.

On arriving in New York City, Maxine was shuttled to Hunters College in the Bronx. The train she had been transported on from the West Coast to New York had a pullman car with napkins, china, flowers and uniformed stewards. It was so very exciting... She met Clover (Legler) Jackson on that trip and they are still friends today after fifty years. The two young girls enjoyed dining so elegantly...

At college, the WAVES wore Navy blue uniforms which reached below their knees. For six weeks, they were trained to become acquainted with 'Navy ways.' That meant you did all things according to Navy tradition. There were special rules for Navy correspondence including shorthand and typing. Forty young ladies graduated to become a Platoon of WAVES which had two Officers. They marched and studied and marched some more. From the Bronx, a group was transfered to Yeoman College at Stillwater, Oklahoma Agricultural and Mining College. Maxine believes, "the people there were the nicest people she ever met." She got a library card for $2.00 as a non-resident student and spent the rest of her three months in that location reading more interesting books as well as practicing Navy directed training for a legal shorthand position. Her next destination became the famous Treasure Island in San Francisco Bay, California, where twenty ladies were sorted out and whisked off to Camp Parks at nearby Pleasanton. The base near Pleasanton, California did not expect girls. There were no female separation areas as to facilities. The Naval Training and Distribution Center just changed things around a bit to accommodate their new female counterparts.

It was April of 1944 when all naval activities in Amador Valley, namely the Construction and Replacement Depot, Camp Parks, the U.S. Naval Hospital, the U. S. Naval Disciplinary Barracks and the Receiving Barracks were organized under a single administrative command, the United States Naval Training and Distribution Center, Shoemaker, California. On the date of commissioning about 50 Officers and 400 enlisted men moved into the uncompleted buildings sprawled over 689 acres which just a few weeks before had been a cow pasture.

The turnover of General Detail Personnel during the first month and a half was 2,223 received and 2,495 transferred. The first draft finally arrived and the group launched their mission of being a "Way Station" for Navy men on their way to the Fleet. The turnover of drafted persons grew by leaps and the numbers increased dramatically. On September 30, 1944, one single day's turnover of persons would be 2,223 received and 2,495 transferred and the monthly turnover was in the vicinity of 50,000 persons! This was the first receiving ship activity the Navy had of this proportion and many "trial runs" were necessary for a smooth and efficient staff organization since the work load exceeded the original authorization and staff compliment. Some departments worked a three-shift day to get all work done and the drafts out in good order. Disbursing Officers paid out in the vicinity of a million dollars a month on pay days to sailors in addition to making out thousands of allotments and receiving and transferring pay accounts to all transient personnel. When Ships Company was originally conceived, a Seabees Group was organized to build Base facilities. Following that time, Marines were added as a Disciplinary Detatchment.

Maxine was assigned as Court Reporter to the Disciplinary Office in its legal section. Maxine met her future husband in the same office. The whole facility was geared to send crews to ships. They were in charge of the distribution of men overseas. 'Transient personnel' were the ones sent out on ships from Shoemaker. Navy men called 'transients' were kept at the base until they were transferred to a facility or ship.

The Officers of Ships Company ran the base with an every Saturday morning review. The women wore grey and white summer seersucker uniforms during inland warmer days. Their hats, shoes and other pieces of clothing were universally designed just for WAVES. It was all like a dress parade review. A Paris designer, Mainbocher designed the uniforms.

The Disciplinary Office at the base had a big vault with a walk-in room-sized safe. Liquor was kept there. The Officer in charge of the Base would send a couple of Military Policeman with an order to pick up any liquor which was evidence in such-and-such-case. Often the alcohol was strong whiskey. Morris would then send the whiskey 'evidence' to the higher authorities. They'd drink the evidence!

One case that Maxine was assigned, involved some real sad transient personnel. It was an extra cold night. A bunch of men went into the boiler room to get warm and the boiler exploded and burned them severely. It was believed they had changed the controls on the heater which caused the explosion. The investigation was carried into the hospital for information from remaining survivors. One man, a totally wasted case was so severely burned.

Another investigation involved young boys just inducted into service. They were on a train which carried a Japanese Zero Plane on one of the flatbed cars. The Zero plane was being transported around the country and displayed as a curiosity for the home-bound public. The charge on the six new inductees was that each of them had broken off and taken a little piece of the Japanese plane for a souvenir. The Captain's Mast actually had a court hearing with Maxine taking down the boys' testimonies. The young men were at the point to plead guilty or not guilty. One very short young boy asked Maxine about their plea. She felt the whole thing was an 'overkill'. She told the boy to plead "not guilty." The new Naval recruits did get away with their souvenir taking of the Zero Plane by pleading not guilty. Of course, if too many people took pieces of that plane it would have been a problem. To Maxine, the whole thing was an extreme example on the subject of right, wrong and disciplinary procedure being carried too far.

When Maxine had lived in the barracks before marriage, the WAVES had their own underwear but were required to put printed name tags on it. Her friend's underwear was stolen off their outside clothes line. (This era was also before dryers had become a common laundry appliance.) Her friend was dreadfully embarrassed because she had to report to Captain's Mast to identify her underwear in front of all those men! Maxine stated, "This too, was probably a hearing held for a bit of intimidation on the perpetrators and could have been held privately!" Maxine believed a little bit in situation ethics!

Morris, who was in the Discipline Office simply stated, "Get your liberty and I'll take you out." Morris, Maxine's future husband had been out to sea on the USS Minneapolis before she was sunk. He had received a shoulder injury in the North Atlantic Ocean from a severe storm while carrying out duty. A big wave knocked him down and the fall broke his shoulder. He had previously served on the USS Chicago, Betelgeuse, Little, and Kalk mostly in the Asiatic Pacific Region. Eventually, after the shoulder injury, Morris drew shore duty to work in the Discipline Office. Many of his friends went down on the USS Minneapolis when she was sunk at Pearl Harbor.

Maxine and Morris had a bet about when the war would be over. Maxine bet that if the two married on September 8th, 1945 the war would be ended. (It ended three weeks earlier on August 14, 1945.) If a person is really needed, the Navy can keep an inductee six months later than the time period enlisted. The couple was informed that Morris was needed in Honolulu where thousands of troops were headed for home. Maxine, the new bride was not invited. When they were married it was at High Noon in a Vancouver church. Before he left for Hawaii, they had the best time living together at Camp Parks. Morris had lived in San Francisco. Maxine purchased a book showing all the beautiful places in San Francisco that she wanted to see. Her future husband took her to all places she indicated an interest in depicted in the book. Besides that, Morris worked for two Admirals and he got to use a Jeep. He ordered San Francisco Newspapers for planning other trips. He sometimes received newspapers earlier than other people from the Admirals. Being a San Franciscan, Morris had enlisted for six years in his hometown. He was in the regular Navy before the war in 1940.

The nostalgic differences of the 1940s as remembered by Maxine "were like no other time." The newly married couple was issued ration books for food (even in the service). Morris and Maxine invited some friends for dinner at their little apartment. Maxine's husband had saved up enough coupons to have steaks for dinner with their friends. The young bride put the steaks in a pyrex dish. The dish broke and the steaks fell. The dinner became one with the main steak entree changed to a can of salmon. Their friends still remember and talk about the incident.

Maxine's husband was already attending night school in San Francisco at Golden Gate College while he was at Shoemaker. He studied rules and laws pertaining to real estate. He found selling real estate was lots of fun. Morris used to say when he got older, "Even in my bed, I do more business than others accomplish in the office." He had the old-type lock boxes and sold property when one page contracts were drawn up to sell a piece of real estate.

Morris' brother, Eugene Hoaglund was a bombardier in Europe during the war. While Morris was sent to Hawaii, Maxine went back to Vancouver returning to San Francisco when Morris arrived from Hawaii. Morris sold real estate with his cousin, Frank Renstrom Jr.'s office for eleven years before opening his own firm. He established his own office at 16th and Noe off Market Street in 1957 until 1984. He died in 1988.

Two people were instrumental in helping to choose the Hoaglunds' place in the sun in Sonoma. Brother-in-law, Eugene, a fireman in San Francisco found a little vineyard near the Sebastiani Winery east of Sonoma. Together the brothers and their wives purchased the twenty-two acres. Dick Hurley was Morris' best friend. As a professor, he wrote a book on the transister radio. Dick Hurley also had a chance to live in Sonoma. He purchased property on the west side of town and Morris was his real estate broker. The fellows used to sell their Muscat grapes to Sebastiani, Glen Ellen, Buena Vista and Sonoma Creek Wineries. Morris had an experimental block of Zinfandel and Burgundy from which he made his own wine the last couple of years before he died. He received a gold medal on Muscat Canelli. His wine was made by Buena Vista. The twenty-two acres were eventually re-purchased by Sebastiani in the nineties.

Maxine and Morris raised five children, Wendy, Neil, Meredith, Linnea and Dana. Maxine was very happy with her husband who always provided a comfortable home. They had lived in the heart of San Francisco and saw all those wonderful exciting places in the Bay area. The happy chance of residing in Sonoma brought the family in an area of a lot of nice friendly people. Many exploratory bike rides taken on back roads by the family was highlighted as having unparalleled scenery.

Rememberance of unusual activities during World War II brought another event to Maxine's mind. As mentioned by other World War II Veterans, American servicemen and civilians scribbled graffiti on walls, ceilings, floors (mostly in bathrooms) the words, Kilroy was Here. Recently, in the Magazine, Reminisce, a story was written by Richard O'Donnell of Honolulu Hawaii entitled *There Really was a Kilroy!* According to the article there really was a James J. Kilroy formerly a Boston City Council member. During the war, James Kilroy's job was to act as a "checker" checking the number of rivets driven into shipping hulls. Workers received their pay according to the number of rivets they drove into the hulls. Kilroy counted blocks of rivets and then put a check mark with chalk where he left off counting so the same rivets would not get counted twice. Sad to report, according to the article, "some riveters would erase his mark and have their rivets counted the second time when the next checker came on duty." Kilroy was then instructed by the foreman to find out what was happening...From that time on, after discovering the subterfuge, Kilroy used crayoned letters and in very large print wrote,

"Kilroy was Here!" This crayon message was seen by thousands of service personnel aboard ships. The reason the crayon was not cleaned off was due to the fact "ships were leaving port so fast there was not time for the notation to be painted over." The slogan was picked up and spread all over Europe and the South Pacific as well as by American teenagers. The words *Kilroy was Here* was probably the most repeated words of the century in the world of graffiti.

Maxine looks back to the days of being a WAVE and her marriage to Morris, a Navy man, as a joyful positive experience followed by a lifetime of satisfaction for being a part of wartime experiences.

Reiman Publications, L.P., *Reminisce.* 5400 S. 60th Street, Greendale, Wi. 53129., pps 71. Article *There really was a Kilroy!* By Richard O'Donnell, Honolulu, Hawaii. pp. 19.

Miscellaneous typed notes regarding the U.S. Naval Training and Distribution Center. No date, no reference to source. Memorabilia of Maxine Hoaglund.

William C. Johnson

United States Army Air Force, 1942 - 1947

United States Air Force, 1947 - 1971

Bill, born in the Los Angeles area enjoyed and graduated from High School in 1938. He lived in glamorous Santa Monica near Hollywood. Bill attending University of California at Los Angeles was on the soccer team. He was in his senior year when he withdrew from College to enter the United States Army Air Force, December of 1941. It was immediately after the Pearl Harbor bombing which was catalyst for many a choice like Bills. While a student at UCLA the young man worked at Douglas Aircraft Company on summer vacations. Bill helped to build DC-3s and DC-4s and military A-20 and B-19 aircraft at Douglas. During his twenty-nine years as Pilot with the Air Forces, he mostly flew Douglas planes often wondering whether his bomber was one on which he worked, while employed at the factory. His main activity at the aircraft plant was in the area of production control. Bill moved parts around the building as there were no assembly lines in the factories of the late thirties. He studied Business Administration while at UCLA and took flying lessons at Mines Field now called LAX or Los Angeles International Airport.

In December of 1941, Bill joined a group of aviation cadets for flight training at San Antonio, Texas, graduating August of 1942. He saw no other United States Airfields except Kelly Field before heading toward the Pacific Region. Bill said, "I was commissioned an Officer, Gentleman and Pilot in one swoop when I got my wings." As Second Lieutenant, the Pilot's first venture was on the beautiful Islands of Hawaii. He was a replacement Pilot with promises of a Pacific region activity. He arrived in Hawaii by transport ship.

Bill was in Hawaii for the first time. His first excitement was meeting his future wife at Wheeler Field Officers Club. This happened so quickly, it took his breath away as well as hers. Doneyn was recently given a placque engraved on the 50th anniversary of the Johnson's marriage. It reads as follows: United States of America, Matrimonial Association. The Matrimonial Commendation Medal with Oak Leaf Cluster Has been awarded to Doneyn Adelmeyer Johnson for Meritorious Service, 8 October 1944 to 8 October 1994, displayed outstanding devotion, preserverance, love, patience loyal support, kindness, discipline, Motherhood, entertainment and hospitality. Signed: William C. Johnson, Devoted Husband. Molly Marrier, President Matrimonial Association. Children: Beverly, Douglas and Gayle. The children became Chiropractor, Musician in Hawaii and Medical technician in that order.

In an early assignment in Hawaii, Bill was furnished a very old-fashioned bomber, a B-18. The airplane was flown at night and the job included the art of gunnery practice. Outside the B-18, Bill drug a sleeve for Ground Anti-Aircraft Batteries to practice shoot live ammunition at the moving contraption. There were special codes used for the Pilot to get in and out of the Island of Oahu. During one of the practice sessions, away from the 'Aloha State' an engine died and the radio was also acting up and temporarily out of commission. When Bill turned around, heading back to Base, he was picked up on radar and was considered to be an enemy. He was in a two-engine airplane with one engine out and it was a known fact you needed both engines to fly that airplane! Meanwhile, search lights were played during the night and the antiaircraft batteries were practicing their artillery skills on the lonely flier in his crippled airplane. Finally, the General was stirred out of bed and questioned about this unknown plane trying to come into the island. With search lights on the plane, his radio which finally resumed operation announced that it had been decided, "not to shoot that wayward Pilot from the skies."

Before his next thrilling adventure, Bill and Doneyn spent time ballroom dancing. Originally the Flying Squadron was introduced to girls from nice families through the USO. Since there was a ban on unnecessary traveling at night during the black out environment, the couples would be transported on a bus for afternoon tea dancing. When the afternoon was over, Bill would wave goodbye to Doneyn while she was still on the bus. They wrote letters and Doneyn kept a scrapbook of articles and pictures which became more interesting as time ensued. Actually, Doneyn was not yet out of high school even when Bill came back to the mainland many months later. She had planned to enroll at Reed College but as Bill said, "she got the college of matrimony instead."

In the nineteen forties Doneyn's dad was the Ford Lincoln Mercury Dealer in Hawaii. When the young couple were not romancing, Bill was training to be a dive bomber Pilot. His airplane was referred to as SBD. The S was short for Scout, the B meant Bomber and the D for Douglas. In fact, Bill's airplane was known as a Douglas Dauntless Divebomber! (Army designation was A-24.) As Pilot, he had his own navigational plotting instruments and materials in the airplane. He was generally escorted by a larger lead airplane with a Navigator on that plane, as well. Journies taken were about 300 to 500 miles round trip. They flew from places like Canton Island, referred to "as that little spit of land out of nowhere." They spent a good six months sub-patrolling the area of Canton Island. At first the targets were not combative. With very little war activity at first, they practiced shooting at clay pigeons. As a result of all that practice they were advertised as being most accurate bombardiers as they were averaging their hits at 95% with several missions coming up with perfect scores. It was on the Island of Makin in the Gilberts Islands that combative missions were endured. Their campsite was located in a marshy section of the island and about 75% of the Pilots had dengue fever. Bill bombed the Marshall Islands of Mille and Jaliut. The flights into the Marshalls were for bombing Japanese shipping, airfields and gas installations. In sharp dives, they unloaded A-24s meteor-swift bomb loads upon scared and running Japanese.

Bill was assigned a plane with a two-man crew, just himself and his Gunner. The Pilot fired the forward guns and operated the bomb release along with keeping his airplane on target. The Gunner did not have the privilege of viewing where he was going. He just looked down to see where he had been. He traveled in the plane with his back to the target always ready to swivel his gun into action. The biggest beef the Pilot or his Gunner had was politely called "combat fatigue." After sitting on a parachute pack and watering cans for several hours "they did get pretty sore behinds." Often upon debarkation of the plane, men would shake their legs around a bit and walk a little stiff-legged to get circulation moving into their bodies once more.

When Bill was taken to Makin Island on Aircraft Carrier, USS Long Island, he received the exciting hair-raising thrill of being catapulted off ship. His plane was placed on the carrier deck. The Baby Carrier Catapult was on the under-flight deck. The catapult was actually a steam controlled hydraulic ram which under pressure converts a small force into a much larger force acting in tandem as a thrust of power. The airplane was hooked to slides in a track. Bill exclaimed, "When the catapult was activated, "the mechanical beast utterly threw the plane off the ship!" The pilot was instructed to rev the engine of the plane to maximum power as if for take-off but then he also held the brakes down at the same time. He held his head back in order not to snap his head out of place. The whole procedure was very powerful. Since there was not enough gasoline carried on the planes to fly that far, planes were ferried out to those islands. Twice, Bill experienced this catapulting procedure.

When the young flyer arrived at Makin it had just been taken from the Japanese. It was a thrill to be the first flyer to land on the newly finished airstrip at Makin Field. The bombers were sent there to neutralize the Marshall Islands so other armed forces would not have to invade. Bill did not experience air opposition so only defensive measures were followed on the Marshalls. The Japanese anti-aircraft did blow away one-half of the Squadron. A dive bomber was a hazardous-sitting-duck-operation. One had to fly right through anti-aircraft flak. A typical raid was but a brief moment of plunging through the sky followed by wild seconds in a dive. The air draft from ackack spurting underneath the plane would push it back upward as high as fifteen feet. In a dive, the plane became a howling vacuum in the air as the ship pummeted downward. From intense bombing activity, palm trees became more and more jagged looking causing shorelines to appear desolate.

Bill made a direct hit on a Japanese Freighter in a lagoon at Mille. The ship could still be seen many years later on the lagoon bottom. Lieutenant Johnson was rescued from the sea and in a three day period, his picture was in newspapers over one-half of the world. His story was in the Honolulu Advertiser on the 5th of April, 1944. The news in his home town paper, the Santa Monica Outlook was calendared on the 6th of April 1944. He was written up in the Chicago Daily Tribune on the next day. On the 7th of April, 1944, the Associated Press Wirephoto from the 7th Air Force showed a little bitty picture of a lone man in the ocean. Coming toward that lonely looking man was a group of Natives happily paddling their outrigger canoe. One story read, "Lt. W.C. Johnson floating on small inflated raft after his dive bomber riddled by Jap fire crashed in Pacific after Marshall Islands raid. Natives in outrigger canoe came to rescue and help Johnson climb aboard." The whole lagoon was mined by Americans. The awe of the situation to Bill was "that neither the Natives nor he on that ten mile journey got hit by a mine." They found upon arrival at the island that they had traveled through heavily mined waters. Bill and his Tail Gunner had parachuted out of the plane when gasoline began to pour out of the tanks. Bill was about ten miles from the Base when the plane quit. When the two men parachuted, Bill said "I calmly stepped outside the plane and endured the one and only time I ever spent in a parachute. The plane was so low shroud lines of the chute became entangled in my legs. I fell in the water of the Pacific out where the big fish play." That event was followed by the Native's rescue efforts. When Bill was brought in by the little rescue boat, he was transferred to air rescue. Until the Natives made the effort, the airman was floating on a little life raft which was a part of his parachute. The life preserver, called a Mae West is part of the flotation gear wear used while flying in an airplane today. The life raft inflates and you just get in it. As a flier, one is trained in use of all the equipment and the presence of mind on how to use it. The Gunner bailed out first and simply did not make it. He drowned. Bill spent several hours drifting while he watched a crash boat that did not come for him. The boat just stood off shore because of the mines in the harbor. The Natives delivered the Pilot very triumphantly to the crash boat. Bill received a wound which he considered, "not worth mentioning."

After the loss of his airplane, he was a flyer without a replacement plane. The missions in the Pacific were drawing to a close as the Americans continually battled and won island after island on their march toward Tokyo. He was awarded the Air Medal with two Oak Leaf Clusters, the Distinguished Flying Cross and the Purple Heart among other medals.

During the Air Force occupation on the island, the United States Government, being chastity minded became conscious of the well-endowed unclothed female anatomy on Makin Island. They sent a shipment of brassieres for the islander girls. Some of the pictures in Bill's scrapbook show some pretty buxom young ladies on display. The interesting thing about the new 'bras' was that the Natives wore the undergarments around their waists to carry fruit and trinkets as if they were little pockets on a string. During Christmas amid the palm trees the Natives put on a party with dancing. On special occasions when the Air Force members were present some Native girls wore cast off white tee shirts. In Bill's scrap book it appeared to be a 50/50 choice as to being clothed or unclothed. Male and female Natives wore anything else they could collect from the American cast-offs. Every type of hat from sailor to a snow cap with ear muff gear and broken helmets were prized and worn by the Natives. On Christmas day, "the 7th AAF's only Fighter-Bomber Squadron in the Pacific was flying out and muttering, "Merry Christmas, Tojo."

Back in Hawaiian Islands in April of 1944, Bill and Doneyn were part of a wedding party for Fred and Nita Larson. Nita was an island girl like Doneyn. It was during this wedding that Bill and Doneyn were inspired to plan their own nuptials which took place in Salinas, California in October of that year.

While stationed at Salinas both Bill and Fred Larson were aerial gunnery instructors, teaching other pilots how to shoot at a sleeve being towed over the ocean from Monterey.

The Johnsons and the Larsons were then transferred to Great Falls, Montana where the boys' job was to ferry B-17s and B-29s from the Boeing plant in Seattle to other parts of the country. In essence, during the war, the assembly lines were running so fast new airplanes were ferried to modification centers for changes as the assembly lines were too busy to make changes in the plant. (Another interesting bit of information regarding the assembly of airplanes, the editor learned that during the war when airplanes were delivered to China-Burma-India, they were sent by shipload in crates. The planes, in parts, were then assembled in a huge Zepplin Hanger probably left over from days of the dirigible. The men assembling the planes were skilled in methods of dope and fabric, a throwback to the wood and fabric construction used during the time of the Wright Brothers., Ed.)

Bill loved flying the B-29, but near the war's end, Bill's father-in-law invited him to get out of the service and work for him selling automobiles. Bill remained a Reservist at Hickamfield as a Military Transport Pilot. He was recalled in 1951 during the Korean War as a Military Air-lift Pilot shuttling people while flying the C-54 (was a DC-4) and a C-97 Boeing Stratocruiser. Later, he flew C-118s (was a DC-6) and a C-124 Douglas Globemaster. He continued many hours of military air-lift flights through 1966. The planes moved the injured in what was known as air evacuation hospital ships. They moved the patients back and forth from the war-torn zones to the United States and according to Bill, "it was a hairy business." The patients in litters and many in casts were all strapped down for flights. The route was generally to Travis Air Force Base from Japan and Hawaii.

Again, due to miles covered and limited fuel, crew staging took place at Wake Island and again at Hawaii. One lap would be from Japan to Wake, then fly to Hickam at Hawaii. Each change of crew was after a flight time of eight to twelve hours, depending upon the winds. The motto of the crew was "hours and hours of sheer boredom interspersed by moments of stark terror."

During the atomic bomb testing at Eniwetok, which Bill observed, another job for the fliers was being pony express for air samples brought to the United States. During a bomb testing one of the airplanes at Eniwotok would fly through the mushroom cloud and a collector contraption would scoop up units of air samples from the dirty mushroom cloud. The evacuation plane going to Hickam would pick up the containers of air samples at Eniwetok and shuttle these specimans to yet another plane heading into

Travis Air Force Base, California. Air samples were then taken to Livermore for analysis. The speciman dust was sealed in heavy lead boxes. The farthest the airplanes could travel at that time on one load of fuel was to fly from Eniwetok to California. Bill did that route many times.

The flyer's last two positions entailed that of first being a Commander of Air Force people on Midway Island for two years. He was then appointed Chief of the 22nd Air Force Command Post for control of Military Airlift over the western 1/2 of the world reaching from the Mississippi River to beyond Japan. Travis Air Force Base was his last duty station.

Looking around Northern California for a place to live, Bill and Doneyn decided they did not want Southern California or Hawaii. The couple read an ad in a newspaper placed by Homer Bosse. Homer showed them Sonoma Valley which became a love at first sight. They were shown a parcel of wooded land on Lake Josephine and they built a house overlooking that beautiful piece of property before leaving Travis.

Retiring from the service, Bill felt he had no avocation or profession except for flying. He decided to sell real estate like Homer and obtained a Broker's license in 1974. Both Bill and Doneyn went to Anthony Schools and Bill went to work for Bosse. When Bosse sold out, Bill went for seven years with Mori and Perkins followed by a stint on his own without salespersons for another seven years. He was honored to become Realtor of the Year on two separate occasions. He served the Board of Multiple Listing for a period of six years and became its Vice-President, President and Past-President of the organization based in Santa Rosa, California.

The Johnson home is a comfortable modifed ranch style two story on the beautiful Lake Josephine found on a private road in the posh area of Sobre Vista Estates. Oaks, red toyon and native flora cover the hillsides. Grape vineyards with yellow to copper-colored leaves lead to the property. Many large water fowl play noisily on a small island in the waters. From the big broad redwood deck holding statuary and flowering plants cared by Doneyn's green and deft thumbs, one can watch large ducks congregate on the water's edge. Inside the big island kitchen are knotty pine beamed ceilings with a massive built-in brick fireplace. The woven oval rug adds a touch of friendliness to one of Sonoma Valley's beauty spots not rivalled by too many other places on the earth.

Santa Monica Outlook Newspaper, article entitled, *Lt. Johnson Lucky, He Says Modestly,* May 22, 1944. page and writer not available.

Brief, 7th AAF Publication, Vol. 1, No. 23., Robert G. Price, Article entitled *Fighter-Bombers.,* May 9, 1944, pp.10., and *Little Muggin,* no date or Vol. given., pp. 10.

Misc. other notes from scrapbook kept by Doneyn Johnson.

Carl G. Mead

United States Coast Guard Reserve, 1943 - 1946

Born six miles west of Salem, Oregon on a little farm in 1924, the family had not settled on a name for the newborn baby. Actually there were lists of male and female names but it took the doctor pressing for an answer to enter a designation on the birth certificate which helped the family make the big decision. Carl finished high school and two years of college. Coming from an active Christian-Minister-based-family the young man was a member of male quartet singing groups and a constant participant in Methodist-Baptist-Choirs. In his senior year of high school (1941) he decided to enter a singing contest. He wanted to take lessons from a voice teacher should he win. The teacher he consulted said, "Don't enter the contest! I'll give you some free lessons if you don't enter!"

As a child on the farm, the boy enjoyed the fact that the family furnished their own music. It was too early for television sets to invade homes. Instead, Carl beat upon a trap drum set and played a few piano solos. The farm sprawled upon a little five acre parcel where his parents scrambled for a living. They raised a bit of alfalfa for a cow, had one horse and 400 stands of bees. The production from the honey collected provided extract bottled and sold by Mead Honey Company.

Carl's father was also a traveling evangelist. His father and mother took the family to the Hawaiian Islands for the Congregational Church and ended up freelancing at the Kaa Kaa Akka Mission. In other words, they ran their own missionary program. They came back to the mainland when his grandfather died. Carl wistfully recalls, "I never saw or talked to a grandfather or grandmother."

Carl was drafted while attending Oregon State College at Corvallis. The draft notice led him to Portland, Oregon as per instructions. When the officer in charge asked him, "What would you like to be?" Carl stated, "No slogging in the mud! Nothing in brown. Give me anything in blue." The officer made a choice, "I need a couple of Coast Guards today." As Carl signed on the dotted line, he didn't know what a Coast Guardsman did or didn't do.

In the swashbuckling days of rumrunning for illegal transport of liquor, the Coast Guard was set up to control unlawful subversives and prevent smuggling. The Coast Guards' peacetime activities were placed under the Treasury Department of the United States. But during wartime, the Guard was administered by the Navy. Navy clothing was issued with Coast Guard insignia. Besides the need for guarding the nation's coasts, the Coast Guard was on distress call for aiding vessels in trouble and the group maintained light houses. Carl found out that Coast Guardsmen sometimes had very lonely outposts. The assignment could be anywhere in the world where the United States had an installation for shipping. Alaskan areas were considered very lonely outposts. After being drafted, Carl became a reservist. He found out there was a friction between "old salts" and reservists.

The draftee was given two to three weeks 'hometime' before being ordered to appear at Oakland-Alameda Port in California for training at Government Island. He had seen the Bay Area in California before, so it was not the same thrill as on the previous journey. The Coast Guard had its own facilities. His job description included guarding the California Coastline, taking care of buoys (bobbing floats warning of a dangerous rock, shoal or a shallow edge of a channel) and every type of thing having to do with coastal installations including shipping. (In war time, the description also included assaults made on beaches around the world.) Buoys were interesting as they came in different shapes and had different functions. They were important in regard to the way their presence was indicated and whether they were bell buoys, light buoys or whistling buoys. A device for keeping a person afloat would be called a life buoy. A collection of buoys would be referred to as a buoyage.

Basic training in the Coast Guard included marching, elementary use of gas mask and tear gas releases. The biggest drag was the feeling of idleness due to inactivity. One chore, Carl particulary did not care for was picking up cigarette butts and it was a cigarette puffing society! Some trips for Coast Guardsmen would include two or three men tossing around in surf boats. These little boats generally used for training had six or eight oars. Continual tests were given regarding the use of this type of watercraft.

Carl was sent to Atlantic City, New Jersey for education as a potential radio operator. Receiving innoculations, he was shuttled with others like cattle for a train ride through North Platt, Nebraska on a mid-northern railway. People were fed sandwiches and squashed onto triple-decker pullman cars. Carl was indoctrinated to the rocking and rolling action of his body across country. He was directed to the third highest bunk for sleeping which was 18 inches from the ceiling of the vibrating clickety-clacking railroad car.

There were a lot of people at Atlantic City for indoctrination into the radio experience. The training was for operation of the appliance aboard a ship. The students were not allowed to repair radios. In fact, they were ordered, "not to fool with them!" They were given the keys for Morse Code. Nothing was hidden or coded. They used the open mike and talked back and forth. Ironically, on a small ship when a radio needed repair no one knew how to do it...

While at Atlantic City, Carl experienced a hurricane which hit the area in 1944. Wild sounding winds whipped water into the hotel lobby. The Boardwalk was being ripped apart. He looked down from his hotel room and watched cars floating down the street from the storm. While at his first class in January of 1944, Carl suffered cellulitis, a rapid inflamation of tissues. His malady was an inflamation of the legs. He was diagnosed, then ordered to come back to classes later. He was informed the Coast Guard needed teachers when he did return to training. To be a radio man, one needed basic typing skills, the Morse Code itself, elementary knowledge of how radio equipment worked (no repair stressed) and hearing and sending the Code. For a little more liberty, Carl joined the drum and bugle corps which increased his marching and drilling skills as well as having an activity to enjoy away from school.

Carl became a Petty Officer Second Class upon graduation from radio school. Soon he made it across Pacific waters to the Hawaiian Islands with dire promises of heading ultimately toward Guam. He became a radio operator on a short 150 foot ship which was also considered to be an icebreaker type of vessel. The ship also had a round-bottomed appearance. The radio shack on the ship was located under the Bridge. As radio operator, the young man moved back and forth a great deal while standing watch. Carl had a small chair tied down with ropes to keep it from moving back and forth from the motion of the waves.

Waves reminded the former Coast Guardsman of their rolly-polly storekeeper. No sooner, than out of sight of the Golden Gate Bridge where riptides meet outgoing crosscurrents, the ship started pitching. The rolly-polly fellow was utterly crawling to the Fantail. Men each grabbed a leg and held him from going over the side of the vessel while urping. The poor man never got out of bed from that moment on and didn't care if he died in the water.

As a radio operator, Carl also did storekeeper duty. This meant being involved with anything written, typed and especially concerned with receiving messages. If it was a secretarial job it was covered by him. In 1946, at Hawaii, the boat kept going around the Islands doing buoy business. At that point, Carl was informed his number was up and he had enough points to go back to the States. He typed his own orders for discharge. He did not have to go to Guam after all.

One interesting thing Carl learned from his traveling evangelist family was how to conduct religious services. As a 21 year old aboard ship, he made up his own religious service. For his exercise of worship and with "all hands on deck" he proceeded. Most of the men attended. As Carl looks back, he said, "and to think I had the gall and impudence to do that! I duplicated hymns, led the singing and gave a short sermon."

He was discharged near Seattle, Washington. He was asked to stay on in the Coast Guard with a promotion. As a Petty Officer Second Class, he replied, "Take my name off the list."

While doing a stint as instructor in radio school, in August of 1944 and before going to the Pacific Region, Carl married Mary his first wife. They met at a church and married there. Carl and Mary had five children named David, Helen, Jessie, James and Jon.

After discharge from the Coast Guard, Carl attended the Moody Bible Institute in Chicago. It was not a college but a Christian Education Music School. The fledgling family went to Santa Barbara where Carl attended Westmont College from 1949 to 1951. He graduated with a B A in Christian Education. Carl became a Director of Christian Education at the Stockton, California First Baptist Church.He taught fifth grade in Manteca for 2 1/2 years. He became the Northern California Baptist Convention Director of Children's work. He continued in sixth grade elementary school teaching. At Valley Forge, Pennsylvania, Carl was made Associate Director of Education for the Pennsylvania Baptist Convention.

Next, came ten years of cab driving. As Carl stated, "I needed that ten year period of time to put my head back together." He did a lot of reading of science fiction and philosophical spiritual growth books. During that time while driving cab to yet another destination, he would get map flashes in his head on how to get there. He was totally spacing out as to driving. He considered, "I am quite possibly on auto pilot. I flashed the route in my head and drove there automatically thinking of other things."

Carl was introduced to a person named Dottie who became his second wife. After they got married in Concord, California the newly-weds decided to find a new area in which to live, get new jobs and do things together. They decided to settle in Sonoma.

The couple searched the Valley of the Moon looking for work. They were hired by the Sonoma Development Center. Belonging to the Edgar Cayse Association for research in enlightenment, they felt at home when receiving training for psychiatric technician work. Married eighteen years and working at the hospital for all those years, the couple delivered nursing care for the mentally ill and developmentally disabled. In that kind of work, Carl said, "You are working with mentally, emotionally and behaviorally motivated persons who act by internal and external stimuli causing emotional, linguistic and other anti-social responsive demeanor. You also have to help feed the persons under care. It is a persevering diligent work that is affected by external actions and impressions in constant motion." The theme of the work was "You're my brother." Carl retired from hospital work in 1989, but he stayed on until recently in a part-time service position.

Presently, the ex-Coast Guardsman is a member of a local church and sings in the 150 voice Sonoma Valley Chorale. He and Dottie are members of Alzheimers Respite Group, American Field Service (a teenage exchange program), Canine Companions for Independence, Teen Safe Ride and Sonoma Commission on Community Service. Leisure hobbies include travel, back packing, camping and reading.

Adam Di Gennaro

United States Marine Corps 1938 - 1946

Born in the Adriatic seaport town of Bari Italy in 1920, Adam the fourth child of ten offspring, came to the United States as a one year old. Adam's dad was a residential building contractor in Rochester, New York where Adam spent his boyhood years. The family home was two story with dining room, three bedrooms and one bathroom. His oldest sister, Lena operated a beauty parlor in the dining room, the three bedrooms and kitchen. The family took turns eating. The bath room really got a workout and the door took a constant pounding and was replaced quite a few times. Adam stated, "One can imagine the pandemonium there with twelve people living together in the house."

While yet in high school, Adam's first job was working in a radio store where little old fashioned radios were sold. He made fifty cents for a couple of hours work. On Saturday, the young man earned $1.00 for all day. At the age of eighteen, $21.00 a month seemed enticing for going into the service. Other benefits included "all you could eat and shelter."

It was Adam's first summer after high school graduation when his buddy, Kenny Kreiser talked Adam into joining the Marines. At first the young man said, "No way!" But since times were bad and there was no full time work to be had and the family was struggling, he decided to go for it. Adam figured if he went into the Marines, he would help the family. It would make one less person for his family to care for and nourish.

The closest recruiting office was located in New York City about 350 miles away. In New York, the doctors examined and quickly passed the new inductee. The powers-that-be decided to ship Adam along with two other recruits by train to Parris Island which is the Marine Recruit Camp (bootcamp) off the coast of South Carolina. Adam was designated as the person in charge of the threesome. On the way to their destination, the train stopped for a transfer to another line at Union Station in Washington D.C. Being young and wanting to see "just a little of their nation's capitol" the three young men decided to take "just a little sightseeing walk." They walked about half-way to the Capitol Building and saw the Lincoln Memorial away in the distance. Their train had departed by the time they got back to Union Station. Several hours later, they took the next train heading for Beaufort, South Carolina for transfer by boat to Parris Island.

At the dock, they were met by a Marine Sergeant who later turned out to be their drill instructor. He growled, "Where have you been all this time?" Adam replied, "We missed our train." "What do you mean?!" the drill instructor shot back. "We went for a little walk and didn't get back in time," Adam replied. The drill instructor was working up a sweat, "You should know better! Foolish thing like that!" By then, the drill Sergeant who had been waiting quite a few hours was close to a rage. For six weeks of boot camp, Adam, the designated leader for the journey, was subjected to extra marches, running multiple extra laps with a rifle over his head and, he was detailed to clean latrines.

However, the young man was impressed with the history of the Marine Corps. He discovered that President Thomas Jefferson, the Barbary Coast of Africa, areas of Tripoli, Tunis, Algiers and Morocco, piracy of the new democracy's shipping and a Barbary War with an extraordinary cast of characters including an American patriot named William Eaton established the pride, tradition and distinction of the Marine Corps. All of these high adventure ingredients stirred together in a series of events was responsible for the establishment of the United States Navy and the Marine Corps as a part of the Navy. The Marines accomplished dangerous combat during the War of 1812 in the Mediterranean Sea. They used sabers, swords, and knives for weapons. They wore leather collars to keep their heads from being chopped off. This is how they got the nickname "leather necks."

The Marines Corps developed even more colorfully as battles of scimiter and sword were carried out. Men on a high mast of their ship swung from ropes onto pirates' vessels. Naval bombardments and unusually bizarre military operations took place. A five hundred mile Libyan Desert march by a foreign legion led by William Eaton was spectacular as to dress, demeanor and as to the exhaustive journey itself. Eaton was an Army Captain with only nine other Americans leading the charge across the desert with foreign legion troops. Eaton was known to dress in a hat with plumes. He carried a simitar and rode on a large Arabian stallion. He could live on a horse all day, eat very little and throw a knife with cutting accuracy for eighty feet. With a Lieutenant and eight men dubbed Marines, they actually became the nucleus of the birth of the United States Marines Corps. Thundering broadsides and naval bombardments were the reality of the Barbary War. New and larger ships with more powerful guns were developed by the Americans to stop the dictators ruling in the name of Allah. The African dictators had been taking Americans hostages and enslaving them on rowing benches of watercraft. They were held for ransom or sold as captured Christians on white slave markets.

Adam discovered there was a certain esprit de corps, enthusiastic pride, devotedness and tradition in the fighting tough organization of the United States Marines. When President James Monroe declared the Monroe Doctrine due to trouble in Central and South America, the Marines were sent in. Therefore, *Semper Fidelis* words chosen "From the Halls of Montezuma" (Mexico) "to the Shores of Tripoli" (on the Mediterranean Sea) was written as a Marine theme song. This idea also translated by Navajo instructor, Jimmy King in the book *The Navajo Code Talkers* was further expounded that the Marines really had traveled and "fought in every place they could take a gun." *Semper Fidelis* meaning "Always Faithful" has carried that legacy of the Marines alive and strong throughout history.

In 1938, Marines were trained in bootcamp as if they were part of an Army Infantry Division. In 1940, they were more intensely trained for ground troop fighting. Marine Pilots provided air cover. Officers of the Marine Corps were required to take classes at the Naval Academy. During World War II, Marines were used for Island hopping throughout the Pacific Theatre. According to Adam, "Their own personal missions were bent on getting even with the Japanese because of Pearl Harbor and they wanted to do it immediately!" he continued; "they were short-changed on supplies of military hardware, ships and aircraft."

Adam's first official job as a young Marine was guarding the USS Constitution (Old Ironsides). The ship was moored in Boston (Massachusetts) Navy Yard. Marine guards not only protected the historic vessel but the pier from civilian pranksters or subversives. Adam quickly added, "Its sister ship the USS Constellation was docked at Baltimore Harbor across the bay from Fort Mc Henry where the *Star Spangled Banner* was written."

The young Marine wanted to go to the United States Naval Academy which was normally entered by way of a United States Senatorial appointment. Another path was to spend two years at sea, then take an entrance examination. Adam applied for sea duty and got it. He was assigned to the USS Brooklyn in

1939. The World's Fair was in progress at Flushing Long Island and he was privileged to attend it.

The USS Squalis, a new submarine cruiser was in the Brooklyn Navy Yard. Shortly before leaving for the West Coast via the Panama Canal on a shake-down cruise, it sank off the New England Coast. The USS Brooklyn was designated as the Command Ship for salvage operations. A new diving bell (big steel chamber) with a hatch for opening was lowered over the submarine equipped with lugs you turn to move sailors and passengers from one chamber to another. The diving bell worked off tugboats. The diving bell was conceived as a large hollow inverted vessel with air supplied under pressure. The Squalis had broken in two. One-half of the ship stopped water. The other one-half was damaged and flooded. The Navy saved one-half of the crew on the side, not flooded. Men made news as they came out one by one by way of the newly-invented diving bell.

After that adventure Adam saw more of the world as the Brooklyn passed through the Panama Canal toward the Pacific Ocean. He enjoyed visiting another World's Fair in San Francisco at Treasure Island. The Marine Corps was part of a celebration known as Fleet Week. In the beautiful bay harbor was a fleet consisting of aircraft carriers, cruisers and destroyers. The USS Brooklyn with other warships was anchored in the Bay. One night, the ship's anchor was dragging. The anchor went into some soft material and the tide was causing the ship to move. The ship almost collided with the USS Enterprise Aircraft Carrier. That was one big ship to tangle with! Men marveled at the newly built Golden Gate Bridge. They stayed at port for two weeks. San Francisco was considered as being spectacular.

Next stop was Bremerton Navy Yard Dry Dock in Washington. For three months, barnacles and dry dock repairs were undertaken. Except for a bit of shore leave, Adam spent a lot of time guarding facilities on ship including battle stations. On ship, there were fifty calibre machine guns placed on each side the Bridge. Not only did Marines guard those big guns but they had to maintain them from salt water and dampness. Cleaning guns was followed by gun strikers firing them while in dry dock. Adam also drew guard duty of the Brig (the jail aboard ship).

The only time Adam became seasick was in the Pacific Ocean while on guard watch at the Brig. After leaving Puget Sound while heading for Pearl Harbor, a terrific storm was in progress. The violent atmospheric disturbance required closing down the hatches on the top deck. The Brig was as far down in the ship's hold as you could get. Sailors were sleeping all over the place on various decks. Three levels of beds on stanchions were pushed up at night. There were air scoops on top and motors were used to circulate air but it was stuffy down in the hold during the storm. Adam went topside to heave. There was no need for guarding the Brig as far as he was concerned unless the prisoner was ill. Aboard ship there was no place for an escaped prisoner to go...

For one and one-half years, the ship was based at Pearl Harbor, Hawaii. One interesting trip taken was a goodwill tour of New Zealand. Places visited on the way were Samoa, Tahiti and Auckland, New Zealand. At Samoa and Tahiti there were no docks at the time. People from those areas were very friendly. In Spring of 1941, the USS Brooklyn was re-assigned back to the Atlantic Fleet to convoy supply ships to England. When near Iceland, British war ships came to convoy the supply ships the rest of the way in very dangerous waters.

After being aboard ship for two and one-half years, the young Marine was next assigned to the Marine Barracks at 8th and I Streets in Washington, D.C. He was part of the Presidential Guard Unit. Every Friday, a dress parade took place accompanied by the Marine Band. That summer, President Franklin D. Roosevelt vacationed at Warm Springs, Georgia at the Little White House. While the President was in residence, the Marines guarded the perimeter of the Little White House, belonging to the Roosevelt Family. The setting was a wooded area. Adam was Corporal of the Guard at the front gate working with the Secret Service. He directed operations from a booth-like station.

The President had a 1937 Ford touring car modified especially for his poliomyelitis condition. He had no use of his legs. "A big Secret Service man would pick the President up and place him in the vehicle. There were automatic gear shifts. Everything in the car was operated by hand levers. President Roosevelt would wave at the guards as he drove by. He didn't know his protectors from a bag of beans," according to Adam.

Back in Washington D.C. and on December 7th, 1941, Adam was in the barracks when announcement came over the radio about the bombing of Pearl Harbor. After the news, the Marines stayed around for a count down. Washington D.C. became terribly busy. People seemed actively running around. There was trouble at a South American Airfield where planes were being deliberately sabotaged. The Marines from Adam's group were sent down to Belem, Brazil at the head of the Amazon River to guard American war planes. Planes were there for overnight stays before crossing the Atlantic Ocean to Dakar, Africa. One physical occurrence happened each and every day. The sky opened up with rain followed by steamy humidity. The men endured this weather for three months while on this special assignment.

In the spring of 1942, Adam came back to the United States dispatched from South America to Camp LeJuene, North Carolina and was assigned as a member of the new 21st Marine Regiment of the 3rd Marine Division. The largest unit would be a Division comprised of three Regiments. There were three Battalions in a Regiment. There were three Companies in a Battalion and three Platoons in a Company. There were three squads in a Platoon and a Squad was comprised of ten men. The Third and Ninth Regiments of the Marines were being trained in Camp Pendleton, California. The 21st went across country by train to join the other two regiments and trained there together as a Division. Adam was almost killed while practicing a special exercise to climb a pinnacle and descend by ropes. While absailing (descending) the rope was to be wound around his shoulders and a poncho with a rope around it placed in the crotch. One carried a rifle, a pack, a steel helmet and one's own weight on the ropes. The rope was attached to a tree or sometimes to vehicles. About three-quarters the way down on one of Adam's descents, the poncho slipped out of place and he was "burning down there!" His hands gave away and he landed on his head and shoulders, then rolled on down the rest of the slope. He was lucky he did not break his neck!

The Marines divided up the 21st Regiment which was sent to Auckland, New Zealand. The Ninth Regiment went to Wellington, New Zealand. The Third Regiment were Samoa bound. At Samoa a large part of the regiment got infected by the bloodsucking tsetse fly and caught elephantitus (nicknamed MuMu). That malady amounted to huge swelling of the legs. Those infected were sent back to Klamath Falls' cooler climate for cure.

The first combat amphibious landing for island hopping in the Pacific was Bougainsville, an Island North of Guadalcanal. On Bougainsville, where they were supposed to land, the point of entry ended up taking everyone by surprise. They had expected some forest swamps but the whole area was marshy. The reason for the battle at Bougainsville was to build an airfield. The Marines had a synchronized motor launch landing after crawling down ropes off ships. They received a signal to go in together. The Marines moved around the perimeter area for an airfield for two months. Then, they went back to Guadalcanal to prepare for landings on Guam. Training was changed each time because every island landing was totally different as having unique conditions.

Guam had a coral reef for about a mile out from the shore. The reef would be under water when the tide was in and visible when the tide was out. To get ashore, the troops used amphibious tractors that travel on water and land carrying ten men. The tracks of the tractors have cups built on them to propel the vehicle through the water. The amphibs went through water like a tractor would travel on land. They made landings from a Landing Ship Transport (LST) which would moor itself about two or three miles off shore. The double doors would open while at sea and then a ramp came out to discharge the amphibs with Marines aboard. The amphibians would splash into the water with the troops intact. Marines had landed on Saipan Island three days before Guam. But the 4th Division could not move after landing. That postponed the Third Marines from the Guam landing. The Fourth Division got a foothold but could not move inland because of opposition. Adam's group, the 3rd Marine Division was kept as 'floating reserves' for a whole month until an Army Division was brought in from Hawaii to re-inforce the 4th Division. Before the month was over the Third Division was out of food, cigarettes, and fuel. Their LSTs were pulled back to Eniwetok Atoll. They, then replenished goods from a supply ship and went back to Guam and made the landings as previously planned. Lives were lost because they had to go up then over the side of the amphibs and were needlessly exposed to gun fire. As they rose up out of the machine, "they were shooting ducks in a rain barrel," according to Adam; "the amphibs were later redesigned with a ramp in the rear that could be let down so the men could exit out the back way. It was after that kind of blood bath landing, that the amphibians were re-designed so that men could run from the rear and not become a frontal stationery target."

After the Island of Guam was secure (the enemy defeated) the 3rd Division trained for amphibious landings to be on the tiny volcanic Island of Iwo Jima. That island was in the middle of nowhere between Guam and the Japanese mainland. It had a small airfield located about one hundred yards away from the beach where the Marine Amphibious Force planned to land. Adam was in the first wave of boats to hit the beach. The troops were taken to Iwo in regular troop transport ships. The ships stayed several miles off shore while the Marines were lowered into motor launches with front end ramps. Upon hitting the beach the ramps would be dropped to enable troops to get out on the run. The Beach area consisted of slippery sandlike volcanic material which was hard to walk or run on. When one went to dig a fox hole, the sides would not hold up. It was much the same for the 100 yards from the beach to the edge of the airfield runway and it was fairly steep, making it difficult to climb. In spite of the Marines inability to move on to the airfield, more and more Marines were being brought ashore. Troops were bunched up all over the beach area making them increasingly exposed for the Japs to pick them off one by one or in groups as they were fired upon from nearby Mount Surabachi, on the left flank.

The first objective was tanks were supposed to lead the attack on the airfield. But, the tanks got stuck on the beach because they mucked down in the volcanic material and their tracks were spinning around but not moving. Tank infantry men were all over the small beach area almost shoulder to shoulder unable to dig-in, unable to go over the airfield ridge and receiving heavy mortar, artillery and machine gun fire from Japanese who were heeled down on nearby Mount Surabachi. Someone in command got the bright idea to use the steel mats for traction which supply ships had brought to cover up pot holes in an airfield, (These mats were also used in other parts of the world by airplanes for wet ground.) The steel mats were placed in front of the tank tracks all the way to the edge of the airfield, finally making it possible to move ahead over the volcanic ash. This idea proved successful.

"Iwo Jima became what is called a frontal assault against a strongly fortified island." There were "estimated to be 23,000 entrenched Japanese and that was probably the strongest in numbers that the Americans encountered in the Pacific. It took a month of fierce fighting at a price of 20,000 casualties" according to *American Military History, ROTCM 145-20*. Casualties were estimated as 26,000 Americans in later estimations. Stretchers were so full that ponchos were used for evacuation. When all three divisions had landed, there were more than 50,000 Americans on the island. According to a book named *Iwo*, "dead bodies were littered with tens of thousands of huge green flies buzzing about." It further chronicled, "When the men from the graves registration respectfully raised their slain comrades, they wore heavy rubber gloves reaching to their armpits." Americans slain were buried in the 5th Division Cemetery.

The Japanese caves were outfitted and so well concealed they were hard to spot. The Japanese had been there for over a year and one-half. They were a fierce lot, trained for protecting Iwo Jima to the death. They stayed near their new airfield. At Iwo Jima, the Japanese had a radio station warning when American bombers would be coming in. The Navy wanted to take that station out. Iwo Jima was estimated about two miles long. The island had been bombed for so long the Japanese were holed up in those deep caves. One way found to get them out in the open was by using flame throwers. "Fellows carried a heavy tank of fuel on their backs to operate the flame throwers. Radio men also carried weapons and lots of equipment on their backs," according to Adam; "both were easy targets." The number of men left in the Marine Regiments were so low at one time two companies were combined. Only eight men in Adam's Company survived or were not injured. There were 250 men to the company.

"In spite of all the ships about," and surprising to Adam; "the Japanese were still getting re-inforcements and troops into Iwo at night. They had their best troops on Iwo Jima and top Japanese Generals." Adam felt, "they should have been starved out. There was no sustenance on the island, only volcanic ash." Adam the recalled that "When the tanks couldn't go forward, then the troops couldn't move forward either. As the Marines came to the edge of the plateau, the men were in more trouble. As waves of Marines backed up, so was more reason for lots of gunfire from the enemy and for heavy troop losses. New re-inforcements with even more and more numbers of men made the difference."

While Marines were attacking Mount Surabachi, finally "E" Company of the 5th Marine Division reached the top of the mountain and raised the American Flag. The-all-Marine-operation finally won the island for the United States of America. A photograph taken by Mr. Rosenthal, a civilian photographer, became a famous symbol of struggle showing six Marines straining to plant their flag. Felix de Weldon created a 78 foot tall statue in bronze at Washington D.C. dedicated November 10, 1954 of this picture. It was described on the fiftieth anniversary of this battle by President Clinton, "As the real picture of America. A picture of unity of the nation forged by men who gave their all."

Iwo Jima is about one mile wide and three miles long. It is narrower at the southern end where Mount Surabachi is located. History records a terrible price paid for what Adam calls, "a dinky little useless Island." Adam's Company Commander was killed with a bullet through the neck and his other three Officers were killed also. Adam was "I" Company's 3rd Battalion 21st Marine Regiment, 3rd Marine Division's Ist Sergeant. He and only seven other enlisted men survived of the 250 in the Company. Those men lost had to be replaced (mostly with troops that had never been in battles before).The first reason given for this battle was to obtain the airstrip. The second reason given for the invasion was that the Pacific Command wanted to neutralize the radio station. It had been warning the Japanese homeland that American bombers were headed that way and to be on the alert. During the fifty year anniversary services in Washington D.C., it was stated 26,000 men died on Iwo Jima, but that 25,000 airmen were saved after the battle had been won. Adam was awarded the Bronze star medal for bravery in action on Iwo Jima. He stated, "Next highest award is the Silver Star and the highest is the Congressional Medal of Honor." Many Marines received those high honors from this battle.

After Iwo Jima, Adam was rotated back to America and received a month's leave at home for rest and recreation. He was ready to go back but the Japanese surrendered and the war had ended. Inasmuch, as Adam still had about a year to complete his second four year enlistment, he was assigned to a transport ship tied at one of the piers near 42nd Street near the heart of downtown New York City. The troop transport was going to India to bring troops home. The ship was to go by way of the Atlantic and come home by way of the Pacific making a round the world trip. Adam was eager to see more of the world but didn't get to go. The ship developed engine trouble and the trip was assigned to another troop tansport ship. In India, the troops were straggling in...

Adam had liberty every night while in New York area. He went to see Broadway shows and frequented famous night clubs. His brother, Frank, in the Navy was also in the area. They enjoyed meeting together and went sightseeing a few times. Adam was assigned to the Marine Barracks at Norfolk, Virginia where he was ultimately discharged. Because of the G. I. Bill, Adam went to college. He attended Alfred University located near Rochester on the southern border of New York State. The college chartered in 1836 was known to be the first co-ed college. 'Guys' bragged about being in the first college to have night football. Adam met his wife, Emily at Alfred University. They both graduated in 1950. Adam earned his B.A and Emily her credentials in Education. They were married shortly after graduation. The ex-Marine began to study law at Syracuse, New York. Shortly after Adam started classes at law school, Emily was not feeling too well. She became pregnant and that news was not exactly what the couple had in mind. When their first child was ready to deliver, Adam was scheduled for his contracts examination. He tried to lie down at the hospital for a little rest but a nurse said, "You have to sit up!" Becky was born at 8 A.M. After checking Mother and baby, Adam immediately dashed off for the exam which he passed. By taking summer sessions, he finished law school in two years instead of the usual three years passing the New York State Bar on the first try.

There were three boys and three more girls born after the Bar Exam had been completed. Becky, the first child was killed in an auto accident at age 24. Penelope, Melissa, Rebecca, Timothy, Dale and Bruce have made Adam extremely proud. Five of the children live on the West Coast. Melissa lives near Washington D.C. After becoming a lawyer, Adam set up law practice in Rochester, New York as a private attorney practicing law for 28 years. When Adam's Mother died in 1979, he came to her funeral in Napa, California. In the month of March, it was seventy degrees in California. Four and one-half hours later by plane, near Rochester, the family endured a blizzard. The travelers could hardly see the road, only telephone lines and wind blowing.

The family decided to move to Napa, California where Adam opened his own business that of making home loans. His son, Dale joined the Principal Mortgage Company in 1989 eventually becoming its President after his father suffered a life-threatening illness. As Adam eased into his retiring role, his two daughters, Penny and Amy became loan processors for the family enterprise. When Emily's mother passed, her father moved into Temelec. As Emily's father's health deteriorated, Adam and his wife drove to Sonoma much of the time. They rented a home for convenience and then moved to Sonoma permanently.

In a sun porch, Adam shows a beautiful rock collection. He belongs to the Gem and Mineral Club. The couple have a motor home for fun and camping. Adam and Emily belong to the Valley of the Moon Good Sam Chapter. The retired Marine holds a Real Estate Broker's License issued by the State of California. He has served as Supervisor in Ontario County, New York and Planning Commissioner for the City of Napa, California. He has been Trustee of his alma mater, Alfred University. As a Kiwanis Club member for over 38 years, he served as President for one year. He was an Eagle Scout as a boy and served as Scoutmaster and leader for the Boy Scouts of America. Since retiring from the United States Marines, Adam has felt proud to have been a part of its traditions. He especially remembers those difficult days at Iwo Jima.

Wheeler, Richard, *Iwo,* orig. pub. Lippincott and Crowell, 1980. First Bluejacket Books Printing, The Naval Institute Press, 1994. 118 Maryland Avenue, Annapolis, Maryland. 21402-5035. pps. 243.

Whipple, A.B.C., *To the Shores of Tripoli,* William Morrow and Company, Inc., 1991. 1350 Avenue of the Americas, New York, N.Y., 10019. pps. 357.

Department of the Army, *American Military History.* ROTCM 145-20, 1607-1953., Washington D.C., 1956., pps.510., p. 439.

The Navajo Code Talkers, ibid., p 21

Coyd Taggart

United States Army, 1942 - 1946

Anyone who was an adult at the time, remembers where he/she was on December 7, 1941.

It was early afternoon in the central time zone. Coyd Taggart was in the ballroom studio of KFBI rehearsing a light opera duet with Mary Lee Brower. The Orchestra had completed the theme of the *Intermezzo* from *Cavaleria Rusticana* and the couple had been introduced for their final rehearsal for a three o'clock show. This program was always the highlight of the week for the participants. Sponsored by an insurance company which owned the station, the city's finest musicians were on prime-time schedule. The program had real class and was enjoyed by a large and growing audience.

The happy event ended abruptly when a man from the program department entered the room and announced that the show was cancelled. The Japanese had bombed Pearl Harbor and a response to that announcement was expected from President, Franklin D. Roosevelt at any time. All programs were cancelled to give the matter full coverage. Coyd was a news reporter on the station. There was a lot of extra work to be done with long hours of coverage. KFBI was the only Kansas station that operated 24 hours a day at that time. Life after that news would never be the same!

The young man still had a year and a one-half of college left. He wanted to finish preparation for a career as a singer. Singing with a small opera company the previous summer had strengthened his resolve to become a professional vocalist. A second career in news broadcasting was just opening to him as well. Coyd had also taken some training for the emerging field of television news. In addition, he was enthusiastically leaning toward a serious commitment to a young woman with whom he sang at the University. This war business was not coming along at a good time!

As the next few days and weeks went by, the draft was announced. It became clear to Coyd, he would be called to participate in that war sooner or later. Plans were made. He enrolled in night school to get the radio operator's license. Then, he enlisted in the U.S. Army Signal Corps through a program called the Enlisted Reserve Corps which allowed him to finish college before he went for basic training.

Theota Smith and Coyd Taggart were married six weeks before they both graduated from Friends University in Wichita. It felt good to finish college. In the next few months, Coyd finished some technical courses on radio and electronics. Theota sought a public school music teaching job.

Camp Crowder near Joplin, Missouri was the place. Coyd found himself at that location enmeshed in basic training. Wintertime in that part of Missouri can be cold for early morning reveille. Missouri's dusty rocky hillsides were not exactly cozy or inspiring environmentally. But from other stories GIs told the young recruit, basic training was expected to be miserable... Even in California, those permanent cadre in desert camps could make it more than equally undesirable.

It seemed clear to Coyd right from the start, that one could find good friends and decent people anywhere. He did! There were some really great 'guys' in that first group with whom he was assigned. He continued to find more great buddies everywhere he served during the war and since! Of course, there were things about military life that surprised him. He never did learn to relate well to some of the routine. Corporal Owen snapped in early morning reveille one day, "all men who have a college degree step forward!" Since Coyd had just graduated from college, he moved forward along with two other enlistees. They were ordered to report to a certain building. When they arrived there for further instructions, their immediate assignment was to take a stick with a nail in it and pick up cigarette and cigar butts that had been thrown on the grounds of the company area. After that, Coyd thought more seriously before responding to every invitation from any Officer.

As was true with other basic training staff, Corporal Owen was a thoroughly committed military man. He was a man of short stature from the Kentucky Hills. He was uneducated, but commanded another kind of respect. He knew and followed every rule the Army brass had taught him. The young college graduate resented some of the stupid things Corporal Owen made him do. But Coyd respected him as a man who would do what he promised. You ALWAYS knew where he was coming from. By contrast, the highly educated Second Lieutenant who became Commanding Officer did not know the Army rules and had little patience or experience in staying within their parameters or enforcing them. The Lieutenant was one of those "thirty-day wonders." The men who came out of college ROTC programs also qualified for Officers Candidate School and a quick commission. The rapid expansion of the military in wartime required all sorts of measures to supply leadership for the millions of men who were being drafted.

The six weeks of basic training went by very quickly. Hours were filled with learning about military life, discipline and getting the body in shape. Physical training was not only rigorous but demanding. Even Sundays were filled with training exercises, except for time enough to go to chapel. There was one evening activity which Coyd was committed and that was Chapel Choir. Soon he learned what a resource the military chaplaincy program would also bring into his life.

One other aspect of basic training was the vocational testing received. The Army officers had plans for first assignments out of basic training. As, usually true with musicians, Coyd's math skills were pretty well honed, so it turned out that he was assigned to go to cryptography school. Coyd later found out that this assignment was triggered by a combination of math scores and his IQ placement which was above a certain level. About five men of the original basic training camp were sent to Arlington Hall, a former school for girls located in the State of Virginia. The whole facility had been taken by the Army for training cryptographers. Selected ones entered into a series of 'secret' settings. Coyd would have these type of meetings for the rest of the war. At different times and places, he might work in a silo or at a fire station. The secret settings might be a mountain lookout station, a sugar mill, a farm, or even a race track. The characteristics of each event were part of a pattern to divert suspicion about what the group was doing.

Cryptography School consisted of teaching pupils the basics of encoding and decoding messages. They were taught to experience the work by hand and with use of machinery. Aptitudes and interest of the participant came together in the machine room. Eleven types of machines used were forerunners of today's computer. Many leaders were creative people from IBM and other scientific developing companies. All of those machines singly working together performed much the same function that one single modern microcomputer would accomplish.

In the research aspect of their work, trying to break an unbroken enemy code, a large number of enemy messages were typed on key punch cards. Those perforated cards were then fed into a reader, a sorter, collator or a printer in order to massage that data in different ways to yield patterns which gave away the code. Character frequency was one technique easily utilized by the machines. The character "E" is the most frequently used letter in the English language. If a code is all in numbers, one could count the character frequency of a large data base and discover which symbol denoted the letter "E". The same technique could be used with reference to recurring phrases. There were many other techniques used to break codes. All of them involved typing large volumes of messages. The information was intercepted by Signal Branches of Allied Forces. The data was then studied until the answer was discovered.

By the end of the war, Allied Forces had the capabilities to break Japanese codes in a matter of hours or days. This was partly due to information learned about techniques. The work was facilitated even more by genius scientists who kept improving machinery. This was so dramatic, by the end of the war the machinery had become more compact and at the same time had much greater capacity than when first introduced. The Army had the earliest versions of the IBM computer. It was put together in Stateside laboratories for one process which filled a room. Work which those early room filled machines did, can now be done faster and better by a laptop computer which fits in one's briefcase.

Finishing Cryptography School at Arlington Hall, Coyd was informed by the Commanding Officer that he was going to be assigned to Signal Intelligence in Washington D.C. for the duration. He suggested that the best thing would be for the young married man to send for Theota to move there. So, Coyd called his wife and invited her to come to Washington, D.C. He rented a modest little apartment in Vint Hill Farms, Virginia. Theota asked to be relieved of her teaching contract. The fine people of Sublette, Kansas released her. The day Coyd was to meet her at Union Station in Washington, he got orders to pack his duffel bags, get his shots and depart for unknown points in the South Pacific by noon! Barely having enough time to meet her train, explain how things changed and get her a ticket for returning home, he also had to arrange for a friend to wind things up and settle with the landlady of the newly rented apartment and get back to base in time to depart!! Theota phoned her school superintendent in Sublette and went back to teach. So much for family life for the duration. What a quick lesson the couple learned about some other things and what it meant to be in the military.

Coyd and his buddies flew that night to Hamilton Air Force Base in Northern California. Like so many other instances of the army syndrome of "hurry up and wait," they cooled their heels in "the ready state" at Hamilton Field for five days. It seemed at the time, a period of five months. Looking back upon the whole picture, it seems understandable that a nation which was totally unprepared for war, which had mobilized millions of people, trained them, then deployed them all over the world in a very short time, would bound to have starts and stops in moving them. There were so many places of destination! But in a short time, those five machine cryptographers who were steamed up that they had to sit and wait, would later wish they were *BACK* there rather than be where they wound up!

The five cryptographers were flown to Guadalcanal on an Air Force B-26 "Liberator" bomber. It seemed to be a sturdy aircraft but no match for the tropical storm turned tornado which collided with the plane while approaching Guadalcanal. Three of the four engines drummed out. They came in on a wing, one engine and a prayer right on schedule. After repair and refueling, the group was relieved "this was not to be their final destination because there was a lot of nasty stuff going on there." They flew on to Brisbane, Australia.

A surprising assignment was made to the Signal Intelligence Services of USAFFE (United States Armed Forces, Far East). This was General Douglas MacArthur's Headquarters! He was seen once in awhile. His main home and office were in a downtown Brisbane Hotel. The men were stationed out at the Ascot Race Course in the suburbs of Brisbane. The work was interesting and important. Usually, Coyd worked the 'graveyard shift' from twelve midnight to 8 a.m. All new recruits coming in from the States automatically inherited that post! But it turned out that he had a great compatible group of people on that shift. When time came for eligibility to move to another shift, most of them found that they'd rather stay with the same team. Developing speed and skill at what they were doing, the group enjoyed working together. One other benefit was they seldom had to deal with top and middle Officers, who dominated the day shift. The commissioned men who supervised the graveyard shift were former non-commissioned men who had become Officers in the field. They seemed to handle authority in a much easier way.

While stationed nine months in Brisbane, the group saw a turnaround in the direction of the war. They felt they had an important part in that process. "It was clear from the work they accomplished that the enemy had lost control of its communication system. Every code system change was quickly broken. The messages the enemy sent to each other were almost like reading an open book for our Commanders," Coyd reported. He continued, "I did not aim a gun at an enemy soldier during my time in service but I still had a wrestling match with my conscience and my spirit about what I was doing. Each morning, a courier would pick up the decoded messages which had come in overnight and deliver them to General MacArthur and his staff."

One of the General's aides on delivery detail told Coyd in a reunion, "that the General read all the messages given him which had been translated every day!" If a message told of the expected location of a particular ship with many troops or carrying armament or other matériel, then the General would order planes or ships dispatched to sink or take over that ship. It was clear to the cryptographers that they *were a part of the killing machine,* even though their individual part dealt with a computer instead of a gun or bomb!

While in Brisbane, the men received a few passes. Coyd spent time hiking in the Oba Oba Range of Mountains west of Brisbane. He also took a trip to the beach. But most of his free time was given to musical events and meeting some interesting people. There were music concerts in the city. Actually, they were not very good quality, but given the circumstance, they seemed wonderful at the time. He was able to find a voice coach and kept up his singing lessons. The singing teacher was Les Edye, a renouned singer. He taught Coyd quite a few techniques. The young man also loved the botanical gardens of the sub-tropic climate in the city. People were wonderful. They were a courteous, kind and warm folk. He made acquaintance with several families through church attendance. With his work buddy, Donald Mahler, they met people in hiking expeditions on their days of recreation. On one of those jaunts, they all took a bus to the mountains and stayed in a small hotel overnight. Surprise! They were awakened by a maid opening the door and bringing in a tray of tea at 7 am.

Coyd related, "Our outfit was composed of all units of the Allied Forces. We had British, Canadian, Australian, Filipino, New Zealander and other national service troops. We also had women in many of the units, especially with the Australian Army Air Force and the Women's Corps of the United States Army. Most of the women were stuck with the tedious job of key punching data. They were a nice bunch of people for the most part."

Coyd remembered, "There was an inordinate number of brainy types in our outfit because of the cutting edge nature of the technological work that was going on. We also had more than the population average of Jewish men and women in our unit. There were no African-Americans. Characteristically, a larger percentage of the people had trouble with alcohol. Part of this alcoholism was brought on or exuberated by the regular issue of beer to the enlisted men and hard liquor to the officers. The "club" was the main off duty activity for many men. The three men with whom Coyd was tentmates with in Australia, for most of the nine months, went to the "club" for noncommissioned men every night. They came in drunk about the time Coyd was going on duty each night. He assumed they all felt this was probably a good match. They didn't enjoy a nondrinker and Coyd wouldn't have enjoyed being with them. Two of those men died of alcoholism before they reached the age of 55.

As MacArthur prepared to move northward with his eventual goals capturing the Philippines and Tokyo, he sent advance units to Hollandia, New Guinea and later to the Philippine Island of Leyte. The camp in Hollandia was on a mountain top. Great views of the forest, mountains and ocean were enjoyed. The men did not do any hiking there! No aircraft attacks came from the Japanese but the troops sure had air attacks by mosquitoes. Some seemed the size of a small bomber! In tents, one learned to sleep in the middle of the cot and tie the top of the mosquito bar (net) up so that you didn't touch any part of it while sleeping. Otherwise, the stinger of the mosquito came right through to the sleeper. It was at Hollandia that Coyd got malaria. The malady was controlled with regular doses of medication. Six years later, the patient learned it wasn't cured just controlled. There were several times when the Japanese soldiers in the jungles made their presence known. They had been cut off from their units when they were decimated by heavy shelling. (Coyd would meet one of those Japanese soldiers in Tokyo the following Christmastime.)

During encampment in Hollandia, one team of four men was trained and sent out on a special mission. They left by ship with an armada preparing to shell one of the forward islands. The Allies were prepared to take this island on the way to Manila. Off shore, the night before the heavy shelling was to be accomplished, the special team was dispatched in a small boat in preparation for landing at dawn. Their task was to row to the island unnoticed by the enemy, scramble ashore without being discovered, and then sneak into the Signal Center of the Japanese Camp when the shelling started. The naval guns were prompted to avoid the Signal Center, (they knew where it was) until John O'Brien and three other guys had a predetermined time in minutes to get into the enemy's building to get the code books and then get out!

They did it! They were given medals of recognition of their heroic service. It saved American lives.

In Hollandia for only a brief time, maybe a couple of months, the group of cryptographers were making great progress in their work. The war was turning around now. The men became bored when off-duty. Coyd wrote to the Modern Press in response to some ads he had seen in a magazine. He ordered about 50 books. Basically they were the classics in a wide literary range. For the most part the books were what was then called the Modern Library. Coyd was utterly amazed at how quickly those books arrived in New Guinea! Loaning the books out to anyone interested, the volumes got a lot of use. The men carried them in duffelbags from island to island. Eventually Coyd brought some books home. By then, they were musty and mouldy from their life in the tropics. But they were a great source of inspiration and comfort at the time and at that place.

The young man began experimenting with a metal forming craft. He learned you could take an Australian Florin, (a two shilling silver piece) pound the edge of it with the convex surface of a large spoon borrowed from the mess hall and the coin's circumference would get smaller and smaller. The edge got thicker and thicker. When the Florin was moulded down to the size one wanted, a hole was drilled in the middle and then one patiently filed out the inside of that circle. After a great deal of tedious work you'd have a silver ring! Around the outside edge of that ring, appeared the printing which was originally on the outside edge of the coin. Only with more and more pounding, one could force the metal to turn in so that the writing appeared on the inside of a plain silver ring. Coyd said, "It sounds ridiculous now but it was something creative to do and it kept me busy."

One of the neat things about cryptographers work was that the punched cards used would not function unless they were dry. So in order to make them function in the tropics, the group always got to work in an air-conditioned room. Even in the jungle, compressors were brought along to provide an air-cooled dry environment for the sensitive machinery. Those insulated rooms were very noisy with the machinery, so nobody objected when Coyd came to work early, found an unused corner of cool space to sit and pound on the coin ring he was making. After the ring was done and one was certainly enough! he turned to another metal making project. Finding some spent Japanese shells on the beach, left over from battle, he decided to make something out of that brass. With a saw, he cut about an inch and a half off the bottom of a larger shell. Next, he prepared a five inch shell casing to be the stick of a candle holder and fitted the piece of the larger shell around for a base. He then cut an inch and a quarter off the base of another of these smaller shells to be the candle cup for soldering to the top. He still has one of two candlesticks made while in Hollandia.

By the time the group had moved up to the Philippines the Japanese were definitely getting the worst of it. The end of the war was only a matter of time. Message interception and translations in the unit had become routine. Machine applications to the process made it all very easy. The Japanese Military was still doing all of their code work by hand.

Camp was set up near Tarlac. Starting from scratch, the men erected some temporary buildings and brought in mobile units for the machines. Location of the operation was hid away in a sugar plantation. The weather was extremely hot. Some of the heavy drinkers in the outfit had been rotated back to the states or stayed in other islands. Some men remained in Australia and married Aussie brides. New people were assigned to Coyd's group. There were new friends with a new kind of hope that the war would soon be over. Everybody began to feel hopeful. Volunteers helped the Chaplain erect a beautiful little chapel in the woods. It was completely built of bamboo under the supervision of a local builder. A little gem of a church was completed. The vaulted roof was enhanced by lining white draping parachutes which made the chapel inspiring. The wheezy little reed organ was a portable G.I. field issue. There weren't any Bach Fugues coming from it but the instrument brought a wonderfully new aspect to musical people's lives. Forming a choir and a male quartet afforded many practice rehearsals and a little performance. The quartet thought they were so good, they decided to obtain a pass, go to Manila and make a recording. The men thought the world would be waiting to hear their efforts when they got home and this might open the way for a "big break"! Of course, that was mostly dreaming by four young men whose other dreams had been postponed for four years. The fellow who was responsible for the 'dream record' lost it on his way back to camp.

The men were becoming so comfortable that they neglected to be as watchful as before. Believing the Japanese had all gone, they no longer kept a carbine rifle by their bunks. Wrong! Snipers in the trees around the camp took shots at some people and reminded the group.

News of the bombing of Hiroshima and Nagasaki filled everyone with conflicting feelings. Rejoicing took place because each one knew that this would bring a quick end to the war. Shuddering, also took place to think of the human suffering which had been inflicted upon innocent civilians in that event. Even at that point, the terror of the atom was clear. Full facts came out which affirmed the wretchedness of that awful day.

With no longer much to do as to decoding messages, the men in the unit, who had spent years in the jungle, were now able to get some R & R (Rest and Relaxation). The Commander made arrangements for small groups to have a week's leave in a wonderful resort area in Northern Luzon at Baguio. The setting was like a paradise! The bamboo huts on stilts were very quaint. Sleeping arrangement was on bamboo mats. That did not prove to be the most comfortable bed but the rest of the environment was peaceful and beautiful. There was a lovely beach and a blue ocean with groves of palm trees making it look like the set for the musical, *South Pacific*. It was very different from the trashy beaches of the war-torn islands from which they had come. Of course, *South Pacific* had beaches populated with beautiful women. Baguio was not. But there was plenty of wonderful food and lots of time to rest.

The Commander then reported that our work was done. He announced he would be reassigning us to other military units. Preferring to make his own plans, Coyd asked for a transfer to the Armed Forces Radio Service. Since that had been his work before joining the Army, Coyd received an assignment to AFRS at Radio Tokyo! What a terrific experience that was! He worked at the same microphone "Tokyo Rose" had used to taunt American soldiers just a few weeks earlier. His job was to broadcast news to the troops in the Southwest Pacific Theater. This assignment became a good transition back to the work he was to do when arriving home. Coyd made News Editor of KFBI in Wichita!

Sightseeing in Tokyo proved to be a city whose wartime deprivations had been great. Much evidence of damage from the limited bombing was easily seen. Many of the people were cool but courteous. Former Japanese military people were angry. Coyd was spat upon once by one of them. (He missed!) But the Christian community was open and eager to meet other Christians from America. Coyd was invited into homes of some of those people.

Christmas came and went in Tokyo. It became one of the most memorable holidays that Coyd ever experienced. He was assigned to cover the broadcast of the first Christmas Midnight Mass after the war. He studied the Mass and interviewed the Chaplain-priest who was in charge, in order to be able to do it well. The station executives wanted Coyd to do a modified eucharistic liturgy commentary of the Mass to cover long periods of silence. The Roman Catholic Priest (Chaplain) who was coaching the young American, raised the question of how a Methodist could do this program. He couldn't decide if Coyd was an unbeliever or a pagan! While trying to clarify that mystification, Coyd had his own convictions but still respected the Chaplain's views. The two men worked together extremely well.

In the process of fullfilling that assignment Coyd met Paul Yinger, Chief of Chaplains for MacArthur. The two would meet again and renew a great friendship 36 years later after they both had retired. Paul wanted to arrange for the first peacetime presentation of Handel's *Messiah* during that Christmas Holiday after the war.

This feat was done. The two men secured an outstanding Japanese Choral Conductor, Dr Nakada, and assembled a chorus numbering 300 voices. Half of the singers were from the American forces and half were from the Japanese community. The group was accompanied by the Tokyo Philharmonic Orchestra. Howard Phillipy, another American Soldier sang tenor solos and Coyd sang the bass. Two Japanese women rendered the soprano and contralto solos. Coyd has never had a more emotional singing experience. Coming together after the war, half from each side of the antagonists of the war were singing of "the coming of peace." There were Japanese men in the chorus who had been across the mountains from the cryptographers in Hollandia. The men standing side by side were joining in sound of their voices together, declaring "the good news of peace!"

Within a month after Christmas, orders were received to return home for discharge from the Army. The trip on a Liberty ship was Coyd's first sea voyage. He was not eager to experience it again. Arriving in Seattle, the group went by train to Fort Leavenworth, Kansas where Coyd was mustered out.

Coyd stated, "As you can see by things I have chosen to speak about in these recollections, I tried to find some good things and some enjoyable memories about the military experience. I left out miserable stuff. The whole business and the whole idea of war and killing was and is distasteful for me. But it is for most everyone. We were in a situation which we were convinced, "someone needed to do what we did. Like everything else I do, I entered into it with a positive attitude. I was determined to be a good soldier and to do the job which my country had asked me to do. I think I did it well. I did not seek advancement in rank for I did not see the military as a continuing life for me. I had the rank of Sergeant at the end of the war. I never learned to hate the Japanese. I have always felt that the whole idea of war as a way of settling disputes is stupid!"

Coyd continued, "I found good people and friends everywhere I went. I learned a lot about people and about their cultures. At the end of the service time, I believed I was a better and more mature person. My religious faith had deepened in this period and although I returned home to become News Editor of the radio station from which I had left, it was not long before I made a decision to go to graduate school and study to become a minister. Through the years, I have maintained contact with half a dozen Army friends. I have attended a couple of gatherings of the 'old outfit'. I am grateful for the experience of the war. I hope that young people will never have to go through that again."

Coyd Taggart is retired and living in Sonoma, California. His first wife, Theota died in childbirth about a year after his return to Wichita. His first Son, Michael was born. Coyd married his present wife, Bunny, who had two children, Dan and Timothy. She had lost her first husband in an auto accident. Bunny and Coyd married. They increased the family of boys by two more, Paul and David. They are proud parents of five adult sons, one of whom lives nearby.

Coyd became a United Methodist Church Minister and secured an MBA from the University of Chicago as well as a Master's degree in theology. His career was spent mostly in the Chicago area. He was the Executive Director and Consultant for private child welfare services for thirty years.

Walter H. Purdy

United States Army Air Corp, 1943 - 1947

United States Air Force 1947 - 1965

The United States Army Air Corps was the first career for Walt Purdy. He considered the Army Air Corps "as the dawn of a new life" just as Charles A Lindbergh did when he penned those words reflecting his non-stop cross-Atlantic flight in 1927. In fact, Charles Lindbergh was one of Walt's two idols when he was growing up. The other was the great Yankee first baseman, Lou Gehrig. Little did Walt know that 'fate' would make it possible for him to cross paths with the world's greatest aviator in a few short years. Walt wanted to fly and share Lindbergh's "moon sweeping over oceans and continents." He wanted to feel those "trembling wings," that Lindbergh spoke about. He (like Lindbergh) just wanted to be able to navigate through "dark and unknown skies to a continent never seen." Walt could hardly wait to grow up so he too could watch for "stars to drop through clouds onto the surface of the ocean for a moment of rest" ... Walt yearned to catch those elements of freedom and adventure like his idol, Charles Lindbergh described on mankind's and his first history making non-stop flight across the ocean from the United States of America to France... alone!!! As Walt moved through his life experiences, he also became intrigued with the way 'fate' reserved a place for his continuing essence. Like his idol, Lindbergh, he too would find life overflowing and he too would look for that "unmarked point" on which to navigate airplanes and that "infinitesimal spot on the earth's surface" that the Army Air Corps would dictate for him to chart as a destination. For Walt, that unmarked point might not only be a geographical spot on the earth's surface but his very life itself.

Walt found the city where he was born, Huntington, West Virginia to be a beautiful sight from an airplane. It melted with the States of Kentucky and Ohio on the great Ohio River. In those innocent times of the thirties and forties like most other communities, Huntington was a real secure area with little crime. Houses were left unlocked. It was a virtual patriotic town best described by Walt "as a thread of democracy."

A military background was not unfamiliar to Walt as he was growing up. His Grandfather, for whom he was named, fought in the Spanish-American War and with the United States Army Infantry during the Boxer Uprising. He was First Sergeant for Captain Fremont (son of the great California explorer, John C. Fremont) while in the Philippines. Walt heard numerous stories about his Grandfather's adventures in the service, especially in the Pacific. When the Japanese attacked Pearl Harbor in 1941, Walt, who was an avid geography student, was completely familiar with places like Pearl Harbor, Wake Island, Manila, Corregidor and Clark Field. A knowledge of aviation was also natural to the boy. Before World War II almost every youngster had one or more heroes. There were plenty to choose from. In addition to Charles Lindbergh, Walt followed the likes of Wiley Post, Jimmy Doolittle, Roscoe Turner, Billy Mitchell, Amelia Earhart and Anne Morrow Lindbergh. Every boy who wanted to fly knew these great people as if they were personal friends. Walt followed their feats, adventures and whereabouts constantly.

On December 7th, 1941 when Japan's Air Force attacked Pearl Harbor and prompted Americans to enter World War II, Walt was busy playing football at a school near his home. A neighbor boy screamed, "Hurry home, your grandmother wants you to come home fast!" Walt ran home thinking perhaps something tragic had happened in the family. His grandmother led him to a chair. "Sit down and listen to the radio, this is a great moment in history," she explained. For millions of other American youngsters, it was also a turning point as it forever changed their lives and destinies.

While attending Huntington High School, Walt's ambitions had been defined to be a professional baseball player and to attend Purdue University to get an aeronautical degree. He wanted to be a part of America's growing aviation industry. By the time he graduated from high school in January 1943, at the age of eighteen, he knew that his ambitions would not be immediately realized. Like most young men in America at that time, he felt the need to help his country as best he could and as soon as possible. Walt urged the local draft board to put his name at the top of the list and by April 1943, he was in uniform. There was a fever during those times...

At the induction center Walt was asked, "Which branch of the service do you want to go into?" He heartily replied, "The Army." Later that day, he learned that five or six of his close buddies had chosen the Marine Corps. Walt went back to the Marine Recruiting Officer (a local sportscaster before the war whom Walt knew well) and asked, "May I change and go into the Marines?" "No," the Recruiting Sergeant said. This was Walt's first brush with 'fate.' Some like to call this type of thing which controls other choices of life as an influence due to 'Guardian Angels' !!!

As 'fate' would have it, everyone of Walt's buddies who went into the Marine Corps on that April day, ended up in the Pacific and all were killed in combat in remote places like Pelileu, New Guinea, Iwo Jima, Ie Shima and Okinawa. Before the war's end, Walt would spend awhile at some of his buddies' graves. One in particular was his very special friend, Jerry Van Zant. He had been in the first wave of Marines to invade Peleliu. To protect his fellow Marines, Jerry threw himself on a Japanese grenade and was killed instantly. It was an act of valor not uncommon wherever young Americans were sent to fight for freedom. After the war, Walt was able to spend some time with Jerry's mother and tell her about his courageous act and the supreme sacrifice Jerry made to help save his comrades.

Sworn into the Army as a Buck Private, Walt was first sent to Fort Thomas, Kentucky for indoctrination and classification. He was then transferred to the Army Air Corps at Miami Beach, Florida along with 125,000 other airmen. It wasn't long before 'fate' entered his life's picture again. He was just one of a thousand young men on a warm May day assembled at the classification center in the main ballroom of the Roney Plaza Hotel. Each airman was told to take a number and wait to be interviewed by one of a hundred Sergeants doing the classifications and making assignments. When Walt's number was called, he reported to Sergeant Edwin Powers, Jr. of Bristol, Tennessee who just happened to be Walt's favorite cousin. They had not seen each other for about five years and neither had any idea the other was in the Air Corps or at Miami Beach. After the cousins chatted awhile, needless to say, Walt was assigned to the schools of his choice (Armament and Aerial Gunnery). In the meantime, he was destined to pull KP 54 times and guarded latrines twenty-seven times!!! Over the next couple of months everyone in the original squadron shipped out to aircraft mechanic's or radio operator's school except for Walt and one other young airman. Permanent KP was fast becoming a way of life for the two awaiting to be sent to Armament School in Denver.

Walt noticed procedure was changing at Miami Beach. New recruits were arriving, not being issued uniforms, staying about a week and leaving. Curious to know what was happening and anxious to get off the KP roster, Walt asked the First Sergeant about those young men. The Top Kick explained, "those fellows are going into the Air Corps Aviation Cadet program to learn how to fly as pilots, navigators and bombardiers. If you're interested, take this note to the Roney Plaza. They'll give you a bunch of tests and if you pass you'll be in some college in ten days." Walt and his pal jumped at the chance, took the tests, passed and then appeared before a Board of Officers at the Caribbean Hotel. A Lieutenant Colonel asked all Pilots, "What do you want to be?" What do you want to fly? Europe or Pacific?" Walt responded, "Be a Pilot and fly a P-38 in the South Pacific, Sir!" He had the answers the Board wanted to hear. An Officer got up on the stand waving some blue cards in his right hand and some red cards in his left hand. "People having names on blue cards will be designated as Navigators and those names appearing on red cards will be Bombardiers. Those not receiving any cards will go back to base." Walt had visions for a brief moment of that base unit and KP. "Oh, Good Lord," he petitioned, "let me be a Navigator." His name appeared on a blue card. Going to Pilot training no longer seemed important. Twenty or thirty persons holding blue cards were called at that time. He got his wish and was ushered into a room with some thirty other airmen. A Colonel told the group, "You fellows have been selected to be Navigators. You are really fortunate. The Air Corps has a brand new bomber, the B-29. All of you will be commissioned as Captains and get to fly in the B-29." "Boy, what a deal!" was all Walt and the others could think of at the time. Well, it didn't quite work out that way...the Colonel was simply 'selling the sizzle'.

However, when his buddy was interviewed, he told the officers he wanted to fly helicopters. The Board was in complete disbelief at the response and ordered a psychiatric examination for the young man. After all, there were only a handful of "gyros" in the Armed Forces in 1943 and everyone felt they had little or no role in combat operations. Many times, since Korea and Vietnam, Walt has reflected upon the fact that his young friend from Philadelphia had far more vision than he or the Board of Officers who eliminated him from the Aviation Cadet Program.

After the big build-up by the Colonel, Walt and a new group of buddies were sent to navigator preflight training in Houston, Texas. Then, it was to aerial gunnery training at Laredo, Texas. The gunnery school was demanding but it was also a lot of fun. Each cadet had to specialize in one of the turrets on the B-24 bomber. Walt's was the consolidated tail turret equipped with two calibre .50 machine guns. There was plenty of air-to-air and air-to-ground practice as well as skeet shooting. Walt recalls how much he admired the skills and bravery of the WAF (Women) Pilots who flew a lot of aircraft towing the sleeves during aerial gunnery practice. "They were excellent flyers and really had to be very brave to do that kind of flying. After all, the practice sleeves they were towing weren't that far behind their planes. Gunner trainees could have easily misjudged when shooting from their turrets and hit the tow planes and aircrews," Walt remembered. "It was certainly no bed of roses for those pilots," he exclaimed!

After completing gunnery training, the young cadets arrived at San Marcos, Texas for advanced navigation training. Usually, that course of training took 20 weeks but Walt's particular class went through in 16 weeks on a one time "experimental" basis. The young flyers learned how to guide a plane to any point on the earth by the use of dead reckoning navigation aided by the stars and planets (celestial navigation), the radio compass, pilotage, LORAN and radar.

When the cadets weren't in the air learning their skills, they were in ground school and when they weren't in ground school they were in the air. It was a busy four months with little time off. "After all, this was serious business. Our nation was at war in virtually every corner of the world and the enemy had to be defeated. Airpower was the ultimate means of reaching and destroying the enemies in Europe and in the Pacific," Walt stated. "Getting our bombers to the target was vital to our national survival and navigators were playing a key role as aircrew members in this endeavor."

Graduation finally came for the young airman. Walt was fortunate enough to have his dad (an Army Captain) pin on his new Navigator's wings and Lieutenant's bars. He lost no time in getting to work using his new skills as a Navigator. Within a few hours after graduation, he was navigating a plane carrying himself and his dad to the Huntsville Arsenal where his dad was a Chemical Warfare Officer.

Now a fledgling Navigator, Walt proceeded to Lemoore, California for assignment to a B-24 combat crew. Again, 'fate' played a part in his life. About 500 flyers were assembed in a large field. All were young. All were newly graduated from flying schools (pilots, navigators, bombardiers, flight engineers, radio operators, gunners.) Walt looked across the entire group, spotted one particular fellow and said to himself, "I hope that 'guy' is my Pilot." Not long ago, Walt picked up the phone and called "that guy," whom he had hoped fifty years earlier would be his crew's Pilot. He reminded him of the date their crew was formed. The former B-24 Pilot now lives in Pittsburg, Pennsylvania. The night of Walt's call to Marshall Fox was the fiftieth anniversary of Crew Number 437. Their friendship has lasted half a century. While they exchanged letters and cards each Christmas, they have seen each other only twice since the end of 'War II'. On this special date, Walt felt it necessary to call "Fox" and thank him for being such a fine Pilot during the war and especially for his friendship. "That 6 foot 5 inch fellow turned out to be my Pilot!" exclaimed Walt. "World War II had a way of creating bonds between people such as has never been seen since."

Combat crew training at Muroc was intensive. (Muroc is now known as Edwards Air Force Base.) Most of the young aviators had little more than one hundred hours total flying time when they were introduced to the B-24 Liberator Bomber. Walt's crew was training for action in the Pacific so great emphasis was placed on long range over water navigation. Dead reckoning was the basis for all navigation. Lindbergh had relied upon dead reckoning to make his historic voyage across the Atlantic in *The Spirit of St. Louis*. Like "Lindy," Walt experienced the "tricks of wind" and "false horizons." He too, "viewed the clouds, sky and sea as if they were in a bowl all stirred up together." What Lindbergh didn't have in 1927 were navigational aids like the radio compass, a sextant to help plot his flight's course by the use of the stars and planets, LORAN (LO ng RA nge N avigation) and radar. While new electronic aids became available to our flyers in the latter stages of 'War II' they still were archaic and "somewhat crude and not completely reliable," according to Walt. "The methods used in 1927 and in 'War II' to navigate a plane from point A to point B are now obsolete and are done by sophisticated computers. Today, the Pilot of a large commercial or military aircraft can obtain his position anyplace on earth instantly. Despite the convenience and increased safety in knowing where you are at all times, most "old timers" are willing to bet that flying isn't nearly as much fun as it used to be when the young Navigators set courses by applying the wind factor, speed and altitude and when they enjoyed searching for visual aids on the ground using them as check points."

The Loran Instrument had been developed by a British Master Station. Using one or more slave stations the instrument picks up and returns signals plotted on special charts. Different lines intercede on radio WAVES. The Loran is used as a navigational system for long-range navigation in which the position of a ship or aircraft is determined by recording the time intervals between radio signals transmitted from a network of synchronized ground stations. The word name was chosen for the instrument comes from LO ng RA nge N avigation. The early type of Loran that Walt used had a 35 mile range. If the target was not within 35 miles then he couldn't pick up the information.

Crew 437 was rated one of the top ten crews finishing the combat transition course at Muroc. They were sent to Langley Field, Virginia for specialized training in radar bombardment (H2X-LAB). That was a course on low altitude bombing. The other thirty five crews went directly overseas to the 7th Air Force on Okinawa. The training at Langley concentrated on teaching the aircrews to use radar for high and low altitude bombing. Radar was in its infancy. The low altitude bombing (LAB) missions were flown at fifty feet above the water at night. These "Snooper" aircrews were being taught to seek out and bomb enemy shipping. The radar altimeter was basic and very crude. It was set for snooping at fifty feet as soon as the bomber was over water after takeoff. The plane was flown manually by the pilot at all times on these missions. If the proper altitude was maintained a "green" light stayed on. If the plane went lower than fifty feet a "red" light appeared and if the plane's altitude went above fifty feet a "yellow" light came on. It was essential for the pilot to fly "in the green" to avoid being detected by the enemy's own radar or to avoid crashing into the sea. It was not an enviable assignment but it was just one more thing that was needed to help put an end to the war of wars.

After the Langley training, Walt's crew was FINALLY ready to go to war. They picked up their brand new B-24M's, flew to Mather Field, (Mc Clelland Air Force Base), Sacramento, California and embarked on their Pacific adventure. 2,000 miles overwater the flight to Barking Sands, Kauai lasted thirteen hours and forty-five minutes. After two weeks of survival training, the crews prepared for their next hop from Kauai to Biak, New Guinea via Canton Island, Tarawa and Los Negros (Manus Island).

Once again, 'fate' became the hunter. During a briefing in Hawaii, the Operations Officer asked, "Is Lieutenant Fox's crew here?" "Yes, it is," responded Fox. The Operations Officer then said, "Lieutenant Fox, you and your crew stand down and leave tomorrow instead of today. Oh, by the way, Lieutenant Murfit and his crew will take your place today and they'll also take your plane and you'll take theirs tomorrow." Walt's plane numbered 1706 was exchanged with Lieutenant Murfit. No one could figure the why of the change? Murfit and his crew departed for Canton Island as ordered and from there they headed towards Tarawa. Somewhere between those two tiny atolls the plane and the men aboard disappeared. It was later concluded that the plane blew up and the entire crew was blown away. Lieutenant Fox and his crew left the next day and did not learn of the incident until they arrived on Tarawa...in Murfit's plane. To Walt, to this day, being delayed for an unknown reason was the work of his 'Guardian Angel'. "Why them? Why not us?" has hammered through his brain for fifty years.

Eventually, Walt's crew together with other aircrews worked their way across the vast Pacific to Yontan Air Base on Okinawa via Biak, Pelileu, Tacloban, Clark Air Base and Ie Shima. Once at Okinawa the crews began flying their missions. Then, suddenly, without any forewarning the B-29 Enola Gay dropped the first atomic bomb on Hiroshima. Then a second "special weapon" was dropped on Nagasaki and the Japanese surrendered and the great war was over! Walt described the feeling among the aircrews as one of sober relief. All of those Allied Forces had been gathering at Okinawa for months to prepare for the invasion of Japan and suddenly it all ended! Walt often reflects upon those days realizing that he and hundreds of thousands of others were probably saved as a result of the dropping of the two A Bombs. "All of that flight training for almost two years to get a specific job done without a chance to find out if we had the right stuff," laments Walt in his twilight years.

After the war's end, aircrews with the most missions returned to the States on the "Sunset Project." However, crews with few missions were transferred to Manila, disbanded and assigned to various tasks. Walt 'lucked' out. He was assigned to Headquarters, Far East Air Forces as a Flight Line Navigator and had a chance to continue his flying career and hone his skills. While flying out of Nichols Field at Manila, Walt had the rare opportunity to spend some time with his dad who was also stationed in Manila in the United States Army's Military Government Office. That was short-lived as Walt's Unit was transferred to Tokyo and designated the Pacific Air Command under General Ennis C. Whitehead who reported directly to the Supreme Allied Commander, General Douglas MacArthur. Little did Walt realize that 'fate' would once more enter the scene and with no advanced preparation or knowledge result in his being selected to become General Whitehead's Navigator on the Pacific Air Command's C-54 Flagship, the K.C. Headwind (#42-72569). Walt woke up one morning thinking and becoming aware, "I am in the 'big leagues' of flying. I never knew exactly why, out of some 25 or 30 navigators in our unit, I was selected but it was a great thrill and honor for a 22 year old kid. Suddenly I was part of a fine aircrew flying for the man who with General George Kenney, had directed all the United States Army Air Corps' efforts from Austrailia to New Guinea to the Philippines to Okinawa and finally to Japan during the period from 1942 to 1945. Of course, it was the B-29s from General LeMay's 20th Air Force that dropped the A-Bombs and caused Japan to surrender but the 5th, 7th, and 13th Air Forces under Generals Kenney and Whitehead were on the scene from the very beginning of the Pacific Campaign and fought those great air battles throughout the entire war. After the war ended, General Whitehead replaced General Kenney and was placed in command of all United States Air Forces in the Pacific Ocean Area (Hawaii, Guam, the Philippine Islands, Okinawa, Iwo Jima, Korea and Japan from 1945 to 1950."

After leaving Japan in 1950, General Whitehead was First Commander of the Air Defense Command and then retired in 1952. Walt described him as "a wonderful man who was more like a father to me than my military commander. He came from the farmlands near Newton, Kansas and he had all these great homespun philosophies. He was truly an enlisted man's General."

He kept telling me, "Purdy your first and most important responsibility as an officer is to take care of the men under you. The enlisted men are the backbone of the Air Force. Without them nothing happens. Engines don't run, propellers don't turn, planes don't taxi or get off the ground without them. And don't ever forget it!! According to Walt, General Whitehead could get real tough on his senior officers but he was worshipped by the enlisted men and junior officers.

Walt tells of one incident on Guam when General Whitehead had justifiably 'racked up' a General Officer for failing to follow orders. He and I were on the plane alone and he turned to me and said, "Purdy, the only way junior Officers can learn is by making mistakes but when I put an eagle (full Colonel) or a star (General Officer) on a man's uniform, he better damned well quit making mistakes!!" It was pretty evident that Walt thought the sun rose and set on General Whitehead. He spoke of his crew (Major Charley Glenn as "the best Pilot whoever lived." He referred to Griffith, Underbrink and Howard, the Flight Engineers who kept "569" ready to fly at all times. There was Kelly and Ingram, Radio Operators who later became outstanding Air Force Pilots and Payne, the Flight Steward from Walt's home state of West Virginia, who found out on a trip from Tokyo to Hawaii, why the "Old Man" never won at solitaire. He had a short deck of only 50 cards. Payne merely replaced them, said nothing about it and the "Old Man" began winning! Also, there was Sergeant Hope, the General's Secretary, from Arkansas, who was the crew's Administrative Manager and kept the General supplied with Charles Krug Sherry which he relished!

The K.C. Headwind usually spent 100 hours in the air each month carrying General Whitehead and various military and civilian dignitaries between Tokyo and Manila, Guam, Okinawa and Hawaii. The C-54, the military version of the civilian DC-4 was extremely comfortable in comparison with the War II bombers. The B-17s, B-24s, B-25s and B-26s were not pressurized and the heating systems rarely worked. The air temperature at high altitude during wintertime flights in the higher Northern latitudes often were more than 55 degrees below zero centigrade! Flying in the Southwest Pacific wasn't very uncomfortable but when the air war moved north of Okinawa and into Japan proper, it was pretty testy. The B-29s from Guam, Tinian and Saipan were pressurized and more comfortable, even in combat. As bad as it was in the Pacific, it probably never equalled the discomforts experienced by the aircrews flying out of England to strike German targets. But these were youngsters, most only 18 to 24 years of age, on the adventure of a lifetime with a resolve to destroy the Evil Empire.

A lot of famous people flew in the K.C. Headwind. The plane got its name from General Whitehead's favorite city in his home state of Kansas, i.e, Kansas City combined with the fact that regardless of where it flew the plane always seemed to be bucking headwinds. The most famous person of all was one of Walt's boyhood idols.

One day in early February 1947, General Whitehead called Charley Glenn, the Kansas City Headwind's superb Pilot and Walt to his office. He said, "We have some 'fella' coming in from the States and I want you to take him wherever he needs to go." Charlie asked, "May we ask who this is?" The General replied with a smile, "Oh, some 'guy' by the name of Charles Lindbergh!"

Anticipation ran riot! This was Walt's idol! He had kept track of the great air explorations of Charles Lindbergh and his wife, Anne Morrow Lindbergh all through the 1930s and early 40s. Charles Lindbergh was considered by most to be the greatest Aviator of all times (and still is). Furthermore, he was as great a Navigator in the air as Magellan had been on the seas! He was about to be a guest on the K.C. Headwind! (This was Walt's hero of America!) Here, he, Walt was but 21 years old and all of a sudden, he was going to be with the great aerial Navigator of all times!! Lindbergh was going to be escorted by the Headwind's crew and Walt was going to be Lindbergh's navigator!!!

When Lindbergh first came on board the K.C. Headwind, he told the Pilot, Charley Glenn, "I would like for you to take me to Southern Japan so I can visit Hiroshima and Nagasaki. The Government of the United States wants me to visit both cities and report my observations and conclusions about the effect of the A-bombs we dropped in 1945." Lindbergh was first flown to Itazuke Air Base. He and the Headwind's entire crew were then flown to Iwakuni Air Base in an RAF Dakota C-47. At the time, Iwakuni was the RAF Headquarters in Japan under the command of Air Vice Marshal Boucher (a famous aviator who directed the RAF fighter operations during the Battle of Britain.)

On the first night at Iwakuni, Air Vice Marshal Boucher invited Lindbergh, Charley Glenn and Walt to have dinner with him and stay in his home. When extended the invitation, Lindbergh said to Boucher, "Thank you very much for your kind invitation but I have one request of you." Boucher said, "I'll honor any request you make." Lindbergh then said, "The dinner and meeting tonight will be one of historic significance to the Pilot and Navigator of the crew. If you have no objections, I would like to ask you to invite the enlisted men of the crew to join us, too. After all, Air Vice Marshal Boucher, you and I have made a few contributions to the history of aviation and I would like to have the entire crew present." The Air Vice Marshal assured him that all would be welcome. For four hours the crew of the Headwind was mesmerized by the exchange of stories between Lindbergh and Boucher.

Walt was especially interested in learning about Lindbergh's P-38 combat missions in the Southwest Pacific. Lindbergh had lost his commission in the Army Air Corps before the start of War II but he headed for the South Pacific anyway after the war began and started teaching the P-38 pilots how to practically double the mileage range of their aircraft with no increase in fuel or decrease in armament. Air Vice Marshal Boucher's accounts of the Battle of Britain kept everyone present on the edge of their seats. Those were dark and desperate days for Great Britain and here was the Headwind's Crew getting a first hand personal report from one of the most important leaders of the air battles over England which turned back the Luftwaffe and literally saved Great Britain!

One part of the exchange that February evening in Iwakuni was extremely interesting. Baucher asked Lindbergh, "Tell us about you and President Roosevelt." It was readily apparent that Lindbergh did not have a good feeling about his relations with the President. Lindbergh had gone to Germany in the late 1930s to look at the build-up of their war machine and especially their growing air armada. While in Germany, Lindbergh was awarded the Iron Cross. "President Roosevelt complained about my being given the Iron Cross by Hitler," said Lindbergh. He continued, "The truth is that Goering, who headed the German Luftwaffe presented the medal to me for my contribution to the advancement of world aviation. I never met Hitler. I saw him only once. It was during a mass rally. He was at one end of a vast stadium and I was at the other end of the room. That's the closest we ever came to each other. President Roosevelt insisted that I return the Iron Cross and I disagreed. In the end, I resigned my Army Air Corps Commission." Walt observed that Lindbergh began warning the United States Government about Germany's tremendous growth in air power. He pushed for a major build-up of the United States Air Forces. He became an isolationist and was heavily criticized before and during World War II for his stand on neutrality. General 'Hap' Arnold, who headed up the United States Air Corps during War II knew what Lindbergh stood for and spent a period of time quizzing him about German planes, armament and inventions. During the dinner with Air Vice Marshal Boucher, Lindbergh told the group that he had been sent into Germany by the United States immediately after the war in Europe ended to learn what he could about the production of German Jet Aircraft. Lindbergh commented, "if the Germans had had three more weeks of uninterrupted jet aircraft production and had not had their ball bearing factories bombed out by the 8th Air Force, they would have taken American planes out of the skies with their jets. America had no jets available for combat operations at the time."

From Iwakuni, Lindbergh and the Crew were taken by PT boat to Hiroshima. The airmen spent an entire day discovering the city was still completely devastated. They visited "ground zero" (the exact place in Hiroshima where the world's first atomic bomb detonated and much of the surrounding area where just 18 months earlier, the historic event had occured. During the tour of the totally destroyed city, Lindbergh stopped and looked in every direction and uttered a curious observation. "Every place I look I see only smokestacks standing. The factories and buildings are all gone but the smokestacks are still there. I guess the message is that if we're ever caught in an atomic attack the best thing to do is climb inside the nearest smokestack!"

Japanese survivors of the blast still appeared to be in a daze. A temporary hospital in a partially destroyed building near gound zero was being used to care for surviving victims. Walt recalls the feeling of compassion which came over Lindbergh and the Crew when they saw the extent of the burns and injuries inflicted upon the victims. Many, of course, were terminal. Living conditions in Hiroshima were deplorable. The people in other Japanese cities which were severly damaged by conventional aerial bombing seemed, by 1947, to be recovering somewhat and getting back to the routine of a normal life. "The people of Hiroshima just were not coming around," Walt recalls. In all, it was an interesting opportunity for these airmen, in the presence of Lindbergh, to be able to see the mass destruction wrought by just one 10,000 pound bomb from just one airplane.

Several days later, the Headwind's Crew flew Lindbergh to Nagasaki for an aerial view of that equally devasted city. On the return flight to Tokyo, after setting the Headwind's course, Walt decided to visit with Lindbergh who was relaxing in General Whitehead's cabin quarters. Walt said, "Mr. Lindbergh, "I'm still real young. You have been one of my idols most of my life. I've read about your flight across the Atlantic in *The Spirit of St. Louis*. I'd really appreciate it, if you would tell me first hand some of the things you remember most about that flight." Mr. Lindbergh was totally accommodating. His most vivid recollections included the difficult takeoff from Mitchell Field, New York, encountering icing conditions, fighting to stay awake, falling asleep, being awakened very suddenly by the flashing of a "bright shiny object" when his altitude was just a few hundred feet above the ocean in time to recover before crashing, spotting Ireland and waving to the completely startled people on the ground and finally his arrival in Paris at night and landing at Le Bourget where he was greeted by hundreds of thousands of people.

To this day, Walt never misses a chance to watch Jimmy Stewart's role in the movie, *The Spirit of St. Louis*. The film was made twenty years after Lindbergh told Walt about his flight. Walt maintains that the movie was definitely "in synch" with what he had been told by the great aviator.

As the Headwind approached Haneda Air Base near Tokyo, Charley Glenn, the Pilot, asked Lindbergh if he wished to make the landing and he accepted without the slightest hesitation. As Walt puts it, "He painted it (the plane) on the end of the runway. What an experience! being flown in a plane by the two best Pilots in the world, Charley Lindbergh and Charley Glenn!" Once on the ground, Walt asked one last favor of the great flyer, "Would you mind having your picture taken with our crew?" Walt has that photograph of the Headwind's Crew with Lindbergh in his den, taken nearly 50 years ago and it is historically included in this book! Walt says, "I knew Mr. Lindbergh was a very private person and he and his wife, Anne Morrow Lindbergh had shunned publicity all their lives. But, he was so very famous and I knew if I didn't ask, I would never have another chance in my lifetime, so I made the request and he seemed only too glad to honor the request. I also got him to sign my "short snorter" a one dollar bill carried by aircrew members during World War II, but his autograph has completely faded away after all these years." He remembers Lindbergh "as kind, extremely considerate and understanding. He was a real gentleman in every respect. It would have been an honor just to have met him but to be with him for most of a week and being able to fly with him and to be his Navigator was more than any young man could dream of and ask for in a lifetime! Once more, 'fate' came to play...

Before the year of 1947 was over, Walt met his wife to be, Bettye, who was an 'Army brat." She was living with her family in Occupied Japan. Her father was an Officer in General MacArthur's Headquarters. They were married in Japan and had their first child, Scott born there. On their second tour in Japan ten years later, their last child, Chris was born in the same hospital as Scott. In-between those tours, Walt and Bet were blessed with four other children, Vivian, Bill, Becky and Mark.

Before Walt returned to Japan the second time, he was to be touched one more time by the hand of 'fate'. After returning to the States from his first overseas tour in the Pacific, Walt was trained to be a "triple rated" aircraft observer (Navigator, Bombardier, Radar Specialist) and assigned to the Strategic Air Command's 2nd Bomb Wing in Savannah, Georgia. He was assigned first to a non-combat-ready-crew but required to fly with a combat-ready-crew for special training as a radar bombardier. SAC was in its infancy in 1949. "The Russians were breathing down the free world's back and General LeMay (SAC's Commander) was doing as much as possible, as fast as possible, to get SAC crews trained so they could deliver "The Bomb" whereever and whenever necessary. Those were hectic days, the only thing between us and war with the Soviets was SAC," according to Walt. He continued, "To compound the problem, the Secretary of Defense Louis Johnson, under President Truman, ordered a massive reduction in all the Armed Forces near the end of 1949 and SAC, along with the other Air Commands was reduced to a mere skeleton of what it had once been. America's great Defense Department had most of its muscle ripped out." It was during this frenzied period that the 'Guardian Angel' really banged on Walt's door!!!

The combat ready crew Walt was flying with to attain his own combat ready status was piloted by an overly ambitious young West Point Officer. The fellow was striving to earn a star long before his time. The Radar Observer teacher was Captain Tony Collandro, a great guy! The Navigator was Rogers Hornsby, Jr., son of the great Baseball Hall of Famer Rogers Hornsby. Walt really thought the world of Tony, who reminded him a lot of Detective Sipowicz on TV's *NYPD Blue*. Between September and December, Walt flew thirteen times with this crew and <u>never</u> completed a mission.

To finish his triple-rated-rank, a flight to Florida was set up just for Walt. He had flown those thirteen times and never completed the triple rated missions. In one case the engine caught on fire... next day they threw a prop, then the radar set malfunctioned. It was always something! Finally the week before Christmas (1949) they were scheduled to fly the B-50 (#7110) from Savannah to Tampa for Walt's practice radar bomb runs. It was a lovely afternoon to be navigating a flight. But Number 3 engine kept backfiring so bad, they had to abort. As far as the radar, it had a beautiful picture on the scope. The next evening, Tuesday, number three engine ran okay but the radar set went out. Wednesday evening the flight was set up again. A massive thule ground fog came in with zero ceiling visibility. The control tower would not clear them for takeoff. The crew again failed to complete the flying mission to Florida.

On Thursday, December 22nd, 1949, a magnificently clear day was enjoyed. The crew was briefed at 1630 (4:30 P.M.) for a 7 P.M. takeoff. About ten minutes into the briefing, the Operations Officer Captain Wynn, who was conducting the meeting was called to his office for an "important phone call." He returned to the podium in a couple of minutes and said, "Lieutenant Purdy, do you want to make this flight?" What did Walt have to say? Walt told him he didn't understand the reason for his question since the mission was specifically being flown to train him. The Officer continued, "Because of the Christmas holidays, the Tampa RBS (radar bombsight) classes are closing down early. The radar mission has been scrubbed. They are changing to a long range navigation flight to El Paso and return. You can go along for the ride or you can go home. If you don't want to go, you don't have to." Walt said, "Well, I have some Christmas shopping to do. I have all the flying time I need this month." Walt turned to the crew, wished them a good flight and told them he'd see them tomorrow...The plane took off from Chatham Air Force Base on time. It had no further radio contact with the tower. It was trying to get back to the base but crashed in the unforgiving Georgia Swamps east of Savannah about two miles short of the runway. The Tech Reps who helped investigate the crash determined that shortly after takeoff number three engine caught on fire, burned through the fuel line, set up a blow torch effect which caused the center wing spar to the right wing to weaken. The wing folded and the plane crashed and burned. No one survived. Walt remembers learning about the crash at 5:30 A.M the following morning when he turned on the radio for the local news. "They didn't say anything more than a B-50 from Chatham had crashed shortly after 7 P.M. the night before. I knew immediately, that it was 110," Walt laments. Asked about his thoughts at the time, Walt said, "It was a very sad Christmas for our Squadron. It really hurt me terribly because I had been flying with that crew for three months. I was especially saddened because of Tony's loss. He and his wife had a brand new baby boy. He had just brought his family from Pennsylvania to live in Savannah. It was Christmastime. It was an overwhelming event which I've never forgotton. To this day, I never forget to say a special prayer every December 22nd. In fact, I can never recall a day passing since then that I haven't remembered just how lucky I was. Do I believe in 'fate' and 'Guardian Angels'??? You bet I do!! After the change of planes in Hawaii during the war and the B-50 crash at Savannah, I've got the picture!"

Walt continued, "The ten people on that B-50 had just as much right to live as I did. Most were married and most had children. I have asked myself thousands of times over the past 45 years since 110 crashed, "Why was I spared and they weren't?" I've often wondered, "What if Tony had asked me to go in his place that night because he had just brought his family down from Pennsylvania? Chances are I would have done it for him. Sort of scary when you stop to think about all of it!

While still at Savannah, Walt applied for Pilot training but was told in no uncertain terms that it would not be approved since he was too valuable to SAC as a triple rated Aircraft Observer. Eventually, he said he no longer wanted to fly, so they grounded him and he was transferred to Personnel. He had subsequent assignments in Japan, Texas and California in Personnel and Command. Although he began in the Army Air Corps as a regular Buck Private who did his share of KP and guard duty, Walt eventually retired in 1965 as Air Force Officer Lieutenant Colonel. He wanted to see if he could make another career for himself in the civilian world. With the support, help and encouragement of his wife Bettye and the children, Walt pursued a career with Fireman's Fund Insurance Companies as a Personnel Director in the San Francisco Home Office and then as an Operations Manager in Tampa, Florida. Walt felt, "I had great people to work for and with a superb company. They were all extremely considerate and helpful." When Walt decided to retire from the insurance company in Tampa, Bet thought of nothing but moving back to the Bay Area and specifically to the town of Sonoma. The family moved to Sonoma in 1986 admitting the scenery, climate and history were powerful attractions. New ways to keep this man busy has been easy. Walt has worked on the Pro Shop Staffs at both Bodega Harbour Golf Links and the Adobe Creek Golf Course at Sonoma. He also has a nice hobby of repairing and refinishing golf clubs.

Walt calls himself "just a run of the mill American kid who like 12,000,000 other American kids came to the aid of their country when needed. He states, "I received no special decorations because I did nothing heroic. There were a lot of genuine American heroes who earned their decorations the hard way and we should never forget the sacrifices they made for us. I have a lot of buddies who left the States and never came back. They're the real heroes. Me? I've just been very lucky. I've been blessed to have a fine wife, family and friends. I've had two long term jobs and steady work! Oh, yes, and best of all, I've had a couple of Guardian Angels along the way!"

Lindbergh wrote, "You never see the sky until you've looked upward to the stars for safety. You never feel the air until you've been shaken by its storms." Walt can truly live in his dreams of yesterday, and as Lindbergh stated, "living in those dreams, he dreams again."

Walt's final remark was, "One thing, I truly feel looking at all of the American History, no words can fully express, no words can state, how blessed it is being an American. Looking back through history, our generation had the best of times."

Index

Publications by the Author:

Operation:Memories, Incredible Stories of
World War II Veterans. Copyright 1995.

Book: *Autobiography of a Fire.* Copyright 1989.

A Century of Favorite Recipes.
Conceived and Chairman of a Church Cookbook
with historical background. 1993.

Pictures of the Past. Written, narrated, June 1985.
Forty scene Tableau Historical Review for
Sonoma, California's Sesquicentennial Celebration.

Album: *Infinite Power of Love.*
Recorded at Wilder Brothers Recording,
Los Angeles, 1984.

Available from:
Senior Distributors. P.O. Box 185,
Vineburg, California 95487.